# *The Last 100 Days*

JOHN TOLAND writes: "To gather material for this book my wife Toshiko and I traveled more than 100,000 miles in twenty-one countries, including five behind the Iron Curtain: to a prison in Munich to see SS General Wolff; to the Bernadotte ancestral home near Stockholm; to the site of the Shell House in Copenhagen; to the Citadel in Budapest; to the Warsaw Ghetto; to Dachau, Buchenwald, Auschwitz and Sachsenhausen. . . . We traveled on both sides of the Oder River to visit the battlefields near Frankfurt an der Oder, Küstrin and Seelow. . . . We listened to Major Szokoll's story of the Vienna uprising in the bar of the Hotel Sacher; W. Averell Harriman's in his Georgetown home; Clement Attlee's in the dining room of the House of Lords; Bernard Baruch's in 'Little Hobcaw' in South Carolina; and Admiral Dönitz's in his home near Hamburg."

To reconstruct the dramatic story of the 100 days between Yalta and the fall of Berlin, over 600 people were interviewed—from Hitler's personal chauffeur to Generals von Manteuffel, Wenck and Heinrici; from underground leaders to diplomats; from top Allied field commanders, such as Generals Simpson and Hodges, to GIs. The book is further based on thousands of primary sources: after-action reports, staff journals and many top secret messages and personal documents that have until now been unavailable to historians.

*The Last 100 Days*

---

*Books by John Toland*

ADOLF HITLER

BATTLE: THE STORY OF THE BULGE

BUT NOT IN SHAME

THE DILLINGER DAYS

THE FLYING TIGERS

GODS OF WAR

INFAMY

THE LAST 100 DAYS

NO MAN'S LAND

THE RISING SUN

SHIPS IN THE SKY

# THE LAST
# 100
# DAYS

---

## JOHN TOLAND

BANTAM BOOKS
TORONTO · NEW YORK · LONDON · SYDNEY · AUCKLAND

THE LAST 100 DAYS

*A Bantam Book / published by arrangement with*
*Random House, Inc.*

*PRINTING HISTORY*

*Random House edition published February 1966*

| | | | |
|---|---|---|---|
| 2nd printing ....... April 1966 | 4th printing ........ May 1966 |
| 3rd printing ....... April 1966 | 5th printing ........ May 1966 |

*Literary Guild edition published February 1966*

*A portion of this book appeared in* LADIES HOME JOURNAL
*June 1966*

*Bantam edition / January 1967*

| | |
|---|---|
| 2nd printing .... January 1967 | 5th printing ... November 1970 |
| 3rd printing .... January 1967 | 6th printing ........ July 1972 |
| 4th printing .... January 1967 | 7th printing ..... October 1973 |

*8th printing ...... August 1976*
*9th printing ... November 1977*
*10th printing .... January 1980*

*Bantam Trade edition / August 1985*

*The author is grateful to the following for permission to quote:*
*Doubleday & Company, Inc.—From* Triumph in the West, *Arthur*
*Bryant. Copyright © 1959 by Arthur Bryant.*
*A. D. Peters & Company—From* The Testament of Adolf Hiter: The
Hitler-Bormann Documents, February–April 1945, *edited by H. R.*
*Trevor-Roper, Published by Cassell & Company, Ltd.*
*Time Inc.—From* Memoirs *by Harry S Truman, Vol. 1, p. 6, 63,*
*206. Published by Doubleday & Company, Inc. © 1955 by Time Inc.*
*Weidenfeld & Nicolson—From* The Bormann Letters: the Private
Correspondence between Martin Bormann and his Wife, from January
1943 to April 1945, *London, 1954.*

**Library of Congress Cataloging in Publication Data**

*Toland, John.*
*The last 100 days.*

*Bibliography: p.*
*Includes index.*
*1. World War, 1939–1945. I. Title. II. Title:*
*Last one hundred days.*
*D755.7.T6 1985    940.53        85-6013*
*ISBN 0-553-34208-8 (pbk.)*

*Published simultaneously in the United States and Canada*

*Bantam Books are published by Bantam Books, Inc. Its trademark,*
*consisting of the words ''Bantam Books'' and the portrayal of a*
*rooster, is Registered in U.S. Patent and Trademark Office and in*
*other countries. Marca Registrada. Bantam Books, Inc., 666 Fifth*
*Avenue, New York, New York 10103.*

PRINTED IN THE UNITED STATES OF AMERICA

DH    0  9  8  7  6  5  4  3  2  1

*To My Mother*

# Author's Note

Perhaps no other 100 days in history have had greater significance and consequences than those at the end of World War II in Europe. Within the space of three months Roosevelt, Hitler and Mussolini died, as did Nazism and Fascism. V-E Day marked the end of one era and the beginning of another, with its fantastic hopes and terrors.

I have tried to write of those portentous days as if they took place a hundred years ago and to portray Hitler, Himmler, Göring and their kind not against the background of one who lived through that period but with the objectivity of time.

The book is based on hundreds of interviews with people from twenty-one countries who were directly involved with the events described. Wherever possible the participants are the basic source for what happened and they reveal—and at times condemn—themselves with their own words. It is time for revelation, not accusation.

The book is further based on several thousand primary sources: after-action reports; staff journals and monographs; a number of top-secret messages and personal documents that have until now been unavailable to historians (Lieutenant General Hobart Gay, Patton's chief of staff, for example, allowed his diary—kept at Patton's order—to be used for the first time); finally, numerous published and unpublished books were consulted.

The excerpts of dialogue in this book are not fictional. They come from transcripts, stenographic notes and the memory of the participants. The *Notes* (at the end of the book) contain sources for all the material used, chapter by chapter.

Max Beerbohm once wrote, "The past is a work of art, free of irrelevancies and loose ends." My hope has been to recreate past events after enough time had elapsed to recollect them in relative tranquillity, but not before the "irrelevancies and loose ends," which are the spice of history, have disappeared.

# Contents

AUTHOR'S NOTE ................................. xi

PART ONE—*The Great Offensive*

1  Floodtide East .................................. 3
2  "Five Minutes Before Midnight" ...................... 26
3  "This May Well Be a Fateful Conference" ............. 40
4  "Bread for Bread, Blood for Blood!" .................. 66
5  "Judge Roosevelt Approves" ......................... 85
6  The Balkan Cockpit ............................... 117
7  Operation "Thunderclap" .......................... 130
8  War and Peace .................................... 150

PART TWO—*Drive from the West*

9  "An Iron Curtain Will Go Down" ..................... 171
10  Ebb and Flow .................................... 182
11  "What If It Blows Up in My Face?" .................. 193
12  "I Am Fighting for the Work of the Lord" ........... 226
13  Operation "Sunrise" .............................. 238
14  The Shell House .................................. 248
15  Between Two Rivers ............................... 254
16  "We Have Had a Jolly Day" ........................ 270
17  Task Force Baum .................................. 285
18  Decision at Rheims ............................... 300
19  The Rose Pocket .................................. 320

PART THREE—*East Meets West*

20  "O–5" ........................................... 337
21  "Such Vile Misrepresentations" ................... 356
22  Victory in the West .............................. 383

23 "On the Razor's Edge" ............................... 397

24 "The Führer Is in a State of Collapse!" ................ 421

25 "We Must Build a New World, a Far Better World" ...... 443

PART FOUR—*Wingless Victory*

26 "Pheasant Hunt" ................................... 463

27 An "Italian Solution" ............................... 475

28 Death Comes to a Dictator .......................... 489

29 "The Chief Is Dead" ................................ 514

30 "And Now You Stab Us in the Back" ................ 535

31 "The Iron Curtain in the East Moves Closer and Closer" .. 543

32 Beginning of a Long Surrender ....................... 555

33 "The Flags of Freedom Fly All Over Europe" .......... 570

ACKNOWLEDGMENTS ................................. 591

NOTES ............................................. 595

INDEX ............................................. 611

# PART ONE

✠ ✠ ✠

## *The Great Offensive*

# 1

# Floodtide East

**1.**

On the morning of January 27, 1945, there was an air of restrained excitement among the 10,000 Allied occupants of Stalag Luft III (Air Prisoner of War Camp) at Sagan, only 100 air miles southeast of Berlin. In spite of the biting cold and the steady fall of snow in large flakes, prisoners huddled outside their barracks discussing the latest report: the Russians were less than twenty miles to the east and still advancing.

Two weeks earlier the first news of a great Red Army offensive had begun seeping into the camp from anxious guards. The prisoners were in high spirits until several goons—guards—hinted that orders had come from Berlin to make the camp a *Festung*, a hedgehog fortress to be defended to the end. A few days later another rumor spread that the Germans were going to use the Kriegies (short for *Kriegsgefangenen*, "war prisoners") as hostages and shoot them if the Russians tried to take the area. This story was succeeded by an even more terrifying one: the Germans were going to convert the showers into gas chambers and simply exterminate the prisoners.

Morale dropped so alarmingly that Arthur Vanaman, an American brigadier general and the senior Allied officer at Sagan, sent a directive to the camp's five compounds urging that all rumors be stopped and that preparations for a possible forced march to the west be accelerated.

One of the prisoners wrote in his diary, "Our barracks looks like a gathering of the Ladies' Aid Sewing Circle." Men sat cross-legged on the bunks cutting glove patterns from the bottoms of overcoats, devising snow caps and face guards, and improvising knapsacks out of trousers. A few ambitious ones were even building sleds from odd bits of lumber and bed boards.

But nothing could stop the rumors, and on January 26 Vanaman called a meeting in the camp's largest auditorium. He strode up to the stage and announced that he had just learned from a BBC news report over a contraband radio that the Russians were only twenty-two miles away. He quieted the cheers and said they would all probably be marched across Germany. "Our best chance of survival is to stand together as one team, ready to face whatever may come. God is our only hope and we must trust him."

By the morning of January 27 the prisoners of Sagan were ready. Evacuation kits were stacked near the doors of each barracks. Other equipment lay on the bunks, ready for hasty packing. As the snow piled up, the men waited watchfully, with a strange feeling of peace and calm. Many kept looking out past the high wire fences at the even rows of snow-laden pine trees. Beyond lay the unknown.

**2.**

Once Hitler held almost the entire land mass of Europe as well as North Africa. His troops had ranged deep into Russia and controlled more territory than the Holy Roman Empire. Now, after nearly five and a half years of war, his vast empire was compressed to the very borders of Germany. The combined American, British, Canadian and French armies were poised for the final assault along the Fatherland's western boundary from Holland to Switzerland. And the sprawling eastern front, extending from the warm waters of the Adriatic Sea to the icy Baltic, was being punctured at a dozen points. After liberating half of Yugoslavia, most of Hungary and the eastern third of Czechoslovakia, the Red Army was already in the fifteenth day of the greatest offensive in military history.

On January 12 almost 3,000,000 Russians—more than a dozen times the troops that landed on D-Day—supported by massed artillery and led by seemingly inexhaustible streams of "Stalin" and T-34 tanks, had unexpectedly attacked some 750,000 poorly armed Germans on a 400-mile front extending from the Baltic Sea right down the middle of Poland. At the extreme north Marshal Ivan Danilovich Chernyakhovsky's Third White Russian Front (Soviet equivalent of an army group) thrust toward historic Königsberg in East Prussia, near the Baltic. On his left the Second White Russian Front, led by the young, dynamic Marshal Konstantin Rokossovsky, drove for Danzig and was already approaching Tannenberg, the scene of one of Germany's greatest triumphs in World

War I. To Rokossovsky's left came the most talented of all Red Army commanders, Marshal G. K. Zhukov, whose First White Russian Front had conquered Warsaw in three days and was now encircling Posen; its ultimate goal was Berlin. Finally, at the extreme southern flank of this great offensive came the First Ukrainian Front of Marshal Ivan Konev, and it was one of his spearheads which was approaching the prison camp at Sagan.

Generaloberst (four-star general) Georg-Hans Reinhardt's Army Group North had been the main target of both Chernyakhovsky and Rokossovsky, and within two weeks his forces had been either overrun or by-passed. One of his armies, the Fourth, was already in full retreat. Its commander, General Friedrich Hossbach, well aware that Hitler expressly forbade such action, had started moving west on his own initiative. Rokossovsky had already knifed nearly 200 miles past him and Hossbach knew that if he didn't make a fighting retreat, his troops would be wiped out. More important, he felt it was his duty to open an escape corridor for the half million East Prussian civilians fleeing west in wagons and on foot.

His immediate superior, Reinhardt, had approved but Generaloberst Heinz Guderian, Army Chief of Staff and also commander of the entire eastern front, was furious when he learned that the bulk of East Prussia had been given up with scarcely a struggle—and without his consent. Born on the Vistula River in East Prussia, Guderian was raised to regard Russia as the deadliest enemy. Prussian to the core, he was determined to save his land from the Bolsheviks. Nevertheless, he stoutly defended both Hossbach and Reinhardt when Hitler summoned him to the Reich Chancellery and accused them of treason. "They deserve to be court-martialed," said the Führer. "They are to be dismissed immediately, along with their staffs."

"I'd be willing to offer my right arm as security for General Reinhardt," Guderian replied, and as for Hossbach, he went on, under no circumstances could he be considered a traitor.

Hitler ignored Guderian. He relieved Reinhardt at once and replaced him with a most unusual man who had recently told his beleaguered troops, "When things look blackest and you don't know what to do, beat your chest and say, 'I'm a National Socialist—that moves mountains!' " This was Generaloberst Lothar Rendulic, an Austrian and a talented military historian with a charming manner and a taste for gracious living. He was clever, subtle and knew how to handle Hitler; fortunately for the troops, he was also competent.

The commander of Army Group Center, on Dr. Rendulic's right, had previously been relieved by Hitler and then, too, Guderian had objected violently—particularly when the replacement was Generaloberst Ferdinand Schörner, one of Hitler's favorites.

Schörner was a robust, sanguine Bavarian who needed these qualities to cope with the chaotic situation he had inherited. His left wing was already shattered by Zhukov and the right was being rolled up by Konev. He began roaming the front and rear, changing commanders, reorganizing supply systems and generally shaking up whatever unit he visited. In the rear, where he routed men from desk jobs and gave them rifles, he was hated. At the front, where combat soldiers and the younger officers had never before seen an army group commander that far forward, he was esteemed. He threatened to shoot anyone on the spot who fled; he promised to bring the best food and clothing up front; he slapped backs in a comradely manner distasteful to officers of the old school; he insulted generals he felt needed insulting; and he passed out cookies and candy to privates.

He was to Hitler what Marshal Ney was to Napoleon, and by January 27, through his highly unorthodox methods, Army Group Center had been patched up into a front—shaky and jigsaw, but still a front that was holding back a tremendous tide of Russians. What he couldn't do, of course, was close up the dangerous hole that Zhukov—the Russian most feared by the Germans—had punched between him and Dr. Rendulic.

This was the problem that worried Guderian most of all and he had told Hitler that there was only one way to stop Zhukov's overwhelming armored attack: an emergency army group would have to be formed immediately and thrown into the gap between Schörner and Rendulic. Guderian wanted this force to be commanded by Generalfeldmarschall Maximilian von Weichs; he was a brilliant and daring officer. Hitler agreed to form the new army group but thought Weichs was too exhausted. "I doubt if he's still capable of performing such a task," he said, and suggested that the job go to Reichsführer Heinrich Himmler*—the second most powerful man in Germany.

Outraged, Guderian protested that Himmler had no military experi-

---

* Himmler's principal role was that of Reichsführer SS (national leader of the Black Shirts). The SS (Schutzstaffel) was originally organized by Hitler as an elite bodyguard of about 280 men sworn to absolute personal obedience to the Führer. Using this small group as a nucleus, Himmler had built the Black Shirts into a vast, efficient organization completely dedicated to the Führer. Its members were carefully chosen according to National Socialist eugenics, and recruitment was open not only to Germans but to Aryans of other nations.

The SS comprised a number of arms, each with different duties and characteristics:

1. Allgemeine (General) SS. Strictly civilian. Most diplomats, top-level state employees, industrialists, lawyers, doctors, etc., held high ranks in the Allgemeine SS.

2. RSHA (Reichssicherheitshauptamt, National Central Security Office). Civilian and paramilitary. Of its seven departments, the most important were: Bureau III, the SD (Sicherheitsdienst, Security Service inside Germany); Bureau IV, the Gestapo (State Security Police); Bureau V (Criminal Police); and Bureau VI (Foreign Intelligence). Reinhard Heydrich, head of the RSHA until his assassination in Czechoslovakia in 1941, had been succeeded by Dr. Ernst Kaltenbrunner after one year of interregnum.

3. Waffen-SS. Armed; strictly military. Some of its elite divisions were composed

ence. Hitler replied that the Reichsführer was a great organizer and administrator, whose name alone would inspire a fight to the end. Determined to prevent "such an idiocy being perpetrated on the unfortunate eastern front," Guderian continued to object with a dogged bluntness that shocked Feldmarschall Wilhelm Keitel, chief of OKW (Oberkommando der Wehrmacht, High Command of the Armed Forces), and derisively nicknamed Lakeitel—for *Lakei,* "lackey"—by fellow officers.

Hitler was just as adamant, contending that Himmler, as commander of the Replacement Army, was the only man capable of forming a major force overnight. He didn't say that Himmler was one of the few he could still trust implicitly.

Himmler accepted the job with the blind enthusiasm he showed to any proposal by the Führer and announced that he would halt the Russians at the Vistula River. Appropriately his new force was named Army Group Vistula. He started east in his special train. Fifty miles out of Berlin he crossed the Oder River, then continued almost to the Vistula at a point just south of Danzig. To stop Zhukov he had a few staff officers and one outdated situation map. Except for several scattered units, the rest of Army Group Vistula existed only on paper. As new divisions arrived, Himmler ill-advisedly began forming an east–west defense line running from the Vistula to the Oder, which merely served as protection for Pomerania to the north. In other words, he was carefully barricading the side door while leaving the front gate wide open.

Zhukov, who had no intention of being sidetracked, simply by-passed Himmler's lateral line and kept racing due west, impeded only by isolated groups, and on January 27 his advance units were 100 miles from Berlin. Ahead lay the Oder, the last major natural obstacle they would have to hurdle before reaching the Reich Chancellery.

## 3.

The Kriegies in camps east of Sagan were already being evacuated to the west and they were now trudging through the snow alongside civilian caravans. One group of Americans had been on the road a week; many had been captured in the Battle of the Bulge and since then had lost an average of thirty pounds apiece in the constant shift from camp to camp, and consequently were easy prey to pneumonia and

---

of volunteers from Belgium, France, Holland, Norway, Lithuania, Denmark, Sweden, Hungary, Rumania, etc., who had joined primarily to fight Bolshevism.

4. Totenkopfverbände (Death's Head units). Paramilitary. Concentration camp guards. At this time, most were elderly or wounded soldiers unable to fight in the front lines. In 1940 the youngest and healthiest were formed into an elite front-line unit, the Totenkopf Division, and thus became a part of the Waffen-SS.

dysentery. Fourteen hundred had left camp at Szubin, not far from the Vistula. By January 27 there were only 950.

It was so cold that when Lieutenant Colonel James Lockett's scarf momentarily blew from one ear, the exposed skin came off as if it had been burned. Late that afternoon the prisoners were led to a farm where they bunked down in drafty hay barns and pigsties. Too sick to continue, 118 were put on a freight train. The others built little fires and dried their shoes and socks. Amazingly, their morale was high and all were resolved to march to their goal—wherever that was.

After a watery meal of hot barley-and-potato soup, the men tried to sleep, daydreaming not of women but of food. Several had memorized a poem written by a former advertising copy writer, Lieutenant Larry Phelan. He had dedicated it to his wife, "the loveliest girl in the world—who won't like it a bit."

> I dream as only captive men can dream
> Of life as lived in days that went before;
> Of scrambled eggs, and shortcakes thick with cream,
> And onion soup and lobster Thermidor;
> Of roasted beef and chops and T-bone steaks,
> And turkey breast and golden leg or wing;
> Of sausage, maple syrup, buckwheat cakes,
> And chicken broiled or fried or à la king.
> I dwell on rolls or buns for days and days,
> Hot corn bread, biscuits, Philadelphia scrapple,
> Asparagus in cream or hollandaise,
> And deep-dish pies—mince, huckleberry, apple.
> I long for buttered creamy oyster stew,
> And now and then, my pet, I long for you.

Hundreds of thousands of German civilians, fleeing from their farms in Poland, traveled the same route in wagon trains. The young, old and sick rode in horse- or cattle-drawn vehicles while the hardy shuffled along by the side, potato sacks over their heads with holes cut for eyes. There were large farm wagons, dog carts, sleds—anything that could move on wheels or runners. Few vehicles were covered and passengers huddled together in wet hay or under soggy feather comforters, in a vain attempt to fight the biting wind and swirling snow.

The caravans crept slowly, battling through the rising drifts in an unbroken line, urged on, in many cases, by young slave laborers from farms. They were French, Polish and Ukrainian, and as eager to get away from the Russians as their masters. Moreover, many of them had been so well treated that they were now determined to bring "their" families to safety.

But these refugees were fortunate compared to the ones trying to escape from East Prussia, 250 miles farther east. Their Gauleiter (district

Party leader) Erich Koch, had declared that East Prussia would never fall into the hands of the Russians and had forbidden flight to the west; but once Chernyakhovsky smashed across the border, a few courageous district officials openly defied Koch and ordered their people to escape. They had left at a moment's notice and now struggled through knee-deep snow, poorly clad and hungry; their hope was to stay ahead of the onrushing Red Army.

One of these groups was entering the village of Nemmersdorf when Russian tanks abruptly appeared, bulldozing everything in their path. Dozens of carts were smashed, sideswiped, rolled over. Baggage spilled out, people were crushed. The tanks rolled ahead obliviously, but in a few minutes Dodge trucks appeared. Infantrymen jumped out and began pillaging and raping. At The White Mug restaurant four women were raped many times, dragged outside naked and nailed through the hands to a wagon. Not far away, at The Red Mug, another naked woman was nailed to a barn. When the Russians moved off, they left behind seventy-two dead civilians.

A few miles to the west, Russians were breaking into the village of Weitzdorf. A young woman, Lotte Keuch, watched in horror as her father-in-law and six male neighbors were shot. Next a dozen French slave laborers at the manor were rounded up and their rings taken away— by slicing off their fingers. Then the Frenchmen were lined up, executed. And the raping began.*

Similar scenes were re-enacted in a thousand villages all over the east that day as troops of the four Red Army fronts looted, raped and killed. The principal motive for this savagery was vengeance for over four years of systematic and unrelenting Nazi brutality; the ignominious peak had perhaps been attained at the concentration camp complex of Auschwitz in the southwest corner of Poland, which one of Marshal Konev's units had now reached. It was innocent-looking, not unattractive, with neat rows of solid brick barracks on tree-lined streets and a slogan in large letters over the front gate: WORK BRINGS FREEDOM. Once filled to capacity with more than 200,000 prisoners, there were only 5000 left when the Red Army troops arrived and these were so weak that they could barely cheer. The other survivors had long since been marched off or shipped to other camps in the west to prevent their liberation. For the past week SS guards had been burning storehouses of shoes, clothing and hair to hide traces of mass extermination. In the summer

* It has been estimated that 5,000,000 Germans were uprooted and driven west at the time of the gigantic Russian offensive. Details of the above and other events dealing with the treatment of German civilians by the Red Army come mainly from the files of the Bundesarchiv in Koblenz. However, no final figures have been released, since the Statistisches Bundesamt in Wiesbaden (the official bureau of statistics) has not been able to account for the fate of 1,390,000 refugees. Until such time as individual cases are solved, the rest of the missing must be presumed dead.

of 1941 Himmler had told the commandant of Auschwitz, Rudolf Hoess, "The Führer has ordered that the Jewish question be solved once and for all, and that we, the SS, implement that order." The biggest death camp was to be Auschwitz, since it was isolated from public view and yet had excellent rail and road facilities.

Hoess was so conscientious a member of the SS that he personally supervised as many executions as possible in the three large camps and thirty-nine subcamps of the forty-square-kilometer Auschwitz complex. He wanted to set a good example for his men and "escape the censure of expecting others to do what I myself avoided," and so was everywhere, ubiquitous and efficient, from the moment a trainload of Jews arrived at the railroad siding, to the burning of their bodies. Some 2000 men, women and children would be selected at the track, told they were going to the bathhouse, and herded naked into a gas chamber. Those guessing the truth and hanging back were beaten with sticks and chivvied by dogs.

Efforts to obliterate all traces of the murders had continued until the morning of January 27 with the final blasting of the gas chambers and five crematoria, but even this could not wipe out the grisly proof of what had gone on for the past four years. In spite of fires and detonations, the Red Army found tons of toothbrushes, eyeglasses, shoes and artificial limbs, and the mass graves of hundreds of thousands of human beings.*

4.

The first refugee caravans reached the outskirts of Berlin with stories of the brutal behavior of the Red Army, and a wave of terror swept through the city. Many citizens, however, still had faith in Goebbels' promise that wonder weapons would save Germany at the last moment. Fortunately for the Allies, the V-2 had not been ready for wide use until the previous fall, otherwise the Allied invasion of France, according to General Eisenhower, "might have been written off." But now V-2s, developed at the experimental rocket station in Peenemünde under the leadership of thirty-four-year-old Dr. Wernher von Braun, were causing havoc in London, Antwerp and Liège, and recently Braun had reviewed preliminary designs for a multi-stage rocket with a winged V-2 as upper stage. This stage, placed on top of a booster rocket, could put a satellite into orbit, or hit New York City—a more popular notion at that time.

* The Soviet government puts the figure at 4,000,000 but Gerald Reitlinger, in his study *The Final Solution* estimates that 600,000 were killed in the Auschwitz crematoria and 300,000 others died of disease and starvation or were shot. In an affidavit Rudolf Hoess testified that 2,500,000 prisoners had been murdered and another half million had died of starvation and disease; but later at his trial in Warsaw he amended the total figure to 1,135,000.

One of the men responsible for creating these *Wunderwaffen,* General-major (Brigadier General) Walter Dornberger, was holding a conference in Berlin. He had just been entrusted with the job of producing a missile that would unerringly destroy any plane attempting to attack Germany, and bring an end to Allied air superiority. The ten members of "Working Staff Dornberger," after reviewing the many experiments made in this field—from nonguided anti-aircraft rockets to remote-controlled missiles for launching from ground or air—concluded that their only chance for success was to concentrate on a few projects. They agreed to retain only four guided anti-aircraft rockets: Professor Wagner's "Butterfly"; a similar rocket capable of supersonic speed; Dr. Kramer's X-4, a missile to be fired from a plane; and the "Waterfall," the large radio-controlled rocket being developed at Peenemünde. The Dornberger group further agreed that all factories, technical institutes and development centers involved in production of these weapons would have to be moved inside Germany, as far from the battle areas as possible. Peenemünde, on the Baltic, for example, might be overrun by Zhukov within a few weeks.

A few blocks away, those scheduled to attend that afternoon's Führer conference were entering the Reich Chancellery, the military through one door, Party members through another. General Guderian and his aide, Baron Bernd Freytag von Loringhoven—a major—walked up the dozen steps to the heavy oak main door. Once inside, they took a long detour to the Führer's office; direct passage was closed off by damage from Allied bombs. They passed windows covered by cardboard, through corridors and rooms barren of pictures, carpets and tapestries, finally reaching an anteroom where guards stood poised with machine pistols. An SS officer asked them politely to hand over their side arms and carefully examined their briefcases. This had become regulation since Count Claus von Stauffenberg planted a time bomb near Hitler's chair just before the start of the Führer conference on July 20, 1944. When the bomb exploded, two conferees were killed but Hitler, amazingly, was only slightly wounded. From that day extreme security measures applied even to Guderian, Army Chief of Staff and commander of the eastern front.

By four o'clock the room was filled with military and political leaders, including Göring, Keitel and his able Chief of Operations, Generaloberst Alfred Jodl. A few minutes later the doors to the Führer's office were opened, revealing a spacious room sparingly decorated. At one end French windows were draped with gray curtains, and carpets covered most of the floor. In the middle of one wall was Hitler's massive desk; behind it was a black upholstered chair facing the garden. The high-ranking conferees seated themselves in heavy leather chairs while their aides and the lesser members either stood or found straight chairs. There were twenty-four men in the room.

At 4:20 P.M. Adolf Hitler shuffled in, shoulders stooped, left arm hanging loose. He greeted a few with a limp hand shake before slowly moving to his desk. An aide pushed forward his chair and he sank into it heavily. Those who saw Hitler only occasionally assumed that his almost useless left hand was a result of Stauffenberg's bomb, but it was the right arm that had been slightly injured by the explosion, and it had long since healed. Hitler had had a bad case of grippe in 1942, and the partially paralyzed left hand was the ultimate effect of injections he had been given by Dr. Theodor Morell, his seedy personal physician. The grippe disappeared all right, but his left eye began to tear and run occasionally. A few weeks later numbness appeared in his left leg; then it moved to the left hand. Hitler often told his private chauffeur, SS-Obersturmbannführer (Lieutenant Colonel) Erich Kempka, that the hand was just a nuisance, and had lately fallen into the habit of simply sticking it in his pocket.

Since the bombing Hitler had aged greatly,* not because of any lasting physical injuries but because of the bitter revelation that the plot had involved so many high-ranking officers. Though scores of suspected conspirators had already been executed in a ruthless purge and scores of others were awaiting trial, Hitler still felt uneasy, distrusting almost the entire officer corps. Conversely, he extravagantly rewarded those who had shown their loyalty on July 20. He made Major Otto Remer, for one, a general, and never ceased thanking Keitel in sentimental terms, simply for leading him out of the wreckage. His suspicions of the military only drew him closer to the so-called inner circle—his secretaries, servants, military adjutants and other members of the household. He listened patiently to their personal problems, advised and scolded them like a father. He was considerate of their comfort, treating them with dignity and politeness. "I'm the first and best democrat of the Reich," he often told Kempka.

The conference opened with Guderian reporting realistically on the growing disaster in the east. Hitler interrupted him to say that measures must be taken to evacuate all the prisoners of war at Sagan before the Russians could liberate them. As an adjutant left to carry out this order, Guderian continued his report. Hitler made remarkably few suggestions, but when the western front came up for discussion he showed a far

* Several months after the bombing Dr. Erwin Giesing—an eye, ear, nose and throat specialist who had been brought in to examine Hitler—discovered that Morell had been relieving the Führer's chronic pains the past two years with "Dr. Koester's Antigas Pills," which contained strychnine and belladonna. The pills were simply given in gross lots to Hitler's personal servant, Heinz Linge, who handed them out at the Führer's request. Giesing reported his findings to Dr. Karl Brandt, Hitler's principal surgeon, who warned him he was being slowly poisoned. Brandt was rewarded by being summarily discharged from his position. There is little doubt that heavy consumption of these pills contributed greatly to Hitler's deteriorating physical condition in 1945.

livelier interest. He listened patiently while Reichsmarschall Hermann Göring explained in language spiced with slang terms why Generaloberst Kurt Student should retain command of Army Group H in the Netherlands and Lower Rhine. Student's detractors, Göring said, couldn't see that the general's extremely slow speech was just a mannerism. "They think he's a fool but they don't know him like I do . . . I'd be happy to take him back because I know he can put the old spirit into his paratroopers." Then he imitated Student's drawl: "He says, 'The . . . Führer . . . told . . . me!' I know him and others don't. . . . The other day somebody asked if he was a dope. I said, 'No, he's no dope. He's always talked like that . . .' "

"He *has* done some extraordinary things," Hitler admitted.

"Well, I'll be happy to have him, because I know that when there is a crisis you'll get angry and call him back. I'm looking forward to that day."

"I'm not," Hitler retorted dryly.

Göring pursued the subject. "So maybe he'll get to speak even more slowly later on, that's possible, but he'll also retreat a lot more slowly."

"He reminds me of Fehrs, my new servant from Holstein," Hitler said. "When I tell him to do something it takes minutes for him to get it. He's dumb as an ox but he certainly works hard. It's just that he's so slow."

Talk shifted to another commander in the west, SS-Oberstgruppenführer (General) Paul Hausser.

"He looks like a fox . . . " mused Hitler.

"He's smart as a whip," Guderian interjected.

"Very quick on the trigger," said Keitel.

". . . with his crafty little eyes," Hitler continued, his thought unbroken. "But perhaps he's been affected by the serious wound he just received." (Part of Hausser's face had been shot away by a shell fragment.)

"No, it wasn't too bad," said SS-Brigadeführer (Brigadier General) Hermann Fegelein, Himmler's liaison officer at the Chancellery. He was a clownish ex-jockey, grown flabby in his quick rise in the Waffen-SS. This had come about through a good military record on the eastern front and his recent marriage to Gretl Braun, sister of Hitler's long-time mistress, Eva. "The Reichsführer [Himmler] wouldn't have suggested his [Hausser's] appointment unless he was entirely sure it would be all right—otherwise he would get the blame. The Reichsführer is very sensitive about such things."

"Aren't we all," said Hitler, not without humor.

"But the Reichsführer is always criticized," Fegelein persisted. Several of the younger officers tried to keep from smiling. Behind his back they called him Flegelein, after *Flegel,* "lout."

"Only if something goes wrong," Hitler muttered.

Not realizing that the Führer was getting annoyed, Fegelein continued his blundering defense. "Besides, Hausser thinks that a sixty-five-year-old soldier can do nothing better than die gallantly at the front."

"But I don't want that," Hitler said. "That's a poor kind of philosophy."

"That isn't quite true," Guderian objected. "Hausser is a man who enjoys life."

"Anyway, he takes all kinds of chances," Fegelein went on. "He walks right through artillery fire . . ."

"I'd surely take cover," Hitler said. Then he turned the conversation, as he frequently did, to World War I. "I had just one general who wouldn't take cover—and he couldn't hear very well." A few minutes later something else reminded him of the past. "Usually, in the First World War, in 1915 and 1916—we really had an ammunition allowance that would make your hair stand on end." He went on and on, reminiscing about his old regiment's artillery fire as if unwilling to return to the military catastrophes at hand. "Most of the time we were quite restricted, but when an attack was laid on we really pumped it out. I remember on May ninth, Major Parseval's battery fired almost five thousand rounds. They fired as hard as they could all day, and that means over a hundred rounds per gun."

Jodl tried to turn the subject to the quiet Italian front.

"I don't know . . . " Hitler muttered absently. Apparently he had been mulling over another subject, for he then said abruptly, "Don't you think that deep down the English really are unhappy about the Russian successes?"

"Certainly not," said Jodl, who felt Churchill was almost as aware of the danger of Bolshevism as they were.

"If this continues we'll get a telegram in a few days," Göring asserted. "They [the English] didn't expect us to defend ourselves step for step and hold them off in the west like lunatics while the Russians drove deeper and deeper into Germany until they got most of Germany." There was more than a touch of irony in his voice, for he, like Guderian, considered it ridiculous to fight so tenaciously in the west when the east was collapsing.

Ignoring the Reichsmarschall's sarcastic tone, Hitler told with rising enthusiasm how Foreign Minister Joachim von Ribbentrop had let a report fall into English hands revealing that the Russians were sending an army of 200,000 captured Germans "completely infected with Communism" into Germany. "That'll make them [the English] sit up and take notice!" he concluded.

"They declared war to keep us from going into the east," said Göring, "but not to have the east come to the Atlantic."

"That's apparent. It really doesn't make sense. English newspapers are already asking bitterly, 'What is the purpose of the war, anyway?' "

The conference went on, the talk flitting haphazardly from Jodl's report on the fighting in Yugoslavia to a dissertation by Hitler about a new Russian tank and the construction of a new shell to destroy it, until a sharp argument suddenly sprang up between Hitler and Göring about the status of those officers who were called out of retirement to active duty, at a reduced rank. They had always clashed on this point. Göring, the last commander of the famed Richthofen "Circus" in World War I, always saw things as an officer; Hitler, the former corporal, as an enlisted man. Moreover, Hitler had become even more distrustful of the entire army system since the attempt on his life. "This whole bureaucratic structure has got to be cleaned out at once," he said sharply, "because it's been so overstaffed that compared to civilian bureaucracy it's like a dinosaur compared to a rabbit."

Göring ignored this to argue heatedly that an officer should be put into a job he could fill, yet keep his former rank.

"But I can't use him in his old rank. If such a man were a colonel it would mean the murder of three thousand men to give him a regiment. He may not even be able to lead a squad now."

"In that case he can pull guard duty. I've given that choice to some of my generals . . . " Göring refused to back down and the two began bickering like schoolboys. When Hitler repeated that rank and job should be commensurate, the Reichsmarschall said, "Only a complete bastard would take a demotion. If he weren't one, he'd shoot himself."

Hitler tried to mollify him, promising not to lower a retired officer's pay even if he was drafted again as a sergeant, but Göring burst out, "*I'd* chuck the pay in their face and say, 'You are robbing me of my honor!' You know that until now this has been considered an officer's worst humiliation."

The "until now" was not lost on Hitler. "But that isn't really true," he said touchily. "That's merely how *you* people look at it."

The argument went on and on as Guderian shifted uneasily, impatient to get back to his General Staff headquarters at Zossen and the desperate problems from the eastern front that were piling up on his desk.

"We are in a state of emergency today," Hitler intoned. "And I must consider what it's like to be a company commander. The company commander is a lieutenant perfectly able to lead the company; over him is a colonel absolutely incapable of leading a company because he hasn't done it for twenty-five years. So this man leads a platoon, perhaps not even that—in a colonel's uniform. What kind of a mess will that lead to? Does the company commander salute the colonel?"

"It's a basic change that will overthrow and destroy everything that has existed until now," Göring insisted. "An idea inconceivable until now."

"In the rest of the world," Hitler replied, "it's that way already."

Guderian kept fidgeting as Keitel and General Wilhelm Burgdorf, head of Army Personnel, supported the Führer with involved arguments that —with three million vengeful Russians battering at the eastern borders of the Fatherland—approached the bizarre.

Finally Hitler began itemizing his arguments. "First, I cannot let these people go home. I can't draft partially unfit men almost fifty-six years old, while I discharge forty-five-year-old men who have always been soldiers. That's impossible. Second, I simply can't hand over units to people unfit to lead them."

Göring interrupted, "And third, *I* can't tell people once capable of leading units . . . that they won't get units again . . . "

The argument had swung full circle. "If they are competent," said Hitler, "they'll get them."

"They were once . . . "

"In that case they'll soon be able to again. All they'll have to do is learn it again. That's no disgrace. After all, didn't I have to learn to be Reich Chancellor? I was Party leader and my own boss, and yet, as Reich Chancellor I was subordinate to the Reich President. For a time I was even a government official in Brunswick." In 1932 a Nazi minister in Brunswick had appointed Hitler to a post in the state government so that he would automatically acquire German citizenship, but he didn't like to be reminded of it.

"But not on active service," said Göring, doing just that. There was an abrupt, embarrassed silence.

"How dare you say that!" Hitler bridled. "I did plenty for that part of the country." In spite of rumors that Göring had lost all standing with the Führer with the decline of the Luftwaffe, such an exchange indicated how close their relationship still was and underlined the fact that the Reichsmarschall remained the Führer's legal successor.

A messenger entered and handed Fegelein a report. The pudgy general got Hitler's attention. "Those ten thousand officers and noncommissioned officers—the Englishmen and Americans in Sagan—will be moving off in two hours in a convoy," he said, adding that another 1500 prisoners farther east had been told that they could wait in their camp, to be liberated by the Russians. "They declined," he said excitedly, "and offered to fight for us!"

Even the hard-headed Jodl caught some of Fegelein's excitement. "If we could get Englishmen and Americans to fight against the Russians," he said, "wouldn't that be something!"

But Hitler was skeptical. "Perhaps one of them said something like that and it was exaggerated. I'm very suspicious of the whole thing."

"Good," said Fegelein, as if the Führer had been enthusiastic. "If it's possible, maybe we can work something out!" Two of the younger officers nudged each other.

"But not merely because *one* prisoner made such a statement," Hitler said wearily.

The conference ended at 6:50 P.M., and Guderian and Freytag von Loringhoven started back to Zossen, twenty miles due south of Berlin. The general was disgusted. They had talked and talked for two and a half hours without reaching a single important decision on the critical eastern front.

One of the army group commanders on that front, Ferdinand Schörner, had just made a difficult decision and was trying to get Hitler on the phone. He had managed to patch up his own shattered northern flank, where Zhukov had driven through to the Oder, but then another crisis arose, this time on his southern flank, where the Seventeenth Army was being heavily attacked by Konev.

A hurried visit to the critical point convinced Schörner that the entire unit would be smashed to bits if it weren't pulled back immediately. Yet a withdrawal meant giving up the key industrial area of Upper Silesia which, except for the Ruhr, was the last great manufacturing and coal-producing region of the Reich. Hitler had already sent Schörner several telegrams forbidding him to abandon it under any circumstances. It would be lost no matter what he did, however, and Schörner ordered the commander of the Seventeenth Army to retreat. He told his chief of staff, Generalleutnant (Major General) Wolfdietrich von Xylander, to listen on an extension while he phoned Hitler.

"My Führer," Schörner began, coming to the point at once, "I've just ordered the evacuation of the Upper Silesia industrial area."

Xylander, who was jotting down their conversation, expected an explosion and a rescinding order, but not a sound came from Berlin.

"These troops have been fighting a heavy battle for two weeks and now they're finished," Schörner continued. "If we don't relieve them we're going to lose the whole Seventeenth Army, and the road to Bavaria will be wide open. We're moving back to the Oder and there we will stop."

There was a long pause and finally a tired voice said, "Yes, Schörner, if you think it's all right, I'll have to agree with you."

## 5.

At Sagan some of the prisoners were reading a pamphlet entreating them to fight against the Bolsheviks:

SOLDIERS OF THE BRITISH COMMONWEALTH!
SOLDIERS OF THE UNITED STATES OF AMERICA!

The great Bolshevik offensive has now crossed the frontiers of Germany. The men in the Moscow Kremlin believe the way is open for the conquest of the Western world. This will certainly be the decisive battle for us. But it will also be the decisive battle for England, for the United States and for the maintenance of Western civilisation. . . . Therefore we are now addressing you as white men to other white men. . . . WE ARE SURE THAT MANY OF YOU SEE WHAT THE CONSEQUENCES OF THE DESTRUCTION OF EUROPE—NOT JUST OF GERMANY BUT OF EUROPE—WILL MEAN TO YOUR OWN COUNTRY . . .

We think that our fight has also become your fight. . . . We invite you to join our ranks and the tens of thousands of volunteers from the communist crushed and conquered nations of eastern Europe, which have had to choose between submission under a[n] most brutal asiatic rule—or a national existence in the future under European ideas, many of which, of course are your own ideals. . . .

Please inform the convoy-officer of your decision and you will receive the privileges of our own men for we expect you to share their duty. This is something which surpasses all national boundaries. The world today is confronted by the fight of the east against the west. We ask you to think it over.

ARE YOU FOR THE CULTURE OF [the] WEST OR THE BARBARIC ASIATIC EAST?

MAKE YOUR DECISION NOW!

The Kriegies of Sagan reacted just as others farther east—and just as Hitler had suspected. No one volunteered, and those who carefully stowed the pamphlet in their packs merely wanted a souvenir or toilet paper.

That evening most of the prisoners of the five compounds were making last-minute preparations for the march, but at South Compound some 500 of them watched a lively performance of their Little Theater's production of *You Can't Take It With You*. The auditorium, designed and erected by the prisoners, had seats made from Canadian Red Cross boxes. All tickets were reserved and the admission was one brick of coal. Footlights and reflectors were constructed from large British biscuit tins, and there was even a catwalk above the wings for movable spotlights. Since the première the previous February, the men of South Compound had produced musical variety shows, one-act plays and Broadway shows such as *Front Page, Kiss and Tell* and *Room Service*. The women's parts were of course played—with no reluctance—by men.

Fires burning in four corner stoves took only some of the chill out of the auditorium, but the men were too absorbed by the Kaufman and Hart comedy to notice their discomfort. At seven-thirty the front door opened with a bang and Colonel C. G. "Rogo" Goodrich, the senior officer of the compound, clomped down the aisle in his hand-carved wooden shoes. He was a stocky American bomber pilot who had broken his back bailing out over Africa. There was immediate silence as soon as he climbed up on the stage.

"The goons have just come in and given us thirty minutes to be at the front gate," he said. "Get your stuff together and line up."

The men scrambled for the barracks. There was little talk as they put on clean underwear, socks and their best uniforms. Lucky ones with extra shoes took them out of storage. What food couldn't be carried was "bashed" in hasty gulps. The men helped one another into overcoats and packs; blankets were tied around the shoulders. Lieutenant Colonel Harold Decker strapped the secret compound radio onto his back; the earphones had already been sewn in his cap. Others were chipping at the hard ground or building fires if it was too frozen, to recover buried code books, maps and money.

Each block formed its own line. Men checked one another, tightening packs, then stood around in the wind, stamping their feet in unconscious rhythm, and waited—something they had got used to since entering the service. Those without face masks suffered from cold so intense that it made their heads ache. After thirty minutes—it seemed like hours—some 100 guards and a dozen yowling sentry dogs pulling fiercely at their leashes began to herd the prisoners out of South Compound. As they filed between West and North compounds, their fellow Kriegies shouted "Good-bye" and "Good luck." It was a little after ten o'clock when the long column of 2000 men was finally beyond the main gate and headed west through snow that whipped around them.

West Compound moved next and each overloaded man received an 11-lb. Red Cross parcel as he marched through the gate. Many kept only special items like chocolate and sardines, and the ditches were soon littered with food.

The men of Center Compound were told by their senior officer, Colonel Delmar Spivey, that General Vanaman would march at the head of their column, and he wanted them to carry out all German orders. "We will be safe if we stick together as a unit," Spivey said and warned the men not to attempt escape.

Because of the slow progress of those already on the road, it was almost four o'clock in the morning on January 28 by the time the last group finally passed through the main gate.

By now the men leading the eight-mile-long line were exhausted; they had been marching for seven hours. A violent wind had sprung up, and this, together with two-foot-high snow drifts, made every step an agony. Even so Lieutenant Colonel Albert Clark, an American fighter pilot shot down in 1942, still would not abandon two huge scrapbooks of stories clipped from German newspapers. Jokingly he had offered a case of Scotch to anyone who would carry the books. Lieutenant Colonel Willie Lanford took him seriously and was now dragging them over the snow on a makeshift sled. Half a dozen others, including Clark, were taking turns pulling, since the shrewd Lanford had made the sled big enough to carry all their packs.

Every few hours the column stopped while men huddled together on the road, legs outspread in toboggan style, each leaning on the man behind. No one spoke; there was little joking. Extra shoes, clothing, souvenirs—jealously hoarded for so long—were dumped on the road and packs rearranged. Some built fires from long-cherished letters and logbooks.

When the men resumed marching, the packs, in spite of the jettisoning, seemed heavier than ever. One man staggered and fell. He was picked up by two comrades who feared he'd be shot, and dragged along, minus pack and blankets. But exhausted prisoners were only loaded in wagons. For by now there was little difference between prisoners and guards, who were also throwing away their packs. One elderly German had been kind to the Kriegies and was now being practically carried by two Americans while a third toted his rifle.

By midmorning the vanguard stopped at a village eighteen miles from Sagan and was quartered in three barns. Those farther back kept marching, and more and more collapsed on the road, their clothes soaking wet from snow and sweat. Usually a comrade would stay behind and rub the exhausted man's wrists to keep him warm until the relief wagon arrived. If it was too full, someone in better condition would get out and give up his place.

The men from Center Compound reached the town of Halbau at three in the afternoon, unable to continue without rest. While they waited in the agonizing cold, a German sergeant looked for quarters. Finally a priest unlocked a Lutheran church seating 500, and then opened up the morgue, a few crypts and a small schoolhouse.

Fifteen hundred men crammed into the church until every inch of space was filled, from basement toilets to balcony. They were packed so tightly in the pews that they couldn't move; others slept under the pews, on the floor. Soon the church became uncomfortably warm from the body heat of so many men. This started a constant, clambering parade to tubs of melted snow placed near the doors. By dark there was even heavier traffic to the toilets, but progress over and around the massed humanity was so slow that sick men were vomiting over sleeping comrades before they reached the doors. The dysentery victims, in agony at the slow progress, shoved into the crowd desperately. In a few hours the smell was sickening and the struggle between those trying to sleep and those elbowing and clawing their way to the outside approached panic.

Suddenly someone shouted, "At ease!" It was Colonel Spivey, standing in his underwear near the pulpit. Next to him was a young Protestant minister, Chaplain Daniel.

"If I catch another man fighting," Spivey said when the uproar finally quieted, "he will stand outside in the snow the rest of the night. Let me tell you that being pushed, shoved, stepped on, even vomited on, is far from the worst that could happen. We're inside now, and three hours ago we were outside, freezing to death." He told them to help the sick and to be courteous to their neighbors. "If you can't sleep, sit there and dream of home. If you can't say something pleasant, keep your damn mouths shut. Good night."

The youthful chaplain came forward and softly said, "Did you ever think that perhaps God is testing our faith?" Then he prayed, asking protection for the sick and weary. "Give us the necessary strength to survive and go ever forward until we find freedom and liberation. Amen."

A calm came over the men, and most of them fell asleep.

Directly in the path of Zhukov's main drive toward Berlin was another group of marching Allied prisoners. They had left their camp at Schokken, Poland, eight days before and were now approaching the village of Wugarten, twenty miles west of the German border. It was an unusual group: 79 Americans and 200 Italians, including 30 elderly generals jailed after the capitulation of King Umberto. The leader of the prisoners was Colonel Hurley Fuller, commander of a regiment of the 28th Division. When he was captured in the Bulge, one of his sergeants had remarked, "The Krauts will sure be sorry they took Hurley." From the beginning Fuller had fulfilled this prophecy. On the first day's march to the east he had suddenly ordered a break as if he were still commanding his regiment, and then reclined in a snow bank. The bewildered guards learned, as had Fuller's superiors, that the forty-nine-year-old Texan was a stubborn man, and when he kept ignoring their threats they put him in charge of the march. Now, for the past week, Fuller had been sabotaging the trek back to the west; he wanted to be liberated by the Russians. As a result the prisoners were entering Wugarten when they should have been across the Oder.

Leutnant Paul Hegel, the German interpreter, found quarters for the prisoners in a schoolhouse and brought them food. He had spent almost five pleasant years in New York City studying to be a banker, so he was already pro-American. "You co-operate with us," Fuller had told him, "and we'll get you back to the U. S. somehow."

That night Hegel heard a reassuring report from Goebbels on the radio: The situation in the east was serious but there was no reason for panic; the Führer's wonder weapons would soon be perfected and the Russians would be easily driven back. But as soon as Hegel turned off the radio the rumble of artillery fire was distinct.

Early the next morning, January 29, Hauptmann (Captain) Matz, the chief guard, heard the not too distant jabbering of machine guns and decided that the only way to stay ahead of the Russians was to leave the prisoners behind. He went to the schoolhouse, woke Hegel, and started writing a note in German. Around seven o'clock he handed it to Fuller. It read: "These American officers had to be left behind because of a breakthrough of heavy Russian tanks and because of their inability to march further."

"When the Russians catch up to us, you bastard, I'm going to borrow a weapon and come after you and shoot you," Fuller snarled, pretending to be angry, but he was happy to be rid of Matz. What he really wanted was an interpreter. He went up to Hegel, who was hurriedly dressing, took away his Walther pistol and pay book and said, "You're staying with us." Then he made him get into a complete U. S. officer's uniform, including GI underwear and socks, and gave him a dog-tag number. "From now on you're an American—Lieutenant George Muhlbauer." Muhlbauer had recently escaped from the group. "Don't worry," Fuller told the dazed Hegel, "you've been decent to us. I'll get you through."

The colonel called the Americans together, told them to remain in the schoolhouse and warned them of the penalty for looting. News of Matz's departure traveled fast and in a few minutes the Bürgermeister of Wugarten arrived and was made solely responsible for all food and supplies. Next came two Polish enlisted soldiers offering the services of 185 Poles. Fuller accepted them; and a few minutes later he signed up seventeen French prisoners, including one who spoke Russian. He set up a command post for his growing army in the mayor's house and ordered all weapons in town turned over. Once armed, he prepared to defend Wugarten from all comers—Germans or Russians.

Three of Fuller's group were already fighting the Germans. Lieutenant Colonel Doyle Yardley and two other Americans had escaped from the march a week before. When they were subsequently overtaken by a Red Army tank unit, the commander threw his arms around Yardley, clapped him on the back and shouted, "*Amerikansky,* Roosevelt, Churchill, Stalin, Studebaker, Chevrolet very good!" He gave the Americans vodka, food and blankets, and insisted that they join his battalion to fight the Germans like good allies.

On January 29 the three Americans were not far from Wugarten, taking part in a Red Army tank attack. Suddenly three ME-109s dived on the armored column. The Americans instinctively leaped into a ditch, much to the amusement of the Russians, who stood nonchalantly in the road, shooting at the planes with rifles, submachine guns and even pistols. The column moved on without pause, leaving its dead in the road, and pushed into the village of Kreuz, where Russian infantrymen were clearing out the last pockets of resistance.

Yardley saw two Germans come out of a house to surrender. A Red Army officer calmly shot them with his pistol, and their bodies were dragged into the middle of the street. Then trucks and tanks began deliberately rolling over them. Yardley was shaken. This was not the same kind of war he had fought on the western front.

While Zhukov was driving west toward Berlin, Rokossovsky was swinging north toward the Baltic Sea and the historic port of Danzig. In front of his spearheads were hordes of German refugees from East Prussia. A man on horseback galloped up to a large caravan bound for Danzig and shouted, "The Russians will be here in half an hour!" Many of those on foot fled across the snow, but the wagons were jammed together on the highway and could only move slowly forward. All at once shells exploded in the nearby fields, and out of nowhere, it seemed, machine-gun bullets swept the road. Josefine Schleiter, a medical student, threw herself in the snow as bullets crackled overhead. Shells exploded with a deafening roar. She was sure her life was over.

Abruptly there was quiet and then just as abruptly great tanks came rolling from several directions. Behind them, plunging energetically through the snow, were Russian soldiers in white suits. One huge tank lunged down the road, plowing aside several wagons, crushing others like a giant steam roller. More tanks followed. Soon wounded horses lay all along the ditches, neighing in terror. People leaped from their wagons into the ditches and fled for their lives.

Josefine heard a young girl begging her father to shoot her. "Yes, Father, and me!" said a sixteen-year-old boy. "I don't have anything to live for." Tears were running down the father's face. "Just wait a little longer, children," he begged.

A Red Army officer rode up on a horse and listened impatiently to the pleas of several German soldiers who were brought up to him. Josefine saw the officer pull out his pistol and closed her eyes. She heard shots. When she opened her eyes the prisoners were lying on the ground, blood gushing onto the snow. Josefine wanted to go to them but was too terrified. Tanks were passing, loaded with big robust soldiers, laughing, waving their arms and calling out, "Hitler kaputt!" A few jumped off and shouted, *"Uri, uri!"*—their version of the German for "watches," *Uhren*. The refugees were stripped of watches, rings, fur gloves. More tanks rolled by, carrying women as well as men. They too looked robust and wore the same good uniforms, boots and fur hats.

Several Polish slave laborers were already making friends with the Russians. "Go back home," they reassured their former masters. "Russians are good people; nothing will happen to you."

By evening Colonel Fuller and his staff had organized Wugarten into a stronghold. In addition to the twenty-six rifles and two machine guns abandoned by Matz and his men, shotguns, rifles, pistols and even swords had been collected from the villagers. Fuller armed the Americans and the 185 Poles, posting guards at either end of the town. East of the village, foxholes were dug and the two machine guns emplaced. By nine o'clock several organized groups of Germans had been frightened off and thirty-six stragglers captured.

An hour later Fuller, Lieutenant Craig Campbell and Hegel, asleep on the second floor of the Bürgermeister's house, were wakened by gunfire. Fuller looked out the window and saw a dozen blacked-out tanks clatter by. They didn't look German; they had the high silhouettes of American Shermans. Before the three men could finish dressing, they heard pounding at the front door. Someone shouted.

"That's not German they're hollering," said Campbell.

"I think it's Russian," said Fuller. "Open the door."

Feet were already clattering on the stairs and Hegel began shouting, "*Amerikansky! Amerikansky!*"

The door swung open and several Russians charged at the three men, ramming submachine guns into their stomachs. Fuller kept pointing at the house next door; finally the Soviets understood and had Alex Bertin, the French prisoner who spoke Russian, brought in. When the Russian in charge, Captain Mayarchuk, was told that the three men were American officers, he laughed sarcastically. "How can Americans be on the eastern front, ahead of the Red Army?" he said and jabbed his gun deeper into Fuller's stomach.

So Bertin explained, and the Russian gave Fuller a bear hug, kissed him on the cheek and said the Americans could have anything they wanted. Fuller said he needed German ammunition and candles; he also wanted to get rid of his thirty-six prisoners. The captain said he'd take them, and tried to kiss Fuller again. Then he said that curfew for all German civilians had to be imposed immediately, and Fuller sent for the Bürgermeister. He was eager to co-operate, said he'd have the town crier make the rounds at once, and hurried outside.

There was a burst of fire and Fuller rushed out. The Bürgermeister was lying in the snow, fatally wounded in the head. Captain Mayarchuk laughed good-humoredly at Fuller's indignation. "We shoot all Bürgermeisters," he said.

The two allies proceeded to the town square, where the Russian tanks —lend-lease Shermans—were grouped around the church. The thirty-six German prisoners were brought out of a cellar, one so badly wounded that he was in a wheelbarrow. While Fuller was being hugged again by the captain he heard another burst of fire, and turned to see the man in the wheelbarrow slumped over, dead.

"This is against the Articles of War!" Fuller protested. "I'll report you to your commanding officer."

When Bertin translated this, Mayarchuk only grinned. "Tell the colonel that we won't shoot any more Nazis in town," he said. "From now on we'll take them out in the country and do it."

All over Wugarten, Russians were drinking vodka in celebration of the chance meeting with the Americans. But Fuller's indignation had made an impression on them. Though they caroused and broke furniture, it was probably the one conquered village on the entire eastern front where not a single woman was raped that night. Only in one house was there any violence. A group of Russians had found pictures of Hitler decorated for next day's celebration of the twelfth anniversary of his rise to power—and shot all ten members of the family.

# 2

# "Five Minutes Before Midnight"

## 1.

Just before five o'clock in the morning of January 30 a big Skymaster—a U. S. C-54 transport—touched down on the island of Malta. It carried Winston Churchill and other British dignitaries who were scheduled to attend "Cricket," code name for a four-day conference with American military and political leaders prior to a Big Three meeting at the Crimean resort of Yalta.

The Governor of Malta, the Commander in Chief of the Mediterranean, and many others, were gathered at the airport as Churchill's personal assistant, Commander C. R. Thompson, peered out of the plane's door; he was wearing a jacket over his pajamas. To his embarrassment he found himself bathed in the glare of floodlights. He was even more embarrassed to learn that the Governor of Malta had been waiting over an hour in the cold—the telegram announcing Churchill's arrival had been based on Greenwich Mean Time.

General George C. Marshall, the U. S. Army Chief of Staff, was also awake. An hour earlier a zealous British Army sergeant had delivered an envelope marked "Very Urgent." It was an engraved invitation to a dinner the next night at the Governor's, and requested an immediate answer.

At ten o'clock Marshall and other members of the U. S. Joint Chiefs of

Staff met at Montgomery House in Valletta, the capital of Malta, to decide what position to take at the first formal session of "Cricket." After some joking about the predawn invitations and considerable griping about the icy stone rooms, they began to discuss the most important military issue facing "Cricket": the final strategy on the western front.

There had been sharp differences between the Britons and Americans on the invasion of Germany ever since the breakthrough in Normandy a few days after Stauffenberg's bomb nearly killed Hitler. From his headquarters in France, Field-Marshal Bernard Montgomery, commander of 21 Army Group, argued for a single thrust into northern Germany through the Ruhr—under his leadership. All he needed, in addition to his own troops, was the American First Army. But American field commanders were just as insistent on launching a simultaneous attack of their own farther south, toward Frankfurt am Main. With the German armies retreating in disorder, both the U. S. and British field commanders had felt, with some justification, that they could gain total victory by the end of 1944—if given a free hand. But the Supreme Commander, General of the Army Dwight D. Eisenhower, was a military statesman rather than a field commander. He compromised: he directed Montgomery to make the main thrust in the north with top priority in supply, but he let Lieutenant General George S. Patton continue attacking in the south with the U. S. Third Army, on a reduced scale.

As a result the Allies pushed eastward on a wide front and reached the German border in September—only to be stopped for lack of supplies. So little happened all along that front for the next three months that Hitler was able to reorganize armies already badly beaten in France, into a stout defense line from Holland to Switzerland. The lull also gave him a chance to mount a tremendous surprise offensive of his own—the Battle of the Bulge. Catching the Americans off balance, the Germans smashed all the way to the Meuse River, and though Hitler's men had been pushed back to the German border, American military morale and prestige were nevertheless greatly impaired.

The argument begun by Montgomery's demand for a single thrust into Germany was aggravated during the Battle of the Bulge when Eisenhower abruptly turned over the northern sector of the Ardennes battleground to the field-marshal. Bradley was shocked to have half his forces taken away just when he felt he had the situation under control, and then angered when Montgomery, once the battle was won, told correspondents how he had "tidied up" the mess. Bradley felt Montgomery had exaggerated his own role and "exploited our distress in the Ardennes."

Only too aware of this unpleasantness, Eisenhower had drawn up his final plan to invade Germany. His lines were much as they had been the previous autumn, stretching along the German border from Holland to Switzerland. At the extreme north was Montgomery's 21 Army Group, comprising three armies: the Canadian First, the British Second and the U. S. Ninth. Then came Bradley's 12th Army Group: the U. S. First and Third armies. At the south was Lieutenant General Jacob L. Devers' 6th Army Group: the U. S. Seventh and French First armies.

Against this background the U. S. Chiefs of Staff were now listening to the Supreme Commander's strategy, presented by Eisenhower's chief of staff, Lieutenant General Walter Bedell "Beetle" Smith: Montgomery would lead his 21 Army Group in the main attack through the Ruhr; Bradley would make the secondary effort with the U. S. 12th Army Group to the south near Frankfurt am Main. Timing, said Smith, was the most important consideration, and the Allies should drive eastward vigorously while the Germans were being so heavily hit by the overwhelming Red Army attack.

At noon the Americans were joined by the British Chiefs of Staff. Together they formed the Combined Chiefs of Staff—and as such were responsible for running the war in the west. Field-Marshal Alan Brooke, Marshall's opposite number, took the chair. Outwardly charming, he reserved his acid wit for the diary he faithfully kept. He was confident that he knew far more about winning the war than Eisenhower but did his best to hide his doubts of the Supreme Commander's judgment. To close friends, however, it was no secret that he regarded Eisenhower as a man overly influenced by the last person he talked with. Brooke also had reservations about Marshall and would have liked it much better if MacArthur—to his mind, the greatest general in the war—had been the U. S. Army Chief of Staff.

He listened politely while Smith outlined Eisenhower's plan, all the time thinking that Bradley's so-called secondary thrust threatened to become almost as important as Montgomery's main attack. Finally he blandly remarked that the British didn't feel there was sufficient strength for two major operations and that it would be necessary to make a choice. Of the two, Montgomery's in the north appeared the most promising.

Smith, with an irascibility aggravated by ulcers, retorted that Eisenhower intended to give Montgomery every single unit he could logistically maintain—thirty-six divisions, with ten more in reserve—and added that "the southern advance is not intended to *compete* with the northern attack." This only quickened Brooke's suspicions. He said he welcomed the explanation but still felt that the Bradley attack might divert too much strength from the north and cause Montgomery to bog down. Marshall was getting visibly annoyed. Curbing his anger, he said—as so many American generals had said before him—that it was not safe to rely on a single pencil-line thrust on Berlin. He felt it was essential to have an alternate advance to turn to *if* Montgomery bogged down.

The British were now sure that the Americans were plotting a second major thrust, and began sharply criticizing Eisenhower's plan to bring up all his forces to the Rhine before making a single crossing. The acidulous Smith retorted that Eisenhower had never intended to sweep the entire area west of the Rhine of Germans before crossings were made. Major General Harold "Pink" Bull, Eisenhower's soft-spoken operations officer, confirmed this. Closing up to the Rhine, he said, wasn't intended if it meant a delay. But Brooke was still secretly convinced this would only be used as an excuse to substitute a general assault all along the river, rather than concentrate on Montgomery's attack. Any secondary operation involving George Patton was bound to become a major one, he thought, so he said politely, if firmly, that rather than approve the Eisenhower plan he would prefer that the Combined Chiefs of Staff simply take note of it at the present time.

Action was deferred. As soon as the meeting was over, Bedell Smith wired Eisenhower at Versailles:

. . . THE BRITISH CHIEFS OF STAFF WILL INSIST ON SOMETHING IN WRITING TO CLINCH THE FACT THAT THE MAIN EFFORT ON THE NORTH IS TO BE PUSHED AND THAT YOU ARE NOT TO DELAY OTHER OPERATIONS UNTIL YOU HAVE ELIMINATED EVERY GERMAN WEST OF THE RHINE. . . .

While this debate was going on, the political leaders of both nations were aboard ship. Churchill was on H.M.S. *Orion,* in Valletta's harbor, confined to bed with a high temperature. President Roosevelt was on the new U. S. cruiser *Quincy,* three days' sailing out of Malta. A single day at "Cricket," he felt, would be enough. For one thing, he didn't want to get into those prolonged debates with Churchill on his cherished scheme for a push through the Balkans to Vienna and Prague.

It was the President's sixty-third birthday and his only daughter, Mrs. Anna Boettiger, was giving him a party. All over the United States the birthday was being celebrated for the benefit of the March of Dimes, the President's favorite charity.

**2.**

January 30 was also a day of celebration in Germany. In 1933—the same year Roosevelt started his first term—President Paul von Hindenburg appointed Adolf Hitler Chancellor of Germany. Today, twelve years later, leading Party members on all fronts were supposed to tell their men of the bright prospects ahead and to assure them the war would yet be won. SS-Obergruppenführer (Lieutenant General) Karl Wolff, head of the SS and Police in Italy, had dutifully called together his key personnel. Formerly Himmler's adjutant, he was a big, energetic, rather simpleminded man who ardently believed in National Socialism and was so close to the Reichsführer that he signed personal letters to him "Wolff-chen."* But as Wolff looked at the words he was supposed to say—words like "ultimate victory"—they stuck in his throat. How could the war possibly be won, short of some miracle? Consequently, he improvised a speech containing not a single mention of brighter days to come.

Before he stopped talking, Wolff had made the most momentous decision of his life—he would see his chief, Himmler, and demand a direct answer to one question: Where are the astounding planes and wonder weapons that Hitler promised would win the war? And if Himmler couldn't answer the question, he would ask the Führer; and if again put off with evasions, he would insist upon an honorable peace. He had developed a great affection for the people of Italy. Why should they suffer a day longer; why should one more SS or Wehrmacht soldier die unnecessarily?

Wolff found out through a telephone call to Himmler's headquarters that the Reichsführer was far to the east commanding Army Group Vistula, but if absolutely necessary, an appointment might be made in the near future. Wolff said he would fly to Germany in a few days.

In the afternoon Martin Bormann—deputy leader of the Nazi Party and the man Hitler now most depended on—wrote another of his frequent sentimental letters to his "darling little Mommy," Frau Bormann, at their home near Berchtesgaden. He advised her to lay in a supply of dried vegetables "and, say, fifty pounds of honey"; he also told her of the atrocities in the east:

The Bolsheviks are ravaging everything. They regard rape as just a joke, and mass shootings—particularly in rural districts—as an everyday occurrence. You and the children must never fall into the hands of these wild beasts. But I hope very much that the danger will never arise, and that the Führer will succeed in

* One such letter was written in 1939, to be delivered by special messenger in case of his death:

My Reichsführer!

Since I do not know whether or not I shall be able to "check out" properly with you before I die, I am doing so in this manner.

I take this opportunity to thank you for the last time for all the friendship and spirit you have given me, and for all that you have meant to me. You personify, not only to me but to the entire Schutzstaffel, all that is good, beautiful and manly and all for which it seems worthwhile striving. All we are today we owe to you and the Führer.

Were I able to make a last wish, it would be that on my next sojourn upon this earth I might be permitted to start by your side again and fight for our Deutschland.

All my best wishes to you and the Schutzstaffel, and may our ideals be attained. Together with all the good spirits, I shall keep faithful watch over you from the lofty heights of Valhalla.

Heil Hitler!

         **Your faithful and very devoted**
         **"Wolffchen"**

parrying this blow, as he has parried the others before it. Among the two or three millions who have been driven from hearth and home there is, as you may imagine, the most unutterable misery. The children are starving and freeze to death, and all we can do is to harden our hearts and strive all the more fiercely to save the rest of our people, and to build up a new defensive line. We *must* succeed.

Your most devoted<br>M.

. . .

More than 30,000 of the people Bormann wrote about were trying to escape back to Germany by sea in four liners. Bound for a port near Hamburg, the convoy was just rounding the Hela Peninsula and leaving the Gulf of Danzig for the Baltic Sea. The biggest of these ships, the 25,000-ton *Wilhelm Gustloff,* had never before carried so many passengers—1500 young submarine trainees and some 8000 civilians—eight times the number on the *Lusitania*. No one knew exactly how many frantic refugees had boarded at Danzig. Though everyone was supposed to have a ticket and evacuation papers, hundreds had smuggled themselves aboard. Some men hid themselves in boxes or disguised themselves in dresses. Refugees had been known to go to even more shameful extremes to escape the Russians. Recently at Pillau, where only adults with a child were allowed to board a refugee ship, some mothers tossed their babies from the decks to relatives on the dock. The same baby might be used as a ticket half a dozen times. In the frenzy some babies fell into the water, others were snatched away by strangers.

As the *Wilhelm Gustloff* headed west into the choppy Baltic, a middle-aged refugee, Paul Uschdraweit, came on deck. He was one of the doughty district officials of East Prussia who had defied Gauleiter Koch and let his people evacuate their towns. He himself had barely escaped the Red Army advance with his chauffeur, Richard Fabian.

The rest of the convoy was skirting the coast of Pomerania to avoid Russian submarines, but the *Wilhelm Gustloff* drew too much water and was on its own, except for a lone mine sweeper. Uschdraweit looked for the other ships of the convoy but could only see the mine sweeper, a mile away. He was glad he'd had the foresight to check the ship for the best exit in case it sank. Just then the ship's captain announced over the loudspeaker that men with life belts must surrender them; there weren't enough for the women and children. No radios would be turned on, no flashlights used.

The Baltic was rough, and most of the women and children became violently seasick. Since it was forbidden to go to the rail, the stench soon became intolerable. The sick were brought amidships, where the pitch was less violent. Uschdraweit found an empty easy chair and settled down. In the past week he had slept little. As he dozed off he wondered if he would ever see his wife again, and if he did reach Germany safely, would he be punished for disobeying Gauleiter Koch's strict orders?

The ship steamed westward, twenty-five miles off the Pomeranian coast. A number of lights were still on, outlining the *Wilhelm Gustloff* sharply against the dark Baltic. At 9:10 P.M. Uschdraweit was wakened by a dull, heavy explosion. He was trying to remember where he was when he heard a second roar. Fabian, his driver, rushed past, ignoring his shouts. Then came a third explosion, and the lights which should have been extinguished hours earlier went out. Off the port side lurked a Russian submarine, waiting to put a fourth torpedo into the liner if necessary—or to sink any ship that came to the rescue.

Uschdraweit thought they had been bombed until he noticed the ship listing to port and realized that it had been torpedoed. He groped his way down a pitch-black passageway and somehow found his baggage; he took out a fur-lined hunting jacket, a ski cap, a pistol and a map case containing official documents. He unlocked a window and jumped to the lower promenade deck. Here it wasn't so dark and he could see a man swinging a chair against a plate-glass window. It wouldn't break. Uschdraweit found a door leading to the bow, ran forward and saw a mob stampeding toward the deck without life belts. At the jammed doorways men were clawing their way through hysterical groups of women and children, punching them, pushing them out of the way. The ship's officers were trying to halt the panic. A few drew pistols and made threatening gestures, but they couldn't bring themselves to fire and were brushed aside.

The ship listed 25 degrees to port. In the engine rooms, men were still at their posts while other crewmen were closing bulkheads, starting pumps. On the decks, crewmen struggled with the lifeboats on the port side but the davits were frozen stiff. Frantic passengers pushed past the crewmen and tumbled into the boats.

At the bow, Uschdraweit saw red rockets—distress signals—shooting into the sky and hoped that ships were hurrying to the rescue. Below him was a wild sight. Hundreds of passengers, shrieking hysterically, scrambled to the rising stern. He started up a staircase toward the remaining lifeboats. An iron girder fell in front of him; he jumped back, detouring around the bridge. The *Wilhelm Gustloff* lurched abruptly and he heard anguished screams. He turned around and saw women and children spilling out of an upturned lifeboat into the black sea.

Someone grabbed his arm. It was a woman he had talked to during the long wait at the pier. She was holding a baby, and two children clutched her skirt. "Help!" she cried. "You're a man, you must know what I should do!" He couldn't think of anything. All the boats were gone; then he remembered the pneumatic rafts. "Stay with me," he said. "I'll try to save you and the children on a raft."

"You're crazy! I can't take my children into the icy water." She glared at him indignantly. "You men just stand around helpless and don't know what to do!" Eyes wide with fright, she herded her children toward the afterdeck.

Her fear unhinged Uschdraweit. He looked down at the raging waves. It was bitter cold, below freezing. He heard several pistol shots above the screams, and spray from the waves drenched his face. Animal fear hit him: he didn't want to die; how could he leave his wife alone in such a world? At last he got hold of himself. "Die respectably," he thought. He remembered a naval officer ordering him not to smoke aboard ship—and he had jokingly replied, "I'll certainly be allowed to smoke if the ship sinks." He decided to smoke one cigarette before dying. After a few drags he threw it overboard; took a second one, threw it away nervously. The third cigarette he smoked to the end.

"How can you smoke at a time like this?" someone asked resentfully. It was a high-ranking officer of the O.T. (Organization Todt) and he wore an Iron Cross.

"You take a cigarette too. It'll all be over pretty soon, anyhow."

The man looked at him as if he were insane, said something and disappeared. A sailor at the rail tore off his uniform and jumped into the water. A tall figure shuffled toward Uschdraweit in the dim light. It was a submarine cadet with a pale face and wide eyes. He pointed to his thigh where a bone was sticking through his fatigue trousers and blood flowed down to the ice-covered deck.

"What's happened to you, son?" Uschdraweit wanted to know.

"I was down below . . . hit by a shell. Now I'm finished. Shit!" He moved away slowly, turned. "Down below . . . thousands are drowned like rats . . . and soon I'll go over the side."

Three vessels were coming to their rescue: two 600-ton destroyers—the *T-36* and the *Löwe*—and a barge. Just before ten o'clock Captain Hering of the *T-36* sighted the sinking ship. As he started to bring his destroyer closer, he saw the barge approach the *Wilhelm Gustloff,* but the swell was so great that the two vessels began grinding together. People jumped in panic from the upper decks of the liner to the pitching barge. Some landed safely; many fell into the water and were crushed between the vessels. Hering realized it would be senseless for him to come alongside too; the sides of his destroyer would be crumpled. He could only stand by and pick up survivors. He shut off his engines so sonar could more easily locate enemy submarines that he knew must be lurking below, waiting for more victims.

Unaware that rescue ships were standing by, Uschdraweit clung to the rail so he wouldn't slip on the canted deck. The bow of the *Wilhelm Gustloff* was almost in the water. He saw a naval lieutenant and called, "It's all over now." The lieutenant crawled closer; it was the officer who had ordered him not to smoke. "Come on, we'll save ourselves," he told

Uschdraweit. "Crawl to port and grab the raft we'll push down to you. Hurry, or it'll be too late."

Wind shrieking in his ears, Uschdraweit started cautiously down toward the bridge. He slipped on the icy deck and slammmed into the rail. "Hurry up!" he shouted. The lieutenant and three cadets had freed a raft and shoved it toward Uschdraweit. Frozen like a rock, it hit him in the shins and only his heavy boots saved him from broken bones. But he didn't even think of his pain.

Just as the five men picked up the raft, a large wave flung them against the window of the bridge. Uschdraweit saw people on the other side of the glass staring at him as from a fish bowl. It was like some weird dream. The next wave washed him into the sea. The abrupt, cold shock gave him a burst of energy and he swam strongly to the drifting raft. For some reason his terror had vanished. He and the other four men grabbed for the raft.

"Paddle, paddle, we're coming into the wake!" the lieutenant shouted. The five men held the raft with one arm and splashed frantically in the water with the other. By the time they had moved fifty yards, Uschdraweit's fur jacket and boots were dragging him down. He tried to climb into the raft but the lieutenant told them all to wait another fifty yards.

At last they clumsily clambered inside. For the first time Uschdraweit thought he might be saved. He looked back and saw the afterdeck of the big liner high above, like a leaning tower. He could hear hundreds of women and children screaming. The terrible sound almost drove him mad. It was the most awful part of this night of terror.

The bow dipped deeper; the big ship trembled. The bulkheads collapsed and water poured through the lower decks. As the *Wilhelm Gustloff* slowly rolled to one side, the screams became even shriller. Uschdraweit, his face wild, also screamed: "If everything doesn't end soon . . . " The lieutenant held him tightly by the shoulder.

The slow roll quickened and the *Wilhelm Gustloff,* siren screeching, flopped heavily on its side. The five men watched the shadow of the ship sink, lower, lower . . . till it disappeared.

"There's one still alive," the lieutenant cried out.

Uschdraweit saw an arm coming out of the sea and grabbed it. He pulled a young sailor into the raft. Now they were six, and they sat trembling in the freezing wind, staring silently into the sea. Dead bodies floated by in their life belts. The survivors were too depressed to talk. Every so often on the crest of a wave, they would see a lifeboat not far away—nothing else. It was the only sign of life around them.

In the raft Uschdraweit noticed that the water was slowly crawling up his legs, but said nothing.

"I believe we're sinking a little," the lieutenant said. When the next high wave brought them in sight of their neighbor—the lifeboat—he ordered everyone to paddle with their hands. The lieutenant asked to be taken aboard, but someone shouted that they were too full already. When the men in the raft continued paddling, the lifeboat was quickly rowed away.

Uschdraweit used a piece of wood as an oar until he realized that his hands were numb. He threw away the wood and used his hands again, and instantly, life seemed to flow back into them. The lieutenant kept nagging the four young sailors to keep moving; they grumbled but obeyed.

The *T-36* and the *Löwe* were drifting around in the darkness, engines still off, landing nets over the sides, hauling aboard survivors. All at once the sonar of the *T-36* picked up a submarine. Hering started the engines and moved out of the path of the marauder.

"Look, our destroyer!" someone in the raft shouted, and they all began to paddle frantically. Uschdraweit couldn't see a thing until a dim shadow appeared 100 yards away; then the beam of a searchlight suddenly swept around and hit them. The next thing he knew, a wave dashed the raft against the *T-36*. The lieutenant hung on to a rope thrown down from the destroyer while the four young sailors scrambled aboard. Uschdraweit urged the lieutenant to climb up, but he clung to the rope and said tersely, "Get moving. I'll be the last one." Somebody grabbed Uschdraweit's arm and he was yanked aboard the *T-36*. As he staggered up from the pitching deck he saw the raft drifting away, with the lieutenant still in it.

Uschdraweit was helped down below. Sailors stripped him, wrapped him in a blanket and laid him like a package in a hammock. His body trembled; the sudden warmth was more painful than the freezing. But all he could think of was the lieutenant in the raft—who had saved their lives.

Hering pulled more than 600 out of the Baltic. Some were already frozen to death; others were dying. Then a second submarine came onto the sonar screen and the *T-36* was forced to flee, zigzagging to avoid torpedoes. At this moment the Führer's voice boomed over the loudspeaker, extolling the great day twelve years before when he took over power; then the voice was abruptly chopped off. A sailor came in and told the roomful of shivering passengers not to be afraid "but we're going to drop some depth charges." He was interrupted by a thudding roar, and the ship shook from the repercussion. Then another roar, and another. The deadly duel went on and on. The submarine loosed another torpedo and once again Hering swung his ship out of danger.

Women and children whimpered; it was even worse than the sinking, for they had thought they would be safe. Next to Uschdraweit was a sixteen-year-old boy, tears running down his face. At the earlier announcement that only women and children could keep life belts, he had given his away. Then his mother had convinced him to take hers, since he could save her if he wore it. But in the panic they became separated. "If I hadn't taken the belt, Mother would still be alive," he kept telling Uschdraweit. "I can swim."

Only 950 were saved by the rescue ships. Over 8000 perished in the greatest of all sea disasters—more than five times the number lost on the *Titanic.*

At dawn, as the *T-36* headed for Kolberg, all male survivors were told to assemble on deck. Uschdraweit climbed up the ladder. There standing in front of him was his driver, Fabian. The two men, speechless, embraced each other.

It had been a night of terror in Wugarten too. A Russian liaison officer, Lieutenant Colonel Theodocius Irshko, had arrived in the village the previous noon with a good supply of food and wine for Fuller's men. Wugarten, he said, would become an assembly point for Allied stragglers, and he named the Texan commander of the town. After exhorting him to maintain local security, Irshko left—taking all the arms Fuller had collected. That night drunken groups of Russians drifted into town. They raped women of all ages and murdered sixteen. Without weapons, the Americans could not answer the piteous cries for help.

The Zhukov spearhead going past Wugarten bound for Berlin encountered almost no opposition. When it reached Landsberg, an important town ten miles farther west, there was a brief skirmish, but by midmorning of January 31 the fighting was over.

Katherina Textor, a middle-aged teacher, saw her first Russians—in white snowsuits—climbing over the fence toward her ten-family apartment house. A minute later they were banging at the doors. As usual they demanded, *"Uri, uri!"* but they were polite and wrote a note in Russian explaining that they had taken all the watches in the house. They only became angry when they found an old hunting rifle and a picture of Hitler. They shouted derisively, "Hitler, Hitler, where, comrade?" but still they molested no one. Katherina and her neighbors were beginning to think that stories of Russian brutality were only Goebbels' propaganda, when two young Red Army men burst in, looking for women. One shoved Katherina and two older women into the kitchen and offered them cigarettes while his friend dragged away a young girl named Lenchen and raped her. When Katherina complained to a Soviet officer, he only smiled indulgently and said, "You can't control amour, mother."

The Zhukov spearhead continued west and approached Küstrin, a city on the Oder only a fifty-two-mile drive to the Reich Chancellery via a paved highway. Just before noon American enlisted men from Stalag IIIC were hastily marched out of their camp, five abreast; 75-mm. shells began falling just in front of them and machine-gun bullets swept their ranks. The Americans saw three Sherman tanks heading toward them and guessed it was a Russian column. Technical Sergeant Charles Straughn, Staff Sergeant Herman Kerley and T/5 Lemoyne Moore hastily made white flags and started toward the tanks. But for some reason the Russians thought they were Hungarians and fired, killing Moore and wounding Kerley. By the time the Russians discovered that they were firing on allies, five Americans were wounded, another five dead.

At the mouth of the Oder, ninety-five air miles to the north, Dr. Wernher von Braun, the technical director of the Peenemünde rocket station, was holding a secret meeting with his chief assistants. Together they had developed the A-4, a rocket they regarded as the first step to space flight. But Hitler saw it as a long-range weapon and Goebbels had renamed it the V-2, Vengeance Weapon-2.

Braun explained to his assistants that he had called the meeting because of conflicting orders received that day—both from SS officials. SS-Obergruppenführer (Lieutenant General) Dr. Hans Kammler, named special commissioner of the project by Himmler, had sent a teletype directing that the rocketeers be moved to central Germany, while Himmler himself, as commander of Army Group Vistula, had dispatched a message ordering all of Braun's engineers to join the Volkssturm, the People's Army, so that they could help defend the area from the approaching Red Army.

"Germany has lost the war," Dr. von Braun continued, "but let us not forget that it was our team that first succeeded in reaching outer space . . . We have suffered many hardships because of our faith in the great peacetime future of the rocket. Now we have an obligation. Each of the conquering powers will want our knowledge. The question we must answer is: To what country shall we entrust our heritage?"

A suggestion that they stay and turn themselves over to the Russians was emphatically rejected; they finally voted unanimously to surrender to the U. S. Army. The first step was to obey Kammler's order and evacuate to the west. There was no time to lose; preparations for the move would take more than two weeks and they could already hear the faint rumble of Zhukov's artillery to the south.

In spite of the bad news from the eastern front, Hitler was not depressed. After the evening's meeting, some of the conferees stayed while Hitler talked informally of the political situation. The Führer occasionally held these off-the-record sessions in an effort to persuade his military leaders—particularly men like Guderian, who thought only in hard military terms—that modern war was also a question of economy, geopolitics and ideology.

Very few people were aware that Hitler had a photographic memory, and they were invariably impressed by his seemingly profound grasp and knowledge of complicated matters as he interspersed his talk with facts and figures which he had simply retained from cursory reading. The atmosphere was relaxed and Hitler spoke like a professor to a group of favorite students, first explaining why he had launched the Battle of the Bulge. He had come to realize, he said, that the war could no longer be won by military means alone. The solution was an honorable peace with the West so that he could throw all of Germany's power against the East. But to get this peace he had to be in a good bargaining position. Therefore he had attacked through the Ardennes with every division he could scrape together, in an attempt to reach Antwerp and thus drive a physical wedge between England and America. Churchill had always feared Bolshevism almost as much as he, and this military setback would be an excuse for the Prime Minister to insist that some sort of arrangement be made with Germany. He admitted that this gamble had failed militarily but an unexpected psychological victory had been won. Already the Americans and British were publicly wrangling bitterly over the conduct of the battle, and a split between the Allies was imminent.

Guderian kept looking impatiently at his watch, but the younger officers—like the six-foot-five Otto Günsche, the Führer's Waffen-SS adjutant —seemed mesmerized as Hitler explained why he had sent SS-Oberstgruppenführer (General) Josef "Sepp" Dietrich's Sixth Panzer Army from the Ardennes to Hungary in spite of Guderian's insistence that this powerful force be thrown against Zhukov or Konev. The reasons, he said, went far beyond the military. First, Dietrich was about to launch a surprise attack that would not only save their last oil resources in Hungary but would regain the oil of Rumania. Second, and more important, he was buying time. At any moment the West was bound to realize that Bolshevism was their real enemy and they would join Germany in the common crusade. Churchill knew as well as he that if the Red Army conquered Berlin, half of Europe would immediately become Communist and in a few years the other half would be gobbled up.

"I never did want to fight the West," he said with sudden bitterness. "They forced it on me." But Russia's program was becoming more and more obvious every day, he went on, and even Roosevelt must have had his eyes opened when Stalin recently recognized the Communist-backed Lublin government of Poland. "Time is our ally," he added. That was why he had decided to let Army Group Kurland stay in Latvia. Wasn't it obvious that when the British and Americans finally joined them, this would be an invaluable bridgehead for a joint attack on Leningrad, only

350 miles away? Wasn't it obvious that every *Festung* they hung on to in the east would eventually be a springboard in the German-American-British crusade to wipe out Jewish Bolshevism?

This joint attack, Hitler said with rising excitement, was close at hand. With a red pencil he dramatically underlined a Foreign Office report about domestic troubles in the United States and Great Britain. "See here, here and here!" he exclaimed. The people were opposing the present policies of Roosevelt and Churchill more and more every day, and would soon demand peace with Germany and war against the common enemy, Communist Russia. His voice rose in passion as he reminded his listeners that in 1918 the Fatherland had been stabbed in the back by the General Staff. But for their premature surrender, he said, Germany would have gained an honorable peace and there would have been no postwar chaos, no Communist attempts to seize the country, no depression.

"This time," he begged, "we must not give up at five minutes before midnight!"

# 3

# "This May Well Be a Fateful Conference"

## 1.

Hitler's prediction that there would be a widening rift between the British and Americans was not based on wishful thinking. As in 1944, the British wanted a single northern thrust into Germany while the Americans still called for a broad assault. Once again Eisenhower compromised: Montgomery was to have the star role, leading the main attack while Bradley launched a secondary drive to the south. And as before, compromise only made both sides unhappy.

At the second meeting of the Combined Chiefs at Malta, on January 31, Bedell Smith read a telegram from Eisenhower assuring them that he still planned to let Montgomery cross the Rhine in the north "with maximum strength and complete determination" before waiting for Bradley and Devers to close up to the river, but added that this could be done only when "the situation in the south allows me to collect necessary forces without incurring unreasonable risks."

Brooke was frustrated. To him the message was just another attempt to please both sides, only confusing an already confused situation, and convinced him more than ever that Eisenhower was a "second-rate player." That night he wrote in his diary, "So we were again stuck!"

It would be interesting to know Marshall's views on the day's proceedings but he kept no diary; in fact, he rarely even discussed such problems with his staff. Once he told Major General John E. Hull, the relatively youthful head of the Operations Division and one of those closest to the Chief of Staff, that he would never write a book, since he could not bring himself to speak frankly about some people.

Marshall's one great disappointment was not being chosen Supreme Commander in Europe. Churchill had wanted him, but Roosevelt—on advice from Leahy, King and Arnold—decided that he was needed more at the Pentagon. Marshall, in turn, recommended a distinguished aviator, his former operations officer, Lieutenant General Frank M. Andrews. But he was killed in an airplane accident in Iceland, and Marshall's second choice was Dwight D. Eisenhower, a relatively unknown brigadier general at the time of Pearl Harbor. Some said Eisenhower merely echoed Marshall. Close associates like Hull, however, claimed that if the two had assumed a father-son relationship, Marshall was certainly never authoritarian, and anyone privy to the frequent messages between them could have confirmed this. Eisenhower and his staff *were* making the decisions, with Marshall approving almost every time; and even in disagreement the Chief of Staff seemed to question rather than criticize.

Though Marshall looked as imperturbable as ever at the Malta meetings, he was only concealing a mounting irritation with the British lack of trust in Eisenhower. This, he feared, could be an opening for their reiterated request to give Eisenhower a deputy who would command all ground operations. The British had long contended that such an appointment would give him more time to perform his chief role as Supreme Commander. Marshall always opposed the idea and only a few days before had told Eisenhower, "As long as I'm Chief of Staff I'll never let them saddle you with the burden of an overall ground commander."

Brooke was getting ready for bed that night when Bedell Smith stopped by for a chat. After a few minutes of casual talk Brooke said he wondered if Eisenhower was "strong enough" to be Supreme Commander. This prompted Smith to suggest that they speak candidly—man to man, off the record. Brooke had of course made the overture and he now bluntly voiced his grave doubts about Eisenhower because he paid too much attention to the wishes of his field commanders. Smith replied that Eisenhower presided over a group of highly individualistic generals and that men like Monty, Patton and Bradley could only be managed with a combination of diplomacy and severity.

This didn't impress Brooke in the least and he said that Eisenhower had too often in the past been deflected from his objective by the opinions of others. Granted that he was peculiarly qualified as a co-ordinator of Allied differences, his sympathy to all points of view made him dangerously susceptible to the opinions of the last man he spoke with. Smith retorted sharply that they had better put the whole matter of Eisenhower's competency before the Combined Chiefs. Brooke quickly backed down and admitted that Eisenhower had many excellent qualities. Hadn't Brooke originally approved his appointment as Supreme Commander? What he hoped, he said, was that Smith personally realized how necessary it was to concentrate in the north and not permit Bradley to turn a "secondary" thrust toward Frankfurt into a major operation.

The two men parted reassured. Brooke was confident that Smith, who drafted and executed Eisenhower's plans, agreed with Brooke's own policies. Smith was sure Brooke felt Eisenhower was more qualified than any other man to be Supreme Commander. Both were mistaken.

2.

At the large formal dinner at Government House earlier that evening Edward Stettinius, Jr.—the recent replacement for the ailing Cordell Hull and at forty-four the second youngest Secretary of State in United States history—had been talking with Churchill. More exactly, he had been subjected to a violent verbal attack. In the scorching language the Prime Minister so often used—and which recording secretaries so assiduously censored from history—he wanted to know what in hell Stettinius thought he was doing by publicly assailing Churchill's recent stand on Italy. Harry Hopkins, Roosevelt's chief adviser, had already warned Stettinius that Churchill "would beat us all up" over the matter. Even so, the new Secretary of State was hardly prepared for the violence of the Prime Minister's attack. Stettinius was imposing to look at, with his shock of snow-white hair and heavy dark eyebrows, and he had been a capable chairman of the board for the U. S. Steel Corporation, at $100,000 a year. While attending the University of Virginia, he had taught Sunday school and in his spare time read the Bible to congregations of mountain people. He didn't smoke, drink or engage in athletics—and had still been popular enough to be elected president of his class. He was sincere, earnest and had no political ambitions, only a desire to serve his country—which he did for $1 a year. But this hardly qualified him for the job as Secretary of State. Thrust into complex international issues with little preparation, he was poorly equipped to deal with professionals like Churchill, Eden, Stalin and Molotov.

At the State Department he almost always deferred to the opinions of his advisers. Once when an outgoing document was presented to him for approval and signature, his only comments had to do with the width of the margins. But if some of the paid professionals made fun of him, regarding him as a pedestrian, hard worker with not much insight, he was universally liked for his modesty and good nature. Perhaps it was these very qualities that made him Roosevelt's choice. Because of Hull's illness, the President had been his own Secretary of State for some time, and rather than choose someone forceful like James Byrnes, perhaps he had wanted a personable man to carry out his wishes without argument. This might explain why Roosevelt had instructed his faithful and astute right hand, Harry Hopkins, to accompany Stettinius to Malta and closely oversee his actions. Enemies of the Administration already were charging that Stettinius was merely Hopkins' "front man" and referred to him disparagingly as "The White-Haired Boy."

Churchill also attacked Stettinius as if he had been personally responsible for the flood of American criticism heaped on the Prime Minister for ordering British troops in Athens to fight Communist partisans, who had recently been battling the Nazis. If the British hadn't had troops in Greece, said Churchill, the Greek Communists would simply have taken over the government.

The next morning, February 1, started more peacefully for Stettinius. He and Anthony Eden, the British Foreign Secretary, left the British light cruiser H.M.S. *Orion* for a stroll down the pier and for a friendly discussion of the problems that would come up at Yalta. Unlike his uncle by marriage, Eden was an even-tempered and pleasant host. Not that he too didn't have his emotional moments. Though the general public imagined that he was a passive, mild-mannered, even suave gentleman, he was indeed capable of outbursts of temper. The lamb who suddenly roars like a lion can be most disconcerting.

Later that morning Eden, Stettinius and their assistants met on the *Sirius,* where the Americans were quartered, to review the stand they would take at Yalta. Eden felt that the Americans gave too much weight to the proposed world organization and too little to Poland, and that there would not be a United Nations "worth much" unless the Soviets could be "persuaded or compelled to treat Poland with some decency."

Although the Polish problem had its genesis in the distant past, the present crisis could be traced to August 23, 1939, when, to the consternation of most of the world, Russia and Germany signed the Moscow Pact. Ribbentrop and Molotov agreed to divide Poland in exchange for Russian nonintervention, and on September 1, German tanks were rolling toward Warsaw. Two days later Britain and France declared war on Hitler's Germany, and World War II had begun.

To Poland, the entry of their allies into the war meant no more than moral support. Within three weeks the entire country was occupied by Germany and Russia, and hundreds of thousands of Poles were thrown into Nazi or Soviet concentration camps. The Polish government, however, after fleeing to England by way of Rumania and France, was recognized as the legal government-in-exile by the Western democracies.

On June 22, 1941, Hitler again startled the world by turning on his ally and invading the Soviet Union. A few weeks later Roosevelt and Churchill revealed to the world the terms of their Atlantic Charter. It brought new hope to Poles of all political persuasions—here at last was the basis for a truly free Poland. And when Russia later agreed to the Charter's principles, promising to "seek no aggrandizement, territorial or other," Polish optimism seemed to have a realistic basis. But once the tide of battle turned and the Red Army began fighting Germany on equal terms, Stalin insisted that the Russian-Polish border be pushed east to the demarcation line, proposed at the Paris Peace Conference of 1919 by Lord Curzon. This meant that Russia would retain almost all the territory the Red Army had seized in 1939. The Poles were incensed, but their arguments failed to impress Churchill. He, like Stalin, believed that the dramatic change in the military situation naturally changed politics. So did Roosevelt, and at Teheran in 1943 these two had secretly promised Stalin that they would accept the Curzon Line.

The Polish Premier, Stanislaw Mikolajczyk, of course didn't know about this agreement and came to America to get Roosevelt's personal assurances that he would stand up for Poland's rights. When the two met on June 6, 1944, D-Day, Roosevelt said nothing about the Curzon Line, only promised that Poland would be free and independent.

"What about Stalin?" asked Mikolajczyk.

"Stalin is a realist," said the President, lighting a cigarette. "And we mustn't forget when we judge Russian actions that the Soviet regime has had only a few years of experience in international relations. But of one thing I'm certain: Stalin is not an imperialist." He went on to say that the Poles must come to an understanding with Stalin. "On your own, you have no chance to beat Russia, and let me tell you now, the British and Americans have no intention of fighting Russia." Noticing Mikolajczyk's obvious concern, he added, "But don't worry, Stalin doesn't intend to take freedom from Poland. He wouldn't dare do that because he knows that the United States government stands solidly behind you. I will see to it that Poland does not come out of this war injured." The President urged Mikolajczyk to see Stalin at once and strive for an understanding. "When a thing becomes unavoidable," he said, "one should adapt oneself to it."

Mikolajczyk, the leader of the powerful Peasant Party, was not insisting, like so many Poles, that not a single concession be made to the Russians, and he agreed to fly to Moscow. En route, however, he almost turned back in anger upon learning that Stalin had arbitrarily given Polish territory liberated by the Red Army to the newly formed Lublin Polish Committee of National Liberation, whose leaders were either Polish Communists or sympathizers.

His arrival in Russia on July 30 could scarcely have come at a more dramatic moment. The Kosciusko radio station in Moscow had just broadcast an appeal to the people of Warsaw to help the rapidly approaching Red Army "by direct active struggle in the streets." When Polish underground leaders heard the final stirring exhortation of this broadcast, "Poles, the time of liberation is at hand! Poles, to arms. There is not a moment to lose!" they put into effect Operation "Tempest," a general revolt against the Nazis, and the commander in chief of the underground Home Army, General Bor (his real name was Tadeusz Komorowski), ordered hostilities to start on August 1. On that date some 35,000 ill-armed Poles of all ages attacked the German garrison in Warsaw. SS and Police units—including convicts on probation and renegade Russian prisoners who hated the Poles—were rushed to the city and, under SS-Gruppenführer (Major General) Erich von dem Bach-Zelewski, opened a brutal campaign designed to raze Warsaw completely as well as crush the uprising.

The Poles fought on, confident that Red Army troops just across the Vistula River would soon liberate Warsaw. But several days passed and these Russians didn't even fire at German planes which dived on the Home Army's positions and were well within their range.

Four days after his arrival Mikolajczyk at last talked with Stalin, who grudgingly agreed to a few concessions if the Poles in London could reach an understanding with the Poles in Lublin. Consequently, Mikolajczyk had several talks with the Lublin Poles, who offered to make him Prime Minister of a coalition government but insisted that Boleslaw Bierut, an avowed Communist, be President and that fourteen of the seventeen cabinet posts go to other Communists or their sympathizers. All this time Mikolajczyk was desperately trying to get military help for Warsaw. On one occasion Stalin told him that the Red Army could not cross the Vistula because of an attack by four new German tank divisions, and then remarked that he had heard there wasn't any fighting going on inside Warsaw, anyway.

In Britain and America, public opinion was so aroused by the plight of the Poles that Roosevelt approved a proposal to send American planes to Warsaw; after dropping supplies to the Home Army, they would continue on to Russian territory to refuel. But the Soviets even turned down this plan and claimed that the Warsaw uprising was a "purely adventuristic affair in which the Soviet government cannot lend a hand."

"If the position of the Soviet government is reflected . . ." Ambassador W. Averell Harriman wrote Washington, "its refusal is based on ruthless political considerations—not on denial that the resistance exists nor on operational difficulties." In spite of rebuffs, Roosevelt and Churchill kept pleading for help to Warsaw. But Stalin stood firm, wiring both of them:

. . . SOONER OR LATER THE TRUTH ABOUT THE HANDFUL OF POWER-SEEKING CRIMINALS WHO LAUNCHED THE WARSAW ADVENTURE WILL OUT. THOSE ELEMENTS, PLAYING ON THE CREDULITY OF THE IN-HABITANTS OF WARSAW, EXPOSED PRACTICALLY UNARMED PEOPLE TO GERMAN GUNS, ARMOUR AND AIRCRAFT. . . . NEVERTHELESS, THE SOVIET TROOPS, WHO OF LATE HAVE HAD TO FACE RENEWED GER-MAN COUNTER-ATTACKS, ARE DOING ALL THEY CAN TO REPULSE THE HITLERITE SALLIES AND GO OVER TO A NEW LARGE-SCALE OFFENSIVE NEAR WARSAW. I CAN ASSURE YOU THAT THE RED ARMY WILL STINT NO EFFORT TO CRUSH THE GERMANS AT WARSAW AND LIBERATE IT FOR THE POLES. THAT WILL BE THE BEST, REALLY EFFECTIVE, HELP TO THE ANTI-NAZI POLES.

If the Red Army was truly unable to liberate Warsaw—and this was very doubtful—Stalin's clumsy attempt to turn the uprising into an "adventuristic affair" indicated that he wanted the Germans to destroy the Home Army completely. With such Poles eliminated, it would be far easier for the Communist-controlled Lublin government to take over postwar Poland.

When General Bor finally surrendered on October 2, 1944, after sixty-three days of gallant resistance, some 15,000 of his army were dead, 200,000 other Poles died with them and Warsaw was in ruins. A week later Churchill arrived in Moscow to try and find satisfactory solutions to the new problems being raised by Soviet expansion in eastern and south-eastern Europe. Since the London Poles were still bitterly denouncing Stalin's betrayal of Warsaw, Churchill feared they might upset the working relations of the Big Three. He telegraphed Mikolajczyk, who had flown back to London in disgust, and insisted that he fly right back with a delegation to continue discussions with the Lublin Poles.

Though reluctant, Mikolajczyk and a group of London Poles arrived in Moscow a few days later, only to receive another shock. At a meeting on October 14 Molotov revealed that Roosevelt had agreed at Teheran to the Curzon Line frontier. Mikolajczyk turned in disbelief to Churchill and Harriman for denial. Their embarrassed silence was eloquent and the London Poles did what they were so good at—protested violently. Churchill just as violently replied that their pigheadedness would "wreck the peace of Europe," and spark a war with Russia which would take 25,000,000 lives. "What are you fighting for?" he shouted. "The right to be crushed?"

Mikolajczyk indignantly asked permission to parachute into Poland so he could join the underground. "I prefer to die fighting for the independence of my country than to be hanged later by the Russians in full view of your British ambassador!"

In spite of this outburst, Mikolajczyk soon realized that a compromise must be made, and upon his return to London, urged the government-in-exile to make a new agreement with Moscow. Predictably, they refused to budge from the Atlantic Charter, and predictably, Churchill then told Mikolajczyk, "If you had followed our counsel in January and accepted the Curzon Line, you would not have had those horrible Poles in Lublin today!" After Churchill threatened to "wash his hands" of the London Poles because of their stubbornness, Mikolajczyk was stung to ask, "Why is Poland, alone among the United Nations, to bear territorial sacrifices, and so soon?"

"All right, then," Churchill answered sarcastically, "let the Lublin Poles continue to hold the leadership of Polish affairs in their hands, since you don't want to take it away from them. Quisling Poles, dirty, filthy brutes will be at the head of your country!" The only way the London Poles could control postwar Poland, he said, was to compromise at once on the Curzon Line. If so, they would have the backing of England and America. "Unless you give me an answer by today or tomorrow, I shall consider everything finished. There is indeed no Polish government if it is unable to decide anything."

"I cannot persuade my colleagues of the necessity to accept the heavy conditions made without proper guarantees," Mikolajczyk replied.

"I've had enough of this!" Churchill shouted. "You are all able to bargain about one thing only—the Curzon Line . . ."

"Enormous and extremely difficult things are demanded of us," Mikolajczyk pointed out. "After all, this concerns the transfer of five to six million Poles into the sphere of the new regions of Poland, as well as the removal from them of seven million Germans."

"What did you return to London for?" Churchill stamped his feet like a furious little boy, made a few more threats, and then abruptly asked, "Are you prepared to leave tomorrow evening for Moscow?"

"No, I couldn't do it."

"And the day after tomorrow?"

Mikolajczyk thought that it might take longer to get approval from the government-in-exile for a new compromise.

All restraint gone, Churchill flailed his arms wildly and yelled, "If your attitude is negative, then have the courage to say so! I shall not hesitate to stand up against you. You have fruitlessly wasted two whole weeks in continuous debates without any results! Where does this lead? Today I'm telling you for the last time. After tonight I shall not speak to you any more!"

When Mikolajczyk reported all this to his Cabinet, they, as he knew they would, indignantly refused to be rushed. Beset on both sides, Mikolajczyk handed in his resignation.

•  •  •

It was against this background of contention, suspicion and intrigue that Stettinius and Eden discussed the Polish question aboard the *Sirius* on the morning of February 1. Stettinius felt that recognition of the Communist-controlled Lublin National Liberation Committee as the government of Poland would be greatly resented in the United States and Eden concurred: the British could not recognize Lublin, either. To him, the only remedy was the creation of "a new interim government in Poland, pledged to hold free elections as soon as conditions permit." After the meeting Eden wrote in his diary that there had been "complete agreement on all major points" and he had done his best "to urge upon Ed that it was their [the Americans'] turn to take up the burden on this issue. We would back them to the full but a change of bowling was needed, and we would both have to do all we could."

The harmony among the diplomats was followed by renewed friction among the military when the Combined Chiefs met in the afternoon and again discussed the campaign on the western front. Marshall requested a closed session so that they could talk more frankly. With recording secretaries out of the room, Marshall urged that Eisenhower's plan of attack be accepted without further fuss. Brooke flatly refused and merely agreed to "take note" of it.

It was one of the rare times Marshall lost his temper. With a vehemence that startled the conferees, he expressed his blunt opinion of Montgomery, whom he assumed to be behind the British objections, and then declared that if the Eisenhower plan was not accepted, he would recommend to Eisenhower that he resign as Supreme Commander; no other course was possible.

This meeting to prepare the way for Yalta had itself created a crisis.

A few hours later Stettinius and Hopkins were dining on the *Orion* with Churchill and Eden. Churchill expressed concern for suffering humanity; contemplating the world, he could see only sorrow and bloodshed and he concluded that postwar peace and stability depended on the close harmony of Britain and America.

This was not just an isolated instance of pessimism. Three weeks earlier he had telegraphed Roosevelt:

. . . THIS MAY WELL BE A FATEFUL CONFERENCE, COMING AT A MOMENT WHEN THE GREAT ALLIES ARE SO DIVIDED AND THE SHADOW OF WAR LENGTHENS OUT BEFORE US. AT THE PRESENT TIME I THINK THE END OF THIS WAR MAY WELL PROVE TO BE MORE DISAPPOINT-ING THAN WAS THE LAST.

And since that message, not only the Big Three but the Western partners had become even more divided, and unless Britain and America could resolve their differences the next day, hopes of achieving any lasting success at Yalta would be negligible.

### 3.

Difficult as it was at times for the Americans and British to understand one another, they at least had a common heritage, a common legal philosophy and a common belief in democracy. Just as important, they had a common language and a common standard of human behavior. Between them and the Russians, however, lay a vast chasm, not alone in politics but in culture, personality and, most important, human behavior—treatment, for example, of enemy civilians.

Until the morning of February 1 the people of Kurzig, a German border settlement not far from Colonel Fuller's village, had yet to see a Russian, since this was not on the main road to Küstrin or Frankfurt an der Oder. There was no electricity in Kurzig and therefore no radio broadcasts, otherwise the people would have known that Zhukov's spearheads were already west of them. But they could hear the rumble of guns and wondered what they should do. Friedrich Paetzold, a police official, was in the Town Hall with his cousin Otto, the mayor, hastily burning all Nazi Party papers. At noon the two men went home to eat, but Paetzold soon became restless and walked outside to see a group of people coming from the forest. The leader was wearing a white snowsuit. Every 100 yards he would kneel and peer through field glasses.

Paetzold ran back to the farmhouse. "The Russians are here!" he cried and ran upstairs to his room. From the window he watched four men approach, cradling submachine guns. When the first aimed his gun, Paetzold jumped back. Splinters of glass spattered his face, then a second shot broke a downstairs window. The Russians jogged forward and shot out the kitchen windows. The women inside screamed.

The Russians took all watches, then went from room to room smashing to bits treasured dishes and glassware passed down many generations. Paetzold watched in dismay as the marauders destroyed everything they could lay their hands on, with the sheer delight of vandalism, even uprooting the telephone and tossing it through a window. They were like children, he thought.

Suddenly a Red Army man burst into the room with the flag of a local rifle club and a saber belonging to his cousin Otto. The Russian threw down the flag and tried to break off the eagle on its shaft. He couldn't. He tried to rip the flag with his hands; the material was too strong. When in frustration he began swearing and jumping about furiously, Paetzold couldn't help laughing. A soldier of another nationality would perhaps have shot Paetzold but the Russian only quieted down sheepishly.

These Russians moved out of town without further incident but another group arrived, found a distillery and, once drunk, began burning, raping and murdering. Frau Lemke, the young wife of a soldier, took her husband's pistol and shot her two children and herself. Her father cut his wrists. The widow Rettig's farm was burned and she was shot in the garden. By dusk almost every building in Kurzig was aflame, and the main street lined with the corpses of the inmates of the old folks' home. Paetzold, his relatives and a dozen people from the village were thrown in the farmhouse cellar, where they lay huddled on straw, waiting for they knew not what.

Two young Red Army men finally descended and grabbed the woman nearest the door, the widow Semisch. "Come on, cook for us," said one of them. "There are young women here!" she cried and tried to point out two young married women hiding under the straw. As she was dragged to the door, Frau Semisch's ten-year-old daughter clung to her, crying, "*Mutti, Mutti!*"

An hour later the widow staggered back into the cellar; most of her clothes had been ripped off. Weeping loudly, she clung her arms to her sides and moaned, "My waist! My waist!" Her daughter ran to her in tears. "Mother dear, what have the soldiers done to you!"

No one else in the cellar said a word.

Paetzold was worried about Otto, who was being kept upstairs, and sneaked up into the house, first checking the kitchen with his flashlight, then the other rooms. But every corner was empty. All was quiet. Finally he came to the two rooms belonging to Otto's mother. The first was empty; in the second the mayor was slumped in a corner next to the wardrobe, which was peppered with bullet holes. Paetzold laid Otto's body on the floor; there were two bullet holes in his head.

Paetzold sank down in a chair, unable to go back and tell Otto's mother and wife what he had found. He sat in this deathwatch hour after hour, remembering how he and Otto had played together as children almost every day and how much Otto was loved by everyone, even the Polish slave laborers. He wondered how God could have allowed such a thing. Why hadn't He let it happen to Hitler, who had destroyed the life and happiness of so many people? There were no answers, and at dawn he finally returned to the cellar. Everybody looked up as he entered and silently sat before Otto's mother.

"He is dead," she said quietly. "I can see it in your face."

Paetzold nodded and after a long silence he told her that Otto was lying in her bedroom.

"I will never be able to sleep there again," said the old lady. "I would always have his image before me."

## 4.

At 9:35 A.M., February 2, the U.S.S. *Quincy* passed through the submarine net gate at the entrance of Valletta's harbor. It was a warm, cloudless morning. Great crowds lined both sides of the channel; all had come to see the man in a brown coat and tweed cap seated on the bridge. The *Quincy* steamed slowly past the moored *Orion,* and Winston Churchill —dressed in naval uniform, cigar jutting out his mouth—waved. The figure on the bridge waved back. There was an abrupt silence as everyone turned toward Roosevelt. It was, thought Eden, "one of those moments when all seems to stand still and one is conscious of a mark in history."

Suddenly the silence was broken: an escort of Spitfires roared overhead, guns boomed in salute and bands of the ships in the harbor began playing "The Star-Spangled Banner."

Franklin Delano Roosevelt broke into his crooked smile, visibly enjoying the reception. This was the beginning of what could be the apogee of his life. In the next few days he and two other men would have an unparalleled opportunity to create a brave new world.

Age and pain were written on his face, but there was also determination and a look of his own destiny. When he was saying good-bye to Mrs. Roosevelt in Washington, he had reaffirmed his high hopes in the conference at Yalta. "I can make real progress in strengthening the personal relationship between myself and Marshal Stalin," he told her.

In spite of his illness, he was determined to proceed with the business of assuring a permanent and just peace for the world. The relationship between him and Churchill was remarkable, intimate as two brothers' and with the mixed feelings of brothers. In 1940, when Britain was in mortal danger, Roosevelt had risked his political future by sending lend-lease aid. Yet after helping save his elder, he was forever lecturing him on the immorality of colonialism. Roosevelt was not at all impressed with official British assurances that "self-government should be achieved within the British Commonwealth," and remained determined to assist dependent peoples—including those of the British Empire—to ultimate self-government.

"I believe you are trying to do away with the British Empire," Churchill once told him in private. Of this there was no doubt. "The colonial system means war," Roosevelt had confided to his son Elliott. "Exploit the resources of an India, a Burma, a Java; take all the wealth out of those countries, but never put anything back into them, things like education, decent standard of living, minimum health requirements—all you're doing is negating the value of any kind of organizational structure for peace before it begins."

But colonialism was only one of the problems he faced at Yalta, and just before leaving America, he had summoned Bernard Baruch for advice. "Bernie, I had too many with the boys last night," he said to explain his trembling hands, and expressed the hope that he could lay the foundation for world peace at the Crimea Conference.

Baruch, who once candidly characterized himself as "the master of the obvious," was prepared and handed him a letter of advice:

. . . The bible and history are filled with missions upon which countless men have set forth to help their fellow-men.

Never has one been fraught with such possibilities as the one upon which you are about to embark.

You carry not only the hopes of the world, but you have an opportunity to make successful all previous attempts by making a peace in which their efforts can bear fruit. . . . We can learn from the mistakes of the past. Your mission must succeed. Above all go my hopes and prayers for all who look to you and I know you will not fail them.

Deeply touched, Roosevelt said he would have Major General Edwin "Pa" Watson, his secretary, read him the letter before each meeting. "I'm not going to take you, Bernie," he said. "You get seasick. But I promise I'm not going to make any terms for a peace treaty. When I do, you'll be sitting right next to Papa."

"Don't make any proposals," Baruch counseled and put his arm around the President's shoulder—it was the first time he had ever been moved to such familiarity. "And remember," he added, "wherever you sit is the head of the table."

Tears came to Roosevelt's eyes, and dropping his head to hide this unusual display of emotion, he sat silent.

George Marshall reported to the President shortly after eleven in the morning of February 2. They were joined by Fleet Admiral Ernest King. Both Marshall and King were stunned at the President's gaunt and haggard face. Unaware of their concern, Roosevelt listened with interest as they described the bitter meetings with the British Chiefs of Staff and the violent reaction of the Britons to a crossing of the Rhine by Bradley.

The President asked for a map, and after carefully examining it, remarked that he knew the terrain well, having once made a bicycle tour through the Bonn-Frankfurt country, and could, therefore, heartily approve of Eisenhower's plan. Marshall and King did not want to tire their Commander and left after half an hour. Once aboard the barge taking them ashore, they were still so appalled at the President's appearance that they looked at each other in mutual consternation, but in the presence of the crew, only shook their heads.

Just before noon Churchill boarded the *Quincy* with his daughter
Sarah and Eden. At the lunch that followed, the Prime Minister, though
still not completely recovered from his own illness, dominated the conversation with his sharp wit and flow of brilliant discourse. At one point
Roosevelt remarked that the Atlantic Charter had never been signed by
Churchill—he himself had penned the Prime Minister's name on his own
copy. He jokingly expressed the hope that Churchill would countersign
the document and make the Charter bona fide. Churchill facetiously
replied that when he had recently read the Declaration of Independence,
he was delighted to find it embodied in the Charter.

After lunch Eden told Stettinius that he thought the President looked
more relaxed than at the Quebec meeting the previous fall, but wrote in
his diary, ". . . he gives the impression of failing powers." Stettinius,
however, was not comforted by Eden's words of reassurance. He still
vividly remembered how Roosevelt's whole body as well as his hands had
trembled during the recent inaugural address. And only at lunch Roosevelt had remarked that he had slept ten hours a night on the sea voyage
to Malta, but still didn't feel "slept out."

That afternoon the President and his daughter were taken on a leisurely thirty-mile tour of the island by the Governor-General. The President's log later noted that "the weather was delightful." Refreshed by
this pleasant interlude, Roosevelt met Churchill and the Combined Chiefs
of Staff for the first time in the wardroom of the *Quincy* at six o'clock.
As usual Churchill did most of the talking, with Roosevelt nodding rather
than speaking. The explosive question of strategy on the western front
was disposed of with surprising ease when Churchill readily approved
Eisenhower's plan. But the Prime Minister had settled one problem,
only to bring up the one Marshall had long feared was coming: he
suggested making Field-Marshal Harold Alexander, who was heading all
Allied forces in Italy, Eisenhower's deputy in charge of all ground operations. The U. S. Chiefs bluntly said no. Undeterred, Churchill suggested
that Montgomery command the greater part of the troops once the Rhine
was crossed. Again the American Chiefs said no. Churchill took the rebuffs good-naturedly and the meeting was adjourned.

While Marshall was waiting to go ashore he was called back to see
Roosevelt, who said Churchill was still most anxious to have Alexander
appointed deputy. Marshall replied that he would never approve the
measure, and was dismissed.

### 5.

Earlier in the day in Spa, Belgium, Bradley had told the commanders
of the U. S. First, Third and Ninth armies—Lieutenant Generals Court-

ney Hodges, George Patton and William Simpson—of the Eisenhower plan. When they learned that Montgomery would lead the main attack and that Simpson's Ninth Army would remain under the field-marshal's command, their reactions were predictable.

The three were old friends with many experiences in common, and the start of their military careers had been equally inauspicious. At West Point, Simpson had finished low in his class, whereas Patton and Hodges flunked as plebes in 1905. Patton finally graduated with Simpson in 1909, but Hodges, found "deficient" in mathematics, started at the bottom again, as a private in the Regular Army. All had chased Pancho Villa in Mexico and fought at the front in World War I. Though widely divergent in personality, they all were aggressive, extremely competent and eager to smash the Germans without delay.

They listened with growing dismay as Bradley went on to explain that Hodges and Patton could continue their present limited attacks against the Siegfried Line—the Germans called it the West Wall—until Montgomery's big drive got under way. After that, the battle would be played by ear.

Patton exploded. He and Hodges both had a far better chance of getting to the Rhine first, he said. What's more, he—and he felt sure Hodges agreed—didn't hold a very high opinion of the offensive drive of British troops. To Patton, this was a foolish and ignoble way for Americans to end the war. Every damn division should be attacking, and if they did, the Krauts wouldn't possibly have the resources to halt them.

## 6.

Both Eden and Churchill were concerned that Roosevelt had avoided talking to them about the political matters to be considered at Yalta, and a small dinner on board the *Quincy* that evening was arranged specifically to remedy that situation. Stettinius felt that at the dinner "the American and British attitudes" regarding Poland, the United Nations and the treatment of Germany had been clarified, but Eden was gloomy. To him, nothing had been accomplished. He wrote in his diary:

. . . Impossible even to get near business. I spoke pretty sharply to Harry [Hopkins] about it, when he came in later, pointing out that we were going into a decisive conference and had so far neither agreed what we would discuss nor how to handle matters with a Bear who would certainly know his mind.

The President was "unpredictable," thought Eden, and both he and Churchill were "uneasy" that there had been no real Anglo-American consultation at the top level.

After dinner Roosevelt and Churchill drove to Luqa Airport to fly to the meeting with Stalin. The Prime Minister boarded his four-engine Skymaster and went to bed. The President, still in his wheel chair, was put in a special elevator which was raised inside his plane, a remodeled C-54.* It was the first time he had ever used the plane. Besides disliking the monotony of flying, Roosevelt considered a plane built solely for his personal use an unnecessary expense. He was, nevertheless, buoyant and excited. Ahead lay new adventures. He was told his plane wouldn't leave for several hours, so he too turned in.

It was cold and starry as the 700 conferees bound for Yalta boarded twenty U. S. Skymasters and five British Yorks. The atmosphere of the blacked-out airfield was tense following a report from U. S. Intelligence that Hitler knew the exact location of the Big Three meeting. Three nights earlier a test run by Lieutenant Colonel Henry T. Myers had almost ended in disaster. Upon landing at Saki Airport on the Crimean Peninsula, Myers found many small flak holes in his plane. Either the tail wind had brought him over German-held Crete, or Turkish gunners had mistaken him for a German.

At eleven-thirty, as a light, cold drizzle settled over Luqa, the first plane took off for the 1375-mile trip to Saki. Others followed at regular intervals, their flight plan calling for a three-and-a-half hour run due east, followed by a 90-degree turn to the north to avoid Crete. The President's plane took off at about three-thirty in the morning, just ahead of Churchill's. Unescorted, the big transport, lights out, soon disappeared in the drizzly gloom. When the drone of its engines faded, the fate of the President of the United States would be unknown for almost seven hours; all planes were to maintain strict radio silence.

The first half of the flight was uneventful. But soon after six P-38 fighters had joined Roosevelt's C-54 over the mountains of Greece, ice began to form on the wings of all seven planes. A P-38 peeled off, one of its engines dead, and returned to Athens. Secret Service men became so concerned by the ice that they thought of waking the President and fitting him with a Mae West life belt, but the danger passed and just after noon, Crimean time (two hours ahead of Maltese time), the pilot executed a 90-degree turn at a radio transmitter near Saki Airport— the maneuver which indicated he was a friend.

At 12:10 P.M. the Roosevelt plane touched down on a runway of concrete blocks resembling a tile floor and came to a stop almost at the end of the ice-coated strip. The countryside was treeless, flat and grim. As the plane taxied to the parking area, those aboard could see Russian soldiers in smart-looking uniforms stationed all around the airfield, sub-machine guns at the ready. An elite Red Army regiment stood at attention while a large military band played martial music. Foreign Commissar

* Later nicknamed *The Sacred Cow* by Bernard Baruch.

Vyacheslav M. Molotov, Ambassador Harriman and Stettinius came aboard to greet the President and to let him know that Marshal Stalin had not yet arrived in the Crimea.

At 12:30 P.M. the Prime Minister's Skymaster landed, escorted by six P-38s. Churchill walked over to Roosevelt's plane and watched as he was lowered in the elevator and lifted into a lend-lease American jeep by the chief of his Secret Service bodyguard, Michael Reilly. The commander of the honor guard gave a speech of welcome to the two Western leaders and the band broke into "The Star-Spangled Banner." The jeep drove down the ranks, with Churchill keeping pace on foot, an eight-inch cigar sticking out like a small cannon.

Roosevelt got into a sedan for the seventy-five-mile drive to Yalta. There was no other traffic at all and armed sentinels in long, heavy, neatly belted coats lined the road at 100-yard intervals. Some wore astrakhan hats, others caps with bright green, blue or red tops. Each guard executed a brisk rifle salute as the President's limousine passed. Anna Boettiger tugged at her father's sleeve. "Look," she said in surprise, "how many of them are girls!" Stationed at intersections were other uniformed girls, each with a red and a yellow flag. If the way was safe, the patrol girl pointed her yellow flag at the car, tucked both flags under her left arm and saluted smartly with the right. It impressed the Americans and made them feel easier about the security of their President.

The first third of the drive stretched over gently rolling, treeless, snow-covered land reminiscent of the great American plains. But unlike America, the countryside was littered with gutted-out tanks, burned buildings, wrecked freight cars and other monuments of battle. After passing through Simferopol, the capital of the Crimea, the road began winding its way over a rugged mountain range. The motor caravan drove down the other side past many country estates to the Black Sea, then turned south, skirting the coast. It passed through Yalta around six o'clock and continued south another two miles until it finally reached Livadia Palace, which was to be Roosevelt's headquarters. The fifty-room palace, designed by Krasnov in Italian Renaissance style, was built during Czar Nicholas' reign, in 1911. Standing some 150 feet above the sea, the white granite edifice looked out on both water and precipitous mountains. To Stettinius it was a breath-taking sight, reminding him of parts of the Pacific coast.

Livadia had been turned into a tuberculosis sanitarium for workers after the Revolution. The Germans had pillaged it efficiently, even stripping it of its paneled walls. They left only two small pictures and an infestation of vermin. In the past ten days—under the supervision of Ambassador Harriman's daughter Kathie—the Russians had filled the palace with furniture and fixtures from Moscow's Hotel Metropole and imported a large group of plasterers, plumbers, steam fitters, electricians and painters to repair the broken windows and defaced walls, and renovate the central heating plant. The vermin were left to the sanitary-minded Americans, and men from the U.S.S. *Catoctin,* a naval auxiliary ship moored at Sevastopol, had completely de-bugged the palace.

Roosevelt was given a suite on the first floor with a private dining room; this had once been the Czar's billiard room. Marshall was assigned the imperial bedroom; the salty Admiral King occupied the Czarina's boudoir and his colleagues never let him forget it. With all this luxury, however, there was one drawback for the 216 Americans: only Roosevelt had a private bathroom. Russian chambermaids walked into all the other bathrooms without knocking, completely oblivious to the embarrassment of startled American males.

Churchill and his party didn't leave the airfield immediately, but followed Molotov to a large oval, heated tent, where buffet tables were loaded with hot tea, vodka, brandy, champagne, dishes of caviar, smoked sturgeon and salmon, hard- and soft-boiled eggs, butter, cheese and bread.

Once under way, the drive to Yalta took more than twice as long as Roosevelt's. After lunching on sandwiches provided by some prudent staff officer, the Churchill party was stopped at Alushta, a small coastal town north of Yalta, and treated by Molotov to an elaborate lunch. The polite British did their best to feign hunger. Filled to bursting, they drove past Roosevelt's headquarters at Livadia Palace, and six miles farther on came to the palace of Prince Yusopov, Rasputin's assassin, where Stalin would stay. They continued south along the seacoast for another four miles to their own quarters, Vorontsov Palace. Though not as large or lavish as Livadia, it was comfortable and luxurious. From one side it looked like a Scottish castle, from another like a Moorish palace. Appropriately, carved lions flanked the entrance, and in the dining room Churchill saw a painting which looked familiar. "I know I have seen that before," he told Commander Thompson. It was a family portrait of the Herberts which he had seen at Wilton; Prince Vorontsov's sister had married into the Herbert family.

Like at Livadia, all the furniture, fixings and staff had been imported from Moscow. As General Hastings Ismay, Churchill's chief of staff, entered the palace he recognized two waiters who used to serve him at the Hotel Nationale in Moscow. When they ignored his smile of recognition he was puzzled, but once alone with him they dropped to their knees, kissed his hand—only to get up quickly and leave without saying a word.

## 7.

On the eve of the conference that was to decide the fate of Hitler's Germany, the Nazis themselves were still trying men who had earlier attempted and failed to end the Third Reich. The People's Court had already convicted hundreds accused of complicity in the July 20 bomb plot, among them Karl Goerdeler, former Oberbürgermeister of Leipzig. It was he who had written the secret letter to the German generals in 1943:

. . . It is a great mistake to assume that the moral force of the German people is exhausted; the fact is merely that it has been deliberately weakened. The only hope of salvation is to sweep away the secrecy and terror, to restore justice and decent government and so to pave the way for a great moral revival. We must not be shaken in our belief that the German people will want justice, honesty and truthfulness in the future, as they have in past. And as in the past too, the few degenerate elements who do not so wish must be kept in check by the legal power of the state.

The practical solution is to bring about the conditions, even if only for twenty-four hours, in which the truth can be told, to restore confidence in the resolve that justice and good government shall again prevail.

The proceedings on February 3 were conducted as usual by Roland Freisler, president of the People's Court. He was shrewd, sharp-tongued and able. An ardent Bolshevik in his youth, he was characterized by Hitler as "our Vishinsky" and for the past six months had been living up to that title. Acting as prosecutor and judge, he ridiculed, attacked, threatened and when all else failed, shouted at the top of his lungs. His shrill voice could be heard far down the halls as he attacked Ewald von Kleist-Schmenzin, a landowner. Unperturbed, Kleist admitted proudly that he had always fought against Hitler and National Socialism. Other prisoners in the dock listened and hoped that they would face the court with equal dignity. Disconcerted by Kleist's answers, Freisler suddenly dismissed his case and resumed the trial of Fabian von Schlabrendorff, a young staff officer and former lawyer. He was not only one of the participants in the July 20 plot but he had planted a time bomb in Hitler's plane in March 1943 which, however, failed to explode. Since his arrest a variety of tortures had not managed to wring a confession from him or the name of an accomplice. He had been beaten with heavy clubs; pins had been pressed into his finger tips by a screw device; and instruments shaped like stovepipes lined with needle-sharp nails had been shoved up his bare legs and a screwing mechanism turned to impale his thighs and shanks.

Freisler began by waving a folder containing evidence against Schlabrendorff, shouting, "You are a traitor!" Then air-raid sirens sounded and the court hastily adjourned. The prisoners were fettered hand and foot and herded down to the same shelter as Freisler. Some 25,000 feet overhead, almost 1000 Flying Fortresses of the U. S. Eighth Air Force began unloading their bombs. Schlabrendorff heard a deafening crash and was sure it was "the end of the world." As the dust cleared he saw that a huge beam had fallen on a court official and Freisler. A doctor was called; but Freisler was dead. When Schlabrendorff saw the lifeless

Freisler still clutching the folder containing his evidence, bitter triumph swept through him. He said to himself, "The way of God is miraculous. I was the accused; he was the judge. Now he is dead and I am alive."

Gestapo men hustled Schlabrendorff, Kleist and another defendant out of the cellar and into a small car and headed for the Gestapo prison. It was still early afternoon, but the sky was dark from smoke and falling ashes. Flames were everywhere. Even the Gestapo building at 9 Prinz Albrechtstrasse—their destination—was burning. But the bomb shelter was only slightly damaged, and as Schlabrendorff passed another prisoner, Admiral Wilhelm Canaris—former head of OKW Intelligence and a long-time conspirator against Hitler—he shouted, "Freisler is dead!"

The good news was passed along to other prisoners—Generaloberst Franz Halder, former Army Chief of Staff, Judge Advocate Carl Sack, and others. With luck, the Allies would free them before the next trial.

# 8.

At Livadia Palace, Roosevelt—who had never believed there was much of a German underground—spent a restful night in preparation for the opening of the conference. The next morning, on a sun porch overlooking the sea, he met with his military advisers for a final briefing before the first Big Three meeting that afternoon. Admiral William Leahy said they all felt Eisenhower should be allowed to communicate directly with the Soviet General Staff, and Marshall pointed out that going through the Combined Chiefs, as the British insisted, was no longer practical—it took too much time and the Russians were already only forty miles from Berlin.

The Joint Chiefs were getting up to leave when Ambassador Harriman and Stettinius came out on the porch with three State Department officials: Freeman "Doc" Matthews, Charles "Chip" Bohlen and Alger Hiss. Stettinius urged the Joint Chiefs to stay and hear the diplomatic position of the State Department. Frequently prompted and advised by Matthews, Stettinius enumerated the topics he felt the Big Three should consider. The most important were Poland, the establishment of a United Nations organization, the treatment of Germany, and the settlement of differences between the Chinese government and the Communists. The only one who took no part in the discussions was Hiss.*

The President agreed with the delegation that the Lublin government should not be recognized and asked for a paper on Poland he could hand to Churchill and Stalin.

---

* Later it was widely believed that Hiss, as a Soviet spy, had persuaded Roosevelt to make concessions to Stalin at Yalta. There is no evidence that he gave any such advice during the conference to either the President or his counselors.

Stalin had arrived that morning after a long tedious rail trip from Moscow. At three o'clock, on his way to the first plenary meeting at Livadia, he stopped off at Vorontsov Palace to pay Churchill a courtesy call. Stalin expressed his optimism about the war; Germany was running out of bread and coal, and her transportation system was breaking down.

"What will you do," Churchill asked, "if Hitler moves south—to Dresden, for example?"

"We shall follow him," Stalin replied calmly, and added that the Oder was no longer a barrier. Moreover, Hitler had fired his best generals, except for Guderian—"and he's an adventurer." The Nazis were stupid to leave eleven armored divisions around Budapest. Couldn't they see Germany was no longer a world power and unable to have forces everywhere? "They'll understand in time," he concluded grimly, "but too late."

Stalin excused himself and drove on to Livadia Palace in the large black Packard with Molotov and an interpreter, to pay similar respects to Roosevelt. It was four-fifteen, forty-five minutes before the scheduled opening of the conference, by the time they were admitted to the President's study. Bohlen, who spoke Russian fluently, was the only other American present. After thanking Stalin for the great efforts made for his comfort and convenience, Roosevelt jokingly remarked that many bets had been made on the sea voyage: would the Russians get to Berlin before the Americans reached Manila? Stalin acknowledged that the Americans would probably reach their goal first, because "at present, very hard fighting is going on for the Oder line."

Roosevelt told Stalin that he had been so struck by the devastation on the trip across the Crimea that it made him "more bloodthirsty" regarding the Germans than he'd been a year before. "I hope you'll again propose a toast to the execution of fifty thousand officers of the German Army," he said. Stalin replied that everyone was more bloodthirsty regarding the Germans, and that the destruction in the Crimea was nothing compared to the Ukraine. "The Germans are savages and seem to hate with a sadistic hatred the creative work of human beings."

After briefly discussing the military situation, Roosevelt asked how Stalin had got along with General de Gaulle at their December meeting in Moscow.

"I didn't find de Gaulle a very complicated person," Stalin replied. "But I feel he's unrealistic in the sense that France hasn't done very much fighting in this war and yet demands full rights with the Americans, British and Russians, who've carried the burden of the fighting."

Roosevelt, who disliked the French leader and regarded him only a necessary nuisance, revealed with a grin that at Casablanca, de Gaulle had compared himself with Joan of Arc. Stalin appreciated the anecdote so much that he smiled slightly. Only correctly polite with Churchill, he was warming to the President. In fact, the two got along so well that they began swapping confidences. Roosevelt informed Stalin of a recent rumor that France didn't plan to annex any German territory outright but was willing to have it placed under international control. Stalin shook his head and repeated what de Gaulle had told him in Moscow: the Rhine was the natural boundary of France and he wanted French troops there permanently.

This exchange inspired such reassurance in Roosevelt that he announced he would now say something indiscreet, something he wouldn't say in front of Churchill: After the war the British wanted a force of 200,000 French soldiers stationed along the eastern border of France; this force could then hold off any attack from Germany while the British were assembling their own army. "The British are a peculiar people," he added cryptically, "and want to have their cake and eat it too."

Stalin was all ears as Roosevelt went on to disclose how much trouble he had had with the British regarding the zones of occupation in Germany. "Do you think France should have a zone of occupation?" he asked the President.

"It's not a bad idea," Roosevelt replied, adding, "but only out of kindness."

"That would be the only reason for giving them a zone" was Stalin's firm reply. Molotov, quiet until now, echoed Stalin with equal firmness. He was a stolid, phlegmatic negotiator, nicknamed "Stone-Ass" by Roosevelt, since he could sit interminably at a conference repeating the same proposal over and over.

The President noticed that it was three minutes to five, so he suggested that they all proceed to the adjacent conference room, where the Big Three military staffs were already gathering; he preferred to have as few as possible witness his arrival at such meetings. Seated on a small stool on casters, he was rolled into the vast room, formerly used by Czar Nicholas as a banquet hall and ballroom. On reaching the large round conference table, Roosevelt hoisted himself to a chair with his muscular arms. Bohlen sat next to him as his interpreter.

By now military photographers were snapping pictures as Stalin, Churchill, Stettinius, Eden, Molotov, Marshall, Brooke and other military and political leaders and interpreters found their places. Advisers moved up chairs behind their chiefs. In all, ten Americans, eight British and ten Russians crowded around the table to begin the fateful conference. The import of their job struck them all. Several coughed nervously, others cleared their throats.

Stalin opened the meeting by suggesting that the President make the introductory remarks, as he had done at Teheran. Those Americans who had never seen Stalin before were surprised that he was so short—only five foot six—and that his manner of speech was so affable.

Spontaneously Roosevelt thanked Stalin and went on to say that the people he represented wished for peace above all and an end to the war as soon as possible. Since they understood each other better now than in the past, he felt safe in proposing that the talks be conducted in an informal manner in which each would speak his mind frankly and freely. He suggested that they first discuss the military questions, "particularly those on the most important front of all, the eastern front."

Colonel General Alexei Antonov, Soviet Deputy Chief of Staff, read a statement on the development of the new offensive, followed by a concise summary of the western front by Marshall. Stalin then broke in to say that the Red Army had 180 divisions in Poland against 80 German divisions. Soviet artillery supremacy was overwhelming—4 to 1. There were 9000 Soviet tanks on the breakthrough sector, and 9000 planes on a relatively narrow front. Stalin concluded by asking what wishes the Allies had regarding the Red Army.

Churchill, also speaking with spontaneous informality, expressed the gratitude of England and America for the massive power and successes of the great offensive and asked only that the Red Army continue the attack.

"The present offensive was not the result of Allied .wishes," Stalin replied a bit testily, and made a special point of the fact that the Soviet Union had not been bound by any agreement at Teheran to conduct a winter offensive. "I mention this only to emphasize the spirit of the Soviet leaders, who not only fulfilled formal obligations but went further and acted on what they conceived to be their moral duty to their allies." At Churchill's personal request he had launched the great Soviet offensive ahead of time to take some pressure off the Americans in the Battle of the Bulge. As for continuing the advance, he added tersely, the Red Army would do it, weather and road conditions permitting.

Roosevelt had called for frankness and he was getting it. He quickly made several placating remarks, and Churchill joined by expressing his complete confidence that the Red Army would press the attack when possible.

With this single exception, the general tone of the first plenary, as Stettinius recorded in his notes, "was most co-operative," and everyone was in a friendly mood when they adjourned at ten minutes to seven. A moment later the two NKVD men detailed as Stalin's bodyguard lost track of him. Quiet panic spread as they scurried silently through the corridors looking for him—until he calmly stepped out of a washroom.

The first day ended with a formal dinner at Livadia given by the President for his two colleagues, the Foreign Ministers and a few key political advisers—fourteen in all. The dinner was mixed Russian and American: caviar, sturgeon and Russian champagne, fried chicken Southern style, vegetables and meat pie. Dozens of toasts were proposed and

Stettinius noted with amusement that after Stalin drank half his vodka, he would furtively fill up the glass with water. The observant Stettinius, who was keeping a detailed record of the conference, also noted that the Marshal preferred smoking American cigarettes.

When Molotov toasted Stettinius and expressed a hope to see him in Moscow, Roosevelt jokingly said, "Do you think Ed will behave in Moscow as Molotov did in New York?" and implied that "Stone-Ass" had spent a gay time there.

"He [Stettinius] could come to Moscow incognito," Stalin jibed.

The banter grew even more permissive and Roosevelt finally said to Stalin, "There's one thing I want to tell you. The Prime Minister and I have been cabling back and forth for two years now, and we have a term by which we call you and that is 'Uncle Joe.' "

Stalin's jaw hardened and he asked stiffly what the President meant. The Americans couldn't understand the words but the tone of his voice was unmistakable, and the necessary pause for translation made the moment even more awkward. At last Roosevelt said it was a term of endearment and ordered another round of champagne.

"Isn't it time to go home?" Stalin asked. When Roosevelt exclaimed, "Oh, no," the Marshal coldly said it was late and he had military duties to take care of. James Byrnes, director of U. S. War Mobilization, tried to save the situation. "After all," he said, "you don't mind talking about Uncle Sam, so why should Uncle Joe be so bad?"

Molotov, in his unusual role of pacifier, turned to them and laughed. "Don't be deceived. The Marshal is pulling your leg. We have known this for two years. All of Russia knows that you call him 'Uncle Joe.' "

It was still not clear whether Stalin was offended or merely pretending, but he promised to stay until ten-thirty. Churchill, a master at such moments, toasted their historic meeting. The entire world was watching, he said, and if they were successful, a hundred years of peace would follow. The Big Three who had fought the war would have to maintain this peace.

The toast and perhaps the timing struck a particularly responsive note in Stalin. Holding up his glass, he declared that the Big Three had borne the brunt of the war and had liberated the small powers from German domination. Some of the liberated countries, he added sarcastically, seemed to think the three great powers had been *forced* to shed their blood to liberate them. "Now they are scolding the great powers for failing to take into consideration the rights of the small powers." He was ready to join America and Britain in protecting these rights. "But I'll never agree to having *any* action of *any* of the great powers submitted to the judgment of the small powers."

For the moment Stalin and Churchill were in agreement—and Roosevelt was the outsider. "The whole problem of dealing with the smaller powers is not too simple," he said. "We have, for instance, lots of Poles in America who are vitally interested in the future of Poland."

"But of your seven million Poles only seven thousand vote," retorted Stalin. "I looked it up and I know I'm right."

Roosevelt was too polite to say that this was ridiculously inaccurate and Churchill, in an apparent attempt to change the subject, toasted the proletarian masses of the world. But it only touched off a lively discussion on the rights of people to govern themselves. "Though I'm constantly being beaten up as a reactionary, I'm the only representative present who can be thrown out of office at any time by the universal suffrage of my people," the Prime Minister said. "Personally, I glory in that danger." When Stalin chidingly remarked that Churchill seemed to fear these elections, he answered, "I not only do not fear them but I'm proud of the right of the British people to change their government any time they see fit."

A bit later Stalin acknowledged that he was ready to co-operate with Britain and the United States to protect the rights of small powers, but again asserted that he would never submit to their judgment. This time Churchill chose to disagree. There was no question of the small powers dictating to the big powers, he said. But the great nations of the world had a moral responsibility to exercise their power with moderation and great respect for the rights of smaller nations. " 'The eagle,' " he paraphrased, " 'should permit the small birds to sing and care not wherefor they sang.' "

Now he and Roosevelt stood together—and Stalin was the outsider. But this was only good-natured sparring, a testing, under the glow of wine and vodka, of things to come. Stalin, in fact, was in such good spirits that he stayed until eleven-thirty, and when he and Roosevelt left the room, they were still in an exuberant mood.

Eden, however, was gloomy. To him it had been "a terrible party." Roosevelt had been "vague and loose and ineffective," while Churchill made "too long speeches to get things going again." As for Stalin, his attitude to small countries struck Eden as "grim, not to say sinister," and the Foreign Secretary was greatly relieved when the "whole business was over."

But the discussions were not quite over. As Eden and Churchill walked to the car, escorted by Bohlen, the Prime Minister remarked that they should let each republic in the U.S.S.R. have a vote in the United Nations —something the Americans opposed. Eden's temper flared and he spiritedly defended the American point of view. His voice raised, Churchill sharply replied that everything depended on the unity of the three great powers. Without that, he said, the world would be subjected to inestimable catastrophe and anything that preserved that unity would have his vote.

"How could such an arrangement attract small nations into joining such an organization?" Eden asked, and added that he personally believed "it would find no support among the English public."

Churchill turned to Bohlen and wanted to know what the American solution was to the voting question.

Bohlen diplomatically answered with a joke. "The American proposal reminds me of the story of the Southern planter who gave a bottle of whiskey to a Negro as a present. The next day he asked the Negro how he liked the whiskey. 'Perfect,' said the Negro. The planter asked what he meant, and the Negro said, 'If it'd been any better you wouldn't have given it to me, and if it had been any worse I couldn't have drunk it.'"

Churchill looked thoughtfully at Bohlen. Finally he said, "I understand."

# 4

# "Bread for Bread, Blood for Blood!"

**1.**

Germany, under attack from east and west, was also being blasted from above. Whereas the full extent of the disaster in the east was still being concealed from the public—and Hitler—almost everyone in Germany, including Hitler, was in the front lines of this air war. On February 4 Deputy Party Leader Martin Bormann wrote to his wife, Gerda, about the woeful state of the Führer headquarters.

My beloved girl,

I have just this minute taken refuge in my secretary's office, which is the only room in the place that has some temporary windows and is reasonably warm . . . The Reich Chancellery garden is an amazing sight—deep craters, fallen trees, and the paths obliterated by a mass of rubble and rubbish. The Führer's residence was badly hit several times; of the winter gardens and the banquet hall only the fragments of the walls remain; and the entrance hall on the Wilhelmstrasse, where the Wehrmacht guard was usually mounted, has been completely destroyed . . .

In spite of it all, we had to go on working diligently, for the war continues on all fronts! Telephone communications are still very inadequate, and the Führer's residence and the Party Chancellery still have no connection with the outside world . . .

And to crown everything, in this so-called Governmental Quarter the light, power and water supplies are still lacking! We have a water cart standing before the Reich Chancellery, and that is our only supply for cooking and washing up! And the worst thing of all, so Müller tells me, is the water closets. These *Kommando* pigs use them constantly, and not one of them ever thinks of taking a bucket of water with him to flush the place . . .

Later that day he wrote his "darling little Mommy" about the collapse in the east, telling her more of the growing peril than was even revealed to the Führer himself.

. . . The situation has so far not stabilized itself at all. We have, it is true, thrown in some reserves, but the Russians have many times more tanks, guns and other heavy weapons of all kinds, and against them even the most desperate and determined resistance of the Volkssturm is powerless! . . .

I would not write all this to you if I did not know that in you I have a very brave and understanding National Socialist comrade. But to *you* I can write quite frankly and tell you how very unpleasant—indeed, if I am completely honest, how desperate—the situation really is, for I know that you, like myself, will never lose your faith in ultimate victory.

In this, my darling, I know I am not demanding of you more than is in you to give, *and it is for this very reason* that I realize, in these most anxious days, what a treasure I have in you! . . .

Until now I have neither realized what a great thing it is to have so stanch-hearted a National Socialist as my wife, my life's companion, my sweetheart and the mother of my children, nor have I properly appreciated my immense good fortune in having you and your children . . . You, my beloved, my most beautiful, you are indeed the treasure of my life!

Complete devotion to all things Nazi made their love strange. After seducing the actress "M," for example, Bormann told Gerda all the details in a long letter, declaring himself a lucky fellow who was now "doubly and unbelievably happily married." She replied that the news delighted her and that it was "a great shame that such fine girls should be denied children," and went on to say it was a pity that she and "M" could not compare notes and work as a team, thus keeping the Führer supplied with a steady crop of Party members. The ten children she and Martin had already produced were, apparently, not enough.

Colonel Fuller—in the eye of the great storm Bormann wrote about—was writing a letter to the commander of the nearest Red Army headquarters, at Friedeberg:

. . . I am anxious that you know of our presence here, and that you report it to a Russian staff officer charged with our repatriation to our own forces.

We are not at present in need of food. However, we are running short of flour for bread, due to the electric current being disconnected to this village. The flour mill here is operated electrically . . .

I desire to take this opportunity to commend to you Capt. Abramov who in this village on February 3 took prompt and aggressive action in preventing an act of violence . . .

Abramov was an affable Soviet liaison officer who had arrived in Wugarten the day before, just in time to save a German woman from being raped by a drunken Red Army lieutenant. A few hours after Abramov had left for Friedeberg, the roar of battle increased to the north. A Russian colonel told Fuller that German tanks were counterattacking and ordered foxholes dug north of the village to help repel any assault.

By dusk the roar of heavy guns was so close that Fuller, taking Bertin along as interpreter, left the village in search of the colonel who had ordered him to dig in. After a mile the two were stopped by a suspicious sentry who herded them through the deep snow to a large number of Russian tanks coiled up in the drifts. Here they were stopped by two more suspicious sentries and an officer who talked in a loud, threatening voice.

Bertin grabbed Fuller's shoulder. "Colonel, they're going to shoot us!" he said. "They think we're partisans."

After a long argument the officer said they could proceed to his headquarters. "But if anything happens to a Russian soldier tonight, *he*"— pointing to Fuller—"will be shot!"

Headquarters was a nearby farm. Everyone was drinking and some of the staff lay on the floor in a stupor. The commander, a captain, thought they were partisans too, but when he was finally convinced that Fuller really was an American he began proposing toasts to Stalin and the Red Army.

However, since the entire area was about to be cut off by German tanks, he thought he had better escort them back. They were walking toward Wugarten when a sentry on horseback galloped up, wildly waving a submachine gun. *"Amerikansky!"* the captain shouted as the sentry aimed his gun at Fuller. But the man was too drunk to understand and began threatening the captain himself. Only after another long, loud argument did the sentry ride off, and the two allies returned safely to Wugarten.

The next morning a small Russian biplane landed in a nearby field. Two officers stepped out and asked for repatriation lists, by name, of every Allied prisoner of war in the village. The newcomers also revealed that ten American officers from their original group were already on the way to Odessa for repatriation—and one was George Muhlbauer, whose name their former guard-interpreter Hegel had been using. Fuller hurriedly rechristened the German 1st Lieutenant George F. Hofmann, Army serial number 0–1293395, and made him memorize a new biography: he had trained at Fort Benning, Georgia; gone to OCS in Virginia; served on Fuller's staff in the 109th Regiment; and been captured in the Battle of the Bulge. From that day Fuller kept quizzing Hegel, often waking him from a sound sleep for his catechism, but no matter how many times he was corrected, the German kept insisting he was trained at Fort Benny.

**2.**

Three thousand other Americans captured in the Bulge had recently arrived at Stalag IIA, located on the heights above Neubrandenburg, some 100 miles north of Berlin. Besides the Americans there were, in separate compounds, more than 75,000 Serbs, Dutch, Poles, French, Italians, Belgians, Britons and Russians. This was a camp for enlisted men and there were only two American officers there: one a doctor, the other Father Francis Sampson, a Catholic chaplain captured near Bastogne while trying to scavenge medical supplies behind the German lines. He had been a solid, hearty man full of good humor; now he was skinny, thin-faced, sick—but still good-humored. The Germans had allowed him to stay with the enlisted men only because a co-operative Serbian doctor had made the camp commandant believe that Father Sampson had double pneumonia and could not be moved.

One morning in early February, Father Sampson led a delegation of Americans to the warehouse to pick up the first U. S. Red Cross parcels to arrive in camp. The emaciated group clustered around the huge cartons, all with thoughts of food. Father Sampson remembered his first meal in camp: cabbage soup, with a few pieces of turnip and numerous little worms floating in it; one man, swilling his portion from a shoe, had looked up at the priest and said, "The only kick I have is—them worms ain't fat enough."

Eagerly they ripped open the Red Cross cartons. There was a strained silence, then a torrent of profanity surpassing anything Father Sampson had heard in eighteen months with paratroopers: before them were badminton rackets, basketball shorts, ping-pong sets, hundreds of games and a dozen football shoulder pads.

In the afternoon Father Sampson visited the *Lazarett* for the first time— the hospital, which was located some distance outside the American compound and staffed with Serbian and Polish doctors. He watched as a Pole amputated both legs of a young American and then applied toilet-paper compresses and newspaper bandages. Gangrene had set in after his feet were frozen during the long march and train journey across Germany. With tears rolling down his cheeks, the doctor told the chaplain that this was the fifth American to lose both legs; eighteen others had each lost one leg.

While Father Sampson was talking to other American patients—most of them suffering from dysentery or pneumonia—a German guard with a Hitler mustache strutted in; he was the most hated man in camp. They called him Little Adolf, and though only a corporal, he was a Party official—even the camp commandant was respectful. At Stalag IIA, Little

Adolf's word was law, and the other guards, who generally treated the prisoners well, claimed that he was in back of every atrocity that occurred.

Little Adolf, who reminded Father Sampson of a ribbon clerk, liked to discuss "culture" and "civilization," so now he turned to the chaplain and asked, "What do you think of the Bolsheviks? How can you justify being allies of the godless Russians?"

"To my mind, the Communist government and the Nazi government are two dogs of the same breed," the priest answered. "At the moment the Nazi is the most dangerous and we'll use any help to get rid of him."

"You must be mad!" Little Adolf cried. "But if you won't believe the truth, let me show you what pigs the Russians are!" He pointed to the Russian compound. It was filthy, its stench permeating the entire camp.

"They live in a pigsty," Father Sampson admitted. "But how could they possibly keep clean?"

"You don't get the point. Other races keep clean. There are professors in the Russian compound. I've talked to them. These are their finest minds and they can't tell the difference between culture and civilization."

"It's only a matter of semantics."

"No, no, you don't get the point. Those people simply can't see the difference. Those Russians are not human. Do you know that when a man dies in there, they keep him for days?"

"To draw the dead man's rations," the priest pointed out. Of 21,000 Russians who had entered the camp, only 4000 were alive; most had died of starvation.

"Your own Dr. Hawes has examined those bodies and verified cannibalism," said Little Adolf. Captain Cecil Hawes *had* confirmed the story. Even so, Father Sampson could not hold the Russians responsible for their actions. After his own seven weeks of hunger he realized that there was little a starved man wouldn't do to stay alive.

Little Adolf led Father Sampson to that part of the *Lazarett* reserved exclusively for Russians. It was a chamber of horrors. Dying men lay sprawled on the filthy floor, so tightly packed that their limbs were intertwined. They hawked and spat on one another, weakly shoved and clawed one another. They gazed up at Father Sampson with empty eyes, not pleading; all knew they would soon die. The only attendant was a French priest with young, unwrinkled skin; he appeared to be in his early twenties. It was known throughout the camp that he gave all his own food parcels to the dying Russians and spent every possible moment with them. Father Sampson watched as the French priest tenderly cared for them, ignoring their complete lack of gratitude.

"See, they are only animals!" was Little Adolf's parting comment. The minute he disappeared, the "young" priest—he was almost fifty—came up to Father Sampson and told him that a wagonload of bodies was about to be hauled out. "Father, some are still alive—they get rid of them as fast as they can!" The Germans wouldn't let him accompany the wagon and he begged the American to do something—anything. Father Sampson hurried out just in time to see a large wagon loaded with bodies roll toward the graveyard. He saw arms and legs move feebly. Men were going to be buried alive—and all he could do was watch.

Horrified, he started back toward the main gate, where a Russian was being searched by a guard. He made him undo his trousers, and a loaf of sour German bread fell out. The guard picked it up but the Russian snatched the bread from him, and even though a bayonet was jabbed into his neck, refused to give it up. The guard smashed the butt of his rifle on the Russian's head, and when he fell, kicked and pounded him. Still the Russian hung on doggedly to the bread. Father Sampson could only think, *Which is the animal?*

In halting German he pleaded with the guard. "I am a priest," he said over and over again, pointing to his crucifix, but the beating continued. Father Sampson knelt beside the Russian in prayer. The guard hesitated, either shamed by the priest's cross or awed by his captain's bars, and signaled two mates to take the Russian into the guardhouse. Dragged off, the prisoner still clutched the loaf of bread.

A few miles east of Frankfurt an der Oder, the Red Army had just overtaken another caravan of fleeing civilians and were dragging them from their wagons. Some thirty girls and boys were separated from their parents and lined up in a ditch while a Russian officer shouted, *"Khleb za khleb, krov za krov!"* One of the Germans, sixteen-year-old Irwin Schneider, knew this meant "Bread for bread, blood for blood!"

The elders fell on their knees, weeping and pleading, when they saw several soldiers aiming their submachine guns, but the officer ignored them and bullets began ripping into the youngsters. Young Schneider felt something sting his upper arm and saw children crumpling on all sides; pale red splashes appeared on the snow. Then a huge egg came floating toward him, and before he realized that it was a grenade, there was a deafening explosion and he felt himself being lifted up as in a nightmare. Hours later—it was seconds—the clanging in his head stopped and he managed to wiggle his fingers. Then he could move the rest of his body, and masked by smoke, he slowly, cautiously crawled away from the pile of bodies—some still writhing—into a nearby clump of bushes. He heard savage shouts, followed by single bursts of fire as those still alive were methodically eliminated. At last the din was over and the only sound was the wailing of parents.

These Russians had killed in cold blood, inspired by propagandists like Ilya Ehrenburg to take revenge:

German towns have no souls . . . All the trenches, graves and ravines filled with corpses of the innocents are advancing on Berlin . . . The boots and shoes and babies' slippers of those murdered and gassed at Maidenek are marching on Berlin. . . . We shall forget nothing. As we advance through

Pomerania, we have before our eyes the devastated, blood-drenched country-side of Byelorussia. . . . A German is a German everywhere. The Germans have been punished, but not enough. The Fritzes are still running, but not lying dead. Who can stop us now? . . . The Oder? The Volkssturm? No, it's too late. Germany, you can whirl around in circles, and burn, and howl in your deathly agony; the hour of revenge has struck!

But soldiers from Mongolia and other eastern regions were raping and looting and even killing, not particularly for revenge but only because they obeyed the primitive urge and conviction of their fathers that to the victor belongs the spoils. For the past few days this had been going on in Landsberg, the town near Fuller's village. On February 6 two young Soviets shot a girl in the stomach, more by mistake than by design, and then ran away in fright when schoolteacher Katherina Textor came to her aid. Katherina and two elderly women found a baby carriage and used it to take the girl to the hospital. By the time they crossed the frozen Warthe River and entered the hospital it was dusk, and Dr. Bartoleit had to remove the bullet without any anesthetic and by flashlight.

Katherina and her two friends decided to stay in the hospital to be safe from the dread Russian order *"Frau, komm!"* but they couldn't have found a worse refuge. Red Army men roamed the hospital corridors all that night looking for women. Several burst into the room where the three newcomers were trying to sleep and peered at them by flashlight. One Russian said disgustedly, "Old—dying," and left.

But all the nurses were raped before being put into trucks bound east. When the Russians finally broke into Dr. Bartoleit's apartment they found him dead on the floor, a pistol beside his hand. Sprawled near by were his wife and daughter.

### 3.

In Berlin that same day, February 6, the Führer was telling his intimates that the Big Three intended to "crush and annihilate" Germany.* "We have reached the final quarter of an hour," he said somberly. "The situation is serious, very serious. It seems even to be desperate." But he insisted there was still a chance for victory if the soil of the Fatherland was defended step by step. "While we keep fighting, there is always hope, and that, surely, should be enough to forbid us to think that all is already

* Hitler's private talks from February to April, 1945, were faithfully copied down by Bormann at the Führer's request so they could be preserved for posterity. On April 17, 1945, Hitler entrusted the documents—labeled Bormann-Vermerke (the Bormann Notes)—to a visiting Party official with instructions to hide them in a safe place. It was not until 1959 that these remarkable dissertations, each page authenticated by Bormann's signature, were finally published under the title *The Political Testament of Adolf Hitler, The Hitler-Bormann Documents.*

lost. No game is lost until the final whistle." He recalled the dramatic change of fortune when Frederick the Great was saved from defeat by the sudden death of the Czarina. "Like the great Frederick we, too, are combating a coalition, and a coalition, remember, is not a stable entity. It exists only by the will of a handful of men. If Churchill were suddenly to disappear, everything could change in a flash!"

His voice rose with excitement. "We can still snatch victory in the final sprint! May we be granted the time to do so. All we must do is to refuse to go down! For the German people the simple fact of continued independent life would be a victory. And that alone would be sufficient justification for this war, which would not have been in vain."

SS General Karl Wolff—Himmler's "Wolffchen" and SS chief in Italy—arrived at the Reich Chancellery to get satisfactory answers to his questions about wonder weapons and the future of Germany. His chief, the Reichsführer, had not been able to supply them and now he had gone to the Führer himself. With them was Foreign Minister Joachim von Ribbentrop, and the three men were pacing back and forth. "My Führer," Wolff said, "if it's not possible for you to give me a date for the wonder weapons, we Germans must approach the Anglo-Americans and seek peace." Hitler's face remained a mask as the fast-talking Wolff revealed that he had already established two contacts for this purpose: Cardinal Schuster of Milan, a close friend of the Pope's, and a British Secret Service agent.

Wolff paused. Hitler said nothing but began snapping his fingers. Wolff took this as permission to continue and suggested that the time had come to select one of these mediators. "My Führer," he went on, "it's obvious from evidence I've gathered from my own particular field that there are natural differences among these unnatural allies [the Big Three]. But please don't be offended if I say that I don't believe this alliance will split up of itself without our own active intervention."

Hitler cocked his head as if in agreement and continued snapping his fingers, then smiled, indicating that the twenty-minute interview was over. Wolff and Ribbentrop left, excitedly talking over the Führer's apparently receptive attitude toward the daring proposition. True, he hadn't said a word and hadn't given any specific directives, but he hadn't said no. They separated, Wolff to explore possibilities in Italy, and Ribbentrop in Sweden.

A block away Bormann was in his office writing another letter to Gerda, this time describing yesterday's birthday party held for Eva Braun, with Hitler, naturally, present:

E. was in a happy mood, but complained that she didn't have a good dancing partner; she also criticized various people with an asperity which was not like her at all.

She was upset because the Führer had just told her that she and other ladies would have to leave Berlin in a few days. This chatty letter crossed an ecstatic one from Gerda on the glories of National Socialism:

. . . The Führer has given us our idea of the Reich, which has spread—and is secretly still spreading—throughout the world. The unbelievable sacrifices our people are making—sacrifices they are capable of making only because they are imbued and possessed with that idea—are proof of its strength and show to all the world how just and necessary our struggle is.

One day the Reich of our dreams will emerge. Shall we, I wonder, or our children, live to see it? In some ways, you know, this reminds me of the "Twilight of the Gods" in the *Edda*. The giants and the dwarfs, the Fenris wolf and the snake of Mitgard, and all the forces of evil are in league against the gods; the majority have already fallen, and already the monsters are storming the bridge of the gods; the armies of the fallen heroes fight an invisible battle, the Valkyries join in, the citadel of the gods crumbles, and all seems lost; and then, suddenly a new citadel rises, more beautiful than ever before, and Baldur lives again.

Daddy, it is always astonishing to me to see how close our forefathers in their myths, and particularly in the *Edda,* are to our own times . . .

My beloved, I am wholly and utterly yours, and we will live to fight on, even if only a single one of our children survives this awful conflagration.

Your

Mommy

## 4.

To citizens in a democracy the Nazi philosophy was incomprehensible, a twisted fantasy, but not to the Germans who had seen Hitler rescue their country from a near state of Communist revolution, from unemployment and starvation. Though relatively few Germans were Party members, never in the history of the world had one man so completely hypnotized so many millions. Hitler had sprung from nowhere to completely dominate a great nation, not through force and terror alone but also by ideas. He offered Germans the proud place in the sun they felt they deserved, with the constant admonition that this would come about only if they crushed the Jews and their sinister plot to rule the world by Bolshevism.

Above all, hatred of Bolshevism had incessantly been pounded into the Germans for more than a decade, and it was this hatred that inspired the soldiers of the eastern front to resist so desperately. Hitler had told them over and over what the Reds would do to their wives and children, their homes and the Fatherland, and now they were fighting against hopeless odds—driven by hatred, fear and patriotism. They fought not so much with machines and weapons as with determination, desperation and raw courage. And in spite of the gigantic surge of the Red Army, overpowering in tanks and guns and planes, the eastern front was beginning to stabilize. A week earlier this would have seemed impossible.

The epitome of the fighting spirit in the east was Oberst (Colonel) Hans-Ulrich Rudel, leader of a group of Stuka dive bombers. Of average height, he impressed one most with his vitality. He didn't walk, he bounded; he didn't talk, he spouted words in a high-pitched voice. He had wavy, light brown hair, light olive-green eyes and strong features that looked chiseled out of stone. He believed without reservation in Hitler, yet no one was more openly critical of the mistakes of Party members and military leaders alike. After almost 2500 combat missions in six years, his accomplishments were already legendary. He had sunk a Soviet battleship and knocked out some 500 tanks.

On February 8 his men were fighting along the Oder River between Küstrin and Frankfurt at the apex of the spearhead Zhukov had driven past Himmler's army group. Himmler, in truth, had little to stop the Russians with except the Oder, a few scattered ground units behind it, and Rudel's Stukas, which, appropriately, were decorated with the emblem of the Teutonic Knights who had battled against the East six hundred years before. The Stuka, no longer the terror of the skies, was slow and clumsy—an easy target as it staggered out of a dive. Rudel himself had been shot down a dozen times and his left leg was still encased in plaster of Paris from machine-gun-bullet wounds. For the past two weeks his men had been racing up and down the river, like an emergency fire department, trying to stop the tide of onrushing Red Army tanks. They destroyed hundreds, but thousands more moved relentlessly up to the river banks.

During the Battle of the Bulge Rudel had been summoned to the Führer's headquarters on the western front to receive a special decoration.

"Now you have done enough flying," Hitler said, grasping his hand and looking into his eyes. "Your life must be preserved for the benefit our German youth might derive from your experience."

To Rudel there was nothing worse than being grounded, and he said, "My Führer, I cannot accept the decoration if I'm not allowed to go on flying with my wing."

Hitler—still clasping Rudel's right hand, still looking deeply into his eyes—extended a black, velvet-lined case with his left hand. In it, sparkling with diamonds, was a decoration he himself had designed for Rudel alone. Hitler's grave face slowly relaxed and he said with a smile, "All right, you may go on flying," but a few weeks later he changed his mind and ordered Rudel grounded. Rudel was incensed and tried to call Reichsmarschall Göring. He was out. Rudel tried Keitel, but he was in conference. There was only one thing to do: call Hitler himself. When he asked to be put through to the Führer, a suspicious voice asked what his rank was.

"Corporal," Rudel joked. He heard an appreciative laugh and a moment later was talking to Oberst Nicolaus von Below, Hitler's Luftwaffe aide, who said, "I know what you want but I beg you not to exasperate the Führer."

Rudel decided to make a personal appeal to Göring, who was at his country place, Karinhall. The Reichsmarschall was wearing a brilliant robe with loose sleeves that flopped like the wings of a huge butterfly.* "I went to see the Führer about you a week ago," Göring told him, "and this is what he said: 'When Rudel is present I haven't the heart to tell him he must stop flying; I just can't do it. But what are you head of the Luftwaffe for? You can tell him; I can't. Glad as I am to see Rudel, I don't want to see him again until he has reconciled himself to my wishes.' I am quoting the Führer's exact words and I don't want to discuss the matter any further. I know all your arguments and objections!"

Accordingly, Rudel said nothing but returned to the front as determined to keep flying as ever. He did, in secret, until a communiqué commended him for destroying eleven tanks in a single day and he was ordered to report to Karinhall immediately.

Göring was angry. "The Führer knows you are still flying," he said. "He has told me to warn you to give it up once and for all. You are not to embarrass him by forcing him to take disciplinary action for disobedience to an order. Furthermore, he is at a loss to reconcile such conduct with a man who wears the highest German decoration for gallantry. It is not necessary for me to add comments of my own!"

Now, on February 8, two weeks later, Rudel was still flying, and in the evening he was visited by Albert Speer, Hitler's most capable and in-

* According to Robert Kropp, Göring's butler since 1933, the Reichsmarschall's great extravagance in clothing was his vast store of dressing gowns. He amassed them as some people collect stamps. They were great voluminous affairs, made after his own design, of velvet or brocade in blue, green, purple; one was covered with Egyptian hieroglyphics. For each coat there were matching leather boots in the same design and color; around his middle he wore a belt and an old Germanic knife.

To Kropp, Göring was a good family man who played for hours with his nephews, particularly with the intricate electric train system in the Karinhall bunker. Kropp is still annoyed at the lurid stories that his employer was a drug addict, put on make-up and wore fantastic costumes at wild bacchanalian parties. It is true that after World War I, Göring was for a time addicted to morphine. However, he received hospital treatment while in Sweden and was cured. According to Kropp, he never reverted to his former drug addiction. Moreover, he drank very little, his main vice being candy. Nor did Göring ever put on make-up or have his hair curled; his complexion was naturally rosy and his long hair was naturally wavy. Nor could there have been any wild orgiastic parties, declares Kropp, or he would at least have seen signs of them.

Kropp is not alone in these opinions. To many in Berchtesgaden, Göring is still regarded as a jovial figure, whereas they wholeheartedly detested Bormann. The Reichsmarschall to them was a man of heart and those who worked for him called him *Vati* (Daddy).

telligent minister, head of Armament and War Production. "The Führer is planning attacks on the dams of the armament industry in the Urals," Speer began. "He expects to disrupt the enemy's arms production, especially of tanks, for a year." Rudel was to organize the operation. "But you are not to fly yourself; the Führer repeated this expressly."

Rudel protested. There were others far more qualified for the job; he was trained in dive bombing. To these and other objections Speer only replied, "The Führer wants you to do it," and said he would send details of the Ural project. He was saying good-bye when he confided to Rudel that the vast destruction of German industry made him pessimistic for the future, but that he was hoping the West would recognize the situation and not let Europe fall to the Russians. Then he sighed and said, "But I'm convinced the Führer is the right man to solve the problem."

## 5.

Prior to the daily Führer conference on February 9, General Heinz Guderian, the Army Chief of Staff and commander of the eastern front, was studying the situation reports with a feeling of utter frustration. Defense was not his forte, nor was command on this level. He was basically a leader of troops, a straightforward, hot-blooded soldier of effervescent nature who fought with such ability and gusto that his men—from staff officers to privates—followed with devotion. After four years at the Prussian Military Academy he had joined a rifle company commanded by his father and served in World War I as a signal officer, as a staff officer of the 4th Infantry Division and finally as a General Staff officer.

He became ardently interested in tanks. Unlike the British and French, who believed the tank's primary features were superior fire power and armor, he averred that these only reduced tanks to the tempo of infantry. The essence of panzer warfare, as he saw it, was speed and maneuverability. Then came fire power and, lastly, armor. To him a panzer division was not just a group of tanks but a completely independent task force, including flak and antitank guns, motorized infantry and engineers. Such divisions should be grouped in panzer armies operating together as a tremendous force, capable of lightning advances.

But the German General Staff agreed with the British and French experts and Guderian's dreams were only realized when Hitler, who was excited by the possibilities of blitz warfare, came into power. Guderian's theory had at last been put into practice in Poland and in the armored dash across Belgium, where, if Hitler hadn't abruptly stopped him, he would probably have reached the English Channel in time to prevent the Dunkirk evacuation.

The first great successes after the attack on Russia in the summer of

1941 also owed much to the Guderian principle, but when the snows began to fall and he implored Hitler to let him race hell-bent for Moscow, the Führer ordered him instead to encircle and take Kiev. This was done but at the cost of valuable time, so Guderian asked for permission to wait until spring to take Moscow. Once again Hitler disagreed and an immediate drive was launched on the Russian capital. Disaster followed and Hitler relieved Guderian of his command; only the Stalingrad debacle two years later brought him out of retirement. In spite of his promotion to Chief of OKH (Oberkommando des Heeres, Army High Command), the rupture between General and Führer was only superficially patched together and with each conference it threatened to break apart again— so much so, in fact, that Guderian's aide, Baron Freytag von Loringhoven, feared for his chief's life.

Guderian fretted and fumed during the twenty-mile drive north from Zossen to Berlin for the February 9 Führer conference. Something had to be done, he said. Far to the north the twelve divisions of Army Group Kurland, cut off on the coast of Latvia, were sitting out the battle because Hitler wouldn't evacuate them by sea. In the Königsberg area 125 miles down the coast, Army Group North was also cut off. Like their comrades farther north, they were being supplied by air and sea only—and neither group was contributing anything to the battle for Germany. Next came Himmler's Army Group Vistula, little more than a paper force as yet and doing almost nothing to stop Zhukov's drive on Berlin. In spite of this direct threat to the capital, Hitler was starting a big offensive far to the south, in Hungary. It was ridiculous, Guderian muttered, and added something about having a final showdown with the Führer that very day.

As usual the SS guard scanned their tight-fitting uniforms with humiliating thoroughness before admitting them into Hitler's office. No sooner had the conference started than Guderian abruptly asked Hitler to postpone the Hungarian drive and instead launch a major counterattack against Zhukov's Berlin-bound spearhead. Zhukov had already outrun his supplies, and simultaneous attacks against both flanks of his spearhead could cut it in two.

Hitler listened patiently until Guderian came to the requirements for such a counterattack: the divisions in Kurland as well as those in the Balkans, Italy and Norway would have to be pulled out at once. This brought a curt refusal, which only made Guderian continue his argument. "You must believe me when I say that it's not stubbornness that makes me keep insisting on the evacuation of Kurland. I can see no other way left to us of accumulating reserves, and without reserves we can't hope to defend the capital. I assure you I'm acting solely in Germany's interests."

Hitler rose from his chair, his left side trembling, and cried, "How dare you speak to me like that? Don't you think *I'm* fighting for Germany? My whole life has been one long struggle for Germany!" Göring went over to Guderian, and taking him by the arm, led him to the next room, where the two drank coffee while Guderian struggled to control his temper. Once back in the conference room, he confounded everyone by repeating his demands for the evacuation of the Kurland troops. Hitler angrily struggled to his feet and shuffled up to Guderian, who sprang from his chair. Face to face the two men glared at each other. Even when Hitler began shaking his fist, Guderian refused to budge. Finally General Wolfgang Thomale, one of Guderian's staff officers, grabbed the tail of his jacket and pulled him back.

By now Hitler had regained control of himself, and to everyone's surprise quietly agreed to let Guderian launch his counterattack. Of course, he added, it couldn't be on quite the scale the general wanted because it was impossible to withdraw troops from Kurland—and then outlined what he had in mind: a very limited attack from the north with troops that Himmler was already using to protect Pomerania.

Guderian started to object but decided that it was better to have a small attack than none at all. At least it would save Pomerania and keep open a path to East Prussia.

Unconcerned about the possibility of any such counterattack, Zhukov was pushing his spearhead even farther into Germany. He had already established a bridgehead on the west bank of the Oder between Küstrin and Frankfurt and was preparing to use it as a springboard to Berlin.

On the morning of February 9, Luftwaffe headquarters advised Rudel that Russian tanks had just crossed the river at this bridgehead. The High Command could not bring up heavy artillery in time to keep these tanks from careering down the highway to Berlin; only Stukas could stop them. In a few minutes Rudel was in the air with every available pilot, heading up the frozen Oder. He ordered one squadron to attack a pontoon bridge near Frankfurt, and then swept down with the antitank flight toward the west bank.

He saw tracks in the snow. Tanks or anti-aircraft tractors? He went down lower through heavy flak toward the village of Lebus, where he spotted a dozen or more well-camouflaged tanks. Then flak slammed into his wings and he climbed as quickly as possible. Below he could see at least eight anti-aircraft batteries and realized that it would probably be suicide to go after tanks in flat country with no tall trees or buildings to give approach cover. Ordinarily he would simply have chosen a better target but today Berlin was in peril, so he radioed that he and his rear gunner, Hauptmann (Captain) Ernst Gadermann, were going down alone to attack the tanks. The others would wait until they saw the telltale blinking of flak guns, then try and knock them out.

Rudel scanned the area and finally saw a group of T-34 tanks creeping out of the woods. "This time I'll have to trust to luck," he told himself and pushed over the nose of his Stuka. Flak began to burst on both sides but he kept going down. At about 500 feet he pulled up slightly and swung toward one lumbering tank; he didn't want to attack from too steep an angle in case he overshot the target. He fired his two cannon and the tank burst into flames. Immediately he had a second T-34 in his sights. He fired at its stern and there was a mushroom explosion. In the next few minutes he destroyed two more tanks. Then he flew back to his base for more ammunition and returned for a second sweep. After knocking out several more tanks he limped home, wings and fuselage torn by flak, and changed to another plane.

By his fourth mission he had destroyed twelve tanks and there was only one left, a big "Stalin." He climbed above the flak, abruptly tipped over into a steep, screaming dive, weaving violently from side to side to avoid the flak. As he neared the tank he straightened the Stuka and fired, then zigzagged until he was out of range of the guns and it was safe to climb again. He looked down and saw the Stalin smoldering but still moving. The veins in his temples were throbbing. He knew it was a dangerous game and the odds against him grew with every pass, but something about the solitary tank enraged him. He had to destroy it. Then he noticed the red-light indicator of one cannon winking—breech jammed! And the second cannon had only a single round left. By the time he got back to 2500 feet he was arguing with himself. Why risk everything on one shot? But the answer was: perhaps it needs just this one shot to keep that tank from rolling on through Germany. "How melodramatic!" he said to himself. "A lot more Russian tanks are going to roll on through Germany if you bungle it now—and you will bungle it, you may depend on that."

He was already in a screeching dive. He saw the spitting of many guns as he twisted and writhed. Abruptly he straightened out, fired. The Stalin burst into flame. Jubilantly Rudel swept by and started a spiral climb. There was a crack and a stab through his right leg like red-hot steel. He couldn't see; everything was black; gasping for breath, he fought to keep control of the plane.

"Ernst," he gasped over the intercom to his gunner, "my right leg is gone!"

"No," Gadermann answered evenly. "If it were, you wouldn't be able to speak." He was a doctor by profession and a natural fighter by avocation. As a medical student he had fought a number of duels and he loved combat so much that he had become a rear gunner. "The left wing is on fire," he said calmly. "You'll have to come down. We've been hit twice by flak."

"Tell me where I can crash-land!" He still couldn't see a thing. "Then get me out quickly so I won't be burned alive."

Gadermann guided the blind pilot. "Pull up!" he cried.

Tree or telephone wires? Rudel wondered. And when is the wing going to fall off? By now the pain in his leg blotted out everything else and he was only reacting to shouts.

"Pull up!" Gadermann yelled again.

The words hit him like a dash of cold water in the face. "What's the terrain like?" he asked.

"Bad . . . hummocky."

He might black out at any moment and just knew he had to get down. He felt the plane swerve and kicked the left rudder. Searing pain stabbed his left foot and he screamed. Wasn't it his right leg that had been hit? he wondered, forgetting that his left was already in a plaster cast.

The plane was burning as Rudel brought up its nose gently to make a pancake landing. He felt a jarring crash, a lurch, and heard a screeching skid. There was abrupt silence. Relieved, he passed out; he was wakened by a wave of pain; again he passed out. When he came to, he was on the operating table of a dressing station a few miles west of the Oder. "Is it gone?" he asked weakly.

A surgeon peering down at him nodded. Rudel thought, No more skiing, diving, pole-vaulting; then, What's the difference when so many comrades have been wounded more seriously; what was the loss of a leg if he had helped save the Fatherland?

The surgeon was apologizing: ". . . except for a few scraps of flesh and some fibrous tissue there was nothing there, so . . ." A little later Göring's personal physician appeared and said that the Reichsmarschall wanted Rudel brought to the hospital in Berlin's Zoo bunker. He also told Rudel that Göring had reported the crash to Hitler, who, after expressing relief that Germany's greatest hero had escaped so lightly, said, "Of course, if the chicks want to be wiser than the hen."

If Rudel was Hitler's ideal warrior, the forty-seven-year-old Dr. Josef Goebbels was his ideal intellectual. An operation at seven had left Goebbels' left leg three inches shorter than the right. In school he turned to mental pursuits, and while still in his twenties, he became in quick succession an amateur novelist, scenario writer, playwright—only to fail in each instance. Gifted with a variety of small talents and embittered by frustrations, he became an ardent spokesman for Hitler's ideas. If a German Communist of Hitler's genius had come along at the same time, Goebbels could just as well have become his willing and capable tool, for he was essentially a spirit in revolt and it was the revolutionary in the Nazi philosophy that appealed to him.

Martin Bormann was as zealous a Nazi as Goebbels and the two men were probably Hitler's most ardent followers. Both were willing to do anything for the Führer; both distrusted and were distrusted by Himmler

In spite of these similarities, their differences were even more marked. Bormann was short and heavy-set, with a wrestler's bull neck. His round face and broad nose accentuated this grossness, giving him a ruthless, almost animal look. Colorless and dour, he preferred to stay in the background. Goebbels was slender, quixotic, as flamboyant as a matinee idol and happiest in the spotlight. He had a keen sense of humor and could sway a large audience or a single listener with his charm and sharp wit. Whereas Bormann was plodding, exact and indefatigable in details, Goebbels was imaginative, yet possessed, according to Speer, a Latin rather than Germanic mind, which helped make him a spell-binding orator and a master of propaganda.

Bormann had probably been drawn into National Socialism by its denunciation of the Church, its nationalism and the chance for personal advancement. As the assistant to Rudolf Hess, he had been a nonentity and even now, as head of the Party Chancellery, he was almost unknown in Germany. He had become Hitler's faithful shadow, always on hand to do the most trivial and arduous jobs—with a casual remark from the Führer bringing instant action. One day at the Berghof, his villa above Berchtesgaden, Hitler looked out the huge picture window at a nearby cottage and called it an eyesore; he wanted the place torn down when its elderly owners died. A few days later Hitler discovered that the eyesore had magically disappeared. The literal-minded Bormann had simply torn it down and moved the owners to a much finer house which they detested.

He was the most mysterious of all the National Socialist leaders. He spurned decorations and public honors. In fact, he shunned any publicity, and pictures of him were so rare that few Germans would have been able to identify him. What he wanted above all was to be the one man Hitler could not do without.

In April, 1943, Bormann was officially named Secretary to the Führer, and in this capacity he wielded tremendous power. It was he who determined whom Hitler should see and what documents he should read. Bormann was present, moreover, at almost every interview.

After the July 20 bombing Hitler came to depend more and more on the few he felt he could trust completely, and of these few Bormann alone was able to reduce ideas and projects to clear, simple propositions. "Bormann's proposals," Hitler once said, "are so exactly worked out that I only need say yes or no. With him I dispatch a pile of papers in ten minutes over which other men would take hours of my time. When I tell him to remind me in six months of this or that business, I can be sure he will do so." And when someone complained of Bormann's ruthless methods of carrying out these duties, Hitler replied, "I know he's brutal, but what he undertakes he finishes. I can rely absolutely on that."

The two high priests, with such similarities and such differences, competed vigorously for the affection and ear of the Führer, but their duel was covert and silent. Goebbels, realizing how much the Führer depended on Bormann, was too clever to be obvious, and Bormann, who knew that Goebbels was still a close personal friend of the Führer's, followed his instinct not to bring the fight into the open.

In addition to his duties as Minister of Propaganda, Dr. Goebbels was also Defender of Berlin and early in February he addressed a small group in his office in that role. Present were Generalleutnant (Major General) Bruno von Hauenschild, military commander of Berlin; the city's Lord Mayor; the Chief of Police; State Secretary Dr. Werner Naumann, Goebbels' assistant; and Hauptmann (Captain) Karl Hans Hermann, detailed by Hauenschild to act as liaison officer with Goebbels. For the past nine days young Hermann had been staying in the Goebbels' home, occupying the bedroom of Frau Goebbels' son by an earlier marriage. After all the stories Hermann had heard of Goebbels' love life,* he was surprised to find him a thoughtful, attentive husband and it seemed to him that despite these affairs, the Goebbels' had a close and harmonious relationship. One night when the household was in the shelter during an air raid, Hermann noticed that Frau Goebbels took her husband's hand and fondly laid it against her cheek.

At the February meeting Goebbels announced that he was about to reveal a state secret and made everyone present take a vow of silence. "I have just seen the Führer," he said and paused dramatically. "No matter what happens, he has now definitely made up his mind not to leave Berlin!" Everyone was dismissed, duly impressed by the urgency of defending the capital, but to Goebbels it was also proof of his first great triumph over Bormann. Goebbels had long maintained that Hitler's end, if it had to come, should be in Berlin with all his chief associates in attendance, while the practical Bormann wanted Hitler to flee to Berchtesgaden. In truth it was no triumph at all. Though Goebbels pulled one way and Bormann the other, Hitler had made up his mind to stay in Berlin for reasons of his own—and was just as likely to reverse himself the next day if conditions changed.

Of all the rulers in Europe, Hitler was the only indispensable one because of his peculiar hold on his people. He was a man of destiny, and he knew it. To him the miraculous escape from the bomb was proof of this, and he still believed what he had written in Landsberg Prison in 1924:

At long intervals in human history it may occasionally happen that the practical politician and the political philosopher are one. The more intimate the

* In 1938 Goebbels would have divorced his wife to marry the Czech actress Lida Baarova if Hitler had not been so morally offended.

union, the greater his political difficulties. Such a man does not labor to satisfy the demands that are obvious to every philistine; he reaches out toward ends that are comprehensible only to the few. Therefore his life is torn between hatred and love. The protest of the present generation, which does not understand him, wrestles with the recognition of posterity, for whom he also works.

At this time his ends were "comprehensible only to the few," but millions still followed with blind loyalty.

# 5

# "Judge Roosevelt Approves"

**1.**

It was a crisp 40 degrees when the second plenary began at 4 P.M. in the great hall of Livadia, and a log fire was burning at the end of the room. Churchill, cheeks rosy, was wearing a colonel's uniform and smoking his eternal cigar. Harry Hopkins, the man closest to Roosevelt, was making his first public appearance at Yalta. He was suffering from hemochromatosis, and in the past week had lost twelve pounds. He sat behind the President, alert and eager in spite of spasms of pain.

Roosevelt opened the meeting with the suggestion that they discuss political matters affecting Germany. The dismemberment of Germany after its defeat was a large part of this problem, and it had already been dealt with at length by the European Advisory Commission, composed of representatives from the U.S.S.R., the United States and Britain.* The E.A.C. had already recommended that postwar Germany be divided into three zones for occupation, allocating the eastern third to Russia, the northwestern to Britain and the southwestern to America. Both Britain and Russia had approved the plan, but Roosevelt, unhappy with the less accessible southwestern zone, had yet to sign.

After the President's opening remarks, Stalin made it plain that he wanted the question of dismemberment of Germany solved at once. To

---

* In October, 1943, the American, British and Russian Foreign Ministers had met in Moscow, and one of their decisions was to establish a standing committee of diplomatic experts, with headquarters in London, to study the problems to be settled after Germany's defeat.

the surprise of several conferees, it was Churchill and not Roosevelt who opposed any hasty decision. "If asked today, 'How would you divide Germany?' " he said, "I wouldn't be prepared to answer." This required very searching study. "I have no fixed opinion. I would like the matter explored and possibly settled in agreement with my two great allies." When Stalin kept insisting that the matter be decided then and there, Churchill stoutly replied, "I do not think it possible to discuss the exact form of dismemberment. That would come at the peace conference."

"You're both talking about the same thing," Roosevelt interjected smoothly, separating the two antagonists like a referee, and added that it might be a good idea "to divide Germany in, perhaps, five states or seven : . ."

"Or less," Churchill muttered; he wanted it cut only in two. "I see no need to inform the Germans at the time of surrender whether we will dismember them or not!"

Harry Hopkins scribbled a note and handed it to Roosevelt:

> Mr. President:—
>
> I would suggest that you say this is a very important and urgent matter and that the three foreign ministers present a proposal to-morrow as to the proceedure * by which a determination as to the dis-memberment can be arrived at an early date
>
> Harry ·

No sooner had Roosevelt put down this note than Stettinius handed him another, in neat handwriting, his signature ending in an optimistic upward sweep:

> Mr. President:
>
> We can readily agree to referring this—the 1st meeting of Foreign Ministers.
>
> Ed

"If this question is discussed all over the world there will be a hundred plans for dismemberment," said Roosevelt. "Therefore, I ask that we confine it to ourselves and that the three Foreign Secretaries bring in tomorrow a plan for dismemberment."

"You mean plan for the *study* of the question of dismemberment, not a plan for dismemberment itself?" the Prime Minister asked quickly.

"Yes, for the study of dismemberment."

If Churchill was placated, Stalin certainly was not. "I think the Prime Minister's plan not to tell the Germans is a risky one; we should say this to them—in advance."

"The Marshal's idea, which is somewhat my own," Roosevelt clarified, "is that it will make it easier if it be in the terms, and tell them."

---

* All notes, messages, letters (in English), are reproduced exactly as written.

"But you don't want to tell them," Churchill retorted. "Eisenhower doesn't want that. That would make the Germans fight all the harder. We should not make this public."

Roosevelt asked Churchill if he would agree to add the word "dismemberment" in the articles of surrender which the E.A.C. had also drawn up.

"Yes, I would agree," Churchill grumbled.

"The question of the French zone remains to be decided," Roosevelt continued. Churchill and Stalin eyed each other like two fighting cocks. Recently—at de Gaulle's insistence and with Churchill's enthusiastic backing—France had been admitted to membership in the E.A.C. but was not given a zone of occupation because of Stalin's firm opposition. The previous night Churchill had told Eden that anything preserving the unity of the Big Three would have his vote, but today he was obviously willing to risk that unity for a good cause—such as a zone for France.

He rose now, on the face of it to champion France, but in fact to stop Russian aggression. He was sure that as soon as Hitler's Germany was defeated, the balance of power would be mightily upset and Russia would attempt to communize western Europe as she was already doing in the southeast. Giving France a zone in Germany would only strengthen the wall against Communism. "The French want a zone and I am in favor of granting it to them. I would gladly give them part of the British zone."

"I think there might be complications in our work if we have a fourth member," Stalin retorted, playing the same game of innocence.

"This brings up the whole question of the future role of France in Europe," Churchill went on. "And I personally feel that France should play a very important role. . . . They have had long experience in occupying Germany. They do it very well and they would not be lenient. We want to see their might grow, to help keep Germany down." He looked meaningfully toward Roosevelt and said, "I do not know how long the United States will remain with us in occupation."

"Two years," Roosevelt answered promptly, not realizing what repercussions such an admission would have.

"Doc" Matthews, sitting behind the President, saw Stalin's eyes glint when M. Pavlov translated this. As if to make sure Pavlov had heard "two years" correctly, Stalin asked the President to elaborate, which he did:

"I can get the people and Congress to co-operate fully for peace but not to keep an army in Europe a long time. Two years would be the limit."

Stalin's quiet exultation was obvious. Harriman, who knew the Marshal as well as any American, wished the President had not so unthinkingly given Stalin such an advantage.

"I hope that would be according to circumstances," Churchill rumbled, striving to hide his dismay. "At all events, we shall need the French to help us."

"France is our ally," Stalin said in a manner that reminded one American of a fat cat gulping down a mouse. "We signed a pact with her. We want her to have a large army." He could afford to be magnanimous.

A few moments later Roosevelt caused Churchill further consternation by remarking, "I should be just as satisfied if the French are not in on the control machinery." What he meant wasn't clear even to Hopkins, since France had recently been made a member of the E.A.C., so he began writing another note.

Stalin chose to think that Roosevelt was backing him against Churchill, and said heartily, "I agree that the French should be great and strong, but we cannot forget that in this war France opened the gates to the enemy. . . . The control and administration of Germany must be only for those powers standing firmly against her from the beginning and *so far* France does not belong to this group."

"We were all in difficulties early in this war," Churchill noted wryly. "But the fact remains that France must take her place. We will need her defense against Germany. . . . After the Americans have gone home I must think seriously of the future."

Stalin undoubtedly knew what he meant and repeated that he was against France taking part in the control machinery. As Churchill continued to argue the point, Harry Hopkins finished his note and passed it to his Chief:

1. France is on the European Advisory committee now. That is only body considering German affairs now.
2. Promise a zone.
3. Postpone decision about Control Commission.

Roosevelt looked up from the note and said, "I think we have lost sight of the French position on the European Advisory Commission." Hopkins had averted what could have developed into a grievous problem. "I suggest that the French have a zone of occupation but that we postpone discussion on control machinery."

"I agree," Stalin answered with a surprising lack of hesitation. To Stettinius it was obvious that the Marshal wanted no clash with Roosevelt, and equally obvious that he was determined to haggle each point with Churchill, who said, "I propose that the three Foreign Secretaries sketch out the kind of commission for control to be set up." Eden leaned over and whispered something in his ear. "He [Eden] says it has all been worked out and I withdraw my question."

The problem of reparations came next, and when Ivan Maisky—who impressed Stettinius with his neatly clipped, pointed beard, scholarly manner and fluent English—ably presented a Soviet demand for $10,000,-000,000, it was Churchill who opposed such heavy payments, pointing out the unfortunate results of World War I reparations. He also brought up the specter of famine in Germany. "If eighty million are starving, are we to say, 'It serves you right,' and if not, who is going to pay for feeding them?"

"There will be food for them, anyway," said Stalin.

Roosevelt, again the conciliator, took a position somewhere in the middle. "We don't want to kill the people. We want Germany to live but not to have a higher standard of living than that of the U.S.S.R. I envision a Germany that is self-sustaining but not starving. . . . In rebuilding, we must get all we can but we can't get it all. Leave Germany enough industry and work to keep her from starving."

A few minutes later the meeting adjourned, leaving some Americans, such as Bohlen, concerned that the President hadn't stood squarely behind the British on the question of reparations. Though Roosevelt had already publicly abandoned the Morgenthau Plan, which would have robbed Germany of the Ruhr and Saar industrial sections and converted her into a "country primarily agricultural and pastoral in its character," its vestiges remained, and to Bohlen and others who understood the history of central and eastern Europe, a suddenly pastoral Germany would mean almost certain domination of the entire area by Russia.

The next day's plenary meeting opened with a discussion of the matter closest to Roosevelt's heart—the United Nations organization.

Churchill declared that though peace depended on the three major powers, free expression of grievances by the many smaller nations of the world should be assured. "It might look as if we [three] are claiming to rule the world . . . whereas our desire is to serve the world and to preserve it from renewal of the frightful horrors which have fallen upon the laps of its inhabitants. Therefore I feel that we [three] great powers . . . should make what I would call a proud submission to the communities of the world."

The observant Stettinius noted that Churchill's horn-rimmed glasses kept slipping down his nose and that Stalin, who had switched back to Russian cigarettes, was doodling incessantly on a piece of paper.

"It's not a question of one power or three powers desiring to be masters of the world," Stalin retorted. "I don't know of any great nation which intends to master the world. Perhaps I'm mistaken," he added with a touch of sarcasm, "and don't see everything. I would like to ask my friend Mr. Churchill to name which powers might intend to dominate the world. I'm sure Mr. Churchill and Britain don't want domination. I'm sure the United States hasn't a desire of this kind. And the U.S.S.R. hasn't. That leaves only one power—China!"

"I was speaking of the three great powers gathered here, collectively lifting themselves so high that others would consider they were trying to dominate the world," Churchill replied.

The problem was much more serious, Stalin explained. "As long as we three live, none of us will allow our countries to get involved in aggressive actions. But after all, ten years from now, none of us may be present. A new generation will come which did not experience the horrors of war and will forget what we have been through. We would like to secure peace for at least fifty years. I have such an idea. I think we have now to build up such a structure which will put as many obstacles as possible to domination of the world. . . . The greatest danger for the future is the possibility of conflicts among ourselves."

The President diverted this trend of thought by bringing up Poland—the touchiest subject of all. For months Churchill had put pressure on a reluctant Roosevelt to force the London Poles to make concessions to Stalin in the name of co-operation with Russia, but now it was Churchill who went to the defense of Poland.

"Great Britain has no material interest in Poland," he began. "Her interest is only one of honor because we drew the sword for Poland against Hitler's brutal attack. Never could I be content with any solution that would not leave Poland as a free and independent state." He glared awesomely over the rims of his glasses. "Our most earnest desire, which we care about as much as our lives, is that Poland be mistress in her own house and in her own soul." He suggested that the three of them make a government then and there. "A provisional or interim government, as the President said, pending free elections so that all three of us can extend recognition. . . . If we could do that, we should leave the table with one great step accomplished toward future peace and the prosperity of central Europe."

Stalin suggested a ten-minute break and the President's butler entered —he was the maître d' at the Hotel Metropole—followed by tail-coated waiters carrying silver trays of cake, sandwiches and scalding hot tea in tall thin glasses. To the amusement of the Russians, the Americans shifted their glasses from hand to hand so gingerly that silver holders had to be brought out.

The meeting reopened with an impassioned speech by Stalin, pointing out that in the last thirty years Germany had passed through Poland twice to invade Russia. He did not mention, of course—nor were Roosevelt and Churchill rude enough to remind him—that the German march across half of Poland in 1939 had coincided with their allies, the Russians, marching across the other half to meet them. He did emphasize, however, that the Curzon Line was invented by foreigners, not Russians, and that he could not return to Moscow with less than Curzon and Clemenceau had once offered.

"Now, about the government," he continued. "The Prime Minister has said that he wants to create a Polish government here. I'm afraid that was a slip of the tongue. Without the participation of Poles we can create no Polish government. They all say that I am a dictator," he added with a little smile, "but I have enough democratic feeling not to set up a Polish government without Poles."

At the end of this long speech Roosevelt, looking exhausted, suggested that since it was already a quarter of eight, they adjourn. But Churchill wanted to have the last word. "Perhaps we are mistaken, but I do not feel that the Lublin government represents even one third of the Polish people. . . . I cannot feel that the Lublin government has any right to represent the Polish nation."

A communiqué was issued to the world, announcing that there was "complete agreement for joint military operations in the final phase of the war against Nazi Germany" and that "discussions of problems involved in establishing a secure peace have also begun." The communiqué sounded reassuring, but a number of Americans who had dealt closely with the Russians were greatly concerned. The former ambassador to Russia, William C. Bullitt, for one, feared that Roosevelt was being taken in. Roosevelt, he remembered, had once told him in private that he would convert Stalin from Soviet imperialism to democratic collaboration by giving him everything he needed to fight the Nazis. Stalin needed peace so badly, the President had said, that he would willingly pay for it by collaborating with the West. Bullitt predicted that Stalin would never keep his agreements.

"Bill, I don't dispute your facts," Roosevelt replied. "They are accurate. I don't dispute the logic of your reasoning. I just have a hunch that Stalin is not that kind of a man. Harry [Hopkins] says he's not and that he doesn't want anything but security for his country, and I think that if I give him everything I possibly can and ask nothing from him in return, *noblesse oblige*—he won't try to annex anything and will work with me for a world of democracy and peace."

When Bullitt remained adamant the President said he was reminded of the time the Germans broke through the French and British armies in 1918. He had begged Woodrow Wilson to send American soldiers into the breach; if not, the Allies would be beaten. "Wilson looked at me and said, 'Roosevelt, I don't want to put our troops in to stop up that hole. What you predict may happen but my hunch is that it won't happen. It is my responsibility and not yours; and I'm going to play my hunch.' That's what I say to you, Bill. It's my responsibility and not yours; and I'm going to play my hunch."

Roosevelt still believed what he had told Bullitt, but he was also heeding the best available advice from his military and political experts. The military were urging him to get the strongest possible commitment for continued co-operation with the Red Army, which was still an important factor in the forthcoming all-out attack in the west. When Marshall met Eisenhower just before Malta, the Supreme Commander had emphasized that the success of his final drive across Germany would largely depend on the continuance of the great Russian offensive in the east.

George Marshall was even more concerned about the war in the Pacific. He had already warned Roosevelt that it would cost at least 500,000 and perhaps 1,000,000 American casualties to conquer Japan unless Russia joined the battle, and begged him to get a definite promise from Stalin at Yalta. Being a sensitive interpreter of public opinion, Roosevelt knew that most American citizens would enthusiastically support such a program of saving American lives, and he had decided to follow Marshall's advice.

For the past weeks Roosevelt had been more receptive to State Department advice than before. The influence of men such as Secretary of the Treasury Henry Morgenthau and other adherents of a hard policy against the Germans was waning, and the more tempered reasoning of career diplomats like Bohlen and Matthews was already having some effect. The President was particularly receptive to reports from Averell Harriman who had warned him that though Stalin seemed frank and blunt, most people made the mistake of taking his first statements on a question at face value. "Ask him three or four questions," Harriman cautioned, "until you find out what his real price is." He knew that Stalin was a tough man, with an enormous capacity for work. Stalin was a student of theology and the son of a priest, yet his religion was Communism, and he would go to any lengths to propagate it. Harriman had heard him remark without a flicker of emotion that he had purposely starved millions of kulaks just to get control of the peasants.

Harriman had also reported that contrary to popular belief, personal relationships were important to Stalin. He admired Churchill as a dogged fighter but trusted him only as long as the battle would last, and once said to Harriman, with mixed feelings, "He's a desperate fellow." But he was awed by the President, and listened carefully to everything Roosevelt said, recognizing his New Deal program as an original concept, which confounded the theories of Marx or Lenin.

It was with all this in mind that Roosevelt was playing his hunch at Livadia Palace. In addition, he could never forget that in early June, 1944, there had been four times as many Germans in the east as in the west, and without the Red Army there could have been no landings on D-Day.

That night, after discussing the third plenary with his advisers, the President decided to write to Stalin about Poland, for it was obvious that because of this problem the conference might be wrecked. With the help of Harry Hopkins and the State Department, a message was drafted. Harriman brought a copy to Vorontsov Palace, where Churchill and Eden read it. Eden thought it was "on the right lines but not quite stiff enough," and suggested several amendments. Both Churchill and Harriman approved the changes and later that evening Roosevelt incorporated them into the final draft:

My Dear Marshal Stalin:

I have been giving a great deal of thought to our meeting this afternoon, and I want to tell you in all frankness what is on my mind.

In so far as the Polish Government is concerned, I am greatly disturbed that the three great powers do not have a meeting of minds about the political setup in Poland. It seems to me that it puts all of us in a bad light throughout the world to have you recognizing one government while we and the British are recognizing another in London. I am sure this state of affairs should not continue and that if it does it can only lead our people to think there is a breach between us, which is not the case . . .

You must believe me when I tell you that our people at home look with a critical eye on what they consider a disagreement between us at this vital stage of the war. They, in effect, say that if we cannot get a meeting of minds now when our armies are converging on the common enemy, how can we get an understanding on even more vital things in the future.

I have had to make it clear to you that we cannot recognize the Lublin Government as now composed, and the world would regard it as a lamentable outcome of our work here if we parted with an open and obvious divergence between us on this issue . . .

He suggested that Bierut and Osobka-Morawski of the Lublin government be invited to Yalta at once, as well as Mikolajczyk and other representatives of the London Poles.

I hope I do not have to assure you that the United States will never lend its support in any way to any provisional government in Poland that would be inimical to your interests.

It goes without saying that any interim government which could be formed as a result of our conference with the Poles here would be pledged to the holding of free elections in Poland at the earliest possible date. I know this is completely consistent with your desire to see a new free and democratic Poland emerge from the welter of this war.

Most sincerely yours,

Franklin D. Roosevelt

That night Americans of much lower echelon invited themselves to a dance at Yalta, and soon turned folk dancing into a jitterbug contest. It ended in a draw. No one could tell who was more adept at throwing a partner around—the perspiring Americans or the husky Russian girls.

### 2.

While the conferees were getting arranged around the big round table for the fourth plenary meeting the next afternoon, Churchill dragged a chair behind him and wedged himself between Roosevelt and Stettinius. "Uncle Joe will take Dumbarton Oaks," he said in a husky whisper. This meant that Stalin would agree to the U. S. proposal for voting in the Security Council of the United Nations. At the Dumbarton Oaks Conference the previous fall, where the blueprint for a World Organization had been drawn up, American delegates had urged that to preserve the world's peace, the five permanent members of the Council (Great Britain, the United States, the U.S.S.R., China and France) must vote unanimously. The Americans had also insisted that all members of the organization, large or small, get a fair hearing.

The meeting began with Roosevelt's suggestion that they return to the Polish question. Stalin said he had received the translation of the President's letter just an hour and a half before and had been trying unsuccessfully ever since to get Bierut and Osobka-Morawski on the phone. "Meanwhile," he went on, "Molotov has prepared a draft to meet, to a certain extent, the President's proposal. Let us hear it when the translation is finished. While we're waiting, let's talk of Dumbarton Oaks."

For once Roosevelt knew what Molotov was about to say. "We believe the decisions taken at Dumbarton Oaks and the modifications suggested by the President will secure collaboration by all nations, great and small, after the war. Therefore we consider the proposals presented as acceptable to us."

The President beamed—until Molotov added that the Soviet Union would be satisfied with the admission of three or at least two of the Soviet republics as original members of the United Nations. Roosevelt's face fell and he hastily wrote, "This is not so good," and passed the note to Stettinius. Nevertheless he commended the Soviets for their great step forward, and began a lengthy but polite criticism of the request just made by Molotov.

Hopkins interrupted him with a note:

> Mr. President   I think you should try to get this referred to Foreign ministers before there is trouble.
>
>                    Harry

Roosevelt glanced at the note, then told the conference that it was important to set up the new United Nations without delay and suggested that the whole matter be referred to the Foreign Ministers, who could also select a date for the first U. N. meeting, perhaps in March.

"I don't disagree with the President's suggestions," Churchill said, "but I feel that the Foreign Secretaries have already had a good deal of work thrust upon them." He also thought March was much too early for the first meeting; the battle was at its height and the state of the world was much too uncertain.

Stettinius slipped a note to Roosevelt:

Stimson takes this same view.

But Roosevelt was more interested in a note from Hopkins:

. . . There is something behind this talk that we do not know of its basis.

Perhaps we better to wait till later tonight what is on his mind.

Under it Roosevelt wrote, "All this is rot!" then scratched out the word "rot" and put down, "Local politics."

In the midst of this, a messenger handed Molotov the draft on Poland and the Foreign Commissar began to read it aloud. Both Roosevelt and Churchill frowned when Molotov came to the third section: "It was deemed desirable to add to the Provisional Polish Government some democratic leaders from Polish emigré circles."

"There is just one word I don't like," Roosevelt observed, "and that is 'emigré.'" Churchill concurred and explained, as if giving Stalin a lesson in history, that it originated during the French Revolution and means a person who has been driven out of a country by his own people.

Roosevelt wrote another note to Hopkins in his cramped style: "Now we are in for half an hour of it." Roosevelt had already jokingly complained in private about the long speeches of "dear old Winston," which he felt were sometimes irrelevant and which obviously irritated Stalin.

Churchill was saying that he wanted Poland to receive territory in eastern Germany to compensate for land the Soviet Union was going to take from eastern Poland, but warned that the Poles should not get too much of eastern Germany. "I do not wish to stuff the Polish goose until it dies of German indigestion," he said, and warned that many Britons would be shocked at the transfer of some six million Germans by force.

"There will be no more Germans there," Stalin replied crisply. "When our troops come in, the Germans run away."

"Then there's the problem of how to handle them in Germany," Churchill continued. "We have killed six or seven million and probably will kill another million before the end of the war."

"One or two?" Stalin interrupted archly.

"Oh, I'm not proposing any limitation on them," Churchill retorted just as archly, and asked if Stalin would be willing to add the words "and some within Poland" to the section on forming a provisional Polish government.

Stalin, in very good humor, answered, "Yes, that is acceptable."

"Well," Churchill concluded, "I'm in agreement with the President's suggestion that we should sleep on this till tomorrow."

"I likewise find this acceptable," said Stalin.

After the meeting was adjourned Leahy voiced the opinion that it was the most promising so far, and several Americans commented on Roosevelt's adroit handling of the frequent arguments that had cropped up between the other two leaders.

The British were not as complimentary and somewhat resented Roosevelt's role as self-appointed mediator; a few were even outspoken about what they considered his appalling ignorance of the history of eastern Europe. Eden felt that Roosevelt was too anxious "to make it plain to Stalin that the United States was not 'ganging up' with Britain against Russia," and this only caused "some confusion in Anglo-American relations which profited the Soviets." To him Roosevelt was a consummate politician who could clearly see an immediate objective, but "his long-range vision was not quite sure."

Late that night Churchill dispatched a long telegram to Clement Attlee, head of the Labour Party and his Deputy Prime Minister:

TODAY HAS BEEN MUCH BETTER. ALL THE AMERICAN PROPOSALS FOR THE DUMBARTON OAKS CONSTITUTION WERE ACCEPTED BY THE RUSSIANS, WHO STATED THAT IT WAS LARGELY DUE TO OUR EXPLANATION THAT THEY HAD FOUND THEMSELVES IN A POSITION TO EMBRACE THE SCHEME WHOLEHEARTEDLY. THEY ALSO CUT DOWN THEIR DEMAND FOR SIXTEEN MEMBERSHIP VOTES OF THE ASSEMBLY TO TWO . . . IN SPITE OF OUR GLOOMY WARNING AND FOREBODINGS YALTA HAS TURNED OUT VERY WELL SO FAR . . .

He also mentioned the letter Roosevelt had sent to Stalin about the new, more representative Polish government. If eight or ten democratic Poles like Mikolajczyk could be included in the new government, it would be to Britain's advantage to recognize this government at once.

. . . WE COULD THEN GET AMBASSADORS AND MISSIONS INTO POLAND, AND FIND OUT AT LEAST TO SOME EXTENT WHAT IS HAPPENING THERE AND WHETHER THE FOUNDATIONS CAN BE LAID FOR THE FREE, FAIR, AND UNFETTERED ELECTION WHICH ALONE CAN GIVE LIFE AND BEING TO A POLISH GOVERNMENT. WE HOPE THAT ON THIS DIFFICULT GROUND YOU WILL GIVE US FULL FREEDOM TO ACT AND MANOEUVRE . . .

Attlee was pleased with the long message. Though he and Churchill were at opposite political poles, Britain's wartime government-by-committee worked with an almost complete absence of politics. Hiding outstanding ability behind a colorless mask, Attlee looked like an insignificant little clerk. He was fond of the flamboyant Churchill and had respect for his considerable abilities, even if he felt that the Prime Minister occasionally did "go off the rail." "Winston," he once said, "is about ninety percent genius and ten percent bloody fool. What he needs is a good strong woman secretary who would say, 'Don't be a bloody fool!' "

He always remembered Lloyd George's comment about Churchill. "There's Winston; he has half a dozen solutions to every problem and one of them is right, but the trouble is he doesn't know which it is."

### 3.

That day, February 7, Lieutenant-General H.D.G. Crerar, commander of the First Canadian Army, called war correspondents to his tactical headquarters in Tilburg, Holland. He secretly briefed them on his plans for Operation "Veritable," the first step in Montgomery's drive toward the heart of Germany.

"Veritable" would be launched the next morning from Montgomery's northern flank; the battlefield was determined by two rivers. The Rhine, flowing north through Germany, abruptly turned west into Holland, and as it passed Nijmegen, was only six miles north of the Maas (Meuse), which came up from Belgium. The Canadian attack would begin at this narrow six-mile strip and continue southeast, flushing out all Germans between the two rivers.

"This operation may be protracted and the fighting tough and trying," Crerar told the correspondents. "All ranks are quite confident, however, that we will carry through to a successful conclusion the great task which we have been given the responsibility and the honor to fulfill."

The plan was theoretically simple and straightforward, but much depended on the weather and the peculiar terrain Crerar would have to conquer. In the afternoon the man he had chosen to lead the initial assault, Lieutenant-General Brian Horrocks, commander of XXX British Corps, drove up to a forward observation post near Nijmegen, where so many Americans had died in the previous fall's unsuccessful airborne attempt to turn the northern end of the West Wall. To the southeast he saw a small valley rising some 150 feet into the forbidding darkness of the Reichswald, a state forest of pines so closely planted that visibility was limited to a few yards. Horrocks had to attack the sinister-looking Reichswald head-on. He would also attack above the forest, along a paved road which ran southeast from Nijmegen. This went through low country for five miles before it began a three-mile ascent to the fortified town of Cleve on the German side—home of Anne of Cleves, Henry VIII's fourth wife.

Horrocks' initial problem had been to bring 200,000 men, tanks, guns and vehicles into the wooded area behind Nijmegen without their being observed. For the past three weeks, but only after dark, 35,000 vehicles had moved men and supplies into position, even though a sudden thaw and heavy rains had washed out a number of supply roads.

As Horrocks scanned the horizon he could see no unusual enemy movement, but this didn't diminish his concern. The woods and outskirts of Nijmegen were so jammed with troops that if Jerry dropped a pea in the area it was bound to hit somebody. What if there was a sizable air raid or it started to rain again?

Crerar had not told the correspondents that once the Germans rushed up reserves from the south to stop "Veritable," Montgomery's right flank would advance into the area just emptied of troops. This was Operation "Grenade," designed to force the German High Command to send the reserves back south. In the ensuing confusion, Horrocks would quickly filter through to the Rhine.

To lead "Grenade," Montgomery had selected General William Simpson, commander of the U. S. Ninth Army. "Big Simp"—to distinguish him from "Little Simp," another American officer with the same name— was tall and rangy, with a bald head and strong features. Though he looked like a fierce Indian chief, probably no other army commander was less feared by his staff and more admired. He was soft-spoken, rarely lost his temper and was effective with a simple word of reproach.

About sixty miles south of Nijmegen, Simpson was cautioning his commanders not to mix their units. "Keep your battlefield orderly. Keep units intact," he said, and then told them that D-day would be in three days, February 10. But no matter how carefully Simpson planned, his ultimate success depended on a general in another army group—and a river. The river was the Roer, which ran north from the Ardennes and which was the first barrier Simpson would have to pass on his way to the Rhine. The general was Courtney Hodges, and his troops were now trying to capture the Roer dams intact. If the Germans destroyed the huge dams, millions of tons of water would, by overflowing the banks of the Roer, prevent Simpson from getting to the other side for two weeks at least—or worse, isolate any troops that had already crossed.

Therefore, the outcome of "Veritable," in the north, depended on water: dams ninety miles to the south, and rain. By dusk the skies were still clear and quiet descended over the Nijmegen area. At nine o'clock Horrocks heard the dull roar of planes—769 heavy British bombers were heading for Cleve and Goch on either side of the Reichswald.

Just before dawn on February 8 he climbed to a small platform halfway up a tree—his command post—and watched a curtain of shells from over 1000 big guns explode all across his front. It was a cold gray dawn and to Horrocks' disgust it began to rain. But he could still see most of the battlefield. Even to one accustomed to war, it was awesome. Then, abruptly, the cannonading stopped, and tanks and "kangaroos"—tanks with tops sheered off to carry infantry—rumbled forward through the mud.

At 9:20 a covering barrage began to fall on the German front lines, increasing until, after forty minutes, it reached full force. At H-hour the barrage was moved forward 100 yards every four minutes, while a protective white smoke screen blanketed the assault battalions of four divisions advancing into the valley. If the enemy couldn't see them Horrocks could, and he watched intently as scattered groups of men and tanks approached the woods against little resistance. But after an hour the tanks slowed down, then seemed to be standing still. They were getting bogged down in mud.

Mud was by no means the worst of "Veritable's" troubles. To the south the assault on the Roer dams by Hodges' 78th Infantry Division was also slackening. Hodges phoned the commander of V Corps, Major General Clarence Huebner, and expressed his displeasure with the progress of the 78th. The attack was supported by 780 big guns and Hodges couldn't see why so much artillery couldn't blast a road straight to the dams. "I have to have them by tomorrow," he said.

Huebner knew that the 78th Division had run out of steam; a fresher unit had to be thrown in. "I've got to use the 9th Division," he told Hodges.

"I want the dams in the morning," Hodges repeated. "How you get them is your own business."

Huebner turned to Major General Louis Craig, commander of the 9th Division, who had just come in, and asked how soon he could move.

"In short order," he replied.

## 4.

The American Chiefs of Staff were far more preoccupied with the war in the Pacific. They were sitting across the table from the Soviet Chiefs of Staff at Yusopov Palace, Stalin's headquarters, trying to iron out military problems in the Far East and in particular what steps Russia should take once war with Japan was declared.

While this meeting was still in session, Roosevelt and Stalin were considering the same matter on a higher level, in the presence of Molotov, Harriman and the two interpreters, Pavlov and Bohlen. Roosevelt favored intensive bombing, which would bring about Japanese surrender and obviate the actual invasion of the islands. To this Stalin replied, "I'd like to discuss the political conditions under which the U.S.S.R. would enter the war against Japan." These conditions, he explained, had already been enumerated in a conversation with Harriman.

Roosevelt felt there would be no difficulty regarding Russia's getting the southern half of Sakhalin Island and the Kurile Islands as a reward. As for giving the Soviets a warm-water port in the Far East, what about leasing Dairen from the Chinese or making it a free port? Stalin paused noncommittally, aware of his good bargaining position, and countered by asking for something else—the use of the Manchurian railways. This seemed reasonable to Roosevelt and he suggested leasing them under Russian operation or under a joint Russian-Chinese commission.

Stalin was satisfied. "If these conditions are not met," he said pointedly, "it would be difficult for me and Molotov to explain to the Soviet people why Russia was entering a war against Japan."

"I haven't had an opportunity to talk to Marshal Chiang Kai-shek," Roosevelt replied. "One of the difficulties in speaking with the Chinese is that anything said to them is broadcast to the world in twenty-four hours."

Stalin conceded that it wasn't necessary to speak to the Chinese yet, then remarked affably, "Regarding the question of a warm-water port, we won't be difficult; I won't object to an internationalized free port."

When the talk switched to trusteeships in the Far East, Roosevelt admitted that the Korean problem was quite delicate. In a confidential tone he added that while he personally felt it wasn't necessary to invite the British to participate in the trusteeship of that country, they might resent not being asked.

"They most certainly would be offended." Stalin also became so confidential that he grinned and said, "In fact, the Prime Minister might kill us." Eager to please Roosevelt, who had been so eager to please him, he said to everyone's surprise, "I think the British should be invited."

It was now almost four o'clock, time for the fifth plenary, and they started toward the big ballroom. The other conferees were already there, chatting in little groups. Alger Hiss was talking to Eden about the controversial voting procedure for the United Nations. That morning Eden had helped draft the Foreign Ministers' report on the matter, and Hiss wondered if he could have a glance at it before the plenary started. Eden hesitated, finally handed over the report. The reason for his hesitation became obvious to Hiss when he read, with mounting amazement, that the United States now supported Stalin's request for extra votes. It was a mistake, Hiss exclaimed; the United States hadn't approved any such thing.

"You don't know what has taken place," Eden said quietly, and sat down at the table without telling Hiss that Roosevelt had privately approved the measure.

The fifth plenary opened with Eden accepting the American invitation to hold the first meeting of the United Nations in the United States on April 25. After a lengthy discussion as to who should participate, Molotov changed the subject by saying, "We think it would be useful to discuss the Polish question on the premise that the present government be extended. We cannot ignore that fact—that the present government exists in Warsaw. It is now at the head of the Polish people and has great authority."

Churchill jutted his jaw. "This is the crucial point of the conference," he said. The whole world was waiting for a settlement, and if they left Yalta, still recognizing different Polish governments, it would be obvious that "fundamental differences" still existed between them. "The consequences will be most lamentable, and will stamp our meeting with the seal of failure." Further, according to his information the Lublin government simply did not have the backing of the majority of Poles and if the Big Three abandoned the London Poles to give full support to those in Lublin, the 150,000 Poles fighting for the Allies would regard it as a betrayal. "His Majesty's Government would be charged in Parliament with having altogether forsaken the cause of Poland," he said and suggested that a "free and unfettered general election" be held. "Once this is done His Majesty's Government will salute the government that emerges, without regard to the Polish government in London. It is the interval before the election that is causing us so much anxiety."

Stalin retorted that the Lublin government—which he called the Warsaw government—really was very popular. "They are the people who did not leave Poland. They have come from the underground." Historically, he said, Poles hated Russians, but a remarkable change in their attitude came once their country was liberated by the Red Army. "Now there is good will toward Russia. It is only natural that the Polish people should be delighted to see the Germans flee their country and to feel themselves liberated. My impression is that the Poles consider this a great historic holiday. The population is surprised, even astounded, that the people of the London government do not take any part in this liberation. They see members of the provisional government there, but where are the London Poles?"

He admitted that it was better, of course, to have a government based on free elections but war had prevented them, and the provisional government must first be settled. "It is like that of de Gaulle, who also is not elected," he pointed out shrewdly. "Who is more popular, de Gaulle or Bierut? We have considered it possible to deal with de Gaulle and make treaties with him. Why not deal with the enlarged Polish provisional government? We cannot demand more of Poland than of France . . ."

"How long before elections can be held?" Roosevelt asked.

"In about one month, unless there is a catastrophe on the front and the Germans defeat us," Stalin replied with another display of heavy-handed humor, and smiled. "I do not think this will happen."

Even Churchill was impressed, or appeared to be. "Free elections would of course settle the worries of the British government at least."

"I move that we adjourn our talks until tomorrow," Roosevelt suggested.

He was openly pleased with this display of harmony and asked that the matter be referred to the three Foreign Secretaries.

"The other two will outvote me," Molotov said with one of his rare smiles.

Stalin's good humor continued even as he asked why they hadn't yet talked about Yugoslavia. And what about Greece? "I have no criticism to make, but I should like to know what is going on," he said with a sly look at Churchill, for it was covertly understood between them that Greece lay in the British sphere of influence.

Churchill said he could talk for hours about Greece. "As for Yugoslavia, the King has been persuaded, indeed forced, to agreement with regard to the regency." The leader of the Yugoslav government-in-exile, he understood, was leaving London immediately to help form a coalition government in Belgrade with Tito. "I am hopeful that peace will come on the basis of amnesty, but they hate each other so much that they cannot keep their hands off each other in Yugoslavia."

This brought another smile from Stalin. "They are not yet accustomed to discussions. Instead they cut each other's throats." As for Greece, he added with elephantine coquetry, "I only wanted to know for information. We have no intention of intervening there in any way."

This air of joviality carried over to the formal dinner at Yusopov Palace, as toast after toast was downed. Stalin proclaimed that Churchill was a man born once in a hundred years. In return the Prime Minister praised Stalin as the mighty leader of a mighty country which had taken the full shock of the German war machine, broken its back and driven the tyrants from her soil.

Next Stalin toasted Roosevelt with a warmth that was more than political. The decisions made by Churchill and himself, he said, had been relatively simple, but Roosevelt had joined the fight against Nazism although his country was not even seriously threatened with invasion, and had become "the chief forger of the instruments which led to the mobilization of the world against Hitler." Roosevelt's lend-lease project, he said gratefully, had saved the day. As the evening progressed Stalin began jestingly to pick on Feodor Gusov, one of his own diplomats, for never smiling. Stettinius felt that the Marshal carried the joke almost to ridicule.

Mosquitoes constantly attacked Admiral Leahy's ankles and irritated him almost as much as the endless toasts. He watered his own drinks so he could stay alert, but the whole thing, he thought, was an unwarranted waste of time. Why couldn't they go home and get the rest they needed for next day's work?

Churchill was on his feet again, making another eloquent toast, this one so optimistic that Stettinius, recalling the Prime Minister's depression at Malta, was taken aback. Churchill said that they were now on the crest of the hill and before them was the prospect of open country. "My hope is in the illustrious President of the United States and in Marshal Stalin, in whom we shall find the champions of peace, who after smiting the foe will lead us to carry on the task against poverty, confusion, chaos and oppression. That is my hope, and speaking for England, we shall not be behindhand in our efforts. We shall not weaken in supporting your exertions. The Marshal spoke of the future. That is the most important of all. Otherwise the oceans of bloodshed will have been useless and outrageous. I propose the toast to the broad sunlight of victorious peace."

A few minutes later the forty-fifth and final toast was proposed and drunk. It was, thought the weary, water-logged Leahy, about time.

The Combined Chiefs met at eleven o'clock the following morning to discuss their final military report. It was agreed that for planning purposes the earliest date to expect the defeat of Germany was July 1, 1945, and the latest, December 31, 1945, and the fall of Japan was set at eighteen months after Germany's defeat.

At noon they were joined by Churchill, and fifteen minutes later the President arrived, delayed by a treatment for sinus trouble. Since the military Chiefs had already come to complete agreement, there was no need for the Western political leaders to resolve any problems, and what followed was largely a genial conversation between Prime Minister and President. After almost an hour Roosevelt turned to Churchill and said with a mischievous smile, "This has been a fine conference, Winston, unless you go back to Paris and make another speech and tell the Frenchmen that the British intend to equip twenty-five more French divisions with American equipment."

With a laugh Churchill denied that he'd ever done such a thing, but the President said he had "a stack of papers" to prove that Churchill had indeed made that statement after the Quebec meeting.

"Whatever I said in Paris I said in French," parried Churchill. "And I never know what I'm saying when I talk in French, so pay no attention to it."

Just before the sixth plenary that afternoon, the Big Three and their principal advisers assembled in the courtyard of Livadia to be photographed. Upon their return to the ballroom, Stettinius started to read the plan the Foreign Ministers had drawn up that morning for dealing with territorial trusteeships in the United Nations. Before he was halfway through, Churchill angrily cried out that so far he had not agreed with one single word of the report. "I have not been consulted nor heard the subject until now!" he shouted, so wrought up that his horn-rimmed glasses slipped to the end of his nose. "Under no circumstances will I ever consent to the fumbling fingers of forty or fifty nations prying into the life's existence of the British Empire! As long as I am Prime Minister I shall never yield a scrap of Britain's heritage!"

At last Churchill quieted down enough to let Stettinius finish reading the report but he continued to fume, and the moment Molotov's proposal on a government for Poland was raised, he stirred in his seat as if getting ready to do battle again. In his role as mediator, Roosevelt said he thought they were near agreement on Poland and that it was "only a matter of drafting." On the other hand, it was also important for him to make a gesture to the 7,000,000 Poles in America, to assure them that the United States would have a hand in securing free elections in Poland. Churchill said he too had to answer to the House of Commons in similar fashion, and added irritably, "I do not care much about Poles myself."

Stalin took quick advantage of this careless remark to say self-righteously, "There are some very good people among Poles," and praised them as scientists, fighters and musicians. He even went so far as to say there were "non-Fascist and anti-Fascist" elements in both the London and Lublin governments. Churchill at once attacked the use of such terms and began a semantic quibble with Stalin, who finally said that the Declaration on Liberated Europe used the same terminology.

The Americans were instantly alert. This Declaration was the brainchild of Roosevelt and had been prepared for him by the State Department, calling for "the right of all peoples to choose the form of government under which they will live." Now that he had everyone's attention, Stalin said in an almost offhand manner, "On the whole I approve it."

Roosevelt was elated. If Stalin signed the Declaration, world peace and the universal rights of man could follow. "This is the first example for use of the Declaration," the President said eagerly. "It has the phrase 'to create democratic institutions of their own choice,' " and with growing excitement he began to quote part of the third paragraph of the Declaration: " '. . . to form interim governmental authorities broadly representative of all democratic elements in the population and pledged to the earliest possible establishment through free elections of governments responsive to the will of the people.' "

"We accept that Paragraph Three," said Stalin.

Roosevelt looked at him warmly. "I want this election in Poland to be the first one beyond question. It should be like Caesar's wife. I did not know her, but they said she was pure."

Caught up in Roosevelt's mood, Stalin rejoined with equal levity, "They said that about her, but in fact she had her sins." It was almost as if two comrades had burst into song.

The third man, Churchill, was left out and showed it. "I do not dissent from the President's proposed Declaration," he said a bit glumly, "as long as it is clearly understood that the reference to the Atlantic Charter does not apply to the British Empire." But a moment later he regained the center of the stage and his good humor when he dramatically said, "I should like to announce that British troops began an attack at dawn yesterday in the Nijmegen area. They advanced about three thousand yards and are now in contact with the Siegfried Line. . . . Tomorrow the second wave will follow and the American Ninth Army comes in. The offensive will continue without cessation."

## 5.

"Veritable" encountered more difficulties than the most pessimistic of its commanders had envisioned. The troops made little progress over fields turned into swamps by the continuing downpour; tanks bogged down in muddy roads; and when the key Nijmegen–Cleve highway became inundated, a monumental traffic jam developed.

To the south Simpson too was beset by water. The Roer River was rising, and though engineers assured him that this was only due to run-off, not because of a breach in the Roer dams, all except one of his corps commanders urged postponement of Operation "Grenade." Simpson told them that he would make up his mind by four o'clock. It was a difficult problem: the success of "Veritable," already off to a slow start, depended largely on his attack the next morning; but what if he sent his assault troops across the Roer and then found it flooded behind their backs? Just before four o'clock he learned that the river was still rising, albeit slightly. Was this really run-off or was it water from the dams? Should he take the calculated risk? His career would probably be finished if he called off the attack and the Roer did not overflow its banks. He sat alone, agonizing, vacillating. At exactly four o'clock something told him, "Postpone the attack." He did.

Craig's 9th Division had not yet reached the dams. The Germans, retreating slowly, were making every yard of advance costly. It was not until nine o'clock—hours after Simpson's decision—that the 1st Battalion of the 309th Regiment groped its way clumsily through the darkness to the biggest of the dams, which held back 81,000 acre-feet of water. The battalion split, part heading for the crest of the dam, the rest descending to the lower level and the powerhouse.

At midnight, in the face of enemy fire, a team of engineers raced across the top of the dam toward an inspection tunnel. Finding the spillway blasted and their way blocked, they slid down the steep 200-foot face of the dam to get in by the tunnel's bottom exit. It was all in vain. The Germans had already destroyed the machinery in the powerhouse and blown up the penstocks. A steady stream of water gushed into the Roer River—just heavy enough to keep the entire Roer valley flooded for the next two weeks.

It is odd that those who had designed "Veritable" so carefully to depend on "Grenade" did not realize that what actually took place was bound to happen. It mattered not that Craig's men had not arrived at dawn—an impossibility—the Germans would simply have done then what they did at dusk. As a result 200,000 Canadians, Englishmen, Welshmen and Scots were now mucked down in one of the most grueling, punishing battles of the war. The responsibility would have to be shared by many— but chiefly by those at the top: Eisenhower and Montgomery, Marshall and Brooke.

All the next day, February 10, Horrocks' men continued their slow, gallant push through flood and mire, against a stubborn enemy. Horrocks should have been relieved of pressure by "Grenade," but of course there was no attack by Simpson, and those Germans sent north as reinforcements remained to make life even more miserable for the men of "Veritable."

By now most of the Nijmegen–Cleve road was under water and four ferries had to transport priority traffic up front. In addition, the first rush of water from the Roer dams had not only overflowed the Roer River but was spilling into the Maas, and in a few hours Horrocks would face still another calamity: the low ground below the Reichswald would also be flooded.

The Allied army that was making the best progress that day was stopped by order—not by the enemy. Bradley called Patton and asked when he could switch over to the defensive. Patton replied heatedly that he was the oldest commander in age and combat experience in the whole Army, and said he would ask to be relieved if forced to go on the defensive. Bradley's arguments only made Patton suggest sarcastically that it might be a good idea if some of the 12th Army Group staff came up front once in a while. To Patton, the trouble with Bradley was that he didn't stand up to Eisenhower and fight for his beliefs firmly enough.

Before long Bradley called again. This time what he had to say gave Patton a strange satisfaction. Monty's "alleged attack," Bradley confided, was the biggest mistake Eisenhower had made yet; he predicted that it either had bogged down or would soon do so completely. Simpson had not kicked off as scheduled, and it was Bradley's understanding that they would now go back to the original plan advocated by Patton—just as soon as weather permitted.

This was all wishful thinking. In spite of the difficulties encountered by "Veritable" and the postponement of "Grenade," Eisenhower had no intention of changing his plan. Montgomery would still lead the main assault across the Rhine and on to Berlin while Hodges and Patton played their supporting roles.

## 6.

Ambassador Harriman met Molotov at Russian headquarters in the afternoon and was handed an English translation of the Soviet Union's political conditions for going to war with Japan. Stalin wanted the status quo preserved in Outer Mongolia, and territory seized by Japan after their war in 1904—principally the southern part of Sakhalin Island, Port Arthur and Dairen—returned to Russia. He also asked for control of the Manchurian railways and the Kurile Islands. In return the Soviet Union would conclude a pact of friendship and alliance with Chiang Kai-shek, as well as declare war on Japan.

Harriman read the draft and said, "There are three amendments I believe the President would wish to make before accepting." Dairen and Port Arthur should be free ports, and the Manchurian railways should be operated by a joint Chinese-Soviet commission. "In addition, I feel sure that the President wouldn't wish to dispose of these two matters in which China is interested, without concurrence of Generalissimo Chiang Kai-shek."

As soon as Harriman had returned to Livadia he showed Roosevelt the draft of Stalin's proposal, with the amendments he himself had brought up. The President approved them and asked Harriman to resubmit them to Molotov, confident that he was doing the best thing for America. The Joint Chiefs had unanimously insisted that he somehow get Russia into the war against Japan, primarily to fight the 700,000-man Japanese Kwantung army in Manchuria. It was Marshall's opinion that in a conquest of this army without Russian help, hundreds of thousands of American boys would perish. A few U. S. naval intelligence officers believed that this Kwantung army existed only on paper, since most of the men had already been transferred to other sectors, but these experts were not heeded—though they happened to be correct—and so, on February 10, Roosevelt was taking steps to do what almost anyone possessing the same information would have done.

Soon after Harriman had left, Roosevelt was wheeled into the ballroom for the seventh plenary—the meeting that would establish the success or failure of the entire conference. The most important questions to be solved were reparations, a zone of occupation for France, and Poland— whose fate would indicate the future of the other liberated nations of eastern Europe.

Roosevelt was in his place promptly at four o'clock, his back to the big log fire. Churchill arrived somewhat breathless. He apologized to

Roosevelt; then, lowering his voice, he said mysteriously, "I believe that I have succeeded in retrieving the situation," and walked off without explaining that Stalin had just agreed informally to a new wording on the question of elections in Poland.

When Stalin came in, he too apologized to the President. Eden opened the meeting, this time with a progress report. He announced that the Foreign Ministers had agreed on the future government of Poland, according to the following new formula:

"A new situation has been created in Poland as a result of her complete liberation by the Red Army. This calls for the establishment of a Polish Provisional Government which can be more broadly based than was possible before the recent liberation of Western Poland. The Provisional Government which is now functioning in Poland should therefore be reorganized on a broader democratic basis with the inclusion of democratic leaders from Poland itself and from Poles abroad. . . .

"This Polish Provisional Government of National Unity shall be pledged to the holding of free and unfettered elections as soon as possible on the basis of universal suffrage and secret ballot. . . ."

Roosevelt handed his copy to Leahy. The admiral frowned as he read it. Handing the paper back, he said, "Mr. President, this is so elastic that the Russians can stretch it all the way from Yalta to Washington without ever technically breaking it."

"I know, Bill," the President answered in an undertone. "I know it. But it's the best I can do for Poland at this time."

While Churchill brought up the fact that the formula made no mention of frontiers, Hopkins handed a note to Roosevelt:

Mr. President:

    I think you should make clear to Stalin that you support the eastern boundary but that only a general statement be put in communique saying we are considering essential boundary changes. Might be well to refer exact statement to foreign ministers.

                       Harry

The communiqué referred to was the one the Big Three would issue when the conference was over, making public their final decisions.

"I think we should leave out all references to frontiers," Roosevelt interjected, ignoring Hopkins' note.

"It is important to say *something*," Stalin emphasized.

For once Churchill and Stalin stood against Roosevelt. The Polish frontier settlement simply had to be in the communiqué, said the Prime Minister.

Roosevelt disagreed. "I have no right to make an agreement on boundaries at this time. This must be done by the Senate later. Let the Prime

Minister make some public statement when he returns, if that's necessary."

Molotov stirred. "I think it would be very good if something could be included about the complete agreement of the three leaders regarding the eastern frontier," he said in a low voice. "We could say that the Curzon Line is generally representative of the opinion of all present. . . . I agree that we need say nothing about the western frontier."

"I agree we must say *something*," said Churchill.

"Yes, but less specific if you wish," the Foreign Commissar suggested. "We must say that Poland is to get compensation in the west."

"Very good," said Molotov.

Roosevelt abruptly brought up a new subject—and caused a sensation. "I should like to say that I have changed my mind with regard to the position of the French on the control council for Germany. The more I think of it, the more I think that the Prime Minister is right." France, he declared, should have a zone of occupation. Before Stettinius could recover from this surprise, he got an even greater one when Stalin said, "I agree." This turnabout had been arranged behind the scenes. Hopkins had privately persuaded Roosevelt that it would be prudent to let France have a zone, and the President then told Stalin privately, through Harriman, that he had changed his mind. Stalin promptly replied that he "would go along" with the President.

Churchill was as exultant at this as Roosevelt had been the day before. "Of course," he observed with a straight face, "France may say that she will have no part in the Declaration and reserve all rights for the future." Everybody laughed. "We must face that," Churchill added with a pixy grin. Even the somber Molotov joined the fun. "We must be prepared to receive a rough answer," he said.

This camaraderie collapsed as suddenly as it had started when Churchill returned to the subject of reparations. He thought $20,000,000,000— half going to Russia—was ridiculous but put it more politely. "We were practically instructed by our government not to mention figures," he said. "Let the [Moscow Reparations] Commission do it." Stalin was expecting this from Churchill and showed no emotion, but he looked genuinely hurt when Roosevelt remarked that he too was afraid the mention of a specific amount of money would make many Americans think of reparations only in terms of dollars and cents.

Stalin whispered angrily to Andrei Gromyko, who nodded and walked over to Hopkins. After a short huddle Hopkins hastily scribbled:

Mr. President:

    Gromyko just told me that the Marshall thinks you did not back up Ed relative to Reparations—and that you sided with the British—and he is disturbed about it. Perhaps you could tell him privately later.

Harry

Stalin was saying with great emotion, "I think we can be quite frank." His voice grew louder, even more charged, as he avowed that no amount of goods taken from Germany could compensate for the tremendous Russian losses. "The Americans already agreed to take as a basis twenty million dollars!" he said, too wrought up to realize he had made a slip of the tongue. "Does it mean the American side withdraws its agreement?" He looked at Roosevelt, affronted as well as disappointed.

Roosevelt quickly retracted; the last thing he wanted was a bitter agrument over what he considered a relatively minor side issue. Only one word bothered him, he said. " 'Reparations' mean only 'money' to so many people."

"We can use another word," Stalin conceded, getting out of his chair for the first time since the meetings had started. "The three governments agree that Germany must pay in kind for losses caused by her to the Allies in the course of the war!"

If Roosevelt was in a placating mood, Churchill was not. "We cannot commit ourselves to the figure of twenty billion dollars, or any other figures, until the [Reparations] Commission has studied the matter," he said, and continued the argument with such ardor and eloquence that Stettinius wrote in his notes that it was always a pleasure to listen to Churchill's "beautiful phrases" rolling out "as water in a running stream."

His words had the opposite effect on Stalin. "If the British don't want the Russians to receive reparations," he said, gesturing emphatically, "they should say so frankly." He sat down heavily and glared.

Churchill took exception to the innuendo, with the result that Stalin jumped to his feet again. Roosevelt got everyone's attention: "I suggest that the whole matter be left to the Commission in Moscow."

Somewhat mollified, Stalin sat down to let Molotov have the floor. "The only differences arise between the United States and the Soviet delegation on the one hand," he said calmly, "and the British on the other in regard to the naming of a sum." Stalin relaxed noticeably. The deft phrasing made him partners with Roosevelt against Churchill.

"Rightly or wrongly, the British government feels that even the naming of a sum as the basis of discussions will commit them," said Eden in a conciliatory tone and proposed that the Reparations Commission be instructed to examine the report recently drafted by the three Foreign Ministers.

Stalin had completely regained his composure. "I propose, first, that the three heads of government agree that Germany must pay compensation in kind for losses caused during the war," he said. "Second, the heads of the three governments agree that Germany must pay for losses to the Allied nations. Third, the Moscow Reparations Commission is given the task to consider the amount to be paid." He turned to Churchill. "We bring our figures before the Commission and you bring yours."

"I agree," said Churchill. "How about the United States?"

"The answer is simple," the President answered, vastly relieved. "Judge Roosevelt approves and the document is accepted."

They recessed for hot tea in the usual big glasses, with silver holders for the Americans. The brief rift between Stalin and Roosevelt apparently worried the Marshal, so he took Harriman aside to say that he was willing to meet the President halfway on the agreement to join the war against Japan. "I'm entirely willing to have Dairen a free port under international control," he said. "But Port Arthur is different. It's to be a Russian naval base and therefore Russia requires a lease."

"Why don't you discuss this matter at once with the President," Harriman suggested, and soon after, Stalin and Roosevelt were conversing in hushed voices. Complete agreement was quickly reached. When the conferees returned to the plenary meeting, the general sense of relief that an ominous cleavage had been avoided resulted in a round of quips. Even Churchill chided Roosevelt about his famous phrase "Freedom from want," as he speculated on what exactly the third word meant. "I suppose that it means 'privation,' not 'desire.' "

At last they got back to business, the most important business of the day: the drafting of the statement on the Big Three position regarding Poland that would appear in the final communiqué. Hopkins was worried that Roosevelt might commit the United States to a treaty establishing the new Polish boundaries and wrote another note:

Mr. President:

You get into trouble about your legal powers & what senate will say.

Harry

After reading the note, Roosevelt suggested that the wording of the statement be changed lest it violate the American Constitution.

A new draft was quickly made and read aloud:

"The three Heads of Government consider that the Eastern frontier of Poland should follow the Curzon Line with digressions from it in some regions of five to eight kilometres in favour of Poland. It is recognized that Poland must receive substantial accessions of territory in the North and West. They feel that the opinion of the new Polish Provisional Government of National Unity should be sought in due course on the extent of these accessions and that the final delimitation of the Western frontier of Poland should thereafter await the Peace Conference."

Hopkins now handed the President a final note:

Mr. President:

I think we are through when this discussion is concluded.

Harry

While Roosevelt was reading this, Molotov suggested that to the second sentence should be added "with the return to Poland of her ancient frontiers in East Prussia and on the Oder."

"How long ago were these lands Polish?" Roosevelt asked.

"Very long ago."

Roosevelt turned to Churchill with a laugh and said, "Perhaps you would want us back?"

"Well, you might be as indigestible for us as it might be for the Poles if they took too much German territory."

"The change would give great encouragement to the Poles," Molotov urged.

"I prefer to leave it as it is," Churchill demurred.

"I withdraw my suggestion," Stalin said equably, "and agree to leave it as drawn."

It was already eight o'clock and Roosevelt was tired. He suggested that they adjourn until the next morning at eleven, when they could write their joint communiqué in time to bring the entire conference to a close by noon. This would enable him to leave Yalta at three o'clock.

Churchill frowned and said that he did not think it would be possible to clear up all their problems so quickly. Moreover, the communiqué was to be broadcast to the world and should not be drawn up hastily. Stalin agreed. Roosevelt, without saying yes or no, nodded to Mike Reilly, chief of his bodyguard, and was wheeled out of the room.

This hasty exit left a number of the British and Russian delegates disturbed, but they had little time to brood. In one hour they all were due to appear at the final formal dinner at Yalta, this time with Churchill as host at his headquarters in Vorontsov Palace. The grotesque Moorish-Scottish villa had already been thoroughly searched by Russian soldiers—they had even crawled under the tables.

During vodka and caviar before dining, Molotov ambled over to Stettinius and said, "We have agreed on the date. Can't you tell us where the conference is to be held?" He was referring to the first meeting of the United Nations organization.

Stettinius had been fretting about the location for some time. A number of cities had been suggested and dropped: New York, Philadelphia, Chicago, Miami. At three o'clock the previous morning he had been wakened by a dream of San Francisco so realistic that he could almost feel the fresh Pacific air. Convinced that this was the perfect location, he went to Roosevelt's bedroom after breakfast, and outlined the advantage of San Francisco, only to get a noncommittal response.

Stettinius left Molotov and walked over to Roosevelt, seated in his ambulatory wheel chair. "Molotov is pressing me on a decision as to a place for the conference. Are you ready to say San Francisco?"

"Go ahead, Ed. San Francisco it is."

Stettinius returned to Molotov and gave him the news. The Foreign

Commissar waved to Eden and a moment later the three Foreign Ministers were drinking a vodka toast to the San Francisco Conference, which would open in eleven weeks.

At dinner Stalin leaned over and told Churchill that he was not happy with the way the reparations question had been settled. He was afraid to tell the Soviet people they weren't going to get adequate reparations because the British were opposed. Stettinius guessed that Molotov and Maisky had privately convinced him he'd conceded too much at the last plenary.

Churchill retorted that he very much hoped Russia would get large reparations, but he couldn't help remembering the last war, when they had placed the figure higher than Germany could pay.

"It would be a good idea," Stalin persisted, "to put some mention in the communiqué of the intention to make Germany pay for the damage it has caused the Allied nations."

Both Roosevelt and Churchill agreed, and the latter proposed a toast to the Marshal. "I have drunk this toast on several occasions. This time I drink it with a warmer feeling than at previous meetings, not because he is more triumphant, but because the great victories and the glory of the Russian arms have made him kindlier than he was in the hard times through which we have passed. I feel that, whatever differences there may be on certain questions, he has a good friend in Britain. I hope to see the future of Russia bright, prosperous and happy. I will do anything to help, and I am sure so will the President. There was a time when the Marshal was not so kindly towards us, and I remember that I said a few rude things about him, but our common dangers and common loyalties have wiped all that out. The fire of war has burnt up the misunderstandings of the past. We feel we have a friend whom we can trust, and I hope he will continue to feel the same about us. I pray he may live to see his beloved Russia not only glorious in war, but also happy in peace."

Stettinius turned to Stalin in an excess of sentiment and enthusiasm. "If we work together in the postwar years, there's no reason why every home in the Soviet Union couldn't soon have electricity and plumbing."

"We have learned much already from the United States," Stalin replied without the trace of a smile.

A moment later Roosevelt told a story about the Ku Klux Klan. Once he had been dinner guest of the president of the chamber of commerce in a small Southern town. When he asked if the two men sitting on either side—one a Jew and the other an Italian—were members of the KKK, his host replied, "Oh, yes, but they're all right; everyone in the community knows them." It was a good illustration, Roosevelt remarked, of how difficult it was to have any prejudices—racial, religious or otherwise—if you really knew people.

"Very true," Stalin agreed, and Stettinius thought it was an example to the world that people of far different backgrounds could find a common basis of understanding.

The discussion turned to English politics and Churchill's problems in the coming elections. "Marshal Stalin has a much easier political task," the Prime Minister remarked mischievously. "He has only one party to deal with."

"Experience has shown," Stalin replied with equal good humor, "that one party is of great convenience to a leader of state."

The atmosphere remained relaxed until Roosevelt told them that he had to leave the next day.

"But, Franklin, you can't go," Churchill said urgently. "We have within our reach a very great prize."

"Winston, I have made commitments and I must depart tomorrow as planned." Earlier the President had told Stettinius he would have to use such an excuse to prevent the conference from dragging on and on.

"I too think more time is needed to consider and finish the business of the conference," Stalin concurred. He walked over to the President and said quietly that he didn't see how they could possibly finish everything by three o'clock the next day, Sunday.

Roosevelt acceded graciously. "If necessary, I'll wait over until Monday."

After the dinner Roosevelt returned to his room at Livadia. Exhausted as he was by the eventful day, he still had two important notes to write. James Byrnes and Edward Flynn—two astute politicians—had warned him that there would be much criticism at home when it was revealed that Russia was getting two extra votes in the United Nations, but it would help to get, in return, two extra votes for America.

Roosevelt now wrote Stalin a frank note explaining the problem and asking if he would agree to extra votes for America at the United Nations. The President also wrote Churchill a similar letter, then went to bed.

## 7.

The next morning, Sunday, February 11, Stalin and Roosevelt showed Churchill and Eden their agreement on the Far East. Churchill was about to sign the paper, but Eden called it "a discreditable by-product of the conference" right in front of Stalin and Roosevelt. Churchill replied sharply that British prestige in the Orient would suffer if he followed Eden's advice, and signed the agreement.

Nothing could dampen Roosevelt's high spirits, for he had just received answers to his two letters about the extra votes. Churchill had replied,

"I need hardly assure you that I should do everything possible to assist you in this matter," and Stalin wrote, "I think that the number of votes for the USA might be increased to three. . . . If it is necessary I am prepared officially to support this proposal."

At the eighth and final plenary that noon, Roosevelt's mood was catching. Not a single problem arose and the drafting of the communiqué took less than an hour. Everyone appeared pleased but Churchill. He began to grumble, predicting that he would be heavily attacked in England on the Polish decision. "It will be said we have yielded completely on the frontiers and the whole matter to Russia."

"Are you serious?" Stalin asked. "I can't believe it."

"The London Poles will raise a dreadful outcry."

"But the other Poles will predominate," Stalin retorted.

"I hope you're right," Churchill said grimly. "We're not going back on it. It's not a question of the numbers of Poles but of the cause for which Britain drew the sword. They will say you have completely swept away the only constitutional government of Poland." He seemed almost depressed. "However, I will defend it to the best of my ability."

If he was a bit gloomy, the luncheon that followed certainly was not. Here the general feeling was one of relief that everything had gone so well. Roosevelt was expansive. His cherished Declaration on Liberated Europe, the promise of world freedom and democracy, was accepted and Stalin had agreed in writing to enter the war against Japan two or three months after the fall of Germany.

Harriman was pleased. Stalin had also agreed to support Chiang Kai-shek and recognize the sovereignty of the Chinese Nationalist government over Manchuria; it was a very solid diplomatic triumph. As for Poland, the ambassador was sure Stalin had meant what he said when he promised a free election. But behind this optimism was nagging doubt, for he remembered the old saying "You have to buy the horse twice with a Russian." The problem now, he thought, was to keep the Russians to their word.

Bohlen felt that it had been "a necessary conference and it really afforded the United States the possibility of judging the Soviet Union by the degree in which they observed the agreements reached." At times Stalin had yielded to Roosevelt, showing evidence that the President had skillfully played on the awe in which Stalin held him. The touchiest problem, Poland, could have had no better solution under the circumstances. Churchill and Roosevelt had only three alternatives: do nothing; stand uncompromisingly behind the London Poles; or try to get as many London Poles as possible into the reorganized government. The first course was out. Anyone who knew Stalin was aware that the second choice would have been turned down flatly. The third, while not the happiest solution, was the only realistic choice for the Western leaders.

There was already some talk by the British that the President's poor health had been an adverse factor at the meetings. Bohlen had spent every minute at Roosevelt's side, and though he could see some truth in this, particularly in the final minutes of a long meeting, he doubted that Roosevelt's physical condition had weakened his resolution.

During the luncheon, final copies of the recently drafted joint communiqué were passed around. Churchill, Stalin and Roosevelt studied their copies, found no flaws and signed. The conference, except for a few formalities, was over.

There was a feeling of quiet satisfaction among the Americans as they were getting ready to leave. Universally it was believed that what the United States had sought at Yalta she had got, with more to spare. Harry Hopkins was sure in his heart that this was the dawn of the new day everyone had been praying for and talking about for so many years. The first great victory of the peace had been won, he felt, with the Russians proving they could be reasonable and farseeing.

It was true that Roosevelt and Churchill had accomplished what the great majority of Westerners prayed they would. There had been bitter arguments, but these were overshadowed by a remarkable number of agreements—some of which, unfortunately, would not be kept. An impartial observer at the Livadia meetings could only have concluded that on paper at least, the West had scored a substantial triumph. And the greatest victory had been won by Roosevelt alone—without a fight—when a reluctant Stalin and a dubious Churchill raised no objections to the United Nations.

That night Roosevelt dined aboard the U.S.S. *Catoctin* in the Sevastopol harbor. The entree was steak and it was "a real treat" to everyone after eight days of Russian food. The President was worn out but happy.

It wasn't until six o'clock that the three hard-working Foreign Ministers signed the protocol of the conference, and after the final word of this document had been radioed to Washington through the communications facilities of the *Catoctin,* "Doc" Matthews said to Stettinius, "Mr. Secretary, our last message has been sent. Can I cut the connections to the ship?"

"Yes," said Stettinius. The Yalta Conference was over.

# 6

## The Balkan Cockpit

**1.**

At Yalta the argument centering on Poland only dramatized a problem facing all the liberated countries of Europe, and nowhere was this problem more acute than in the Balkans. In the spring of 1944 the Russians had surged so suddenly into the Ukraine with three powerful Soviet fronts that within a week the Balkans were laid open to conquest.

This alarmed Churchill almost as much as Hitler, since he had long regarded the Balkans as one of the cornerstones in a stable postwar Europe. Even when the Soviet Union sent a formal note to Britain and America promising not to change by force the existing social system of Rumania—the first Balkan country in the path of the Red Army—Churchill nevertheless believed that Stalin secretly intended to convert all of southeastern Europe to Bolshevism. He therefore asked Eden to draft a paper for the Cabinet on "the brute issues" between West and East in the Balkans. "Broadly speaking," Churchill said in his memorandum to Eden, "the issue is, Are we going to acquiesce in the Communization of the Balkans?" If not, ". . . we should put it to them pretty plainly at the best moment the military events permit."

At the same time, Churchill felt it was impossible to stop the Russians everywhere and was willing to make an agreement with Stalin dividing up the Balkans in spheres of influence—for example, let Russia dominate Rumania while Britain dominated Greece. The rub was that the mere thought of such a "deal" morally offended Secretary of State Cordell Hull and many other Americans. As for Roosevelt, he was strongly opposed to involving the United States in the postwar burden of re-constituting Europe, and particularly the Balkans. "That is not our natural task at a distance of 3500 miles or more," he wrote Stettinius. "It is definitely a British task in which the British are far more vitally interested than we are."

He also made these feelings bluntly clear to Churchill, cabling him that he was opposed to the division of the Balkans into spheres of influence, and cautioning him that America would never use military power or any kind of force to achieve diplomatic victories in southeastern Europe. Late in August, 1944, after the last German-Rumanian defenses had been crushed by the Red Army, King Michael dismissed the Antonescu government and called for an end to hostilities. A coalition government of Conservatives, Socialists and Communists was formed. But the coalition had little meaning when an armistice was signed a few days later which put Rumania under the direct authority of the Soviet High Command. Ambassador Harriman let Washington know that this gave the Soviets immediate police control of Rumania and eventual political control. The State Department told Harriman that he could protest, but this protest, and a similar one from Britain, had as much effect on Stalin as King Canute's command to the sea. And within a few weeks Western observers in Bucharest began reporting that Rumania was being dragged closer and closer to Communism.

The case of Bulgaria was a variation on the same theme. Though its government had never declared war against Russia, Bulgarian troops were helping Hitler control the Balkans, and as soon as Rumania was conquered the Red Army pushed up to its boundary. Bulgaria's Cabinet promptly fell and a new one denounced the pact with Hitler, promising unconditional neutrality, but this was not enough for Stalin, who sent his troops across the border. It was a bloodless conquest, with the Bulgarians not only receiving the Red Army enthusiastically but setting up a new government, a coalition representing many factions, including the Communist Party. As in Rumania, the Red Army was in full control and this coalition too was only a fiction, with each succeeding day bringing more power to the Communists.

### 2.

The next target for the Red Army was Yugoslavia, a study in contradictions. The leader in its fight against Hitler was a Communist, disliked and distrusted by the world's leading Communist, yet admired and endorsed by one of the world's leading democrats. To Stalin, Tito was an egotistical upstart; to Churchill, he was a gallant warrior waging a patriotic battle against Hitler.

The problems of Yugoslavia were unlike those of any other Balkan country. A kingdom created artificially after World War I out of Croatia, Serbia, Montenegro, Macedonia and Slovenia, its government had signed a pact with Rumania and Bulgaria on March 25, 1941, aligning the three nations with Hitler's new European order. The infuriated people rose spontaneously, and two days later the regent, Prince Paul, and his Prime Minister were taken into custody by a group of Air Force officers who formed a patriotic government. When Hitler first heard of this coup d'état, he was incredulous. Assured that it was indeed true, he ordered Yugoslavia invaded, and in a few days bombers pounded Belgrade as German, Hungarian, Bulgarian and Italian troops struck from several sides. Twelve days later Yugoslavia capitulated and was carved up by the victors.

There was little organized resistance in the country for two months until Hitler's surprise attack on Russia, when the Comintern radioed Josip Broz, secretary-general of the Yugoslav Communist Party:

ORGANIZE PARTISAN DETACHMENTS WITHOUT A MOMENT'S
DELAY. START A PARTISAN WAR IN ENEMY'S REAR.

Broz—his party name was Tito—was a handsome, virile man of fifty-three. The seventh of fifteen children, he was born to parents who were peasants and he had inherited the sturdy body of one. For the past twenty-eight years he had been a dedicated Communist. He was also a dedicated patriot, and within a few months he combined his two loyalties so ably and energetically that most Yugoslavs acknowledged him as the leader of their united front against Fascism.

One large partisan group refused to accept his leadership. These were the Chetniks, heirs to a historical tradition of resistance, whose ancestors had led guerilla fights against the Turks. Commanded by Colonel Draja Mikhailovich of the Royal Yugoslav Army, they still wore the traditional fur hat and emblem of crossed knives, and still sang old bloodthirsty songs of throat-cutting, with a few modern variations:

> My fur cap trembles, my knife also trembles during
>   the march.
> We shall kill, we shall cut the throats of everybody
>   who is not for Draja.

Mikhailovich, a former intelligence officer, was a staunch Monarchist, longing for the authority of the old days. In spite of some schooling, he retained many of the primitive qualities of his forebears, and to further complicate matters, was an irresolute man who disliked making decisions. He refused to join Tito's partisans because of his hatred of Communism, so within months what had started as a patriotic fight against Hitler turned into a political war against Tito, a war so bitter Mikhailovich began secretly collaborating with the Germans. Once their country was rid of Tito, he told his lieutenants, they would turn their arms against the Germans. Ironically, his son and daughter were fighting for Tito.

The London government-in-exile denounced as a Bolshevik lie the charge that Mikhailovich was collaborating with the Germans, promoted him to general and appointed him Minister of War and commander in chief of the Royal Yugoslav Army. These London Yugoslavs were so persuasive that Britain and America began parachuting extensive supplies to Mikhailovich, and it wasn't until the middle of 1943, after a revealing report from Captain F. W. Deakin, a young Oxford don traveling with Tito, that Churchill began to doubt that all the aid going to Mikhailovich was being used against the enemy it was intended for. To determine if Tito, rather than Mikhailovich, should get the bulk of Allied aid, the Prime Minister dispatched Brigadier Fitzroy Maclean, a thirty-two-year-old former career diplomat, to Yugoslavia as head of the military mission to the partisans.

Maclean, a Conservative Member of Parliament, discovered that Tito had united patriots of many political shadings into an aggressive, effective force. The partisans, he reported, were self-disciplined, austere. There was no drinking, looting or dalliance. All seemed bound by an ideological and military vow to drive out the Fascists—and then set up an equitable government for all the peoples of their jigsaw country. What particularly surprised Maclean was Tito's intense national pride, a characteristic seemingly incompatible in an ardent Communist. Other things were also unexpected: Tito's broad outlook; his sense of humor and naïve delight in the small pleasures of life; his violent rages; his thoughtfulness, generosity and willingness to look at both sides of a question.

More important, Maclean learned first-hand that Tito's partisans, by late 1943, were tying down upward of a dozen German divisions; also, that he was constantly harassed by Mikhailovich as well as by a nationalist group of Croatians called the Ustachi. They were fervent Roman Catholics bent on a campaign of terror, bloodthirsty even by Balkan standards. The Ustachi hated the Serbs, the Jews, the Communists and, particularly, members of the Greek Orthodox Church. Though most of the ecclesiastical officials in Croatia were hostile to the Ustachi, the rank-and-file Catholic priests joined in the bloody purges with enthusiasm, and often led attacks in which entire villages were massacred, whether the people renounced their religion or not. One of the favorite Ustachi methods was to burn down Orthodox churches with their congregations inside.

Largely because of Maclean's reports, Churchill persuaded Stalin and Roosevelt at Teheran to give Tito the major support in Yugoslavia. Two months later the Prime Minister wrote Tito:

. . . I am resolved that the British Government shall give no further military support to Mihailovic and will only give help to you, and we should be glad if the Royal Yugoslavian Government would dismiss him from their councils. King Peter the Second however escaped as a boy from the treacherous clutches of the Regent Prince Paul, and came to us as the representative of Yugoslavia and as a young prince in distress. It would not be chivalrous or honourable for Great Britain to cast him aside. Nor can we ask him to cut all existing contacts with his country. I hope therefore that you will understand we shall in any case remain in official relations with him, while at the same time giving you all possible military support. I hope also that there may be an end to polemics on either side, for these only help the Germans. . . .

In reply Tito thanked Churchill for the military aid, but pointed out the political future of his country was more complex than the British seemed to realize.

. . . I quite understand your engagements towards King Peter II and his Government, and I will contrive, as far as the interests of our people permit, to avoid unnecessary politics and not cause inconvenience to our Allies in this matter. I assure you, however, your Excellency, that the internal political situation created in this arduous struggle for liberation is not only a machine for the strivings of individuals or some political group, but it is the irresistible desire of all patriots, of all those who are fighting and long connected with this struggle, and these are the enormous majority of the peoples of Yugoslavia. . . .

At the present moment all our efforts turn to one direction . . . to create union and brotherhood of the Yugoslav nations, which did not exist before this war, and the absence of which caused the catastrophe in our country. . . .

In spite of political differences, Churchill and Tito continued their co-operation so successfully that by D-Day the partisans, with the help of weapons from the West, were fighting perhaps twenty-five enemy divisions on almost even terms, and by the time the Red Army—after its easy conquests of Rumania and Bulgaria in September—crossed into Yugoslavia, the Germans were already withdrawing.* Tito arranged to go to Moscow, for the purpose of co-ordinating the operations of his partisans with those of the Red Army. The Russians asked him to leave secretly, so with his dog, Tigar—head muffled in a sack—he slipped past British guards at the airfield on the island of Vis, just off the coast of Yugoslavia, and boarded a Soviet-manned Dakota.**

It was Tito's first visit to Russia since 1940, when he was an obscure member of a not very important underground party, with the prosaic code name of Walter. Now a victorious marshal and the leader of a resurgent party which would undoubtedly soon take over the country,

* Mikhailovich continued to fight Tito to the end. He was captured by the partisans, tried and executed.

** Maclean got this information from Yugoslav sources and believes the Russians might have urged secrecy only to break up the close relationship between Tito and Churchill. If this was the case, they succeeded. Churchill was extremely annoyed at Tito's secret departure, and in an indignant radio message to Hopkins, called it "graceless behaviour."

he was driven to the same *dacha* used by Churchill. The short, stocky Stalin embraced Tito, and to his surprise, lifted him off his feet. Tito responded to these overtures with respect, if not obeisance, and Stalin cooled perceptibly. He was already more than annoyed by recent messages from Tito, particularly one which began, "If you cannot help us, at least do not hinder us." The aging Stalin must also have resented Tito's striking appearance and magnificent uniforms—and the spate of good publicity he was getting in the Western press.

"Be careful, Walter," Stalin said condescendingly at one of their meetings, "the bourgeoisie in Serbia is very strong."

"I disagree with you, Comrade Stalin," retorted Tito, who resented being called Walter. "The bourgeoisie in Serbia is very weak."

There was an embarrassed silence, not helped by the fact that Tito was right. When Stalin asked about a certain non-Communist politician in Yugoslavia, Tito answered, "Oh, he's a scoundrel and a traitor; he collaborated with the Germans."

Stalin mentioned another man and got the same curt answer. "Walter," Stalin said peevishly, "to you they are all scoundrels."

"Exactly, Comrade Stalin," Tito replied with a touch of righteousness. "Anyone who betrays his country is a scoundrel."

What was only an awkward situation threatened to become serious when Stalin declared that he was in favor of restoring King Peter to avoid clashes with Britain and America—at this point in the war, he still needed their military help badly. Tito, who needed help but not at that price, replied sharply that it was impossible to restore the monarchy. The people wouldn't stand for it, he said, and impetuously branded such action outright treason.

Stalin held his temper and his tongue. "You need not restore him for good," he said slyly. "Take him back temporarily. Then you can slip a knife into his back at a suitable moment." Just then Molotov reported that the British had landed on the Yugoslav coast.

"Impossible!" Tito exclaimed. "What do you mean 'impossible'?" Stalin said testily. "It's a fact." But Tito brushed it off by explaining that it was undoubtedly only the three batteries of artillery which Field-Marshal Harold Alexander had promised to land near Mostar to support a partisan operation.

"Tell me, Walter," Stalin asked him, "what would you do if the British *really* tried to land in Yugoslavia against your will?"

"We would offer determined resistance."

Tito showed the same independence in the military discussions, unequivocally stating that he would permit the Red Army to enter the country only at his invitation, and making it clear that he needed only limited assistance: one armored division would be enough to help him liberate Belgrade; moreover, the Red Army would not be permitted to usurp civil and administrative functions in Yugoslavia, as it had in Rumania and Bulgaria. Stalin agreed to these restrictions with apparent grace, and said that he would send Tito a corps instead of a division—that is, about four times what he asked.

Tito flew home just as the promised Red Army corps entered Yugoslavia, and about three weeks later his partisans, with this support, finally took Belgrade. It marked the end of Tito's military struggle, for the Germans now wanted only to escape into Hungary. Tito's political life also changed, the former outlaw taking up residence in Prince Paul's White Palace on the outskirts of the capital. First he repaid his great debt to Churchill by signing an agreement with the London government-in-exile to have free elections determine the permanent government of Yugoslavia. This recompense cost Tito nothing. Unlike Communist leaders of other countries in eastern Europe, he was a genuine hero, the savior of Yugoslavia, and there was no doubt at all that the overwhelming majority of his countrymen would vote him their postwar leader.

A few days after Tito's departure, Churchill arrived in Moscow. He wanted very much to see Stalin—"with whom I always considered one could talk as one human being to another"—about the postwar status of the liberated countries in Europe. The two men were discussing the Polish question when Churchill abruptly said, "Let us settle about our affairs in the Balkans. Your armies are in Rumania and Bulgaria. We have interests, missions and agents there. Don't let us get at cross-purposes in small ways. So far as Britain and Russia are concerned, how would it do for you to have ninety percent predominance in Rumania, for us to have ninety percent of the say in Greece, and go fifty-fifty about Yugoslavia?" He was scribbling on a piece of paper, then shoved the note across the table to Stalin, who saw that in addition to the percentages on Rumania, Greece and Yugoslavia, Churchill proposed that Hungary be split 50-50 and that Russia have a 75-percent predominance in Bulgaria. The Marshal paused, then made a large blue pencil mark on the paper.

In the space of a few seconds history was made. "Might it not be thought rather cynical if it seemed we disposed of these issues, so fateful to millions of people, in such an offhand manner?" Churchill said after a while. "Let us burn the paper."

"No, you keep it," Stalin replied.

The two allies sent a joint telegram to Roosevelt announcing that they had agreed on a policy about the Balkans. Churchill also sent a private message to the President:

. . . IT IS ABSOLUTELY NECESSARY WE SHOULD TRY TO GET A COMMON MIND ABOUT THE BALKANS, SO THAT WE MAY PREVENT

CIVIL WAR BREAKING OUT IN SEVERAL COUNTRIES, WHEN PROBABLY YOU AND I WOULD BE IN SYMPATHY WITH ONE SIDE AND U.J. [Uncle Joe] WITH THE OTHER. I SHALL KEEP YOU INFORMED OF ALL THIS, AND NOTHING WILL BE SETTLED EXCEPT PRELIMINARY AGREEMENTS BETWEEN BRITAIN AND RUSSIA, SUBJECT TO FURTHER DISCUSSION AND MELTING DOWN WITH YOU. ON THIS BASIS I AM SURE YOU WILL NOT MIND OUR TRYING TO HAVE A FULL MEETING OF MINDS WITH THE RUSSIANS. . . .

### 3.

After Marshal Feodor Ivanovich Tolbukhin's Third Ukrainian Front had helped Tito capture Belgrade in October, 1944, it pushed northwest to help Marshal Rodion Yakovlevich Malinovsky's Second Ukrainian Front liberate Hungary. Once a Holy Roman emperor was king of Hungary as well, and for many years the emperors of Austria, the Hapsburgs, ruled as kings, but of all the bizarre governments endured by its exuberant people, none was more bizarre than the present. Today Hungary was a kingdom without a king, governed by an admiral without a navy, the regent Miklós von Horthy—who was subject to the whims of Adolf Hitler.

After World War I the Hapsburgs were exiled but this brought no relief to the landless peasants, for feudalism remained under Horthy's kingless monarchy. Consequently, nowhere in Europe did there exist such abject poverty amid such arrant luxury. Hungary had joined Hitler in his crusade against Communism with some enthusiasm, but when this began to wane Hitler put an end to the fiction of Horthy's independence when, several months before D-Day, he occupied the country.

The present de facto ruler was the German minister in Budapest, SS General Dr. Edmund Veesenmayer, but with the Red Army less than 100 miles from Budapest, Horthy figured it was at last time to surrender the sizable Hungarian Army—which was still fighting the Russians, if reluctantly and not well—in payment for political considerations. Since a secret in Budapest was usually discussed loudly in cafés, the Russians learned almost immediately of Horthy's decision and assigned a Red Army colonel named Makarov the task of hastening matters. Makarov wrote two letters filled with such extravagant promises that Horthy hastily dispatched a deputy to Moscow to negotiate. It was typically Hungarian that the Admiral forgot to give his deputy written authorization and had to rush off a well-known impressionist painter with the proper papers; and it was typical of the Russians to pretend they knew nothing about Colonel Makarov and his beguiling letters. The result, of course, was confusion and delay; and the more confused and delayed things became, the sterner were the Russian demands.

It was also typically German that Hitler knew perfectly well what was going on. While the Hungarian deputies' negotiations in Moscow went from bad to worse, Hitler sent thirty-six-year-old SS-Sturmbann-führer (Major) Otto Skorzeny to Budapest to bring the Hungarian leaders back in line. The six-foot-four Viennese was, apart from his size, an imposing figure: he had a large scar on his face from a student duel over a ballet dancer, and he carried himself with the air of derring-do of a fourteenth-century condottiere. In late 1943 he had abruptly dropped out of the sky with half a dozen gliders to rescue Mussolini in a commando operation that made him famous with friends and enemies alike.

Having an almost mystical faith in men such as Skorzeny, Hitler had simply sent him to Budapest with a single parachute battalion, with instructions to prevent Horthy from changing sides. Skorzeny was to seize the Citadel, where Horthy lived and ruled, in a fairly bloodless coup, Operation "Panzerfaust." But complications were a way of life in the Balkans, and Skorzeny was faced with another plot: the surrender of Hungary by another Horthy, young Miklós "Miki" Horthy, the Admiral's son, who was doing it with his father's consent. Miki was the *enfant terrible* of the Horthy clan, notorious for his wild parties on Margit Island, and now that his elder brother István, a flier, had died on the eastern front, he was the hope and despair of his father. When Skorzeny learned from a German intelligence agent that Miki had already met with a representative of Tito to negotiate his own peace with Russia, he agreed to help the Gestapo kidnap the young man the next time he met the Yugoslav. The plan was called Operation "Mickey Mouse."

On October 15, 1944, Miki met Tito's agent, only to be seized immediately by Skorzeny and Gestapo men, wrapped in a carpet and smuggled to the airport. When the Admiral was told that his son had just been bundled off to Germany, he denounced the Nazis and told the Crown Council that they should instruct their negotiators in Moscow to surrender to the Russians regardless of terms.

That afternoon Dr. Veesenmayer, the German minister, called at the Citadel and was summarily informed by Horthy that he was negotiating with the Allies for a surrender, and a little later a recording of the Admiral's voice repeated announcements over the radio that Hungary had concluded a separate peace with the Russians. Of course, nothing of the sort had occurred—it was all talk, and the Soviets themselves were quite annoyed; they radioed Horthy that there would be no armistice unless he accepted their terms by 8 A.M. the next day. Far into the night Horthy and his ministers argued without reaching agreement, and the Admiral finally went to bed in disgust. At last the ministers agreed among themselves that they should seek asylum in Germany, and a messenger named Vattay was sent to inform Horthy of their decision. But any student of Hungary could have guessed the result: Horthy huffily refused to abdicate and went back to bed. What followed was again purely Hungarian: Messenger Vattay apparently disliked bearing · bad news and simply told the ministers that Horthy had accepted their plan "in its entirety."

The Minister President consequently sent a note to Dr. Veesenmayer informing him that the Crown Council was resigning and that Horthy was abdicating. It was about three o'clock in the morning when Veesenmayer received the message, and it took him another hour on the telephone to rouse Foreign Minister von Ribbentrop in Berlin, who said he would have to get Hitler's personal approval. This took two more hours and it was not until 5:15 that word at last came that Hitler would accept the abdication of Horthy. About twenty minutes later Veesenmayer drove up to the Citadel. Inside, Horthy was still resisting all attempts to make him abdicate, but the moment he heard the bugle sound announcing the arrival of Veesenmayer he gave in, and walked out to the courtyard.

"I have the unpleasant duty of taking you into custody," Veesenmayer said and looked at his watch. "The attack will begin in ten minutes." He was referring to Operation "Panzerfaust," which was to start at 6 A.M. He took Horthy's arm and escorted him toward his car. As the two men drove away it was 5:58 A.M. At the German legation someone was already telephoning Ribbentrop that the affair had ended without bloodshed.

Unfortunately nobody told Skorzeny. At 5:59 A.M. he waved his arm —the signal to start motors—then stood up, pointed toward the Citadel, and the column began climbing a steep hill. Within half an hour, at the cost of seven lives, Skorzeny captured the Citadel—needlessly.

Even though the country was now more firmly under Hitler's control than ever, the combined German-Hungarian forces were steadily driven backward by the Red Army. On Christmas Eve, 1944, Russian tanks burst into the suburbs of Buda—on the west side of the Danube; Pest was on the east—and a few got almost as far as the famed Hotel Gellert. Holiday shoppers on trolley cars calmly watched the Russian tanks rumble by, in the belief that they were German; when the red stars were finally noticed there was panic. Within sight of terrified churchgoers, Tiger tanks crossed the Danube bridges and knocked out the advance Russians.

These were from the spearhead of Tolbukhin's Third Ukrainian Front, which had pushed across the Danube below Budapest. Although this first probing into the city was easily repulsed, Tolbukhin increased the pressure from the south while Malinovsky's Second Ukrainian Front was crossing the Danube above Budapest. On December 27 the two great forces met west of the city, and nine divisions—five German and four Hungarian— were encircled, together with 800,000 civilians. Though Tolbukhin's attack on hilly Buda was easily thrown back, a much stronger one by Malinovsky on Pest, which was flat, could not be stopped and by January 10, 1945, the Red Army cleared eight city districts with the help of Rumanians who had switched sides. This was achieved mainly by hand-to-hand fighting because the Red Army did not want to endanger the city's waterworks with all-out bombing or artillery barrages.

Early in the morning of January 17 the defenders of Pest retreated into Buda across the Danube. The Hungarian soldiers refused to blow up their historic bridges; they said that the ice over the Danube was thick enough to hold tanks, anyway. The Germans replied that it was no time for history and blew up the bridges themselves.

In Pest, cowering citizens awaited the looting, rape and murder the Germans had told them to expect from the Bolsheviks. But to their surprise, the Red Army passed out flour, barley, coffee, black bread, sugar and whatever else they could spare. There were no murders and few rapes. The Soviet soldiers had been told that Hungary was "a good country in spite of a lack of culture" and consequently were friendly to its people. They loved to give presents and would sometimes rob one house only to pass on the booty to the next-door neighbors. Curiously, on leaving the city some of these soldiers took away the toys they had given children. "We take your children's teddy bears," one Russian told an irate grandmother. "Those following us will bring them more." They simply wanted to have presents for the children up ahead.

By February 11, the last day of the Yalta Conference, the battle for the west side of the river had turned into a bitter siege. Securely entrenched in Buda's hills, German-Hungarian troops shelled any attempts to cross the ice-covered Danube. But the 70,000 defenders were trapped; other Russian forces were closing in from the west.

About the time Roosevelt was enjoying his steak dinner on the *Catoctin,* the Nazi commander in Buda, Karl von Pfeffer-Wildenbruch, ordered his men to try and break through the Soviet ring in three separate groups. It was obvious that there was almost no chance of escaping, but few objected. It was better to die fighting than to be exterminated. The odds for escape were even slimmer than imagined. The Red Army commander knew all about the breakout and was already covertly withdrawing his men from the first buildings surrounding the German-Hungarian troops.

As the three groups were about to move off in different directions, Russian rockets began blasting the recently evacuated buildings. Nevertheless, they surged out of their hiding places armed only with machine pistols and met a withering wall of rocket and artillery fire. Most of them were cut down in the first few minutes. The others kept coming, desperately trying to break through. Those surviving the rockets and artillery were met by such masses of Russian infantrymen that it seemed impossible for a single man to survive, let alone escape; but in the darkness and confusion almost 5000 German-Hungarians filtered through.

Since 1st Lieutenant Gyula Litteráti of the 12th Hungarian Division knew every street in Buda, he managed to lead one group—eleven Hungarians and four German SS men—up the snowy Swabian Hill by following the tracks of the funicular railway. Near dawn on February 12, as Litteráti came to a small woods, he was startled by a whistle. Two yards ahead was a Russian covered with a sheet. Other camouflaged figures jumped out. As Litteráti reached for the machine pistol strapped on his back, he got a glimpse of a savage, barbarian face and felt something crash into the side of his head. He passed out.

By dawn the fighting was over and Russians searched the rubble of Buda for survivors of the desperation breakout, butchering Germans where they lay exhausted or wounded. Sound trucks drove up to the woods of the Buda hills and broadcast appeals to those hiding to come out and be "treated decently." If Germans emerged, they were shot down; Hungarians were usually given the choice of being interned or joining the Soviets. Those changing sides pinned strips of red cloth to their uniforms and were marched off to help round up other Hungarians.

By this time young Litteráti had regained consciousness. He raised his head and saw the four SS men of his group standing naked before a line of Red Army soldiers laughing at some joke. Then, almost casually, the Russians lifted up their submachine guns and began firing. Afterward one of the Russians walked over to Litteráti and said accusingly, "You are a German officer."

Litteráti tried to convince him that he was Hungarian, but to no avail; the other called him a liar and pointed to the German and Hungarian medals on his chest. Litteráti's men backed him up, but the Russians reloaded their guns.

"Fascist, you die!" said a Soviet soldier.

Litteráti looked around desperately. He saw a tall man in a Hungarian uniform, wearing a red strip of cloth around his arm. "Comrade, tell those crazy Russians that the rest of us are Hungarians, not Germans!" Miraculously he had found a man whom the Russians believed, and he was brought to a nearby forester's house. Weak from his wound, Litteráti stretched out on a bed with a handkerchief under his head to keep the blood off the covers.

He saw a familiar face staring down at him. It was the "barbarian" who had hit him. While a Russian nurse washed his wound, the ferocious-looking Soviet soldier broke into a grin, handed Litteráti two packages of cigarettes and pumped his hand enthusiastically.

Of Pfeffer-Wildenbruch's 70,000 men, little more than 700 escaped to the German lines. Most of the rest were killed in battle or murdered. The

Soviet commander claimed that his men had captured 30,000, and since there were only a few thousand prisoners on hand, he simply arrested about 25,000 civilians from the streets of Buda. But the true story of the butchery of prisoners as well as numerous reports of widespread rape and looting all over Buda could not be suppressed, and the people on the other side of the Danube began to wonder if liberation was such a blessing, after all.

That same day the *Catoctin,* with Roosevelt aboard, left the Crimean port of Sevastopol. As far as the President was concerned, the future of the Balkans had been assured the moment Stalin accepted the Declaration on Liberated Europe. Roosevelt was aware that Communist-dominated governments were already being forced on the people of Bulgaria, Rumania and Hungary, but he assumed that this would stop—in compliance with the terms of Yalta.

# 7

## Operation "Thunderclap"

### 1.

When the communiqué of the Crimea Conference was published on February 12, almost all Britons and Americans approved it enthusiastically. In England leading articles in such varied newspapers as the *Manchester Guardian,* the *Daily Express* and the *Daily Worker* praised the decisions reached by the Big Three. Joseph C. Harsch of *The Christian Science Monitor* expressed the heartfelt reaction of most Americans:

. . . The Crimea Conference stands out from previous such conferences because of its mood of decision. The meetings which produced the Atlantic Charter, Casablanca, Teheran, Quebec—all these were dominated, politically, by declarative moods. They were declarations of policy, of aspirations, of intents. But they were not meetings of decision. The meeting at Yalta was plainly dominated by a desire, willingness and determination to reach solid decisions.

There was similar acclaim throughout the Soviet Union. *Pravda* devoted an issue solely to the conference; in its opinion the decisions reached there indicated that "the alliance of the Three Big Powers possessed not only a historic yesterday, but also a great tomorrow," and *Izvestia* asserted that it was "the greatest political event of the present day."

The communiqué also delighted Goebbels, for it gave him an opportunity to strengthen his propaganda about the Morgenthau Plan and unconditional surrender, and to declare that the Big Three decisions at Yalta to dismember Germany and force her to pay crushing reparations only proved that Germany must fight with renewed vigor—or be wiped out.

In France the enthusiasm over the decision to let her have an occupation zone in Germany with representation on the central machinery of control was tempered by de Gaulle's personal bitterness. The general's annoyance was understandable. Not only had his request to attend the conference been rejected out of hand, but he had been in the dark about its results until Jefferson Caffery, the American ambassador to France, handed him a memorandum on February 12. R. W. Reber, a political officer in France, cabled Roosevelt that de Gaulle had received him "frigidly" and must have "expected a bigger role for himself out of the communiqué." This report and de Gaulle's refusal to meet him at Algiers were shrugged off by the President, who already disliked the general. "Well, I just wanted to discuss some of our problems with him," he told Leahy. "If he doesn't want to, it doesn't make any difference to me."

De Gaulle, at least, was outwardly polite about Yalta, but the Poles in Britain and America were vituperous. Led by Prime Minister Tomasz Arciszewski, Mikolajczyk's replacement, they claimed that Roosevelt and Churchill had, in effect, handed over Poland to the Soviet Union as a sacrifice to unity among themselves. One Pole did more than accuse. Lieutenant General W. Anders, commander of the II Polish Corps, which had played such a gallant part in the seizure of Monte Cassino, threatened to pull his troops out of the battle line. He radioed Wladyslaw Raczkiewicz, President of the Republic, that he could not accept

. . . THE UNILATERAL DECISION BY WHICH POLAND AND THE POLISH NATION ARE SURRENDERED TO BE THE SPOIL OF THE BOLSHEVIKS.
. . . I CANNOT, IN CONSCIENCE, DEMAND AT PRESENT ANY SACRIFICE OF THE SOLDIERS' BLOOD . . .

A Pole who could have made a far more sensational protest, yet said nothing, was Count Edward Raczynski, ambassador to the Court of St. James. Shortly before, Sir Owen O'Malley had shown Raczynski the final report of his exhaustive investigation into the massacre of 11,000 Polish officers in the Katyn Forest. It proved beyond a doubt that the atrocity had been committed not by the Nazis but by the Russians. Sir Owen also told the count that after the British Cabinet had read this damning report, it was ordered suppressed and another was written which wouldn't offend the Soviet Union. But Raczynski had given O'Malley his pledge of secrecy, and as a gentleman, felt he must join in the conspiracy of silence.

Just before noon General Guderian entered Hitler's office in the Chancellery, where a large group was already settling in the chairs facing the Führer's big desk. On the trip to Berlin, Guderian had told his youthful chief of staff, General Walther Wenck, "Today, Wenck, we're going to put everything at stake, risking your head and mine." The limited counterattack against Zhukov's spearhead on the Oder would fail miserably if directed by Himmler, who was an amateur. "We can't let the troops flounder around up there without at least one professional soldier."

Himmler—a man of average size, with thin, colorless lips and somewhat Oriental features—looked uneasy, as he usually did at such conferences. It was no secret that he disliked facing Hitler, and once had even told General Wolff that the Führer made him feel like a schoolboy who hasn't done his homework.

In Himmler a constant battle raged between what he was and what he wanted to be. He was a Bavarian, yet fervently admired Prussian kings like Frederick the Great and constantly praised Prussian austerity and hardness. He believed fanatically that the ideal German was Nordic—tall, blond, blue-eyed—and preferred such people around him. He admired physical perfection as well as athletic skill, and often said, "You have to exercise to stay young," yet was perpetually suffering from stomach cramps and presented a ridiculous figure on skis or in the water—and once collapsed trying to win a lowly bronze sports medal in the mile run. He had more personal power than anyone in the Reich except Hitler— but was an unpretentious if conscientious pedant with the intellectual scope of a German elementary school teacher. He relentlessly attacked Christianity and yet, according to one of his closest associates, had rebuilt the SS on Jesuit principles, assiduously copying "the service statutes and spiritual exercises presented by Ignatius Loyola . . ."

Like the man he both feared and revered, he was indifferent to things material and lived in frugal simplicity. He ate moderately, drank little and restricted himself to two cigars a day. Like Hitler, he worked with an intensity that would have killed most men, was fond of children and treated all women with the prim respect he gave his mother. And like Hitler, he had a mistress. Rather, he had at least two. When he was nineteen he lived with a prostitute, Frieda Wagner, who was seven years older. She was found murdered, and young Himmler was brought to trial for her death but freed for lack of evidence. He married another woman seven years his senior, a nurse named Margarite Concerzowo. With her money he started a chicken farm near Munich, which failed. So did the marriage.

The couple had a daughter, Gudrun, but Himmler wanted a son. However, his views on divorce were in accordance with his strict Catholic upbringing; that Hitler's attitude was the same must have helped influence him to lead, instead, a double life. He began a lengthy liaison with his personal secretary, Hedwig, who bore him a boy, Helge, and a girl, Nanette Dorothea. A romanticist, Himmler regularly wrote his mistress— he fondly called her Häschen, "little rabbit"—long and sentimental letters while he maintained, outwardly at least, a respectful and affectionate attitude toward his legal wife. And as a man of responsibility, he provided for each family in a style which kept him continuously in debt.

His stern father's son, he cluttered his office with moralistic slogans, such as: "One path leads to liberty. Its milestones are called obedience, application, honesty, sobriety, cleanliness, a spirit of sacrifice, order, discipline and love of country." As his boyhood friend Dr. Karl Gebhardt once said, "He believed what he was saying at the moment he said it and everybody believed it too." Some of his beliefs, however, were so eccentric that even his faithful followers found them difficult to accept: glacial cosmogony, magnetism, homeopathy, mesmerism, natural eugenics, clairvoyance, faith healing and sorcery.

Cleanliness was a fetish with him, and he gargled and washed himself throughout the day. He was a man of exact habits—parsimonious, neat and careful—and blessed with no originality, common sense or intuition. His receding, stubborn chin was evidence of an obstinacy bordering on the absurd. All this, combined with his love of secrecy, his issuance of vague orders, and an almost perpetual Mona Lisa smile, kept him shrouded in mystery. In short, in the acid words of SS General Paul Hausser, who had helped him organize the Waffen-SS, the one-time chicken farmer was "a fantastic idealist with both feet planted firmly several inches above the earth—a mighty queer bird."

This was the most feared man in Germany, perhaps in the world, but at the Führer conference now in session, Guderian welcomed Himmler's presence. Without preliminaries he turned to the Reichsführer and demanded that his counterattack begin in two days. Blinking his small blue-gray eyes behind his pince-nez, Himmler said he simply had to have more time. All ammunition and fuel hadn't yet been issued to the frontline units. He took off his glasses and began to wipe them assiduously.

"We can't wait until the last can of gasoline and the last shell have been issued!" Guderian cried. "By that time the Russians will be too strong."

Hitler took this as a personal criticism. "I will not permit you to accuse me of procrastinating."

"I'm not accusing you of anything. I'm simply saying that there's no sense in waiting until the last lot of supplies have been issued—and the favorable moment to attack has been lost."

"I just told you I will not permit you to accuse me of procrastinating!"

Guderian proved that he was a poor diplomat by choosing this inopportune moment to say, "I want General Wenck at Army Group Vistula as chief of staff. Otherwise there will be no guarantee that the attack will be successful." Looking over at Reichsführer Himmler, he added, "The man can't do it. How could he do it?"

Hitler hoisted himself painfully from his chair and said angrily, "The Reichsführer is man enough to lead the attack alone!"

"The Reichsführer doesn't have the experience nor the right staff to lead the attack without help. The presence of General Wenck is absolutely necessary."

"How dare you criticize the Reichsführer! I won't have you criticize him!" There was fury in Hitler's words but also a theatrical quality. He protested too much.

Guderian would not back down, but repeated, "I must insist that General Wenck be transferred to the staff of Army Group Vistula to properly lead the operation." Guderian's continued defiance now genuinely aroused Hitler. The two men began to argue so heatedly that one by one the conferees unobtrusively left the room until only Himmler, Wenck and a few blank-faced adjutants remained.

Hitler turned his back to Guderian and strode up to the big fireplace, where a portrait of Bismarck was hanging. To Guderian, Bismarck seemed to be glaring accusingly at Hitler, and across the room a bronze bust of Hindenburg was asking reproachfully, "What are you doing to Germany? What will become of my Prussians?" This distressing hallucination hardened Guderian's resolve, and for more than two hours the argument went on. Each time Hitler shouted "How dare you!" and took a deep breath, Guderian would reiterate his demand that Wenck be made Himmler's assistant. And each time the demand was made, Himmler seemed to get a shade paler.

Finally Hitler broke off his nervous pacing, stopped in front of Himmler's chair and said with a sigh of resignation, "Well, Himmler, General Wenck is going to Army Group Vistula tonight to take over as chief of staff." He turned to Wenck. "The attack will start on the fifteenth of February," he said and sat down heavily. Then he looked at Guderian and murmured, "Let us please resume the conference." He smiled winningly. "Herr Generaloberst, today the Army General Staff won a battle."

A few minutes later Guderian went to the anteroom and, exhausted, sat down at a small table. Keitel came up to him. "How dare you contradict the Führer like that?" he cried. "Couldn't you see how perturbed he was getting? What if he'd had a stroke?"

Guderian looked at him coldly. "A statesman must expect to be contradicted and to hear the hard truth. Otherwise he can't be called a statesman."

Others began echoing Keitel's accusation, but Guderian turned away and told Wenck to issue the orders for the February 15 attack.

**2.**

Air Chief Marshal Sir Arthur T. Harris was a chunky, forceful and energetic man of fifty-three who had enlisted at the outbreak of World War I as a bugler in the Rhodesian Infantry. After record marches in German

Southwest Africa he swore that he'd never march again and joined the Royal Flying Corps. Now he headed Bomber Command, and that night his men were scheduled to launch an attack on Dresden; this was to be the first in a series of large bombing raids on the principal cities of eastern Germany, designed to deliver the final blows to German morale. Operation "Thunderclap," the code name for all the raids, was just another step in the British War Cabinet's planned campaign of area bombing—to Harris, the best way to end the war. He was popularly known as Bomber Harris, a nickname he didn't mind at all, and a few newspapermen referred to him as "Butcher" Harris, which he ignored. It was his job, he felt, to help wipe out German war production and for this to be accomplished, cities had to be destroyed and people killed, but the plan to do so was not his.

His prickly personality and aggressive advocacy of pattern bombing made him disliked by some, but this same militancy made him beloved by his airmen, since he fought just as stoutly for the best possible equipment and the safest possible methods to carry out bombing raids.

The background of "Thunderclap" was long and complex. Two months after D-Day, Sir Charles Portal, chief of the Air Staff, had suggested that the moment Germany approached military collapse, a series of heavy air raids be launched against east German population centers; these raids might even precipitate total surrender. The Joint Intelligence Committee —a group of British intelligence experts—was cool to "Thunderclap," since it was not likely "to achieve any worth-while degree of success," and the American air leaders deemed it imprudent to be diverted from precision bombing. Besides, General H. H. "Hap" Arnold, chief of the U. S. Air Force, was against such bombing on principle, and Eisenhower's Psychological Warfare Division went so far as to call it terroristic.

Consequently, "Thunderclap" was shelved until ten days after the great Soviet offensive on January 12, 1945, when the director of Bomber Operations suggested to Portal's deputy, Sir Norman Bottomley, "If the operation were launched at a time when there was still no obvious slackening in the momentum of the Russian drive, it might well have the appearance of a close co-ordination in planning between the Russians and ourselves."

Asked to re-evaluate "Thunderclap" in this light, the Joint Intelligence Committee reported that a four-day, four-night series of bombing attacks could very well cause a heavy flow of German refugees that "would be bound to create great confusion, interfere with the orderly movement of troops to the front and hamper the German military and administrative machine" and "materially assist the Russians in the all-important battle now raging on the eastern front and would justify temporary diversion from attacks against communications or indeed from any targets other than oil plants and tank factories." Moreover, there could possibly be a "political value in demonstrating to the Russians, in the best way open to us, a desire on the part of the British and Americans to assist them in the present battle."

On January 25 Bottomley telephoned Harris to discuss putting "Thunderclap" into effect at last. "Berlin is already on my plate," Harris replied, and passed on a request from his SHAEF liaison officer that the other targets for the operation be Chemnitz, Leipzig and Dresden, three cities which were not only the main housing centers for refugees from the east but key communication points along the crumbling eastern front.

Simultaneously, Churchill happened to be talking about just such raids with Sir Archibald Sinclair, Secretary of State for Air, and asked what plans the Royal Air Force had for "basting the Germans in their retreat from Breslau [on the Oder]." It really wasn't much of a coincidence, since "Bomber" Harris, a frequent visitor at Chequers, had often discussed "Thunderclap"-type attacks with Churchill and informally urged their inauguration.*

The next day Sinclair passed on the query to the Air Staff. But Portal, the originator of "Thunderclap," now had little enthusiasm for the operation, and in his report pointed out that oil targets should continue to have priority, with jet factories and submarine yards next on the list. Once these three items had been taken care of, he said, "we should use available effort in one big attack on Berlin and attacks on Dresden, Leipzig, Chemnitz . . ."

After reading this half-hearted approval and after consulting others on the Air Staff, Sinclair was cool to the whole project. "You asked me last night whether we had any plan for harrying the German retreat from Breslau," he wrote Churchill and suggested that this was a job better suited to Tactical Air Forces. The bombers, he went on, should continue hitting oil targets, weather permitting; if not, area attacks could be launched on cities in eastern Germany.

This memorandum brought a quick, sarcastic reply from Churchill, who apparently forgot his own words:

I did not ask you last night about plans for harrying the German retreat from Breslau. On the contrary, I asked whether Berlin, and no doubt other large cities in East Germany, should not now be considered especially attractive targets. I am glad that this is "under examination." Pray report to me tomorrow what is going to be done.

Perhaps Churchill's sudden interest in "Thunderclap" was prompted by the conference that would soon take place at Yalta; perhaps he was anxious to show Stalin how valuable the Allies' strategic air forces could

---

* Recently Harris commented: "Originally 'Thunderclap' was intended for Berlin by daylight British and U. S. bombers together. But at the last moment Doolittle said the U. S. could not give us the necessary close long-range fighter cover and I refused to take on Berlin by daylight without it."

be to the current Russian offensive. After the Battle of the Bulge, the West certainly needed all the military prestige it could muster at the conference table. Whatever inspired Churchill, the ironical urgency of his note to Sinclair brought immediate results, and Harris was ordered to attack cities such as Berlin, Dresden and Chemnitz as soon as possible, "where a severe blitz will not only cause confusion in the evacuation from the east but will hamper the movement of troops from the west."

Harris' deputy, Air-Marshal Sir Robert Saundby, however, had personal qualms, and upon reading the order, wondered why Dresden was included. Its importance, he felt, was overrated. Though a key rail center, there was little to indicate its importance as an industrial center or that it was being used for troop movements on a large scale. He therefore asked the Air Ministry to reconsider the inclusion of Dresden as a target. Such requests were usually answered promptly through a personal telephone call. This time Saundby was told that higher authority had to be consulted. Saundby had to wait several days before receiving verification that Dresden would be bombed. The delay, he was told, was due to Churchill's personal interest in "Thunderclap"—and he was then at Yalta.

Now it was only a question of weather. On the morning of February 13 conditions were at last reported favorable, and just before nine o'clock Harris ordered No. 5 Group to attack Dresden that night, to be followed closely by a second strike of a combined force from four groups. Early in the morning American Flying Fortresses would hit the city a third time. About noon, however, meteorologists reported that conditions had changed. Clouds were drifting over all of central Europe and the skies over the target would not clear until ten at night.

To Harris this was not reason enough to scrub the raid, and that afternoon Wing Commander Maurice A. Smith, Master Bomber for the first wave, reported to the Intelligence building of 54 Base at Coningsby for briefing. His dangerous assignment was to remain over the target, often at low level, and direct the bombing. He would pilot a Mosquito, an all-wood, fast twin-engine plane, relatively safe at the high altitudes it could fly but almost completely unarmored. Smith had controlled raids on Karlsruhe, Heilbronn and other large German cities, but under more promising auspices. Even the target map for Dresden could not be found, and he had to settle for a district target map based on poor aerial photos taken in 1943.

Smith was told to concentrate No. 5 Group's bombs on railways and communication centers in Dresden's Altstadt (Old Town), famed for its beautiful buildings and monuments. The Base Commander remarked that he had once stayed at a hotel on the Altmarkt, the square in the center of the Old Town, and been cheated. He hoped, he added facetiously, that this injustice would soon be taken care of.

Because of the weather, success depended on split-second timing. The first planes to reach Dresden would be the primary markers, two squadrons of Lancaster bombers. At 10:04 P.M. they would drop green parachute flares and green indicator bombs to mark out the general position of the city. A few minutes later, eight Mosquitoes would follow, and guided by the green markers, would drop red indicator bombs on the sports stadium which was right next to the main target—the railroad yards. Finally at zero hour, 10:15 P.M., the main force—with the call name "Plate Rack" —would arrive to bomb the target outlined in red.

Just before 5:30 P.M. the eight Mosquitoes took off. Their pilots were perturbed by instructions to avoid a forced landing east of Dresden at all costs; instead, they were to head back west and come down in enemy territory rather than let recently developed electronic equipment fall into the hands of their ally, the Russians.

A few minutes later the first of 244 Lancasters began to leave the No. 5 Group fields in the Midlands, and by 6 P.M. all bombers were airborne. At 7:57 P.M. Wing Commander Smith, the Master Bomber, left Coningsby in his Mosquito. After about an hour a stiff west wind began to blow, and this helped him catch up with the other eight Mosquitoes, which had flown an indirect course. Above 15,000 feet over northwestern Germany, the nine planes picked up an 85-knot tail wind. It wasn't until 9:49 P.M. that the navigators first saw a beam on "Loran," the American-built electronic navigational guide which would lead them directly to their target. But Smith's navigator could not pick up the second beam on his Loran screen and two were needed for a positional fix. He looked at his watch. It was 9:56. In eight minutes the primary markers should be dropping their green flares. At about 10 o'clock the second beam finally appeared and Smith's navigator located their position: fifteen miles due south of Chemnitz.

All nine Mosquitoes swung northwest, looking ahead for the green flares that were to drop in less than four minutes. As they descended the clouds slowly began to clear—just as predicted. It was as if the protective cover over Dresden was being pulled back by design.

Though Dresden was not an open city, it had experienced only two relatively small air raids, one on October 7, 1944, when 30 U. S. bombers hit the railroad yards, killing 435, and again on January 16, 1945, when 133 U. S. Liberators attacked almost the same target and killed 376. Subsequently there were several alerts, but since they all turned out to be false alarms, the feeling was prevalent that a secret agreement had been made with the Allies: if Oxford was spared, Dresden would not be attacked. After all, the city had little military value and its numerous museums, churches and other baroque buildings were recognized as a world treasure of architecture.

A rumor—false, of course—was abroad that leaflets had been dropped by the Allies promising that Dresden would not be bombed, since it was to be the capital of postwar Germany. All this had lulled the 630,-000 permanent inhabitants to complacency, and in spite of the catastrophe in the east there was even a festive air throughout the city on that night of February 13. It was *Fasching** Tuesday, a favorite German holiday, with many children still dressed in gay carnival costumes, and there was little excitement when the first alert—the "cuckoo"—sounded about ten o'clock. Few were concerned that there wasn't a single concrete-and-steel air-raid bunker in the entire city.

This feeling of security of the citizens had spread to the hundreds of thousands of refugees from the east as well as those from Berlin and western Germany. The railroad waiting rooms were filled with these no-mads and their piles of property. Public buildings were crowded with makeshift sleeping accommodations. The overflow was so great that the city's lovely Grosser Garten—about the size of New York's Central Park was dotted with tents and hastily constructed shacks for about 200,000 refugees and slave laborers.

The station was jammed with the last trains from the east, but the roads from the front were still black with refugees on foot, in horse-drawn carts, cars, trucks; the city was becoming more swollen with every hour and there were now about 1,300,000 human beings in Dresden, including hundreds of American and British prisoners of war.

The city's air defense was pitiful. The fearsome-looking flak guns, showily mounted on the surrounding hills, were only papier-mâché. The real guns had been commandeered for the eastern and western fronts, and only their empty concrete pads remained.

Luftwaffe defense was not much better. The Central Early Warning communications system in France had long since been captured, and when the 244 Lancasters of No. 5 Group began to appear on the screens of the warning system inside the German borders, it was im-possible to determine their targets. Suddenly 300 Halifax bombers also appeared on the screens; they were heading for a raid on the oil refinery just south of Leipzig, but the real purpose was to create a diversion. They were successful, for the Germans still had no idea which was the main assault. There was also the possibility that both were diversionary, since "Bomber" Harris had another 450 bombers at his disposal.

The 1st Fighter Division, stationed at Klotzsche a few miles north of Dresden, was prepared to defend the city, but since the Germans did not know where to send their few fighters, they had to wait until a definite pattern emerged. Only after the 244 Lancasters had by-passed Leipzig and turned directly toward Dresden were the defenders able to commit themselves, and it wasn't until 9:55 P.M. that the 1st Fighter Division

* This was an impromptu Lenten festivity; there had been no official *Fasching* celebration since 1939.

got orders to scramble its night-fighter squadron. By the time these planes were airborne, it was too late. The primary markers had already dropped their green flares.

Master Bomber Smith was just then approaching Dresden and for the first time he broke radio silence: "Controller to Marker Leader. How do you hear me? Over."

The Marker Leader in the lead Mosquito said he could hear clearly.

"Are you below cloud yet?" Smith asked.

"Not yet" was the reply. The Master Bomber asked if the green primary flares were in sight.

"Okay, I can see it. The cloud is not very thick," the Marker Leader answered, and was soon flying over the target, amazed to find not a single searchlight or burst of flak. Below he could see a number of bridges gracefully spanning the Elbe, which meandered through the center of Dresden, separating the new section from the old. The whole area reminded him of Shropshire, Hereford and Ludlow.

As he swept low over the railroad yards, he saw a single puffing locomotive near a large building which he guessed was the Central Station of the Old Town. From 2000 feet he began diving toward a sports stadium (there were two others near by.) "Marker Leader, tallyho!" he called. At 800 feet the bomb-bay doors opened and his 1000-lb. target-indicator bomb tumbled out, leaving a brilliant red trail. When another Mosquito pilot saw a burst near the leader's plane, he cried, "My God, the Marker Leader's been hit!" but it was only the flash of the bulb in Marker Leader's camera.

The Master Bomber was hastily checking Dresden's three stadiums on his map. "You've marked the wrong one," he said tersely. He checked the map again, then said with relief, "Oh, no, that's all right, carry on." He could see a red flare burning near the correct stadium, and said, "Hello, Marker Leader—that target indicator is about a hundred yards east of the marking point."

It was almost 10:07 P.M., eight minutes to zero hour. The other Mosquitoes began dumping their indicator bombs onto the first. The Master Bomber's next concern was whether the markers could be seen by the oncoming bombers through the thin layer of cloud. He called to one of the Lancasters which had dropped the green primary flares and still hovered 18,000 feet above the city, "Controller to Check 3. Tell me if you can see the glow."

"I can see three TIs [target indicators] through cloud."

Smith thought the other had said "green TIs" and replied, "Good work. Can you see the reds yet?"

"I can *just* see reds" was the reassuring answer.

It was not until 10:09 P.M. that a Dresden radio announcer cried,

"*Achtung, Achtung, Achtung!* An attack is coming! Go to your cellars at once!" The citizens did as they were told, but reluctantly, for most even doubted that this was a real raid. At the Old Town railroad station all lights had been extinguished. Most of the peasants from the east had never heard an alarm and were milling around in confusion, trying to find shelters that a booming loudspeaker voice kept telling them about.

At 10;10 P.M. the Master Bomber was saying over and over again to the main force of bombers approaching Dresden, "Controller to Plate Rack Force. Come in and bomb glow of red TIs as planned." There was not a gun flash from the ground, not a burst of flak. Since the city was obviously undefended, Smith ordered Plate Rack to come in even lower than scheduled.

Large high-explosive bombs—designed to blast off roofs and smash windows as a preparation for incendiaries—were soon ripping up the Old Town.

"Hello, Plate Rack Force," said the Master Bomber from his vantage point 3000 feet directly over the city. "That's good bombing."

Fourteen miles to the northwest, fifteen-year-old Bodo Baumann, a student in the cadet school at Meissen, watched the "Christmas trees"— red flares—falling while masses of bombers roared overhead, their exhausts spitting fire. He had experienced two heavy bombings in Berlin, but he had a feeling this was going to be the largest of them all. Even from Meissen, young Bodo could see great flames leap up. The windowpanes in a nearby building shook violently, and the entire horizon was crimson and violet. At first Bodo could distinguish single bombs exploding into a small cone, but in a minute there were so many explosions that everything became a reddish blur. The earth shook under Bodo and he stood transfixed. The city is doomed, he told himself, and nobody can come out alive.

Another fifteen-year-old, Joachim Weigel, was on the roof of the apartment house where he lived just across the Elbe from the Old Town. He and other Hitler Youth were throwing sand on four blazing incendiaries, but when high-explosive bombs began to fall in the street, the boys ran to the cellar and slammed shut the iron door. The man in charge of the youthful wardens almost immediately routed them out: the fifth floor was burning. The five boys and one girl scrambled upstairs to begin throwing rugs, furniture—anything that might add fuel to the fire—out the windows.

Hans Köhler, fourteen, was on duty at the Altstadt police station as assistant to a lieutenant whose job it was to dispatch some reserve fire engines and those from several nearby towns to the biggest fires. The lieutenant was supposed to wait in the police station cellar until the raid was over before driving up to the reserve engines which were parked on a hill several miles away, but the bombing was so tremendous that he knew a dozen fires must have started already. "We might be able to make it to the engines," he told Hans.

The two ran into the street just as a bomb crashed into a nearby building. Debris suddenly billowed up like in a slow-motion movie and began falling all around them. The heat was almost unbearable. They jumped on a motorcycle and headed west. As they raced past the railroad yards, Hans could see only a few small fires. It was the Old Town itself that had been so hard hit.

They continued west up a hill to the Löbtau section of town, sped past Hans's home and finally reached the parked fire engines. While the lieutenant was dispatching these trucks to specific buildings in the Old Town, the first vehicle from outlying areas arrived. Its driver knew little about Dresden, and Hans volunteered to guide him back to the heart of the fire.

At 10:21 P.M. the Master Bomber saw the Old Town engulfed by flames. He called one of the Lancasters and told him to relay the following radio message to England:

TARGET ATTACKED SUCCESSFULLY STOP PRI-
MARY PLAN STOP THROUGH CLOUD STOP

A few minutes later the great bomber formation wheeled west, dropping great quantities of metal-foil strips to jam radar. Then they ceased this "windowing" and quickly descended to 6000 feet, just under the horizon of the German radar system.

The second wave—529 Lancasters, more than twice the size of the first—was already well on its way. When the crews had first learned the destination, there was general uneasiness. It was a long trip, about as far as a Lancaster could go, and many wondered why the Russians didn't hit it themselves if it was so important to their advance. Intelligence officers gave various explanations to various groups: they were attacking German Army headquarters; destroying a German arms-and-supply dump; knocking out an important industrial area; wiping out a large poison-gas plant.

On the way to the target the temperature dropped so precipitously that many planes began to ice up; others were forced to fly by manual control, their automatic pilots out of order. Heavy clouds protected the raiders until they neared Chemnitz, then the skies abruptly cleared and flak guns picked off three Lancasters. By now the primary markers for the second wave could already see blazing Dresden. The city was so illuminated that they had no trouble dumping flares across the aiming point at 1:23 A.M., but by the time their Master Bomber arrived five minutes later, heavy smoke had blotted out all of east Dresden and the Old Town was a solid mass of leaping flames.

A fire storm, like that in Hamburg, had generated. This was a meteorological phenomenon caused when many fires abruptly joined to heat the air to a temperature as high as 1100 degrees Fahrenheit. This fantastic heat created a violent updraft which sucked fresh air into the center of the fire, and this suction, in turn, created a wind of tremendous velocity. The final result was a roaring inferno.

The Master Bomber realized that it was impossible to bomb with any accuracy, so he decided to concentrate on those areas not covered by Plate Rack. He radioed his main force, "Press On," to bomb left, then right, and finally directly over the section already ablaze. A few minutes later, bombs began to drop. Unlike the first attack, blockbusters were now used to spread the fires and keep the fire wardens under cover; then 650,000 incendiaries, including 4-lb. thermites, were scattered over the city, and the fire storm increased to incredible ferocity. The bombers watched in awe; never before had they seen such clear details. It was fantastic, unearthly; a shocking sight, with entire streets etched in fire.

The eighteen German night fighters from Klotzsche who had taken off too late to stop the first attack were sitting in their cockpits, eagerly waiting for word to go after the next wave of attackers. They heard the roar of approaching Lancasters, but still no word came. Instead, lights marking a path to the runway began flashing. Apprehensive, the fighters phoned Control to douse the lights before the enemy bombers spotted them and wiped out the entire field. But the answer was that a flight of transports from besieged Breslau was scheduled to land at any moment.

As time passed and the bombs rained on Dresden, the fighter pilots' anxiety turned to frustration and rage. Was it sabotage? Defeatism? Why weren't they allowed to get up and at least try to defend Dresden? The base commander was just as frustrated. All radio and telephone communications were out and he had not yet been able to get permission from Central Control in Berlin to send up the fighters.

Young Bodo Baumann was in a rescue convoy just entering Dresden with 200 other students of his school when the second attack started. The trucks stopped and the boys ran for shelter. Bodo jumped behind a stone wall. Between explosions he could hear the eery roar of the burning city. The ground was shaking as in an earthquake.

When the bombing stopped, the boys continued on foot toward the center of town until they came to burning buildings and falling debris. They reached a bridge crossing the Elbe to the Old Town—now an eleven-square-mile furnace. Even on Bodo's side of the river the heat was tremendous. The boys had orders to get people out of their cellars before they died of suffocation, so they held hands and moved single file to the middle of the bridge, then edged cautiously forward. Suddenly the man leading the human chain screamed—and was sucked into the voracious flames. The boy behind him grabbed for something so he wouldn't be dragged in. The fire roared like cannon, the wind shrieked, and the dust and smoke swirled furiously around them.

The boys stumbled back across the bridge, found a rope, and using it as a life line, again tried to cross, but the heat was too intense and they fell back a second time. Bodo saw dead firemen lying in the street, their clothes smoldering. Clouds of black smoke drove the boys to the river, where they soaked handkerchiefs and put them over their faces.

On the other side of the burning city Hans Köhler was walking back to the fire engines on the hill when he heard the sirens warn of the second raid. He found a bicycle and began pedaling to his destination. Halfway there, he saw the primary flares dropping. He stopped and began taking pictures with a box camera. He heard the banshee screech of falling bombs and dived into a ditch. There was a shattering explosion 100 yards away. He looked up and saw the apple trees which had lined the road gone as if by magic. He ran across the road to an apartment house. As he was going downstairs to the cellar another bomb struck. He felt himself being picked up, flung to the floor. People were choking from the dust and smoke; women were moaning. Someone lit a candle.

A middle-aged woman said calmly, "I'm going upstairs to see what's going on." The others shouted for her to come back, but the woman slowly disappeared up the stairs of the shaking building as if sleepwalking. In ten minutes she returned just as stolidly and said, "Oh, there's a lot of noise up there but it looks pretty." Hans wondered if she was insane or simply trying to calm everyone.

The roar of engines was shattering as the bombers passed overhead. Then there was abrupt silence except for the crackle of flames and the crash of falling walls. Back outside in the street, Hans became aware of a distant unearthly moan, unlike anything he had ever heard. He looked down at the Old Town; it was a solid sheet of flames. Enthralled, he walked compulsively a mile toward the fire storm and stopped at the Yenize cigarette factory. It was shaped like a mosque and its exotic silhouette seemed to dance weirdly in the surrounding blaze.

Close to the edge of the inferno he looked for fire engines: None were there. What should he do? People were staggering toward him like specters: faces black, hair burned off, clothes smoldering. They were clutching babies, suitcases, even incongruous things like pots and pans. A few moaned but the majority were unnaturally silent, staring blankly with wide eyes as if unaware of what had happened. These ghosts reminded Hans of his own family and he turned back to find them. Part way up the hill to Löbtau he stumbled into a restaurant. People were stretched on the floor, clothes in tatters. He peered into the black faces hopefully but recognized nobody. Then someone touched his arm. He swung around and saw his mother, her long hair hanging loose.

"Everything is gone," she said.

"Where's Father?"

"He's in the apartment trying to recover some things. But don't go there. It's horrible." She tried to reassure him. "He'll be all right. *They* won't come again."

She looked at the sky and began to mumble incoherently.

Inside Altstadt, most people still huddled in their cellars, not realizing that the oxygen would soon be gone. Some who had tried to escape in between raids were caught in the open by bombs; others tried to find shelter inside the round metal advertising kiosks but were literally roasted to death.

Circus Sarassini was aflame. The alarm for the first raid had come in the midst of a gala performance while clowns were riding donkeys. Now much of the audience was still trapped in the big cellars under the arena, and the famed Arab horses wearing colorful trappings were milling in terror outside the building. Not far away, in the Grosser Garten, the zoo animals were out of their damaged cages and ranged wildly around the park, but only the vultures were to escape with their lives.

The huge crowd of refugees in the Grosser Garten was just as helpless. In a desperate attempt to escape the unbearable, suffocating heat, they scrambled frantically into the large water tanks kept in reserve to help combat air-raid fires. They were saved from the flames, but drowned like rats in the deep water.

The Central Station at the edge of the Old Town had only been lightly damaged by the first raid, after which railway officials immediately began loading all the trains for evacuation, giving children priority. However, before any of these trains could move out of the station, the markers for the second raid began dropping, followed by clusters of incendiaries which smashed through the glass station roof, and the entire structure burst into flames. Rescue workers fought their way into the fiery building. Hundreds of people were slumped along the station walls as if asleep, but they had been suffocated by carbon monoxide. The children in the trains were found huddled in heaps; they too were dead. In the cellars where thousands had rushed for shelter, the floors were covered with lifeless bodies.

Just north of the station, Annemarie Friebel, whose soldier husband was fighting Russians, climbed out of a smoke-filled cellar with a wet towel over her head. She wrapped damp rags over her year-old baby's face and pushed him in the carriage down the street, followed by her mother. Blocked by a huge pile of rubble, Annemarie wrapped the baby in a blanket, picked him up and stumbled across the mound. The baby made not a sound; during the bombing he hadn't even whimpered. Burning pieces of debris rained on their heads, setting the baby's blanket afire. Her mother beat out the flames with her hands.

Others were trying to get out of the same cul-de-sac; a few carried personal possessions but most were only interested in saving their lives. One woman pushing a baby carriage was caught by a draft and sucked like a leaf down a side alley into the flames.

Annemarie and her mother, sweat pouring down their faces, finally reached the edge of Altstadt and started up the hill to the west. All at once Annemarie realized that she was freezing and led the way into a workman's shed. In the doorway she turned and saw the city burning like a lake set on fire; it was beautiful, awesome. Others came into the shed. Nobody knew what to do. Annemarie herself felt dazed, numb; she didn't quite know what had happened.

## 3.

At 4:40 A.M., crews of the U. S. Eighth Air Force were briefed on their two major targets: Dresden and Chemnitz. The 1st Air Division was assigned Dresden: 450 Flying Fortresses would hit the marshaling yards and the Neustadt railroad station on the north side of the Elbe. The navigators were told to set course for the city of Torgau and then merely go up the Elbe River for another fifty miles: the next big city would be Dresden. The crews were in their planes by 6:40 A.M., but word came for them to hold, and it wasn't until 8 o'clock that the first Fortress took off.

The bombers were joined by 288 P-51 Mustangs over the Zuyder Zee. Half of these fighters were to stay with the bombers to stave off Luftwaffe attacks while the rest went down on the deck at Dresden to strafe targets of opportunity. Bombardiers wondered, as they flew over Germany, if visual bombing would be possible. There wasn't much cloud cover above, but the undercast was almost complete. Because of these clouds the entire 298th Bombardment Group got lost and at noon was about to bomb Prague, 75 air miles to the southeast.

And so only 316 Flying Fortresses were approaching Dresden and almost half of these, the 457th Bombardment Group, were slightly off course and missed the IP. The 457th circled around to make another pass. Staff Sergeant Joe Skiera, a gunner trained also to drop bombs, looked up to see a B-17 400 feet overhead. Their new course had taken them directly under another group. The bomb bay of the plane above was wide open and Skiera could see a cluster of 500-lb. bombs dangling, ready to drop.

The 457th circled a second time and a third, still not finding an opening in the clouds below. Their gray contrails formed a bowl and Skiera thought it was like someone painting a huge dirty halo. On the fourth pass the bombardiers found a gap in the undercast.

Below, fires in the Old Town were still raging from the first two attacks. Yellow-brown clouds of smoke and fume drifted south toward Prague, scattering cinders of clothing and paper for miles. It was Ash Wednesday.

People were staggering along the banks of the Elbe with damp pillowcases around their heads. Bodo Baumann, who had seen his leader sucked into the flames by the bridge, was in a group of youngsters trying to help bewildered survivors. One deranged man jumped into the river, and when the boys pulled him out, jumped back in again. Not far from the Marienbrücke, Bodo came to rows of barbed wire. Human debris— arms, legs, torsos, apparently blown through the barbed wire—was strewn near the river bank. It was a nauseating sight.

At noon Bodo and several friends went into a burning building for food. They found a bottle of cognac upstairs; they were drinking it when the flames rekindled and cut off their escape. As the boys shinnied down a rope from the second floor, the first American bombs began to fall. In this part of the city there were no air-raid warnings and Bodo saw a group of fifty elderly people sitting in the courtyard as if nothing was going on. Surrounded by their belongings, they sat immobile, staring fixedly ahead, but as the boys passed they held out beseeching arms. One of them cried, "Take me along!"

Whizzing bomb fragments forced Bodo to duck behind a cement post. One hand still clutched the bottle of cognac and he wondered how he had managed to climb down the rope with it. A bomb exploded close by and a building bulged dangerously toward him, so he scrambled into the nearest cellar.

The Mustangs, looking for their targets of opportunity, dived at the crowds fleeing along the banks of the Elbe. Youngsters recognizing their silhouette shouted *"Jabos!"* and scrambled for cover, but their elders kept running in the open and many were cut down by machine-gun bullets. Other Mustangs swooped down on trucks, carts and masses of refugees streaming out of town on the main highways.

After the Americans had left, Annemarie Friebel and her mother decided to get as far from Dresden as possible. Together with a friend they loaded a few belongings into a wagon, put the baby and another small child on top and joined several hundred thousand in their exodus to the south. The endless column moved slowly, without hysteria.

Hans Köhler and his father were also pushing a cart filled with family belongings rescued from their gutted apartment. Hans suddenly stopped and said he really ought to stay on duty with the fire engines. His father approved.

On his way back to Altstadt, Hans went by a burning butcher shop where hundreds of sausages were roasting on the shelves. He grabbed a long string and continued. He passed a Nazi scrubbing a sidewalk on which had been scrawled with paint, "Thank you, dear Führer!" Outside the Grailing cigarette factory he saw soldiers fire at two men who were filling burlap bags with cigarettes which by some freak had not burned and were covering the street like a foot-deep snowdrift. He passed a large apartment house where some tenant with foresight had placed a sign: "We are alive. Get us out." Rescuers were now trying to break into the cellar but the heat was still too intense.

At last he came to the Old Town itself. Something out of a fairy tale before, it was now a chaos of charred wreckage giving off a sickening smell. The famous opera house—where *Tannhäuser* had first been produced—was only a glowing shell; the Zwinger Palace, one of the world's most beautiful examples of baroque architecture, a smoldering ruin; as were the castle and the Hofkirche. Only the Kreuzkirche, its dome shrouded in smoke, by some miracle seemed to be almost intact.

At the half-ruined police station Hans was sent off on a bicycle with a message. On his return he was accused by a policeman of sabotaging the rescue effort by dawdling. He burst into tears, swore at the policeman and ran outside. He found the Lindenauplatz littered with naked corpses, their clothes burned or blown off. Near the entrance of a public toilet he saw a nude woman lying on a fur coat; a few yards away were the bodies of two young boys, also naked, clinging to each other. Near the Seidnitzerplatz several hundred people were slumped in a shallow pool—all dead.

A woman staggered toward Hans, dragging something in a white sheet. Inside, he saw the charred remains of a man, probably her husband. As she passed, a leg and two arms fell out. She laughed. He could hear her still laughing when he ran away.

He saw others carrying loved ones, looking distractedly for a place to bury them. Finally he came to the Grosser Garten. Some of the biggest trees had been uprooted; others had burst apart or were snapped in two like matchsticks. The lawns were covered with bodies. Many looked as if they were sleeping, but all were dead. When rescuers lifted them their limbs moved around like windmills. Scattered among the people were dead animals from the zoo. A leopard was draped over the top of a small tree, suspended over two naked women. Dazed and suddenly exhausted, the boy started back toward the wreckage of his own home. Behind him lay 1600 square acres of complete devastation—almost three times the damage done London during the entire war.

Since there was no communication between Dresden and the outside world, details of the ghastly story did not reach Berlin until later in the day. The preliminary official report stated that at least 100,000*

---

* U. S. Air Force historians estimate the dead at 25,000 to 30,000. In *The Destruction of Dresden*, David Irving places the number at 135,000. Irving's figure seems far more realistic.

people and probably many more had been killed in two successive air raids and that one of the most ancient and revered cities of the Reich was utterly destroyed. At first Goebbels refused to believe the report. Then he began to weep uncontrollably. When at last he found his voice it was to castigate Hermann Göring.

"If I had the authority I would have this cowardly and good-for-nothing Reichsmarschall tried!" he shouted. "He should be put before the People's Court. What a burden of guilt this parasite has brought on his head by his slackness and interest in his own comfort! Why didn't the Führer listen to my earlier warnings?"

Britons first heard about Dresden from the 6 P.M. news broadcast which announced that this was one of the great attacks promised by Roosevelt and Churchill at Yalta. "Our pilots report that as there was little flak they were able to make careful and straight runs over the targets without bothering much about the defenses," said the announcer. "A terrific concentration of fires was started in the center of the city."

# 8

## War and Peace

Early in the morning of February 14, Goebbels and his press officer, Rudolf Semmler, drove to see Himmler at the sanatorium of his old friend, Dr. Gebhardt. This retreat at Hohenlychen, seventy-five miles north of Berlin, had become an unofficial headquarters for Himmler, who loved its quiet surroundings and solitude. For the record, Himmler was being treated for tonsillitis but it was his nerves that bothered him—he was still shaken by yesterday's explosive Führer conference, when Guderian and Hitler had almost come to blows over him.

Over dinner at the Goebbels' several days previously, Goebbels had intimated to Semmler that he was going to seek Himmler's support for a far-fetched plan to reconstruct the Cabinet, with himself as Reich Chancellor and Himmler as head of the Armed Forces. Just then a tenor on the radio began singing Lehar's "Don't Reach for the Stars, My Dear." Frau Goebbels burst into laughter and Goebbels touchily said, "Turn that thing off!"

Semmler was not allowed to be present at the meeting with Himmler, and as they rode back to Berlin in silence, the press officer guessed that the discussion had not gone well.

At noon Himmler had another visitor, General Wenck, the chief of staff just foisted on him by Guderian. Now the actual commander of Army Group Vistula, Wenck was eager to get back to the front where the limited attack into Zhukov's right flank was about to be launched, but first, Himmler said, they would have lunch. "Then we can talk about the general situation."

"After we eat," the outspoken Wenck remarked, "I won't be available to talk. I'm going to the other side of the Oder—where I belong."

Aware that his enemies in Berlin were circulating jokes about the great distance from his command post to the front lines, Himmler said testily, "Are you implying that I'm a coward?"

"I'm not implying anything, Reichsführer. I just want to go where I can operate as a soldier." He explained that he would wage a battle east of the river to gain time for improving the defenses west of the Oder and to give the refugees a chance to escape.

The problems facing Wenck had no precedent in military manuals. Army Group Vistula was in fact two separate fronts: first and most important, the 150-mile-long Oder River line defending Berlin; second, the line protecting Pomerania—a weak, tortuous affair starting at the Oder in the west and running generally east to the Vistula River. Farther east lay German pockets of resistance—some small, some huge—all the way to Kurland in Latvia. One of the largest was Danzig, and several caravans of refugees from East Prussia were trying to escape to this dubious refuge, but Rokossovsky's troops, also bound for Danzig, had cut between them; their only hope now was to cross the ice of the Frisches Haff, a fresh-water inlet, to the Nehrung, the narrow tongue of land that separated the Haff from the Baltic Sea. Once on the Nehrung, the refugees could proceed west to the mainland and Danzig.

A sudden thaw had softened the ice of the inlet, and the only safe route was marked by signs at fifty-yard intervals. The night before, hundreds of wagons had broken through when the drivers lost their way in the dense fog, and the crowds still waiting on the south bank were almost too frightened to move forward. But the growing rumble of Russian fire was even more terrifying, and as soon as the fog cleared, thousands ventured onto the ice and headed toward the Nehrung, five miles away. By midmorning the first group could see sand dunes just ahead and the shout went up, "To the Nehrung! To the Nehrung!" They slogged forward frantically, for the ice was melting fast in the rising sun. Suddenly Russian shells began exploding on all sides, and panic broke out. The refugees ignored the marked route and ran pell-mell toward the shore. Many reached safety but almost a third fell through paper-thin patches of ice.

Wenck's limited counterattack into Zhukov's right flank would come in two blows: the first at a point some fifty miles east of the Oder, and the second, fifty miles farther east. The Eleventh Army would drive due south toward Wugarten and continue a few miles, to the confluence of the Warthe and Oder rivers. A day or so later, depending on the progress of the first attack, the Third Panzer Army would strike the main blow and force Zhukov to retreat, or at least postpone his assault on Berlin.

When the young, impulsive commander of the Eleventh Army, SS-

Obergruppenführer (Lieutenant General) Felix Steiner got his orders he was flabbergasted: it was impossible to smash south all the way to the Warthe with only 50,000 men and 300 tanks. He decided that it would be better to strike southwest—and with a more limited objective. This would leave him less exposed to the Zhukov counterattack that was sure to follow, and he would be in a better position to defend Pomerania. By-passing Wenck, he phoned Guderian directly and a violent argument broke out.

Finally Steiner shouted, "Accept my plan or relieve me!"

"Have it your own way," Guderian answered, and slammed down the phone.

On the morning of February 16, Steiner left his railroad-train headquarters and moved south to a villa overlooking Stargard, about forty miles northwest of Wugarten, so he could be at the starting point of the attack. By dark all roads around Stargard were jammed with columns of armored vehicles. Cannon, trucks and tanks were brought into place, ready for the dawn assault. Troops were read an urgent proclamation from the puppet commander of Army Group Vistula, Reichsführer Himmler: "Forward! Forward across the mud! Forward across the snow! Forward in daytime! Forward at night! Forward to free the soil of the Reich!" Masking his own pessimism, Steiner had signs erected: HERE IS THE ANTI-BOLSHEVIST FRONT! and personally encouraged each of his division commanders.

"This year we'll be at the Dnieper again," he told Colonel Léon Degrelle, commander of a division of Belgian volunteers, and slapped him affectionately on the back. Their attack from the north in conjunction with another from the south, he added, would snip off Zhukov's spearhead. At first Degrelle thought, What audacity! What a *coup de théâtre!* Then he noticed the sober faces of Steiner's staff officers as they made last-minute preparations. The atmosphere was as it must have been at Montmirail when Napoleon launched his final attacks.

Degrelle was the leader of the Rexist Party in Belgium, an impassioned man of thirty-eight, the prototype of a million other non-German volunteers who believed the future of all Europe was now at stake. Enemies in Belgium called him Fascist and Nazi, but he regarded himself as neither. Rexism to him was a reaction against the corruption of the times; a movement of political renovation and political justice; a battle against disorder, incompetence, irresponsibility and uncertainty.

When Hitler invaded Russia in 1941, Degrelle told his comrades that the people of the conquered countries like Belgium and France would have to volunteer in Hitler's legions and take an active part in the fight against Bolshevism. Only out of such a brotherhood of battle could a new and just Europe emerge. His fanaticism went even further: he maintained that unless the non-Germans joined this holy fight against

Bolshevism they would have no say in the New Europe, and Germany would become too powerful. He then enlisted as a private, even though he was offered a high rank. "I will see Hitler," he told his followers, "only when he pins the Ritterkreuz on me. At that moment I will have won the right to talk to him on equal ground. Then I will ask him, 'Are you going to make a United Europe or only a Big Germany?' "

In four years of fighting on the front line Degrelle was wounded seven times, and when he finally won the Knight's Cross he did indeed press the Führer about a United Europe. Hitler listened to the compulsive Degrelle and predicted that in one generation all the young people of Europe would know one another and be brothers. Russia would be a vast laboratory, peopled by all the youth of Europe, living in experimental unity.

Degrelle often became carried away in subsequent talks, but Hitler always listened indulgently and one day remarked fondly, "If I had a son, I'd want him to be like you." Their relationship became so intimate that Degrelle once went so far as to say, "I've often heard people call you a lunatic." Hitler only laughed. "If I were like everyone else, I'd just sit in a café and drink beer."

At dawn on February 16 Degrelle led his men into battle on foot. After seizing the ridge that was his objective, he climbed to a machine-gun nest to watch Steiner's tanks carry out the main attack. As the Tigers and Panthers rolled across the snow he reflected that the élan of former years was gone: they moved ahead cautiously toward a woods. He saw several German tanks burst into flames before reaching it, but the rest disappeared among the trees and a few minutes later came out on the other side, driving Red Army men before them. Now German infantry started into the woods; this was the most crucial moment. If they advanced with vigor the positions would be consolidated, but they hung back, and the frustrated Degrelle felt like booting them.

Steiner had pushed only eight miles by nightfall, and though Zhukov's Sixty-eighth Army was retreating, it did so slowly, in an orderly fashion. Shortly after midnight Degrelle was ordered to report back to Eleventh Army headquarters. Stargard was already burning from Soviet bombing as he drove up the hill to Steiner's villa. He stood in a garden and looked down on the blazing city, the plain towers of its medieval Lutheran churches rising straight and somber, silhouetted against the red-and-gold background. Poor Stargard, he thought. These austere Protestant towers of the east were sisters of the great gray Catholic towers of Saint-Rombaut of Malines and the Belfry of Bruges. He felt the tragedy here was his tragedy, and he began to weep.

The battle raged all the next day, February 17. A handful of Stukas made pass after pass at the horde of Russian tanks thrown into the battle. Hundreds were set afire but hundreds more plowed forward through the snow. Still, Steiner kept moving forward doggedly, and by dusk had driven such a dangerous wedge into Zhukov's flank that two Soviet tank armies bound for Berlin were recalled to stem further advance.

Late at night Wenck was ordered to come immediately to Berlin and brief Hitler on his progress. It was dawn before the exhausted Wenck left the Reich Chancellery. Anxious to get back and oversee the Third Panzer Army operation which was to start in two and a half hours, he told his driver, Hermann Dorn, to head for Stettin. Wenck had gone without sleep for three nights and was just dozing off when Dorn pulled the big BMW to the side of the road. "Herr General," he said. "I just can't stay awake."

"We've got to get back to the front," Wenck said and took the wheel. As they raced at 60 miles an hour along the dark Autobahn, he put an unlit cigarette in his mouth and chewed the tobacco to keep awake. But within an hour he fell asleep and they smashed into the abutment of a railroad bridge. Dorn and a major who was asleep in the back seat were both thrown out of the car at the impact and tumbled down an embankment to the railroad tracks, but Wenck was wedged behind the wheel, unconscious. The car, hung up on the bridge, suddenly burst into flames. Several loaded machine pistols in the back seat began to explode, and the noise of the shots roused the dazed Dorn. Though badly injured, he clawed his way up the embankment, smashed a window and pulled out Wenck, whose clothes were ablaze. Dorn tore the coat off his chief and rolled him on the pavement to extinguish the flames.

When Wenck awoke he was on an operating table, with a fractured skull, five broken ribs and numerous contusions. Without him, hope for success in the desperation counterattack was out of the question.

## 2.

The other claw of the pincers, which was to drive up into Zhukov's left flank from the south, never even got under way. The Germans who were to launch it had all they could do to stave off attacking Russians. Those entering newly won Bunzlau, a city eighty air miles east of Dresden, made up a colorful, exotic column. On top of oil-splattered Stalins and T-34s, greasy tankers squatted on brightly colored rugs, drinking and singing. Then came a line of heavy guns, their crews astride embroidered cushions, playing German harmonicas and accordions. Behind was an old-fashioned carriage with crystal lanterns, crammed with heavily armed young officers and men wearing top hats and holding umbrellas; in drunken solemnity they peered through lorgnettes at the foot troops. Another carriage, with its top folded back, was filled with laughing and carousing soldiers.

A Russian captain, Mikhail Koriakov—a short, stocky Air Force correspondent relegated to the infantry for attending a Requiem Mass in a village church—watched this wild, undisciplined scene with dismay. Control posts set up to maintain order ignored the passing drunken parade, and officers speeding by in American jeeps were apparently too busy to notice what was going on. He had seen only one senior officer, a colonel, try to stop the mobile orgy—and he was drunk himself. He halted a carriage loaded with stolen chickens and a hog, and pulled out a soldier wearing a huge flowered woman's hat.

"So you want chicken?" the unsteady colonel shouted and poked a gloved fist into the young man's face. "Do you know about Comrade Stalin's order of January nineteen?" The soldier knew of this strict code of behavior for troops in German territory. "Have you heard of the commanding general's order?" The soldier had. "Then what more do you want!" The colonel grabbed a chicken hanging from a lantern and slammed it in the soldier's face. "I'll teach you to respect Comrade Stalin's order!" he shouted, then stumbled to his jeep beside a huge straw-covered bottle of alcohol.

In Bunzlau, Koriakov visited a small square to pay homage to the monument of General Kutuzov, the Russian hero who had died there while pursuing Napoleon. Engraved in the marble was the German tribute:

PRINCE KUTUZOV-SMOLENSKY LED THE VICTORIOUS RUSSIAN
TROOPS TO THIS SPOT. HE FREED EUROPE FROM OPPRESSION
AND ITS PEOPLE FROM SLAVERY. HERE DEATH PUT AN END
TO HIS GLORIOUS DAYS. HIS MEMORY WILL LIVE FOREVER.

He was thinking sadly how Russians had changed when he heard a shriek and saw a girl run into the square, dress torn, stockings hanging around her ankles. She stopped and looked at him beseechingly. Two soldiers in black tank-corps helmets came dashing around the corner and smiled cheerfully at the captain as if asking him to join their fun.

"Are you from the Third Army?" Koriakov asked. They proudly said yes. Their commander, Colonel General Rybalko, personally led every attack. He had sworn to avenge his daughter who had been carried off by Germans, and at the border of the Reich he told his men, "The long-awaited hour, the hour of revenge is at hand! We all have personal reasons for revenge: my daughter, your sisters, our Mother Russia, the devastation of our land!"

This army always left behind it a path of blood, and Koriakov asked the tankers what they wanted with the girl. To work in the company kitchen, one of them answered. "She is not going to work for you." Koriakov said firmly.

A drunken sergeant grabbed the girl's arm. "Our own officers are waiting for her," he shouted.

But Koriakov refused to be cowed, and the sergeant reluctantly released the girl, muttering, "Headquarters' rat!" as he walked off.

The incident reminded Koriakov of a recent conversation with a Polish blacksmith. "Why does war have to rage in this world, Captain?" the Pole had asked. "Six years of this. It came out of Germany, right through here. It traveled through Russia, through the heart of Russia, as far as the Volga. Then it turned back and came through here again. Now it is traveling toward the heart of Germany, to Berlin and Dresden. Why? One half of Russia has been gutted; Germany is aflame now and will continue to burn until there is nothing left."

The answer, thought Koriakov, was simple: The Germans had scorched Russia, murdering millions of women and children and old people with unbelievable cruelty; now the Russians—inflamed by Ilya Ehrenburg's slogans, "Two eyes for an eye" and "A pool of blood for a drop of blood"—were repaying Germany.

Even Stalin had become concerned by the brutality. "Hitlers come and go," he declared, "but the German people go on forever." His misgivings were echoed on February 9 in a *Red Star* editorial:

"An eye for an eye, a tooth for a tooth" is an old saying. But it must not be taken literally. If the Germans marauded, and publicly raped our women, it does not mean that we must do the same. This has never been and never shall be. Our soldiers will not allow anything like that to happen—not because of pity for the enemy, but out of a sense of their own personal dignity. . . . They understand that every breach of military discipline only weakens the victorious Red Army . . .

This monition was practical as well as moral.

Our revenge is not blind. Our anger is not irrational. In an access of blind rage one is apt to destroy a factory in conquered enemy territory—a factory that would be of value to us. Such an attitude can only play into the enemy's hands.

Five days later, criticism of Ehrenburg's propaganda came from an even more significant source when G. F. Alexandrov, leading ideologist of the Central Committee, in an article in *Pravda* entitled "Comrade Ehrenburg Is Oversimplifying," stated that it was un-Marxist and unwise to think all Germans were Nazis, to be treated only as subhumans. There were good Germans, Alexandrov said, and the Soviets would have to co-operate with them after the war.

But this article had had little effect on front-line troops, and several days after its publication Koriakov's good friend Stoliarov, an amiable man, suggested that they burn a large hardware store.

"Are you crazy?" Koriakov exclaimed. "What for?"

"What do you mean—what for?" Stoliarov's good-natured face was distorted. "Revenge! They burned us out and we'll burn them out!"

## 3.

Four days after the triple raid on Dresden, parts of the city continued to smolder and thousands of rescue workers, including British prisoners of war, were still digging out a few survivors.

Fifteen-year-old Joachim Barth was wandering the city alone, mainly out of curiosity. Dressed in a girl's coat and shuffling around in wooden shoes, he watched with morbid fascination as flame throwers burned a huge pile of bodies in the Altmarkt square. He saw a man and woman—caught stealing bracelets, rings and watches from corpses—lined against a wall and shot.

Young Bodo Baumann was in front of the Altstadt railroad station helping to stack bodies in a huge pile over 100 yards long, 3 yards high and 10 yards wide. Thousands of corpses were packed in boats and sent down the river; others were sprinkled with lime and removed to Brühler Terrassen, where they were burned with flame throwers; still others were put in trenches or piled on side streets and covered with straw, sand or rubble so the survivors wouldn't see them.

After the station area was cleaned up, Bodo and his detail were sent to the Grosser Garten to dispose of more than 10,000 bodies. It was a loathsome task to pick them up barehanded. What nauseated Bodo most was the sickly sweet smell of burned flesh mixed with smoke and the stench of decomposition.

Earlier in the day Hans Köhler had returned to Dresden with his father. As they were about to cross a bridge into the Old Town a man said, "Don't go over. They're putting everyone in the Volkssturm."

"Now is the time for you to go west until you get to the American lines," Herr Köhler told his son. "Then wait until it's all over."

They embraced and the youngster started west, without food or money, through a cold drizzle.

Goebbels was able to use the holocaust at Dresden to engender a feeling of moral indignation in Switzerland, Sweden and other neutral countries. But the bombings represented more than an opportunity for propaganda. At a conference with his department chiefs on February 18 he declared emotionally that the Geneva Convention "has lost all meaning when enemy pilots can kill a hundred thousand noncombatants in two hours." Because of the Convention, the Germans could not take reprisals on enemy air crews for their "terror tactics" but if it were invalidated, he argued, they could prevent another Dresden simply by executing all the British and American Air Force prisoners on the charge that they had "murdered civilians."*

Most of his listeners objected, particularly Rudolf Semmler, who cautioned against the "enormous risks that we would run by such an act and of the reprisals which might fall on our own men in enemy hands." Goebbels ignored their monitions and told his press officer to find out how many Allied airmen were in German hands and how many German airmen in Allied hands. Semmler started to protest again, but Goebbels' adjutant kicked him under the table and he closed his mouth.

That evening Goebbels took the matter to the Führer, who agreed in principle but decided to wait before making the final decision. Fortunately Ribbentrop and others were able to dissuade him.

---

* The morality of the Dresden bombings was questioned not only by the Germans and neutrals but by the Allies themselves. Three days after the raids C. M. Grierson, an RAF air commodore, told reporters at a SHAEF press conference in Paris that the air forces planned to bomb large population centers in an attempt to bring about the collapse of the German economy. Grierson referred to the German charges of "terror bombing" and the next morning the dispatch from the Associated Press correspondent, featuring this phrase, was widely read in the United States:

> Allied air chiefs have made the long-awaited decision to adopt deliberate terror-bombings of German population centers as a ruthless expedient of hastening Hitler's doom. . . .

This story stirred a controversy in Great Britain which reached its climax two weeks later when, in the House of Commons, Richard Stokes denounced indiscriminate bombing of large cities. He quoted a recent report in the *Manchester Guardian*:

> What happened on the evening of 13th February? There were a million people in Dresden, including 600,000 bombed-out evacuees and refugees from the East. The raging fires which spread irresistibly in the narrow streets killed a great many for lack of oxygen.

Stokes then noted with pointed sarcasm that the Russians appeared to be taking cities without destroying them utterly. "What are you going to find, with all the cities blasted to pieces, and with disease rampant?" he asked. "May not the disease, filth and poverty which will arise be almost impossible either to arrest or to overcome? I wonder very much whether it is realised at this stage. When I heard the Minister [the Secretary of State for Air, Sir Archibald Sinclair] speak of the 'crescendo of destruction,' I thought: What a magnificent expression for a Cabinet Minister of Great Britain at this stage of the war." Stokes called attention to the A.P. report based on Grierson's SHAEF press conference and wondered if "terror bombing" was going to be government policy from now on.

This speech made such a deep impression on the conscience of the West that Churchill felt impelled to write a minute to General Hastings Ismay and the Chief of the Air Staff Sir Charles Portal:

> It seems to me that the moment has come when the question of bombing of German cities simply for the sake of increasing the terror, though under other pretexts, should be reviewed. Otherwise we shall come into control of an utterly ruined land. We shall not, for instance, be able to get housing materials out of Germany for our own needs because some temporary provisions would have to be made for the Germans themselves. The destruction of Dresden remains a serious query against the conduct of Allied bombing. I am of the opinion that military objectives must henceforward be more strictly studied in our own interests rather than that of the enemy.

## 4.

Other Germans were striving for peace rather than vengeance, and reports of negotiations appeared on February 18 in newspapers of four European countries. Those from Portugal and Spain were false but the ones from Sweden and Switzerland were the fruit of the recent meeting in Berlin when Hitler, by his silence, gave both SS General Wolff and Ribbentrop the impression that he wanted them to arrange a peace with the West.

It was not so strange that the SS and the Foreign Ministry were trying to accomplish the same thing independently. Since the early days in Munich, Hitler had set one subordinate against another to inspire both to greater efforts. Himmler and Ribbentrop had been rivals for years and shared one physical peculiarity: after a single word of censure from the Führer each would get sick to his stomach. Their current rivalry was centered on the transactions for peace and had become so intense that there was almost a state of war between the two offices.

Interwoven with these peace moves were negotiations by both men to save the prisoners in concentration camps. Himmler's efforts in particular were not motivated by humanitarianism but were a form of blackmail, since it was obvious that millions of lives could be a strong bargaining factor in a negotiated peace. He was being encouraged by two men in this pursuit. One was his masseur, Dr. Felix Kersten, who was a Balt, born in Estonia in 1898. Kersten had no medical degree. A mild-looking man with a sensual mouth, he was short, fat and moved clumsily, but he became so adept at "manual therapy" that the wealthy and famous of Europe sought him out. Just before the war Himmler was stricken with severe stomach pains—probably aggravated by the battle going on within himself. Kersten was summoned and treated the Reichsführer with such success that by now Himmler was completely dependent on him. Kersten had already used this influence to save a number of concentration camp prisoners from death. "With every massage he gives me," Himmler once said, "Dr. Kersten deprives me of a life."

---

The Foreign Secretary has spoken to me on this subject, and I feel the need for more precise concentration upon military objectives, such as oil and communications behind the immediate battle-zone, rather than on mere acts of terror and wanton destruction, however impressive.

The Prime Minister apparently forgot that it was he who had triggered the Dresden raid with his ironic and forceful note to Sinclair. After Portal read the minute, he reminded the Prime Minister that Bomber Command should not be blamed, even by inference, for faithfully executing a government policy.

Churchill withdrew the minute and composed another. Changing "terror bombing" to "area bombing," and without reference to Dresden, he quite reasonably observed, "We must see to it that our attacks do not do more harm to ourselves in the long run than they do to the enemy's immediate war effort."

The second man was Himmler's chief of espionage, SS-Brigadeführer (Brigadier General) Walter Schellenberg. He sympathized with everything Kersten was doing and had just about convinced Himmler that a show of humanity to political and war prisoners would prove to the world that he was no monster. Though officially subordinate to SS General Dr. Ernst Kaltenbrunner, chief of the RSHA and Himmler's second-in-command, he had managed things cleverly and now dealt directly with Himmler. Schellenberg was a small, good-looking, fastidious man of thirty-three who had been educated in a Jesuit school. He had long been convinced that Hitler was leading the Reich to complete destruction and had tirelessly urged Himmler to explore every possible opportunity for peace.

This was no easy task, since all negotiations had to be conducted without Hitler's knowledge; nor did it help that Kaltenbrunner was a faithful Nazi who disliked and distrusted Schellenberg. He continuously urged Himmler not to get too involved in schemes that might result in Hitler's displeasure—or worse. These warnings were enhanced by Kaltenbrunner's formidable appearance. He was a burly man of six foot seven, with a great flat forehead and small, brown, piercing eyes. He had a huge lantern jaw, a saber cut across one of his cadaverous cheeks, massive shoulders and dangling, simian arms. Born in 1903 near Hitler's birthplace, he came from a family of scythe makers. His father had broken the pattern to become a lawyer, and the son followed. At twenty-nine he joined the Austrian Nazi Party, and by diligence and persistence rose to his present job, bringing to it legal logic and mediocrity.

His chief, Himmler, had first opposed the annihilation of the Jews and later admitted to Kersten that "the extermination of people is un-Germanic." Violence was repugnant to the Reichsführer—even though he had ordered his own nephew shot for homosexual activities—and when he witnessed his first execution he vomited; only his almost mystical belief that everything Hitler did was right, together with his deep dread of the Führer, had made him stay and watch grimly till the last victim toppled over. In notes for a lecture to Wehrmacht officers, he once wrote in his spidery handwriting, "Execution of all potential resistance leaders of resistance. Very hard, but necessary. . . . We must stay hard, our responsibility to God."

This sometimes ludicrous, always tortured man, squeamish by nature, had finally accepted violence as his way of life, to become the world's greatest executioner. In 1943 he told a group of SS generals:

"Among ourselves it should be mentioned quite frankly—but we will never speak of it publicly. . . . I mean cleaning out the Jews, the extermination of the Jewish race. . . . Most of you must know what it means when a hundred corpses are lying side by side, or five hundred or a thousand. To have stuck it out and at the same time (apart from exceptions caused by human weakness) to have remained decent fellows, that is what has made us so hard. This is a page of glory in our history which has never been written and will never be written."

And a year later he spoke frankly to officials in Posen of the difficulties of exterminating the Jews:

"We were forced to come to the grim decision that this people must be made to disappear from the face of the earth. To organize this assignment was our most difficult task yet. But we have tackled it and carried it through, without—I hope, gentlemen, I may say this—without our leaders and their men suffering any damage in their minds and souls. That danger was considerable, for there was only a narrow path between the Scylla and Charybdis of their becoming either heartless ruffians unable any longer to treasure human life, or becoming soft and suffering nervous breakdowns. . . . That's about all I want to say at the moment about the Jewish problem. You know all about it now, and you had better keep it to yourselves. Perhaps at some later, some very much later period we might consider whether to tell the German people a little more about all this. But I think we had better not! It's we here who have shouldered the responsibility, the responsibility for action as well as for an idea, and I think we had better take this secret with us into our graves."

But in spite of these words Himmler himself was tortured by the horrendous crimes he was forced to commit. "It is the curse of greatness that it must step over dead bodies to create new life," he told Kersten. Hadn't the Americans ruthlessly exterminated the Indians? "Yet we must create new life, we must cleanse the soil or it will never bear fruit. It will be a great burden for me to bear."

The burden of mass murder, indeed, became so great that his stomach convulsions increased in severity, putting him even further under the influence of the only man who could bring him relief—Kersten. And now Kersten, with the help of Schellenberg, was using this power to inveigle Himmler into saving the Jews he had not yet murdered. A born follower, he was being forced to act on his own; a true believer and faithful disciple, he was being tempted to betray his leader; a natural coward, he was being inspired to heroics. At the same time, he kept brooding over the dire consequences that might follow such action and vacillated between the slight and charming Schellenberg and the towering Kaltenbrunner, almost perpetually in a state of anguished indecision. Recently Schellenberg had dominated in this struggle and persuaded Himmler to meet secretly with Jean-Marie Musy, former President of Switzerland. Musy promised to pay a bounty in Swiss francs for each Jew released and also attempt to soften the free world's feelings about Germany. Himmler had readily agreed to send 1200 Jewish prisoners to Switzerland every two weeks.

One of Ribbentrop's subordinates, Dr. Peter Kleist, also began tentative negotiations with the World Jewish Congress and had already met with Gilel Storch, one of its important representatives. At their first conference in a Stockholm hotel, Storch proposed that they negotiate for the release of about 4300 Jews from various concentration camps.

Bargaining for human beings affronted Kleist. He said that even a half-civilized Central European couldn't lend his name to such trading. The only *quid pro quo* he was interested in was a solution to the war that would not ruin Germany.

"This is not a business transaction," said Storch. "It is simply a deal to save human lives."

"I cannot and do not want to be involved in this 'deal,' because it just seems repulsive and dirty to me," Kleist answered. "Also, it's not possible to solve the whole Jewish problem by such individual operations." He maintained that it could only be done politically. In his fight against the anti-Semitic Third Reich, Roosevelt was being egged on by influential Jewish businessmen like Morgenthau, he said, and this as well as the unconditional-surrender formula was only intensifying Germany's anti-Semitism; as a result all Jewry would be destroyed along with all of Europe, leaving the Continent to the Bolsheviks. "If the preservation of Jewry can be traded for the preservation of Europe," Kleist went on, "then we have a real 'deal' here that's worth the risk of my own life."

"You have to speak with Ivar Olson," Storch interjected. "He is an American diplomat in the Stockholm embassy who is the personal adviser to President Roosevelt for the War Refugee Committee of Northern and Western Europe. He has direct contact with the President."

A few days later Storch, visibly excited, told Kleist that according to Olson, President Roosevelt was willing to redeem the lives of the 1,500,000 Jews in concentration camps "with politics." This was exactly what Kleist wanted—a political solution to the war—and he was so elated that he repeated Storch's words to Count Folke Bernadotte, vice-president of the Swedish Red Cross. But the Count only made an incredulous face. Kleist next tried the story on Dr. Werner Best, the Nazi commissioner of Denmark, who, like Kleist, belonged to the General SS. Unlike Bernadotte, Best was impressed enough to advise Kleist to take up the touchy subject directly with Himmler's assistant, Kaltenbrunner.

Kleist knew Kaltenbrunner personally and upon his return to Berlin informed him that Storch promised "a political solution to the war," in return for 1,500,000 Jews. Kaltenbrunner knew of Storch's connection with the World Jewish Congress, and he began pacing back and forth. Suddenly he stopped and said in his heavy Austrian accent, "You know very well what you've stuck your nose into! I have to report this to the Reichsführer immediately. I don't know what he is going to decide about the matter—and you." Kleist was placed under house arrest, to keep him from talking to Ribbentrop. "Don't even step out of your garden gate until this matter has been clarified," Kaltenbrunner warned him.

After several days Kaltenbrunner sent for Kleist and pumped his hand affably. "The Reichsführer is definitely willing to take up this Swedish possibility!" he said, then added, to Kleist's surprise, "There are not one and a half million Jews in our hands. We have two and a half million." There was a second surprise: Kleist himself was to go to Stockholm to start negotiations, and as a token of good faith would bring some 2000 Jews to Sweden.

Kleist had no sooner returned home than he was recalled to police headquarters, but this time Kaltenbrunner glowered at him and said, "The case with the Jews is finished for you. Don't ask me why. You have never had anything to do with this matter and you never will have anything to do with it in the future. It doesn't concern you any more. That's it!" Kaltenbrunner did not bother to explain the reason for this sudden change in plans: Schellenberg had just talked Himmler into sending Dr. Kersten to handle the transaction. Why share credit with Ribbentrop?

Kersten went to Sweden to begin negotiations with Christian Günther, the Swedish Minister of Foreign Affairs, for the freedom of Scandinavian prisoners in concentration camps. Himmler had told him that if this preliminary step went well, Kersten could negotiate directly with Storch. The talks with Günther went so smoothly that it was agreed that Bernadotte should come to Berlin and make final arrangements with Himmler personally.

Ribbentrop knew nothing of these events until the Swedish ambassador in Berlin innocently sent an official message to Himmler requesting that Bernadotte be granted an interview with the Reichsführer—and being official, of course, it had to go through the Foreign Office. For the first time Ribbentrop realized that negotiations in Sweden were being carried on by his rival behind his back.

Himmler feared that Ribbentrop would tell Hitler. Close to panic, he phoned Kaltenbrunner and implored him to tell the Führer offhand about the visit of Bernadotte to Berlin and get his reactions. For further insurance Himmler also phoned SS General Fegelein, Eva Braun's brother-in-law, and asked him to "sound out" Hitler on the same matter.

The next day, February 17, Fegelein called to say that the Führer had made only one terse comment: "One cannot accomplish anything with this sort of nonsense in total war."

Himmler was confounded, afraid to go ahead, yet realizing that this might be his only chance to show the world he was a humanitarian. Fear won out. He decided to have nothing to do with Bernadotte, and when Schellenberg telephoned to announce that the Count had just arrived from Sweden, Himmler said he was "too tied up" with the counteroffensive of Army Group Vistula to see anyone. But Schellenberg again pointed out the great personal advantages that such a meeting would hold for the Reichsführer. Himmler had rarely been able to resist Schellenberg's persuasions, nor could he this time. He agreed to see the Count but insisted on taking one precaution: Schellenberg would somehow have to persuade Ribbentrop to see Bernadotte first, which would prevent the Foreign Minister from carrying tales to Hitler.

Schellenberg "leaked" a story that prospects of the Bernadotte-Himmler negotiations were so bright that the Reichsführer might do what no one else had been able to do: save Germany from disaster. The ruse worked. The following morning, February 18, Ribbentrop summoned Kleist. "Count Bernadotte is in town to see Himmler," he announced reproachfully, and said he wanted to talk to the Count as soon as possible.

At the Swedish legation Kleist chanced to meet Bernadotte in the hallway, who promised to see Ribbentrop. But the Count had a previous engagement with Kaltenbrunner and Schellenberg, an appointment set up by the Reichsführer. Himmler was still waiting to see what Ribbentrop would do, before he committed himself personally.

Bernadotte was driven to Kaltenbrunner's luxurious home on the outskirts of Berlin. The Count, whose father was King Gustav V's brother, was a man of elegance and simplicity, of sophistication and naïveté. He wore his rather individualistic Red Cross uniform smartly and carried a baton as if born with it, yet his favorite picture showed him slumping exhausted against a tree in Boy Scout shorts. Some friends believed his American wife, the former Estelle Manville, had taught him to laugh at himself.

He was peculiarly qualified for his present mission. Although by no means an intellectual, he had an even more valuable quality: eminent common sense. In negotiations, he never gave up. He could go on hour after hour without losing his good humor and if things became tense he would start telling stories. But perhaps his most valuable assets were a simple desire to help the unfortunate and his firm belief that almost every man was basically decent and could be persuaded to do the right thing.

With aloof politeness Kaltenbrunner offered his guest Chesterfield cigarettes and Dubonnet. Doubtlessly looted from France, the Count thought as he accepted graciously. Kaltenbrunner fixed Bernadotte with cold, inquisitorial eyes and asked why he wished to see Himmler. A meeting at such a crucial time would be most difficult to arrange. Couldn't he transmit the Count's message? He lit another cigarette—he smoked up to four packs a day, and his relatively short, stubby nicotine-stained fingers reminded the fastidious Schellenberg of a gorilla's.

"Are you acting under official instructions?" Kaltenbrunner asked.

Bernadotte understandably wanted to negotiate directly with Himmler, and decided to tell him as little as possible. "No, but I can assure you that not only the Swedish government but the whole Swedish people share the opinion I have just indicated."

Kaltenbrunner said that he deplored the situation, as did Himmler, who was most anxious to bring about good relations between their two countries, but strong measures, like taking hostages, were necessary to combat sabotage.

"It would be a great misfortune for Germany" Schellenberg observed, "if Sweden were to be dragged into the war against her." The Count had immediately been impressed by the spy chief's gentlemanly manner and thought he looked more like an English don than a German. Schellenberg was equally impressed by the Count. Here was a man of the highest standing in international circles, whose motives were beyond doubt. With him as a contact perhaps Sweden, which had a special interest in the pacification of northern Europe, could be persuaded to mediate a peace with the West. It was an exciting possibility.

Kaltenbrunner asked Bernadotte if he had any concrete suggestions. The Count proposed that the Swedish Red Cross be allowed to work in the concentration camps, and was surprised when Kaltenbrunner not only nodded his head but also said he "quite agreed" that Bernadotte should see the Reichsführer personally. Within the hour the Count was talking to Ribbentrop at the Foreign Office, or rather, he was listening: from the moment he sat down near a cheerful fire, the Foreign Minister had begun an oration. Curious as to how long this would go on, Bernadotte surreptitiously set his stop watch.

Ribbentrop started with a dissertation on the differences between National Socialism and Bolshevism, postulating that if Germany lost the war, Russian bombers would be over Stockholm within six months and the Reds would shoot the royal family, including the Count. He went from one subject to another, parroting Nazi platitudes without pause—like a worn phonograph record, the Count thought. Finally Ribbentrop declared that the living man who had contributed most to humanity was "Adolf Hitler, unquestionably Adolf Hitler!" He fell silent and Bernadotte snapped the stop watch at sixty-seven minutes.

The next day, February 19, Schellenberg drove Bernadotte to Dr. Gebhardt's sanatorium. Constant Allied air attacks made it a dangerous journey, particularly for the Count, who suffered from hemophilia. A minor cut could be fatal. On the way Schellenberg confided with unexpected frankness that Kaltenbrunner could not be trusted and that Himmler was a weak man, susceptible to the arguments of the last one who talked to him.

At Hohenlychen the Count was first introduced to Dr. Gebhardt, who gloomily remarked that his hospital was filled with eighty refugee children from the east, undergoing amputations because of frostbite or bullet wounds. Bernadotte surmised that this prologue had been arranged to play on his sympathies. Schellenberg then introduced him to a little man in a green SS uniform without decorations, a man with small, delicate hands and carefully manicured nails—Himmler. Bernadotte found him extremely affable; he even joked when the conversation lagged. There was nothing at all diabolic in his appearance. He seemed to be a vivacious man, with an inclination to be sentimental whenever the Führer's name was mentioned.

Other Scandinavians had been puzzled by the contradictions in Himmler's character. Professor Didrik Seip, head of the University of Oslo and a stanch Norwegian patriot, had recently told Bernadotte that he thought Himmler was "a kind of idealist, with a particular liking for the Scandinavian countries."

"Don't you think it's meaningless to go on with the war, since Germany cannot possibly win?" Bernadotte asked.

"Every German will fight like a lion before he gives up hope," Himmler replied. The military situation *was* grave, he said, very grave, but not hopeless. "There is no immediate risk of a Russian breakthrough on the Oder front."

Bernadotte said that what had aroused indignation in Sweden was the seizure of hostages and the murder of innocent people; when Himmler denied the latter, Bernadotte listed specific examples. The Count obviously was misinformed, Himmler replied heatedly and asked if the Count had any concrete proposals.

"Wouldn't it be better for you to suggest some measures that might improve the situation?"

After a brief hesitation the Reichsführer said, "I can suggest nothing."

Bernadotte proposed that Himmler release Norwegians and Danes from concentration camps for custody in Sweden. This modest request touched off a stream of vehement accusations against the Swedes that made no sense at all to Bernadotte but had probably been inspired by one of Himmler's sudden flashes of fear. "If I were to agree to your proposal," he said, his eyes blinking spasmodically, "the Swedish papers would announce with big headlines that the war criminal Himmler, in terror of punishment for his crimes, is trying to buy his freedom." But he said he just might do what Bernadotte asked—if Sweden and the Allies assured him that sabotage would stop in Norway.

"That's unthinkable," the Count replied, and changed the subject. "The Swedish Red Cross is very anxious for your permission to work in the concentration camps, particularly in those where Norwegians and Danes are interned."

"That would probably be very useful, and I see no reason why permission should not be granted," Himmler replied.

The Count was getting accustomed to Himmler's quixotic changes and asked for several other small concessions, which were promptly granted. Encouraged, Bernadotte wondered if Swedish women married to Germans could return to their homeland.

"I don't feel inclined to send German children to Sweden," Himmler replied with a frown. "There they will be brought up to hate their country and their playmates will spit on them because their fathers were German."

The Count pointed out that their fathers would be comforted to know that they were safe.

"Their fathers would doubtless much rather see them grow up in a hovel than have them given refuge in a castle in a country as hostile to Germany as Sweden is," Himmler retorted, but agreed to do what he could. Bernadotte had pushed him to the limit, and his mood changed. "You may think it sentimental, even absurd, but I have sworn loyalty to Adolf Hitler, and as a soldier and as a German I cannot go back on my oath. For that reason I cannot do anything in opposition to the Führer's plans and wishes." Only a moment before, he had granted concessions that would have infuriated Hitler, but now he began to echo his Führer at length on the "Bolshevik menace" and prophesied the end of Europe if the eastern front folded.

"But Germany was allied to Russia during part of the war," the Count said. "How does this fit in with what you have just said?"

"I thought you'd say that," Himmler replied, and admitted it had been a mistake. He began talking nostalgically of his youth in southern Germany, where his father had been tutor to a Bavarian prince, about his service as a sergeant major in World War I, and his enrollment in the National Socialist Party at its inception. "Those were glorious days!" he said. "We members of the movement were in constant danger of our lives, but we were not afraid. Adolf Hitler led us and held us together. They were the most wonderful years of my life! Then I could fight for what I regarded as Germany's rebirth."

Bernadotte politely questioned the treatment of the Jews. "Won't you admit there are decent people among the Jews, just as there are among all races?" he said. "I have many Jewish friends."

"You're right," Himmler replied, "but you in Sweden have no Jewish problem and therefore can't understand the German point of view."

At the end of the two-and-a-half-hour conference Himmler promised to give definite answers to all of Bernadotte's requests before he returned to Sweden, and Bernadotte presented Himmler, who was greatly interested in Scandinavian folklore, with a seventeenth-century work on troll-drums.

Himmler said he was "deeply touched" and asked Schellenberg if he had chosen a good chauffeur for the Count. Schellenberg said he had picked the best man available and the Reichsführer grinned. "Good. Otherwise the Swedish papers might announce in big headlines: WAR CRIMINAL HIMMLER MURDERS COUNT BERNADOTTE."

In Berlin, Schellenberg briefed Kaltenbrunner about the meeting. The RSHA chief accused him of exerting "undue influence on the Reichsführer," and SS-Gruppenführer (Major General) Heinrich Müller, head of the Gestapo, grumbled that it was "always the same thing when the gentlemen who consider themselves statesmen talk Himmler into agreeing to one of their ideas." And this particular notion, Müller said, was "completely Utopian."

Bernadotte returned to Ribbentrop's office. The Foreign Minister seemed more eager to help the Count than before, but his overbearing good humor only rankled Bernadotte, who politely excused himself as soon as he could.

Ribbentrop immediately called in Dr. Kleist and told him to sit in the armchair near the fireplace just occupied by Bernadotte. "Who exactly is Bernadotte?" he asked. "Who is backing him up? And what does he *really* want besides saving the Scandinavians?"

Kleist noticed a large leather billfold bulging with papers in the upholstery of the chair. As he lifted it up, a passport fell out.

"What's that?" Ribbentrop asked.

"The billfold of your last visitor." Kleist handed it over, assuming that Ribbentrop would examine the papers inside, but Ribbentrop merely put the billfold in a large plain envelope. "Please return this to Bernadotte," he said. "I'm sure he will miss it."

Kleist was impressed. It seemed a unique "gesture of chivalry amidst the dissolution of a total war."

Even as Himmler was making negotiations that he hoped would lead to a favorable peace, his army group was disintegrating. Steiner had been forced to pull all his troops back to their original starting point, and the main attack by the Third Panzer Army—without Wenck on hand to oversee the operation—was making no progress. Total disaster in the east seemed so imminent that other important Germans, besides Himmler and Ribbentrop, were also beginning to think that the only hope for the Fatherland lay in diplomacy—or unconditional surrender.

# PART TWO

※ ※ ※

## Drive from the West

# 9

## "An Iron Curtain Will Go Down"

**1.**

On February 14 Eisenhower met Montgomery at his tactical headquarters in Zonhoven, Belgium. The controversial problem of command was still very much on Eisenhower's mind. He complained of "always being bullied by Marshall and the U. S. Chiefs of Staff for being too British, or by the P.M. [Churchill] and the British Chiefs of Staff for being too American." What did Monty think of the situation? As usual the field-marshal's views were definite: if allowed to make the main attack aided by Simpson's U. S. Ninth Army, Montgomery would consider the present setup satisfactory. He recorded in his diary:

Ike was delighted that I was happy about the present command situation. There is no doubt that he was worried about something when he arrived at Zonhoven, and appeared so during our talk.

I have even now no idea what is at the bottom of his worry. But it was very obvious that as soon as I had said I was very well satisfied with the present situation about command, he became a different man; he drove away beaming all over his face.

He also wrote Brooke, expressing his delight that "Ike agreed with everything I was doing" and had promised to leave Simpson under his command for the rest of the war. "All this is very good and I do believe that we are at last all well set with a fair wind to help us into harbour. We have had a few storms, but the sky is now clear."

Nine days later the Roer River—flooded when the Germans destroyed the dams—subsided enough to start "Grenade," a tremendous operation involving 303,243 men. At 2:45 A.M. on February 23 Simpson's Ninth Army opened up a heavy artillery barrage. Forty minutes later it stopped and the initial wave—four infantry divisions—began crossing the still swollen Roer in assault boats. There was little enemy resistance at first, but the violent river swamped numerous boats and hampered bridge building.

To the north Montgomery had achieved what had appeared impossible a week before—brought order out of chaos. Operation "Veritable," momentarily thrown off balance by the postponement of "Grenade," had regained its first momentum and was now moving slowly but steadily across flooded plains through thick stretches of woods. Horrocks' XXX Corps smashed through fortified villages and towns and took its two main objectives, Cleve and Goch, in some of the fiercest hand-to-hand battling of the war.

Montgomery was relieved by the fall of Goch, supposedly the last great bastion of the West Wall. But the next town proved to be another "Goch," and the next and the next. There was to be no breakthrough. The eleven German divisions jammed in the narrow strip between the Roer and the Rhine meant to stand and fight—until destroyed. It was evident, however, that the hard-won successes of the British and Canadians had made Simpson's way far easier. By nightfall the Americans were safely across the river on a wide front, at the cost of only ninety-two dead. The next day German air and artillery tried to stop Simpson's engineers, but seven Class 40 bridges, capable of carrying tanks, and twelve lighter bridges were thrown across the Roer.

The following morning, February 25, the 30th Infantry Division fought its way through the Hambach Forest. Little lay before Simpson now except the flat open country of the Cologne Plain—and this, traversed by a network of hard-surfaced roads, was a tanker's paradise. Combat commands from the 2nd and 5th Armored divisions burst through the holes made by the infantry and raced toward the Rhine. Sidney Olson of *Time* watched the 2nd Armored spearhead from a Piper Cub: he saw great waves of American tanks scurry like heavy dark beetles across the green cabbage fields; then, as Thunderbolts swooped down on German strong points, countless trucks loaded with infantry rolled forward in a massive mop-up. To Olson it was "one of War's grandest single pictures of united and perfectly functioning military machines in a supreme moment of pure fighting motion."

**2.**

Although the German reaction to "Veritable" had been slow, the crossing of the Roer by Simpson clarified the Allied aims, and Feldmarschall Gerd von Rundstedt, the aged commander of the western front, finally realized that with "Veritable" the anvil and "Grenade" the hammer, two of his armies would be destroyed unless he pulled back quickly. Catastrophic as these two attacks against his northern flank were, he felt that the unpredictable George Patton presented an even more dangerous threat in the south, and on February 25 he asked Hitler for new directives. Unless there was a general retreat across the Rhine, he declared, the entire western front would crumble.

This desperate appeal was ignored and Rundstedt sent a second, calling for a modest withdrawal near the juncture of the Roer and Maas rivers. This time Berlin answered with a curt negative, followed on February 27 by a personally signed message from Hitler informing Rundstedt that general withdrawal behind the Rhine could not even be considered.

At his conference several days later Hitler ridiculed Rundstedt's persistent requests to withdraw. "I want him to hang on to the West Wall as long as humanly possible. Above all, we must cure him of the idea of retreating here. Because at that very moment the enemy will have the entire Sixth English Army [he meant the Second British Army] and all the American troops free, and will throw them all in over here. These people just don't have any vision. It would only mean moving the catastrophe from one place to another. As soon as I move out of here, the enemy will have that whole army free. He can't tell me that the enemy will stay here instead of moving over here." It was almost as if he had overheard the plans made at Yalta to launch the main attack in the north while holding in the south.

For all that, Hitler was nagged by some doubt and suggested sending observers to the western front. "We have to get a couple of officers down there—even if they only have one leg or one arm—officers who are good men, whom we can send down there so that we get a clear picture." He said he didn't trust official reports. "They are made only to throw dust in our eyes. Everything is explained and later we find out that nothing happened."

As for the eastern front, Hitler urged that Himmler build up a front by any means, even by mustering women. "So many women who want to shoot are volunteering now, that I really think we ought to take them immediately." The idea of using women was revolting to a soldier like

Guderian but he said nothing. "They are braver, anyway," Hitler continued. "If we put them into the second line, the men at least won't run away. Here behind the Rhine nobody can go over to the enemy. That's the beauty of it. From here they can only take off to the rear."

## 3.

Both Hodges and Patton had been making good advances, yet both were being restrained by Eisenhower: until Montgomery reached the Rhine, Hodges could not attack Cologne, nor Patton seize Koblenz. A bitter Patton told Bradley that history would criticize the American High Command for its lack of energy. He kept asking Bradley to let him "make a rush at Koblenz," and was finally told he could—if the opportunity presented itself. This came on February 27, when the 10th Armored Division, temporarily loaned to Patton, drove to within six miles of Trier, an ancient city located so strategically on the Moselle River that once the Germans were dislodged, they would have to fall all the way back to the Rhine.

At dusk Patton phoned Bradley that he was within sight of Trier and requested permission to keep going, even though the 10th Armored Division was supposed to be returned to SHAEF reserve that night. Bradley said to keep on, that is, at least until Eisenhower personally ordered him to return the division. Then he chuckled and said he would stay away from the telephone. Patton thought he and Bradley were "putting one over" on Eisenhower, but Bradley's insubordination was a pretense. He and Eisenhower had privately decided to let Patton make a surreptitious push all the way to the Rhine, an agreement so secret that Bradley's own staff knew nothing of it.

Thus the 10th Armored Division continued its drive toward Trier, and just after midnight of February 28 the task force of Lieutenant Colonel Jack J. Richardson quietly entered its southeastern suburbs and captured a company defending a railroad crossing with four antitank guns, without firing a shot. One of the prisoners revealed that it was his job to warn demolition teams at the two bridges over the Moselle River of the arrival of Americans. Deciding to try and capture them intact, Richardson sent half of his men to the northern bridge, which was blown up before they arrived, and half to the southern, the Kaiserbrücke, built in Roman times.

Richardson himself headed for the Kaiserbrücke. In the full moonlight he could see his men pinned down by small-arms fire from the other side of the Moselle. He swept the far end of the bridge with fire from his own .50-caliber machine gun, then ordered a platoon of infantry and five tanks to cross. Six drunken Germans tried to blow up the opposite approach, but the Americans were upon them before they could set off the charge.

By dawn two combat commands of the 10th Armored, reinforced by elements of the 94th Division, were swarming over the city, rounding up dazed, sleepy German soldiers. With Trier and its bridge in his hands Patton could either follow the Moselle up to Koblenz and the Rhine, or turn southeast to the Saar industrial region. Whatever course he chose, who could stop him? Just then Patton was handed a message from SHAEF ordering him to by-pass Trier, since it would take four divisions to effect its capture. With relish he replied: HAVE TAKEN TRIER WITH TWO DIVISIONS. WHAT DO YOU WANT ME TO DO? GIVE IT BACK?

That same day, March 1, the infantrymen of Simpson's 29th Division seized Mönchen-Gladbach, the largest German city yet conquered and only twelve miles from the Rhine. To Simpson, "Grenade" had been "like a football game with every play working perfectly."

Eisenhower visited Ninth Army headquarters and said that he was most interested in any plans Simpson had for capturing a bridge over the Rhine. There were eight in his zone and bold, rapid pursuit might win at least one. Simpson said he was planning to make a run the next day for one of the three Neuss–Düsseldorf bridges. They drove up front in the rain in an open jeep to inspect a regiment of the division that had just captured Mönchen-Gladbach, and Eisenhower continued, "I want to tip you off. In a few days you can expect Prime Minister Churchill. What kind of an automobile have you?"

Simpson only had a Plymouth; someone in the rear apparently kept "short-stopping" cars meant for him.

"I'll take care of it," Eisenhower said. "Another thing. Churchill likes Scotch. Be sure and have a good supply on hand."

Soldiers recognized Eisenhower in the front seat of the jeep and began shouting, "There's Ike!" The two generals walked through mud up a slope where some 3600 infantrymen were gathered. Simpson introduced the Supreme Commander, who talked movingly for five minutes, but as he turned to leave, his feet slipped and he sat down hard in the mud. There was a roar of laughter. Eisenhower struggled to his feet, grinned and gave a boxer's salute. There was another roar from the men—this one an ovation.

Eisenhower also visited Montgomery that day and intimated that he knew all about Brooke's maneuvering to have Alexander made his deputy in charge of ground operations. Again, what did Monty think of the whole idea? The end of the war was in sight, Montgomery replied, and Alexander's appointment would only stir up resentment in certain American quarters. "For goodness' sake, let us stop any further causes of friction at all cost. We are just about to win the German war. Let Alex remain in Italy. And let Tedder see the thing through to the end as Deputy Supreme Commander."

Montgomery had another important visitor, the Prime Minister, who had come to the Continent to partake personally in the great victories of 21 Army Group. On the morning of March 3 Churchill, Brooke and Montgomery motored in two Rolls-Royces for a visit with Simpson at Maastricht. The group, accompanied by a large number of correspondents, began to load into cars for a trip to the battle area, and Simpson wondered if Churchill wanted to visit the men's room first.

"How far is the West Wall?" the Prime Minister asked. When he learned that it was only half an hour's trip he said he would wait.

At Montgomery's suggestion Simpson sat beside Churchill. A jeep overtook them and a messenger handed the Prime Minister a small package. Churchill unwrapped his bridgework, matter-of-factly shoved it in his mouth and began regaling Simpson with stories from the early days of the war. He had flown to Paris during the German invasion of 1940 to offer perpetual union with Britain; the French leaders turned down the proposal. About Dunkerque he said, "I think we were lucky to get over fifty thousand back."

As they approached a bridge over a small ravine Simpson remarked, "Mr. Churchill, the boundary between Holland and Germany runs under that bridge ahead of us."

"Stop the car," Churchill said. "Let's get out." He walked across the bridge and climbed down the bank toward the river to a long row of "dragon's teeth," the German tank defense system. There he waited until Montgomery, Brooke, Simpson and several other generals joined him. From the bridge a crowd of correspondents and photographers watched expectantly.

"Gentlemen," Churchill said sonorously, "I'd like to ask you to join me. Let us all urinate on the great West Wall of Germany." He wagged a finger at the photographers, who were aiming their cameras, and called out, "This is one of those operations connected with this great war which must not be reproduced graphically."

Brooke stood next to the Prime Minister and was particularly impressed by "the childish grin of intense satisfaction that spread all over his face as he looked down at the critical moment."


## 4.

Just before flying to the western front, Churchill had asked the House of Commons, in the face of bitter controversy, for approval of the Crimea Conference decision on Poland. "It is quite evident that these matters touch the whole future of the world," he said. Somber indeed would be the fortunes of mankind if some awful schism arose between the Western democracies and the Russian Soviet Union . . .

"The ties that bind the three Great Powers together and their mutual comprehension of each other have grown. The United States has entered deeply and constructively into the life and salvation of Europe. We have all three set our hands to far-reaching engagements at once practical and solemn."

The House of Commons overwhelmingly endorsed the Yalta decisions, only twenty-five voting against the government.

The following day, March 1, Roosevelt left the White House for the Capitol Building, with Mrs. Roosevelt, their daughter Anna and her husband, where he would try to emulate Churchill and win approval of Yalta from both Houses of Congress.

Mrs. Roosevelt had noticed a marked change in her husband since his return. She found that he needed a rest in the middle of the day and that he was less and less willing to see people for any length of time. Only when he talked to her about Yalta did his old enthusiasm return. "Look at the communiqué from the Crimea," he said. "The path it charts! From Yalta to Moscow, to San Francisco and Mexico City, to London and Washington and Paris. Not to forget it mentions Berlin! It's been a global war, and we've already started making it a global peace!"

Sam Rosenman, who had been working with Roosevelt on the Yalta speech, thought the President was listless, "all burnt out," and that the crushing effect of twelve years as President had become increasingly evident. But when Frances Perkins, the Secretary of Labor, saw the President enter the Speaker's Room, she was pleasantly surprised. His face was gay, eyes bright, skin again a good color. That Roosevelt man is a wonder, she said to herself. He gets tired, but just give him a little rest and a sea voyage and he comes right up again.

Roosevelt had always addressed Congress from the rostrum of the House of Representatives. Now a table, bristling with microphones, stood only a yard from the first curved row of seats. Roosevelt entered, followed by Vice-President Harry S Truman and Speaker of the House Sam Rayburn. For the first time Roosevelt didn't stand to speak. "Mr. Vice-President, Mr. Speaker and members of the Congress," he said. "I hope that you will pardon me for the unusual posture of sitting down during the presentation of what I want to say, but I know that you will realize it makes it a lot easier for me in not having to carry about ten pounds of steel around on the bottom of my legs, and also because of the fact that I have just completed a fourteen-thousand-mile trip."

This was the first time Roosevelt had publicly mentioned his affliction and many Americans listening on the radio were staggered. A surprising number had no idea their President was crippled. Mrs. Perkins thought he said it in such a casual, unself-pitying and debonair manner that no one was uncomfortable. And she was impressed by the speech that followed. It answered whatever unspoken fears she might have had. Truman, on the contrary, missed the famous Roosevelt manner and delivery. Rosenman was not only dismayed at Roosevelt's halting, ineffective delivery but thought some of his extemporaneous remarks bordered on the ridiculous and must have popped into his head at the moment.

The President outlined the two main purposes of Yalta: "To bring defeat to Germany with the greatest possible speed and the smallest possible loss of Allied men" and "to continue to build the foundation for an international accord that would bring order and security after the chaos of the war, that would give some assurance of lasting peace among the nations of the world." He told of the new United Nations organization and its first conference, to be held at San Francisco on April 25.

"This time we are not making the mistake of waiting until the end of the war to set up the machinery of peace," he said. "This time, as we fight together to win the war finally, we work together to keep it from happening again."

If the speech lacked the usual Roosevelt eloquence, Congress was stirred and almost everyone present deeply impressed by the President's show of courage and will power. At the end he received a sincere, affectionate ovation.

"As soon as I can," he wearily told Truman a moment later, "I will go to Warm Springs for a rest. I can be in trim again if I stay there for two or three weeks."


Even while Churchill and Roosevelt were telling their people of the accomplishments of the Crimea Conference, a crack in the vaunted unity of the Big Three was appearing in Rumania. America's political representative in Bucharest reported that "the violent element of the Communist Party increases its demands, distorts facts, and levels charges as the government's position with the people improves." Local Communist papers labeled police efforts to break up mass demonstrations against the Radescu coalition Cabinet as "bloody massacres" and demanded the government's immediate dissolution.

British and American members of the Allied Control Commission for Rumania asked for a meeting to resolve the crisis, but the Soviet chairman refused to call it. In protest Harriman wrote Molotov an official letter declaring that the political developments in Rumania should follow the Declaration on Liberated Europe, as agreed at Yalta. Stalin's answer was to send to Bucharest Deputy Foreign Commissar Andrei Vishinsky, best remembered for his vituperous prosecution at the Moscow Trials. At Yalta he had grinned benevolently, and outwardly at least, was charming. In Bucharest he chose to be threatening and ordered the King of Rumania to dismiss the Radescu government at once—and gave him exactly two hours and five minutes to find a new Premier and publicly announce the appointment. When Foreign Minister Visoianu protested that the King must follow constitutional practice, Vishinsky shouted "Shut up!" and left with a slam of the door.

The next day, about the time Roosevelt was addressing Congress, the King appointed Prince Stirbey as Radescu's replacement. But the Communists refused to join his government, and Vishinsky instructed the King to make a new choice—Petru Groza, a man closely associated with the Communists.

A more amiable diplomacy was being practiced in a nameless Hungarian village by a soldier—Marshal Tolbukhin, commander of the Third Ukrainian Front. In the past few months Field-Marshal Harold Alexander had sent him several messages requesting a meeting to discuss military problems: their two forces were rapidly approaching and Alexander wanted to keep them from colliding head-on. Apparently acting on instructions from Moscow, Tolbukhin at first simply ignored the messages, but when Alexander politely persisted he was at last invited to come to Third Ukrainian Front headquarters in Hungary, with a small party of British and American experts. The Allied group was flown in a Soviet C-47 to a secret air base just across the Hungarian border, then driven over bad country roads for an hour and a half. Lieutenant Colonel Charles W. Thayer, head of the American Military Mission to Yugoslavia —a career diplomat and a graduate of West Point—asked the Russian general accompanying him where they were. The general said he didn't even know if it was Yugoslavia or Hungary. Finally they came to a large village, luxuriant with flowers and fruit trees.

"This," said the general, "is Marshal Tolbukhin's headquarters."

Thayer counted about 100 small cottages. There was no traffic and only a few sentries, nor were there telephone lines or any of the paraphernalia one expected to find at an army group headquarters. The Allied party was led into the cottage that was Tolbukhin's command post. After a short wait the marshal strode in; to Thayer, he seemed to have stepped "fresh out of *War and Peace*." He was tall, bulky and moon-faced, with thinning hair. British Major-General Terence Airey, Alexander's chief of intelligence, also thought he looked like the typical pre-Revolution imperial officer—impressive and expansive.

Tolbukhin hid any annoyance he might have felt at being forced, as it were, to confer with Alexander, and greeted his guests with gusty warmth. First he suggested a light breakfast and led them to a dining room where they started with pickled herring, ham, sardines, cheese and vodka. Thayer noticed that the Soviet marshal was having his own glass filled from a special carafe. When Tolbukhin saw he had been observed, he jovially fined Thayer three glasses of vodka for prying, and a moment later fined him four more for noticing another Russian use the same carafe.

After breakfast, while the military specialists were in conference, Thayer and Brigadier Fitzroy Maclean—sent to Yugoslavia by Churchill —strolled around the village. It was the most curious military installation either had ever seen. It looked as if Tolbukhin and his staff, together with a group of the prettiest Russian female soldiers in the area, had only arrived a few hours earlier. Thayer was reminded of the fake villages Catherine the Great's favorite statesman and adviser, Potemkin, had built to please his mistress.

Alexander found the official session friendly but fruitless. He apologized for the accidental killing of a Red Army corps commander by Allied fighter pilots. If Tolbukhin would only inform him of the front lines, he said, such regrettable accidents could be prevented. The dead corps commander had been one of his best friends, Tolbukhin replied, and added resignedly, "There's no use talking about giving you our front-line positions. Moscow says no."

At a banquet that evening, enormous sturgeon, roast turkeys and whole stuffed suckling pigs were served along with vodka, sweet Crimean champagne and sticky brandy from the Caucasus. At last an elaborate iced cake, decorated with allegorical statuettes and patriotic symbols, was ceremoniously carried in. Toast followed toast until the mood became so relaxed that everyone was shouting to each other around the huge table. A four-star Red Army general asked Maclean where he had learned to speak Russian so well. When the brigadier said he had spent the years of the Moscow Trials in the Soviet Union, the Russian's friendly face clouded abruptly. "They must have been difficult years for a foreigner to understand," he said, and turned to his other table partner.

After the party a Soviet lieutenant general escorted Alexander to his quarters and Thayer went along as interpreter. They walked into Alexander's cottage, where an attractive blonde in uniform was asleep on a couch.

"Who, may I ask, is this?" Alexander inquired politely.

The Russian general stammered unconvincingly that he didn't know. "As a matter of fact," he added quickly, "she ordinarily lives in this cottage. Must have come back by instinct."

"Like a homing pigeon?" Alexander retorted.

The girl was wakened and sent off. Thayer also found a girl soldier in the quarters he was sharing with Major General Lyman Lemnitzer, an American on Alexander's staff.

"What the hell goes on here?" Lemnitzer asked. "What's the WAC for?"

Thayer explained that she was ostensibly an orderly. "She'll be sleeping in the outer room, so don't worry."

In that room she had made up a bed on the couch for Thayer. She tucked him in as if he were a child, brought him a glass of hot milk, then wrapped herself in an overcoat and lay down on the floor. Thayer was wakened at five in the morning when she mopped his face with a cold, wet rag. After shaving him, she said, "Now open your mouth and I'll brush your teeth."

Breakfast with Tolbukhin again started and ended with vodka, and most of the Allied party remembered little by the time they woke up in Belgrade the following day. Undoubtedly Moscow had planned it that way.

In Bucharest several days had passed since Vishinsky had told the King of Rumania to form a new government headed by Groza, the Soviet choice, but the King's ministers were still hesitating. Finally, on March 5, Vishinsky's patience wore out and he summarily ordered the King to announce the formation of the Groza government that very day. Failure to do so, he shouted, would be considered by the Soviet Union as a hostile act. At seven o'clock the new Cabinet—thirteen supporting Groza, and four representing all other parties—was sworn in. By threat and without benefit of election, Communism had, in effect, come to Rumania.

Harriman objected, as he had done since the crisis started, only to be told blandly that the old government had been Fascist. Posing as the only true defenders of democracy, the Soviets further declared that "the terroristic policy of Radescu, which was incompatible with the principles of democracy, has been overcome by the formation of the new government."

By an irony of history, Dr. Josef Goebbels had recently written an article entitled "The Year 2000," warning the West of just such duplicity. But who could believe an enemy, particularly when he freely mixed fact and fiction?

. . . At the Yalta Conference the three enemy war leaders, in order to carry out their program of annihilation and extermination of the German people, have decided to keep all Germany occupied until the year 2000. . . .

How empty must be the brains of those three characters, or at least the brains of two of them! For the third, Stalin, has planned much farther ahead than his two partners. . . .

If the German people surrender, the Soviets will occupy . . . the whole east and southeast of Europe in addition to the larger part of Germany. In front of this enormous territory, including the Soviet Union, an iron curtain will go down. . . . The rest of Europe will fall in political chaos which will be but a period of preparation for the coming of Bolshevism . . .

If Goebbels did nothing else, in "iron curtain" he invented a phrase for Westerners to ponder over—and eventually claim as their own.

# 10

# Ebb and Flow

## 1.

A lull had descended on the eastern front. It was partly a simple case of logistics—the tremendous Soviet thrust had at last outrun its supplies—and partly a result of the gallant, if sporadic, German defense. Konev's First Ukrainian Front encountered increasing resistance from Schörner's troops. And though Zhukov had driven three small bridge-heads across the Oder, he was meeting firm opposition at Frankfurt, Küstrin and Schwedt; moreover, Steiner's limited attack in the north had caused such apprehension in the Red Army High Command that the main drive on Berlin had been postponed until the trouble spots were wiped out.

The measure of Hitler's preoccupation with the Russian threat was clearly shown when he transferred one of his best field commanders to the east—from a front that was about to give way. Hitler ordered Baron Hasso von Manteuffel, whose Fifth Panzer Army had been the spearhead of the Battle of the Bulge, to take over an important sector on the Oder River. Manteuffel was a forceful young general and grandson of a great military hero. Only a few inches more than five feet, he had at one time been an expert equestrian and German pentathlon champion, and he typified the best in Prussian military tradition. He was one of the few who dared disagree with Hitler, and had even disobeyed a direct Führer order. Albert Speer, Minister for Armament and War Production, an old ac-quaintance, had begged him not to follow the injunction to destroy the bridges, dams and factories in the important industrial Cologne-Düsseldorf area; otherwise the people of Germany would suffer after the war. Manteuffel needed no urging; he would destroy bridges only if it were necessary for strategic purposes.

On March 3 Keitel met Manteuffel in the anteroom of the Reich Chancellery and said anxiously, "Manteuffel, you are young and impetuous. Don't make him nervous. Don't tell him too much." A moment later the little general was led into the Führer's office, where he found Hitler sitting slumped over like an old man. Before the Battle of the Bulge, when they had argued about plans for the attack, Hitler had appeared to be in poor physical condition. Now he looked worse.

Hitler glanced up, and instead of greeting Manteuffel with the usual warmth, cried, "All generals are liars!"

It was the first time Hitler had ever shouted at him and Manteuffel resented it. "Has the Führer ever known General von Manteuffel and his officers to be liars? Who said so?"

The only witness, Hitler's Army adjutant, was standing there, mouth agape. Hitler himself blinked, and explained that he hadn't referred to Manteuffel or his generals, then calmly and politely began talking of the overall situation. Manteuffel was appalled at Hitler's ignorance of Allied air superiority, and had to explain that nothing could move in the Rhineland in the daytime—not convoys, nor even lone vehicles—without being shot up by Allied planes.

"That's hard to believe" was the Führer's comment.

"I've personally had three jeeps shot out from under me by Allied planes in the past few months," Manteuffel retorted, and Hitler was so impressed that his mouth fell open.

He then told Manteuffel that the lull in the east was only momentary. Zhukov stood at the Oder, an hour's motor drive from Berlin, with more than 750,000 troops. To protect the capital, Himmler had completely reorganized Army Group Vistula. All available forces had hastily been assembled into two armies: one behind Frankfurt and Küstrin, commanded by General Theodor Busse, and one to Busse's left, holding a line all the way to the Baltic Sea. This latter army needed a man who knew how to fight Russians, Hitler said, and told Manteuffel to report at once to Reichsführer Himmler at his headquarters. Manteuffel had heard that Himmler was in nominal command of the army group, but it seemed too ludicrous and he couldn't help asking why such a man had been selected.

Hitler merely shrugged his shoulders and said apologetically, "Himmler was made commander in chief just as a political gesture."

As Manteuffel passed briskly through the anteroom, the harassed Keitel tagged after him. "I heard what you told the Führer in there," he scolded. "You shouldn't do such things. He has enough troubles!"

**2.**

On the other side of the Oder, tension in Wugarten had subsided; the Allied prisoners under Colonel Fuller no longer feared a German counterattack from the north. Their main concern now was the Russians who were preparing for the final drive to Berlin. Every few days a different unit would pass through town, carousing and raping. Once Fuller voiced his strong objections about the unsoldierly behavior of the Soviets to a Russian general, only to be told, "You must remember, Colonel, that all women are the property of the Red Army. Don't you interfere any more with these Russians."

To make matters worse, the food situation in the village had reached a critical level. And when on March 4 the long-promised Soviet supply wagon rolled into town, it brought only sixteen packages of tobacco and a letter from Army headquarters informing Fuller that trucks would come to Wugarten in a few hours to transport the American prisoners to the east for eventual repatriation. At dawn the villagers watched silently as their protectors climbed into five Dodge trucks. Just before leaving, Fuller recommended that Captain Foch, a relative of the famed maréchal, be placed in command of the remaining prisoners. To the Italians, this was the final insult to their General Geloso.

Fuller put Hegel—the German guard-interpreter masquerading as an American—in his own truck and warned him to stay out of sight when going through towns. At one of the rest stops Captain Donald Gilinski noticed a dead Russian soldier lying in the ditch and told a Red Army sergeant to get the man's name and serial number.

"Why?" the sergeant asked.

"So his death will be reported back to Division."

"Why?"

"So his parents can be notified."

"When he doesn't come back," the sergeant said, "they'll know he's dead."

The closer they came to Posen, the more excited Hegel became at the prospect of seeing his wife and children. Fuller and the other American officers in the truck again warned him not to call any attention to himself. If he was discovered they would all be in trouble. But as they drove down Hegel's street he could not resist peeking out at his house. A young officer jerked him back.

They continued through the city to a large prisoner-of-war camp at Wrzesnia, which was overflowing with Americans, British, French, Poles, Yugoslavs, Rumanians, Italians and one lone Brazilian. A group of GIs who had landed with Fuller in Normandy greeted him enthusiastically.

But the British reaction was cool, and one enlisted man even jumped the unwary Fuller and knocked him to the ground.

"What's wrong with that crazy bastard?" Fuller asked.

"Oh, he hits anyone who looks like an officer," another British soldier explained.

The following night all the Americans and British in camp boarded a train bound for Warsaw and then Odessa. From there they would sail on British ships to Italy.

As the Fuller group approached the Polish capital, two young Poles also seeking freedom were escaping from Warsaw to avoid execution by the Russians. One was eighteen-year-old Jan Krok Paszkowski, son of a division commander captured by the Germans in 1939 and still a Nazi prisoner. Jan's brother, a lieutenant, had fought the Russians while his father was battling the Germans. He then joined the Polish underground, but was captured by the Nazis and executed in Maidenek. Like his brother, Jan went underground. He fought in General Bor's doomed Home Army in the Warsaw uprising and was wounded twice. In a desperate last attempt to break out, he and 300 others tried to escape through the sewers but were flooded out—directly in front of a German police headquarters. On the way to his execution Jan managed to slip away, and with the help of peasants reached the family summer home near the city.

As soon as the great Soviet offensive of January 12 started and the Russians crossed the Vistula, the Home Army disbanded—Poland would soon be free. But after several weeks it became obvious that Stalin intended to make Poland a Communist satellite—not liberate her—and most of the Home Army, including Jan, again went underground.

Early in March, Jan learned that the Russians were about to arrest him because of his participation in the Warsaw uprising, and decided to escape to the west. There was a rumor that the Germans were about to mount a counterattack near the Polish-Czechoslovakian border. Jan and another young partisan hoped to slip through the battle lines in the confusion, and boarded a train to Katowice in southern Poland. Jan was wearing a shiny, worn tuxedo (issued by the underground along with two gold pieces worth $10) and high black cavalry boots, but caused no comment—that year the bizarre in clothing was commonplace.

Katowice had become a bustling Mecca for displaced persons and opportunists. The curiosity of the two friends was piqued by a sign outside a store: WESTERN TERRITORIES SOCIETY. Inside, they discovered that for a few bottles of vodka they could get new identity cards, entitling them to settle in the German territory promised Poland at Yalta. Jan was sure it was a racket. It was—but those in line told him that for some reason the Russians were accepting such identification.

The next morning the two young men, armed with new identities, approached a bridge at the Oder River. They were stopped at a Russian check point and herded with others to an enclosure on the east side of the river, where they told an NKVD officer that they had been sent by the Western Territories Society to organize quarters for settlers in Neisse, an old German city about forty miles to the west on the river of the same name, near the Czech border. The Russian believed their story and issued them special passes allowing them to ride any Soviet vehicle; by midafternoon the two were again heading west across the Oder, in a Russian truck. At dusk the truck stopped near the bridge leading to Neisse, and they were told to dismount. Walking up to the bridge, they could see the city in flames across the river; they also heard occasional staccato shots.

There were two barriers on the bridge; they passed the first but were stopped at the second, and were told that this was the new border between Poland and Germany. Jan pointed to the burning city—famed as the Silesian Rome—and asked if he could help save the historic buildings in Neisse, which would eventually be part of the new Poland. This argument so impressed a Russian major that he not only gave them permission to pass but ordered a private and a lieutenant to escort them. As they walked toward the city the private—a heavy-set, pasty-faced young man—said, "I used to be an officer but I shot another officer who was raping a Polish girl." Jan thought he was an NKVD man putting on an act, since the officer treated him so respectfully.

In town the little party tried to round up soldiers to put out fires, but they were busy looting. They reeled drunkenly around the streets, shooting at their own images in plate-glass windows.

"We Communists shouldn't act like beasts!" the pasty-faced private shouted. "You're a Communist. I'm a Communist. You shouldn't burn a Polish town. We are true brothers!"

With no help the four could only save a few buildings during the hectic night, and by dawn Jan's tuxedo was no longer recognizable. The Russian private found new clothes for the two Poles and gave them red-and-white cockades to wear so they wouldn't be shot by mistake.

In the evening they were brought to an officers' mess for a celebration and introduced as representatives of the "First Polish Administration." Jan sat between two good-looking Red Army women officers who spoke only in broken Polish but were most friendly. While they ate, seven musicians—captured German civilians, each with an armband reading "An Artist"—played Western popular music. After dinner a strange performance began: men dancing alone or with each other, but rarely with women. This merriment went on with unceasing vigor until three in the morning, and by that time the two young Poles were so caught up in their fraud that they almost believed it themselves.

In the light of day, however, they decided to get away while they still had the chance, but before they reached the western edge of town, two black sedans pulled up, followed by a truckload of soldiers waving Polish flags. One of the sedans stopped and the two Red Army female officers stepped out in civilian clothes. To Jan's further consternation, one of them addressed him in perfect Polish. "We're happy you're here," she said. "We've come to install the first group of Communist authorities." She introduced the others in the car as fellow Communists and asked if she could help the two Poles.

Jan's friend did some quick thinking and said, "We're in the cultural department and our job is to safeguard the buildings and museums." This spontaneous ruse must have sounded logical to the Communists, because it was not long before they set up an office for the two young Poles, gave them a truck and permission to travel as far as Czechoslovakia to bring back plundered museum pieces; they even provided them with comfortable quarters aboard a yacht on the river. All they had to do now was relax and wait for victory.

### 3.

The rumor that Jan had heard about a German counteroffensive near Czechoslovakia was close to the truth. Hitler was indeed planning a surprise offensive farther south—in Hungary, where the Russians themselves were preparing an attack on Vienna. Hitler was hoping to thwart this by striking first. He ordered the First and Sixth Panzer armies to launch an attack from Lake Balaton to a point on the Danube River south of Budapest, and thus split Marshal Tolbukhin's Third Ukrainian Front in two. The Germans were then to turn north and crush Marshal Malinovsky's Second Ukrainian Front. The task of the Sixth Panzer Army, commanded by the colorful SS General Sepp Dietrich, was simple, if preposterous. In a recent futile attempt to save besieged Budapest, his army had lost at least 30 percent of its tanks and infantry; now he was supposed to drive beyond the Danube.

On March 3 one of the men who would lead the attack, SS-Obersturmbannführer (Lieutenant Colonel) Fritz Hagen,* reconnoitered the jumping-off position of his battle group. It was pouring, and young Hagen, winner of a dozen medals and one of the most aggressive tank commanders in the Waffen-SS, told his driver to stop the jeep. He pointed dramatically to the vast morass of mud stretching to the east, and said, "Gentlemen, we are now at the jumping-off point!" At first they laughed at this but then they swore.

---

* Not his real name.

As soon as Hagen had slogged his way back to Veszprém, north of the lake, he phoned Corps headquarters and said, 'I have tanks, not submarines. You can kiss my ass but I won't do it."

"Keep calm," he was told. "We're doing something about it."

They had already brought up the unfavorable weather conditions to Army Group South's commander, General Otto Wöhler, who promised to talk to Hitler about delaying the attack. Hagen was ordered to move his people to the jumping-off point and wait for the Führer's decision. However, the weather was not Hagen's only problem. On his left two Soviet officers had just surrendered to Leutnant Erich Kernmayr. One, a Ukrainian, was fed up with the Bolsheviks; the other, an Uzbek, was an ardent Communist who believed Stalin had betrayed Marx and Lenin by turning imperialist. They revealed that about 3000 Red Army armored vehicles were massed for attack. If the Sixth Panzer Army drive was not called off, the Germans would be smashed through that rare possibility dreaded by every military man: a meeting engagement in which two great assaulting forces collide with devastating impact.

Kernmayr personally escorted the two Russians back to Army Group South headquarters, but Wöhler's intelligence officer, Oberstleutnant (Lieutenant Colonel) Graf von Rittberg, didn't share his alarm. Rittberg said it was "most interesting" and he would "tell the general over lunch." Hours passed as Kernmayr waited—while Rittberg rode, played chess and attended a birthday celebration. It was almost dusk when he finally reappeared. "The general was most interested in that story of yours," he said cheerfully. "Really most interested. Give my regards to General Gille." When he saw Kernmayr's look of consternation, he said, "Was there anything else?"

"But what's going to be done about it? What am I to report? After all, this is an extremely dangerous threat to our flank."

"Oh, my dear fellow," said the count, "don't worry! You've got the 25th Hungarian Hussars . . ."

Kernmayr reminded him that the Hungarians had only two machine guns to a company.

"Everything's under control, my dear fellow. Army Group will do all that's necessary."

But apparently nothing was done, and on March 4 Hitler radioed Wöhler to begin the offensive as planned. The next day the three tank divisions which would spearhead Dietrich's attack moved forward to their positions, followed by the sixteen divisions that would exploit the breakthrough. A new slogan spread from unit to unit: "Present the Rumanian oil fields to the Führer for his birthday!"

By midnight Battle Group Hagen neared its point of departure. Its tanks, water up to the bellies, churned slowly ahead as the supporting infantry marched silently single file, hand in hand, through the pitch dark. Gray dawn dimly revealed plains covered by water. Suddenly German shells flew over their heads in a heavy barrage. The tankers looked at one another proudly—just as salvos from Russian guns and rocket launchers blanketed the area in a barrage that made their own seem puny. It was spectacular and terrifying. The infantrymen were trapped, unable to dig foxholes in the foot-deep water, and most of them were killed or wounded.

Hagen phoned his commanders that they must not wait and attack at 8 A.M. as scheduled, but would have to move out as soon as possible. He had no idea what lay ahead. Hungarian outposts sitting atop crude wooden towers reported that they could see nothing. Even so, Hagen gave the order to crank up. But none of the engines would start—the gas had become diluted with water. Volunteers crawled under the tanks, holding their breath when the chilly water submerged their heads, and drained the contaminated gas from the belly containers while other volunteers in scout cars scoured the area for more fuel. At noon Battle Group Hagen, powered by gas commandeered at pistol point from another unit, finally roared into the attack.

### 4.

At 9 P.M. on March 4 an American was given the first direct order to storm the Rhine if possible. Colonel Edward Kimball of Combat Command B, 8th Armored Division, was told to take Rheinberg, a small town only two miles from the river, at the extreme north of Simpson's line. "Keep rolling, and if things aren't too tough at Rheinberg, push on, cross the Rhine and establish a bridgehead on the other side." Kimball had to take Rheinberg by dark of the next day, before the Germans dug in. He was eager to attack; CCB had done well lately, but this was the first time he was on his own with priority on all roads.

In the gray morning light the first elements passed through the line held by the 35th Infantry Division en route to Kamp-Lintfort, eight miles northwest. Another five miles beyond it lay Rheinberg. Task Force Roseborough, which was predominantly an infantry unit, was leading, and it was to clear Kamp-Lintfort and push on to Rheinberg. Task Force Van Houten, a tank unit, would follow and lead the main attack on Rheinberg. Spirits were high as word went around that according to G-2, only 3 self-propelled guns and 300 demoralized Germans stood between them and the Rhine. By night they could make history.

Task Force Roseborough met little resistance at Kamp-Lintfort, but at three o'clock Kimball got disquieting news from out front: Captain Kimball Tucker, commander of the reconnaissance troops, reported that "all hell has broken loose" as his men approached Rheinberg. Obviously a lot more than 300 Germans and 3 guns were defending the little town.

Kimball decided that it was too late in the day to call for an air strike. The only solution was a quick, smashing drive with tanks and armored infantry. Artillery support was hopeless, since all forward observers were pinned down with the recon troops. He told Lieutenant Colonel John Van Houten about the unexpected resistance at Rheinberg, and ordered him to pass his main force through the pinned-down recon units, then attack and secure the town. Van Houten was soon charging down the road over the flat country in his tank. It was bad terrain for armor, with many canals winding through barren fields and only small patches of bare trees to conceal any maneuvering.

A few minutes later Van Houten ran into the man who had reported the trouble at Rheinberg—Captain Tucker. "Double the reconnaissance and continue striking on," Van Houten ordered.

Tucker started east and almost immediately drew fire. But he returned it and continued. Van Houten saw him wheel north, and radioed, "Get over to the right!"

"I'm killing Germans left and right!" was Tucker's cheerful answer. "Just got a Mark IV tank and am having a hell of a good time." But the infantrymen with him were not, and within half an hour they were pinned down. When Van Houten learned this he ordered Tucker to get in front of the infantry with his tanks. "Move on to Rheinberg and attack it from the southwest." Tucker did as he was told, moving toward town parallel to a canal, with infantry perched on the tanks until chased off by intense antitank, mortar and artillery fire.

On his right another unit, Company B, was also attacking Rheinberg. Captain David Kelley led his column in a quick rush into the southern outskirts of town. It was a narrow section with winding streets and old houses surrounded by the remnants of an ancient wall. As soon as anti-tank fire began to explode on all sides, Kelley pulled back to rally his somewhat confused company, which was strung out along the road.

"May I hold my position here?" he radioed Kimball, and said he needed infantry assistance before trying to assault the town again; he had only seven tanks left. Kimball okayed the request. A moment later Van Houten called Kimball to say that he didn't want any more tanks inside Rheinberg itself; two had already been hit and were blocking the road, and he was sending his exec, Major Edward Gurney, with the light tanks of another company to assault the town from the west.

Less than fifteen minutes later Kimball got a desperate call from Gurney himself: he had already lost nine tanks and would soon be overwhelmed unless he got help. Kimball quickly collected as many infantrymen as he could find and put them in half-tracks. "For God's sake, get some help up here!" he phoned his own executive officer and jumped into the first vehicle. He came to a blown-out bridge and signaled the men to follow as he started forward on foot through heavy mortar, bazooka, machine-gun and rifle fire. Ahead lay a grim sight: Gurney's nine burning tanks with bodies hanging out of the hatches as if still trying to escape.

Kimball kept walking until he came upon Gurney, who was preparing another assault on Rheinberg with his remaining eighteen tanks and three half-tracks. Kimball waved his own men on and jumped into one of Gurney's half-tracks. The whole group headed toward Rheinberg. Suddenly Germans in camouflaged pillboxes on both sides of the highway opened up with bazookas and machine guns in a withering cross fire. Kimball vaulted out of the half-track and crawled into a light tank. "Step on it," he told the driver. "Catch up to those other tanks." Three light tanks bound for Rheinberg were the only vehicles still moving ahead, but after only 500 yards an 88-mm. shell put Kimball's vehicle out of commission. He and the driver scrambled out of the smoldering tank, and as machine-gun bullets spattered the road, dived into a ditch.

The survivors of Gurney's forces were also in the ditch, with the commander himself stretched out, wounded in the stomach. It was 4:30 P.M.

"If you want to live, get the hell out of here!" someone shouted.

Kimball saw a farmhouse fifty yards away. He ran toward it, followed by an enlisted man. An 88-mm. shell smashed into the wall only four feet over Kimball's head and he dropped to the ground; so did the soldier. Then bullets started digging up the dirt, and they both scrambled through a cellar window.

The soldier lit a cigarette and handed it to Kimball as the two caught their breath. "Colonel," he said, "thank God we made it."

Kimball shook his hand. "You betcha."

Less than thirty miles to the south, Hodges was also approaching the Rhine—and Germany's fourth largest city, Cologne. In two weeks Lieutenant General J. Lawton "Lightning Joe" Collins' VII Corps had not only provided steady protection for Simpson's right flank, but had spearheaded a First Army drive all the way to the Rhine. The operation, started with modest aims, had developed so unexpectedly that Hodges wisely gave the aggressive Collins free rein.

Two of Collins' divisions—the 104th Infantry and the 3rd Armored—were converging on Cologne with such relentless efficiency that the German LXXI Corps defending this area was falling back in confusion. Its commander, General Friedrich Köchling, now had at his disposal only two worn-out divisions—the 9th Panzer and the 363rd Infantry.

Spearheads of the 3rd Armored Division began to attack Köchling's advance command post, about eight miles north of Cologne. The general watched remnants of the 9th Panzer overrun by the oncoming American tanks and he was forced to evacuate his own command post. Under fire, Köchling drove several miles to Merkenich. In the cellar of a brewery he found the commander of the 9th Panzer, who said his division was falling back in some order. But there was no news of the 363rd.

By early afternoon Köchling had retreated all the way to Cologne, to a bunker one kilometer north of the Hohenzollern Bridge, and took over command of the city itself. In the center of Cologne almost every building was gutted, but miraculously the twin towers of the famed dome were still standing. The cathedral had been saved by an enemy—General Collins had forbidden its towers to be used for registration fire.

The former commander of the city told Köchling that the local situation was desperate: there were no forces or equipment to defend Cologne except a few Volkssturm troops. While they were talking the local Gauleiter burst in and shouted, "Cologne must be defended to the end! The Volkssturm can stop the American tanks with bazookas." The military men watched in amazement as the civilian official went from one officer to another, pleading, demanding and finally threatening. After this strange performance he urged Köchling to move to his own command post, but Köchling refused. Of the Gauleiter's promised 1200 Volkssturm "elite" troops, only sixty reported for duty.

The next morning, as units of the U. S. 104th Division were closing in on the center of the city, Köchling was relieved of his command and arrested, probably at the instigation of the Gauleiter. But before leaving the besieged command post, he wrote a bitter report predicting that it would be "only a question of hours" before the city and the great Hohenzollern Bridge across the Rhine were captured. Because of the hopeless situation west of the Rhine, "the willingness to fight has given way to resignation and apathy on the part of the command as well as the completely worn-out troops . . ." He signed the report and placed himself in the custody of his chief of staff; the two went back across the Rhine, where Köchling was scheduled to stand trial for dereliction of duty and possibly treason.

It was hardly a surprise when the Hohenzollern Bridge blew up in the face of American troops, but the behavior of the townspeople was totally unexpected. Braving sniper fire, thousands of drably dressed civilians emerged from their cellars to greet the Americans, not as conquerors but almost as if they were liberators.

Some were extremely outspoken in their denouncement of Hitler, and one man wearing baggy trousers and a dirty celluloid collar called out to war correspondent Iris Carpenter, "We've been waiting for you to come for a long time!" In the wrecked square in front of the opera house, citizens pointed derisively at a sign in both German and English:

GIVE ME FIVE YEARS AND YOU WILL
NOT RECOGNIZE GERMANY AGAIN.

—ADOLF HITLER

# 11

## "What If It Blows Up in My Face?"

**1.**

The Rhine, not crossed by an invader since Napoleon, had long been considered by the Allies as the last great barrier to the heart of Germany. In the months of planning, no one seriously counted on the possibility of seizing a bridge intact. That would be too fantastic.

It still seemed fantastic—until March 2, when Simpson's Ninth Army closed up to the river and his 83rd Division learned that fifteen miles ahead there was an intact bridge leading into Düsseldorf. A task force was hastily organized, its tanks disguised to look like German panzers, and just after dark the column set out with German-speaking GIs mounted on the fronts of the vehicles while infantry walked inconspicuously behind. The Americans boldly passed through enemy lines without being challenged and continued for ten miles, once even crossing paths with a German infantry column going the other way.

By dawn the task force could see the bridge, but then a German soldier on a bicycle in a passing column recognized American uniforms and refused to stop when challenged. The Americans quickly wiped out the German column, but by then a siren was shrieking a warning. As the first U. S. tank lumbered onto the bridge there was a great explosion, and four tremendous water spouts rose from the Rhine. When the water and debris finally settled, most of the bridge had disappeared.

Also on March 3, Simpson's 2nd Armored Division came even closer to seizing a Rhine bridge fifteen miles north of Düsseldorf. Besides speed-ing up Montgomery's drive toward Berlin by several weeks, its capture would have caused the Führer intense personal embarrassment—it was named after him. Colonel Sidney Hinds of Combat Command B, 2nd Armored Division, outlined the plan to Captain George Youngblood of the 17th Armored Engineer Battalion: A company of infantry from Task Force Hawkins would dash across the Adolf Hitler Bridge at Ürdingen and overwhelm the guards on the other side while Youngblood's engineers were disarming demolition charges on the bridge itself. It was a gamble with small chance of success, but Hinds felt that it had to be taken.

The first unit of Task Force Hawkins—Lieutenant Peter Kostow and his tank section—reached the Rhine around noon. Stretching before Kostow was the huge three-span Adolf Hitler Bridge, 1640 feet long. Shells were bursting rhythmically at both approaches: for fifteen and a half hours the U. S. 92nd Armored Field Artillery Battalion had success-fully prevented the Germans from blowing it up. Kostow dismounted, and before Germans who were dug in on the west shore could fire, ran up to the bridge and started across, his excitement mounting with each step. Kostow was the first invader over the Rhine. It was a historic moment, but he was only interested in returning to the west bank and getting word back to Hawkins that the bridge was still intact.

True, the bridge was standing, but the Germans were nevertheless determined to fight off the Americans until it could be blown up. Hawkins' first four tanks were knocked out before they even reached the bridge. Momentarily stalled, he sent two battalions of infantry forward. They reached the bridge, only to be pinned down by concentrated fire. More tanks were moved up but were stopped by something else: in the middle of the road leading onto the bridge was a gaping thirteen-foot crater.

As soon as it was dark Lieutenant Miller of the 41st Infantry Regi-ment crept forward to scout the bridge. It was a moonless, cloudy night. He circled the hole in the road and headed across the bridge. Like Kostow, he went all the way to the east shore, where the bridge's tar approach road was burning. Small-arms fire suddenly came from a nearby house and he scrambled back to the west shore. He was in the midst of telling Hawkins that only infantry could get across the bridge until the crater was fixed, when there was a sudden explosion. Two minutes later the sky behind the bridge blazed from a second explosion, the loudest Hawkins had ever heard. He guessed the Germans had destroyed the bridge but it was too dark to see what had happened, so he ordered three enlisted men to scout the structure and find out if it could be negotiated.

Captain Youngblood decided that he could wait no longer for infantry cover and headed for the bridge with his engineers. He dropped off three men as a rear guard and led the others into a darkness relieved only by bursting American and German shells. Several rounds hit the bridge but the engineers crept forward, methodically cutting every wire and inspecting critical columns, joints and suspension members. At the east shore they too saw the bridge's tar roadway burning and, like Kostow, turned back. The bridge was intact—there was still a chance to make the incredible come true.

While Hawkins reorganized his men for a dawn attack, the Germans crept back onto the bridge, working feverishly to replace severed demolition wires. Just after daylight there was a tremendous explosion—then another and another. The Americans who were about to launch their assault stood in awe as the eastern half of the great bridge swayed, then thundered into the river.

Of all the Rhine bridges still standing, the one least considered for capture was, of course, the least desirable. In the lengthy planning of the storming of the Rhine, the Ludendorff railroad bridge at Remagen, fifty-five miles south of Düsseldorf, had never been mentioned as a possible crossing point. The roads leading into Remagen from the west were poor, and once across the river the invaders would immediately be faced with a 600-foot basalt cliff. Beyond this, for about twelve miles, were heavily forested mountains, traversed only by inadequate roads, making armored advance against any kind of determined defense almost impossible. But to seize any bridge across the Rhine would be one of the great military feats of the war, so on March 4 General Hodges discussed this possibility with Major General John Millikin, III Corps commander. It was only a remote possibility, however. After the Germans' narrow escape at Ürdingen, they would be more alert than ever.

Hodges' opposite number, General Gustav von Zangen, was more than concerned about this threat. He had a premonition. His Fifteenth Army was successfully holding a long section of the West Wall some twenty-five miles west of Remagen. But his neighbor on the north, the Fifth Panzer Army, had been driven back to the Rhine, leaving a sixty-mile gap between them, and Zangen had had recurrent nightmares of Hodges bursting through to seize the Ludendorff Bridge from the rear. He told his army group commander, Feldmarschall Walther Model, about this potential danger and asked permission to withdraw three of his divisions from the West Wall and plug up the breach. Fiery and brilliant, Model was a zealous disciple of Hitler, resolved to carry out his order to hold every foot of ground until the last moment.

"How can you justify such a drastic relocation of forces?" he asked sarcastically.

"The Americans would have to be stupid not to take advantage of this hole and push tanks toward the Rhine. I think they will use this valley like water flowing downhill."

"That's nonsense," Model snapped. Hodges would attack north of

Remagen, since only a fool would try to cross the Rhine at a point where steep bluffs rose like a wall on the east bank. "None of your troops will be withdrawn from the West Wall," he continued, but he must have seen some merit in Zangen's argument because a moment later he said, "Of course, I would not object to a slight weakening of the West Wall."

Encouraged, Zangen suggested that they also send some troops back to the Ludendorff Bridge to strengthen its notoriously weak defenses.

"You should not look back so much," Model replied curtly, and forbade him to send a single man back to Remagen.

Zangen resignedly returned to his command post, where he learned that one of Hodges' spearheads had taken Cologne while another was racing toward the sixty-mile gap on his right. He decided to risk his career and perhaps his life by disobeying orders. He ordered his right flank, the LXVII Corps of General Otto Hitzfeld, to swing back northeast and make a fighting retreat to Bonn, fifteen miles north of Remagen, where it would link up with the Fifth Panzer Army. This would slam the door to Remagen.

Surprisingly, Model was not angry at Zangen and even promised to launch a drive from Bonn with a battle group of the Fifth Panzer Army, to meet Hitzfeld. For the first time in a week Zangen felt relieved. If the Hitzfeld maneuver didn't stop Hodges, it would at least delay him for a few days and give the commander of the second line of defense, General-leutnant (Major General) Walther Botsch, a chance to strengthen the weak forces at Remagen.

Botsch was just as distressed about the Ludendorff Bridge as Zangen, and had even wrung a promise from Model to send reinforcements to shore up Remagen's defenses. But before these reinforcements arrived, Botsch was summarily transferred by Model. Direct command of the Ludendorff Bridge was now in the hands of General von Bothmer, to whom Bonn, the birthplace of Beethoven, was the place to be defended and Remagen not even important enough to warrant a visit by him. In his stead Bothmer sent a liaison officer who was a stranger to the area, and he unsuspectingly headed directly for the American unit closest to Remagen.

This was the 9th Armored Division, commanded by Major General John Leonard. Model mistakenly thought he had destroyed it in the Battle of the Bulge; now it was the spearhead of a drive Hodges had launched to meet a Patton column from the south, in a great pincers movement designed to entrap some 250,000 Germans—including all of Zangen's Fifteenth Army. Leonard would sweep through Remagen and then turn south along the west bank of the Rhine for about thirty miles, until he met Patton's spearhead near Koblenz.

By noon of March 6 Leonard's division had already penetrated the sixty-mile gap between the two German armies, just as Zangen had feared. On the right was Combat Command A, and on the left, the north, Combat Command B, led by Brigadier General William Hoge. At four o'clock Hoge's unit rolled into the town of Meckenheim, twelve miles from Remagen and its important railroad bridge, after a lightning ten-mile thrust. Usually a laconic and calm man, Hoge had been driving his men relentlessly the previous week, taking advantage of the crumbling enemy resistance. "If something in the other man's zone is in your way, you have to get it out," he told his unit commanders. "Infantry battalions will leapfrog. By-pass towns if possible . . . Get help from tanks as you can. If there are no antitank guns, shove tanks out front. I will give you additional objectives as the thing develops." These were the days, he felt, to take advantage of every break.

Hoge never tried to be popular with his men but was liked and respected. A graduate of West Point—as were two brothers and two sons—he, Leonard and Hodges had served in the same division in World War I. His achievements since then had been outstanding: he was in charge of the pioneer stage of the Alcan Highway, commanded the unloading of supplies at Omaha Beach and fought his combat command with distinction at St. Vith, in the Battle of the Bulge. Others of far less ability—and less frankness—had long since outranked him.

Hoge sent for his operations officer, Major Ben Cothran, and told him to pick a good route toward Bonn, fifteen miles north of Remagen; Combat Command A, on the right, was scheduled to take Remagen and then swing on south. But at six o'clock Hoge told Cothran that plans had been changed, and to stand by for new orders. Almost sleepless the past week, the exhausted Cothran—formerly city editor of the Knoxville *Journal* and a public relations executive—stumbled into bed.

A few hours later Leonard received a phone call from his immediate superior, Millikin of III Corps. They discussed Leonard's mission for the next day, and at one point Millikin remarked almost casually, "Do you see that little black strip of bridge at Remagen? If you happen to get that, your name will go down in glory." Millikin hung up and promptly forgot what he had said; attempting to seize every bridge was routine military procedure but he didn't seriously think the opportunity would arise.

**2.**

The commander of the bridge's security company, Hauptmann (Captain) Willi Bratge, was also on the phone, trying to strengthen its feeble defenses. On paper he had over 1000 men: 500 Volkssturm troops; 180 Hitler Jugend; 120 Russian volunteers; about 220 anti-aircraft and rocket men, and his own company of 36 men.

Bratge was a prim, meticulous man, originally a teacher who in 1924 had been forced into the Army by unemployment. He knew that in an emergency he could depend only on his own thirty-six men, and these were all convalescents from the front. Of the Volkssturm only six had not fled and many of the flak people—those who manned guns on the Erpeler Ley, the cliff rising with startling abruptness some 100 yards beyond the eastern end of the bridge—had already mysteriously disappeared. He had tried to erect simple wooden barricades at the highway entrances to the bridge on the Remagen side, but the irate townspeople invoked an old edict forbidding the destruction of a single precious German tree. Incredibly, Bratge's superiors refused to interfere.

Now Bratge was on the phone telling an ordnance lieutenant named May in Model's headquarters that the four-day job of laying planks across one of the two railroad tracks had just been completed and that the Ludendorff Bridge was finally ready to carry eastbound vehicular traffic. Bratge then urgently requested reinforcements, since the Americans were so close that he could actually hear tank fire.

"The Americans aren't coming to Remagen," Leutnant May said, echoing Model. They were bound for Bonn. He belittled the tank fire Bratge had heard: it must have come from a small American force protecting the main body's flank.

"I've been a soldier for a long time," Bratge replied; he had fought in Poland, France, Russia and Rumania. "Those aren't small forces; they're strong."

He hung up in frustration and went outside, groping through the dense fog to the western end of the bridge, where he met Hauptmann (Captain) Karl Friesenhahn, a slight, gray-haired middle-aged man who commanded the 120 engineers detailed to destroy the bridge at the very last moment. He was looking south toward his home town of Koblenz where the sky was dull red from fires. Obviously worried about his family and in a bad mood, Friesenhahn criticized Bratge for sending almost his entire security company of thirty-six men to Viktoriaberg, the hill just west of Remagen. Why weren't they down here protecting the bridge? Bratge bristled—his men were posted on the hill to warn of approaching Americans so that Friesenhahn and his engineers would have plenty of time to blow up the bridge. Both captains were small men, about five foot five, and they glared at each other like bantam roosters. Friesenhahn was not satisfied, but all he could do was shrug his shoulders and walk away.

Hitzfeld, who had failed to close the sixty-mile gap through which Leonard's division was pouring, had just been given an additional task: the defense of the Ludendorff Bridge. Like Zangen, he realized its importance; he summoned his adjutant, Major Hans Scheller, whom he regarded as a competent and prudent man. Of all those available he was best qualified to cope with such a critical situation. He told Scheller to assume command of all forces at the bridge and take care of the final preparations for its destruction. "If necessary," he added, "depending on the situation, you will give the order for demolition yourself."

Scheller was elated. "Get the car ready," he called to his orderly. "This will be worth at least a Knight's Cross!"

### 3.

At Hoge's command post, Colonel John "Pinky" Growdon, Leonard's operations officer, arrived at 2:30 A.M. with new orders for CCB: at 7:00 A.M. it was to move in two columns on Remagen and Sinzig, a town three miles south of it. Growdon also said that there were no definite directives regarding the Ludendorff Bridge except that it should be fired on only with time (posit) fuzes. Such shells would explode before hitting the bridge and prevent German traffic from crossing, without seriously damaging the structure itself.

By dawn on March 7, light rain was falling as cleanup crews hurriedly removed debris from the streets of Meckenheim so that Hoge's armor could move out of town. The general had gathered his commanders for a briefing: CCB would be split up into two task forces. Lieutenant Colonel Leonard Engeman would take his 14th Tank Battalion and the 27th Armored Infantry Battalion directly east to Remagen and secure the town. The other task force, Lieutenant Colonel William R. Prince's 52nd Armored Infantry Battalion, would supposedly have a much more difficult mission. Prince was to drive below Remagen and establish a bridgehead over the Ahr River, a tributary to the Rhine, by taking the town of Sinzig.

Task Force Prince got off on schedule, but rubble at the eastern edge of town held up Task Force Engeman and it didn't leave until 8:20 A.M. Leading was a platoon of Company A, 27th Armored Infantry Battalion, and right behind was a platoon of big M-26s, the new Pershing tanks with 90-mm. guns.

Back at Meckenheim, Hoge was studying a map with a lighted magnifier when General Leonard walked in and said, "Bill, how's it going?"

Hoge looked up, his blue eyes characteristically half closed. "John, how about this bridge across the river?" He drew a circle around the Ludendorff Bridge.

"What about it?"

"Your Intelligence can't tell me if it's still standing. Suppose I find that the bridge hasn't been blown here, should I take it?"

"Hell, yes," Leonard said without hesitation. "Go across it." Seeing Cothran buckle on his pistol and start for the door, he said, "Where the hell are you going?"

"If Engeman is supposed to cross that bridge, somebody better tell him," Cothran replied in his Southern accent. "I don't think we ought to put it on the horn. It's too close to the Krauts."

Leonard grinned. Like everyone else, he felt there was little likelihood of grabbing the bridge. "Yeah, go up there and maybe you'll get your name in the papers."

"General, I don't want my name in the papers," said Cothran. "I just want to finish the damn war and go home."

At 10:30 A.M. Lieutenant Harold Larsen, an artillery liaison pilot, was flying in a light plane through clouds and mist toward the Rhine. His mission was to find passable roads and bridges for Hoge's two task forces and to locate artillery targets. With dramatic suddenness the river appeared and a bridge loomed out of the haze. Disregarding possible flak, he continued toward a town for a closer look. It was Remagen. Larsen dipped lower to find out if the bridge was still carrying traffic. The bridge was intact! He banked away and headed back to report.

## 4.

German vehicles had been crossing the bridge since daylight, each one checked by Bratge. Already exhausted and in a bad mood, he fumed when he saw gangs of men slowly dragging anti-aircraft guns up to the bridge approach late that morning. They were to replace guns on the Erpeler Ley that had been sent down to Koblenz to stop Patton. For the first time Bratge realized that there were almost no flak guns on the strategic cliff. He looked up at the steep hill across the river. "On the double," he shouted at the sweating crews. "The Americans are coming!" Then he returned to his command post, a cloister several hundred yards from the western end of the bridge. It was a gloomy day and he felt a strange sense of depression.

Then a tall, tired-looking officer walked in and announced that he was Major Scheller, the new combat commander of Remagen. Bratge assumed that he had brought the promised reinforcements and asked where they were. Scheller said he had no idea what the captain was talking about, and Bratge suspected he was a spy until he checked his identification. Scheller's immediate concern was the final preparation for demolition. About sixty separate explosive charges had been placed at key points in the bridge, and just before noon the two men began to connect the charges to a main cable that led to a detonating device located in the tunnel across the river.

Simultaneously, Task Force Engeman passed through Bierresdorf, a tiny village three miles from Remagen. The column then turned almost directly east and entered the woods on the plateau overlooking the Rhine. Near the head of the column the acting sergeant of Company A's 1st Platoon became suspicious of the deadly quiet in the woods and fired several machine-gun bursts into the trees, just to make sure. He was Carmine Sabia, a short, stocky, mustached twenty-five-year-old from Brooklyn. The column stopped and Sabia, with nine other men from Company A, piled out of their half-tracks and moved ahead cautiously. Sabia went up the road. Around 1:00 P.M. he reached a sharp bend to the right, and suddenly, spreading out far below him, was the magnificent view of the winding Rhine and the town of Remagen. He shouted, "Jesus, look at that!" and then just stood there, speechless. Finally he asked the man nearest him, "Do you know what the hell river that is?"

Staff Sergeant Joseph De Lisio hustled forward to find out what was holding things up. Like Sabia, he was short, chunky, mustached and twenty-five years old, but he came from the Bronx. When he saw the Rhine he couldn't say a word; he too was struck by the beauty of the sight. The war momentarily ceased, but then, through the haze to his right, he saw an unbelievable sight: a bridge with traffic moving across it. Instinctively De Lisio felt it was a trap. Usually nothing bothered him and he fought as if the Germans couldn't possibly kill him. For example, his favorite trick to flush out a sniper was to stride into the open with a brilliant yellow scarf around his neck. But he wanted none of that bridge. Once they were on it he knew the damn thing would be blown sky-high.

The discovery brought their company commander, Second Lieutenant Karl Timmermann, and platoon leader, Emmet Burrows, hurrying up to the bend in the road. Like the others, they were stunned by the panorama stretching before them. Surveying the bridge with field glasses, they could see cows, horses, soldiers, vehicles moving across.

Burrows called to his mortar squad, "Set up and blast the retreating line." But Timmermann decided it was a job for tanks and artillery. This was no time for a mistake in judgment—it was his first day in command. He was tall, blond, serious. Most of his men liked him but some of them thought he was too exacting, and at battalion meetings he had already antagonized several of his superiors with outspoken comments.

The task force commander, Colonel Engeman, was speeding toward the head of the column in his jeep and in a minute he too stood surveying the scene. He was short, stocky and quick-moving. This was luck, incredible luck, but he had always been lucky—at the University of Minnesota he had won a Pierce-Arrow on a fifty-cent chance. He watched the traffic creeping across the bridge and told his artillery forward observer to ask the supporting artillery for posit fire.

Meanwhile Task Force Prince had been speeding southeast virtually unopposed, greeted in each village by German civilians waving white flags. Several miles west of the Rhine they turned abruptly south and stormed across the Ahr River into Sinzig so unexpectedly that defenders in concrete emplacements were taken completely by surprise. Three hundred soldiers were taken prisoner. Lieutenant Fred De Rango began interrogating local citizens, and one of them informed him that the Ludendorff Bridge was going to be blown up at 4:00 P.M. De Rango sent a messenger back to Hoge's new headquarters at Bierresdorf and also tried to reach Task Force Engeman directly by radio. When this failed, De Rango started toward the bridge with his platoon and hoped he could disarm the dynamite charges in time.

## 5.

Engeman ordered Company A to go into Remagen on foot, with Company C following a few minutes later in half-tracks. He then told Lieutenant John Grimball of the 14th Tank Battalion, a lanky lawyer from South Carolina, "I want you to barrel down through Remagen, John. Cover the bridge with tank fire. Get rid of anyone who tries to blast it."

At 1:50 P.M. Timmermann sent all but a platoon of Company A down the winding road to Remagen, with Lieutenant Burrows' platoon in the lead. The remaining platoon, led by the aggressive Sergeant De Lisio, took a short cut straight down the hill, along a steep footpath, past vineyards. They passed behind the famous four-towered St. Apollinaris Church, rebuilt in the thirteenth, seventeenth and nineteenth centuries from a chapel going back to Roman days, and came to the paved Bonn–Remagen highway which skirted the west bank of the Rhine. Here De Lisio found an abandoned German roadblock. Leaving one machine-gun section to man the position, he pushed on boldly to the edge of the river. Here he turned right, heading for the town—and the bridge which was just beyond it. A few rounds of small-arms fire from the outlying dwellings made them quicken their pace, but by the time the platoon reached the houses they were empty.

A private ran toward De Lisio. "Sergeant Foster just caught a German general!" he shouted excitedly. De Lisio followed the private to a house where Foster and his whole squad were surrounding a uniformed German and two women.

"Whaddya think of this, Joe?" Foster asked.

De Lisio began to laugh. "Let the man go," he said. "That's a railroad conductor you've got."

De Lisio pushed along the river bank through Remagen. Half a mile farther on he saw what looked like two castle towers—the western terminus of the Ludendorff Bridge.

Hidden from De Lisio's view behind the Becher furniture factory, Captain Friesenhahn and four volunteer engineers were on the western approach to the bridge, squatting around a demolition charge. This was designed to blast a hole big enough in the road to stop any American vehicle. A retreating artillery unit was scheduled to arrive at any moment and Friesenhahn was waiting until the very last moment before setting off the charge.

There was the crackle of small-arms fire as the main body of Company A neared the bridge, and rounds from Grimball's tanks began to fall near the German engineers. Still Friesenhahn hesitated, but when he heard a whistle blow and saw the glint of American helmets in the furniture factory, he cried, "Fire the charge!" An engineer yanked the cord and everyone took cover. Six seconds later, at 2:35 P.M., there was an explosion. When the smoke cleared Friesenhahn saw, with satisfaction, a thirty-foot hole in the approach road. He signaled his men and started running back across the bridge. A shell from a Pershing burst a few yards away and the concussion knocked him unconscious. Fifteen minutes later he came to and staggered toward the east shore.

Behind him two other figures scrambled onto the bridge. They were Sergeant Gerhard Rothe, in charge of the lookouts on Viktoriaberg, and a noncom. Only they had been able to break through. They circled the thirty-foot crater in the approach road. Already wounded three times in the leg, Rothe fell just as he reached the bridge. Bullets spattered on the bridge framework around him as he crawled toward the other shore. It was only 1069 feet away but it seemed endless.

General Hoge had been told about the bridge by Cothran and was driving up to the bend overlooking the Rhine. When he saw the bridge still standing he could hardly believe his eyes, and he suddenly recalled what Leonard had told him earlier that morning about taking it intact. Neither of them had really believed it could be done. Perhaps it couldn't. The Germans might just be waiting until all of Engeman's men crossed before blowing it.

"Grab that bridge," he shouted to Engeman. Suddenly everything seemed to be working too slowly. "Take some tanks and put them on each side of it and fire across the river. Send your infantry across when you establish fire superiority." Those on top of the hill had never before seen Hoge so agitated. Ordinarily quiet, he was storming at what he felt was unpardonable delay. He impatiently asked Engeman why he hadn't already taken Remagen. Engeman explained that two infantry companies followed by Lieutenant Grimball's tanks had been sent down the hill some time before. Hoge didn't want explanations; he wanted Remagen, and without delay. Suddenly his face became thoughtful. "Be nice to have a bridge," he muttered.

"Yes, sir!" said Engeman, and immediately radioed his men to move faster.

At 3:15 P.M. Hoge's radio man handed him a message. It was De Rango's warning that the bridge would probably be blown up in forty-five minutes.

"You've got to hurry," the general shouted to Engeman. "They're blowing the bridge at 1600. Put some phosphorus and smoke around that bridge but don't hit it. I don't want the Krauts to see what we're doing. Cover your advance with tanks and machine guns and bring up your engineers to pull out those wires on the bridge!"

Engeman replied that he had already called for smoke. His words were punctuated by blooms of white phosphorus exploding across the river. But they were landing in Erpel, the town half a mile north of the eastern terminus of the bridge, and even on top of Erpeler Ley. There was smoke everywhere, it seemed, except on the bridge. Hoge scanned the bridge with his glasses. No activity. What was holding up the attack? He told Major Murray Deevers, the happy-go-lucky armored-infantry-battalion commander, to get down the hill and move his men across, then swung back to Engeman. "I want you to get to that bridge as soon as possible."

"I'm doing every damn thing possible to get to the bridge!" Engeman answered and jumped into his jeep. As he entered the outskirts of Remagen he radioed Grimball, "Get to the bridge."

"Suh, I'm already there."

"All right, cover the bridge with fire and don't let the Krauts do any more work on it," Engeman ordered, and sent a messenger for Lieutenant Hugh Mott of the 9th Armored Engineer Battalion. Within minutes the two met behind a hotel near the bridge. "Mott," the colonel said, "get on the bridge and clear it of explosives and cut all wires, and let me know how soon you can repair it so I can get the tanks over." When young Mott saw the thirty-foot crater made by Friesenhahn, he realized that no tanks could cross for several hours. He called two of his sergeants and all three got ready to follow the first infantry assault group onto the bridge.

By now Major Deevers had arrived and was preparing this assault. He found Lieutenant Timmermann near the furniture factory and said, "Do you think you can get your company across that bridge?"

Timmermann glanced up. Rifle and machine-gun fire was coming from the two towers on the other side of the river, but it was a big opportunity. "Well, we can try, sir."

"Go ahead."

Timmermann looked at the bridge again. Shells from flak guns on top of Erpeler Ley were exploding on the superstructure. In the smoke the bridge looked wobbly, ready to collapse. "What if it blows up in my face?" he asked.

Deevers didn't answer. Timmermann slid into a shell crater where his platoon leaders were waiting. "We got orders to go across," he said calmly. "Alpha Company leading. The order of march: 1st Platoon, 3rd Platoon, and 2nd Platoon."

Sabia, who liked the tall lieutenant, said, "It's a trap. Once we get in the middle, they'll blow up the bridge."

De Lisio, who didn't like Timmermann much, didn't like his order much, either, but he didn't say anything.

Timmermann hesitated, then said, "Orders are orders. We're told to go. All right, let's go." He scrambled out of the crater.

On top of the hill, Hoge had just received a message from III Corps. It canceled his present mission. Patton had almost broken through to the Rhine and Hoge was ordered to drive south at once to Koblenz to meet him.

It was a jolt. Before Hoge lay one of the great opportunities of the war, and now he couldn't take it—if he followed orders. He scanned the bridge with his glasses. Deevers' infantry assault hadn't yet started across. It was not too late to stop the entire operation. He hesitated, but only a moment. It was a hard but clear choice for a soldier. If he succeeded, he would be a hero; if he failed, he could very well lose his command and ruin his military career.

He decided to try to take the bridge—and to hell with the consequences.

On the other side of the river Captain Friesenhahn, still dazed, staggered to the railroad tunnel, which started at the base of the cliff. Seeing Bratge at the tunnel entrance, he gasped, "The Amis are at the Becher factory!"

"Blow up the bridge," Bratge urged excitedly.

Friesenhahn hesitated. An hour earlier he had begged Scheller to let him blow up the bridge, only to be forcefully reminded of Hitler's recent order to court-martial any man who blew up a Rhine bridge too soon. "Major Scheller has to give the orders," the bewildered Friesenhahn replied.

Sergeant Rothe too had just crawled off the bridge and was helped inside the tunnel. He confirmed that the Americans were swarming all over the other end of the bridge. Bratge impatiently told Friesenhahn that he was taking matters into his own hands, then started toward Scheller's command post at the other end of the tunnel, a quarter mile away. He groped through the darkness along railroad tracks, his progress slowed by crowds of terrified townspeople. Finally he reached the rear mouth of the tunnel, only a few hundred yards from Erpel. "We've got to blow up the bridge!" he shouted to Scheller and told him the Americans were at the furniture factory.

But Scheller still remembered Hitler's orders and hesitated.

"If you don't give the order," Bratge said impetuously, *"I'll* give it!"

The major sighed and said, "All right, blow up the bridge."

Bratge laboriously made his way back toward the other end of the tunnel. As soon as he could see Friesenhahn he called out, "Blow up the bridge!"

Friesenhahn hesitated, then turned to those near by and told them to drop to the ground and keep their mouths open to protect their eardrums. He then knelt by the detonating device connected to the sixty-odd charges scattered over the bridge, grasped a key—like that of an old-fashioned clock—and gave it a turn. Bratge braced himself for the explosion, but nothing happened. Friesenhahn kept twisting the key frantically. Still nothing happened. He realized that the main circuit had been broken, probably by an American shell. He ordered a special crew out to the bridge, but when the men got to the mouth of the tunnel they were driven back by a fusillade of tank fire. Friesenhahn asked his NCOs for a volunteer to run out and hand-light an emergency charge—300 kilograms of "Donerit"—located just beyond the two towers on the east shore. For a long while the men were silent, then a Sergeant Faust said he would try to do it. At 3:35 P.M. he crept out of the tunnel in face of a deadly flurry of machine-gun bullets and made a break for the emergency primer cord eighty yards away.

Friesenhahn impatiently ran out of the tunnel to see what was going on. A shell exploded and he leaped into a crater. He peered up and was dismayed to see Faust coming back. Something had gone wrong with the emergency charge too. While he cursed this second failure—forgetting how long it took for the primer cord to burn—he heard a roar and saw timber leap into the air. Thank God, the bridge was out of commission!

Hoge heard only a faint explosion, but when he saw the bridge rise in the air he was sure that the structure was destroyed. It was a great disappointment, relieved only slightly by the realization that there was no longer a need to make a difficult choice. As the smoke cleared he saw to his amazement that the bridge was intact. He jumped into his jeep and headed down the hill to tell Engeman to throw the whole task force across the river at once.

Lieutenant Timmermann too saw the bridge heave up from the explosion and shouted, "As you were! We can't cross the bridge, because it's just been blown!"

De Lisio thought, Now we get five days' rest.

Then someone exclaimed, "She's still standing!"

Timmermann signaled his three platoon leaders. "All right, we'll cross the bridge," he said in his ordinary voice. "Let's go."

He started for the bridge, but the men were hesitating. Major Deevers —always ready with a quip—cheerily called out to the 1st Platoon, "Come on, fellows, let's get across. I'll see you on the other side and we'll all have a chicken dinner."

This drew several obscene remarks and nobody budged. "Move on," Deevers yelled, no longer joking. "Get going!"

Sergeant Anthony Samele turned to Sergeant Mike Chinchar, the acting leader of the 1st Platoon. "C'mon, Mike, we'll just walk it across." Chinchar moved cautiously onto the bridge. Right behind them was PFC Art Massie. Then came Lieutenant Mott, who had been ordered to clear demolitions and cut all wires. Big Samele was fourth.

Chinchar turned and shouted, "Okay, let's take off," and started forward on the double. The others, still afraid that the bridge would disintegrate at any moment, hurried after him. "Massie," Chinchar called, "you leapfrog me up as far as that blown hole." He pointed about two thirds of the way across, where Faust's explosion had blasted a hole in the bridge surface.

"I don't want to go but I will," said Massie. Bullets began to sing around them. Not far behind, Lieutenant Timmermann was prodding the next group to go faster. "Get going! Get going!" he kept shouting. From the bank Chaplain William T. Gibble was taking movies of the assault with his 8-mm. camera.

Mott was now joined by his two sergeants, and the three engineers began cutting every cable in sight. They found no explosives until they were halfway across, when they discovered four charges of about 25 lbs. each, tied to I-beams under the decking. They snipped the connecting wires and moved forward. Chinchar led his men along the left side of the bridge, and bullets from machine guns in the two stone towers on the bridge, about 100 yards from the tunnel, began to spatter in front of him. He halted near the left tower. De Lisio caught up to him and wanted to know what the hell was holding things up.

"Sniper fire," said Chinchar.

"Goddamn, why let a couple of snipers hold up the whole battalion? Let's get off this damn bridge. If it goes, we all go." The aggressive De Lisio sent back word for his second squad to come forward, and started running. Still expecting an explosion at any moment, he led the way up the left side of the bridge until he heard someone call out, "Who's got the right tower?" He crossed over to the right, charged up to a big archway and began pushing aside several bales of hay blocking the tower entrance.

Sabia was behind him. The trip across the bridge had seemed endless— as if he were running on a treadmill. He couldn't help looking down occasionally at the swirling river eighty feet below. He wasn't the best swimmer in the world and he wondered how long it would take for his heavy pack to drag him under. He saw a bullet hit the archway and cried, "Joe, you're hit!"

De Lisio felt himself. There was no pain. "You're crazy."

"I saw that shot go right through you," Sabia insisted and darted to the other tower. Now alone, De Lisio rushed into the right tower and discovered five Germans huddling around a jammed machine gun. He fired two shots into the wall with his M-1 and yelled, "*Hände hoch!*"

The surprised Germans spun around and threw up their hands. De Lisio leaned down and with one hand closed the tripod of the machine gun, then heaved it out the window so his comrades would know the gun was out of action. He asked in broken German, "Anyone else upstairs?"

"*Nein.*"

"Let's go up and see." He prodded the five prisoners up the winding stairway ahead of him. At the top they came upon two men—a private and a lieutenant. The former remained frozen to the floor but the officer, who seemed to be drunk, made a wobbly leap toward a detonating device in the corner. De Lisio fired in front of his feet, then pushed him and the others back down the stairs.

Outside, Alex Drabik—a tall, lanky, shy Ohioan with sad eyes—was looking for his platoon leader, De Lisio. It would be just like him to be up at the railroad tunnel already. He shouted to the rest of the squad, "De Lisio must be over there all alone. Let's go!"

"Go ahead," said Sabia, who had helped Chinchar, Samele and Massie subdue a machine-gun crew in the left tower. He then followed the charging Drabik. Seconds later De Lisio pushed his seven prisoners out of the tower, pointed them back to the American side of the bridge and ran after Sabia.

Drabik was running so fast that his helmet fell off but he didn't stop, and he was the first American to get across. Immediately behind him was Marvin Jensen, a plasterer from Minnesota, who kept shouting over and over, "Holy crap, do you think we'll make it?" At their heels were Samele, De Lisio, Chinchar, Massie and Sabia.

Timmermann was the first officer over the bridge. He pointed to the yawning railroad-tunnel mouth some 100 yards away. "Reconnoiter, but don't get in a fight," he told Sabia. "Take Joe and a couple of others."

Characteristically, De Lisio had already decided to poke his nose into the tunnel. Sabia warned him to walk on the railroad ties so that they wouldn't make noise and "invite any trouble." Followed by several others, they crept into the black tunnel, not knowing what to expect. They walked past barricades but drew no fire. Cautiously they followed the sharp curve of the tracks past a line of freight cars. Ahead they could hear muffled voices. De Lisio fired a volley into the ceiling, causing a ricochet.

Two German soldiers came forward, hands raised. The Americans escorted them back, out of the tunnel, and motioned them toward the bridge.

## 6.

Once Bratge learned that Americans were crossing the bridge, he hustled back to Scheller at the rear of the tunnel and told him that he needed engineers for a counterattack. Scheller gave his okay and the captain started back, rounding up men on the way. At the bridge end of the tunnel a sergeant came running after him and told him that Scheller and two other officers had disappeared. With Scheller gone, Bratge considered himself in command. He tried to lead his men up to a ridge overlooking the bridge so that he could reorganize and mount a proper attack, but gunfire from the first Americans off the bridge drove everyone back. The civilians in the tunnel had panicked. They begged Bratge to stop fighting, and even tried to disarm the engineers. Bratge gathered the remaining officers—Friesenhahn and three lieutenants.

"Major Scheller and two other officers have left us," he said in his stilted manner. "I don't know why. We can't afford to fight any longer." He reminded them of a recent order of Hitler's: " 'Whoever wants to fight, even if only a private, can command the others,' " and asked, "Does any of you want to fight? If so, he will have the command."

Nobody answered.

He started to tell the same thing to the troops, but a group of civilians surged forward carrying a white flag. Bratge turned back to the soldiers and said, "I order the fighting to stop. I ask you to destroy your arms and leave the tunnel last."

Several hundred yards past the tunnel exit, Sabia led his squad to the little railroad station of Erpel. A train was serenely pulling in from the north. Sabia motioned his men to crouch in a ditch and watched, absorbed, as middle-aged German soldiers, armed with rifles, awkwardly spilled out and were gruffly brought into neat lines by a spruce young lieutenant. It was, Sabia thought, like a Mack Sennett comedy. Once all the soldiers were in line, the Americans in the ditch simply stood up and said, *"Hände hoch!"* Not one of the elderly soldiers tried to resist— nor did the spruce lieutenant.

The rest of Company A was trying to scale the almost vertical and slippery slopes of Erpel Ley under such deadly anti-aircraft fire that it was spontaneously renamed Flak Hill. It was far worse than crossing the bridge.

In the meantime C Company had circled around Flak Hill and headed for the rear end of the tunnel, guarded by a solitary German armed with a *Panzerfaust* (bazooka). A GI shouted at him to come forward. He did, and within a few minutes Bratge and some 200 of his men were rounded up.

Lieutenant Colonel Sears Y. Coker, the division engineer, was waiting at Hoge's Bierresdorf command post when the general returned from Remagen. Upon learning of Hoge's dilemma, Coker volunteered to drive back to Division headquarters and explain why Hoge had ignored the new orders. Shortly after Coker's departure the division commander himself drove up, and before General Leonard could get out of his car, Hoge said, "Well, we got the bridge."

"What the hell did you do that for?" Leonard replied, but Hoge knew he was joking. "Now we've got the bull by the tail, and caused a lot of trouble." Then Leonard said seriously, "But let's push it, and then put it up to Corps."

Hoge held out the message he had received from III Corps to continue south. "Here're my new orders. What'll I do?" he asked. "I've already got troops on the other side."

"You've disobeyed orders," Leonard said, then added with a wry grin, "but you were absolutely right and I'll back you up."

Hoge had been sure Leonard would say that, but he felt a great relief all the same.

"Hold on to what you've got and I'll send you everything I've got," Leonard went on decisively. "The division will be responsible up to the bridge."

Leonard suddenly wondered if the Germans had put delayed time bombs on the bridge. "Suppose they blow up the bridge?" he asked. If it went up within thirty-six hours, everything on the east side would be lost.

Hoge thought it was well worth the risk. "We've only got a task force on the other side," he said. "And the war is almost over."

Leonard sighed. It might be an enemy trap, but he too decided the risk was worth taking. "Disobeying orders is a bad thing to do," he said. "But I'll stay with you, Bill. I think you're right."

Colonel Harry Johnson, Leonard's chief of staff, had just learned about the bridge from Colonel Coker and was phoning III Corps. He got Colonel James Phillips, Millikin's chief of staff, on the other end of the line and told him about the bridge. Phillips' reaction was a burst of laughter. Johnson tried to prove that he wasn't joking. "I have a West Point lieutenant colonel standing at my elbow who's just come from Hoge's headquarters and personally talked to Hoge himself!"

Phillips sobered instantly and said that Millikin was out on inspection and wouldn't be back for several hours. Johnson refused to be put off; Hoge should be allowed to hang on to the bridge. "This could well be the turning point in the war!" he said.

"Well," Phillips conceded at last, "hold it lightly." But after some "vehement and skillful persuasion" by Johnson, he agreed to let Hoge throw everything he had across the Rhine.

Now that Phillips had committed III Corps, he had to get approval from First Army for his own actions. But General Hodges too was out on inspection and his operations officer could not, on his own, give permission to expand the Remagen bridgehead. For the first time there was delay in approving what had already been done. And for the first time there was some question about taking full advantage of such an unexpected stroke of luck. There was even the possibility that Hoge, Leonard and Phillips, who had already ignored specific orders to send an entire task force across the Rhine, might suffer for the initiative expected of all good soldiers.

Engineer Mott and his two sergeants had thoroughly examined the bridge. They had been harassed by sniper fire from a half-submerged barge 200 yards upstream until a tank lobbed several shells amidships. A little after 4:30 P.M. Mott reported to Engeman that the bridge had been cleared of explosives, including a 500–600-lb. charge with a blown fuse cap. A crew was already repairing the crater in the approach road. "We'll have the bridge ready for vehicles in two hours," Mott said.

"Do you mean tanks?" Engeman asked.

"Yes, tanks in two hours."

To get positive confirmation of what he had done, Engeman radioed Hoge: BRIDGE INTACT. AM PUSHING DOUGHS TO OTHER SIDE. PREPARING BRIDGE FOR TANKS TO CROSS. WHAT ARE YOUR PLANS? ADVISE AS SOON AS POSSIBLE.

A few minutes later he sent another message: BUILDING UP ON OTHER SIDE OF RIVER. WHO IS GOING TO PROTECT OUR REAR? WHAT ARE YOUR PLANS? WOULD LIKE TO KNOW AS SOON AS POSSIBLE.

Hoge replied: WE ARE BACKING YOU WITH EVERYTHING WE HAVE. BUILD UP DEFENSES ON OTHER SIDE.

## 7.

As yet the German general in direct command of the Remagen area, Hitzfeld, knew nothing about the capture of the bridge; nor did his superior, Zangen, who had predicted what actually happened; nor even Zangen's superior, Model, whose headquarters was being moved east of the river. Model's operations officer, Günther Reichhelm—at thirty-one probably the youngest full colonel in the Wehrmacht—had already arrived there with an advance guard. Then he heard the news by chance from one of Rundstedt's officers who had picked it up from an antiaircraft officer near Koblenz. Unable to locate Model or his chief of staff, Reichhelm took charge. He immediately tried to find someone close to the bridge, but the nearest he got was the commander of Army Communication Troops, General Praun, who, when told to mount an instant attack on Remagen, protested that he was only an administrator. "I'm not the right man," he asserted. "I wouldn't know what to do."

Reichhelm finally reached General Wend von Wietersheim, commander of the 11th Panzer Division in Bonn, and told him to assemble all troops. "Take them under your command. You will be responsible for the attack." Wietersheim was willing but had no fuel to move his 4000 men, 25 tanks and 18 artillery pieces down to the bridgehead.

Reichhelm then phoned General Joachim von Kortzfleisch at the castle of Bensberg, twenty miles north of Bonn, and placed him in overall command of the entire bridgehead operation. Until this time Kortzfleisch had been in charge of the rear line of defense, which was manned only by scattered groups of Volkssturm units and half-trained replacement troops. It was such a farce that not long before, he had sarcastically told Model, "Supplying them with weapons is an indirect delivery of weapons to the U. S. A." Now Kortzfleisch was told to borrow two frontline armored divisions: the 11th Panzer and Panzer Lehr. Kortzfleisch and his operations officer, Oberst (Colonel) Rudolf Schulz, drove south through the rain toward the bridgehead. It would take time to transfer the front-line units to Remagen. What they needed was a unit ready to move and equipped with fuel.

At a village on the Rhine just across from Bonn they suddenly came upon the answer to their problem. Lined up in the street was a full-strength armored infantry battalion: sixteen tanks, loaded with extra gas tanks and ammunition. Its commander, Oberstleutnant (Lieutenant Colonel) Ewers, said the unit was part of the 106th "Hall of Generals" Armored Brigade, bound for Bonn, but readily volunteered to help throw the Americans back into the Rhine. For an hour Kortzfleisch tried unsuccessfully to get approval to change Ewers' mission. Finally, in desperation, he phoned Feldmarschall Model. "If Ewers, with his combat-experienced men, doesn't throw back the Americans tonight," he said, "then it must be presumed that the inner door to Germany will remain open for the Americans."

To Kortzfleisch's surprise Model replied that he knew all about the situation and that he had even discussed it with Hitler. The Führer did not consider Remagen that important and had ordered the 106th to continue to Bonn. Ordinarily calm, Kortzfleisch lost his temper. "Herr Feldmarschall," he shouted, "I feel obligated to point out that this order will be of decisive consequence in the war!"

As Ewers reluctantly moved on to Bonn, Kortzfleisch and Schulz drove south. Five miles from Erpel a tall, haggard artillery major staggered up to them. It was Scheller. He said hoarsely that he had to phone Model and then told them about his experience at the bridge. Schulz thought he looked like a man "who had just emerged from the thickest mire, and whose soul was heavily burdened."

Scheller reported that the American infantry on the east shore was still weak and could easily be wiped out if an attack was launched at once. He begged Kortzfleisch to act immediately. A delay of even a few hours could be disastrous. But the unit that Reichhelm had long since ordered to make this first attack—the 11th Panzer Division—was still trying to scrounge gasoline and would not be fully ready for another day.

It was long after dark when Model's headquarters finally phoned Zangen and ordered him to continue holding all positions west of the Rhine despite what had happened at Remagen. Zangen wondered if the "world had gone mad." But disobeying orders was becoming a habit, and he immediately ordered all dispensable units and part of his artillery to cross to the east shore of the Rhine.

Nothing since the July 20 bombing had agitated Hitler so much as the capture of the bridge at Remagen—his deprecating words to Model notwithstanding. To him it was another betrayal and he was determined to punish those responsible. It also gave him an excuse to get rid of the aging Rundstedt, who seemed only to want to retreat. He phoned Feldmarschall Albrecht Kesselring, his commander in Italy, and ordered him to report to Berlin at once. Kesselring asked why, but was only told to hurry.

Hitler also sent an urgent call for the man he was depending on more and more in such emergencies—Otto Skorzeny. By the time the big Austrian reported to the Reich Chancellery, Hitler was in bed, and it was Jodl who told him that Hitler wanted him to destroy the Ludendorff Bridge with his special group of frogmen. For the first time in his military career Skorzeny was not too eager. The temperature of the Rhine, he said, was almost zero, and since the Americans were already extending the bridgehead upstream, he saw extremely little prospect of success. He promised to dispatch his best men from Vienna to Remagen but stipulated that it be left to the frogmen alone to decide, after studying the situation, whether they should take the risk.

## 8.

The hesitation at First Army to approve Hoge's crossing was ended the moment Hodges returned to Spa at dusk. Here at last was the opportunity to break open the whole western front and he could do it by shoving ten divisions into the bridgehead. He immediately ordered his staff to push everything available across the bridge. Then he phoned Bradley at his headquarters in the Château de Namur and said with his usual calm, "Brad, we've gotten a bridge."

"A bridge? You mean you've got one intact on the Rhine?"

"Leonard nabbed the one at Remagen before they blew it up."

"Hot dog, Courtney, this will bust him wide open! Are you getting the stuff across?"

"I'm going to give it everything I've got."

"That's fine."

"I'm having the engineers throw a couple of spare pontoon bridges across to the bridgehead," Hodges said and added that he was sending over the 78th and 9th Infantry divisions immediately, then asked if he could also push across the 99th Division.

"Shove everything you can across it, Courtney, and button the bridgehead up tightly," Bradley replied as he scanned his own big map board. "It'll probably take the other fellow a couple of days to pull enough stuff together to hit you."

The capture of the bridge at Remagen caused more excitement in the various western front headquarters than anything since the Battle of the Bulge, but when Bradley sat down to eat that night he still had not phoned Eisenhower. By coincidence, however, his dinner guest was Eisenhower's operations officer, Major General Harold "Pink" Bull, who was also one of Bradley's closest friends. Bull was an unobtrusive but highly competent staff officer, a small, mild-mannered New Englander with pale reddish hair. He had arrived at Namur just before dinner to discuss Eisenhower's plan to divert four of Bradley's divisions to General Jacob Devers for the 6th Army Group's impending drive into the Saar. He also wanted to see first-hand what help was needed to keep Bradley's present attack going and, particularly, what logistics were needed to support a possible Patton breakthrough.

As soon as Bull stepped into the castle, one of Bradley's staff officers excitedly asked him, "Have you heard the good news?" and told him about the bridge. Bull appreciated its enormous possibilities but reflected to himself about its effect on the main attack across the Rhine by Montgomery in two weeks. During dinner all he could think of was the bridge and its problems, but to his surprise Bradley did not even mention it. Bull wondered what decision Eisenhower and Bradley had come to.

After dinner the two men went to Bradley's war room and for the first time the subject of the Remagen bridge was mentioned. Grabbing the bridge was "a great and heroic" military coup, Bull said, but it was certainly no one's first choice, because of the miserable terrain on the other side. "You're not going anywhere down there at Remagen," he said. "Besides it just doesn't fit into the overall plan."

"Plan, hell!" Bradley exclaimed. "A bridge is a bridge, and mighty damn good anywhere across the Rhine."

"I was only saying that Remagen wasn't the ideal position to cross that we've been looking for."

"But I don't want you to give up your plan," Bradley said impatiently. "Just let us develop this crossing with four or five divisions; perhaps you can use it as a diversion. Or maybe we can employ it to strengthen our pincers south of the Ruhr. At any rate, it's a crossing. We've gotten over the Rhine. But now that we've got a bridgehead, for God's sake let's use it."

"But once you get across, Brad," Bull persisted, "where do you go?"

Bradley led him to the map board and demonstrated a route on a terrain study. After Hodges got ten miles past the bridge to the Bonn–Frankfurt Autobahn, he could turn southeast toward Frankfurt for fifty-five miles, then swing due east. Bull examined the map, tapped it with his finger and said jokingly, "I'll bet you fellows just had it made up."

"Six months ago," Bradley replied; he didn't think Bull was joking. Bull reiterated that it would be difficult to change the overall plan.

"Change—hell, Pink," Bradley said brusquely, "we're not trying to change a thing. But now that we've had a break on the bridge, I want to take advantage of it."

Bull was surprised at the sharp tone from his old friend. After all, he didn't see what was wrong with an operations officer pointing out the inescapable complications just created, "as well as several marked advantages." Why did Brad keep asking *him* for permission to take four divisions over the bridge? Ike was the one to decide such a question. Suddenly it dawned on Bull that Bradley had not yet talked to Eisenhower about the bridge—and the news was almost two hours old! "You can talk to me all night, Brad, and it won't make any difference," he said. "I can't give you permission to send four or five divisions across."

It was about eight o'clock when Eisenhower sat down to dinner in his house at Rheims. His guests were his naval aide, Captain Harry Butcher, Lieutenant-General Frederick Morgan and a group of American airborne commanders, including Major Generals Maxwell Taylor, James Gavin and Matthew Ridgway, who had been alerted for an airdrop over the Rhine in the coming massive Montgomery drive.

Just before the first course was over, Eisenhower was called to the phone. When Eisenhower heard what Bradley had to tell about Remagen he could "scarcely believe my ears" and shouted, "How much have you got in that vicinity that you can throw across the river?"

"I have more than four divisions but I called you to make sure that pushing them over would not interfere with your plans."

Bradley need not have been concerned. "Well, Brad, we expected to have that many divisions tied up around Cologne and now those are free.

Go ahead and shove over at least five divisions instantly, and anything else that is necessary to make certain of our hold." Eisenhower was exultant and would always remember it as one of his "happy moments of the war."

"That's exactly what I wanted to do," Bradley answered gleefully, "but the question has been raised here about conflict with your plans, and I wanted to check with you."

Everyone at the table was listening eagerly to Eisenhower as he said, "To hell with the planners. Sure, go on, Brad, and I'll give you everything we got to hold that bridgehead. We'll make good use of it even if the terrain isn't too good."

Ridgway leaned over to Butcher. "Butch, couldn't you get us in on this show? It sounds good."

Eisenhower returned to the table fairly beaming. "Hodges got a bridge at Remagen and already has troops across." Butcher said the airborne generals would like to get in on the show. Eisenhower replied that they were out of luck on this one but that there was still plenty of work to do elsewhere.

At Flak Hill, rain was falling in a steady, saturating drizzle. While the three infantry companies of the 27th Armored Infantry Battalion were clinging grimly to the slippery sides of the cliff, engineers frantically planked up part of the big hole on the bridge flooring and filled in the crater at the western approach. Tankers waited tensely, a few hoping that the bridge would blow up before it was repaired.

By now, reinforcements were pouring in and trucks, tanks, self-propelled guns and other vehicles jammed the entrance to the bridge, with more traffic piling up every minute. Not far away at his wine-cellar command post, Colonel Engeman told his officers that he didn't know if the bridge would hold tanks even after the repairs. "But," he said, "we've got to try." He explained that engineers would string white tape across the bridge to guide the drivers in the pitch-black night. On reaching the other side of the bridge, the tanks would coil up until dawn and then attack.

Captain George Soumas, commander of the tanks making the night crossing, turned to First Lieutenant C. Windsor Miller, a real estate man from Washington, D. C., whose platoon of tanks would lead the column. Soumas said, "I think you'd better have a tank in front of you tonight." It was Miller's practice to ride in the first tank. Miller said nothing; he still planned to go first. Somehow Engeman sensed this and said, "Miller, that's an order. You will have a tank go ahead of you. I'll not have one of my officers lost, first crack out of the box."

Miller picked his way through the darkness to the commander of his Number Two tank, Sergeant William Goodson, nicknamed Speedy since he was so easy-going and deliberate. "Speedy, I've got the toughest order to give you that I've ever given. You and I are changing places tonight." Goodson said nothing but asked himself sardonically, Why am I selected for this great honor?

The tankers mounted their Pershings and waited. The minutes dragged on and on. Finally, at midnight, Soumas got word that the bridge was ready and waved his column around a line of big tank destroyers. As Goodson's tank clattered onto the bridge there was an ominous, nerve-racking creak. Goodson heard Miller's cautionary voice on the intercom. "Take it easy . . . slowly. Don't go too far ahead of me." Halfway across in the total blackness Miller lost sight of the tank ahead. "Where are you?" he asked.

"Did you notice that thumping?" Goodson replied. "You're bumping into my tank."

Miller recalled the expression "so dark you can't see your hand in front of you." He put up his hand and couldn't see it. He leaned far out looking for the white tape but couldn't see that, either.

There was no gunfire while the tanks crossed, but as soon as they turned off the bridge onto the famous scenic highway running along the Rhine, they were met by machine-gun bullets. The tanks continued north toward Erpel and Miller kept looking for the infantry guides who were supposed to meet him. He was surrounded by Germans; some were shouting *"Kamerad!"* but the rest were shooting.

Miller radioed back: "Enemy firing at us. Many trying to surrender. Send infantry to take prisoners."

Engeman's answer was: "You will hold that position until the last tank is shot from under you."

Miller was in more trouble than he imagined. There would be no more armored reinforcements for several hours. The tank destroyers had followed the Pershings at a brisker pace, but when the first one came to the hastily repaired crater made by Faust's explosion, its right steel tread slipped into the unplanked part of the hole and the big vehicle now hung precariously over the Rhine, part of it blocking the bridge.

Colonel Coker, the division engineer, reached the T/D and intended shoving it through the hole into the river some seventy-five feet below. Then he realized that the substructure might keep it from falling through, in which case it would remain a roadblock for days.

He climbed under the T/D, uncomfortably aware of the cold waters of the Rhine below, and felt for horizontal members that could be floored with crossties so the vehicle could be towed back to safety. He found one suitable member immediately, but couldn't locate a second one in the pitch black. Each passing second "seemed like an eternity." As he searched desperately he couldn't help thinking of the approaching dawn. If traffic wasn't flowing before then, it would be the end of the bridgehead.

In the middle of this crisis a stream of infantrymen began running back toward the west shore in panic, past the toiling engineers. A rumor had started on Flak Hill that all troops were to withdraw at once. Since the rumor originated with an officer, it carried weight, and by the time Deevers' staff learned what was going on, a third of the men on the cliff had fled back to Remagen.

At 4:30 A.M. the first infantry reinforcements sent by Hodges were assembled, ready to march across and strengthen the little bridgehead. Lieutenant Colonel Lewis Maness, who would lead the first group, was told, "There's no problem across the bridge. There's nothing there but demoralization." Maness hoped that meant German demoralization. He led his battalion—about 700 men—onto the bridge, wondering if he should close up tight and get across fast or open the column wide, but after a few steps on the creaking bridge the choice was obvious. "Let's get across here as quickly as possible!" he called.

Coker—muddy all over, but triumphant—had at last found a second suitable horizontal member. Within half an hour, flooring was nailed across and the tank destroyer safely towed to the rear. Soon the hole was completely covered, and tanks, trucks and other vehicles began rolling east again in a steady stream.

Dawn was breaking as infantrymen from the 78th Division began filing across, many looking with uneasy fascination at the muddy, swirling waters far below. They immediately ran into 100 German engineers, sent by their commander, Major Herbert Strobel, to blow up the bridge. There was a brief, fierce fight and though several Germans actually reached the bridge with 1 1/2 tons of explosives, they were captured.

At 8:00 A.M. Hoge and Cothran jeeped across, followed by the communications half-track. Near the tower De Lisio had taken, the general noticed an American helmet. He stopped the jeep and picked it up. It was Drabik's. German mortar shells were falling on both sides, and Hoge could hear American and German machine guns chattering near by. He continued into Erpel and established a command post in the cellar of the Bürgermeister's home.

Half an hour later Captain Soumas, who had already set up a roadblock just south of the bridge with five of his tanks, decided it was time to push up the river. The five Pershings moved south along the Rhine River highway for several miles. At the suburbs of Linz they were met by Captain Gibble, the chaplain who had taken movies of the first crossing. Early that morning Gibble had set up a field altar at the mouth of the tunnel, but feeling that he should do more, had jeeped up the river to Linz, where the local officials readily surrendered their town to him. They said that Linz had been declared an open city because of a large hospital, and that only wounded and medical German personnel were there. Soumas remained suspicious, however, and set up a roadblock on the spot. Minutes later they were pinned down by bazooka and small-arms fire from Linz.

Linz was the headquarters for Major Strobel, who had launched the daring but unsuccessful attempt to blow up the bridge. Now he was caught between two generals with completely different ideas: one who wanted to rescue and one who wanted to attack. Generalleutnant (Major General) Richard Wirtz, Model's engineer officer, instructed him to get the German troops west of the Rhine across the river before they were trapped. Generalleutenant Kurt von Berg, commander of the Combat Area XII North, ordered him to throw every man into a counterattack against the bridgehead.

Strobel obeyed the latter order and assembled all his engineers, including those operating ferries, for the assault. Wirtz discovered this and angrily sent the ferry engineers back to their proper duties. When Berg found the ferries still operating he exploded, and the squabble of command started all over again. As a result of this and similar conflicts of interest, only sporadic forays were being made against the Remagen bridgehead, and by midafternoon over 8000 Americans had crossed the Rhine.

Eisenhower telephoned Montgomery and tactfully queried the field-marshal about enlarging the bridgehead. Excellent move, replied Montgomery. "It will be an unpleasant threat to the enemy and will undoubtedly draw enemy strength onto it and away from the business in the north." He hung up to continue his own methodical plans to cross the Rhine *en masse*.

Although Allied newsmen had heard rumors of the bridge and several were already in Remagen, only at nightfall were they given the official story, and it wasn't until the following morning that newspapers in the United States headlined the story. Not since D-Day had Americans been so excited or proud.

The *New York Times,* quoting an A. P. dispatch, said:

The swift, sensational crossing of the Rhine was a battle feat without parallel since Napoleon's conquering legions crossed the Rhine early in the last century.

Hal Boyle of the Associated Press probably expressed best what every GI felt:

With the exception of the great tank battle at El Alamein, probably no tank engagement in World War II will be remembered longer than the dashing coup which first put the American Army across the Rhine at Remagen.

It was accomplished by the U. S. Ninth Armored Division.

It is no exaggeration to say that the speedy fording of the Rhine at a comparatively undefended point by tanks and infantrymen and engineers who knew there was strong likelihood the dynamite-laden bridge would blow up under them at any moment has saved the American nation 5000 dead and 10,000 wounded.

## 9.

On March 8 ten German planes attacked the Ludendorff Bridge, but hastily emplaced American anti-aircraft units drove them off before real damage was done. German shells could not be stopped, however, and although Flak Hill protected the bridge itself, explosions on the west shore were killing Americans and dangerously jarred the weakened structure.

Already the rapidly expanding bridgehead had created organizational problems. Hoge's combat command staff and communications were not equipped to cope with the situation and Hodges replaced him with a division commander. Just before midnight General Louis Craig of the 9th Infantry Division started across the bridge, and although he couldn't see it, he passed a sign:

CROSS THE RHINE WITH DRY FEET
COURTESY OF THE 9TH ARM'D DIVISION.

Like the previous night, it was so dark that Craig had to lie on the hood of a jeep and feel the way by hand, calling back instructions to the driver. He hoped nothing was coming the other way.

The tense trip over the bridge convinced Craig that it should only handle eastbound traffic, but even this one-way traffic was halted the following afternoon when a German shell hit an ammunition truck just starting to climb the western approach. Nevertheless, Craig kept pushing his bridgehead forward and to either side, and the Germans—still a grab-bag force—continued to fall back slowly but steadily.

The fate of the bridgehead, however, was being decided not in battle but back at Rheims. Eisenhower's spontaneous enthusiasm about Remagen had begun to cool. He was committed to Montgomery's attack, which would need ten additional divisions after the first had crossed the Rhine, and he decided to let only five divisions be sent to Remagen. When Hodges arrived at 12th Army Group headquarters to receive a French decoration, Bradley relayed the bad news, which meant that Hodges could only expand his bridgehead about 1000 yards a day, "barely enough to keep the enemy from mining and entrenching around that foothold." Moreover, when Hodges reached the Bonn–Frankfurt Autobahn, he was to hold in place until Ike gave the green light.

For once Hodges was vocal in his protests. First Army had just pulled off one of the greatest coups of the war, he said, and tremendous possibilities lay ahead. Bradley felt exactly the same, but they would simply have to wait until Ike made up his mind about a plan just submitted: there would be a second crossing of the Rhine, this one by Patton, who was waiting farther south, and a simultaneous breakout from the Remagen bridgehead; when Hodges and Patton converged they would both turn north to meet Montgomery on the east side of the Rhine and thus encircle the entire Ruhr industrial area. It was a bold, imaginative plan and Eisenhower had promised to give it every consideration.

Kesselring arrived in Berlin that noon, and while he was waiting for Hitler to see him privately after lunch, someone mentioned casually that he was going to relieve Rundstedt. Kesselring thought it was a joke and turned to Keitel and Jodl, but they confirmed it. Kesselring, nicknamed Smiling Albrecht because of his unwavering optimism, frowned. He was needed in Italy, he said, and besides, he wasn't yet fully recovered from a serious automobile accident. Such arguments, Keitel and Jodl assured him, would "hold no water" with the Führer.

They were right. Hitler told Kesselring that the loss of the Ludendorff Bridge necessitated a change in command. "Only a younger and more active commander who has had experience in fighting the Western Powers and enjoys the confidence of the men in the line can perhaps still restore the situation," Hitler said pointedly, without mentioning Rundstedt by name, and ordered Kesselring to "accept this sacrifice" in spite of his poor health. "I have confidence you will do everything humanly possible." The man who, only hours earlier, had considered Bonn more important than Remagen, now said that the most vulnerable spot was the Ludendorff Bridge. "It is urgent to restore the situation there. I am confident it can be done."

Hitler's lengthy exposition greatly impressed Kesselring, who thought it was "remarkably lucid and showed an astounding grasp of detail." It also clarified his own role in the complex puzzle: all he had to do was "hang on."

But Hitler's initial rage at the Americans' capture of the Ludendorff Bridge had not abated—and for good reason. The loss of the bridge also meant the loss of his last natural defense in the west—the Rhine River. He was now more determined than ever to punish "those responsible," although he was, of course, the real culprit. His stubborn insistence that the western front be held at all costs had opened the door to Remagen, and his own order forbidding Rhine bridges to be blown up until the last moment had forced Scheller to delay so long. It was he and Model who were most responsible, but Hitler had summarily relieved Rundstedt —the experienced professional soldier who had realistically proposed an orderly retreat behind the Rhine, which would have forestalled a Remagen.

Following the same logic, Hitler now prepared to deal with those more directly concerned, like Scheller and Bratge. If such as they were tried and punished immediately, it would discourage the growing cowardice and lack of discipline on the western front. Hitler therefore established the "Flying Special Tribunal West," a mobile court that would conduct on-the-spot trials of soldiers of any rank and was empowered to carry out its judgments immediately. He appointed SS-Gruppenführer (Major General) Rudolf Hübner, a faithful Party member, to head it.

On March 10 Hübner reported to the Reich Chancellery; he was to start court-martial proceedings at once against the "cowards and betrayers" of Remagen. In the evening Hübner and two assistants, none with legal training, arrived at Kesselring's command post near Bad Nauheim and explained their mission. The Feldmarschall heatedly claimed that such a drumhead tribunal would weaken morale along the entire western front, and excused himself to attend to more pressing matters. The first of these was a telephone call to OKW, Keitel's headquarters. His impressions of the front, Kesselring reported, were not good; the odds were too great. "Seen at close quarters," he said, "the situation appears to be much more serious than I was led to believe," and insisted that his requirements, therefore, be met fully and quickly.

The next morning Kesselring and his chief of staff, Generalleutnant (Major General) Siegfried Westphal, headed for a tour just north of Remagen, to see Model. As they passed great numbers of troops heading eastward with carts loaded with baggage, Westphal remarked, "This is the situation as it really is in the west." Kesselring shook his head and muttered, "If I'd only come three months ago!" which antagonized Westphal, who felt it was a slur on Rundstedt. Kesselring antagonized Model as well. "Throw the Americans back across the Rhine," he told the Army Group B commander, who took it as a slur on himself. "I'll try," Model answered testily, "but I don't think my forces are sufficient."

In the afternoon the commanders concerned with Remagen brought their complaints to Kesselring. Generalleutnant Fritz Bayerlein said that every time he made up a plan of attack, he would learn that the Americans had just captured the jump-off point.

"The jump-off positions for attack are, by now, hardly up to the German command, in view of the American progress," Zangen pointed out sarcastically, and urged Kesselring to let him counterattack in strength at once. "For every day that we delay a counterattack we'll have to throw in twice as many men; otherwise the counterattack will only lead to new reverses and to a fruitless expenditure of our forces!" He then predicted that the Americans, after reaching the Autobahn, would do what Bradley in fact planned to do: swerve down toward Frankfurt, and after fifty-five miles abruptly turn east toward the heart of Germany.

By the end of the day Kesselring was convinced that Remagen alone was swallowing up almost all the replacements and supplies fed to the western front. The fate of the whole Rhine front hung on wiping out or containing the bridgehead. But how could he do it with the shattered forces at his disposal? Frustrated, he felt "like a concert pianist asked to play a Beethoven sonata before a large audience on an ancient, rickety and out-of-tune instrument."

Earlier in the day Hübner's first court-martial had opened in a farm-house about thirty miles east of the Rhine. The three judges sat side by side on a couch in the living room, with Oberst (Colonel) Felix Janert, Army Group B's legal officer, perched on an old chair. Bratge was tried *in absentia* and sentenced to death. Then a pale and nervous Major Scheller was escorted into the room. Under rapid-fire questioning from Hübner he became rattled, and it took him some time to give satisfactory answers. Hübner shouted, "Do you admit your cowardice and guilt?" Scheller mumbled that he did and was taken away. The three-man court sentenced him to death.

An anti-aircraft lieutenant, Karl Peters, was next. He testified that he had brought most of his Flakwerfer 44 battery across the Ludendorff Bridge but admitted that he might possibly have left one of these top-secret weapons west of the Rhine. Before Peters could explain the circumstances, Hübner shouted, "You are guilty of high treason and deserve to be shot for your cowardice!"

The dazed Peters mumbled, "Yes, sir," and in a few minutes he too was sentenced to die. Hübner then tried and condemned to death Major Strobel, the engineer from Linz who had launched the daring attempt to blow up the bridge, and Major August Kraft, Friesenhahn's imme-diate superior, who hadn't even been in the area.

Kesselring, who had decried the trials, was compelled to publicize the results. He sent out a special message as a warning to every man on the western front. "Who does not live in honor," he said, "will die in shame."

## 10.

On the same day that Bradley told Hodges that for the time being he could only push five divisions into the Remagen bridgehead, Patton hap-pened to be in Namur to receive a French decoration. He told his chief of staff, Major General Hobart "Hap" Gay, of Bradley's remark at one point during the day that Eisenhower wasn't in favor of the all-out Montgomery attack but "was afraid it had to be done." Patton's disgust was enlarged upon by Gay in his diary:

. . . A commentary, which is purely on the part of the author of this Diary, is to the effect that if the Supreme Commander did not believe in it, then why did he not say "No"—perhaps looking back into history when another Amer-ican commander pounded on his desk and said, "No, goddamit, no!", and thereby made history. It was further stated that the First Army had authority to enlarge the bridgehead at REMAGEN so that it was approximately nine miles deep and twenty-two miles wide. This is a peculiar statement when one thinks that the main effort of the American Armies should be to defeat the German forces, and that the RHINE before them is the last formidable natural barrier to the east in this zone . . .

The man most affected by Eisenhower's temporary decision—Courtney Hodges—did not allow his great disappointment to diminish his determination to exploit the bridgehead as far and as fast as he could. Things were going too slowly for his taste. He was also concerned about the bridge itself, which was close to collapse. Fortunately the treadway bridge under construction about 500 yards to the north was completed by the morning of March 10. Moreover, the heavy pontoon bridge a mile to the south would probably be ready for traffic that evening. In addition, a number of ferries were also carrying ammunition and gasoline to the east bank and returning with wounded. The fastest—rafts with double outboard motors—could negotiate the dangerous trip in eight to ten minutes.

First Army had only three bridges, and extra parts for two others on the books, but seven more were being rushed up to the Rhine by engineer officer Colonel William Carter. Even Hodges had no idea where the seven mystery bridges had come from. In Antwerp one of Patton's men was surreptitiously chalking "Third Army" on every bridge that came through, but First Army had a "friend" in the Liège regulating station who industriously erased all "Third Army" chalk marks and dispatched everything to Carter. Though Patton's Third Army openly boasted that they were the champion hijackers in the European Theater, the sedate First Army was quietly assuming the title.

In the afternoon on March 10 Hodges drove up to Remagen to see what was going on across the river. As soon as all traffic on the treadway was cleared, the general's jeep raced across. Craig told Hodges that some 20,000 men were in the bridgehead; furthermore, the 99th Division was in the process of crossing and would be operational in a day. Things already looked pretty secure and the 9th and 78th divisions were making 1000 yards a day. Even though this was the limit Bradley had imposed, Hodges insisted on faster progress.

Not long after the general had jeeped back across the Rhine, the Ludendorff Bridge was closed and engineers moved in with heavy equipment to repair the almost severed truss near Faust's explosion. Unless a huge steel plate could be welded in place, engineers predicted the bridge would soon collapse. But it was no longer vital. At 11:00 P.M. the first traffic began to roll east over the heavy pontoon bridge. The bridgehead would soon be glutted with supplies and reinforcements, and it was only a question of time before Craig's troops broke through the wooded hills to the Autobahn ten miles away.

It was a weird battle. A few hundred yards from brisk action there would be utter silence. Strangely the silence was often more nerve-racking and the will to keep pushing on into the unknown forest was hard to sustain.

One of the young officers sent to press the attack was 2nd Lieutenant William McCurdy of the 52nd Armored Infantry Battalion, 9th Armored Division. It was to be McCurdy's first battle command and he was eager to make good. As he reached the east shore, the crews of anti-aircraft batteries lining the bank shouted, "Go back! You'll be sorry!" or "How are things back in the States?" McCurdy and the replacements with him shouted back insults and got more in return, but for some reason it made them feel better. They walked south a few miles to the village of Kasbach, where McCurdy reported to a tall, thin, haggard major named Watts, who smiled wanly and said, "Now, you fellows will have to be firm with these men. They've all been at it steadily for almost two weeks and are very tired. So you'll have to provide that extra push to get things done."

McCurdy was escorted up to his new platoon and a corporal removed the shiny gold bars from his trench coat. "Don't worry, Lieutenant," he said. "We know you're in command here but you'd be a first-class target for snipers with these things on. Most of the officers pin them under their collars, where they don't show." It was new to McCurdy but seemed sensible. His first assignment was to set up a roadblock near the railroad. An entire company had tried to move up there the day before and couldn't make it. McCurdy nodded but wondered how a platoon could do today what a company had failed to do yesterday.

He led his platoon down a stream bed and into a forest trail. Suddenly in front of him he saw two dead Germans near a machine gun. One man was still in firing position but his partner was sprawled backward. Their skin was so unnaturally dark that McCurdy first thought they were wax dummies put there to scare newcomers like him, but when he drew closer he saw that they had once been men and his stomach dropped like an elevator. Then he thought: Why is it so quiet out here?

It wasn't until two days later, on March 13, that Eisenhower at last made up his mind about the plan to let Hodges and Patton loose east of the Rhine—and the decision was negative. He radioed Bradley that Hodges should not be allowed to advance more than ten miles; the Remagen bridgehead would only be used to draw German troops away from the Ruhr area and Montgomery.

To a field commander such an order was ridiculous and Hodges didn't hesitate to say so. He told Bradley that while Monty was ponderously preparing his assault across the Rhine, First Army could be breaking out from the bridgehead. Bradley was sympathetic but said there was no use arguing; the orders from Ike had to be followed.

It was an ironically cautious ending to such a bold beginning.

# 12

# "I Am Fighting for the Work of the Lord"

## 1.

Of all Hitler's acts against humanity his "final solution to the Jewish problem" has most appalled and mystified the civilized world. But his course of action was clearly plotted in *Mein Kampf*. In that book he not only repeatedly predicted the extremes he was willing to go to, but revealed the wellspring of his own prejudice.

When he was eighteen years old he moved to Vienna to study art. "Wherever I went, I began to see Jews," he wrote, "and the more I saw, the more sharply they became distinguished in my eyes from the rest of humanity." At first his bigotry was personal; the mere sight of bearded orthodox Jews in their strange clothes physically repelled him. But when he read "The Protocols of the Elders of Zion," his anti-Semitism burgeoned into an obsession: he must defend the world against the Jews. This document, forged by the Imperial Russian Secret Service in 1905, alleged that the Jews secretly intended to dominate the world through a grotesque combination of capitalism and Marxism. "We shall everywhere arouse ferment, struggle and enmity," one Jewish leader purportedly announced. "We shall unleash a world war—we shall bring the peoples to such a pass that they will voluntarily offer us world domination." The young Austrian, already a fanatical German nationalist, believed every word of the forgery. "In this period," he wrote, "my eyes were opened to two menaces whose names I had scarcely known before and whose terrible importance for the existence of the German people I certainly did not understand: Marxism and Jewry."

He called his five years in Vienna "the hardest, though most thorough, school" of his life. "I had set foot in this town while still a boy and I left it a man, grown quiet and grave. . . . I do not know what my attitude toward the Jews, the Social Democrats, or rather, Marxism as a whole, the social question, etc., would be today if at such an early time the pressure of destiny—and my own study—had not built up a basic stock of personal opinions within me."

His repugnance and fear rapidly grew into an *idée fixe* that was to him "the greatest spiritual upheaval" of his life. "I had ceased to be a weak-kneed cosmopolitan and became an anti-Semite." Much of this obsessive hatred of Jews had its root in Hitler's own failure as an architect and artist. He was embittered by the success of Jews in these fields. "Was there any form of filth or profligacy, particularly in cultural life, without at least one Jew involved in it? If you cut even cautiously into such an abscess, you found, like a maggot in a rotting body, often dazzled by the sudden light—a kike!"

But it was the threat of Marxism, primarily, that fanned his anti-Semitism to action. The most hypnotic orator of the twentieth century, Hitler was able to impart his fanaticism to others. He propounded in speech after speech that once the Jew gained economic control of the world through the stock exchange and finance, he would seize political control. "His ultimate goal in this stage is the victory of 'democracy,' or, as he understands it: the rule of parliamentarianism. . . . With infinite shrewdness he fans the need for social justice, somehow slumbering in every Aryan man, into hatred against those who have been better favored by fortune, and thus gives the struggle for the elimination of social evil a very definite philosophical stamp. He establishes the Marxist doctrine."

After this is done, Hitler warned, the Jew ends the masquerade and reveals what he really is. "The democratic people's Jew becomes the blood-Jew and tyrant over peoples. In a few years he tries to exterminate the national intelligentsia, and by robbing the peoples of their natural intellectual leadership, makes them ripe for the slave's lot of permanent subjugation. The most frightful example of this kind is offered by Russia, where he killed or starved about thirty million people with positively fanatical savagery, in part amid inhuman tortures, in order to give a gang of Jewish journalists and stock-exchange bandits domination over a great people."

He was convinced that the Jewish-Marxist plot would come to a climax in Germany. "The Bolshevization of Germany—that is, the extermination of the Jewish intelligentsia in Germany, to make possible the toil of the German working class under the yoke of Jewish world finance—is conceived only as a preliminary to the further extension of this Jewish tendency of world conquest. As often in history, Germany is the great pivot in the mighty struggle. If our people and our state become the victim of these bloodthirsty and avaricious Jewish tyrants of nations, the whole earth will sink into the tentacles of this octopus; if Germany frees herself from this embrace, this greatest of dangers to nations may be regarded as broken for the whole world."

There is little doubt but that Hitler believed every incredible word he uttered, and in *Mein Kampf* he showed just how far he was prepared to go. "If during World War I twelve or fifteen thousand of these Hebrew corrupters of the people had been subjected to poison gas . . . the sacrifice of millions at the front would not have been in vain. On the contrary: twelve thousand scoundrels eliminated in time might have saved the lives of a million real Germans, valuable for the future."

That a leader of a civilized state could accept as genuine "The Protocols of the Elders of Zion" was improbable enough, but that he could use mass murder to end "the Jewish menace" was so utterly incomprehensible that when the ultimate horrors of the concentration camps were revealed, most Westerners believed Hitler was a madman, the evilest of criminals, the ultimate Antichrist.

But Hitler and Nazism would have seemed most believable, indeed admirable, to many of the medieval prophets of the Millennium—that one thousand years of great happiness, good government and freedom from wretchedness predicted in Revelation xx. Rather than appearing as Antichrist, Hitler would have seemed the very embodiment of Christ Arisen to such as Tanchelm, who started a revolutionary movement in Flanders in the early twelfth century, and John Ball, leader of the English peasants' revolt of 1381, and even Thomas Münzer, who led the German peasants' revolt of 1525. Each of these prophets believed in varying degrees that he was Christ Arisen, destined to overthrow world tyranny and bring mankind a glorious new life, and that the massacre of their opponents was the will of God. Münzer, for example, enjoined his followers to kill without pity. "Don't let your sword get cold! . . . At them, at them, while you have daylight! God goes ahead of you, so follow, follow!" Like these fanatics, Hitler also aimed to shatter and renew the world; he too claimed to have been chosen to bring the Millennium to a corrupt world. He offered boundless aims and promises, and unlike other politicians of his day, he gave social conflicts and national hopes a mystical sense of majesty and purpose.

Behind all this mysticism was a materialistic program that satisfied the aspirations of practically all classes. Hitler promised to revoke the "infamous" Treaty of Versailles and bring back German honor; revive the Wehrmacht and Luftwaffe; save the country from a devastating depression; expand Germany's borders into Asia; and exterminate Bolshevism as well as all "undesirable" elements, such as the Jews.

Hitler did not spring from a void; the excesses perpetrated by him were a culmination of a straight, relentless line of persecution that had been going on for centuries, from the time of the Crusades throught the First Reich—the Holy Roman Empire—in the Middle Ages to the Second Reich of Bismarck and Kaiser Wilhelm II, when a strong belief in German racial superiority was developed. He was the logical heir to the bloodthirsty prophets as well and, like them, he was dynamic and ruthless, obsessed by apocalyptic fantasy and completely convinced of his own infallibility. He did not smoke or drink; he was a vegetarian; he lived with simple, almost ascetic frugality; he was beyond personal corruption. He had a mistress, but he hid her from the public so he could present himself rather as a sexless symbol of purity. His goal too was set above all else; his mission worth any sacrifice, even millions of human beings. Each of the old prophets felt he had to destroy one great corrupting force. In Hitler's case it was the Jews—an ancient target—and their elimination was only a necessary cleansing which would bring the world to its final glory. "[The Jew] goes his baleful way until the day when another power comes to oppose him and in a mighty struggle casts him, the invader of the heavens, back to Lucifer."

It was this inherited apocalyptic vision that inspired Hitler to massacre millions of Jews.* He had no qualms. "I believe that I am acting in accordance with the will of the Almighty Creator," he said. "By defending myself against the Jew, I am fighting for the work of the Lord."

By March, 1945, the shadow of defeat moved Hitler to accelerate his program of annihilation and he ordered the murder of all the remaining Jews in the concentration camps before they could be liberated by the Russians and their allies.

Dr. Kersten, Himmler's masseur, entreated him to countermand the directive. "Those are the Führer's direct orders," Himmler replied, "and I must see to it that they are carried out to the last detail." For a week the two argued stormily, with Himmler maintaining that "the criminals in the concentration camps shall not have the satisfaction of emerging from our ruin as triumphant conquerors." But the indefatigable Kersten would not give up and kept after Himmler until the harried Reichsführer set down on paper a personal promise to Dr. Kersten not to blow up the camps or kill any more Jews; all prisoners were to remain in their present camps and be handed over to the Allies "in an orderly manner."

When he had finished writing this remarkable document, Himmler

---

* There is a wide divergence of opinion on the approximate number. Some Germans regard the figure given at the Nuremberg Trials—5,700,000—as a gross exaggeration. Gerald Reitlinger puts the figure at between 4,194,200 and 4,581,200.

peered at it for a while through his pince-nez, then at last, in his slow, stilted writing, signed it "Heinrich Himmler, Reichsführer SS."

Kersten elatedly grasped the same pen, and on the spur of the moment wrote, "In the name of humanity, Felix Kersten."

Kersten's accomplishment was substantial but it was, after all, only a private compact, and though Himmler had recklessly compromised himself, there was no assurance that he would keep his word.

Ironically, at the same time that Himmler was resisting Kersten's pleas, he was setting up a secret meeting in Austria with Dr. Carl J. Burckhardt, president of the International Committee of the Red Cross, which could result in vastly alleviating conditions in prison and concentration camps. What Himmler hoped for in return was the good will of the world. Moreover, the man Himmler had sent as his agent was Dr. Kaltenbrunner. Enemies such as Walter Schellenberg would have found it nigh impossible to believe that he could have participated in such humanitarian negotiations.*

Dr. Burckhardt wanted to persuade Kaltenbrunner to let the Red Cross visit the concentration camps and bring some relief to the inmates. Ten years earlier he had tried to wring the same concessions from Kaltenbrunner's predecessor, the notorious Reinhard Heydrich, who had become the symbol of Gestapo brutality. Heydrich had parried Dr. Burckhardt's request by defending Nazi policy. The camps, he said, were filled with criminals, spies and dangerous propaganda agents. "You must not forget that we are battling, that the Führer battles, the universal enemy," he said. "It's not only a question of making Germany safe and sound; it's our duty to save the world from intellectual and moral decay. That's one thing you people don't understand." Then Heydrich dropped his voice to a conspiratorial whisper: "Abroad they think we're the damnedest brutes, don't they? For the individual, it's almost too hard to carry it out, but we have to be as hard as granite, or the work of our Führer will perish. There will come a day when they will all thank us for having assumed these responsibilities."

Dr. Burckhardt got more than words from Heydrich's successor. Surprisingly, Kaltenbrunner approved a stepped-up delivery of food parcels to military prisoners and even agreed to let Red Cross observers live in prisoner-of-war camps until the end of hostilities. Encouraged by Kaltenbrunner's "reasonable attitude," Dr. Burckhardt brought up the treatment of civilian prisoners. Kaltenbrunner offered the inmates of the con-

---

* According to Dr. Kleist, Kaltenbrunner was trying to negotiate for peace in 1943 "when it was very dangerous to consider such ideas. Kaltenbrunner did all he could to help me in my negotiations with Gilel Storch. It was the intervention of Schellenberg which delayed the whole thing for months."

Dr. Kleist believes that Schellenberg wanted to take all such negotiations out of the hands of Ribbentrop, Kaltenbrunner and himself for his personal benefit; he was "what we simply call a *Characterschwein*." Storch recently wrote, "As regards the role by Schellenberg . . . Count Bernadotte and I had promised him asylum in Sweden . . ."

centration camps the same concessions just granted to military prisoners. "In fact," he said, "you may even send permanent observers to the Israelite camps."

The next few days Himmler made even more humanitarian concessions. He was persuaded by Kersten to rescind Hitler's order to destroy The Hague and the Zuyder Zee Dam, and to draft an order forbidding any cruelty to Jews. In fact, he had become so tractable by March 17 that Kersten asked him to meet secretly with Storch of the World Jewish Congress.

Himmler gasped. "I can never receive a Jew!" he cried. "If the Führer heard of it, he would have me shot dead on the spot!" But he had already made too many concessions, and Kersten had a signed carbon copy of the promise to disobey Hitler. In a weak voice Himmler gave his consent.

Hitler was aware of a number of the plots revolving around him— some of which he himself may have instigated. He knew, for example, of Ribbentrop's negotiations in Sweden, and of Wolff's in Italy. He even knew that Himmler was dawdling with the Jews. But Hitler continued to allow these men to negotiate as if in his name. If a negotiation failed, he would deny any knowledge of it; if it succeeded, he could take the credit.

But it is doubtful that he knew his proposed "scorched earth" directive was being actively opposed by his ablest minister, Albert Speer, before Speer himself boldly criticized the idea in a memorandum on March 18:

There is no question but that the German economy will collapse in four to eight weeks. . . . After the collapse the war cannot be continued even militarily. . . . We must do everything to safeguard the lives of our people, even if on the most primitive level . . . We have no right at this stage of the war to carry out demolitions which might affect the very existence of the people. If our enemies wish to destroy this nation, which has fought with unique bravery, then this historical shame shall rest exclusively upon them. On us rests the duty of leaving to the nation every possibility of insuring its reconstruction in the distant future . . .

Hitler had always admired Speer as a fellow architect and felt a personal warmth for him extended to few others. Perhaps that was one reason why these words so infuriated him. If he had ever wavered in his determination to scorch German earth, Speer's memorandum spurred him to action. He summoned Speer and said heatedly, "If the war is lost, the Reich will also perish! That's inevitable. It is not necessary to worry about the basic requirements for people to continue a primitive existence. On the contrary, it will be better to destroy these things ourselves because this country will have proved to be the weaker one and the future will belong solely to the stronger eastern nation [Russia]. Besides, those who remain after the battle will be the inferior ones, for the good ones will have been killed."

The Führer peremptorily dismissed Speer and dictated the order Speer had tried to stop. It called for the destruction of all military, industrial, transportation and communication installations, rather than letting them fall into the hands of the enemy. Nazi Gauleiters and defense leaders were to help the military carry out these measures. "All directives opposing this," the order concluded, "are invalid."

Ever since Stalingrad, Hitler had been making similarly rash and arbitrary decisions, and ever since the July 20 bombing, he had become short-tempered and inflexible. Many of his advisers noted with dismay that now he often had only a single desperate solution for a problem, not several alternatives as in the past.

With his chauffeur Kempka and the household servants and secretaries, however, Hitler continued to be considerate and polite, but even they could see he was under increasing strain. "I am lied to on all sides," he told one of his secretaries. "I can rely on no one, they all betray me, the whole business makes me sick. If it weren't for my faithful Morell [the physician who gave him so many pills] I'd be absolutely knocked out—and those idiot doctors want to get rid of him. What would become of me without Morell was a question they didn't ask. If anything happens to me Germany will be left without a leader. I have no successor. The first, Hess, is mad; the second, Göring, has lost the sympathy of the people, and the third, Himmler, would be rejected by the Party."

He apologized for talking politics during lunch, and then said, "Rack your brains again and tell me who my successor is to be. This is the question that I keep on asking myself without ever getting an answer."

He revealed these same doubts to others in one of his last "private talks." After complaining that he was fated to try to accomplish everything in the short span of his own lifetime, he said, "I have now reached the stage where I wonder whether among my immediate successors there will be found a man predestined to raise and carry on the torch, when it has slipped from my hand. It has also been my fate to be the servant of a people with so tragic a past, a people so unstable, so versatile as the German people, a people who goes, according to circumstances, from one extreme to the other." It would have been ideal, he said, if there had been time to imbue German youth with National Socialism and then let future generations wage the inevitable war. "The task I have undertaken of raising the German people to the place in the world that is their due is unfortunately not a task that can be accomplished by a single man or in a single generation. But I have at least opened their eyes to their inherent greatness and I have inspired them to exaltation at the thought of the union of Germans in one great indestructible Reich. I have sown the good seed." And one day, he prophesied, that harvest would come. "The German people is a young and strong people, a people with its future before it."

## 2.

The foundation for the New Europe set up by Hitler's enemies at Yalta was already beginning to crack. The Big Three had drawn the plan in relative harmony but were deeply embroiled over its implementation. Their arguments centered on Poland. The Big Three representatives meeting in Moscow to form a new Polish government had reached an impasse. Molotov proclaimed over and over again that the Lublin government truly represented the people of Poland, whereas Harriman and Sir Archibald Clark Kerr, the British ambassador to the Soviet Union, contended that a more representative government, including such men as Mikolajczyk, must be set up.

While they argued, Poles in London and America attacked Yalta with increasing bitterness. "I consider that a great calamity has occurred!" General Anders accused Churchill, who tartly replied, "It is your own fault."

Churchill's words belied his true position. Secretly he was fighting Poland's battle. He was still trying to persuade Roosevelt to join him in opposing Stalin. Together, he pleaded, they should send a message demanding that the Soviet leader honor the Yalta agreement and help set up a truly democratic government in Poland.

On March 11 Roosevelt finally answered Churchill's pleas:

. . . I FEEL THAT OUR PERSONAL INTERVENTION WOULD BEST BE WITHHELD UNTIL EVERY OTHER POSSIBILITY OF BRINGING THE SOVIET GOVERNMENT INTO LINE HAS BEEN EXHAUSTED. I VERY MUCH HOPE THEREFORE THAT YOU WILL NOT SEND A MESSAGE TO UNCLE JOE AT THIS JUNCTURE, ESPECIALLY AS I FEEL THAT CERTAIN PARTS OF YOUR PROPOSED TEXT MIGHT PRODUCE A REACTION QUITE CONTRARY TO YOUR INTENT. . . .

Throughout the Balkans the Soviets were openly foisting Communist governments on the liberated areas, and unless Communism was stopped now, Churchill saw that it would gain dangerous momentum. Reluctantly he deferred his own message to Stalin, but entreated the President to let Harriman and Clark Kerr raise the points enumerated in his proposed message.

. . . POLAND HAS LOST HER FRONTIER. IS SHE NOW TO LOSE HER FREEDOM? . . . I BELIEVE THAT COMBINED DOGGED PRESSURE AND PERSISTENCE ALONG THE LINES ON WHICH WE HAVE BEEN WORKING AND MY PROPOSED DRAFT MESSAGE TO STALIN WOULD VERY LIKELY SUCCEED.

Bernard Baruch also found Roosevelt reluctant to make a decision when he visited the White House on March 15. They talked about Yalta, and then about the postwar world. "We learned a lot of lessons in World War One," Baruch said. "As soon as the shooting's over, everyone is a hero. The American efforts will be minimized. We must keep ourselves strong and settle problems before we dismiss our troops."

"Bernie, how long do you think it will be before we have real peace in the world?" Roosevelt suddenly asked.

"Five or ten years."

"Good God, no!"

"If we're to have peace we have to find men who know how to wage peace and who know how to get people back to work at jobs of their choosing."

Roosevelt particularly liked the last phrase and repeated it. "Yes, that's what we have to do."

"It also depends on the position we take at the peace table. Are you thinking of running for another term? You can't. You have to make up your mind who should follow you." He mentioned three or four candidates, but Roosevelt only stared out the window at the Potomac River.

"We've got to make up our minds," Baruch pressed. "How to draw up a treaty? What kind of a peace? And who will succeed you?"

But still Roosevelt said nothing. He had many problems not known even to such a close confidant as Baruch. Stimson had recently revealed that an atom bomb would probably be ready soon for testing, and while it looked as if it might work, no one could visualize its implementation or its possible effect on the postwar world.

In these trying days the President was getting more irritable. For the first time his wife realized that he "could no longer bear to have a real discussion." If she disagreed, he got upset. "Franklin was no longer the calm and imperturbable person who, in the past, had always goaded me on to vehement arguments when questions of policy came up. It was just another indication of the change which we were all so unwilling to acknowledge."

This was illustrated by his answer on March 16 to Churchill's second request for a firmer stand against Stalin on Poland. He said he could not agree that they faced a breakdown on the Yalta agreement, and wanted Harriman and Clark Kerr to continue negotiating with Molotov in Moscow. Churchill conjectured that this and other recent messages "were not his own," and sent Roosevelt a personal and nostalgic message which he hoped would "ease the uphill march of official business":

. . . OUR FRIENDSHIP IS THE ROCK ON WHICH I BUILD FOR THE FUTURE OF THE WORLD, SO LONG AS I AM ONE OF THE BUILDERS. I ALWAYS THINK OF THOSE TREMENDOUS DAYS WHEN YOU DEVISED

LEND-LEASE. . . . I REMEMBER THE PART OUR PERSONAL RELA-
TIONS HAVE PLAYED IN THE ADVANCE OF THE WORLD CAUSE, NOW
NEARING ITS FIRST MILITARY GOAL . . .

AS I OBSERVED LAST TIME, WHEN THE WAR OF THE GIANTS IS OVER
THE WARS OF THE PYGMIES WILL BEGIN. THERE WILL BE A TORN,
RAGGED, AND HUNGRY WORLD TO HELP TO ITS FEET; AND WHAT
WILL UNCLE JOE OR HIS SUCCESSOR SAY TO THE WAY WE SHOULD
BOTH LIKE TO DO IT? . . .

ALL GOOD WISHES.

WINSTON

### 3.

The Remagen bridgehead had expanded more than ten miles eastward
and patrols of the 9th Division were approaching their objective, the
Frankfurt–Cologne Autobahn. Despite air and artillery attacks, the
Ludendorff Bridge still stood, and in desperation the Germans brought
up a huge tank-mounted 540-mm. gun, the "Karl Howitzer." This monster, weighing 132 tons, fired a 4400 lb. shell. After a few rounds that
failed to hit the bridge, it had to be pulled back for repairs. Twelve
supersonic V-2s were launched from Holland. They landed in a scattered pattern, with only one causing any appreciable damage when it hit
a house 300 yards east of the bridge, killing three Americans.

The bridge was being jolted as much by reverberations from nearby
American anti-aircraft batteries and 8-inch howitzers as from German
shells. At three o'clock in the afternoon on March 17, engineers were
ready to weld a huge plate over the almost severed arch. Once that was
in place, the bridge would be secure. Lieutenant Colonel Clayton Rust,
commander of the 276th Engineer Combat Battalion, was in the center
of the bridge checking the progress of the work when he heard a sharp
report, like a rifle shot. As he looked up he heard another, and saw part
of the structure break off. Before he could give the alarm, the bridge
trembled and dust rose from the wooden planking. The workers dropped
their tools and dashed for the nearest shore. Rust started to run back
toward the Remagen side as the center span vibrated, then slowly sank
toward the river, dragging the two truss spans off the abutments with a
penetrating metallic shriek. The entire bridge plunged into the Rhine.
Rust and many of his men were swept downstream to the treadway bridge,
where they were pulled to safety. But twenty-eight were killed outright
or drowned.

In Spa, General Hodges had just phoned Millikin to tell him that he
was relieved as commander of III Corps. "I have some bad news for
you," he began.

"Sir," Millikin interrupted, "I have some bad news for you too. The railway bridge has just collapsed."

With the Ludendorff Bridge down, Skorzeny's frogmen decided to destroy the pontoon bridge upstream. Around seven o'clock they plunged into the cold waters of the Rhine, each man clinging to an empty five-gallon can to which were fastened four packages of "Plastit," a plastic explosive. But before they reached their goal, Americans operating the top-secret CDL (Canal Defense Lights—a powerful light beam whose source was undetectable) spotted and fired at the daring swimmers. Two men were drowned, and the rest captured.

Model's entire Army Group B had been smashed and its remnants shoved back across the Rhine by Montgomery and Hodges, who between them had taken about 150,000 prisoners. To the south SS General Paul Hausser's Army Group G was being backed up against the Rhine on the west bank, and was about to be surrounded by Patton's Third Army from the north and Lieutenant General Alexander Patch's Seventh Army from the south. Hausser, a witty and caustic man of sixty-five, realized that he was facing disaster, and urgently asked Kesselring to let him cross the Rhine before it was too late. "The policy of all-out defense west of the river can only end in tremendous losses and probable annihilation."

Kesselring hesitated.

"A decision to withdraw behind the Rhine must be made quickly," Hausser prodded impatiently.

"Rejected," Kesselring answered curtly. "Hold the line."

Hausser repeated his arguments but Kesselring only shook his head, and said, not angrily but almost apologetically, "These are my orders. You must hang on!" As soon as Kesselring had left the room, however, Hausser told his commanders to prepare for withdrawal in utmost secrecy.

Two days later, on March 15, Patton broke through Hausser's northern-most army and swept toward the Rhine. Hausser ordered a withdrawal, then phoned Kesselring and asked permission to do it.

"Hold your positions," Kesselring said, and then, "but avoid being encircled."

This was all Hausser needed. "Thank you!" he blurted and quickly hung up. But it was too late; the bulk of Army Group G was already doomed.

On the day the Ludendorff Bridge fell, Eisenhower told Patton in all seriousness, "The trouble with you people in Third Army is that you don't apppreciate your own greatness. You're not cocky enough. Let the world know what you are doing, otherwise the American soldier will not be appreciated at his full value."

Patton and his aide, Colonel Charles Codman, then flew with Eisenhower to Seventh Army headquarters in Lunéville. On the way the Supreme Commander continued to praise Third Army. "George," he said expansively, "you are not only a good general, you are a *lucky* general, and as you will remember, in a general, Napoleon prized luck above skill."

"Well," Patton replied with a laugh, "that's the first compliment you've paid me in the two and a half years we've served together."

In the meeting at Lunéville, Eisenhower mentioned that the West Wall was still standing in front of Patch's Seventh Army, while Patton had made a breakthrough, and then asked Patch if Patton could attack across the northern sector of the Seventh Army zone. Patch readily agreed. "We are all in the same army," he said.

Back at Third Army headquarters that night, Patton was relaxed and gay at dinner. "I think Ike had a good time," he said. "They ought to let him out oftener."

"What I can't get over was his statement that Third Army isn't cocky enough," Hap Gay mused. "How do you explain it?"

"That's easy," Patton replied and stirred his soup. "Before long, Ike will be running for President. The Third Army represents a lot of votes." Noting the smiles on the faces around him, he said, "You think I'm joking? I'm not. Just wait and see."

# 13

## Operation "Sunrise"

**1.**

Upon returning to Italy, Karl Wolff found that his concern for the future was shared by one of his staff officers, SS-Standartenführer (Colonel) Eugen Dollmann, a handsome, sophisticated man with a caustic tongue. To friends, he was witty; to enemies, merely malicious. His mother was Italian and he had many social and intellectual ties in Italy. Wolff even called him Eugenio. Wolff also had many discussions on this subject with Dr. Rudolf Rahn, the German ambassador to Mussolini's neo-Fascist government. Two years earlier, when he was German plenipotentiary in Tunis, Rahn had helped save the Jewish population of that country from extinction.

The three men were sure that Italian partisans in northern Italy would set up a Communist government if German resistance suddenly collapsed. Together with the French Communists to the west and Tito to the east, they would form a wide belt of Bolshevism stretching across southern Europe. The only solution was to arrange an orderly surrender of German forces so that the West could take over northern Italy before the partisans seized control. Soon after this conversation, Dollmann casually remarked at a party that he was "tired of the damn war" and that it was too bad someone couldn't get in touch with the Allies. This indiscretion could have wrecked the plan but had the opposite effect. Guido Zimmer, a minor SS officer, overheard Dollmann. Luckily, he too felt the war was lost and, as a devout Catholic, wanted to prevent senseless death and destruction. Zimmer concluded that if Dollmann felt this way, so did Wolff.

Zimmer thought he knew just the man they needed as an intermediary: Baron Luigi Parrilli, formerly a representative of the American Nash-Kelvinator Corporation, manufacturers of refrigerators, and son-in-law of a Milan industrialist. Zimmer had heard rumors that Parrilli was secretly helping some Italian Jews escape the country. He called on the baron and repeated what Dollmann had said. Like Wolff, Parrilli feared a Communist take-over in northern Italy, where he had substantial financial interests, and he listened with mounting interest as Zimmer explained that only Wolff could bring such a scheme to a successful conclusion, since it was his task as head of the SS and Police to suppress such plots.

It all made sense to Parrilli and he promised to help. On February 21 he took a train to Zürich, Switzerland, to contact his old friend Dr. Max Husmann, headmaster of a well-known boys' school in Zugerberg. Husmann was sympathetic but didn't feel the Allies would enter into any negotiations inimical to Russia. Nevertheless, he telephoned a friend, Major Max Waibel, a forty-four-year-old career officer who had studied at the universities of Basel and Frankfurt, graduating with a doctorate in political science. Waibel too was aware of the Communist threat in northern Italy. Genoa was the port primarily used by the Swiss, and if it went Communist, his country's economy would suffer. Waibel knew that if he conspired and was caught his career would be ruined, but a plan involving Wolff intrigued him and he promised to co-operate—not officially, of course, since that would have meant violating Switzerland's neutrality.

Husmann could not have chosen a better man to further the plan. Waibel was a top intelligence officer of the Swiss Army who could arrange to bring any German negotiators secretly into Switzerland. He also knew Allen W. Dulles, a mysterious figure who was commonly supposed to be Roosevelt's personal representative in Switzerland.

In 1942 Dulles had opened a Berne office, using the vague title of "Special Assistant to the United States Minister." The Swiss press, however, persisted in calling Dulles "Roosevelt's Special Representative" despite his denials. He was, in fact, neither what he claimed to be or denied being. He was Major General William J. Donovan's OSS representative for the area of Germany, southeastern Europe, and parts of France and Italy. Dulles was the son of a Presbyterian minister, the grandson of one U. S. Secretary of State and nephew of another, and had practiced law for fifteen years in the office of his elder brother, John Foster Dulles. He was a big, relaxed, friendly man who usually wore tweeds and puffed a pipe. He looked like a professor, secure in some endowed chair, but took to political intelligence operations with great zest, and particularly enjoyed slipping in and out of the backs of restaurants or disappearing mysteriously at dinner parties.

The day after Husmann's phone call, February 22, Waibel invited Dulles and his chief assistant, Gero von S. Gaevernitz, to dinner and told them he had two friends who very much wanted to discuss a matter of mutual interest with them. "If you like, I'll introduce them to you after dinner," he said. Dulles, of course, could not commit himself but suggested that his assistant meet the "two friends" first.

Gaevernitz was urbane and handsome, with a dash of mystery about him. His father, Gerhard von Schulze Gaevernitz, a noted Liberal, university professor, author and member of the German parliament in pre-Nazi days, had helped draw up the Weimar Constitution. Throughout most of his life he, together with his political friends, had been working for an American-British-German alliance as the surest way to secure world peace. His final book was a reply to Spengler's *Decline of the West,* and expressed ultimate faith in democracy.

Young Gaevernitz had received his doctorate in economics in Frankfurt and went to New York in 1924, where he worked in the international banking business and became an American citizen. Upon Hitler's arrival to power he put his father's beliefs into practice. It was his particular task, he felt, to build and maintain a close line of contact between the anti-Nazi forces in Germany and the U. S. government. Some of these anti-Nazi leaders already knew and trusted him; he, in turn, felt that if he could convince Dulles of their sincerity, much might be done to overthrow the Hitler regime or shorten the war in some other way. When Dulles opened his office in Berne he asked Gaevernitz to work for him. Gradually a very close association developed between the two men.

Parrilli told Gaevernitz of the situation in Italy. Gaevernitz listened with polite suspicion—it was all too fantastic—but he said he would see Parrilli again if there was a concrete offer. Parrilli asked if Gaevernitz or an associate would be willing to speak directly with Zimmer or Dollmann.

"That might be arranged," Gaevernitz replied, and the meeting was over.

Parrilli returned to Italy, and for the first time Wolff himself was informed of the contact with Dulles. He decided to abandon his efforts to negotiate through the Pope or the English, and sent Dollmann to Switzerland. On March 3 Major Waibel spirited Dollmann and Zimmer across the border at Chiasso, where they were met by Parrilli and Dr. Husmann. To their amazement Dollmann acted as an equal, not a suppliant. At the Bianchi Restaurant in Lugano he announced that he expected the Allies to negotiate a "just peace" that would thwart Communist aspirations in northern Italy. Dr. Husmann replied that Germany was in no position to bargain and that it was folly to imagine that the West could be separated from the Soviet Union until the war ended.

Dollmann listened without comment to what he considered a tedious and condescending lecture until Husmann said Germany's only hope was unconditional surrender. Then the colonel's face flushed and he jumped to his feet. "You mean treason?" he cried. Apparently, surrender to him was not treasonous if the terms were right. He said Germany was in too good a bargaining position to bow to unconditional surrender. There was still an intact and undefeated army of 1,000,000 men in Italy.

"Think it over," Husmann said. "Your situation is hopeless. Speak to your friends."

Dollmann did not care to pursue the argument with a middleman. He wished Dulles' representative would arrive. But when this man—it was a Paul Bloom, not Gaevernitz—finally appeared, he too said the terms would have to be unconditional surrender. He did add that Germans of good will who helped bring about the end of hostilities would be shown consideration, and handed Dollmann a piece of paper. On it were the names of two imprisoned leaders of the non-Communist Italian resistance movement, Ferruccio Parri and Major Usmiani. The whole thing reminded Dollmann of a "game of forfeits at a schoolgirls' party," but he kept a straight face and asked, "What about these two men?"

Parrilli explained that Dulles would consider it a token of good will if they were set free and smuggled from Italy into Switzerland. It was preposterous: Parri would be recognized immediately. Despite these misgivings Dollmann said he would do his best and the second meeting ended with all shaking hands amicably.

The demand for unconditional surrender did not outrage Wolff as much as it had Dollmann; at least negotiations had begun and perhaps in further discussions more honorable terms could be secured. The release of two important political prisoners was another matter. It was a foolhardy risk that might endanger the whole plan, but Wolff decided it was the only way to impress Dulles. Dollmann advised him to go to Switzerland: his presence there as Supreme SS Commander in Italy would carry tremendous weight with the Americans. Wolff said he would have to think it over. It would be extremely dangerous, since he was so well known in Switzerland.

The following day he drove to Kesselring's headquarters. Wolff looked on him almost as an elder brother and hoped this friendship would enable him to get the eventual approval that was needed to surrender. Without mentioning names, he told the Feldmarschall that he had made contact with Americans in Switzerland and hinted that a negotiated peace might be arranged. Kesselring was properly noncommittal, but gave Wolff the impression that if an honorable peace could be arranged, he would be for it.

The next day Parrilli met with Wolff at Lake Garda and, in the name of Dulles, invited him to a conference at Zürich on March 8. Wolff accepted.

It was an eventful March 8. The bridge at Remagen was seized and Kesselring was summoned to Berlin, relieved of duty in Italy and dispatched to the western front. Earlier in the day Wolff and Dollmann, together with Parri and Usmiani—the two Italian partisans—were clandestinely escorted into Switzerland by one of Waibel's men and brought by train to Zürich, where the prisoners were placed in a private room at the Hirslandenklinik in an exclusive suburb. Neither Parri nor Usmiani had yet been told why they had been released from their Italian prisons.

In the evening Waibel brought Dulles and Gaevernitz to the hospital. Parri, who until the previous night had been in the hands of the SS, was certain he was about to be killed, and when he saw his old friend Dulles he burst into tears. It was a moving scene but to Dulles it was even more —a pledge of good faith. He said he was now willing to meet Wolff. About an hour later Husmann escorted General Wolff to an old-fashioned building near the lake where Dulles maintained an apartment for secret meetings.

Gaevernitz was the first to approach Wolff, whom he wanted to put in a relaxed mood before he talked to Dulles. "General, I have heard a great deal about you," he began. When Wolff stared at him he hastily added, "What I heard is greatly to your credit." As it happened, Countess Mechtilde Podewils had some time before told Gaevernitz that an influential Nazi—he was sure it was Wolff—helped her save Romano Guardini from being sent to a concentration camp. "General, I understand that you saved the life of Guardini, the famous Catholic philosopher. I believe we have a friend in common, a lovely lady who has told me a great deal about you." Wolff smiled.

Dulles was introduced to the Germans and Dr. Husmann opened the discussion. "General Wolff," he said, "did it become clear to you in the course of our long talk on the train that the war is irrevocably lost for Germany?"

Wolff had already made up his mind that peace must be bought even at the price of personal humiliation and said yes.

"Was it clear from our discussion that only an unconditional surrender can be considered?" Husmann asked.

"Yes," Wolff answered dutifully.

"Should you nevertheless try to speak on behalf of Himmler," the professor went on, "the conversation would last no more than a few seconds, for Mr. Dulles would have to excuse himself. Wouldn't you, Mr. Dulles?" Dulles puffed on his pipe and nodded.

Wolff said he felt it was a crime against the German people to continue the war. As a good German, he would take any risk to help bring an end to it. There was a tone of sincerity in these words, and for the first time Gaevernitz thought something might come of the meeting.

Wolff said he commanded rear echelon army units in Italy as well as the SS and Police. "I am willing to place myself and my entire organization at your disposal to end hostilities," he continued, but to do this he had to get Wehrmacht approval. He told them about Kesselring's show of sympathy. Once the Feldmarschall irrevocably committed himself, he said, this would influence other commanders on other fronts to capitulate.

Months before, Gaevernitz had told Dulles that many German generals were at the point of turning against Hitler and that he was even then working on a plan to induce five captured German generals to inspire widespread revolt. As Wolff continued to talk Gaevernitz's suspicions vanished; he was convinced of the man's sincerity; Wolff asked nothing for himself and his reasoning made sense. Dulles was just as convinced. Wolff, he felt, was not a creature of Hitler's or Himmler's, and negotiations with him could very well end in a complete German capitulation in Italy.

Wolff had come prepared to give further proof of his good faith. He declared that he was curbing unnecessary destruction in Italy and had already, on his own initiative and at extreme personal risk, saved the famous paintings from the Uffizi and Pitti palaces, as well as King Victor Emmanuel's priceless coin collection. These were all in a safe place, he assured them, and would definitely not be shipped off to Germany.

"These are about half of the paintings," he said. In awe, the Americans studied a list of 300 paintings, including works by Botticelli, Titian and other masters.

Dulles made up his mind. He said he would deal with Wolff, provided the general made no other Allied contacts. This was agreeable to Wolff, who also promised to do his utmost to protect the lives of prisoners and prevent the destruction of factories, power stations and art treasures.

On this note of promise and good will the hour-long meeting ended, and Waibel escorted the German party back to the border. On the Gotthard Express they discussed a possible Cabinet for the new Reich: for President, no one but Kesselring. Foreign Minister? Von Neurath had done well once, why not now? Finance Minister? The old fox, Papa Schacht, of course. Minister of Interior? General Wolff was suggested and, his face reddening slightly with embarrassment, he refused. It might look like a reward for co-operating with the Allies.

But he was returned to reality the moment he crossed the border and learned that Kesselring had just been recalled to Berlin by Hitler himself. Would he be replaced in Italy by someone Wolff could influence?

There was also an ominous message from Kaltenbrunner: Wolff was to report at once to Innsbruck, just on the other side of the Austrian-Italian border. Wolff was sure that Himmler's second-in-command had somehow learned about the negotiations with Dulles and that a trip to Innsbruck would end in jail, or even worse, that he might be killed. He decided to ignore the invitation.

Dulles informed General Donovan of the meeting with Wolff and was instructed to continue negotiations under the code name Operation "Sun-

rise Crossword." The two major generals on Alexander's staff who had
enjoyed Marshal Tobulkhin's hospitality in Hungary—the American Lyman Lemnitzer and the British Terence Airey, the field-marshal's chief
of intelligence—drove up to the Swiss border from Naples on March 15,
posing as American enlisted men but wearing civilian clothes. Their mission was to meet Wolff and make definite arrangements for the surrender.

At the Swiss customs office Lemnitzer satisfactorily answered numerous
questions, but Airey knew little about America. Fortunately it didn't
make any difference. Waibel had already instructed the border guards
to admit the two incognito generals no matter what they said.

After two days with Dulles in Berne they were taken to Lucerne, where
Waibel told them he had just received disturbing news from Italy: Kesselring had been replaced by Generaloberst Heinrich von Vietinghoff. Wolff
was on his way, however, to meet the two Allied generals as planned.

Gaevernitz drove the generals to Ascona, a village near Locarno overlooking Lake Maggiore, and installed them in his home, a picturesque old
farmhouse, where they stayed as his guests. At lunch the next day, March
19, Gaevernitz told them that Wolff had arrived with Dollmann and two
others and was being quartered in a house on the lake shore.

The SS general's meeting with Dulles, Lemnitzer, Airey and Gaevernitz
began at 3 P.M. that day. No one else was present in the small house
on the lake. While Gaevernitz acted as interpreter, and at times intervened
to help the negotiations along, Dulles said he was pleased that a leading
German was negotiating without making personal demands.

Wolff appreciated these sentiments but replied with the realistic prediction that the change of command in Italy threatened the entire operation. Perhaps Kesselring had been relieved of duty because the negotiations
had been discovered? There was even the possibility that they would all
be arrested upon return to Italy. Frau Wolff had already been confined
to her castle by a Kaltenbrunner decree. Wolff, nevertheless, promised
to do everything he could to effect the surrender. He was urged to visit
Kesselring as soon as possible in an effort to persuade him to make a
similar arrangement on the western front. Wolff thought it best if he
simply asked Kesselring to approve the Italian surrender. Kesselring could
then covertly advise Vietinghoff to support Wolff.

Gaevernitz led Wolff aside onto the terrace, and asked how many
political prisoners were in Italian concentration camps. Wolff thought
there were several thousand of various nationalities. "There are orders
to kill them," he said.

"Will you obey those orders?"

Wolff paced the terrace and finally stopped in front of Gaevernitz.
"No," he said.

"Will you give me your word of honor?"

Wolff grasped Gaevernitz's hand. "Yes, you can rely on me."

**2.**

That same day unfounded rumors of peace negotiations swept along the western front. These were given some credence at Hodges' headquarters when Bradley phoned at noon and told the First Army commander to fly immediately to Luxembourg for a meeting with him and Patton.

Hodges found it was only another military conference. Bradley started by announcing that Eisenhower had just given his permission to use nine divisions at Remagen. Hodges could at last enlarge the bridgehead and prepare to attack out of it to the north and northeast.

Patton was about to congratulate Hodges when Bradley added that the attack could not start until after March 23—the day Montgomery was scheduled to cross the Rhine *en masse*. Bradley then told Patton he "felt it better for Third Army not to try a crossing over the Rhine in the vicinity of Koblenz." Instead he should make it in the Mainz-Worms area. In other words, Patton could not attempt an immediate crossing at Koblenz, where he was, but at Mainz, which was still more than ten miles away.

Patton flew back to his headquarters in a gloomy mood, convinced that if Montgomery crossed the Rhine first, the bulk of Allied supplies and reserves would be drawn to the north and Third Army would have to go on the defensive. He had only four days to beat the British across the Rhine; this was not time enough even under ordinary conditions to reach and clear the Mainz area. There was only one solution: make his men do the extraordinary.

At Rheims, "Beetle" Smith had just convinced Eisenhower he "must get some relaxation or face a nervous breakdown," and the Supreme Commander left for a short holiday in Cannes. As usual he thoughtfully filled his plane with extra passengers.

**3.**

From the beginning Ambassadors Harriman and Clark Kerr had kept Molotov informed about Operation "Sunrise," and from the beginning the Foreign Commissar had adamantly demanded that a Russian officer accompany Lemnitzer and Airey to Switzerland. But Harriman advised the State Department that the Russians would certainly not allow any Allied officers to take part in a similar action in the east. Western acquiescence would only be regarded as a sign of weakness and as encouragement to even more unreasonable demands in the future. The Combined Chiefs concurred, and so the historic meeting took place at Ascona on March 19 without Soviet participation.

Two days later Churchill told Eden to inform the Russians of the results reached at Ascona. The reaction was quick and violent. Within hours Molotov handed Clark Kerr a reply couched in terms rarely used by diplomats. Undoubtedly angered by having Soviet political aspirations in northern Italy so dangerously threatened, Molotov accused the Allies of conniving with Germans "behind the backs of the Soviet Union, which is bearing the brunt of the war against Germany," and labeled the whole affair "not a misunderstanding but something worse."

Harriman received an equally insulting letter, which he relayed to Washington. For several weeks he had been urging Roosevelt to take a firmer stand against the Soviets and he hoped this show of Russian venom would at last spur the President to action. The ill-tempered letter, he cabled, proved that the Soviet leaders had drastically changed their tactics since Yalta.

THE ARROGANT LANGUAGE OF MOLOTOV'S LETTER, I BELIEVE, BRINGS OUT IN THE OPEN A DOMINEERING ATTITUDE TOWARD THE UNITED STATES WHICH WE HAVE BEFORE ONLY SUSPECTED. IT HAS BEEN MY FEELING THAT SOONER OR LATER THIS ATTITUDE WOULD CREATE A SITUATION WHICH WOULD BE INTOLERABLE TO US.
I, THEREFORE, RECOMMEND THAT WE FACE THE ISSUE NOW BY ADHERING TO THE REASONABLE AND GENEROUS POSITION THAT WE HAVE TAKEN AND BY ADVISING THE SOVIET GOVERNMENT IN FIRM BUT FRIENDLY TERMS TO THAT EFFECT.

Privately Harriman could not see why Stalin "would have made the agreements at Yalta if he intended at the time to break them so rapidly." He felt that "the Marshal may have originally intended to keep these promises but had changed his mind for a number of reasons." First, some members of the Praesidium of the Communist Party had criticized Stalin for making too many concessions at the conference. Second, Stalin was getting more and more suspicious of everything and everybody; when American shuttle fliers smuggled several Soviet citizens out of Russia, Stalin had branded it part of an official U. S. plot.* Third, and most important, Stalin had confidently believed at Yalta that the Red Army would be accepted as a liberator by the peoples of eastern Europe and the Balkans. It was now obvious, however, that the Lublin Poles could not deliver Poland to Stalin in a free election, and that throughout the

---

* Much later Khrushchev told Harriman, "I am aware that you knew Stalin well and had a certain regard for him. So I feel you should know that in his later years he became more and more suspicious of everyone. When we came into his office, we didn't know if we'd come out alive to return to our families. A man can't live that way."

Balkans the Soviets already were regarded as conquerors rather than purveyors of freedom.

Whatever the reasons,* Stalin had decided to ignore the promises made at Yalta. This was a simple matter for a man who once blandly told Harriman—in connection with another understanding—that he had not broken his word but had simply changed his mind.

Another factor that must have encouraged Stalin's abrupt turnabout was the revelation made by Roosevelt at Yalta that the United States would withdraw its forces from Europe as soon as possible. This was probably the greatest Allied mistake of the conference, for, with this assurance, Stalin could, and did, treat subsequent American protests—including the President's personal appeals—with contempt.

---

* Philip Moseley, U. S. representative on the E.A.C. and one of the most authoritative observers of the Soviet scene, further believes that "the dominant voice in Soviet policy may well have passed from the Foreign Ministry . . . into the hands of the powerful economic ministries, bent on squeezing every bit of economic relief out of Germany, and of the secret police, responsible directly to the Politburo for enforcing Soviet control in occupied areas."

# 14

# The Shell House

**1.**

At 4 A.M. on April 9, 1940, German troops had crossed into Denmark without warning; others landed at a number of ports, including Copenhagen. As bombers flew ominously over the country an hour later, the German minister to Denmark handed the Danish government a memorandum demanding submission. The Germans claimed they had come merely to protect Denmark from invasion by the Western Allies, not with hostile intent. They promised to respect Danish neutrality and refrain from interference in internal affairs.

The Danish government capitulated, but the 4,500,000 hardy and independent Danes refused to accept this humiliation, and it was not long before little groups of resistance fighters sprang up spontaneously. As in Poland, there were no political distinctions and it was common to see Communists working side by side with Conservatives. Leaders emerged from varied sources. There were university professors, businessmen, workers, professional men—even a literary agent.

The Danes went beyond conventional sabotage and work delays; they also waged an imaginative psychological war. In the beginning they walked past the Germans as if they didn't exist, and soon stories began to circulate—probably apocryphal, but nevertheless indicative of the attitude of the Danes—such as this one: A guard standing inside his tiny, shoulder-high circular fortress in the middle of Copenhagen was surprised to find passers-by finally noticing him. They were laughing at a sign some wit had hung on the outside: "He has no pants on." A program of ridicule had begun.

By August, 1943, there were six or seven major acts of sabotage a day. The Germans retaliated by occupying the factories, which touched off a wave of spontaneous strikes. In desperation the Germans flooded the streets with troops, established a curfew and threatened to take hostages, but this only aggravated the situation.

Dr. Werner Best, the chief Nazi administrator, flew to Berlin and pleaded for patience and a more lenient policy. The rising revolt, he said, could be curbed by concessions. But the Führer was not to be dissuaded, and on August 28 sent an ultimatum to the Danish government demanding martial law, direct German censorship, a total ban on strikes and meetings and the death penalty for sabotage. The next day the Danish government, with the full approval of King Christian X, rejected the demands. That night German soldiers openly seized control of Denmark. But Hitler's troubles were only beginning, for the entire country was now unified behind the resistance movement.

The following month the Germans ordered the arrest of Danish Jews, but by the time special police started making the rounds, all except 477 elderly Jews had mysteriously disappeared. The others, about 6000, had been smuggled across the Sound to Sweden by the aroused Danes. For the first time the Nazis had met solid resistance by an entire population to their "final solution."

This clandestine mass operation inspired the Danes to further resistance. Planned by the Freedom Council, a seven-man coalition of the dominant resistance groups, railway sabotage increased until German troop movements fell to 25 percent below normal. The partisans became so aggressive that whole factories were destroyed, including the Globus plant in Copenhagen, which made vital parts for V-2 rockets.

If the Danes were not officially at war with Germany, they certainly acted as if they were, and though occupied, were contributing to the fall of Hitler's regime. By the fall of 1944, however, the Gestapo had collected so much information on underground activities that resistance leaders asked the Royal Air Force to destroy the Gestapo files stored in Aarhus University. The subsequent raid was so successful that the resistance requested another, this time on the Shell House in Copenhagen, which contained the bulk of the Gestapo archives. But the British were reluctant to grant this request; the top floor of the Shell House had been turned into a jail for very important Danish prisoners.

A month later the resistance radio again appealed: the material in the Shell House was so damaging that it had to be destroyed regardless of possible danger to the Danish prisoners. After considerable deliberation the Air Ministry finally reversed its decision, and the planning of the raid began. Models of all buildings within a kilometer of the target were constructed, as well as replicas of the Danish landscape to be overflown. Underground members of the Danish press provided the British with the latest photographs of the area. The revealing pictures were published in Copenhagen's *Berlingske Tidende* as illustrations for an innocuous feature story. The Nazi censors missed their significance and the following day the newspaper was relayed to London via Stockholm.

**2.**

On March 19 Group Captain Bob Bateson told some seventy British airmen in the Norfolk airdrome operations room that the following noon they would bomb the Shell House in three waves. Svend Truelsen, who was not only involved in Denmark's underground espionage but also a major in British Army Intelligence, then described the target: it was U-shaped, four stories high and was conveniently camouflaged with brown and green stripes—the only building in the city so marked. Truelson instructed the fliers to come in low and skip their bombs into the base at the front of the building. That would give the prisoners on the top floor a chance to escape down the back stairs.

The next day the weather was so poor that the operation was postponed. But March 21 dawned clear, and a single Mosquito bomber took off in a strong wind from the Norfolk airdrome. Its pilot, a Wing Commander Smith, gave the signal and eighteen other Mosquito bombers began taking off by twos. Then twenty-eight P-51 Mustang fighters took to the air.

"Smith" was Air Vice-Marshal Basil Embry, who had personally commanded the raid on Aarhus. He would lead the entire formation to the target area, where Captain Bateson was to take over. The bombers skimmed so low across the North Sea that the gale-lashed waters sprayed the windshields, clouding them with salt. But the bombers stayed down, hoping to sneak under German radar.

At the Shell House one of the thirty-two prisoners in the top-floor jail, Chief Inspector Christen Lyst Hansen of the Danish Police, was being led downstairs. He asked where they were taking him.

"I'm not allowed to tell you," the guard said, then whispered, "Frøslev" —a concentration camp near the German border, where, it was rumored, the elite prisoners were to be shot. But Hansen reached the main door just as the car bound for the concentration camp drove away, and he was returned to his cell.

Around nine o'clock a new group of prisoners was being marched up to a room on the third floor of the Shell House. For two hours a German judge and a Danish interpreter interrogated one of these prisoners, Jens Lund, and each time he refused to answer a question he was struck by both the judge and interpreter. At about 11:15 two machine-gun straps were fetched and Lund knew he was going to get a severe beating. All he could think about was the miraculous escape of Pastor Harald Sandbaek from the Gestapo during the air raid on Aarhus. He prayed it might happen again.

The Mosquitoes were approaching Copenhagen at 150 feet. Through the salt-encrusted windshield Captain Bateson saw a large railroad yard and a moment later the landmark he was looking for—the lake just behind Shell House.

In the top-floor jail Professor Mogens Fog, a neurologist and a member of the Freedom Council, thought the roar came from German fighter planes diving at the roof to frighten the prisoners. Even the rattle of machine guns did not convince him that it was an actual attack, and he climbed to the top of his double bunk to peer out a tiny window. The planes were coming straight at him! He jerked his head back and leaped to the floor as bombs began their screeching descent. Scrambling under the bunk, he shielded his face with a suitcase.

On the floor below, Lund too heard the terrible noise of machine guns and asked what was the matter. The judge, his mouth open, said nothing and Lund figured the Germans were merely practicing. Suddenly there was a crash and the room tilted. The judge grabbed Lund and pulled him to the stairway as dust from pulverized walls rose in clouds. People were scurrying down in panic. Lund wrenched himself away from the judge and slid down the banister, past a mass of men and screaming women. At the second floor the stairway was so packed that he had to get off the banister. Part of the stairs collapsed and just in front of him a man vanished in a dark cloud of smoke and dust. To one side he saw a gaping hole in the wall and the street below, so he jumped onto the sidewalk.

The first six Mosquitoes successfully skipped most of their bombs into the base of Shell House, but air-raid sirens did not begin to blast until the second wave started to make its run. One plane came down too low; its wing swiped a railroad tower in the yards and bombs tumbled out just before the plane crashed into the Jeanne d'Arc School. Drenched in high-octane aviation gas, the school burst into flames. The other five Mosquitoes continued, one turning east to Dagmarhus, a structure housing another German headquarters, and the rest skip-bombed the Shell House. Those in the third wave were drawn by a great cloud of smoke rising near the railroad yards. They released their loads into the smoke and headed back for England, thinking they had bombed the target. The smoke, of course, had come from the blazing Jeanne d'Arc School.

As soon as the first attack was over, Professor Fog got out from under the bed and threw himself against the locked cell door. It wouldn't open. Then he heard the second wave and scrambled back under the bed. A few cells away, Police Inspector Hansen clung desperately to a bunk. The building seemed to sway and he was afraid he'd fall through the floor. When the roar of the bombers was gone he lunged at the wooden door; it wouldn't give. He grabbed a stool and battered it down. As he ran into the corridor he looked up and was astonished to see open sky. The entire roof had been blown off. Now he could hear Fog and other prisoners shouting and hammering on their cell doors. "We have to get them out!" he yelled to the lone German guard.

Fog heard all this and immediately shouted through the door, *"Die Nückeln!"*

The guard stood transfixed with fear and Hansen grabbed the keys from his pocket. The released prisoners fled down the back stairs, away from the conflagration in the front. Fog followed the others at first, but then reasoned that the Germans must have gone that way too and would be waiting below to recapture them. On the second floor he went to the front staircase, where he encountered a fellow prisoner, Dr. Brandt Rehberg. It was amusing, he thought, that of all the prisoners only the two professors thought of going to the front.

Rehberg, however, was just standing in shock, surrounded by a dozen dead bodies. Fog slapped his shoulder and said, "Shouldn't we go on?" They made their way through the wreckage to the main door, where they came upon an injured girl lying on the floor. Fog was dragging her into the street when he heard the wailing of sirens. The Hipos—Danish turncoat police—were coming! They abandoned the girl and hurried down the street, away from the sirens. Of the thirty-two prisoners, only six died in the blaze. The rest escaped to freedom.

J. Jalser was leading his six fire engines up to the blazing Shell House. He correctly surmised that most of the prisoners on the top floor would try to escape out the rear and started for the back of the building to save them. He was stopped at a barrier by a German officer who ordered him to take his engines to the front of the building and fight the main blaze. Jalser pretended he couldn't understand German; he wanted to see the fire destroy all the Gestapo records.

A volunteer fireman wearing rubber boots came over and offered to act as interpreter, but when Jalser nudged his foot he understood and left —and so did the disgusted German officer. Moments later several German fire trucks pulled up. Jalser pointed to a concrete shed and yelled "Explosives! Explosives!" Everyone scattered, including the guards at the barrier.

Free at last, Jalser led his men to the back of the Shell House, which they began hosing down. By this time the fire at the front of the building containing the Gestapo records was raging completely out of control. Within an hour the building was gutted.

The Jeanne d'Arc School was still burning when Jalser arrived with his fire trucks. Firemen and nuns were trying to drag out more than 100 children trapped in the blazing cellar. Jalser was appalled by the sight—concrete, chairs, bricks and children all mixed up together—and he heard one fireman saying over and over, "This is cruel, this is cruel!"

A girl hopelessly trapped in the bricks cried out, "My mother doesn't know where I am!"

To soothe her, a fireman said, "I phoned your mother."

"But we have no phone!" the girl whispered.

Another fireman, caught in the wreckage with the children, shouted, "Pull me out!" but his comrades were driven back by dust, smoke and flames.

Most of the children rescued from the inferno were terrified, but one little girl kept saying, "How dirty my dress is!" and dusted herself fastidiously. And one boy just asked for something to eat.

The Danes had rejoiced when they saw the Shell House going up in flames, together with evidence that would have led to the execution of hundreds of resistance fighters. Then they learned of the tragedy at the Jeanne d'Arc School, where eighty-three children, twenty nuns and three firemen died.

The next day the underground *Nordic News Service* spoke for all Denmark:

. . . We meet with gratitude the pilots who destroyed the monument of German infamous deeds and Gestapo terror in the heart of Copenhagen, the Shell Building . . .

Unfortunately, beyond the actual bombing goal a great number of Danes were killed, principally children in the French School in Frederiksberg Allé. . . . For those parents who lost their dearest ones there is no consolation; we can only express our deepest compassion.

The sacrifice which, indirectly, they have made in Denmark's battle should, however, incite the rest of us to bend every effort to the purpose of creating opportunity for other Danish children not only to live, but live in a free, secure Denmark where the war no longer strikes streets and alleys with death because aggressor nations so decided and because barbarians conduct a policy of oppression.

# 15

# Between Two Rivers

**1.**

By March 22 Hitler's Grossdeutschland was pressed between two rivers —the Oder and the Rhine. And from both east and west his enemies were poised for massive attacks which they were certain would bring final victory. Montgomery's assault across the Rhine, Operation "Plunder," was scheduled to start the next day, and unlike American ventures, was planned to the last detail. Everything was in its place and each unit knew exactly what it was supposed to do.

When the field-marshal first drew up the plans in late January he called on Lieutenant-General Miles Dempsey's Second British Army to carry the burden of attack and cross the Rhine just north of Wesel, a city strategically located about twenty miles north of Düsseldorf. Only a third of Simpson's Ninth U. S. Army would be involved and that—the XIX Corps—would play a minor role; it would support the main assault with a crossing at Rheinberg, a few miles below Wesel, and construct all the tactical bridges over the Rhine.

When Simpson received this directive he was "flabbergasted"; his troops were little more than bridge builders. Moreover, they would be under Dempsey, not him. He protested to Montgomery, who finally agreed to let him retain the XIX Corps within his command. On March 4, three days before the seizure of the bridge at Remagen, this corps suddenly burst through the German defenses and reached the banks of the Rhine ahead of schedule. Its commander, Major General Raymond McLain, phoned

Simpson with the rousing news that he had found "a fine place to cross the Rhine" just north of Düsseldorf, well hidden by trees. If he had been under Bradley instead of Montgomery, Simpson would have shoved across and then informed Army Group. But he knew Eisenhower would want him to go through channels, so he again went to Montgomery and asked permission to make an impromptu crossing of the river, pointing out that the Germans were so confused and stunned by the rapid advance that they had not yet built defenses on the east shores.

Without even glancing at the map prepared by Simpson, Montgomery said, "You can only use one division or less over there. There's no room to do anything. I want to stick to my plan." Only by strictly observing his schedule, he said, could he keep himself well balanced and the Germans off balance.

Patton and a number of other American officers felt Simpson was being held back so the British would have the honor of making the first massive assault crossing of the river. But Simpson who was more affected than anyone else considered Montgomery too professional a soldier to make a decision motivated only by national prestige; Monty simply wanted a tidy battle with no last-minute improvisations or changes to disturb the master plan.

But Montgomery decided to insure the success of "Plunder" with an afterthought of his own: an airdrop across the Rhine by two airborne divisions. It was named Operation "Varsity" and its mission was to "disrupt the hostile defenses of the Rhine in the Wesel sector . . ." It would be the first daylight Allied airborne operation and would come a few hours after the initial night crossings by the infantry.

For the task Major General Matthew Ridgway picked the British 6th Airborne and the U. S. 17th Airborne divisions, both part of his XVIII Airborne Corps. The British 'troopers were veterans of the Normandy drop but this would be the first airborne action for the Americans, although they had fought as infantrymen in the Bulge. On March 22 both units, morale high, were "sealed in," the British near East Anglia, England, and the Americans near Paris. The troop areas were surrounded by barbed wire, and special guards patrolled the airfields. If information about the drop zones leaked out, "Varsity" might end in disaster.

Even with these precautions, however, the Germans must have learned that an airdrop was imminent. Commentator Günther Weber broadcast from Berlin: "Allied airborne landings on a large scale, to establish bridgeheads east of the Rhine, must be expected. We are prepared."

George S. Patton was making his own personal plans to cross the Rhine. Instead of mounting a formal frontal assault to the river, he used his armor and armored infantry almost as if they were cavalry, making deep probes that were not only spectacular but netted a great bag of prisoners and saved numerous American lives. They also had brought him to the Rhine sooner than expected.

For the past three days, ever since getting Bradley's permission to cross near Mainz, he had been flying from headquarters to headquarters like a wild man—begging, coaxing, demanding and threatening. He wanted speed and more speed. He knew Montgomery was going over the Rhine the night of March 23 and he wanted to make his own crossing in the Mainz area first. He also felt sure that a quick, unheralded crossing would save lives and place him in position for even more spectacular gains into the heart of Germany.

On March 20 he flew to Major General Manton S. Eddy's XII Corps headquarters near Simmern. Pacing excitedly, he said, "Matt, I want you to cross the river at Oppenheim tomorrow!" Oppenheim was a town about fifteen miles south of Mainz.

"Just give us another day," Eddy replied.

"No!" Patton shouted and waved his arms.

Eddy, a big heavy-set man, stuck out his aggressive chin and stood his ground. But as soon as Patton petulantly stamped out, Eddy telephoned Major General S. Leroy "Red" Irwin of the 5th Division and said, "You've got to get across, Red. Georgie's been tramping up and down and yelling at us."

Irwin pushed his men so hard for the next thirty-six hours that they reached the Rhine at Oppenheim before nightfall on March 22. At ten o'clock they quietly started across the river in assault boats. The first wave landed before the surprised Germans could organize a defense, and by dawn six of Irwin's battalions had crossed. Without preparatory artillery, air bombardment or paratroopers, Patton had made the first assault crossing of the Rhine by boat since Napoleon—and at a cost of only twenty-eight men killed or wounded.

Word of the success was immediately sent to Third Army headquarters, but Patton's deputy chief of staff, Colonel Paul Harkins, suggested that the news be withheld from Bradley until the night of the twenty-third, just before the announcement of Montgomery's crossing. It was the kind of suggestion Patton liked to hear.

2.

The river protecting the other side of Germany, the Oder, had also been breached. Zhukov had three bridgeheads only fifty miles from Berlin, but the unexpected Steiner attack had forced the Russians to regroup before making the final assault on the capital.

Ever since Wenck's auto accident, Guderian had not received a single report from Himmler, the man responsible for holding back Zhukov. By mid-March the frustrated commander in chief of the eastern front drove to Army Group Vistula headquarters. Himmler's chief of staff, SS-Brigadeführer (Brigadier General) Heinz Lammerding, met Guderian at the headquarters entrance and said, "Can't you rid us of our commander?"

"That's purely a matter for the SS," Guderian replied, and asked where the Reichsführer was.

"He's down with the flu and is being treated by Professor Gebhardt at Hohenlychen."

At the nearby sanitarium Guderian found Himmler in apparent good health and urged him to resign as commander of Army Group Vistula. He reminded the Reichsführer that he was also national leader of the SS, chief of the German Police, Minister of the Interior and commander in chief of the Replacement Army. How could one man possibly fulfill the duties of all these posts?

The idea appealed to Himmler but he had reservations. "I can't go and say that to the Führer. He wouldn't like it if I came up with such a suggestion."

"Then you will authorize me to say it for you?" Guderian prompted.

Himmler nodded approval, and in the evening Guderian suggested to the Führer that the overworked Reichsführer be replaced on the Oder. Hitler too must have realized that a change was necessary, because he asked who should take over Army Group Vistula.

Guderian proposed Generaloberst Gotthard Heinrici, commander of the First Panzer Army, who was holding Schörner's right flank.

"I don't want him," Hitler said and suggested several other names.

"He's especially experienced with the Russians," Guderian pointed out. "They haven't broken through him yet." This impressed Hitler, and on March 20 a telegram was sent to Heinrici's Carpathian headquarters appointing him head of Army Group Vistula.

The following day Guderian encountered Himmler and Hitler strolling in the Chancellery garden. Guderian wondered if he could speak with Himmler in private, and Hitler accommodatingly walked off.

"The war can no longer be won," Guderian said without preamble. "The only problem now is finding the quickest way to put an end to the senseless slaughter and bombing. Except for Ribbentrop, you are the only man with contacts in neutral countries. Since the Foreign Minister is reluctant to ask Hitler to open negotiations, you must go with me to Hitler and urge him to arrange an armistice."

Himmler couldn't answer for a moment. "My dear General," he said finally, "it's too early for that."

"I don't understand you. It's not five minutes to twelve now, but five minutes past twelve. If we don't negotiate now, we'll never be able to do so at all. Don't you realize how desperate our situation has become?" But Himmler refused to commit himself; he preferred to carry on negotiations his own secretive way.

After the evening conference Hitler asked Guderian to remain. "I understand that your heart trouble has taken a turn for the worse," he said. The mere sound of Guderian's voice prophesying doom in the east was growing increasingly irksome to Hitler, and he wanted a replacement who wasn't a defeatist. "You must immediately take four weeks' sick leave."

Guderian knew what was behind Hitler's words. "At the moment I cannot leave my post, because I have no deputy." General Hans Krebs, Wenck's replacement, had been wounded in a recent bombing of OKH (Army High Command) headquarters at Zossen. "I'll try to find a deputy as quickly as possible," he said, though he had no intention of doing it, "and then I'll go on leave."

An adjutant interrupted. Minister of Production Speer wanted to talk to the Führer in private. "I can't see the Minister now—not for three days," Hitler said irritably and turned back to Guderian. "When someone asks to see me alone these days, it's because he has something unpleasant to tell me. I can't stand any more of these Job's comforters. His [Speer's] memoranda always begin with the words 'The war is lost!' And that's what he wants to tell me again now. I always put his memoranda away in the safe, unread."

Although Zhukov held three bridgeheads west of the Oder—one below Frankfurt, one above Küstrin and one midway between these two cities—the Germans still had two footholds of their own on the east bank, at Küstrin and Frankfurt. These two areas were obvious targets for Zhukov's final assault on Berlin, since paved highways ran directly to the capital from both cities.

The Küstrin bridgehead was under SS-Oberstgruppenführer (General) Heinz Rheinefarth, a police official little versed in military tactics, but Frankfurt's commander, Ernst Biehler, though only a colonel, was a competent, determined Wehrmacht officer who had turned his native city into a formidable *Festung*. After being wounded in the thigh and leg on the eastern front in late 1944, Biehler was sent to a hospital in Frankfurt. As the Russians surged toward the Oder in late January, he had hobbled out of the hospital on crutches to stop them with a pickup force of convalescents, stragglers, Volkssturm and 3000 artillery trainees.

One day in early February, Biehler was having tea with his wife and four children when he was called to the phone. He came back and said calmly, "Frankfurt an der Oder is to be a *Festung* and I am to make it one."

Five weeks later he had 30,000 men. Half were emplaced on the hills east of the river, while the other half remained on the west side of the Oder for training. Biehler's artillery was a motley collection of about 100 pieces: Yugoslav and Russian cannon, French 75s and German mortars. When twenty-five decrepit Panthers were sent by OKH as reinforcements, he buried them up to their turrets at strategic points. His only mobile armor were twenty-two panzer wagons ingeniously reassembled from wreckage. But he was beset by doubts, his arduous efforts notwithstanding. "What use am I really serving in this hole?" he asked Dr. Goebbels on one of the latter's inspection tours up front.

"We need this bridgehead across the Oder because we are planning to push against the Russians all the way to Posen." Biehler looked incredulous. "We are thinking of making peace with the West," Goebbels explained, "and then the Americans and British will help us fight the Russians. Or at least they'll let us bring all our armies from the western front to the east. And then we'll attack, and retake Posen." Goebbels peered at him urgently. "It does make sense for you to be in this hole! This is the bridgehead for the future."

Reassured, Biehler went from unit to unit, telling the men, "If you don't hold your ground, the Russians will take your motherland—your wives and children! We must all stay here!"

The man chosen to replace Himmler was small and middle-aged. Gotthard Heinrici was the son of a pastor, but on his mother's side the men had been soldiers since the twelfth century. He was efficient, methodical, and reliable, just the man needed to take over a chaotic front. For more than two years his Fourth Army had fought well in the Moscow area, but his promotion to the rank of Generaloberst was delayed by his stubborn insistence that the Gestapo cease interfering with his command. Following his recent successful defensive battles against the Russians, however, he was finally promoted and awarded the Knight's Cross with Oak Leaf Clusters.

He reported to Guderian, an old and trusted friend, on March 22. The streets of Zossen were still littered from an air raid. After greeting him warmly, Guderian said, "I personally called you up here—it's impossible with Himmler. He never executes the orders I issue; he doesn't submit proper reports. I've told Hitler he's incompetent and that he has never led a platoon across the river."

Heinrici asked for an overall picture. Guderian hesitated, then said, "The situation is very difficult and perhaps the only solution can be found in the west."

Heinrici wondered what this meant but dismissed the subject from his mind, and began questioning Guderian's battle tactics. Why, for example, was he still defending Kurland? Guderian became agitated. He recounted Hitler's "mad" insistence that Kurland be held at all costs. "I'm being called to Berlin all the time!" he burst out and listed Hitler's faults as Supreme Commander.

Heinrici listened, but with growing impatience. Finally he interrupted, "What's taking place along the Oder?"

Guderian outlined the deployments: Himmler had two armies along the Oder protecting Berlin—on the left was Manteuffel, and on the right, behind Küstrin and Frankfurt, the Ninth Army of General Theodor Busse. "I don't have too many details," he said apologetically and blamed it on Himmler, who, characteristically, always gave vague answers to direct questions. "But I understand a general counterattack south of Küstrin will start tomorrow," Guderian went on; the most dangerous of the three Russian bridgeheads across the Oder was the one between Küstrin and Frankfurt. It was almost twenty-five kilometers wide and five deep, and contained a tremendous amount of Russian artillery. The Luftwaffe had attacked it again and again, but with little success because of strong anti-aircraft defenses.

Zhukov was about to launch an attack on Berlin from this bridgehead, Guderian continued, and Hitler wanted it wiped out. The Führer's plan was to send five divisions across the Oder into Biehler's bridgehead and drive up toward Küstrin; cut off from the rear, the Russian bridgehead on the other side of the river would then wither and die.

Heinrici was astounded. Any sensible military man could see that these were the tactics of an amateur. For one thing, there was only a single bridge at Frankfurt. How could five divisions cross it in time to make an attack?

"Engineers are also building a pontoon bridge," Guderian explained, but it was obvious that he too disapproved of the entire plan.

"But both bridges will be in range of Russian artillery," Heinrici exclaimed. "This is a hell of a job!"

The general had put his finger on the flaw and Guderian knew it. "You're right," he admitted sheepishly; Busse had also objected, proposing instead to attack the Russian bridgehead directly. But Hitler had disliked Busse's suggestion and dispatched General Krebs up front to see if an attack from the other side of the Oder was feasible. Krebs had reported that it could be done. And it was going to be done. "I have to go see Adolf now," Guderian said sarcastically, and suggested that Heinrici come along and report to the Führer.

But Heinrici said he belonged at Army Group. "I have to get briefed on what's going on. I'm completely uninformed. My report would just be a formality, and I'd lose half a day."

Guderian sighed. Heinrici's pragmatic thinking would have been a welcome relief at the Reich Chancellery. "I'll tell Hitler you're getting yourself briefed," he said.

Heinrici drove to Army Group Vistula headquarters near Prenzlau, some 100 miles northeast of Berlin. It was almost dusk by the time he walked into Himmler's command post, a one-story wooden building, and half an hour later he was still waiting to see the Reichsführer. Finally he demanded to be received at once and was led into a large room, simply but tastefully decorated; facing the door was a huge photograph of Hitler on the wall. Under it sat Himmler at a large desk. It was the first time the two had met, and Himmler rose politely as Heinrici said, "I've come up here to take your place as commander of Army Group Vistula."

Himmler extended a hand and Heinrici shook it. It was limp, like a baby's.

"I'm going to explain what great battles we have fought in delaying action," the Reichsführer began. "I've told a stenographer to come in and take notes, and maps will be brought in." He called for General Eberhard Kinzel, the de facto chief of staff, and Colonel Hans-Georg Eismann, the de facto operations officer.

Himmler began relating his accomplishments but got so involved in details that the sense was lost. Kinzel got up in embarrassment. "I've got important work next door," he said and left. Then Eismann asked to be excused. After forty-five minutes of deepening confusion the phone rang. Himmler listened a moment. He silently handed the phone to Heinrici, who heard General Busse say, "The Russians have broken through and have enlarged their bridgehead below Küstrin."

Heinrici looked questioningly at Himmler, who shrugged his shoulders and said, "You're the new army group commander. Issue the proper orders."

"What do you propose to do?" Heinrici asked Busse.

"As soon as possible I'd like to counterattack to restabilize forces around Küstrin."

"Fine. As soon as I have a chance I'll see you and we'll both look over the front lines."

As Heinrici hung up, Himmler said, "I want to tell you something personal." Then in a conspiratorial tone that struck Heinrici as odd, he said, "Sit next to me on the couch," and disclosed his attempts to contact the West.

All at once Guderian's recent cryptic remark made sense to Heinrici, and he said, "Fine, but what means are available and how do we get to them?"

"By means of a neutral power," Himmler said mysteriously. He looked around nervously and swore Heinrici to secrecy.

The next morning Heinrici inspected the northern half of his army group, which was defended by Manteuffel's Third Panzer Army. Between Manteuffel's front lines and the Oder stretched an area of swamps, and this would be the least likely place to expect the main Russian attack.

Heinrici then drove south toward Frankfurt, across the front held by the Ninth Army. Here Busse, Manstein's former chief of staff, was in command. He was able, reliable and calm under pressure—qualities that would soon be needed, for it was here, along this area, Heinrici concluded, that Zhukov would strike. By dusk Heinrici had not only narrowed down the probable attack zone to the twenty-five-mile sector just west of Frankfurt and Küstrin but had designed a defense. He would establish his main line about ten miles west of the Oder on a small ridge running parallel to the river. Beyond—all the way to Berlin—there were no appreciable natural defense positions.

Heinrici issued his first order: he transferred all the divisions that had already escaped from Pomerania—including the 25th Panzer, 10th SS Panzer, Führer Grenadier and 9th Parachute divisions—to the critical zone behind Frankfurt and Küstrin. His second order was an imaginative one that had nothing to do with troop movements: he ordered the gradual release of the waters of Ottmachau, a large artificial lake more than 200 miles to the southeast which emptied into the Oder. This would flood the ten-mile strip between river and ridge with two feet of water.

Hitler was confident that the present lines of defense could hold back the imminent Russian offensive. But some of his associates lacked his optimism and had begun preparations for an *Alpenfestung,* a National Redoubt in the Alps where National Socialism would make a final Wagnerian stand. Ironically, the whole idea had originated in the minds of Americans. In the fall of 1944 Dulles' office in Switzerland heard rumors that Germany was building an impregnable defense system in the Austrian Alps. The rumors, quite properly, were passed on to Washington and created such apprehension that the story somehow leaked to the press. Goebbels immediately recognized its propaganda value and before long the European press was filled with speculations about the formidable Alpine fortress.

Contrary to Allied fears, no actual defenses had yet been built; no one was even officially in charge of the operation. Unofficially, however, several prominent Germans were making definite plans. One of these most interested was the Austrian-born Kaltenbrunner, who had become increasingly powerful through Himmler. In mid-March Kaltenbrunner summoned Wilhelm Höttl to his new headquarters in Alt Aussee, Austria. Formerly a historian, Höttl was at the time engaged in Operation "Bernhard," the mass forging of British bank notes.* Kaltenbrunner knew that

---

* 160 inmates of the Sachsenhausen concentration camp were put to work as counterfeiters. The purpose of Operation "Bernhard" was dual: to hurt the British economy and to provide additional funds for SS operations. Probably about £150,-000,000 worth of £5, £10 and £20 notes were produced.

Höttl often visited Switzerland and asked if in his opinion the Allies really feared a last-ditch battle in the *Alpenfestung*. When Höttl answered yes, Kaltenbrunner said this fear could be used as a bargaining price for "implicit or explicit permission" for the Germans to continue fighting the Russians even after an armistice with the West. Fear was not enough, Höttl replied; the Allies would eventually discover there was no real *Alpenfestung*. Kaltenbrunner smiled, rang a bell and sent for Dr. Meindl, chief of the Steyr Werke, the greatest munitions works in Austria.

"I can guarantee small-scale production of armaments from workshops tunneled into the mountains by May 1," Meindl said. Kaltenbrunner named several other industrialists who were also co-operating, and revealed that Operation "Bernhard" was now located in Austria and would be able to finance the *Alpenfestung*. The 160 Sachsenhausen experts and their counterfeiting equipment had recently been transferred to Redl-Zipf,* not far from the city the Führer called home—Linz, Austria.

Only one thing was necessary: to get Hitler's permission to continue the battle in the south if Germany was split in two. On March 23 Kaltenbrunner went to Berlin to get this authorization. He expected, indeed he hoped, to find Hitler so concerned about the imminent military collapse that he would at last give his support to a desperation measure like the *Alpenfestung*.

Hitler was bending over a large model of Linz as Kaltenbrunner walked into his office. When he saw it was a fellow Austrian his eyes lit up, and he announced that he was going to rebuild the city completely and make it the metropolis of central Europe. What did Kaltenbrunner, as a native of Linz, think about the ambitious plan?

Kaltenbrunner mumbled an answer and listened with wonder as Hitler continued to talk compulsively of the new Linz. Suddenly Hitler looked up and said with a slight smile, "I know exactly what you've come here to say, Kaltenbrunner. But believe me, if I were not convinced that I'll build up Linz again with your help, as you see it in this model here, I would blow my brains out this very day. *You must have faith*. I still have ways and means of bringing the war to a victorious conclusion."

Like so many others, Kaltenbrunner walked out of the Führer's office with new hope. In five minutes Hitler had convinced him that victory was still possible.

---

* Early in May, 1945, crateloads of the counterfeit money were loaded into two trucks for evacuation from Redl-Zipf. But both trucks broke down almost immediately. One was turned over intact to Wehrmacht troops. The contents of the other truck were dumped into the Traun River. After about ten days, however, the crates burst open and hundreds of thousands of bank notes floated into the Traunsee, where they were salvaged by the inhabitants and American soldiers. This sensational discovery led U. S. investigators to the second truck—and some £21,000,000 worth of notes.

## 3.

Patton's desire to keep word of the Rhine crossing a secret was understandable but, of course, impractical. The next morning, March 23, his chief of staff, General "Hap" Gay, received a phone call from the Seventh Army. There was a rumor that Patton had already crossed the Rhine. Was it true?

"I don't feel at liberty to answer the question," Gay answered, and then urged Patton to tell Bradley at once that Third Army already had seven battalions over the river.

Bradley had just finished his second cup of coffee in the dining room of the Château de Namur when he was called to the phone.

"Brad," Patton said with conspiratorial excitement, "don't tell anyone, but I'm across!"

"Well, I'll be damned! You mean across the Rhine?"

"Sure I am. I sneaked a division over last night. But there are so few Krauts around they don't know it yet. So don't make any announcement. We'll keep it a secret until we see how it goes."

Bradley was delighted, and told Patton that Third Army could put ten divisions in this new bridgehead. He also said he was giving Hodges what he had wanted from the beginning—ten divisions for the Remagen bridgehead.

Montgomery was absorbed with details of preparation for his own great offensive, "Plunder," which was scheduled to begin late that night. Everything was of course moving smoothly at a proper pace, with each assault unit ready to move off at the proper time. Even Montgomery's personal message to the troops had been prepared well in advance:

. . . The enemy possibly thinks he is safe behind this great river obstacle. We all agree that it is a great obstacle; but we will show the enemy that he is far from safe behind it. This great Allied fighting machine, composed of integrated land and air forces, will deal with the problem in no uncertain manner.

And having crossed the Rhine, we will crack about in the plains of Northern Germany, chasing the enemy from pillar to post. The swifter and the more energetic our action, the sooner the war will be over, and that is what we all desire; to get on with the job and finish off the German war as soon as possible.

Over the Rhine, then, let us go. And good hunting to you all on the other side.

May "The Lord mighty in battle" give us the victory in this our latest undertaking, as He has done in all our battles since we landed in Normandy on D-Day.

At three o'clock in the afternoon Churchill and Brooke took off from Northolt Airport in Middlesex and about two hours later touched down at Venlo, on the German border. The Prime Minister, in spite of opposition from Montgomery and Brooke, was going to watch the launching of "Plunder." Brooke had written the field-marshal that Churchill was determined to come "and is now talking of going up in a tank!," to which Montgomery replied, "As regards the P.M. If he is determined to come out for the Battle of the Rhine, I think there is only one course of action: and that is to ask him to stay with me in my camp. I shall then be able to keep an eye on him and see that he goes only where he will bother no one. I have written him a letter; Simpson will show it to you; it should please the old boy!"

The Churchill party—consisting only of his aide, Commander C. R. Thompson, his valet, and Brooke—drove the short distance to Montgomery's headquarters, where they had tea. The field-marshal, dressed in an old pullover and corduroy pants, described his plan of attack: following a bombardment, two corps of the Second British Army and one corps of the Ninth U. S. Army would cross the river. The next morning two airborne divisions would drop a few miles west of the Rhine near Wesel.

For days a seventy-mile sector along the river had been blanketed with smoke to hide these preparations, and by now the men were so sick of it that many said they would rather be seen by the Germans. But because of such precautions a vast concentration of troops, assault boats, "Buffaloes" (amphibious carriers), bridging material and guns were safely and secretly in position.

In the distance Churchill could hear the guns of the opening barrage. These were in the north, where Horrocks' XXX British Corps would make the initial crossing. Just before nine o'clock Horrocks climbed to his observation post on high ground overlooking the Rhine. It was a warm, pleasant night. Though he could see little in the hazy darkness except the flicker of guns, he visualized the leading Buffaloes, loaded with infantry of the 153rd and 154th Infantry brigades, as they lumbered down to the river bank along routes marked with tape. Soon they would be lunging into the Rhine. To the south he could hear bombardment in the XII Corps area, where the Scot commandos would be crossing to Wesel.

Then artillery began to roar all along the entire Second Army sector, in a spectacular display of power. Back at Venlo, Montgomery, an old soldier who knew the value of sleep, had excused himself after dinner and was abed in his trailer, but Brooke and Churchill were excitedly pacing up and down in the moonlight, discussing the momentous situation. It brought back memories of earlier struggles, and they reminisced about Cairo, where Alexander and Montgomery had been given their start and Churchill had had to trust Brooke's selection. Later, back in his quarters, Brooke wrote in his diary:

. . . He [Churchill] was in one of his very nicest moods and showed appreciation for what I had done for him in a way in which he had seldom done before.

We then went into the caravan and examined his Box which had just arrived. It contained a telegram from Molotov which worried him a great deal, connected with the Russian attitude to the peace negotiations which Wolff is trying to open in Berne and their fear lest we should make a separate peace on the Western Front without them being in. He dictated a reply, let his secretary out of the caravan, called him back, considered it, started writing another and finally very wisely left it till to-morrow to think over carefully.

I am now off to bed. It is hard to realize that within fifteen miles hundreds of men are engaged in death-struggles along the banks of the Rhine, whilst hundreds more are keying themselves up to stand up to one of the greatest trials of their lives. With that thought in one's mind it is not easy to lie down and sleep peacefully.

The 1st Commando Brigade was just getting ready to cross the river toward Wesel. On the bank, newsman Richard McMillan was talking with a commando colonel, a young, baldish man. "I wonder what Jerry's got on the other side," he said as he smeared his face with blue grease and drank tea from a mug.

At 10 P.M. the commandos, who wore green berets instead of helmets, started across in the bulky Buffaloes. The scream of shells overhead was deafening. Within minutes, empty Buffaloes were returning for another load. "Not so hot on the other side as we expected," the drivers told McMillan.

At 10:30 P.M., 201 R.A.F. bombers began to drop over 1,000 tons of high explosives on Wesel, and even as they wheeled to head back for England the commandos converged on the pulverized city.

A few miles to the south, near Alpen, Simpson and Eisenhower climbed a church tower to watch the Ninth Army artillery barrage. At 1 A.M. on March 24, 40,000 American artillerymen began rapidly firing from batteries located along the flat plains west of the river. For over an hour more than 2000 guns blasted German targets. Suddenly the incessant din stopped and the first wave of the 30th Division, three battalions abreast, started across the Rhine in assault boats powered by outboard motors. Farther south, to their right, the 79th Division moved down to the west bank, ready to shove off in an hour. None of the assault troops carried gas masks; Simpson, taking a calculated risk, had decided that masks would only increase drownings.

Eisenhower said he wanted to see the crossing and Simpson escorted him to the river bank, where the two generals fell into step with a group

of 30th Division infantrymen, all apparently in high spirits, en route
to their boats. Then Eisenhower noticed that one young soldier looked
depressed. "How are you feeling?" he asked.

"General, I'm awful nervous. I was wounded two months ago and
just got back from the hospital yesterday. I don't feel so good."

"Well, you and I are a good pair then, because I'm nervous too. But
we've planned this attack for a long time and we've got all the planes,
the guns and airborne troops we can use to smash the Germans. Maybe
if we just walk along together to the river we'll be good for each other."

"Oh, I meant I *was* nervous. I'm not any more. I guess it's not so
bad around here."


About the time the first British troops were crossing the Rhine, Bradley
was again called to the telephone by Patton. "Brad," he pleaded shrilly,
"for God's sake tell the world we're across! We knocked down thirty-
three Krauts today when they came after our pontoon bridges. I want
the world to know Third Army made it before Monty starts across."

The Germans were already reacting frenziedly to Patton's crossing
at Oppenheim. Kesselring was dumfounded. He had warned his Seventh
Army commander of a probable attempt to cross in this area and yet
the Americans had done it with ease. Strategically, he thought, this gave
Patton the chance to swing behind the German First Army, which was
still west of the river, and drive deep into the Reich. Remagen had been
the grave of Model's army group. Oppenheim, he feared, was going to
be Hausser's.


## 4.

Earlier that day in Washington, Roosevelt was handed the latest draft
of JCS [Joint Chiefs of Staff] 1067, the directive of United States policy
for the occupation of Germany. In it Morgenthau's original proposal to
make an agrarian nation of Germany was softened; all that remained
was the vague statement that the German government and economic
system would be decentralized. It emphasized, however, that the German
war potential would be destroyed.

. . . As part of the program to attain this objective, all implements of war
and all specialized facilities . . . shall be seized or destroyed. The maintenance
and production of all aircraft and implements of war shall be prevented.

But these were only words and their effectiveness would depend to
a large degree on who enforced them.

At noon Roosevelt talked to the five bipartisan members of Congress
who would represent the United States at the forthcoming United Nations

Conference in San Francisco. Admiral Leahy, Acting Secretary of State Joseph Grew, James Dunn and "Chip" Bohlen from the State Department were also present. "This discussion is off the record," the President began. He then told them about Stalin's request at Yalta for two extra votes in the U. N. Assembly, and explained why he and Churchill had agreed to support this at San Francisco. "I would like, at a later date," he said, "to see the United States get an equal number of votes."

None of the delegates, Republicans or Democrats, made a single objection to Russia's extra votes.

The following day, March 24, Robert E. Sherwood, who had just returned from Manila, called on the President at the White House. The noted playwright said a three-hour discussion with MacArthur had impressed him "with the extent of his understanding of the Orient and the breadth of his views" and had convinced him that the general would be an excellent Military Governor of Japan after the surrender. After listening to MacArthur on the subject, Sherwood felt, victory in the Pacific "appeared a good deal nearer than I had imagined."

"I wish," Roosevelt said, "that he would sometimes tell some of these things to *me*."

Roosevelt wondered about the wisdom of attending the San Francisco Conference. "Steve [Early] doesn't think I ought to open that conference—just in case it should fail," he remarked, laughing. "He thinks I ought to wait to see how it goes and then, if it is a success, I can go out and make the closing address, taking all the credit for it. But I'm going to be there for the start and at the finish, too. All those people from all over the world are paying this country a great honor by coming here and I want to tell them how much I appreciate it."

He asked Sherwood to look up some quotations of Thomas Jefferson's on science, for his speech on Jefferson Day. "There aren't many people who realize it, but Jefferson was a scientist as well as a democrat and there were some things he said that need to be repeated now, because science is going to be more important than ever in the working out of the future world."

Sherwood, of course, knew nothing of the atom bomb and didn't realize the significance of these words. He wished Roosevelt a happy holiday in Warm Springs, where he was going for a rest after a week at Hyde Park, and then walked to the Cabinet Room to compose a memorandum on MacArthur.

Roosevelt had luncheon that day with Anna Rosenberg, one of his most trusted advisers, in the little room on the top floor of the White House. They talked at such length that Mrs. Roosevelt finally entered and said they had to leave for the railroad station to say good-bye to the Canadian Governor-General, the Earl of Athlone, and his consort, Princess Alice.

As the President was wheeled out of the room, flanked by the two ladies, he was handed a decoded cable from Ambassador Harriman. It quoted the "arrogant" letter he had received from Molotov, demanding that Operation "Sunrise" be discontinued at once, together with the Ambassador's recommendation to "face the issue now."

Roosevelt angrily banged his fists on the arms of his wheel chair. "Averell is right!" he cried. "We can't do business with Stalin. He has broken every one of the promises he made at Yalta!" He became so agitated that it was apparent to both women that from now on his dealings with Stalin would take on a new, stronger tone.

The cause of the growing dissension among the Big Three, Karl Wolff, had just arrived in Berlin, summoned by an angry Himmler, who demanded an explanation of his maneuverings. The two met in SS General Fegelein's apartment. Himmler immediately accused Wolff of treason; Kaltenbrunner's spies in Switzerland had found out all about the negotiations with Dulles. Himmler also accused Wolff of stupidity. Hadn't the Führer recently raged at Ribbentrop upon learning of his fumbling efforts to negotiate in Sweden? "How can I tell the Führer you're doing the same thing without specific orders?" he shouted. "Maybe he'll kill us all!"

Wolff made a suggestion that turned Himmler pale; together they should both go to the Führer and tell him everything. For a moment Himmler couldn't speak. Finally he said, "It's impossible for you to deal with Dulles," and flatly forbade Wolff to return to Switzerland. "You don't know enough!"

# 16

## "We Have Had a Jolly Day"

The Führer's evening conference for Friday, March 23, didn't get started until 2:26 A.M. the next day. It was a small meeting. In addition to Hitler's three adjutants—Günsche, Below and Johannmeier—there were Walter Hewel of the Foreign Office, several minor officials and General Wilhelm Burgdorf, the red-faced chief of Army Personnel, who lately had become the faithful echo of Hitler's ideas and earned the contempt of fellow Wehrmacht officers.

Of all reports from the fronts, Patton's unexpected crossing of the Rhine vexed the Führer the most. "I really consider the second bridgehead, the bridgehead at Oppenheim, as the greatest danger," he said.

"Because the enemy managed to bring up his bridge equipment so fast," Burgdorf added.

Hitler pointed at a map. "On a river barrier one negligent man can bring about a terrible disaster. Actually, the upper bridgehead [Remagen] is probably the salvation of some units down here. If it hadn't happened—and then the enemy in the south had pushed across the Rhine with all his strength—nobody would have escaped. As soon as you let yourself get kicked out of a fortified position, it's all over. The leadership acted miserably in this case. They drummed into the troops, from the top down, that they could fight better in open country than along here."

Burgdorf brought up a request from Goebbels, who as Defender of Berlin wished to make a landing strip of the avenue called the East-West Axis that cut through the city's great park, the Tiergarten. "It would be necessary," Burgdorf pointed out a bit anxiously, "to cut down all the lampposts on the sides and to clear away twenty meters more of the Tiergarten on each side."

Hitler wondered why so much had to be cleared away. "They aren't going to land with 'Goliaths' [light tanks]. It's fifty-two meters wide."

"If the JU-52s have to land in the dark," observed Below, the Luftwaffe adjutant, "those street lamps will cause trouble."

"All right, the street lamps. But to chop down twenty to thirty meters of the Tiergarten on the right and left . . ." The idea of cutting down trees troubled him.

"That's hardly necessary," Below conceded.

"They don't need more than fifty meters' width," the Führer went on. "It wouldn't help, anyway, because the strips on the right and left couldn't be paved. They would be completely useless."

"There's just the sidewalk and the slope," said Johannmeier, the chubby Army adjutant.

"I don't consider the cutting of twenty meters necessary, either," airman Below argued. "But the removal of the street lamps—"

"He can remove the street lamps," Hitler repeated.

"Then I can pass that on," Burgdorf concluded.

But Hitler wasn't finished. "It just occurred to me that HE-162s and ME-262s could take off on the East-West Axis."

Below said it was long enough for both jet planes.

"But not with the Siegessäule in the middle," Hewel reminded them. This was the large monument commemorating the victory over France in 1871.

"That would have to be removed," Burgdorf agreed.

"It's almost three kilometers to the Victory Column," Hitler said, reluctant to destroy such a monument. "That's long enough."

The subject was exhausted at last, and Burgdorf asked the Führer what he intended to do about Guderian's sick leave.

"Once and for all," Hitler said, exasperated, "I want the doctor's opinion about Wenck, and I want him to make a definite statement. I'll make him vouch for it with his life: 'By that time Wenck will either be well or not.' Period! They talk and talk, and say that on such-and-such a day he can leave the hospital. Now they don't even know whether they have to operate." It was obvious that Hitler hoped to replace the increasingly irksome Guderian with Wenck.

"The doctor told us that Wenck should stay until April fifteenth," Burgdorf said, "although he himself is getting impatient."

"My Führer," Below interrupted, changing the subject, "when you are not at the Obersalzberg [Berchtesgaden], can't they save the smoke screen down there? Right now they make artificial fog every time aircraft are sighted, and it's using up all of the chemical-smoke supply."

"Yes, but if that goes, everything goes. We've got to realize that. It's one of the last hide-outs we have."

They talked of the OKH bunkers at Zossen and then moved on to a lengthy discussion of special units that could be thrown into the desperate struggle. "We just don't know what's floating around," Hitler complained. "To my amazement, I just heard that a Ukrainian SS division has suddenly appeared." It was sheer insanity, he said, to give weapons to a Ukrainian division that wasn't quite trustworthy. "I'd rather take their weapons away and raise a new German division." Unlike many of his advisers, he was wary of using units made up of captured Red Army men who had volunteered to fight Stalin.

Burgdorf officiously reminded everyone that the Latvian and Estonian volunteer divisions had fallen apart.

"What are they supposed to be fighting for, anyway?" Hitler asked sarcastically; they would have to check all the foreign units. "The Vlasov Division,* for instance, is either good for something or it isn't. There are only two possibilities: if it's any good it must be considered a regular division, and if it's not good it would be stupid to equip a division of ten thousand or eleven thousand men, when I can't even raise German divisions because I don't have the weapons. I'd just as soon raise a German division and give it all those weapons."

"The Indian Legion—" Burgdorf started.

"The Indian Legion is a joke. There are Indians who can't kill a louse and would rather let themselves be eaten up. . . . I think that if we used the Indians to turn prayer wheels or something like that, they'd be the most indefatigable soldiers in the world. But to use them in a real death struggle is ridiculous. How strong are the Indians? But it's all idiotic. If you have a surplus of weapons, you can afford a joke like that for propaganda purposes, but without a surplus of weapons, such jokes for propaganda purposes are completely irresponsible." He continued in this sardonic vein for several minutes, then suddenly said, "I don't mean to imply that you can't do anything with such foreigners. Something could be done with them, but it takes time. If you have them for six or ten years, and if you govern their home territories, as the old Hapsburg monarchy did, then they will become of course good soldiers." But he still had no use for the Indians. "We'd be doing them the greatest favor if we told them they didn't have to fight any more."

Someone noted that the 2300 Indians had 1468 rifles, 550 pistols, 420 machine pistols and 200 light machine guns.

"Just imagine," Hitler interrupted scornfully, "they have more weapons

* General of the Red Army Andrei Andreevich Vlasov denounced Stalin three weeks after his capture in 1942 and helped the Germans mobilize 1,000,000 Russian prisoners into Hitler's service. He was, however, primarily interested in wiping out Communism and not in furthering National Socialism and, consequently, was suspect in the Führer's eyes.

than men! Some of them must carry two weapons." He asked what they were supposed to be doing and was informed that they were in a rest area. Hitler flipped his hand in utter disgust. "These outfits of yours are always resting, never fighting."

At that moment a liaison officer interrupted with an urgent report: "Army Group H reported at 3 o'clock [A.M.] that the enemy has moved up for attack one and a half kilometers south of Wesel and near Mehrum. [This, of course, was Montgomery's Operation "Plunder."] The strength and nature of this attack has not yet been reported. That attack was to be expected. Since 1700 hours [5 P.M., March 23] there has been heavy artillery fire on our main battle line as well as on rear areas."

As they began discussing German strength near Wesel and possible reinforcements for the breakthrough area, a liaison officer named Borgmann reminded Hitler that there weren't even enough reinforcements to halt Patton at Oppenheim: there were only five tank destroyers available and they wouldn't be ready for a least another day. "In the following days two more will be added so that the unit can be raised to seven. Everything else is now committed, and for the time being nothing else is ready."

"Actually they were meant for the upper bridgehead," Hitler said.

"Yes," Borgmann confirmed, "for the 512th battalion at Remagen."

"When do they leave?"

"They'll be ready today or tomorrow. They can probably move tomorrow night."

"Then we'll take that up again tomorrow," Hitler said. He began to muse out loud about how soon a group of "sixteen or seventeen Tigers" could be repaired. "That would be very important." Hitler's concern over a handful of tanks dramatically illustrated the bankruptcy of Germany's armed might.

## 2.

Just before dawn the first planes transporting the 4876 men of the British 6th Airborne Division took off from their base in East Anglia, England. Within an hour 247 C-47s of the U. S. 9th Troop Carrier Command and 429 British planes and gliders were in the air heading for the Rhine River and Operation "Varsity."

In France the men of the 17th Airborne Division had just finished a breakfast of steak and apple pie, and after a final check of equipment, began strapping on their bulky gear and loading into planes and gliders. At 7:17 A.M. the first transports took off. The 507th Parachute Infantry would drop first and seize a strategic woods. Then came the 513th Parachute Infantry and four groups of glider troops, which were supposed to come down just east of the 507th. The last regiment, the 194th Glider Infantry, would land near Wesel and seize the Issel Canal bridges.

It was almost 9 A.M. before the last plane took off, and the huge column—226 C-47s, 72 C-46s and 610 C-47s towing 906 gliders—extended farther than the eye could see. The 9387 American paratroopers flew northwest to the final rendezvous point southeast of Brussels, where they joined the smaller British air column.* Side by side, in a gigantic sky train two hours and eighteen minutes long, the two groups headed for Wesel with 213 Royal Air Force fighters and 676 9th U. S. Air Force fighters flitting protectively on all sides.

To all but a few of the American 'troopers in the cargo planes, jumping in combat was a new experience. Many shared a common reaction: a lump in the throat which grew until it threatened to strangle. Those in the gliders were even more apprehensive as their flimsy craft jerked and bucked in the slip streams of the tow ships ahead.

In his plunging glider, Howard Cowan of Associated Press tried to forget the vivid pictures he had seen of gliders smashed and splintered in Normandy and Holland. He looked to the left and saw the right wing tip of a sister glider, hitched to the same C-47, as it swayed dangerously close. What would happen if the two locked wings? He gritted his teeth and tried not to notice a neighbor vomiting into his helmet.

Lieutenant Colonel Allen C. Miller, commander of the 2nd Battalion, rode in the lead plane of the 513th. He was only five foot four; his helmet came down over his eyebrows and his jump boots almost reached to his knees. His fellow officers called him Ace, but to the GIs who had followed him through the Battle of the Bulge he was "Boots and Helmet."

The plane was a big C-46, faster than the old C-47. Miller walked to the open door and looked out at the greatest air display he had ever seen. It was awesome. He was in the midst of a massive swarm of planes: long, straight columns of transports carrying 'chutists; strings of gliders, swaying back and forth behind their tow planes like great unruly kites; and hundreds and hundreds of fighters darting in and around like angry bees. Miller checked his men, took a Dramamine pill and settled back for a good sleep.

At 9:30 A.M. Montgomery's aide, Noel Chevasse, escorted Churchill and Brooke to a hill overlooking the Rhine, near Xanten. They were there to watch the airdrop but it was so hazy that they could see only a few of the boats ferrying troops across the river. All around was the din of batteries firing rapidly at German emplacements. But at 9:40 A.M. they heard another sound—the distant but penetrating roar and rumble of an approaching aerial armada.

* 17,255 British and American airborne troops landed in Normandy on D-Day.

The paratroopers knew they were getting close to the Rhine. Ahead they could see great clouds of smoke where the British had screened almost seventy miles of the river.

Richard C. Hottelet of CBS and *Collier's* was watching from a C-47. Ahead black columns rose from the drop areas, which were being saturated by Allied medium bombers. Only one thing worried Hottelet: he wasn't worried.

Wing Leader Johnnie Johnson, one of the most experienced fighter pilots of the war, was awed by the seemingly endless parallel lines of transport aircraft and gliders approaching the river. So was the pilot in the plane next to him, who radioed, "Greycap. You can see Uncle Sam is on the ball today!"

At 9:46 A.M. the first planes of the 507th neared the Rhine. Red signal lights began flashing, and the 'troopers hooked up and checked equipment. As heavy fire from 20-mm. and 40-mm. anti-aircraft guns grew in intensity, those near the open doors could pick out German batteries even through the clouds of smoke. Some Germans were scattering like chickens chased by a hawk, while others looked up defiantly and fired rifles, submachine guns and pistols.

At 9:50 A.M. green lights flickered and the 'troopers began to tumble out of the transports. The 1st Battalion floated down more than a mile north of its drop zone. After Colonel Edson Raff, the regimental commander, had hit the ground, he assembled his men and wiped out a nest of Germans in a nearby woods. He saw a battery of 150-mm. guns firing from among trees almost a mile away. He captured this battery intact and moved southeast through the woods, clearing them as he went.

The 513th approached its drop zone just before 10 A.M. and Colonel Miller was wakened. He yelled down the aisle, "Stand up. Hook up. Check your equipment." He walked up to the cockpit and patted the pilot on the back. The pilot, without turning, gave a V-sign. Miller had started back toward the jump door when flak began exploding on all sides. From the open door he could see the majestic sweep of the Rhine. Above it, Allied bombers and fighters seemed to fill the sky. He looked back. The slower C-47 groups were coming on in perfect formation and it seemed likely that they would make the final assault in a V of Vs, as planned. But where were the other C-46 groups and the big British column?

Miller's plane was down to 350 feet and small-arms fire squirted up through the steel matting on the floors. Several 'troopers were hit. The crew chief ran back, yelling that the pilot was badly wounded. The C-46 veered to the left, straightened out.

Other 513th planes were also in trouble. The flak hitting Lieutenant Paul McGuire's C-46 reminded him of hail on a corrugated-iron roof. But he was so busy checking his jump equipment that he didn't realize the plane was badly damaged until smoke began to pour from one of the wing tanks. The plane's crew chief hustled down the aisle, buckled on an emergency parachute and asked a paratrooper, "Say, bud, what's the password tonight?"

Miller could make out railroad tracks ahead. "Jump!" he shouted. He stood aside and let several men go out the door, then leaped himself. As his chute cracked open he glanced back and saw the left wing of his C-46 burst into flame. The 'troopers' camouflaged chutes were blossoming by the hundreds, interspersed with blue, red and yellow supply parachutes. The staccato of fire from the ground sounded to Miller like a rifle range. Just below a man who had preceded him was inert. His head flopped back, blood gushing out.

Miller was drifting down directly onto the railroad tracks. He slipped his chute and landed in a small fenced pigpen. He turned the metal coupling of the new British quick-release device and pressed. Nothing happened. As he struggled with the mechanism, machine-gun bullets began digging the spring sod a yard from his face. He rolled away, grabbed his jump knife and cut himself loose from the chute.

The firing came from a nearby farmhouse. Miller yanked out his pistol and headed for what appeared to be a small windowless shed. As he reached it, a big paratrooper vaulted the five-foot fence and plopped down beside him. The little colonel, startled by the newcomer's abrupt appearance and annoyed by his obvious look of fright, kicked him in the rear as hard as he could. Neither said a word.

Cautiously Miller peered around the corner of the little building. Not two feet away was the profile of a German firing rapidly across the railroad tracks into the open field. Beside him were three others. The field was utter confusion, with 'troopers and their chutes littering the ground and others landing on top of them. It suddenly occurred to Miller that if he had landed where he was suppposed to—just across the tracks— he would probably be dead.

Though he wasn't a good pistol shot, how could he miss at this distance? He took aim at the nearest German. They were so intent on their own shooting that Miller killed three of them before the last one turned around—and gasped. Miller fired.

He came to a cement doorway; the shed was a camouflaged bunker. He signaled the big paratrooper to follow and jumped into the bunker, ready to shoot. To his relief it was empty. But there were steps at the rear, leading into a dark tunnel. He groped his way into the dimly lit cellar of the farmhouse. Miller beckoned the paratrooper to follow, but he was alone and didn't know it; the big man had not even entered the tunnel. Miller made out a figure slumped in a corner. He almost fired but something stopped him. It was an old woman, deathly pale. She remained motionless as he started up the steps into the kitchen.

At a sandbagged window three Germans were firing a machine gun. The colonel crept from room to room. Almost every window was manned by a machine-gun crew. The house had been converted into a fort commanding the surrounding fields—and he remembered the German broadcaster saying, "We are prepared."

A figure ducked out the back door. Miller hastily bowled a thermite grenade down the hall toward the kitchen and skidded a fragmentation grenade into the dining room. Before they exploded he was running out of the house toward the railroad tracks, past the bunker he had recently entered. Suddenly he almost stumbled over a friend, Captain Jack Lawlor. He was dead. Miller hesitated and for the first time noticed that the big 'trooper was not with him. He crossed the tracks to the field. There were dead and wounded everywhere, and the carnage reminded him of pictures of Pickett's charge.

Captain Oscar Fodor, the assistant battalion surgeon, looked up from the wounded and recognized Miller. He pointed to a woods where some of the 513th were trying to assemble. Just then British gliders loomed over the edge of the field, swooping toward a group of Americans who were floating to the ground. Miller watched in horror as a Horsa, far bigger than American gliders, belly-landed into a string of 'troopers that had just come down. The glider skidded to a stop near Miller, its tail blew off and an armored car rolled out. Germans in the house opened concentrated fire on the car. It blazed. But the British gunner kept firing his Bren gun doggedly until overcome by flames.

In the woods Miller found twenty men, including a few pilots and several British paratroopers. He led them to a farmhouse which Captain Fodor was using as an aid station. Blood was running down the doctor's own leg. He calmly dropped his trousers and applied a tourniquet. "I've just been shot in the ass," he said, and started back to the open field.

There was a shattering roar overhead. Miller looked up at B-24 Liberators brushing the treetops with incredible boldness as they brought in the first medical and ammunition resupply. They were so close he could see the pilots' purposeful faces; the sight thrilled him. The men on the ground cheered and waved and Miller felt glad he was an American.

One of the daring Liberators burst into flames, then another and another. Supply bundles in four-foot-long steel cylinders, attached to parachutes, drifted down in large clusters. One broke from its chute and hurtled at Miller like a bomb; it buried itself in the soft earth at his feet. He remembered it as his closest brush with death in the war.

A moment later the regimental commander of the 513th, Colonel James Coutts, ran up with a handful of men. "I want you to attack south from here with your left on the railroad!" he gasped out to Miller and pointed to an open field. Sporadic machine-gun fire began coming from that direction and everyone hit the ground.

The little colonel stood up. "Follow me!" he yelled. Not a man moved. Rarely profane, Miller lost his temper. "Goddamnit!" he shouted. "Get moving!" He ran back and forth, bellowing the same thing over and over. Two men reluctantly rose to a crouch, as if embarrassed, and started forward tentatively; then several others followed. Finally everyone was moving. When the Germans saw that Miller and his men kept coming toward them in the face of their fire, they turned and fled.

The third unit of airborne Americans, the 194th Glider Infantry, neared its target, the Issel Canal bridges, at 10:20 A.M.

"It won't last long," a sergeant told A. P. correspondent Howard Cowan. The two shook hands, wished each other luck. Cowan kept his eyes glued on their pilot, waiting to see him push the lever that would cut the glider loose.

"Going down!" the pilot shouted.

As the clumsy craft pitched forward steeply, the sergeant said, "Now is when you pray."

People have been praying ever since leaving, Cowan thought. The gliders penetrated a huge cloud of acrid smoke, and Cowan felt as if he were in a burning building. Below, dozens of gliders were parked at crazy angles. All at once the ground came racing toward him. There was a splintering crash as they went through a fence and bounced across a gully. Then a wing tip smashed into another fence, and there was a sudden silence. They were in a pasture—safe. He clambered out of the glider and looked around.

Cowan watched, intrigued, as little cupfuls of green turf danced about him—bullets! He rolled into a shallow ditch filled with red slimy water. It felt good, so he stayed there. A glider swooped over his head. It clipped off the top of a nearby tree and crumpled to a safe landing 100 yards away. Cowan eased out of the ditch and looked cautiously around. The shooting was over—for the moment. He offered a prayer of thanksgiving. He would never, never ride in a glider again.

Many gliders had collapsed like match boxes, their occupants being killed or maimed; a few were shot down. But at least the 194th had landed in the designated area, well grouped. For them everything had gone as planned, a rare occurrence in battle. Artillery pieces were set up as the regiment assembled and moved toward the Issel Canal to seize the bridges.

From their vantage point Churchill and Brooke had a perfect view of the air columns as they flew directly overhead, but the planes disappeared in the fog and smoke before the 'troopers tumbled out. Moments later the transports came streaming back, with doors open and ripcords fluttering behind.

Just before noon Churchill and Brooke were taken ten miles north by armored cars to high ground near Kalkar, where they watched the 51st Highland Division cross the river. Their guide, Chevasse, had orders from Montgomery: "Get rid of the whole party until well after tea—and make certain no one is killed." But as soon as lunch was finished the Prime Minister made a reckless request: he wanted to cross the Rhine. Chevasse anxiously conferred with Churchill's aide, Commander Thompson, and was advised to refer the matter to Montgomery.

That evening the amused Brooke recorded in his diary:

> Winston then became a little troublesome and wanted to go messing about on the Rhine crossings and we had some difficulty in keeping him back. However, in the end he behaved well and we came back in our armoured cars to where we had left our own car, and from there on back to the H.Q. P.M. went off for a sleep which he wanted badly; he had been sleeping in the car nearly all the way home, gradually sliding on to my knee.

At dinner Churchill was in such high spirits that he entertained Montgomery and the others with dramatic readings from Maeterlinck's *Life of the Bee.*

It was 1:04 P.M. by the time the last paratrooper jumped, three hours and fourteen minutes after the first. Less than an hour later, the American paratroopers made contact with the British 1st Commando Brigade, which had fought its way into Wesel the night before. About the same time, the British 'troopers of the 6th Airborne Division met the British 15th Division at Hamminkeln, a town about seven air miles east of the Rhine.

General Matthew Ridgway crossed the Rhine in an Alligator immediately after he had learned that his troops were linking up with the ground units. As the clumsy vehicle waddled up the river bank, its British machine-gun team fired precautionary bursts at every patch of grass. There was no answering fire. The XVIII Airborne Corps commander and his four companions climbed out and started ahead on foot, looking for Major General William "Bud" Miley, commander of the 17th Airborne Division. As usual, several hand grenades dangled from Ridgway's belt. Clutching a 1903 Springfield rifle in one hand, he led the way into a woods. A commander who relentlessly drove everyone, including himself, his philosophy of battle was, "Be aggressive and then more aggressive." At a bend in a path he came upon a German soldier in a foxhole. The general stopped and stared. The German stared back wide-eyed—he was dead.

The little party pushed forward again until Ridgway saw a flicker in the woods ahead and heard a heavy thumping. He signaled everyone to take cover. A bulky, heavy-footed farm horse pounded down the path. Astride was a U. S. 'trooper, rifle slung over his back, wearing a high silk hat and a satisfied smile. Ridgway stepped out abruptly in front of the rider. At the sight of Ridgway's two stars he began to thrash around, apparently not knowing whether to salute, descend, present arms, or take off the top hat. But when he saw Ridgway starting to laugh, he relaxed and grinned.

Ridgway reached the 17th Airborne Division command post soon after, and together with General Miley, he jeeped to the command post of the 6th Airborne for a conference with General Eric Bols. On their way back to Miley's field headquarters in a three-jeep convoy, they approached the hull of a burned-out truck and slowed down to make a detour. In the darkness ahead, Ridgway saw scurrying figures. He jumped to the ground and began firing the Springfield from his hip. A yelp—and one of the shadows collapsed. Ridgway dropped behind the jeep to get another clip; there was a deafening roar and he felt a burning sting in his shoulder. A grenade had exploded under the jeep only two feet from his head—but on the other side of the wheel.

In the silence Ridgway could hear men breathing all around him. He held his fire, afraid he'd hit a friend. Then he saw a slight movement across a ditch in a clump of willows. "Put up your hands, you son of a bitch!" he shouted.

"Ah, go shit in your hat!" a very American voice answered.

Ridgway took his finger off the trigger.

When it looked as if the German patrol had fled, Ridgway called out to Miley, "How are you, Bud? I think I got one of them." He didn't mention he'd been hit.

The party moved forward in two jeeps until Miley saw something moving on the dark road ahead. He fired his pistol; there was no reply. He got out of his jeep and found a 17th Airborne 'trooper manning a .30-caliber machine gun. "Damn it," said Miley, "you got orders to shoot. Why didn't you shoot me?" The 'trooper only smiled sheepishly and Miley, not knowing whether to bawl him out or thank him, did neither.

Some 150 miles up the Rhine, George Patton and his two aides—the Groton graduate, Colonel Charles Codman, and the Texas gun fighter, Major Alexander Stiller—were crossing the pontoon bridge at Oppenheim. "Time out for a short halt," Patton said, peering over the edge of the bridge. Then, without another word, he emulated the peculiarly Anglo-Saxon rite performed by Churchill on the "dragon's teeth." "I've been looking forward to this for a long time," he said contentedly as he buttoned his trousers.

The little group continued toward the east bank. As the history-minded Patton stepped off the bridge, he deliberately stumbled onto the soft ground in imitation of William the Conqueror, who is supposed to have said, as he fell on his face upon stepping out of a boat, "See, I have taken England with both hands."

The general scooped up some dirt and scrambled to his feet. Letting the dirt sift through his fingers, he said, "Thus, William the Conqueror."

## 3.

On top of the ridge that Heinrici had selected as his major line of defense behind the Oder River was the village of Seelow. It was here, on Palm Sunday morning, March 25, that he first met Theodor Busse, the big, confident commander of the Ninth Army. Busse explained that his hastily prepared attack launched two days previously had failed, as he had prophesied to OKH. His armor had rolled through the Red Army lines, but his inexperienced infantrymen didn't know how to consolidate the gains and he had been forced to pull back the tanks.

Heinrici reluctantly ordered him to launch another attack at once; there was little chance of success but the situation was desperate. The brief meeting with Busse ended Heinrici's inspection of Army Group Vistula; then he headed for Berlin and his first meeting with Hitler.

It was midafternoon when he walked into the Reich Chancellery, where those who would attend the conference were already milling in the corridor. There were about thirty, including Keitel, Jodl, Guderian and Burgdorf. Before they had finished sandwiches and coffee someone said, "The Führer is coming," and everyone hastily made for the small briefing room. The curtains were drawn, the light subdued. A door at the opposite end of the room was flung open and Hitler entered. He walked forward with stooped shoulders and seemed shrunken.

Heinrici was introduced, and when they shook hands he was dismayed by the feebleness of Hitler's grasp. The Führer waited behind a large desk until an aide pushed a chair under him. He flopped into it and lifted his palsied arm onto the table with his right hand. Another aide handed him dark green glasses.

Someone whispered to Heinrici to sit at the Führer's left; he didn't hear very well with his right ear. Without preamble Heinrici began to give his account of the situation in the east, speaking as frankly now as he had with Guderian. In the middle of his review he was handed a message from Busse: the second attack had also failed.

Hitler scowled at this information and jerked himself to his feet. "Reattack again and by all means re-establish lines with Küstrin." He wanted to know why the first two attacks had failed. "Not enough artillery?"

"I got there in time to see iron flying on both sides," Heinrici replied.

"The Russians have iron too." Hitler ignored this sarcasm and repeated that Küstrin must be retaken.

"In that case we won't be able to launch an attack from the Frankfurt area," Heinrici said, with mixed feelings. The proposed attack from that *Festung* seemed even more stupid.

"*First* we will retake Küstrin," Hitler corrected him.

### 4.

By dawn this Sunday morning, Ridgway had thrown back two strong German counterattacks. Operation "Varsity" was already a smashing success. The cost, however, was heavy. The Americans suffered about 10 percent casualties and the British at least 30 percent, but together they had almost destroyed the three German divisions in the drop area—the 84th Infantry and the 7th and 8th Parachute divisions—as well as numerous artillery and anti-aircraft units. Even more important, they had also assured the success of Montgomery's main attack, "Plunder."

Following Palm Sunday services Churchill, Montgomery and Brooke drove to a rendezvous with Eisenhower, Bradley and Simpson at a château overlooking the Rhine, near Rheinberg. The conversation was spirited, with everyone jubilant at the success of the immense operation. Over and over Churchill exclaimed to Eisenhower, "My dear General, the German is whipped! We've got him! He is through."

"Thank God, Ike, you stuck by your plan," Brooke said. "You were completely right and I am sorry if my fear of dispersed effort added to your burdens. The German is now licked. It is merely a question of when he chooses to quit. Thank God, you stuck by your guns."

At least that is what Eisenhower recalled he said. Brooke himself only remembered that he politely congratulated Eisenhower on his success and told him his policy was now the correct one. He could not have admitted that Eisenhower was "completely right," he wrote, since he was still convinced that the Supreme Commander was "completely wrong."

After a pleasant lunch on the lawn, Eisenhower suggested that they all drive down to a sandbagged house on the edge of the Rhine where they could observe the activities. They stood on a porch extending over the river and watched landing craft flit back and forth. "I'd like to get in that boat and cross," Churchill remarked.

"No, Mr. Prime Minister," Eisenhower said. "I'm the Supreme Commander and I refuse to let you go across. You might be killed."

But once Eisenhower had left for another appointment, Churchill drew Montgomery's attention to a small launch which had just landed, and said, "Why don't we go across and have a look at the other side?"

"Why not?" the field-marshal rejoined, somewhat to the Prime Minister's surprise.

Simpson returned from escorting Eisenhower to his plane, to find Churchill, Montgomery and several other officers climbing into a U. S. Navy LCM. "Now that General Eisenhower is gone," Churchill called out with a boyish grin, "I'm going across!"

The sun was shining brilliantly when they stepped onto the east bank, and German shells were bursting intermittently. Before anyone could stop him, Churchill began striding rapidly toward the battle, violently puffing his cigar.

"This is no place for the P.M.," Simpson said to Montgomery. "I'd hate to have anything happen to him in my army area." He quickened his pace to catch up to the Prime Minister, who looked as if he would never stop. "If we keep on going," Simpson called out tactfully, "we'll soon be in the front line."

On the return trip across the Rhine, Montgomery was infected by Churchill's spirit of adventure and asked the captain of the launch, "Can't we go down the river towards Wesel where there is something going on?"

This was impossible because of a chain across the Rhine to stop floating mines, but as soon as the west bank was reached, the field-marshal leaned over to Churchill, as one conspirator to another, and said, "Let's go down to the railway bridge at Wesel, where we can see what is going on on the spot."

This large iron bridge had been partially destroyed and was still under enemy fire. Again in the lead, Churchill scrambled spryly onto the structure. Shells were falling closer and closer, creating great geysers of spray. Finally one salvo hit on the other side of the bridge, almost as if the Germans knew Churchill was there.

A junior officer approached Simpson and worriedly noted that the Germans had direct observation for a mortar battery. "We're bracketed already," he said. "One or two more tries, and they may hit you."

Simpson caught up to Churchill. "Prime Minister," he said, using the correct form of address, "there are snipers in front of you; they are shelling both sides of the bridge and now they have started shelling the road behind you. I cannot accept the responsibility for your being here and must ask you to come away."

A look came over Churchill's face that reminded Brooke of a small boy being called away from his sand castles on the beach. Grasping a girder with both arms, he peered over his shoulder at Simpson with a pout, as if defying him to pry him loose.

Then, to everyone's relief, he let go the bridge and reluctantly dragged his way back to shore. Churchill had repeatedly told Brooke, "The way

to die is to pass out fighting when your blood is up and you feel nothing."
It seemed now to Brooke that the Prime Mininster was determined to
take every possible risk, as if a sudden and soldierly death at the front
would be a suitable end and free him from the worries in the postwar
world with the Soviet Union.

It had been an adventurous day for the Prime Minister but even at the
front he couldn't escape the Russian problem. A message from London
was waiting for him at Montgomery's headquarters. It was from Eden,
who was wondering if there would be any point in going to the San
Francisco Conference in view of Soviet suspicion and arrogance. "How
can we lay the foundations of any new World Order when Anglo-American relations with Russia are so completely lacking in confidence?"

Churchill immediately replied that he too thought "the whole question
of the San Francisco Conference hangs in the balance," and then changed
the subject to remark nostalgically, "We have had a jolly day, having
crossed the Rhine." Later that evening Churchill wrote Eden again. Stalin's
abrupt decision to send Gromyko to San Francisco in place of Molotov, he
said, was "the expression of the Soviet displeasure" over Operation
"Sunrise," and opined that "quite definite forming up by Britain and the
United States against breach of Yalta understandings now is necessary if
such a meeting is to have any value."

But Churchill was still afraid that Roosevelt might not back him in a
strong united stand against Russia. Two messages from Roosevelt to
Stalin that very day had done little to allay the Prime Minister's misgivings. In one, Roosevelt politely regretted Molotov's absence from the
San Francisco Conference, and in the other he defended Operation "Sunrise"—with conciliatory words. Roosevelt's very real anger upon reading
Molotov's rude message was not yet indicated in these official communications and as yet Churchill had no hint that the President was at last in
the mood to join him in a firmer stand against Stalin.

# 17

## Task Force Baum

On March 24 Patton threw his 4th Armored Division across the Rhine. Now under the command of William Hoge, the captor of the Remagen bridge, the division raced about twenty-five miles toward the next barrier, the Main River—with Combat Command A scheduled to cross east of Frankfurt at Hanau, and Combat Command B some twenty miles to the southeast at Aschaffenburg.

The XII Corps commander, Major General Manton Eddy, telephoned Hoge and gave him a strange mission: Patton wanted a special expedition sent about sixty miles behind enemy lines to free "900 American prisoners" in a PW camp at Hammelburg. Hoge thought it was curious but made no comment.

Later in the day Patton himself telephoned Hoge and in a voice pitched even higher than usual said, "This is going to make MacArthur's raid on Cabanatuan* peanuts!" Hoge said nothing to Patton but told Eddy he didn't like the idea. Sending a task force to the east would only further disperse his division, which was already spread along a twenty-mile front with orders to drive north after crossing the Main. Why take such a risk at this late stage in the war? There were many PW camps—what was so important about Hammelburg? Eddy said he would take up the matter with Patton.

Hammelburg was a good-sized town on the winding Fränkische Saale River, fifty-five air miles due east of Frankfurt am Main. Twenty air miles

* A prison camp in the Philippines recently liberated by MacArthur.

farther east lay Schweinfurt, the famous ball-bearing center. Oflag XIIIB (*Offizierslager,* Officer Prisoner of War Camp) was located on a saucer-shaped plateau atop a steep hill three miles south of Hammelburg. In one compound there were about 3000 officers of the Royal Yugoslav Army, captured after the short campaign in 1941. The Yugoslavs—they preferred to call themselves Serbs—were proud, swarthy and volatile, with shabby but ornate uniforms. They were extremely kind and generous to the 800 U. S. officers who arrived in January, 1945, and by popular vote donated 150 of their own food packages to their allies.

Most of the Americans had been forced to surrender early in the Battle of the Bulge; consequently they felt no pride in their unit and showed their senior officers little respect. There was almost no internally organized activity except for Sunday church services. Unlike the camp at Sagan there were no athletic, musical or dramatic programs. Few thought of escape, since it was obvious that the war would last only a few more months. Red Cross parcels were issued only once a month—not sufficient to appreciably bolster their regular starvation diet, which, even though supplemented now and then by the camp delicacy, tomcat stew, led to an inordinate number of influenza and pneumonia cases. Dysentery was almost universal.

The entire compound, in short, was in a desultory state and remained so until March 8, when about 430 U. S. prisoners, commanded by Colonel Paul "Pop" Goode, arrived from Szubin, Poland. The middle-aged colonel, a former instructor at West Point, was sick and exhausted from the rigorous trip. But when he shambled into camp, carrying his cherished bagpipes, there was such a defiant look on his worn face that the Bulge prisoners felt a quick surge of pride.

Overnight, Goode and his competent chief of staff, Lieutenant Colonel John Knight Waters, brought back discipline and order, and "Pop" became a magic name to those young officers who had been disgusted with the past state of affairs. Uniforms were cleaned, shoes shined, hair trimmed, beards shaved off. Assemblies became more military, barracks were cleaner. Goode then turned his attention to the German camp commander, Generalleutnant (Major General) Günther von Goeckel. The food improved, roll calls were canceled in bad weather, fuller use was made of camp facilities—and "Pop" Goode was a hero to all but a few who resented his autocratic manner.

On March 25 Major Alexander Stiller, one of Patton's aides, unexpectedly arrived at Hoge's headquarters. A taciturn former Texas Ranger with a hard, leathery face, he had been a sergeant on Patton's staff in World War I. Stiller tersely announced that he was supposed "to go along" on the expedition to Hammelburg. Hoge was surprised; he had thought that the whole operation was shelved, so he again protested to Eddy, who told him not to worry; he would handle Georgie.

The following morning Patton flew up to Eddy's headquarters. When he walked in, Brigadier General Ralph Canine, the corps chief of staff, told him that Eddy was out.

"Pick up the phone and get Bill Hoge," Patton said impatiently. "Tell him to cross the Main River and get over to Hammelburg."

"General, the last thing Matt told me before he left was that if you came by and told us to issue that order I was to tell you I wasn't to do it."

Patton showed no anger at such insubordination. "Get Hoge on the phone," he said quietly, "and I'll tell him myself." A moment later he was ordering Hoge to "carry out the plan." Hoge said he couldn't spare even a single man or tank.

"I promise I'll replace every man and every vehicle you lose!" Patton wheedled.

Hoge was embarrassed by the almost pleading tone in Patton's voice. With a baffled look he turned to Stiller, who had been listening. Stiller explained in a low voice that the "Old Man" was absolutely determined to free the prisoners of Hammelburg—and revealed that John Waters, Patton's son-in-law, was one of the prisoners.*

Forced to obey Patton's direct order, Hoge reluctantly sent the assistant division commander, Brigadier General W. L. Roberts, to Lieutenant Colonel Creighton Abrams, whose Combat Command B had just seized a railroad bridge across the Main. When Abrams learned that it was up to him to send a special task force to Hammelburg, he phoned Hoge and assured him that a reinforced company alone would be wiped out. If it had to be done, the entire combat command should go. Hoge told him that Eddy had already refused to divert a combat team for such a mission; the orders stood.

### 2.

On the afternoon of March 26 Captain Abraham Baum of the Bronx was sleeping on the hood of a half-track when he was wakened and told to report at once to Combat Command B headquarters. Baum, formerly a pattern cutter in a blouse factory, was the intelligence officer of the 10th Armored Infantry Battalion. He was six foot two, rangy and, like his

---

* About a month before, three American officers who had hitchhiked across Poland and western Russia had told Major General John Deane, head of the U. S. Military Mission in Moscow, that Waters and other Americans were being marched to the west by the Germans. Deane wired the information to Eisenhower, who passed it on to Patton.

Combat Commander, extremely aggressive. His crew-cut hair, mustache and grin added to his already cocksure appearance.

Baum was still yawning when he entered the command post, but he snapped out of it the instant Abrams told him to take a task force behind enemy lines and bring back 900 American prisoners. No reason was given and Baum expected none. He only turned to his battalion commander, Lieutenant Colonel Harold Cohen, and jokingly said, "This is no way to get rid of me. I'll be back."

He was told to pick his own men and get moving.

By 7 P.M. Task Force Baum was set to go: 307 men, all battle-tested and full of fight, though dog-tired. The column consisted of ten Shermans and six light tanks, three 105-mm. assault guns, twenty-seven half-tracks to haul back the prisoners, seven jeeps and a medic "weasel."

Baum reviewed his problem. He was to plunge more than sixty miles through enemy lines with a reconnaissance force. Not strong enough to withstand a heavy attack, he would have to cause confusion as he sped through an area which was a complete blank to him—he didn't even know the location of enemy strong points. So he had to go into unknown country, fight God knew what, and come back with 900 extra passengers.

Already uneasy about the whole operation, Baum got another jolt when Abrams told him that a Major Stiller would go along. "What's the story?" Baum asked suspiciously. Abrams assured him that Stiller would only be an observer with no command function, and suggested that perhaps Patton wanted to "indoctrinate" Stiller into battle. But one look at Stiller was enough to make him realize that no indoctrination was needed. Once Patton had ruefully told Colonel Codman that he wished to hell he had a real fighting face like Al Stiller's.

Like Hoge, Abrams knew the real purpose of the mission. Although Stiller had told Cohen and several others, "I'm going for the laughs and thrills," he had just admitted to Abrams in confidence, "I think Patton's son-in-law is in there." Baum's men, of course, knew nothing of all this. In fact, some didn't even know they were going behind the lines to liberate a PW camp.

Abrams' plan to shove Task Force Baum through the thin crust of German defenses was simple. Combat Command B would cross the recently taken railroad bridge in force and clean out the little town on the other side. Then Baum would rip through the hole they had blasted and make a break for Hammelburg, sixty miles away. He should get there by early afternoon of March 27 and, with luck, be back the same night.

At 9 P.M., March 26, CCB crossed the Main River. Though Intelligence had predicted that there would be little opposition, Abrams immediately ran into trouble and was forced to throw in everything he had before he could finally open up a road for Baum. It was midnight, several hours behind schedule, when Task Force Baum finally rumbled across the bridge—with infantrymen perched on tanks, extra ammunition and gas in the half-tracks—and headed east. It was dry and warm, with a high overcast. There was no moon. The column sped through the first villages so unexpectedly that they met almost no resistance. The tankers sprayed all possible targets, and the infantrymen tossed grenades into doors and windows to keep snipers down.

But by now the German Seventh Army knew that an armored unit had broken through—probably as much as a division—and guessed that it was Patton. Because of such daring and unexpected tactics, most German field commanders both feared and respected him more than any other American commander. Villages and towns farther along the way were warned and told to block the force, but Baum was moving so fast and violently that although he encountered small-arms and bazooka fire in each blacked-out town, only a few men were lost.

Just before dawn the task force, after progressing twenty-five miles, roared up to the city of Lohr. When the light tanks came to a barricade across the highway, they pulled aside and let the Shermans smash through. A panzerfaust fired at short range and knocked out one of the Shermans, but the crew transferred to a half-track and the column pushed on, only to run head-on into a German truck convoy driving unsuspectingly into Lohr from the east. The Americans machine-gunned the trucks without stopping. When a young officer saw that some of those killed were girls in uniforms, he vomited.

The invaders turned northeast, following the left bank of the twisting Main River. As they passed a flak train running along the river, they destroyed the engine and threw thermite grenades into its multibarreled 20-mm. anti-aircraft guns. Not long after dawn, the task force approached Gemünden, a hilly town on the Main, at the confluence of the Sinn and Saale rivers. To Baum it looked like a perfect place for an ambush. He sent back word not to use radios or even talk.

At 6:30 the column rolled into Gemünden. Sergeant Donald Yoerk in one of the last tanks was amazed to see German soldiers walking nonchalantly in the street carrying briefcases. This town, unlike all the others, seemed to be completely unaware that an American task force was on the loose. To the right of the highway, Yoerk saw a train come out of marshaling yards, heading in his direction. In the next tank Frank Malinski hit the engine with his first shot, and then began blasting the cars. Suddenly an ammunition car blew up. When the smoke cleared, Yoerk could see only four wheels sitting on the track. Farther ahead, the light tanks had already set fire to several barges on the river and ripped apart a combination passenger-freight train. Now the Shermans moved up and knocked out a dozen more trains, tying up the entire yards. By chance a German division was just detraining and was thrown into confusion.

Baum told Lieutenant William Nutto to send his Shermans through town, raking both sides of the road as they went. Two platoons of infantry accompanied them on foot, but as the first two men stepped onto a bridge in the center of town it blew up, killing them both. The Shermans milled around, cut off from the rest of the column behind them, and Germans began firing panzerfausts from windows and roof tops. Baum and Nutto were several hundred yards to the rear, talking over plans. Hearing noise of battle ahead, they ran toward the wrecked bridge just in time to see one Sherman aswarm with Germans swing its turret around as if trying to swipe them off. Suddenly a panzerfaust round exploded, throwing Baum and Nutto to the cobblestone street. Momentarily blinded, Nutto clutched his chest; he was also hit in the legs. Baum felt pain in his right hand and knee, and blood seeped through his pants leg. He yelled, "Let's get the hell out of here!" and pulled back the column.

The main road to Hammelburg was cut off and Baum quickly selected a new route.* He detoured north along the west bank of the Sinn River, looking for a crossing. At 8:30 A.M. he sent his first message: a request for an air attack on the Gemünden marshaling yards.

The German Seventh Army had just learned about the destruction in Lohr and Gemünden, and immediately ordered all available forces to stop the rampaging Americans. It was a German, however, who helped Baum solve his immediate problem: a paratrooper home on sick leave and tired of war readily divulged that the best place to cross the Sinn River was at Burgsinn, eight miles above Gemünden.

Within a mile the Americans captured another German of more importance but less use—a leather-coated general whose Volkswagen blundered into the column. "Who the hell are you?" Baum asked when the general proudly walked forward, pulling on his gloves. He started to explain, in German, but Baum interrupted, "Get the son of a bitch up in a half-track and let's get going."

The column crossed the Sinn, then struck off southeast on a mountain trail. The terrain was hilly and heavily wooded, but the ground was firm enough for the tanks and vehicles. In a few minutes they came upon a road gang of about 700 Soviet prisoners, who at the sight of American tanks jumped their guards and seized their weapons. Yoerk saw one Russian brandishing a bayonet as he chased a guard into the woods. Baum turned over the 200 prisoners he had already collected to the Russians, who

---

* A few minutes after Baum had left Gemünden, a three-man Combat Propaganda Team arrived, headed by T/3 Ernst Langendorf. Langendorf had been told simply to help Baum get through town and had no idea he was already thirty-five miles behind enemy lines. The Langendorf team broadcast appeals in German, and some 300 soldiers promptly surrendered. Langendorf told them to wait for the next American unit and returned home without a shot fired at him—still unaware that he had been in German territory for hours.

assured him that they would continue guerilla warfare in the area until the Americans arrived in force.

The task force then crossed the Fränkische Saale, and they were only five miles from their goal when a German liaison plane droned overhead. Baum stopped the column. In the relative silence he could hear armored vehicles not far away. There was no use trying to hide, so he decided to head northeast, straight for Hammelburg. Shortly thereafter he saw his first German tanks—only two, which after a few harmless shots pulled away, but Baum knew others had to be near by. At 2:30 P.M. the town of Hammelburg finally came into view. Half a mile short of the outlying houses, the American column turned off the main highway and started up the steep hill to the prison camp.

Suddenly a German tank stuck its nose around the corner ahead, then another and another. Baum ordered his remaining six Shermans to attack and radioed Sergeant Charles Graham to move up his three self-propelled guns. The fight for Oflag XIIIB was on.

### 3.

The prisoners heard the first brief exchange of tank fire in the distance, and Colonel Goode joined the rush to the barbed-wire fence at the edge of the camp. Across fields dotted with grazing sheep Father Paul Cavanaugh, a Jesuit chaplain of the 106th Division, watched two platoons of German guards scramble into prepared positions along the crest of the hill while an entire company hastily manned prepared positions astride the road from Hammelburg. On the side of the road were two 40-mm. Bofors guns.

For thirty minutes the prisoners waited; then all at once a cacophony of machine guns, panzerfausts, rifles, 76s and mortars rattled across the meadows. "That's the way a tank battle starts, Padre," Colonel Goode said. "I've heard enough of them to know. General Patton's boys are getting close—and the Germans are going to move us out of here." He said he had already stalled Goeckel twice that morning and hoped to keep holding him off until the Americans arrived.

As the noise of battle grew louder, some of the men drifted away from the fence toward the kitchen to break open the hoarded supplies for one final "bash." About 100 others were heading for Father Cavanaugh's barracks where he was about to hear confessions before Mass. At 3:50 P.M. there was a staccato series of blasts on the camp siren, and word was shouted from doors and windows: "All men stay in the barracks where you are!" A few stragglers darted across the compound to get to the Mass.

"Since no more can get here," Father Cavanaugh said a moment later,

"I will start Mass immediately and give you General Absolution before Holy Communion." While he was putting on the vestments he kept hidden in a cardboard box in the storeroom, several American shells landed near by. He hastily began the prayers at the foot of the altar—a table. He was frightened and hoped it didn't show.

At the Gospel, another shell landed in the area and everyone dropped to the floor. After waiting a moment, Cavanaugh crawled out from under the altar, and though he felt he wasn't giving them a very good example, asked them to be calm and remain kneeling. "If anything happens, just stretch out on the floor. I'll give you General Absolution now." With trembling hands he made the sign of the cross over the kneeling congregation. "Men, be calm. I am going to shorten this Mass as much as possible so that everyone may get to Holy Communion." Facing the altar, he read the "Hanc igitur" prayer. Never before had the words seemed so meaningful. "Graciously accept, O Lord, this offering of our subjection to you. Give us peace today. Save us from eternal damnation and number us in the flock of your chosen ones, through Christ our Lord."

Norman Smolka wasn't a Catholic but was present because he happened to be quartered in the barracks. As he looked up from the floor, sun rays burst through the window, illuminating the priest. The padre looked "as if he were God."

The object of the battle outside, John Waters, was watching the action from the ground floor of Goode's headquarters. Waters was a handsome man of thirty-nine from Baltimore. He had attended Johns Hopkins University for two years, majoring in both the arts and sciences, and then transferred to West Point. In 1931 he graduated as a second lieutenant of Cavalry. He was a quiet, soft-spoken soldier of outstanding ability, and was executive officer of the 1st Armored Regiment when captured in North Africa in February, 1943.

Waters could see several American tanks roll across the fields, firing into the Serbian barracks. Just then General von Goeckel burst in. He was now Goode's prisoner, he said, and the war was over for him. He asked if any American would volunteer to go out and stop the fire. Apparently the attackers were mistaking the Yugoslavs for Germans because of their uniforms.

"Okay, I'll go out," Waters said. "We ought to take an American flag and a white flag so we won't get shot." He then went through the main gate, past the imposing sentry house. Beside him was Hauptmann (Captain) Fuchs, a German interpreter. A step behind came two more U. S. volunteers, one carrying an American flag, the other a white sheet on a pole. They intended to skirt the battleground and make contact from the side.

Task Force Baum was just coming directly over the ridge onto the high ground where the German guards were dug in. The tank battle on the hill had been brief but fierce. Baum lost five half-tracks and three jeeps, but his six Shermans had knocked out three German tanks and three or four ammunition trucks.

Great clouds of smoke were billowing as the Waters party continued toward Task Force Baum. About a half mile from the main gate they came to a barn enclosed by a plank fence. Fifty yards away a soldier in camouflage uniform started running toward them. Waters wasn't sure he was a German or an American in paratrooper uniform, and called out, "*Amerikanisch!*"

The soldier was German. He ran up to the fence, stuck his sniper's rifle through it and fired before Fuchs could explain. Waters felt as if he had been hit with a baseball bat, but strangely, there was no pain. Lying in the ditch where he had fallen, he thought, "Goddamn it, you've ruined my hunting and fishing."

The German vaulted the fence, backed Fuchs against a shed and yelled that he was going to shoot—and it took Fuchs several harrowing minutes to make him understand that they were parliamentaries. Then Patton's son-in-law was put in a blanket and carried back to camp.

Inside the compound, Americans were packed behind the windows, cheering as if they were watching the World Series. A stray bullet spit through the glass and everyone hit the floor, but they immediately got back to the windows. From the second floor of the infirmary the camp surgeon, Major Albert Berndt of the 28th Division, saw Sherman tanks heading up over the plateau. Suddenly .50-caliber machine-gun slugs began tearing through the roof. Fearing an assault on the unmarked U. S. infirmary, Berndt ran down to Goode's office and suggested that a team of doctors and corpsmen set up a second aid station at the other end of the building—a solid partition divided the structure and there was no way to get from one end to the other without going ouside. Goode told Berndt to do it, but he decided to wait until the heavy fire ouside died down. Half an hour later Goode learned that the second aid station had not yet been set up and sent for Berndt, who explained that he didn't think it was advisable to send his men out under fire. To Goode this was rank insubordination and he accused Berndt of disobeying a direct order. "I am hereby relieving you of your duties as camp surgeon."

At that moment the door was flung open and Waters was carried in.

Father Cavanaugh was distributing Holy Communion. His trembling hands made him fear he would drop the Consecrated Host. As he finished the last line of communicants, a spontaneous shout of joy came from outside.

The priest turned to the altar and finished Mass. Then he asked, "What happened?"

"Father, we're free! We're liberated!" General von Goeckel had surrendered to Goode.

"Wasn't it wonderful!" Major Fred Oseth exclaimed. "While Mass was going on, we were liberated. You're not a Kriegie any longer, Father."

Still clad in vestments, the priest looked out the window and watched an American tank grind to a stop. Prisoners crowded around it, trying to touch their liberators. Father Cavanaugh noticed how sharply the newcomers contrasted with the emaciated prisoners. The priest slowly removed his vestments, packing them away—for the last time, he thought—in the cardboard box. When he stepped outside he saw white sheets hanging from all the windows. Americans and Serbs were shouting in wild jubilation, shaking hands and hugging one another.

While the prisoners were eating the most sumptuous meal ever served at Oflag XIIIB, orders came from Goode to pack up. At dusk the Americans formed in a column of fives on Hermann Göringstrasse, blankets on backs, and keepsakes of prison life in an odd assortment of sacks and bags. Father Cavanaugh filled a flour sack—given to him by a Serb to be used as a towel—with socks, woollen shirt, bath towel, breviary and several pounds of food. A few were even carrying their Smoky Joes—stoves made from tin cans.

Illuminated by the flames of a burning building, the Americans triumphantly passed cheering Serbs. They filed through a great hole in the wire fence torn open by Baum's tanks, and headed across a field past the empty guard towers. About a mile from camp they reached the main body of Task Force Baum atop the dark plateau, its tanks silhouetted like giant ducks against the sky.

Exhausted by the excitement of the day and the exertion of climbing, they sat on the chill, damp earth as free men. They laughed and joked. Suddenly two rifle shots rang out and the tenseness returned. Word went around: "No smoking, no lights." For almost two hours they sat shivering as the moon darted in and out of clouds. Goode was conferring with Baum, who had learned to his surprise that there were not 900 prisoners but 1291, far too many to bring back. Baum, disheartened, turned to look at the men sitting on the hill, expecting to go home. He told Goode that he could only take those who were physically able to ride on the tanks or in the half-tracks.

Goode walked over to his waiting men and told them they would be divided into three groups: those who wanted to escape on their own, those who could ride tanks and half-tracks and fight their way back, and those who felt they should return to camp because of poor physical condition. "We have been liberated and are free," he said. "But until we can get within the American lines each man is on his own. Sixty miles is the distance we will have to make—without food or supplies, and we are in a weakened condition. . . . Each man is free to do as he thinks best."

It was quite a blow to them to learn that this was not the vanguard of Patton's army, only a tiny, exhausted armored force which had knifed its way far behind enemy lines and was now going to try to fight its way back. But at least it was a chance to escape, and about 700 of the prisoners began roaming up and down the column, searching and even battling for vacant places aboard vehicles. Personal gear and extra equipment were dumped to make room for more riders. While they were loading up and being handed weapons, a group of Germans crept up under cover of darkness and fired several panzerfaust rounds. One tank burst into flames. Baum took tighter control of the motley group and re-formed the column along a dirt road.

Some of the prisoners hadn't yet made up their minds and were wandering aimlessly around the field, talking about what to do. Bruce Matthews, a chaplain of the Disciples of Christ, went up to his former regimental commander, Colonel Theodore Seely, and asked if he had any orders.

"None, Chaplain—each man is on his own."

"Do you have any advice to share?"

"None, Chaplain."

"Do you mind telling me what you plan to do, sir?"

"I'm going back in, Chaplain," Seely replied, starting for the camp.

"Thank you, sir," Matthews said and climbed onto the left fender of a half-track. The heat of the motor felt good in the chilly night.

Lieutenant Alan Jones, Jr., son of the commander of the 106th Division, was perched on a tank and glad to ride, since his feet had been frozen in the icy boxcar ride from the Ardennes. Then the tank commander decided that some of the passengers were in the path of the gun traverse, and Jones and several others were put off. Jones hobbled away alone across the plateau, guided west by the stars.

Hundreds of others had already formed escape teams and were also disappearing into the darkness. Lieutenant Alexander "Bud" Bolling, Jr., a close friend of Jones's and the son of Major General Alexander R. Bolling, commander of the 84th Division, joined with three others and headed west down the hill. They heard dogs barking. The hunt was already on.

More than a third of the men were in no shape to march or fight and headed slowly back to camp. Father Cavanaugh joined this sad, silent retreat. Just after midnight he again passed through the gaping hole in the barbed wire around the Serbian compound. The Serbs, who had given the Americans such a rousing farewell a few hours before, gazed in silent dejection at the returning parade.

When the priest walked into his barracks someone said, "We are not free yet, Father."

"Well, let's get some sleep, anyway," he replied and rolled into his bunk. But a few minutes later someone shouted, "The Germans have taken over and are marching us out of here! Be ready in fifteen minutes."

At 1:30 A.M. on March 28 the 500 Americans who had been unfit to march to freedom were lined up on Hermann Göringstrasse by forty guards and herded out the main gate. Their pockets were stuffed with the only food left in camp—potatoes. As the disheartened group started down the winding road to Hammelburg, there was mist in the air and a chill dampness. In the darkness they could make out clusters of German soldiers waiting quietly on either side of the road. A few minutes later a motorized column approached and the prisoners were shunted to one side to let it pass through. Some of the vehicles stopped and Father Cavanaugh could hear the convoy troops talking with the guards in confused undertones.

## 4.

The exhausted Task Force Baum was slowly moving down the other side of the hill along a deeply rutted cart trail. Baum's men had been traveling and fighting for almost twenty-eight hours and they faced an even more arduous journey back to the American lines. The trail grew narrower. Finally the three medium tanks in the lead could go no farther, and doubled back a mile until another trail to the west was found. Faint marks on the rocky surface showed that the light tanks sent ahead on reconnaissance had gone that way.

As the main body fumbled its way down this dark path, they met the light tanks returning. The reconnaissance leader had good news to report: the little road ran almost all the way to Hessdorf, a town on the Hammelburg–Würzburg highway. Now Task Force Baum rumbled ahead once more, making good progress in spite of frequent stops to let the vehicles close up.

It was almost 2 A.M. by the time the column entered Hessdorf. Near the town square the column was blocked by two abandoned German trucks. Ex-Kriegies jumped off the tanks and pushed the trucks aside, and the column roared on. The commotion so alarmed the townspeople that white sheets began flapping from windows and doors. The column milled around in the dark and finally turned back north toward Hammelburg. Now Baum was on a main highway. He could return the way he had come but he knew that would be a hornet's nest of Germans, so he decided to head northwest until he made contact with the 4th Armored Division.

His reasoning was good, but Germans were waiting for him a mile ahead, in the next town. At the outskirts of Hollrich the lead tank creaked to a halt to avoid running into a roadblock. Suddenly, blinding flashes spurted from both sides of the highway as panzerfaust rounds slammed into the stalled tank, killing the commander and one of the ex-prisoners. The dazed gunner blindly sprayed the street with his .50-caliber machine gun.

Other panzerfaust rounds were flashing by like deadly Roman candles. One escapee clinging to the turret of the second tank was killed by a grenade, and several others cringing on the deck were wounded. It took a moment before the fatigued Americans reacted. Then the men from Hammelburg leaped into the ditch while the tankers fired machine guns into the roadblock and toward the field on both sides.

There was wild confusion as red and yellow tracers streaked across the sky. Then the fight was over just as abruptly as it had started, and only the idling motors and cries of the wounded could be heard. To Baum, it would be suicide to continue through the darkened town, and the tanks and vehicles clumsily backed down the narrow highway until they could turn around safely. A few minutes later the column moved off the road to reorganize on top of a commanding hill. The flurry of action had stimulated the ex-prisoners and they deluged the tankers with eager advice. Baum's weary men told them, with much profanity, "to take off," and a number indignantly started toward the highway.

Baum took stock of his force. He had started with 307 men and now had only 100 who could fight, and he himself was wounded in the hand and knee. He had six light and three medium tanks, three assault guns and twenty-two half-tracks. He ordered the gas siphoned from eight of the half-tracks into the tanks and radioed a final message stating simply that his mission was accomplished and that he was heading back.

The useless half-tracks were set on fire and the seriously wounded put in a stone building marked with the Red Cross emblem. Then Baum gathered the rest of the men and told them what they were up against. They were going back cross-country and would even use half-tracks as bridges, if necessary, to ford streams. In the distance Baum could hear the roar of enemy tanks and other vehicles coming from the east. He finished with a short pep talk and shouted, "Mount up!"

Task Force Baum was almost surrounded. To the south and northeast, self-propelled guns were approaching; two infantry companies and six tanks were closing in from the southeast, together with six Tigers from the north, and a column of armored vehicles from the northwest.

Baum was just stepping into his jeep when the fastest automatic tank fusillade he had ever heard opened up; the burning half-tracks made the task force a perfect target. Then, heavy small-arms fire came from the darkness. Baum's three assault guns fired smoke in a vain effort to throw up a protective screen, but the German barrage continued with deadly accuracy. Two assault guns, a light tank and several half-tracks were hit directly and the resultant blaze attracted even more withering fire from three sides.

Major Don Boyer of the 7th Armored Division was manning a tank's .50-caliber machine gun. Cursing continually, he enjoyed himself thoroughly for the first time since his capture in the Battle of the Bulge. But bravery was not enough. Task Force Baum was being annihilated by an enemy it could not see. Within fifteen minutes every American vehicle was ablaze, and the German tanks and infantry began to close in. With all his tanks gone, Baum himself headed for the woods, where he reorganized the remnants of his force. Several times he tried to lead an attack back to the area to see what could be salvaged from the holocaust, but each time the handful of Americans was driven back.

"Break up in groups of four and take off!" Baum yelled. He gave hasty directions and then started off with a Kriegie and Major Stiller, who had proved to be a silent but efficient fighter. The three tried to hide in a pine grove, but in minutes they were tracked down by dogs. In the ensuing melee Baum was shot in the leg—his third wound in two days.

Everything happened so quickly that Baum just had time to throw away his dog tags lest the Germans find out that he was Jewish. As he and six others were herded back toward the barn by a single guard, Baum took off his steel helmet and was about to bash the unsuspecting German on the head, when Stiller stayed him by grabbing his arm.

Baum's men were separated from the Hammelburg inmates for immediate questioning, but several Kriegies told the guards that Baum was one of them and he was allowed to join the group marching back to the camp. Supported by Stiller and another man, he hobbled down the road.

The first light of day revealed a hill littered with wrecked, smoldering tanks and half-tracks. The surrounding trees were smashed or shell-scarred; the barn marked with the red cross lay in ruins. This was the graveyard of Task Force Baum.

The mission to Hammelburg was a complete failure, but the gallant force had accomplished something quite different and even more important than Patton intended. Task Force Baum had left a path of destruction in its wake. Every town it had passed through was in a state of confusion and hysteria. The German Seventh Army headquarters still did not know what had happened, and had already diverted the equivalent of several divisions to guard strategic crossroads and bridges while another large force was scouring the hills with dogs, trying to round up about 1000 liberated Americans and Russians.

The cost was not small. In addition to Baum's own losses, John Waters, the gentlemanly cavalryman from Baltimore, the husband of Patton's daughter, "Little B," was lying in the hospital at Hammelburg, badly wounded. The bullet had entered Waters' right thigh and torn through his left buttock. A Yugoslav doctor, Colonel Radovan Danich—equipped only with paper bandages and a table knife—was skillfully keeping the wound drained.

The Third Army press officer merely told correspondents that a task force had been lost and gave no details. Some time later, however, bits of the story were revealed and Patton called a press conference. He told newsmen categorically that he had not known until nine days after Baum reached Hammelburg that his son-in-law was among the prisoners. To prove his statement, he displayed his official and private diaries and said, "We attempted to liberate the prison camp because we were afraid that the American prisoners might be murdered by the retreating Germans."

Hoge, Abrams and Stiller knew differently but as good soldiers kept silent. Stiller died without revealing the truth and the other two waited for almost twenty years.

# 18

## Decision at Rheims

**1.**

For many years Danzig had played a vital role in the history of eastern Europe. It was not only Poland's chief water outlet but the most important port on the Baltic. At this time it was vital not only as the greatest outlet for escape for those Germans cut off by the Russian offensive but as one of the last few *Festungen* in the east—one so important to Hitler that he ordered the entire area defended to the last man. More than 225 air miles northeast of Zhukov's deepest bridgehead on the Oder, this *Festung* had become the haven of so many civilian and military refugees from East Prussia that almost 1,000,000 human beings were now jammed in Danzig and her sister port, Gotenhafen, fifteen miles to the north.

By early March, Marshal Rokossovsky had swung his Second White Russian Front behind Danzig, completely cutting off escape to the Reich —except by sea. On March 22 he suddenly drove a wedge between Danzig and Gotenhafen—"Gdynia" to Poles. Two days later pamphlets signed by the marshal were dropped from Russian planes, calling on the defenders to cease resistance. Rokossovsky warned that he was setting up artillery to blast the two ports. "Under these circumstances your resistance is foolish and will only result in your destruction and that of hundreds of thousands of women, children and old people. . . . For all who are going to surrender, I guarantee your life and your personal belongings." The others would be killed in battle.

The answer came that night from the Führer headquarters: EACH SQUARE METER OF THE AREA DANZIG-GOTENHAFEN MUST BE DEFENDED

TO THE END. It was the death sentence for two cities already on the verge of starvation. Red Army planes began dropping incendiaries and high-explosive bombs as heavy artillery systematically pounded the area. Within hours a wall of smoke and flame almost three miles high encircled Danzig.

There was also terror from within the city. To stiffen resistance, SS men were hanging scores of soldiers from the trees. Signs around their necks read, "I am a Traitor," "I was a Coward," "I am a Deserter" or "I disobeyed my Commander." And when refugee carts blocked traffic, their owners were often dragged out and strung up as a warning to other "culprits." Wehrmacht officers denounced this terrorism so bitterly that open conflict among the defenders threatened to erupt.

On Palm Sunday evening, March 25, Frau Klara Seidler, an elderly widow, huddled with friends in the cellar of an apartment house near the center of Danzig. All at once the building shook like a ship at sea, the lights went out and rubble rained down. There was an awesome explosion, the door blew open and there was a burst of flames. The little group, faces covered in wet towels, finally found a way to the street, each person carrying as many possessions as possible. They ran down the dark, smoky streets, looking for refuge from the increasing rain of bombs and shells. The Johanniskirche was crowded and they hurried to the Langen-brücke, only to find it on fire. They turned back and scrambled into a house just as a shell exploded in the entrance. They panicked and ran into the street over the bodies of five people, then tried in vain to push their way into the huge bunker at the dam, where people were already jammed to the very top of the stairway.

A few minutes later the Hochbunker was a mass of flames. With their clothes and hair on fire, people staggered out screaming. The Seidler group dropped all possessions but their suitcases. They hurried down the streets, which were littered with luggage and dead or dying, and at last found refuge, with 2000 others, in the cellar of the gas works office. Here they huddled in terror all night as shells landed overhead with terrifying regularity.

By morning most of the able-bodied had fled the cellar, but the Seidler group stayed all day. At midnight there was an abrupt silence, then they heard military music blasting from a loudspeaker, and at 2 A.M., March 27, someone from above shouted, "Do you surrender down there?" A white cloth was hastily stuck out the cellar doorway. After a tense half-hour several dozen good-looking Russians in new uniforms came into the cellar, and politely told everyone to return home; there would be no more shelling or bombing; it was all over.

At the Seidler apartment a vehicle draped with carpets drove up and four Red Army officers climbed out and asked for water. They were afraid anything else might be poisoned and refused coffee or tea. Like the Russians in the cenan they were correct and offered the frightened civilians cigarettes. One German went to the piano and played all the Russian music he could remember, while the women sewed buttons on some of the officers' uniforms.

All over Danzig, Red Army soldiers were plundering and raping but the Seidler party was safe—until their Soviet protectors left at dark. Then groups of soldiers burst in, shouting their favorite phrases: *"Uri, uri!"* and *"Frau, komm!"* Frau Seidler told Inge Bart, a girl of thirteen, to sit on her lap and act like a small child. They were spared, but many women of all ages were dragged out of the apartment and raped.

But there was worse to come. At noon, artillery again began to fall on the city. In panic the Seidler group grabbed what was near at hand— this time it was butter and sugar—and ran down the street, dodging crumbling walls. One of the men, Inge Bart's father, suddenly remembered that his pet bird had been left behind, so he returned to where he found drunken Russians smashing furniture and singing raucously. Several were sitting on the piano, pounding the keyboard with their feet. They had already killed the bird.

Bart left the apartment and rejoined the group, and they finally found a building that was not burning. The bombardment stopped and they came out—to meet another terror. Russian soldiers were rambling down the street, raping and murdering. An eighteen-year-old soldier, a bottle of wine clutched in one hand, shoved the elderly Frau Seidler into a phone booth.

"Grandmother is too old," she pleaded.

"Grandmother must!" he cried over and over.

Near by, a young mother with three small children tried to sneak into a cellar. Several Russians grabbed the woman and her children began screaming, "Mama, Mama!" A huge soldier suddenly seized one of the children and threw him headfirst against the wall, then the second and the third. Frau Seidler would never forget the terrible sound of crashing skulls.

When the Russians had gone, Frau Seidler helped the hysterical mother to her feet, but she crumpled to her knees and had to crawl. Another gang of Russians approached and eight of the refugees crowded around the woman to hide her, but she was discovered. The soldiers flung her down and one by one began raping her.

Frau Seidler's own troubles were far from over. A Pole and his girl friend noticed the wedding ring on her finger, and when it wouldn't come off, the man took out a knife as if to sever the finger. Frau Seidler somehow tore off the ring.

That night her group found another refuge—no safer than the others. They were lying face-down, not moving, letting themselves be trampled, as Russians roamed around, looking for women. At dawn all Danzig was burning. The smoke was suffocating; buildings collapsed. The little group found a small truck and decided to escape to the outskirts. They drove through the smoldering ruins, and overheard one woman, looking like a ghost, saying over and over, "My jewelry and gold is in the cellar!" They continued slowly through the burning streets, their throats parched by the heat and smoke. Their eyes stung and it was painful to keep them open.

By dusk they finally reached the suburbs and tried to sleep on the ground even though it rained, then snowed. But when artillery shells began falling again, they scurried into a damaged house almost filled with refugees. Safety was again only temporary; the Russians soon found the house, and their cry *"Frau, komm!"* began echoing through the rooms. The women—even sixty-seven-year-old Frau Mietke—were dragged into the halls. Here, to the roar of exploding shells and clatter of machine guns, they were raped and their breasts bitten badly. This time Frau Seidler escaped by crawling into a child's crib and covering herself with books and rubble. Even this hiding place was discovered by a Russian who asked her if she was sick. When she nodded and he went away, she decided to keep using the same subterfuge.

## 2.

The deteriorating situation in the east was also bringing about a deterioration in the personal relations between Hitler and his commander of that front. As Guderian and Major Freytag von Loringhoven drove up from Zossen to Berlin on the morning of March 28, the aide was sure the meeting would be a stormy one, since it was obvious that Guderian had reached the breaking point. What a crime, he thought, that one of Germany's greatest field commanders was wasting his talents in a conference room, arguing futilely with the Führer.

"Today I will tell him all!" Guderian burst out. What upset him particularly was that 200,000 German soldiers were needlessly trapped hundreds of miles behind Russian lines in Kurland.

Their car was now crawling through the rubble-littered streets of Berlin, past row after row of gutted, smoldering buildings, past harried citizens scrounging for scraps of food. They parked near the partially destroyed Reich Chancellery and walked along several corridors. Finally they were escorted by a guard down a flight of stairs to a steel-reinforced door guarded by two SS men. This was the entrance to Hitler's new home: the huge bunker way below the Reich Chancellery garden.

They went down more stairs to a narrow corridor, which was covered with a foot of water. This passage was actually a pantry and was referred to as Kannenbergallee after Hitler's butler, Artur Kannenberg. They balanced their way across duck boards to a door, then down another short flight of stairs to the upper level of the bunker. Twelve small rooms opened on a central vestibule which also served as the general mess hall.

Guderian and his aide went through this passageway, then down a curving stairway and a final dozen steps to the lower level, the Führer bunker. Here were eighteen cubicles, separated by an entrance hall which was divided into a waiting room and the conference room. Beyond these, in a small vestibule, was the emergency exit to four steep flights of concrete steps leading up to the Chancellery garden. On the left of the conference room was a small map room, a rest room for the Führer's bodyguard and the six-room suite of Hitler and Eva Braun. On the right were quarters for Drs. Theodor Morell and Ludwig Stumpfegger (he had replaced Dr. Karl Brandt as Hitler's surgeon), and a first-aid station. The whole bunker was protected by a twelve-foot-thick reinforced ceiling, topped by thirty feet of concrete. This would be Hitler's tomb or his bastion of victory.

The two officers were searched by more guards and admitted to the conference room, which was already filling up with important personages. The air was stuffy despite a ventilating system whose shrill, monotonous whine penetrated every room of the bunker.

A moment later Hitler shuffled in from his adjoining apartment, and the noon conference opened with a report by General Busse on his unsuccessful attempts to relieve Küstrin. When Busse tried to explain why the three counterattacks had failed, Hitler broke in sharply, "I am the commander! Responsibility for orders lies with me!"

This irrelevant interruption did not perturb Busse, who had attended many such conferences with Manstein. But Guderian could not control himself. "Permit me to interrupt *you*," he said. "Yesterday I explained to you in detail—both verbally and in writing—that General Busse was not to blame for the failure of the Küstrin attack." He seemed to whip himself into a fury with each word. His voice rose and his manner became violent. "Ninth Army used the ammunition that had been allotted to it. The troops did their duty—the unusually high casualty figures prove that. I therefore ask you not to make any accusations against General Busse!"

Stung by this direct attack, Hitler struggled to his feet. But Guderian was not intimidated. He boldly brought up the subject he and Hitler had fought about for weeks. "Is the Führer going to evacuate the Kurland army?" he asked accusingly.

Never! bellowed Hitler, waving his right arm. His face became deathly white, while Guderian's became red. The general advanced threateningly toward Hitler. General August Winter, Jodl's deputy, held Guderian from behind while Burgdorf tried to escort Hitler back to his chair.

Both Winter and Jodl were now shepherding Guderian away from Hitler, trying to walk off his fury, but he kept shouting at the Führer in a loud, uncontrolled voice. Freytag von Loringhoven was afraid that Guderian would be arrested, so he ran into the anteroom and telephoned the general's chief of staff. He hurriedly told General Krebs what was happening and asked him to hold the wire, then went back into the conference room and told Guderian there was an urgent call. For the next twenty minutes Krebs talked to Guderian, and by the time he returned to the conference room he had control of himself.

Hitler was back in his chair, face pinched, and though his hands trembled, he too had regained his poise. "I must ask all of you gentlemen to leave the room," he said quietly, "with the exception of the Feldmarschall and the Generaloberst." When Keitel, Guderian and Hitler were alone the Führer said, "General Guderian, the state of your health requires that you immediately take six weeks' sick leave."

Guderian extended his arm in a stiff salute. "I shall go," he said, starting to leave.

"Please stay here until the end of the conference," Hitler said evenly.

Guderian sat down too and the conference continued as if nothing had happened. After several hours, which seemed interminable to Guderian, the meeting was over. But he was not free yet; the Führer wanted him to remain. "Please take good care of yourself," he said solicitously. "In six weeks the situation will be very critical. Then I shall need you urgently. Where do you think you will go?"

Keitel suggested a spa in western Germany, Bad Liebenstein, but Guderian sarcastically informed him that the Americans were already there. "Well, what about Bad Sachsa in the Harz?" Keitel suggested good-naturedly.

Guderian said he would pick a place that wouldn't be overrun in the next forty-eight hours. He raised his arm in salute and, accompanied by Keitel, walked out of the Chancellery to his car. Keitel said he was glad Guderian had not opposed Hitler's suggestion to take a leave, and they parted.

It was evening by the time Guderian reached his private quarters in Zossen.

"The conference lasted terribly long today," Frau Guderian remarked.

"Yes," said the exhausted general, "and that is the last one. I have been dismissed." They embraced.

### 3.

By now every neutral capital in Europe had its own peace rumor. Stockholm had more than its share, some so fantastic that they quickly died. Probably the most fantastic was that Germany now sought peace with Russia, and about the only ones who gave it credence were those actively engaged in the operation.

These negotiations had started in mid-March when Foreign Minister von Ribbentrop invited the Japanese ambassador to Germany, General Hiroshi Oshima, to his office. "As a politician, I can do nothing now for my country except arrange peace with the Soviet Union," Ribbentrop told him, but neglected to add that Hitler knew nothing of the matter. "This will allow our forces on the eastern front to be used in the west for a great concentrated effort against the British and Americans."

In Oshima's opinion it was too late for any such move, but he listened without comment as Ribbentrop pointed out that since Japan and the Soviet Union had a neutrality pact, Russo-German peace would enable both Germany and Japan to channel their strength toward defeating the British and Americans.

"Contact can be made in Tokyo or Moscow through Japanese diplomatic circles," Ribbentrop went on. "But I'd rather avoid Tokyo and Moscow." It would be best, he said, to meet Foreign Commissar Molotov somewhere else, through Major General Makoto Onodera, the Japanese military attaché in Stockholm. "Then the matter could be settled at one stroke." Oshima remained dubious but promised to sound out Onodera.

On March 25 Lieutenant General Mitsuhiko Komatsu, the military attaché in Berlin, radioed Onodera:

AMBASSADOR OSHIMA WANTS TO HAVE EARNEST DISCUSSION WITH YOU. PLEASE COME TO BERLIN IMMEDIATELY. THE GERMAN AIR FORCE GUARANTEES SAFE-CONDUCT ON YOUR FLIGHT. . . . FURTHERMORE, KEEP IT STRICTLY CONFIDENTIAL FROM OUR MINISTER IN STOCKHOLM AS WELL AS TOKYO THAT AMBASSADOR OSHIMA SENT FOR YOU.

Three days later, on March 28, Onodera landed at Tempelhof in a Swedish plane and was driven to the Japanese embassy. Here he conferred with Ambassador Oshima, General Komatsu and three embassy officials.

"As you know, Germany is pressed from both west and east, and the situation is growing desperate," Oshima began, and then described his strange meeting with Ribbentrop. The consensus was that the proposal had little chance of success, but all agreed that with Stalin the most fantastic things were possible. At any rate, it was worth a try, and they decided that Onodera should return to Stockholm and get in touch with the Soviet ambassador to Sweden.

The next day Oshima reported to Ribbentrop that Onodera had agreed to approach the Soviets. Now for the first time Ribbentrop revealed that Hitler was ignorant of the proposal, and he asked the Japanese ambassador to do nothing until he got the Führer's approval. Oshima returned to his embassy and waited, and about midnight he was asked to come to Ribbentrop's office at once. "Hitler refused [*kategorisch abgelehnt*]!"

Dresden—after the three controversial bombings of February 13-14, 1945.

The Yalta Conference, February 4-11. At one of the plenary meetings at Livadia Palace (clockwise from left) Vishinsky, Molotov, Stalin, ———, Gromyko, Leahy, Stettinius, Roosevelt, Bohlen, Byrnes, ———, Eden, Churchill. Hopkins is bending over behind Roosevelt.

East meets West *en passant*. After Stalin broke promises made at Yalta, Harriman constantly urged a harder policy toward the Soviet Union.

The Big Three in the patio of Livadia Palace, February 10.

*(Below)* Stettinius proposes a toast to the momentous conference which has just ended.

The Führer and a member of his inner circle, his private chauffeur, Erich Kempka. This picture, taken at Rastenburg in 1942, has never before been published.

KEMPKA

The man who exercised the greatest influence on Hitler in the last 100 days, Martin Bormann *(right)*, little known even in Germany and rarely photographed. With him is Foreign Minister Joachim von Ribbentrop.

Reichsführer Heinrich Himmler, the most powerful man in Germany next to Hitler.

Himmler met clandestinely four times with Count Bernadotte. The Count's mission was purely humanitarian; Himmler's, personal and political.

The role of Kaltenbrunner in these and similar negotiations is still clouded in mystery.

Ernst Kaltenbrunner, chief of the Sicherheits-dienst (the SS Security Service).

Count Folke Bernadotte, vice-president of the Swedish Red Cross.

Commanders on the eastern front. Upon these men fell the task of stemming the Red Army drives on Berlin and Dresden.

General Theodor Busse, Ninth Army *(right)*, and Colonel Ernst Biehler, commander of the Frankfurt an der Oder *Festung*.

WALTER K. NEHRING

General Gotthard Heinrici, Army Group Vistula.

General Walther Wenck, Twelfth Army.

Baron Hasso von Manteuffel, Third Panzer Army.

Generalfeldmarschall Ferdinand Schörner, Army Group Center.

On April 29 Hitler drew up his political testament and named Grossadmiral Karl Dönitz his successor.

The Führer's favorite commando, the legendary Otto Skorzeny, most famed for his rescue of Mussolini.

U. S. ARMY

Four American generals discuss strategy in the Rhineland. George S. Patton, Jr., though lowest in rank, is, as usual, dominating the conversation. The others are *(left to right)* Omar Bradley, Courtney Hodges and Dwight Eisenhower.

The most famous bridge of 1945—the railroad span at Remagen—just after its collapse on May 17. General William Hoge (*inset*) called for its capture despite a conflicting order. Across the Rhine are the two towers stormed by GIs and the precipitous Erpeler Ley.

Against Eisenhower's orders, Churchill crossed the Rhine just after Montgomery's assault. Everyone, including Montgomery and General William Simpson (three stars), is in a jovial mood, except Field-Marshal Alan Brooke (*extreme right*) whose apprehension was justified. Upon landing, Churchill struck out east and had to be restrained by Simpson.

The three key figures in Operation "Sunrise," the clandestine plan for surrender of all German forces in Italy by Obergruppenführer Karl Wolff, head of the SS in Italy *(left)*.

Allen Dulles, head of the OSS in Switzerland *(above)*, discusses the plan with his chief assistant, Gero von S. Gaevernitz.

Count Pier Luigi Bellini, the Italian partisan leader whose men captured Mussolini, his ministers and his mistress, Claretta Petacci, at Lake Como.

After their execution by Communist partisan leaders—over the protests of Bellini—the Fascist leaders, as well as Miss Petacci, were hauled to Milan, mutilated and strung up on the girders of a partially constructed gas station.

WIDE WORLD

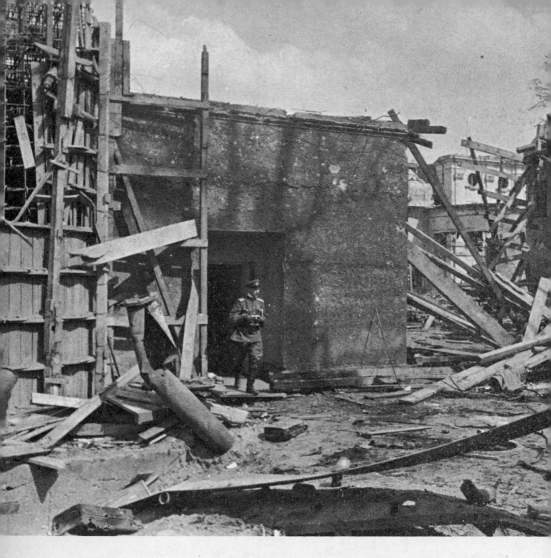

A Soviet officer stands in the emergency exit from Hitler's bunker facing the blasted garden of the Reich Chancellery. Here the bodies of the Führer and his wife were cremated for hours with gasoline on the afternoon of April 30.

The next day Joseph Goebbels and his wife walked up to the garden and ordered an SS man to shoot them. Their bodies too were doused with gasoline and set ablaze; a few days later Russians found the charred remains (right).

Hitler and Eva Braun at the famed tea house on top of Kehlstein Mountain.

Reichsmarschall Hermann Göring.

The end of Hitler's Thousand-Year Reich. Red Army man plants flag atop the ruins of the Reichstag on May 5.

One of the last pictures taken of the Führer; he is decorating a Hitler Youth just outside the bunker.

Marshals Grigory Zhukov (*left*) and Konstantin Rokossovsky, who, with Ivan Konev, led the Red Army attacks on Berlin.

VICTORY . . . Eisenhower a few moments after the first signing of the German surrender at Rheims, May 7. *(Left to right)* General Walter Bedell Smith, Lieutenant Kay Summersby (Eisenhower's secretary), Captain Harry Butcher, General Eisenhower and Marshal of the Royal Air Force Sir Arthur Tedder.

. . . AND DEFEAT: Generalfeldmarschall Wilhelm Keitel after the second and final surrender ceremony in Berlin, May 8. To his left is Admiral Hans Georg von Friedeburg; to his right, General Hans Jürgen Stumpff.

Ribbentrop greeted him excitedly. "Then he told me, 'I am absolutely convinced that I will win final victory against both east and west.' " Ribbentrop said, however, that another opportunity to negotiate might come later. "Have General Onodera bear this in mind."

Walking through the dark streets of the wrecked city, Oshima wondered why Ribbentrop had ever thought up such a silly idea. What impressed him was Hitler's point-blank answer to Ribbentrop and his unalloyed conviction of victory. Oshima was so impressed by the Führer's optimism that he decided to report the whole matter to Tokyo.*

## 4.

On the day that Guderian was relieved of command, March 28, Dwight Eisenhower was preparing to make a decision—a decision that became one of the most fateful of the war. The tremendous military events of the past two months were causing the Supreme Commander to re-evaluate his plans for the final assault on the heart of Germany. Who could have envisioned six months earlier that Zhukov would now have bridgeheads across the Oder River, forty air miles from the Reich Chancellery, or that Hoge would grab intact a bridge across the Rhine or that Patton would surge so dramatically through the Palatinate and leap the Rhine at Oppenheim?

Eisenhower reasoned that the Germans could hold Berlin for only a few more weeks. How could he possibly reach the capital first, when Simpson's spearhead at Dorsten was still 285 air miles from the center of Berlin and in between were the Harz Mountains and the Elbe River? Furthermore, if Eisenhower continued the main attack toward Berlin, as his field commanders expected, he was sure this would lead to "the practical immobilization of units along the remainder of the front."

An attack on Berlin, therefore, was out of the question. Instead, he would surround the Ruhr area and launch his main attack to the southwest, toward Munich and Leipzig. The troops bound for Leipzig would push on to meet the Russians as quickly as possible, while the others drove into southern Bavaria and Austria to wipe out the National Redoubt, where Hitler was rumored to be preparing a last desperate defense. And instead of going to Berlin, Montgomery would swing to the northwest and seize Lübeck, the important Baltic port just above Hamburg—and cut off German troops in Denmark and Norway.

This was Eisenhower's official reasoning for his decision not to seize

---

* Though Oshima did inform his country of this peace feeler, his message was never recorded and this information is revealed for the first time. It was confirmed by General Onodera.

Berlin, but he could also have been influenced by more personal motives. He knew that some senior American generals—Bradley, Patton, Simpson and Hodges in particular—felt that they had not been utilized to the full extent of their capabilities since the Battle of the Bulge. This new plan would give him the excuse to transfer the initiative to the Americans. A drive to Leipzig and Munich would have to be led by Bradley and would necessitate the return to him of Simpson's Ninth Army once the Ruhr was encircled.

Perhaps there was one other factor that helped shape Eisenhower's thinking. Recently Churchill had shown him the barbed message of suspicion from Molotov regarding Operation "Sunrise." What more open and conciliatory move could he now make than reveal his new plan to Stalin? It would surely prove that Americans could be trusted to wage war with no ulterior purpose.

Whatever the reason, Eisenhower considered it so important that on the afternoon of March 28 he sent a personal message to Stalin—without first checking it with the Combined Chiefs of Staff—via General Deane in Moscow, asking him to transmit it to Stalin and get "a full reply."

Eisenhower told Stalin of his decision to launch his main attack south of Berlin—and to leave the capital to the Russians:

. . . BEFORE DECIDING FIRMLY ON MY PLANS, IT IS, I THINK, MOST IMPORTANT THEY SHOULD BE CO-ORDINATED AS CLOSELY AS POSSIBLE WITH YOURS BOTH AS TO DIRECTION AND TIMING. COULD YOU, THEREFORE, TELL ME YOUR INTENTIONS AND LET ME KNOW HOW FAR THE PROPOSALS OUTLINED IN THIS MESSAGE CONFORM TO YOUR PROBABLE ACTION.

IF WE ARE TO COMPLETE THE DESTRUCTION OF GERMAN ARMIES WITHOUT DELAY, I REGARD IT AS ESSENTIAL THAT WE CO-ORDINATE OUR ACTION AND MAKE EVERY EFFORT TO PERFECT THE LIAISON BETWEEN OUR ADVANCING FORCES. I AM PREPARED TO SEND OFFICERS TO YOU FOR THIS PURPOSE.

Six months earlier Eisenhower had written Montgomery that Berlin clearly was the main prize. "There is no doubt whatsoever, in my mind, that we should concentrate all our energies and resources on a rapid thrust to Berlin." And until the night of March 28 Montgomery had imagined that Eisenhower still held the same thoughts. Then he received a message that once the Ruhr area was surrounded, Simpson's army would revert to Bradley, who would deliver the main Allied attack toward Leipzig. Henceforth Montgomery's role would be merely "to protect Bradley's northern flank." Eisenhower's message was, of course, a stupefying blow to a man who was already Berlin-bound with the main Allied force, and it was little consolation to read the last optimistic words: AS YOU SAY, THE SITUATION LOOKS GOOD. . . .

Two American armies were in the throes of encircling the Ruhr industrial area in a huge pincers movement. The northern claw was Simpson, the southern Hodges; and neither general knew that as soon as they met and entrapped Model's entire army group, American hopes would be realized: Simpson would be back under Bradley's command and the Americans would then launch the main Allied attack.

Spearheading the Hodges claw was the 3rd Armored Division, and spearheading the division was Task Force Richardson. Late on the night of March 28, Lieutenant Colonel Walter Richardson was ordered to report to Colonel Robert Howze, commander of Combat Command Reserve, 3rd Armored Division. Richardson was a bit disgruntled. He had been fighting for over a week with almost no sleep and guessed he was about to lose some more. At Howze's command post he met his old friend and fellow Texan, Lieutenant Colonel Sam Hogan. They had fought side by side across France, in the Bulge and over the Rhineland.

Howze, usually a calm man, was excited. "We'll move," he told the two lieutenant colonels. "We'll really go!" He pointed to Paderborn on the map and looked meaningfully at Richardson. It was more than 100 miles north-northeast.

Richardson couldn't believe his eyes. "You mean—get to Paderborn in one day?"

Howze nodded. "Tomorrow morning *you* leave for Paderborn. Just go like hell! Get the high ground at the Paderborn airport." Turning to Hogan, he ordered him to cover Richardson, slightly echeloned to the left. Task Force Welborn, from another combat command, would come up on Richardson's right, with the rest of the division following as best they could. "Get to Paderborn—don't stop," and the general explained that Simpson's 2nd Armored Division would meet them there. This would put the entire Ruhr in a sack.

It was the kind of mission Richardson liked, and he forgot his exhaustion. Back at his own command post he told his commanders that they were going to move out at 6 A.M. He said Howze had given him only one order, "Go!" and they were free to move anywhere—off the road, on trails, on highways—as long as they got to Paderborn in one day. It was typical of Richardson that he got up at 4 A.M. and personally reconnoitered three miles ahead in his jeep so that the task force could start with momentum. When he found nothing out front, he returned and inspected the column to see that extra gas was aboard.

At 6 A.M. Task Force Richardson started north full throttle, at 32 miles an hour, with orders to circle any strong roadblock and move cross-country if necessary. In the lead was a half-track and several jeeps. Then came Richardson's jeep and three Shermans stripped of equipment and riders. Behind them were seventeen Shermans loaded with infantrymen and three big Pershings with their great 90-mm. guns. Next came Richardson's staff, a battery of self-propelled guns, seventeen more Shermans, light tanks and a long line of trucks filled with men, ammunition and food. It was a mobile, battle-tested force, and in spite of general exhaustion, almost everyone was as eager as Richardson himself.

Little happened all morning as they raced north in column. At noon they knocked out a German passenger train without stopping, then rolled through several peaceful-looking military installations. When they finally came to a roadblock Richardson simply smashed his way through, using the lead tanks like battering rams.

Just before dusk Richardson checked his speedometer; it had already clocked seventy-five miles. But fog was rolling in and his radioman could make no contact. There was only one thing to do, push on. Entering Brilon a few minutes later, Richardson received a radio order from the division commander, Major General Maurice Rose: Task Force Richardson was to clear Brilon. Richardson acknowledged the message, but as far as he was concerned he was still going to follow Howze's orders, so he kept going. Paderborn was more than thirty miles away and he didn't yet know which route to take. He went ahead with a few vehicles to find the best road, and sent the main body into Brilon to make a cursory investigation.

It was more than an hour before Richardson learned from a civilian that a good road to Paderborn was just ahead, but it was now so dark and foggy that someone would have to walk ahead and guide the column. He had just started to get out of his jeep to do the job himself when he heard the main body of his force at last catching up; he wondered what had kept them so long in Brilon. A young lieutenant, a platoon leader, leaped from the first tank and hustled up to Richardson through the gathering darkness.

"Follow me," said the colonel, and they started to walk down the road. Richardson noticed the lieutenant was so scared that his face looked white in the gloom. He didn't blame him.

The tanks, their lights shielded by blue tissue, rumbled behind, getting closer and closer. Richardson walked faster but the first tank kept gaining on him. When it nudged him in the back, he jumped aside and jogged across the road into the ditch. Like a faithful dog, the tank followed Richardson into the ditch. He scrambled back on the road and waved his flashlight frantically, but the tank continued to bear down on him. Now he could see the second and third tanks wobbling back and forth in a clumsy effort to follow the leader. And just behind he saw the dim mark of a red cross. What the hell were his ambulances doing up front? Finally, in answer to his signals, the first tank stopped with a lurch. There was a loud clank as the second tank banged into the rear of the first and, a moment later, two more metallic thuds.

Richardson shouted angrily at the driver of the first tank, and turned to the young platoon leader. "What the hell happened to the tank commander?"

The shaken lieutenant climbed up to the turret of the tank and looked in. "Something's wrong!" he called. "There's champagne all over the floor of the tank."

Richardson clambered up and saw the tank commander, eyes glassy, sitting on the floor of the turret clutching two bottles of champagne. The colonel hopped to the ground. "Guide the tanks up the road," he ordered the lieutenant. "Keep them on the road. Throw the champagne out and keep all hatches open." The cold and damp fog, he figured, would sober up his drunken column. As he walked back to the first ambulance, a familiar bundled-up figure shuffled toward him. It could only be Dr. "Scattergood." "We ought to go back to Brilon," said the doctor mysteriously and grinned.

"Scat, what in hell is going on?" Richardson asked suspiciously.

"Colonel, I have to tell you the truth." He confessed he was the one who had found a warehouse full of champagne in Brilon.

Richardson radioed his executive officer to get the rest of the task force out of Brilon immediately, if he had to shoot them out, and again started down the road on foot. After a few miles the fog thinned and the colonel returned to his jeep.

At midnight he again checked his speedometer and found that he had gone 109 miles—and his only casualties were hangovers. But five miles ahead lay Paderborn, site of a tank school and an SS Replacement Army training regiment. He stopped the column, told the men to gas up, eat and get a few hours' sleep. The next morning they would be in for a brawl.

## 5.

The British Chiefs' irate reaction to Eisenhower's decision was predictable. "To start with," Brooke wrote in his diary on the night of March 29, "he has no business to address Stalin direct, his communications should be through the Combined Chiefs of Staff; secondly, he produced a telegram which was unintelligible; and finally, what was implied in it appeared to be entirely adrift and a change from all that had been previously agreed on."

In this indignant mood, and without consulting Churchill, the British Chiefs sent a lengthy telegram to the American Chiefs of Staff. Eisenhower, they claimed, had exceeded his authority by writing Stalin directly. Worse, the decision to change the direction of attack was a grievous political and military mistake. They also pointed out that British Intelligence was not at all concerned with the rumors about the so-called

National Redoubt, which should be dismissed as a factor on which to base future strategy.

Marshall's reaction to this sharp rejoinder was to send a personal wire to Eisenhower listing the main British objections and requesting comments. This inspired Eisenhower to some second thoughts and he immediately wired Deane in Moscow, asking him to hold delivery of the message to Stalin if it was not too late. He must have been relieved when Deane replied that the message had not yet been processed and would be held until further notice.

Like his military leaders, Churchill too felt that Eisenhower had made a colossal blunder. In the first years of the war he had been as eager as Roosevelt to crush Hitler, and consequently often sacrificed political considerations. But since Yalta he had become increasingly convinced that the problems in the east foreshadowed the dangers of the future and that political matters gained in importance as victory neared. To him it was now clear that Russia "had become a mortal danger to the free world . . . that a new front must be immediately created against her onward sweep . . . that this front in Europe should be as far east as possible . . . that Berlin was the prime and true objective of the Anglo-American armies."

Further, he believed firmly that Prague should be liberated by the Americans, Austria regulated by the West on equal terms with the Soviets, and Tito's ambitions curbed. And most important, he realized that major issues between Russia and the West would have to be solved *before* the West surrendered any of the German territory it had liberated and before the Western armies were disbanded.

A remarkable mixture of sentimentality and cynicism, an aristocratic Tory with the common touch, Churchill was proving to be, his faults notwithstanding, the Western leader most capable of realistic judgment. For over a month he had been trying again and again to persuade Roosevelt that they must now stand firm together against Stalin's further aggressions.

"There seems to be only one possible alternative to confessing our total failure," he told Roosevelt in one pleading message. "That alternative is to stand by our interpretation of the Yalta Declaration. . . . In view of this, is it not the moment now for a message from us both on Poland to Stalin?"

Spurred by Churchill's repeated pleas and his own genuine anger at Molotov's insulting letter, Roosevelt at last cabled the Prime Minister on March 29 that the time had come "to take up directly with Stalin the broader aspects of the Soviet attitude . . ." and sent a copy of the message he was dispatching to Stalin. It ran as follows:

I CANNOT CONCEAL FROM YOU THE CONCERN WITH WHICH I VIEW THE DEVELOPMENTS OF EVENTS OF MUTUAL INTEREST SINCE OUR

FRUITFUL MEETING AT YALTA. THE DECISIONS WE REACHED THERE WERE GOOD ONES AND HAVE FOR THE MOST PART BEEN WELCOMED WITH ENTHUSIASM BY THE PEOPLES OF THE WORLD. . . . WE HAVE NO RIGHT TO LET THEM BE DISAPPOINTED. SO FAR THERE HAS BEEN A DISCOURAGING LACK OF PROGRESS MADE IN THE CARRYING OUT, WHICH THE WORLD EXPECTS, OF THE POLITICAL DECISIONS WHICH WE REACHED AT THE CONFERENCE PARTICULARLY THOSE RELATING TO THE POLISH QUESTION. I AM FRANKLY PUZZLED AS TO WHY THIS SHOULD BE AND MUST TELL YOU THAT I DO NOT FULLY UNDERSTAND IN MANY RESPECTS THE APPARENT INDIFFERENT ATTITUDE OF YOUR GOVERNMENT . . .

I WISH I COULD CONVEY TO YOU HOW IMPORTANT IT IS FOR THE SUCCESSFUL DEVELOPMENT OF OUR PROGRAM OF INTERNATIONAL COLLABORATION THAT THIS POLISH QUESTION BE SETTLED FAIRLY AND SPEEDILY. IF THIS IS NOT DONE ALL OF THE DIFFICULTIES AND DANGERS TO ALLIED UNITY WHICH WE HAD SO MUCH IN MIND IN REACHING OUR DECISIONS AT THE CRIMEA WILL FACE US IN AN EVEN MORE ACUTE FORM . . .

If the message wasn't as strong as Churchill might have wished, it was at least a step forward and made Eisenhower's personal message to Stalin even more disheartening. This was the time for firmness on all fronts.

Roosevelt sent this message the day he was preparing to leave for a vacation in Warm Springs. He talked briefly to each member of his Cabinet. To Frances Perkins he said, "I am going out to San Francisco to open the meeting, make my speech, and receive the delegates in a social and personal way." Though they were alone, he dropped his voice to a whisper. "Then we are going to England. Eleanor and I are going to make a state visit." He smiled with anticipation. "I have long wanted to do it. I want to see the British people myself. . . . I told Eleanor to order her clothes and get some fine ones so that she will make a really handsome appearance."

"But the war!" Miss Perkins protested. "I don't think you ought to go. It's dangerous. The Germans will get after you."

Roosevelt put his hand to his mouth and whispered, "The war in Europe will be over by the end of May."

The President also conferred with Byrnes and General Lucius D. Clay, just selected as Deputy Military Governor in Germany. Clay, unhappy at the appointment, since he had wanted combat duty in the Pacific, stood silently at attention while the President said he was glad a general who was also an engineer was going to Germany. And what did Clay think of establishing a TVA in central Europe to relieve the chronic coal shortage? Before the general could answer, Roosevelt spoke of his schooling in Germany, when he had "formed an early distaste for German arrogance and provincialism."

After the meeting Byrnes jokingly told Clay, "General, you talk too much."

"Mr. Justice, even if the President had given me a chance, I doubt that I could have talked to him, because I was so shocked at his appearance."

"Your comment worries me," Byrnes said. He saw the President frequently and not until that moment had he noticed the rapid decline in Roosevelt's health.

As Roosevelt left his office to take the train to Georgia, Admiral Leahy walked beside his wheel chair toward the south entrance of the White House. "Mr. President, it's very nice that you are leaving for a vacation," he said. "It is nice for us too, because when you are away we have much more leisure than when you are here."

Roosevelt laughed. "That's all right, Bill. Have a good time while I'm gone, because when I come back I'm going to unload a lot of stuff on you, and then you'll have to work very hard."


At Okecie, Warsaw's airport, twelve leaders of the Polish underground —wearing a hodgepodge of borrowed clothes, such as striped pants, and hunting and lounging jackets—were boarding a Red Army plane, to attend, they had been assured, a conference with Marshal Zhukov at his field headquarters.

At first several of the Poles had been reluctant to come out of hiding, but the majority argued that Zhukov's invitation indicated that Russia was willing to be reasonable; only such a meeting could bring security to their country. As a token of good will the Soviets had agreed to release imprisoned underground leaders, including Alexander Zwierzynski, chairman of the right-of-center National Democrats. They also promised to fly the eight leading underground delegates directly from Zhukov's headquarters to England to report to the London government-in-exile. The other Poles, of course, would be returned safely home.

Beguiled by such promises and hopes, the twelve Poles boarded the Soviet Liberator at Okecie in all innocence.* Inside, to their surprise, they found Zwierzynski. He was bewildered, and told them he had been kept in a cellar and brutally beaten, and then suddenly brought to the plane. What was going on?

The plane took off and it wasn't long before the Poles realized that they were heading eastward. While they were anxiously speculating on this development, a pleasant young Soviet captain told them that they

---

* Hours earlier, three other Polish underground leaders had been kidnaped by the Soviets and flown to Moscow.

were going to Moscow. Zhukov, he said, had unexpectedly been summoned there.

Some of the Poles were sure they were being kidnaped, but others saw the logic in a meeting in Moscow, where they could deal with the highest Soviet officials. And hadn't the Russians kept their promise by releasing Zwierzynski?

The engines droned on for hours, then suddenly sputtered and coughed, and the plane glided down into a snow bank. No one was hurt, but the passengers were stranded in a white wilderness. After a long wait, several hundred civilians cleared a road in the snow and the group was escorted to a railway station and on to Moscow. They arrived exhausted, hungry.

Zbigniew Stypulkowski, a National Democrat, and two other delegates were put in the first car. They passed the Foreign Office, where they were supposed to stay, finally stopping in front of a stately marble building, patrolled by well dressed NKVD guards.

"To what grand hotel have they brought us?" one impressed delegate asked.

"It's a prison," Stypulkowski told him. The gates were opened and the car entered a yard surrounded by walls with windows covered by steel shutters.

"But it's impossible!" his naïve comrade exclaimed.

The Poles got out of the car and were put in separate cells. Stypulkowski tore up the paper giving him authority to conduct talks with the London Poles and the Anglo-Americans, and began to swallow the pieces. Though his throat was dry, he finally accomplished the job just before a handsome young woman entered and grimly said, *"Rozdiewajtes!"* ("Undress!") When he only took off his overcoat and hat, she stamped her foot and said, "I told you—undress." He took off his shirt. She shouted again and he took off his pants. After a detailed and thorough search of every part of his body, she asked, "Do you have syphilis?" and left.

An NKVD man came in, cut off all the buttons on his clothes, ripped apart his hat, cut the lining of his coat and tore apart the soles of his shoes. After taking Stypulkowski's ring, watch and wallet, a guard ordered him to dress. He was led down long corridors to another cell, where he was searched again. Finally he was taken to the top floor and put in Room 99, a dark green cell with a small window overlooking the gloomy yard—of Lubianka Prison.

"This is your home now," the guard said and locked the door.

## 6.

In making his decision to let the Red Army take Berlin, Eisenhower felt he was avoiding politics and would always insist it was based on "purely military" factors—even when he fulfilled Patton's prophecy and won the highest political post in the United States. But in effect he was doing just the opposite. Military factors in the spring of 1945 involved more than the defeat of Germany, already almost an accomplished fact.

Eisenhower's action had been conditioned by the unique evolution of the American military establishment. Before the war it had been a small, highly professional group which was solely concerned with military threats to the United States regardless of political alliances or friendships. Consciously separating themselves from civilian thinking, the military had only one goal—the military security of the nation. And their job was to prepare defenses against future enemies as well as present ones. Their attitude toward foreign policy was based on one principle: Does it help or hurt the military security? Indeed, the military were performing their classic, proper function, without regard for public opinion or politics.

In the months preceding Pearl Harbor they were conservatively realistic in evaluating the long-range goal of establishing a balance of power in Europe and Asia. They strongly advised the President to proceed cautiously and avoid any break with Japan or Germany. At the same time Hopkins, Ickes, Morgenthau and Secretary of War Henry Stimson were urging Roosevelt to go to the aid of England. Again and again the military opposed embargoes or any other aggressive move that might lead to a two-front war. But Roosevelt was finally convinced that the world could only be saved by intervention and even though the military urged an abstention from the "precipitance of military action" in the fall of 1941, America was precipitated into war with Japan.

All at once the generals and admirals gained undreamed-of power as the civilian leaders willingly turned over unprecedented responsibility to them. Secretary of State Cordell Hull told Stimson, "I have washed my hands of it, and it is now in the hands of you and Knox—the Army and the Navy." And Stimson asserted that his duty now was "to support, protect, and defend his generals."

Soon after Pearl Harbor—at "Arcadia," the first Anglo-American war conference in Washington—it was agreed that a unified command must be created. Thus was born the Combined Chiefs of Staff, comprised of the British Chiefs of Staff and their U. S. counterparts. The British were already organized and the Americans, realizing that they must also present a common U. S. front so they would not be overridden by the British, created the Joint Chiefs of Staff: the Army Chief of Staff, the Commanding General of the Army Air Forces and the Chief of Naval Operations. A few months later a fourth member was added, Admiral Leahy, Chief of Staff to the President and an old comrade of World War I who probably had more personal contact with Roosevelt than any other man save Hopkins. As the war progressed, the Joint Chiefs became more and more political-minded because of their close personal relationships with Roosevelt. As Commander in Chief, the President, like Churchill, enjoyed the intimate association with his military leaders.

It was Harry Hopkins who "discovered" Marshall and recommended him for Army Chief of Staff. At first he was Marshall's contact with the President, but by 1943 the Army Chief of Staff had gained Roosevelt's confidence and needed no intermediary.

With such direct access, Leahy and Marshall had almost complete control of all military matters. Stimson and Frank Knox, the elderly Republican Secretaries of War and Navy, respectively, did not even meet with the Joint Chiefs and Roosevelt. Their influence gradually waned until procurement and logistics passed to the hands of their Under-Secretaries, Patterson and Forrestal.

The voice of the State Department was also muted. Of course diplomacy, not force, was its function, but during the war it confined its attentions mainly to the neutrals, minor allies and plans for the new World Organization. Roosevelt did not even allow Secretary of State Hull to attend the major war conferences. "After Pearl Harbor I did not sit in on meetings concerned with military matters," Hull wrote, aggrieved. "This was because the President did not invite me to such meetings. I raised the question with him several times. . . . The question of where the armies would land and what routes they would take across the Continent in the grand military movement to conquer Hitler was a subject never discussed with me by the President or any of his top military officials, although I was early informed of the decision reached. I was not told about the atomic bomb."

On the other hand, the influence of Marshall and Leahy kept growing to such a degree that only in rare cases was their advice turned down: once in 1942 regarding the invasion of North Africa and again in 1943 over the Indian Ocean offensive. Both times Roosevelt had approved the Joint Chiefs' recommendation but changed his mind, primarily because of British pressure. In short, all the important decisions of the war were being settled by Roosevelt, Hopkins and the Joint Chiefs. This had a curious result—the military became more and more involved with political considerations.

As the U. S. Chiefs grew in power and scope, they supported administration policies since they had done so much to form them. The British Chiefs, on the other hand, still retained their professional military outlook, often differing vociferously from the government view until a decision was reached. Then and only then did they solidly back Churchill.

By now the American Chiefs had generally accepted Roosevelt's concept of the conduct of the war.* In short, they were no longer purely and simply soldiers but statesmen-soldiers, often sharing the same perspective as informed citizens—it was as if ferocious watchdogs had been emasculated. Such opposition as there was rarely reached Roosevelt;

* In March, 1944, however, Marshall and the other U. S. Chiefs had unsuccessfully urged Roosevelt to restate the unconditional-surrender terms in order to reassure the German people.

the Joint Chiefs now had such rapport with him that they instinctively knew what he wanted and screened their ideas before presentation. In other words, the balance between the military and civilian points of view was upset, with no one representing the purely military.

"It may be true that the President formally overruled them on very few occasions," wrote Captain T. Kittredge, Historical Section of the Joint Chiefs, "but this was only because informal discussions of the President with Leahy, Marshall, King, and Arnold usually led them to know in advance the President's views. They, no doubt, frequently recognized the advantages of accepting the President's suggestions with their own interpretations, rather than of risking an overruling by presenting formally proposals they knew would not be accepted."

Thus in the name of expediency and harmony—a most dangerous harmony—the Joint Chiefs were not carrying out their basic function of advising the President on a strictly military basis. They had even become so sensitive to the power of public opinion that they strove for victory with the least possible loss of American lives. And any excursion, such as the attack on Berlin, would only result in casualties unnecessary to victory. That lives lost at Berlin might contribute to the future military security of America apparently was not considered.

The Joint Chiefs, of course, recognized that Russia would become the decisive power in Europe, but at the Quebec Conference of 1943 they had voted not only to help the Soviets but "to make every effort" to win her friendship. And a year later they agreed with Roosevelt that cooperation among the Big Three could replace the balance of power in Europe. They declared that the basic national policy "should seek to maintain the solidarity of the three great powers . . . during which, it may be hoped, arrangements will be perfected for the prevention of future world conflicts."

Though part of this desire for harmony with Russia stemmed from a desire to get Russia's help to defeat Japan, it was just the kind of idealistic reasoning the same men would have derided five years earlier. The Joint Chiefs had neglected their basic military responsibility: to provide first of all for the nation's future security.

This quasi-military thinking eventually led not to final victory but to an armed and uneasy peace. The Joint Chiefs should have warned their President that there would always be a struggle for power in the world of reality; that alliances were temporary and today's foe could be tomorrow's ally and vice versa; and that power politics in Europe and Asia, though highly regrettable from a philosophic and moral viewpoint, would inevitably be a factor for many years to come.

The Joint Chiefs, however, were not to blame. They were forced to change their thinking by the American people. If they had retained their aloof military judgment, insisting that such unmilitary aims as unconditional surrender and co-operation with Russia be curbed or at least tempered, they ran the risk of being relieved of command. America demanded total victory and a brave new world; and Roosevelt's achievements and aspirations had the enthusiastic endorsement of the great majority of the nation.

# 19

# The Rose Pocket

**1.**

The entire western front was at the point of collapse. In the south Hausser's Army Group G was already split in two by Bradley, and in the north Generaloberst Johannes Blaskowitz's Army Group H was being shattered by Montgomery. This meant that three of Eisenhower's armies—Simpson, Hodges and Patton—could now concentrate on the utter destruction of those in the center, Model's Army Group B.

Faced with imminent disaster, all three army group commanders begged the commander of the western front, Kesselring, to let them pull back *en masse,* but he was doomed to the hopeless philosophy forced on him by Hitler—to hold at all costs—and assured them that every day the Rhine was held meant a further "bolstering of the front." To his commanders, however, every day of delay only meant the inevitable loss of more troops and matériel. The man in the middle, Model, never let up in his demands, but Kesselring just as persistently refused; Model had to hold the vital Ruhr area.

On March 29 Model drew up an estimate of the entire situation and teletyped it to Kesselring: his mission to contain the enemy at the Remagen bridgehead and prevent widespread advance across the Rhine had failed; continuation of this defense, therefore, was "absurd, as such a defense could not even pin down enemy forces." A new mission was necessary, since an American armored unit—this was Task Force Richardson—had suddenly appeared out of nowhere and was at the outskirts of Paderborn. If this force was not snapped off at the base, Army Group B would be outflanked. Model asked permission to attack eastward with the LIII

Infantry Corps, from a point about forty miles west of Paderborn. This would cut right through the American spearhead and isolate it from all supplies and reinforcements. Kesselring approved and Model ordered the commander of LIII Corps to attack the following morning, March 30.*

Up ahead, Richardson was preparing his own attack on Paderborn, never suspecting that the Germans were about to attack forty miles behind him and cut him off from the bulk of the 3rd Armored Division. At the first light of dawn he moved out. It was dull, cloudy. At a crossroads, Panthers knocked out Richardson's first two tanks, and two miles farther on, at a village only three miles from Paderborn, a sizable force of Panthers and Tigers darted out, attacking with ferocity. After a brief, savage fight both Richardson and the Germans pulled back. It was a stand-off: neither side could move without being blasted. Richardson radioed for Thunderbolts to attack the Germans who were hiding behind a hill, but heavy clouds made air support impossible. Desperately in need of fan belts as well as ammunition and gas, Richardson radioed for an airdrop. "No aircraft available" was the laconic reply. A few minutes later came even worse news: the Germans had launched a surprise attack forty miles to his rear and he was about to be cut off.

Now Richardson could only dig in and hope that the Germans lying in wait out front would not attack. They were just as leery of him and did nothing, but at dusk Richardson was presented with another problem: "Big Six"—General Maurice Rose, the 3rd Armored Division commander —was coming up to inspect Task Force Richardson and wanted someone to meet him. Richardson radioed back that he couldn't even spare a jeep. "Don't send Big Six this way!" he warned and abruptly signed off.

Rose was about five miles to Richardson's right, temporarily attached to Task Force Welborn. Colonel John Welborn had just been informed by the Air Force that four Tiger tanks ahead had been destroyed by P-47s, and he moved on confidently. Nothing happened for a few miles, but as the Americans were rolling along a barren rise, heavy and accurate 88-mm. fire suddenly hit the column head-on. The four "destroyed" Tigers were very much alive. They had been hit only by napalm and not the usual killers—500-pounders. Welborn and the first three tanks rumbled safely ahead into a defilade of a creek bottom, but the next seven were rapidly picked off like sitting ducks.

* Curiously, on the night of March 29 General von Zangen, Fifteenth Army, and his staff were cut off from their own army, which was a part of Model's army group. Between Zangen and his troops was the main body of Rose's 3rd Armored Division, which was following Richardson, Hogan and Welborn. Zangen hid in the woods with some 200 vehicles until the end of one of Rose's columns rumbled past. He waited a minute; then, using the same dim lights as the Americans, simply joined their column. Sandwiched between the Americans, Zangen stayed in line for several harrowing hours. Finally, near Brilon, he left the Americans by turning off on a dirt road, and was soon reporting to Model, who could only exclaim in disbelief, "You're here?"

General Rose, the son of a rabbi, was an aggressive commander. He had a stern, handsome face and wore riding breeches and shining boots. He was half a mile behind the burning tanks, and after learning that the first three had successfully broken through, he radioed for help from Task Force Doan, which was following.

But seven or eight Tigers had just come out of the southeast, cutting off the rear of Task Force Welborn and blocking Doan's advance. This new German force had already knocked out a tank destroyer and several personnel carriers. Except for the first three tanks, Task Force Welborn was now completely surrounded. Ahead were four Tigers visible on a hill astride the road; behind were at least seven more, firing and slowly moving up the column; and on either side German infantrymen were hiding in the woods.

At dusk, after the last P-47s had departed, a group of nine Tigers, three abreast and three deep, suddenly poked out of the woods to the left and ahead of the cut-off column, and slowly moved down the road, raking all the vehicles and machine-gunning the ditches. Rose and his party were trapped, with Tigers front and rear systematically destroying everything in sight. The only light now was from burning American vehicles. No move was good. However, there was no choice but to move.

It was "a wild scene from Dante's Inferno," thought Colonel Frederic Brown, the division artillery commander. He advised Rose to cut through the woods on the left in spite of small-arms fire, in order to get around the tanks blocking the rear. But Rose pointed out that there was no tank fire ahead where Welborn had turned—the four Tigers ahead must have withdrawn. Therefore, it was safer, he argued, to go right, out of the light of the burning column, and then forward to join Welborn.

So the general's party—two jeeps and an armored car followed by a messenger on motorcycle—swung out of the line of blazing tanks and headed toward Welborn. After a mile they came to a junction. Up a road to the right they could see the dim outlines of one of his tanks. The Rose column turned off the main road—which led to Task Force Richardson—and started over toward the tank. It was disabled and abandoned. Suddenly there was a burst of rapid small-arms fire from a woods ahead. The Rose party quickly turned back to the main road and continued toward Richardson. Brown's jeep, with the colonel driving, was in the lead; then came Rose's jeep, the armored car, and the motorcycle.

The four vehicles were just starting up a rise when Brown saw a big tank lunging down toward them through the gloom. "There's one of Jack's new tanks," he said, thinking the ghostly shape was one of Welborn's new Pershings. But as the tank rolled by, one of Brown's passengers—Colonel George "Seafood" Garton—noticed its two exhausts; a Pershing had only one. It was a Tiger and Garton felt sure others were right behind. "Tigers," he shouted to Brown. "Get off the road!" Brown gunned the jeep past two more Tigers and looked for a place to turn off.

The first three Germans didn't realize that they were passing an enemy column. But the fourth abruptly started to swing across Brown's path. He squeezed the jeep between a tree and the Tiger, tearing off his gas can to get through. As he slowed to see if Rose had also broken through, a fifth Tiger approached. Brown swung to the right, gunned the jeep through the ditch and cleared the road. He stopped in the middle of a field. Behind, German flares were shooting up and he could hear the roar of guns. Everyone scrambled out of the jeep and headed for the woods.

The Rose jeep—with driver T/5 Shaunce and the general's aide, Major Robert Bellinger, also aboard—got past the second Tiger but was blocked by the third. Rose and the others jumped to the road. The Tiger's guns followed them ominously. Then a German stuck his head out the turret. He motioned with a burp gun and said something unintelligible.

"I think they want our guns," said Rose.

Bellinger and Shaunce unbuckled their shoulder holsters. But Rose, who stood between them, had to reach down to release his pistol belt.

Suddenly there was a staccato burst. Rose fell to the road, dead. In the darkness the nervous German tank commander had misunderstood the general's intentions. Shaunce leaped behind the tank out of the line of fire. Bellinger flipped backward in the opposite direction and landed in the ditch. He drew all the German fire but miraculously was not hit; he ran off and hid in the woods. Shaunce had broken his leg but he too escaped. The crew of the armored car, however, and the division operations officer, Lieutenant Colonel Wesley Sweat, were rounded up by the Germans.

Survivors of the first ambush were still scattering all over the countryside. As they ran they rid themselves of Lugers, watches and other German loot. For the most part their fear of reprisal was groundless; few Germans were interested in revenge and even less in hunting down Amis.

That night Sergeants Bryant Owen and Arthur Haushchild, fleeing through the woods, stumbled on almost 100 Germans who greeted them eagerly with hands in the air. The two sergeants took turns standing guard. Owen had slept little the past week and dozed off twice during his tours, but was wakened each time by a prisoner urging him to "get on the stick!" At dawn Owen and Haushchild herded their prisoners on a trail through the woods, hoping it was in the right direction. After several miles they came to a little guard shelter. In the poor light they saw a soldier inside but couldn't tell if he was American or German.

"Je-sus Co-rist!" the guard cried when he saw the gang of Germans, and Owen could have kissed him.

As soon as the two sergeants had handed over their prisoners to a division officer, they were ordered to go back at once and retrieve Rose's body. It took them an hour to find him on the road. The Germans apparently were unaware that they had killed a division commander; the maps and codes in his jeep were unmolested, as were those in the ditched armored car.* Rose's .45 was still in his holster and Owen took it to send back to the general's family. They rummaged through the jeep and armored car till they found a blanket. They roped Rose in the blanket, put his helmet on his chest and began dragging him to the rear. As they approached the American lines, a replacement second lieutenant asked what the hell they were doing. When they told him, the lieutenant criticized them for treating a general so disrespectfully. Owen, who had several friends lying back there on the road, told him off and was turned in for court-martial.

## 2.

On March 30 Bernard Baruch, who had just arrived from America on a special mission, was driving from London through the English countryside, green with spring, listening to Churchill speak fondly of Roosevelt and Harry Hopkins, two dear friends.

Several days before, Hopkins had come to Baruch's suite at the Shoreham Hotel in Washington and hinted at a number of postwar problems Roosevelt was having with Churchill. Hopkins said that neither he nor John Winant, the U. S. Ambassador to the Court of St. James, had been able to "budge" the Prime Minister, and Roosevelt wondered if Baruch would go over and try to influence his old friend.

When Baruch went to the President for more definite instructions, Roosevelt at first seemed more interested in talking of Operation "Sunrise" and Russia's unwarranted and suspicious reactions. Finally Roosevelt got to the point. He wanted Baruch to see Churchill and explore "various problems relating to the peace." Baruch's attempts to get further details were so futile that he felt the President was "almost too weary to make decisions." On one point, however, Roosevelt was clear. "It would be a grand gesture," he said, "if the British restored Hong Kong to China." Baruch did not agree but would, of course, deliver the message.

"Would you like a letter to Winston?" Roosevelt asked.

"I don't need any letter," Baruch observed judiciously. "You may want to repudiate me later."

After briefings by Stettinius, Arnold, Leahy and King, Baruch flew to England in the President's personal plane, which he had nicknamed *The Sacred Cow,* and now, on their way to Chequers, he asked Churchill, "What's all this talk about the boys having difficulties with you?" Then he

---

* There were a number of reports in the Allied press claiming that Rose had been "murdered" by the Nazis because he was a Jew. There is no evidence to support this charge.

brought up the Prime Minister's opposition to UNESCO. Churchill replied that he thought it would be ineffective.

"Will it do any harm?"

"No, but it won't do any good."

"Well, if it won't do any harm, why not give the President what he wants?"

Before they reached Chequers, Churchill had agreed to support the President—who at last was supporting him.

Churchill, however, had just received a radiogram from Eisenhower which revealed, he thought, a complete lack of understanding of the postwar Russian menace. The message was an answer to a personal telephone call from Churchill questioning the wisdom of by-passing Berlin. In his reply Eisenhower repeated his arguments and reaffirmed his determination to leave Berlin to Stalin, and merely drive eastward "to join hands with Russians or to attain general line of Elbe."

The British Chiefs received an even more disturbing message almost simultaneously. It was the American Joint Chiefs' answer to their British counterparts' harsh condemnation of Eisenhower's new decision. It stated flatly that Eisenhower was "the best judge of the measures which offer the earliest prospect of destroying the German Armies or their power to resist," and that his strategic concept was "sound from the overall viewpoint of crushing Germany as expeditiously as possible and should receive full support." There was no doubt at all. The American Chiefs were solidly, even aggressively, behind Eisenhower.

At Rheims, Eisenhower was still explaining to Marshall why he had decided not to take Berlin. It was "no change in basic strategy,"* and Berlin itself was "no longer a particularly important objective." Moreover, he said, his new concentrated attack south of the capital would "more quickly bring about the fall of Berlin . . . than will the scattering around of our effort. . . ."

To Montgomery, Eisenhower was even more specific about Berlin itself and radioed:

. . . THAT PLACE [BERLIN] HAS BECOME, SO FAR AS I AM CONCERNED, NOTHING BUT A GEOGRAPHICAL LOCATION, AND I HAVE NEVER BEEN INTERESTED IN THESE. MY PURPOSE IS TO DESTROY THE ENEMY'S FORCES AND HIS POWERS TO RESIST.

The next day, March 31, Churchill composed a memorandum to the British Chiefs, pointing out inconsistencies in the rather emotional message they had sent to the Joint Chiefs before consulting him. He agreed with them thoroughly, he said, but pointed out that "we have only a

---

* The British reaction to Eisenhower's decision indicates it was a great change, at least in their eyes. It would also be a shock to a number of American field commanders.

quarter of the forces invading Germany, and that the situation has thus changed remarkably from the days of June 1944. . . . In short, I see argumentative possibilities being opened to the United States Chiefs of Staff by our telegram, on which they will riposte heavily. . . ."

Before the note was dispatched he received a copy of the aggressive reply from the Joint Chiefs resoundingly backing up Eisenhower, whereupon he added to his missive: "P.S.—The above was dictated by me *before* I had seen the United States Chiefs of Staff riposte."

He also sent a reply to Eisenhower's message of the day before. With remarkable prescience it parried every one of Eisenhower's arguments— and ended with fourteen words which Churchill was to omit from his own book:

. . . I DO NOT KNOW WHY IT WOULD BE AN ADVANTAGE NOT TO CROSS THE ELBE. IF THE ENEMY'S RESISTANCE SHOULD WEAKEN, AS YOU EVIDENTLY EXPECT AND WHICH MAY WELL BE FULFILLED, WHY SHOULD WE NOT CROSS THE ELBE AND ADVANCE AS FAR EASTWARD AS POSSIBLE? THIS HAS AN IMPORTANT POLITICAL BEARING, AS THE RUSSIAN ARMIES OF THE SOUTH SEEM CERTAIN TO ENTER VIENNA AND OVERRUN AUSTRIA. IF WE DELIBERATELY LEAVE BERLIN TO THEM, EVEN IF IT SHOULD BE IN OUR GRASP, THE DOUBLE EVENT MAY STRENGTHEN THEIR CONVICTION, ALREADY APPARENT, THAT THEY HAVE DONE EVERYTHING.

FURTHER, I DO NOT CONSIDER MYSELF THAT BERLIN HAS YET LOST ITS MILITARY AND CERTAINLY NOT ITS POLITICAL SIGNIFICANCE. THE FALL OF BERLIN WOULD HAVE A PROFOUND PSYCHOLOGICAL EFFECT ON GERMAN RESISTANCE IN EVERY PART OF THE REICH. WHILE BERLIN HOLDS OUT GREAT MASSES OF GERMANS WILL FEEL IT THEIR DUTY TO GO DOWN FIGHTING. THE IDEA THAT THE CAPTURE OF DRESDEN AND JUNCTION WITH THE RUSSIANS THERE WOULD BE A SUPERIOR GAIN DOES NOT COMMEND ITSELF TO ME. THE PARTS OF THE GERMAN GOVERNMENT DEPARTMENTS WHICH HAVE MOVED SOUTH CAN VERY QUICKLY MOVE SOUTHWARD AGAIN. BUT WHILE BERLIN REMAINS UNDER THE GERMAN FLAG IT CANNOT, IN MY OPINION, FAIL TO BE THE MOST DECISIVE POINT IN GERMANY.

THEREFORE I SHOULD GREATLY PREFER PERSISTENCE IN THE PLAN ON WHICH WE CROSSED THE RHINE, NAMELY, THAT THE NINTH U. S. ARMY SHOULD MARCH WITH THE TWENTY-FIRST ARMY GROUP TO THE ELBE AND BEYOND BERLIN. THIS WOULD NOT BE IN ANY WAY INCONSISTENT WITH THE GREAT CENTRAL THRUST WHICH YOU ARE NOW SO RIGHTLY DEVELOPING AS THE RESULT OF THE BRILLIANT OPERATIONS OF YOUR ARMIES SOUTH OF THE RUHR. IT ONLY SHIFTS THE WEIGHT OF ONE ARMY TO THE NORTHERN FLANK AND THIS AVOIDS THE RELEGATION OF HIS MAJESTY'S FORCES TO AN UNEXPECTED RESTRICTED SPHERE.

In Moscow that night General Deane and Harriman, together with their British counterparts, went to the Kremlin and handed Stalin the English and Russian texts of Eisenhower's long-delayed message about Berlin. After reading it, the Marshal remained as poker-faced as ever. He said the plan "seemed good," but he could not commit himself until he consulted his staff. He then asked if Eisenhower had any knowledge of prepared positions toward the center of Germany.

"No," Deane replied.

Would the advance of the secondary attack in the south come from Italy or the western front?

Deane said he understood it would be the western front.

Could they verify Soviet information that there were sixty German divisions on the western front?

The Americans said they had counted sixty-one.

Did the Germans have any additional reserves on the western front? Apparently not.

Harriman now asked about weather conditions in the east. "Considerably improved," Stalin said.

"Does your previous estimate that operations in the east might be bogged down at the end of March still hold good?" Harriman asked.

"The situation is better than I had anticipated." Stalin explained that the floods were early that year and that the roads were already in the process of drying. They continued to talk for some time about the eastern front until Stalin, who must have been mulling over the Berlin message, abruptly said, "Eisenhower's plan for the main effort is a good one. It accomplishes the most important objective of dividing Germany in half." He also felt that the direction was favorable for the juncture with the Red Army. After stating that he, like Eisenhower, thought the Germans would make their last stand in the mountains of Czechoslovakia and Bavaria, Stalin assured his visitors that he would give them a reply to the Supreme Commander's message the next day. It was obvious that he was pleased.

In England, Brooke returned home from a day of fishing with Mountbatten to find a message that the Prime Minister wanted the Chiefs of Staff to meet at Chequers the next day.

His weekend holiday cut short, Brooke left for Chequers the following morning. It was Easter Sunday, April 1. For two hours the Chiefs and Churchill discussed the Eisenhower decision. Brooke felt that the whole matter, including the transfer of Simpson to Bradley, was "due to national aspirations and to ensure that the U. S. effort will not be lost under British Command." But the group realized there was nothing they could do and finally concluded that Eisenhower's fuller explanations made it clear that there was "no very great change" in his plans—except that the main axis of advance was now Leipzig, not Berlin.

After the meeting the Chiefs worked on an answer to what Brooke termed "the American Chiefs' rather rude message." Churchill, in the meantime, dispatched a long cable to Roosevelt. Although conciliatory in spirit, declaring that their two nations were "the truest friends and comrades that ever fought side by side as allies," it still emphasized Churchill's firm belief that the true nature of aggressive Communism should be uncovered and resisted at once, in every way possible.

. . . I SAY QUITE FRANKLY THAT BERLIN REMAINS OF HIGH STRATEGIC IMPORTANCE. NOTHING WILL EXERT A PSYCHOLOGICAL EFFECT OF DESPAIR UPON ALL GERMAN FORCES OF RESISTANCE EQUAL TO THAT OF THE FALL OF BERLIN. IT WILL BE THE SUPREME SIGNAL OF DEFEAT TO THE GERMAN PEOPLE. ON THE OTHER HAND, IF LEFT TO ITSELF TO MAINTAIN A SIEGE BY THE RUSSIANS AMONG ITS RUINS, AND AS LONG AS THE GERMAN FLAG FLIES THERE, IT WILL ANIMATE THE RESISTANCE OF ALL GERMANS UNDER ARMS. THERE IS MOREOVER ANOTHER ASPECT WHICH IT IS PROPER FOR YOU AND ME TO CONSIDER. THE RUSSIAN ARMIES WILL NO DOUBT OVERRUN ALL AUSTRIA AND ENTER VIENNA. IF THEY ALSO TAKE BERLIN WILL NOT THEIR IMPRESSION THAT THEY HAVE BEEN THE OVERWHELMING CONTRIBUTOR TO OUR COMMON VICTORY BE UNDULY IMPRINTED IN THEIR MINDS, AND MAY THIS NOT LEAD THEM INTO A MOOD WHICH WILL RAISE GRAVE AND FORMIDABLE DIFFICULTIES IN THE FUTURE? I THEREFORE CONSIDER THAT FROM A POLITICAL STANDPOINT WE SHOULD MARCH AS FAR EAST INTO GERMANY AS POSSIBLE, AND THAT SHOULD BERLIN BE IN OUR GRASP WE SHOULD CERTAINLY TAKE IT. THIS ALSO APPEARS SOUND ON MILITARY GROUNDS . . .

Later that day Brooke wrote in his diary, "It is all a pity and straightforward strategy is being affected by the nationalistic outlook of allies. . . . But, as Winston says, 'there is only one thing worse than fighting with allies, and that is fighting without them!' "

Brooke was in a rare mellow mood, but Eisenhower was perturbed as he wrote an answer to Churchill's latest message. And what bothered him particularly was the Prime Minister's last fourteen words. After repeating that he had "not changed any plan" and that the only difference was one of timing, he went on:

I AM DISTURBED, IF NOT HURT, THAT YOU SHOULD SUGGEST ANY THOUGHT ON MY PART TO 'RELEGATE HIS MAJESTY'S FORCES TO AN UNEXPECTED RESTRICTED SPHERE.' NOTHING IS FURTHER FROM MY MIND AND I THINK MY RECORD OVER TWO AND A HALF YEARS OF COMMANDING ALLIED FORCES SHOULD ELIMINATE ANY SUCH IDEA. BUT FURTHER TO THIS POINT I COMPLETELY FAIL TO SEE HOW THE ROLE, ACTIONS OR PRESTIGE OF SECOND BRITISH AND THE CANADIAN

ARMIES ARE MATERIALLY AFFECTED BY THE FACT THAT NINTH
ARMY, ADVANCING IN ITS OWN ZONE, IS CONTROLLED BY BRADLEY,
UNTIL I CAN BE ASSURED THAT OUR REAR AREAS ARE SUBSTANTIALLY
CLEANED OUT AND THE THRUST TO LEIPZIG SUCCESSFUL . . .*

QUITE NATURALLY, IF AT ANY MOMENT 'ECLIPSE'** CONDITIONS
SHOULD SUDDENLY COME ABOUT ANYWHERE ALONG THE FRONT WE
COULD RUSH FORWARD AND LUBECK AND BERLIN COULD BE INCLUDED
IN OUR IMPORTANT TARGETS.

If the British were still unhappy with Eisenhower, America's other
ally was more than content. That same day General Deane forwarded to
the Supreme Commander a Personal and Most Secret telegram from
Stalin:

YOUR PLAN TO CUT THE GERMAN FORCES BY JOINING UP THE
SOVIET FORCES WITH YOUR FORCES ENTIRELY COINCIDES WITH THE
PLAN OF THE SOVIET HIGH COMMAND.

I AGREE WITH YOU ALSO THAT THE PLACE FOR THE JOINING UP OF
YOUR FORCES AND THE SOVIET FORCES SHOULD BE THE AREA ERFURT,
LEIPZIG, DRESDEN. THE SOVIET HIGH COMMAND CONSIDERS THAT THE
MAIN BLOW OF THE SOVIET FORCES SHOULD BE DELIVERED IN THAT
DIRECTION.

BERLIN HAS LOST ITS FORMER STRATEGIC IMPORTANCE. THE SOVIET
HIGH COMMAND THEREFORE PLANS TO ALLOT SECONDARY FORCES
IN THE DIRECTION OF BERLIN.

It was ironic that Stalin used Eisenhower's argument about Berlin's
loss of strategic importance—though it was not even mentioned in the
Supreme Commander's message to him—to hide his own intentions while
Zhukov was making last-minute preparations for a final, tremendous assault on Berlin.

---

* This entire paragraph is deleted from Churchill's *Triumph and Tragedy*, nor
does it appear in Eisenhower's *Crusade in Europe*.
** Operation "Eclipse" was, basically, a general plan for taking over the administration of Germany upon its sudden collapse or surrender. Initiated before D-Day
under the code name "Talisman," it charged First Allied Airborne Army with preparing plans for operations against Berlin and/or Kiel, should such prove necessary
to establish Allied control. The plan was to seize airfields near Berlin and Kiel by
parachutists. Though an airdrop on Berlin by Ridgway's XVIII Airborne Corps remained a possibility almost to the end of the war, "Eclipse" dealt primarily with
more mundane matters, such as armistice terms, disarmament, displaced persons,
prisoners of war, and German courts. In April, 1945, it seemed very unlikely that
overall surrender would come before Germany was completely occupied and SHAEF
decreed that there would be no formal transition to "Eclipse."
Ironically, a few days before this decision, the British copy of the "Eclipse" papers
had somehow found its way to Kesselring's headquarters. The documents were
translated and delivered to Hitler, together with one map dividing Germany in Allied
zones of occupation and another indicating Berlin as an enclave within the Russian
zone, to be shared by Britain, America and Russia.

## 3.

On Easter Sunday some Allied prisoners of war were being marched away from the battle fronts to Bavaria; others were kept captive in their compounds, awaiting momentary release by Allied or Russian troops; and still others had already been liberated by the Russians but felt far from liberated. To almost all, however, the day had the same special significance—it was an emotional turning point. Freedom seemed close enough to touch.

The group from Hammelburg was resting after having marched about a third of the way to Nuremberg. Their greatest trepidation was caused by their own aircraft. American planes had already swooped down several times to strafe, only to discover, just in time, panels that the prisoners had spread out on the fields. But how long could such luck hold out?

At eleven o'clock Father Cavanaugh held Mass in a small ancient village church dedicated to St. Joseph. It was the first Catholic church he had entered since his capture in the Bulge. Wearing the village priest's heavy gold vestments, he began the service for the eighty men jammed inside:

"My dear Kriegies, this is the day that the Lord hath made; let us be glad and rejoice in it. . . . During the past four days we have suffered our way of the cross and we have suffered with the Christ who was represented in the wayside crucifixes that flanked our line of march. . . .

"We have many blessings also to ask Our Lord for. We ask Him to continue His protection of us, to keep us free from sin, to help us to be better men."

Tears were running down many cheeks and Father Cavanaugh's own eyes were wet. "Easter is the feast of peace—peace between God and men; peace between nations, peace in political life, peace in home life, peace in the heart of every child of God. Let us offer this Mass and Holy Communion that peace may come quickly to the world."

The enlisted prisoners at Stalag IIA, north of Berlin, had no doubt whatsoever that peace was near; their guards now treated them like equals rather than captives and overlooked offenses that ordinarily would have resulted in severe punishment. The previous Sunday, while holding Mass in the presence of several guards, Father Sampson had leaned against the pulpit—inside, the camp radio was hidden—saying, " 'Seek ye first the kingdom of God and His justice, and all these things shall be added unto you.' " It was as if he had said, "Open, Sesame." The trap door flew open —he had forgotten to secure it with a spike the night before—and the contraband radio tumbled out. As the embarrassed priest stuffed the radio back in place the congregation burst into laughter—all but the guards. They acted as if nothing had happened and did not report the incident.

Now, on Easter Sunday, the guards made only token protests when thousands of prisoners of different nationalities began congregating in a large field around an improvised altar. Father Sampson and the other priests had prepared an outdoor Solemn High Mass without even informing the camp commandant. Sampson had never seen such a huge congregation except at a national Eucharistic Congress. The sermon—preached in French, English, Italian and Polish—was simple but inspiring: Here in prison camp there was no argument, no friction, no hatred, no intrigue or struggle for balance of power; and there was a King whom all could love and obey and in that love and obedience find the happiness and freedom every man longs for.

## 4.

By noon on March 31 Model's desperation attack out of the Ruhr had plunged eight miles into the attacking U. S. 3rd Armored Division—and cut off Task Forces Richardson and Hogan. "Lightning Joe" Collins, commander of the corps including the 3rd Armored Division, did not know this. But he had just learned from prisoners that the Germans were going to launch a counterattack against his left flank. He made a highly unorthodox phone call to an old friend, General Simpson. Collins desperately needed help—even if he had to get it from an army in another army group.

Montgomery's 21st Army Group was scheduled to meet Bradley's 12th Army Group near Paderborn in a few days—and this would sew up the Ruhr pocket. But Collins told Simpson that Monty was moving too slowly and the junction would have to be made soon, or the Germans might "break out toward Paderborn."

"Bill, I'm worried," Collins said. "I'm spread out so thin." He asked Simpson to release a combat command of the U. S. 2nd Armored Division and have it drive immediately toward Paderborn. "I'll send a combat command over to meet them."

Simpson agreed without checking with Montgomery, and at nightfall his 2nd Armored Division began racing southeast. Near the head of the column was 1st Lieutenant William Dooley, commander of Company E of the 67th Armored Regiment. He had no idea he was on a momentous mission, and didn't even know exactly where he was going. He had only been ordered to push fast to Lippstadt, a city twenty-two miles east of Paderborn. It was pitch-black, and though occasionally he could hear a burp gun going off in the distance, he couldn't see a thing. It was nerve-racking. From the south came the steady rumble of explosions so severe that the tanks shook from the vibrations. It was the sound of battle inside the Ruhr.

But Dooley's company ran into only scattered resistance from burp guns and small-arms fire, and at six o'clock on Easter morning, after a road march of fifty miles, it reached the outskirts of Lippstadt. The infantry groggily dismounted from half-tracks, cleared out the first houses and started into town. Just then a German tank appeared and fired at the first American tank. By luck the shell ricocheted off the right side of the turret. The German tank fled. Farther on, the Americans ran into cement building blocks piled in the road, but civilians suddenly ran out and pushed the blocks away.

Second Lieutenant Donald E. Jacobsen, the 1st Platoon leader, was told to get into town; a squad of infantry had been cut off in a hospital and needed help. Jacobsen loaded his platoon on tanks and took off. As soon as this force approached the hospital, about thirty-five Germans came forward, hands raised, and were also loaded onto the tanks. Then Jacobsen headed on through town, looking for a fight. On the far side of Lippstadt he saw tanks approaching from the east. As he prepared to fire he recognized they were M-5s of the 3rd Armored Division.

It was now one o'clock. Model's entire Army group, some 300,000 men, had just been encircled inside Germany's last industrial area,* but to the Americans who made the epic junction it was just another day. They shouted ribald jokes at one another and were relieved that they didn't have to fight for the town.

Jacobsen didn't realize the significance of what had happened until he was interviewed by a group of photographers and correspondents congregated near a church. Then he thought: It's amazing how ignorant the fellows are who really fight the war.

What still concerned Churchill most that day was Eisenhower's decision to leave Berlin to the Russians. The Prime Minister was afraid, however, that the argument would end in bitterness unless cut short, yet was not willing to drop the subject.

He compromised by sending Eisenhower a reasonable and friendly message:

THANK YOU AGAIN FOR YOUR MOST KIND TELEGRAM . . . I AM HOWEVER ALL THE MORE IMPRESSED WITH THE IMPORTANCE OF EN-TERING BERLIN, WHICH MAY WELL BE OPEN TO US, BY THE REPLY FROM MOSCOW TO YOU, WHICH IN PARAGRAPH 3 SAYS, "BERLIN HAS LOST ITS FORMER STRATEGIC IMPORTANCE." THIS SHOULD BE READ IN THE LIGHT OF WHAT I MENTIONED OF THE POLITICAL ASPECTS. I DEEM IT HIGHLY IMPORTANT THAT WE SHOULD SHAKE HANDS WITH THE RUSSIANS AS FAR TO THE EAST AS POSSIBLE . . .

* The Ruhr pocket was later renamed the Rose Pocket in honor of the fallen general.

But this message had no more effect on Eisenhower than the previous ones. He was so firmly committed to his plan and believed so earnestly in its military soundness that he was even "prepared to make an issue of it."

When Kesselring got back to his battle headquarters in the Thuringian Forest, his chief of staff, Westphal, reported that a new order had just come in from the Führer's headquarters. Model was ordered to defend the Ruhr as a fortress—and not to try to break out.

Kesselring found it hard to believe. Didn't OKW know there was only enough food in the encircled Ruhr to feed soldiers and civilians for two or three weeks? Besides, Eisenhower could have no strategic interest in the Ruhr; his objective lay far to the east.

The western front was no longer a front. Blaskowitz in the north was shattered. Hausser in the south was equally shattered, and his remnants were scattering in confusion. And Model in the center was doomed. Kesselring's entire front had evaporated; from now on there could only be a bitter delaying action.

Bormann was writing to his wife for the first time in days, describing the desperation that hung over Berlin like a cloud. He warned his "beloved" that the Army Command in Vienna was "so deplorably bad that one has to expect the worst," and that she should get ready to evacuate from the Obersalzberg to the Tyrol. "It makes me both sad and angry that for the moment I have nothing more cheerful to write about," he concluded, "but I'll make up for it when the good times of peace come."

But some Germans still refused to face the mounting disaster. Himmler for one maintained that the military situation was not hopeless. "I am ready to do anything for the German nation, but the war must go on," he told two listeners, Count Bernadotte and Schellenberg, during a four-hour interview. "I have given my oath to the Führer and that oath is a binding one."

"Don't you realize that Germany has lost the war?" the Count exclaimed. "A person in your position, bearing such an enormous responsibility cannot obey a superior blindly, but must have the courage to accept responsibility for decisions made in the interest of the people."

Himmler was silent and thoughtful; he did not move until he was called to the phone a minute later. He got up and quickly left the room, as if glad for an excuse to get away from Bernadotte's upbraiding. Schellenberg was pleased that his chief had been subjected to such pressure, and urged Bernadotte to press the issue even further.

But when Himmler returned, Bernadotte restricted the conversation to his own mission. He asked that all Danes and Norwegians be transferred at once to Sweden.

A look of apprehension came over Himmler's face. "Personally I would grant your request with pleasure, but I can't possibly do it." He changed the subject abruptly and acknowledged that the German government had made a number of fatal mistakes. "It was a mistake not to be frank with England. As for me—well, of course, I am regarded as the most cruel and sadistic man alive. But one thing I want to put on record: I have never publicly vilified Germany's enemies."

"If you haven't, Hitler has done so all the more thoroughly," the Count replied. "What was it he said—'We shall wipe out every one of the English cities.' Is it then so surprising that the Allies systematically bomb German towns?"

The day after the American juncture at Lippstadt and the collapse of the Ruhr pocket, Hitler finally admitted in a "private talk" that total defeat was not only possible but probable. "Even this prospect, however," he said, "does not shake my invincible faith in the future of the German people. The more we suffer, the more glorious will be the resurrection of eternal Germany!"

Though he personally could not bear to live in a defeated Germany, he now wanted to give those who survived a few "rules of conduct." He advised them "to respect those racial laws which we laid down" and "to preserve indissoluble the union of all the German races."

He then prophesied that only two great world powers would emerge from a German defeat—America and the Soviet Union. "The laws of both history and geography will compel these two Powers to a trial of strength, either military or in the fields of economics and ideology. These same laws make it inevitable that both Powers should become enemies of Europe. And it is equally certain that both these Powers will sooner or later find it desirable to seek the support of the sole surviving great nation in Europe, the German people. I say with all the emphasis at my command that the Germans must at all costs avoid playing the role of pawn in either camp."*

* This was the last of Hitler's "private talks." Fifteen days later, on April 17, the documents were taken out of Berlin for safekeeping.

# PART THREE

### ✠ ✠ ✠

## *East Meets West*

# 20

## "O-5"

**1.**

Hitler's last gamble in the southeast had failed; Sepp Dietrich's ill-conceived offensive which was supposed to split and then annihilate Tolbukhin had begun in desperation—and ended in complete rout.

The battle group of SS Lieutenant Colonel Fritz Hagen, after stealing gas from another unit, had made the deepest penetration through the morass and mud of central Hungary, but after four days and forty-five miles its lead tank, exhaust pipes shot off, was still twenty miles from the Danube. When Hagen reported his position he was only asked what the hell he was doing so far out ahead of everyone else and told to retreat at once. "Don't you know the Russians are attacking toward Vienna?"

Hagen was disgusted, and would be even more so when he learned that no sooner had Dietrich begun his attack than Tolbukhin launched an even greater one. As a result, of course, most of Dietrich's Sixth Panzer Army was destroyed in the crushing meeting engagement and the survivors were falling back in a desperate attempt to stem Tolbukhin's drive toward Vienna.

Hagen retreated with his remaining twenty-five tanks to a position astride the main Budapest–Vienna highway where Tolbukhin's spearhead smashed straight into him with such reckless abandon that the out-gunned German Panthers were able to knock out 125 big "Stalin" tanks.

As Dietrich pulled back to the northwest toward Vienna, he was forced away from the Sixth Army of General Hermann Balck on his right flank, and on April 1 Tolbukhin sent a strong armored force into the widening breach.

Balck, his flank now completely exposed, sarcastically told General Wöhler, commander of Army Group South, "If the Leibstandarte [Dietrich's elite Adolf Hitler Division] can't hold their ground, what do you expect us to do?"

The report of this conversation angered Hitler so much that he said, "If my own Leibstandarte can't hold their ground they aren't worthy of carrying my personal emblem!" and ordered Keitel to send Dietrich this message:

THE FÜHRER BELIEVES THAT THE TROOPS HAVE NOT FOUGHT AS THE SITUATION DEMANDED AND ORDERS THAT THE SS DIVISIONS ADOLF HITLER, DAS REICH, TOTENKOPF AND HOHENSTAUFEN BE STRIPPED OF THEIR ARM BANDS.

The story soon spread that upon reading this, Dietrich called together his division commanders, threw the message on the table and exclaimed, "There's your reward for all you've done these past five years!" He then wired Hitler that he would shoot himself rather than carry out such an order, and sent back all his medals in a chamber pot. The story came close to the truth—but with a different cast of characters. Dietrich had not been angry with the Führer; he was so sure that Hitler had acted on misinformation that he simply ignored the order, something few other commanders would have dared do.

However, the contents of Hitler's message seeped down the chain of command. When it came to Hagen he could not rationalize its contents, as Dietrich had done. The Führer was his idol and he would never forget their first meeting when he and twenty others had lined up in the Reich Chancellery. Hitler mechanically shook hands down the line but after passing the blond, handsome Hagen, he swung around, walked back and again grasped the tanker's right hand in both of his, transfixing him with his blue-gray eyes. From that moment Hagen would cheerfully have put his head on the execution block for the Führer.

Now Hagen was so angry that he called together his officers and said "Let's take a chamber pot, put all our medals in it and tie around it the ribbon of the Division Götz von Berlichingen."* But the heat of the moment passed and Battle Group Hagen returned to combat.

Malinovsky and Tolbukhin were pushing shoulder to shoulder toward Austria. To the north Malinovsky was delayed by rugged hills, but Tolbukhin kept racing along the main highway and by Good Friday, March 30, approached the Austrian border—only forty miles from Vienna.

* Götz von Berlichingen was the crusty knight in Goethe's play, who told the Bishop of Bamberg, "Kiss my ass!"

## 2.

For the past year numerous loosely organized resistance groups had been forming spontaneously all over Austria. At the beginning of 1945 Major Carl Szokoll, an Austrian staff officer in the Wehrmacht, approached a group known as the Committee of Seven. These were civilian resistance leaders of all political complexions, bound by mutual hatred of the Nazis. Szokoll told them that a successful uprising in Austria depended on close co-operation of civilian and military resistance groups; he revealed that he had already organized a strong underground group of Austrian patriots serving in German units.

Szokoll was a slender, fastidious man of thirty, hardly more than five feet tall. He had joined the July 20 conspiracy and had helped imprison Gestapo and SS officials in Vienna. When the plot failed he had somehow managed to convince his German superiors that he had only done his duty.

Szokoll and the Committee of Seven joined forces. They decided to call the coalition "0–5." This was simple code for the first two letters of Oesterreich (or "Österreich, the name for Austria before the *Anschluss* in 1938, when it was called Ostmark), with the "5" standing for the fifth letter of the alphabet. Resistance members began marking "0–5" on all official propaganda posters. The general public only knew that this was the symbol for a resistance movement, and it became a popular sport for Austrians of all ages to chalk and paint "0–5" from one end of the country to the other, giving the impression that the movement was far more widespread and significant than it really was.

By the middle of March, 1945, the leaders of "0–5" were convinced that Hitler was willing to sacrifice Austria in the final struggle and that Vienna would suffer the same fate as Budapest. Besides saving their city, they wanted to show the world that in spite of the long Nazi occupation and the imprisonment of hundreds of their resistance leaders, the will for liberation of the Austrian people had not been broken.

On March 25 Major Szokoll told an "0–5" meeting that Vienna could only be saved by helping the Red Army seize it. "If they accept our terms, we must offer to hand over the city to them," he said, and explained how this could be done. His present assignment at Army District XVII headquarters was to help form the defensive line in front of Vienna, against the attack from the east. This had given him a perfect opportunity to place certain battalions loyal to "0–5" in the Vienna Woods, south of the city. At the moment of final assault, said Szokoll, he would merely withdraw these troops and the Russians could march through the woods near Baden, fourteen miles south of Vienna. They could then unexpectedly enter the capital from the rear, and with the help of "0–5" take it with little bloodshed or damage. Szokoll's plan was enthusiastically approved and a committee selected to organize civilian-military liaison.

Five days later, on Good Friday, the people of Vienna first heard the distant booming of guns as Tolbukhin drew up to the Austrian border. That night the sky to the southeast was purple. Martial law was established. The next morning Allied air attacks on railroad yards, bridges over the Danube and important intersections caused fires to spring up in so many places that the overworked fire brigades could not begin to cope with them. The Viennese took beds into their cellars or shelters, and began to live underground. Traffic could not move through the rubble-filled streets; the city railroad service was discontinued and streetcars ran on few routes. Gas and electricity were available only a few hours a day and in many districts there was no water.

Political collaborators and Party officials who had ruled over the city no longer dared appear in public in their brown uniforms, and by late afternoon the roads were jammed with those who had enough influence to get exit permits.

Most of the people could not flee, but being Viennese, they had not lost their sense of humor and the latest joke was: "On Easter you'll be able to take a streetcar to the front lines." By Easter it was no longer a joke; word came that Tolbukhin had broken through Dietrich's line of defense southeast of Vienna and was only about eight miles from the suburbs. Gauleiter, and now Defense Commissioner, Baldur von Schirach, the former Reich Youth Leader, declared the city a *Festung* and called up the Volkssturm for immediate service. Boys and old men began digging trenches in the outskirts. Civilians were turned out of their homes and forced to build antitank obstacles and throw up hasty street barriers with cobblestones, trees and streetcar tracks. The Hitler Youth were given panzerfausts and told to dig foxholes.

"The hour of Vienna, the time of proof has come!" Schirach proclaimed. The *Little War-Newspaper* declared, "Hate is our prayer, revenge our password." On the radio, Sepp Dietrich pleaded, "It's not for us, it's for the Party! Heil our Führer!"

Later in the day Szokoll finally learned the exact positioning and passwords of Dietrich's last replacements, two SS divisions. With this information Szokoll was ready, and he summoned "0–5" leaders to an emergency meeting in Vienna.

They gathered secretly on the night of April 2 in one of the most unlikely places imaginable—Army District XVII headquarters on the Stubenring, where Szokoll had his office.

"Which of you gentlemen will volunteer to take my plan to the Russian High Command?" he asked. He looked around the room and his eyes stopped at thirty-one-year-old Ferdinand Käs, a broad-shouldered, stocky Feldwebel. The two had known each other for eleven years and their fathers had served in the same regiment in World War I. "The time has come, Sergeant," said Szokoll.

Käs stepped forward. "I am ready, Major."

Szokoll instructed him to circle around the main battle line southeast of the city, then gave him a faked pass and a small map illustrating the plan. The two men shook hands.

Driven by Gefreiter (Corporal) Johann Reif, the major's own chauffeur, Käs headed due south. After fifteen miles they came to the famed spa, Baden, where Tolbukhin would be allowed to pass through the German lines. They continued south another fifteen miles, to Wiener Neustadt. Here they began circling to the southwest over back roads, and just before dawn of April 3 reached a quiet sector where they hoped to make a dash through the German positions. They penetrated the front line unchallenged, but guards at the last German outpost began firing as they raced past. Their Opel was hit, and after several hundred yards came to a dead stop. Käs and Reif leaped into a ditch and began crawling away from another flurry of bullets.

A Russian wearing a fur cap and holding a balalaika stepped from behind a tree and said, *"Rukiv verkh!"* ("Hands up!")

It took hours to pass the two Austrians from one command to another and not until ten in the evening did they reach the headquarters of the Third Ukrainian Front in the village of Hochwolkersdorf, some ten miles south of Wiener Neustadt. After an hour's wait Käs was brought to the living room of a large house. Three generals and half a dozen staff officers sat around a table and eyed him suspiciously. The senior officer, Colonel General Alexei Sergeievich Zheltov, a man with graying hair and a little mustache, courteously told Käs to be seated, then said, *"Nachinaj!"* ("Start!")

Käs outlined Szokoll's plan, but stipulated that it would not be put in operation unless the Russians made several guarantees: all Allied air attacks against Vienna must be stopped; furthermore, members of "0–5" were not to be arrested by the Russians; and Austrian prisoners of war must be released earlier than others.

Annoyed by the Austrian demands, the staff officers showed far less courtesy than Zheltov and began bombarding Käs with questions: What is "0–5"? Do they have arms, ammunition, troops? Who are the leaders? What are they—Social Democrats, Socialists, Communists, Fascists? What is the political situation in Austria? How strong is the present Social Democratic Party? the Communist Party? Aren't all Austrians Nazis? If not, why did they shout so enthusiastically when Hitler marched into Austria?

Käs knew they were trying to trap him and answered cautiously. Finally a large map was laid on the table. Käs pointed to Hochwolkersdorf.

"How do you know where we are?" someone asked in surprise.

"There's a sign over the firehouse," he answered, and everyone laughed.

Käs marked down the German positions on the Russian map, and then said, "The war is over and any soldier who dies now will have died in vain. We Austrians want you to treat Vienna as an open city. The Nazis don't care what happens and have already declared it a *Festung*. The resistance movement is too weak to prevent the ruin of Vienna but we can lead Russian troops into the city without loss of life."

Käs showed how the Red Army could march straight through the Vienna Woods at Baden, then turn and enter the capital from the west. Here members of "0–5" would meet the Russians and lead them into the heart of the city while other resistance forces were seizing key points.

A Russian intelligence officer checked the German positions Käs had drawn and said they confirmed his own reports. This impressed some of Zheltov's staff but several remained suspicious. One, a scowling major general, said he could not believe Käs was only a sergeant major; he was obviously an officer sent by the German High Command to lure the Red Army into a trap. Käs turned to General Zheltov, who struck him as intelligent and objective, and volunteered to lead the first Russian tank in the attack. Zheltov was convinced, but the High Command in Moscow would have to give final approval. An answer should arrive within the next few hours.

Käs was wakened early the next morning, April 4, and escorted back to the meeting room. The atmosphere was more congenial and he noticed several new faces. An older general, who had said little in the first meeting, stood up. After lighting a cigarette he said in German, "The High Command of the Red Army has accepted the conditions of the Austrian resistance organization." On their part, he went on, "0–5" must promise to occupy the most strategic points in the city, such as public buildings and bridges, and also re-establish civil and police administration. "0–5" would lead the Red Army into Vienna but the Russians would do the fighting.

Zheltov interrupted. If Käs agreed to all this, he said, Allied air attacks against eastern Austria would cease immediately and the Red Army would protect the city water supply.

Käs stood up. "I accept in the name of Vienna."

Zheltov also rose and the two shook hands. They again went to the table. On it lay a map of the Red Army General Staff attack plan. An arrow ran through the Vienna Woods to the rear of the capital. Tolbukhin had followed Szokoll's plan. Another arrow swung down on Vienna from the northeast. This was Malinovsky's Second Ukrainian Front.

A telephone rang. Käs was told that it was Field-Marshal Alexander in Italy, who had promised to honor the Red Army High Command request not to bomb Steiermark, Lower Austria and Vienna. Käs felt "a great wave of relief." All he had to do now was get back to Vienna.

## 3.

It was an indication of the importance Hitler gave Vienna that he ordered a panzer division pulled out of the line defending Berlin and rushed to the Austrian capital. The same order also deprived Heinrici's Army Group Vistula of two infantry divisions. These were bound for Schörner's Army Group Center.

Heinrici knew this wholesale transfer could spell the end of his front, already thinly spread out. The loss of three divisions would be catastrophic and his only salvation was to find immediate replacements. He could think of only one source—Colonel Biehler's eighteen battle-tested battalions inside the Frankfurt *Festung*. These would have to be pulled back across the Oder and placed astride the important Frankfurt Berlin Autobahn. And this, of course, meant Heinrici would somehow have to convince the Führer to abandon the *Festung*.

In the afternoon of April 4 Heinrici and his operations officer, Colonel Eismann, approached the Chancellery garden entrance to the underground bunker. The garden was a jumble of trenches, foxholes, felled trees. The two men climbed down the steep stairs to the lower level, the Führer bunker. Two husky SS guards approached and politely asked if the general would consent to a body search. Heinrici nodded and a big guard looked through his pockets, patted his sides and hips. Eismann's briefcase was emptied and searched, and the two were led down a narrow corridor. It was all done correctly, in a dignified manner, but Heinrici thought, How far we have come!

Near the end of the corridor, about thirty high-ranking officials were assembled. After coffee and sandwiches were served, Keitel said, "The following people can go into the briefing . . ." and called out the names of Dönitz, Bormann, Jodl, Krebs, Himmler, Heinrici and Eismann.

Heinrici entered the tiny map room. There were wooden benches on two sides, a map table and a single chair. Everyone took seats on the benches except Bormann, who chose a box in a corner. Then Hitler entered, wearing dark glasses. He shook hands with Heinrici and Eismann, and sat down.

Krebs suggested that Heinrici and Eismann start their briefing so that they could return to the battlefield. Hitler nodded. Heinrici started by drawing a precise picture of the front-line situation. Suddenly he faced Hitler and proposed that Biehler's eighteen battalions be withdrawn from the Frankfurt *Festung*—and waited for the explosion.

Hitler seemed to have no reaction at all. Heinrici even wondered if he was awake, since he could not see his eyes behind the glasses. Finally

Hitler turned drowsily to Krebs and said, "It looks as if the general is right."

Dönitz nodded and Krebs said, "Yes, my Führer."

"Go ahead, Krebs," Hitler mumbled, "issue the orders."

Heinrici marveled that he had won so easily. Suddenly the door opened and Göring strode in noisily. After excusing himself for being late, he pushed his big stomach into the table and pompously announced that he had just visited one of his "airborne" divisions on Heinrici's front. Göring's voice startled Hitler, as if he had been daydreaming. He rose jerkily and said in a loud voice, his hand trembling in excitement, "Nobody understands me! Nobody's doing what I want done! As for the *Festung* matter —we've successfully held out at Breslau and we've delayed the Russians many times before in Russia!"

Everyone was cowed to silence—except Heinrici, who realized that he was about to lose what he had come for. He shook his head and said Volkssturm troops couldn't hold back the Russians. He pointed out almost pedantically that you could look at a *Festung* two ways: its defenders could fight to the last shot and die; or they could delay the enemy and withdraw at the last possible moment, to take up the fight later on.

"Who is the officer in charge at Frankfurt?" Hitler interrupted sharply.

"Colonel Biehler."

"Is he a Gneisenau?"*

"We'll find out after the main Russian attack," Heinrici remarked. "I believe he is a Gneisenau."

"I want to see him immediately."

Heinrici said that was impossible for at least two days, and again urged that the *Festung* battalions be moved back at once.

"All right," Hitler said. "I authorize you to withdraw six battalions. But Frankfurt will remain a *Festung!*"

Heinrici knew that this was as big a concession as he would get and began to present his plan of defense against the coming Zhukov drive. It called for a surreptitious retreat of front-line troops to prepared positions just prior to the first Russian bombardment. Hitler approved the idea, but asked, "Why don't you move back now to those positions?"

Heinrici explained that he wanted the Russians to think that the main line was a few miles to the east. Just before they began bombarding this fake line, his men would steal back to the real defenses, leaving only a skeleton force behind. The shells would fall on empty positions. He admitted that he had learned this trick in World War I from the French.

Hitler smiled appreciatively and Heinrici decided that this was the psychological moment to complain about the transfer of so many units

* An officer in the Napoleonic War who defended a fortress so resolutely that his name became a symbol for dogged resistance.

to Vienna and Schörner. "Now there's not much left of my Ninth Army," he said. "This is a severe blow to me."

"To me also," Hitler retorted sarcastically.

"The Russians are about to attack," Heinrici protested. "What reinforcements can I expect?"

The Führer was puzzled. "Haven't you been told that large forces from East Prussia as well as heavy-tank columns are coming down to reinforce you?"

"That's not too sure," Krebs said uneasily. "Those columns are also going to General Schörner."

"I don't know anything about all this," Heinrici interjected. "I don't know what's going on in Schörner's area."

Hitler did not seem at all worried. "The main attack is not going to be on Berlin, anyway," he said with a certainty that appalled Heinrici. "Berlin is only subject to minor side attacks. The major assault will be on Prague."

Hitler's confidence was based on a report from General Reinhold Gehlen, head of Army Intelligence, whose secret agents had proof that Stalin had already ordered the main Soviet assault to be launched at Prague, largely because Bismarck once said that whoever occupied Prague held Mitteleuropa. Gehlen's agents were correct as far as they went. What they didn't know was that Stalin's order had met with violent opposition from Zhukov and other military leaders who insisted that Berlin should be the main target, since Hitler was there. And so, despite Bismarck and Stalin, the Red Army was, in fact, preparing its mightiest blow against Heinrici.

Heinrici said that from his experience he was certain the Russians would attack Berlin, and then began talking of the Göring "Airborne" Division that had been placed in the line defending Berlin. "They are young men, well armed," he said. "In fact overarmed, and the infantry on their flank is only half armed." Göring smiled as if he had been complimented. "But these air people are not experienced. Most of them are recruits with only two weeks' training, and they are being led by pilots."

"My airborne people are excellent soldiers," Göring blustered.

"I'm not saying anything against your men, but they've had no battle experience yet," Heinrici retorted. He turned to Hitler and said Army Group Vistula was about to be attacked in the north also. Hitler thought this was impossible; the area held by Manteuffel's Third Panzer Army was flat and flooded.

Heinrici ignored Hitler and continued to insist on more men to defend his long front. He pointed out that a division loses at least a battalion in a day's battle. "Where can I draw replacements from?" he asked. "I need at least a hundred thousand!"

There was silence. Suddenly Göring stood up. "My Führer, I'll give you a hundred thousand Air Force men!"

Dönitz rose. "I can give two hundred and fifty thousand crewmen from my ships."

Himmler could not remain seated. He jumped up and enthusiastically shouted, "I will give fifteen thousand!"

"There!" Hitler said. "There are your people."

Heinrici tartly rejoined that that was fine, but he couldn't make war with "just people." He needed organized divisions.

Still buoyed by the spontaneous response, Hitler told Heinrici to use the 100,000 replacements in the second line of defense. "They'll simply annihilate the Russians who break through!"

Heinrici started to say that use of such inexperienced troops would only result in massacre, but someone leaned over and whispered, "Stop your complaining. We've wasted two hours already."

Heinrici could not be quieted. He had inspected the troops along the Oder, he said, and most had no battle experience. "Therefore I can't guarantee they'll withstand the coming Russian attack. And the lack of proper reserves dangerously lessens my chance of holding off the Russian attack."

"You have your hundred thousand new men," Hitler said quietly. "As for holding the line, it's up to you to back up the troops with morale and confidence, and the battle will be won." He seemed in a good mood when Heinrici left the room at five o'clock.

But Heinrici was depressed as he climbed out of the bunker into the garden. He had lost three divisions and in return received only six battalions and 100,000 almost useless replacements—and he still had to hold the Frankfurt *Festung*.

Two days later an exhausted Biehler arrived at the bunker to report on the *Festung* and fell asleep in the foyer. When he was at last ushered into the conference room he stated that he could hold all his positions, but his neighbors on the west bank of the Oder were weak and the Russians would easily break through them. "Then it will be impossible for me to hold Frankfurt." He suggested a withdrawal of all his troops across the Oder at once and a strengthening of his flanks on the west side of the river.

"You must strengthen your sides, as you say," Hitler said in a soft voice. "And you must also build up the rear. But the bridgehead stays and Frankfurt an der Oder remains a *Festung*. That is a direct command." He looked at Biehler for confirmation.

Biehler wasn't sure how to answer. If he began tentatively with a "yes," Hitler would interrupt before he could qualify it, and say, "Biehler has said yes."

"No, my Führer," he blurted out.

The faces around them went stiff with terror.

Hitler struggled up angrily and pointed to the door. "Get out of here!"

Biehler gathered his map and papers and walked out. As he slowly headed for the exit to the garden, Krebs ran out after him and said, "You are relieved of your command! Go and see General Busse; he'll let you know what will happen to you."

The man who had fought so long and well at Frankfurt could not believe his ears. It wasn't possible. Ignoring Krebs's order, he headed for OKH headquarters in Zossen to find out what he should do—they must have gone temporarily mad at the bunker.

At Zossen word of Biehler's disgrace had preceded him and staff officers shrank away when they saw him coming down the halls. Even his old friend General Dethleffsen told him, "You'll have to look out for your own welfare." Still in a daze, Biehler drove to the front, and desperate to find someone who would stand behind him, he phoned Heinrici direct.

"Biehler," Heinrici said without hesitation, "you can be sure that everything will come out all right." These were the first positive words Biehler had heard all day. He could hardly believe what he heard next. "Go back to Frankfurt and take command."

Heinrici knew more about the situation than Biehler realized. Moments earlier Burgdorf had called Heinrici to read a sarcastic message from Hitler: "Biehler is not a Gneisenau." Then Burgdorf told Heinrici that Biehler had been relieved.

"I demand that the order be rescinded," Heinrici had said. "Biehler must be reinstated and given the Knight's Cross." It would be utterly ridiculous, he added, to get rid of the one man who was the spirit of the bridgehead.

"Impossible!" the flustered Burgdorf replied. "Those are Hitler's orders."

"I demand that Biehler stay, or I quit," said Heinrici and hung up.

## 4.

About sixty hours had passed since Sergeant Käs left Vienna on his mission to hand over the city to the Russians. At Army District XVII headquarters, on the morning of April 5, Szokoll had no idea whether Käs had even reached the Russian lines. The previous night there had been a tremendous artillery barrage and Tolbukhin's men were reported already advancing on the southern outskirts of the city. Excited members of "0–5" streamed into Szokoll's office with whispered reports that resistance operations were all ready, and asked anxiously: had Käs succeeded?

Szokoll was also inundated by constant demands from Army Group South and General Rudolf von Bünau, who would command the final *Festung* defense of Vienna, for replacement troops—troops which Szokoll himself needed to storm important centers once the uprising started.

In the forenoon Szokoll's secretary noted that not a single enemy plane had yet appeared in the cloudless sky over the city. Szokoll wondered if this was because of Käs, or because the Red Army assault on Vienna had started and the Western Allies didn't want to hit friendly troops. Just then an officer reported that, curiously, the Tolbukhin advance had stopped. Szokoll began to think that Käs must have succeeded, and sent out messengers to assure the other "0–5" leaders that everything was progressing as planned—with a prayer that he was right.

At that moment Käs and Reif were only about thirty miles south of Vienna. They had walked through the German lines with a large crowd of terrified refugees trying to escape the Russians. Once in German territory, they flagged down a car driven by the Gauleiter of Wiener Neustadt, on his way to see Baldur von Schirach in Vienna. Käs showed their faked passes and demanded a ride. When Käs noticed that they were heading for Baden, which lay directly in Tolbukhin's path, he called, "Turn around. The Russians are already in Baden!"

The district Party leader said there were only German troops there and insisted on going to Vienna the shortest way. Käs grabbed him by the throat and told him to stop. Reif took the wheel and they started toward the capital via a roundabout route.

They entered Vienna at noon. The streets were empty. Streetcars stood idle; stores were closed. Käs and Reif got out of the car near the Kunsthistorisches Museum on Ringstrasse.

"Heil Hitler," said the Gauleiter.

"Heil Hitler," said Käs, and headed for the Hotel Bristol, where he telephoned Szokoll and reported his safe arrival.

That evening the leaders of "0–5" met at Szokoll's office at eleven o'clock for last-minute discussions. Szokoll told Major Karl Biedermann to post reliable units of his 1600-man Greater Vienna Army Patrol—they were Austrians—at strategic points and, above all, to prevent the destruction of Danube bridges. Hauptmann Alfred Huth was to storm the Bisamberg radio transmitter with a motorcycle platoon. Oberleutnant (1st Lieutenant) Rudolf Raschke would defend the Army District XVII building, headquarters for all future "0–5" operations. Szokoll said that he would personally lead a group of officers to General von Bünau's command post and force him to capitulate.

Szokoll told them that Tolbukhin was already moving into the Vienna Woods near Baden. When the Soviets reached the city they would shoot up a red signal light. "0–5" would reply with a green light. As Russian units approached, they would display red-and-white flags. Resistance forces would carry white flags. The password would be a name which sounded almost the same in German and Russian: "Moskva."

Not long after the meeting, red signal lights shot up from the woods south of the city. After a pause, green lights climbed over blacked-out Vienna. Szokoll gave the order to begin the uprising at midnight. At that time the "0–5" code word "Radetzky" would be broadcast over the government radio station: the signal for each resistance group to go into action. Key buildings and bridges would be seized; riots started; prominent Nazis arrested; communications disrupted; and barricades erected south of the city to keep out any of Dietrich's troops falling back from the front.

But even before this signal could be given, the uprising was betrayed. A motorcycle rifleman of Major Biedermann's Greater Vienna Army Patrol happened to mention to a fellow Austrian, Leutnant Walter Hanslick, that his battle group was going to seize the Bisamberg radio transmitter. An ardent Nazi, Hanslick's suspicions were aroused. He reported what he had heard, and within the hour Biedermann was ordered to see General von Bünau at *Festung* headquarters, in the heart of Vienna. Biedermann must have guessed that he had been discovered, but he obeyed; flight would endanger the entire conspiracy.

At *Festung* headquarters Biedermann was questioned. When he revealed nothing, he was tortured. He held out until the early hours of April 6— and finally divulged the names of four of his fellow conspirators: Szokoll, Käs, Raschke and Huth.

At 4:30 A.M. Käs brought the grim news that Biedermann had been arrested to the Army District XVII building. This presented Szokoll with a new problem. He could let the uprising continue as scheduled and hope that Biedermann had not revealed anything important—or make entirely new plans. He decided to continue, and ordered Bünau's command post attacked at once to liberate the prisoner. But by the time Szokoll reached Festung headquarters they had been reinforced by two SS combat units.

It was a double blow. Not only was he unable to rescue Biedermann, but *Festung* headquarters were now impregnable and there was no chance to force Bünau to capitulate. Szokoll realized that his headquarters at the Army District XVII building were no longer safe, so he sent Käs there with orders to double security and to hold the building at all costs until help could be sent.

Käs arrived at about 6:30 A.M., conveyed the orders to Raschke and left. Raschke immediately summoned the guards and ordered them to arrest anyone trying to enter the building with the German password for the night, "Gneisenau." But moments later Major Neumann, Bünau's chief of staff, burst into Raschke's office—he had been admitted with the "0–5" password, "Radetzky"—and asked, "Where is Major Szokoll?"

"The major is at home—he has stomach cramps," Raschke replied.

The entire building was seized by the Germans, but in the midst of all this confusion two women secretaries stayed at their desks and phoned Szokoll and other "0–5" leaders about the unexpected raid.

To Szokoll it seemed as if everything that could go wrong had. Biedermann was captured; Bünau was safe in his command post; the Army District XVII building with its arms and motor pool was lost; and important members of his own staff were under arrest. The military phase of the uprising was kaputt.

But there was still hope. When the civilian conspirators learned of the series of disasters they did not panic. Their local meeting points and battle groups were still undiscovered, and they assured Szokoll that they would carry out their assigned duties. The civilian "0–5" units were joined by Austrian deserters who had been hiding for weeks in the city's allotment gardens, and by the end of the day the uprising was not only alive but flourishing.

While the German command did not yet realize the extent of the conspiracy, the arrests were causing general uncertainty. Could any of the Austrian units be trusted? This concern was suddenly overshadowed by an alarming report: the Russians were attacking Vienna from the rear!

Hasty defenses were ordered set up to the west of the city, but it was too late. Red Army tanks were already moving past the famed outdoor wine gardens of Grinzing and other key points just west and northwest of Vienna. So far the Russians had run into no German troops, and tankers stood carelessly with open hatches. "0–5" men tried to lead them toward the center of the city, and though there was little to stop them, the Soviets either did not understand or were suspicious, and hung back.

All over town, citizens began emerging from their cellars to hang out sheets and pillowcases from windows and doors. They even boldly refused to let little groups of German soldiers make *Festungen* of their apartments. Women with babies in their arms shouted at the Germans to go home. Old men argued with young German soldiers: why fight against women and children?

Austrians in uniform, eager to desert, were hidden in houses and given civilian clothing. Thousands of slave laborers began roaming the streets, looking for weapons. Poles, Ukrainians, Czechs, Serbs, Greeks, French and Belgians bargained with householders for shotguns, rifles, pistols, knives and even offered their trousers in return. Nothing could stop them from settling accounts with their former masters.

Word of the revolt spread to the front and even Germans began deserting. When Dietrich learned that Tolbukhin's troops had swept through his lines and almost encircled Vienna, he knew it could no longer be held. He loved the old city and did not want to see it become a battleground for a hopeless fight. Disregarding the order to hold every foot of ground to the end, Dietrich ordered his troops to move farther west behind the city to form another defense line.

By late afternoon Russians were streaming into Vienna from the west almost at will, while "O-5" men carrying stolen passes and wearing Volkssturm arm bands moved openly throughout the streets, sniping at anyone in German uniform. That evening Dietrich's chief of staff reported to Army Group South: "Firing started already inside Vienna, but it is Austrians shooting at us, not Russians."

The frantic exodus grew as fire brigades, air-raid wardens and even police joined the disorderly mob fleeing the city.

The next day, April 7, civilian and military headquarters of "O-5" were moved to the Palais Auersperg, owned by Princess Agathe Croy, a member of the resistance. From here Szokoll and civilian leaders continued to direct the uprising, which had reached such proportions that General von Bünau radioed Führer headquarters:

THE CIVILIAN POPULATION, BY THE HOISTING OF THE RED-WHITE-RED FLAG, DIRECTS A STRONGER FIRE AGAINST GERMAN TROOPS THAN THE ENEMY DOES.

The answer from Berlin was:

> PROCEED AGAINST THE REBELS IN VIENNA
> WITH THE MOST BRUTAL MEANS. HITLER.

By evening Russian spearheads were pushing against a Vienna which was a patchwork of flames. The few remaining fire brigades were kept running from district to district as they desperately tried to control spreading blazes.

On Sunday, April 8, Tolbukhin's men, delayed by their own supply and organizational difficulties, moved in force deeper into the "Red" suburbs where there was almost no resistance. The Socialists in these areas had persuaded most of the defenders to give up their arms and remove their uniforms. In one district alone the inhabitants helped some 3000 German soldiers become "civilians" by hiding them in attics and cellars.

The first Russians entered the city limits about noon. Their firing was heard by Paula Schmuck-Wachter, who was hiding with her six-year-old child and mother in the cellar of their apartment. When she heard boisterous voices above, she was certain they would all be killed. To calm herself she read Goethe's *Faust*. One part she recited over and over:

> ". . . all seems like an oppressive dream,
> Where in confusion is confusion reigning
> And lawlessness by law itself maintaining,
> A world of error evermore obtaining."

"Babies will be born and life will go on," her mother said, and hid Paula and her child in the coal bin.

As was often the case, there was nothing to fear from these Russians. They were easygoing, and even indulgent with children. They were intrigued by watches, clocks—anything mechanical. Fascinated with the toilets, they would sit on the floor flushing them over and over, laughing delightedly. Some took the toilets for refrigerators and kept food inside. Several soldiers accidentally flushed the food away and killed their hosts in retaliation. They thought the toilets had been booby-trapped.

At a nearby apartment the Russians were friendly until one of them was hit by a German sniper. His enraged comrades forced a young wounded Austrian soldier to set fire to the apartment house. As soon as the Austrian thought the Russians had left he began throwing buckets of water on the blaze. But a Russian in a huge Caucasian hat came back and shot the wounded man through the head. A woman tearfully began calling the Russian a murderer but he only shoved his pistol back in its holster and said, "You good—we good. You bad—we bad."

There was no pattern to the fighting and no front line. German stragglers held isolated positions all over the city but the red-white-red flag of "0–5" flew from hundreds of buildings. Rebels held the Parliament and the Town Hall. Other groups stormed police headquarters on the Schottenring to liberate prisoners.

General von Bünau, however, was still firmly entrenched in the Inner City, which was encircled by the broad, tree-lined avenue called Ringstrasse, or simply the Ring, and the Danube Canal to the northeast. In the afternoon a small convoy of cars sped out of the *Festung* area and up to a nearby square. Biedermann, Huth and Raschke were shoved out of one car by Gestapo and SS troops. Insignia were torn from their uniforms, and their hands tied. A rope was thrown over a traffic sign and looped around Biedermann's neck. He was hanged, then Raschke. As another rope was fastened to a streetcar stop sign and the loop placed around Huth's neck, he shouted, "For God and Austria!"

One "traitor" still remained inside the fortress. He was Leutnant Scheichelbauer, an "0–5" man posing as a loyal Nazi. Earlier in the afternoon he had made a remarkable discovery in the operations office—he stumbled across the new defense plan of the Inner City, which described in detail the exact strength and location of every unit loyal to Bünau.

Scheichelbauer managed to smuggle the plan out to Szokoll. The documents were so important that Szokoll decided to take them to the Russians personally. About 4 A.M., April 9, as Bünau's troops were being slowly pressed back toward the Danube, the major and ten bodyguards crossed into the Russian lines. Two hours later Szokoll was standing before Tolbukhin himself. He told him about the new German positions and showed how the Russians could break into the Inner City through a series of tunnels.

The trip back was hectic. With several high-ranking Russians in his car, Szokoll drove at top speed toward a Danube bridge, only to see too late that it had been destroyed. He careened off into the river, badly injuring two of the Russians. Szokoll, however, was unhurt; he transferred to another car and drove recklessly through the German positions until he safely reached the Palais Auersperg.

## 5.

The next day another Viennese who was worried about the fate of his city returned home. At Hitler's personal request Otto Skorzeny was on an inspection tour of the eastern front. He was lunching with Schörner when an aide rushed in with the news that the Russians had entered Vienna.

Skorzeny's family was still in Vienna and so were two of his commando units, which he didn't want sacrificed in some routine action. He said good-bye to Schörner, and after six hours of fast driving approached the suburbs of his native city. He was appalled to see German soldiers streaming in disorderly retreat from Vienna. His rage mounted as he saw that wounded were walking while able-bodied men sat in trucks loaded with furniture. He tried to halt a horse cart filled with soldiers and a girl. When it didn't, he reached up and grabbed a sergeant by the collar and slapped his face. "Now throw out all that furniture and make way for wounded people!" Skorzeny cried. "If the girl wants to come, she has to walk." He took the sergeant's pistol and gave it to the nearest wounded man. "Load up only wounded," he ordered.

It was dark by the time Skorzeny entered Vienna. He discovered with relief that his two units had already left, and set out to learn the fate of his family. He found his mother's half-destroyed house; she had left several days before. His brother's house too was wrecked and empty. He then drove through deserted streets toward the factory he had established before the war, making scaffolding for contractors. The sounds of battle grew louder as he approached the Schönbrunn Palace. A shell exploded near by. He passed two elderly policemen and asked what the situation was.

They snapped to attention. "Colonel," said one with a grin, "*we* are the defense line of Vienna."

At his factory there was no electricity, and his secretary boiled water for tea over a candle as the workmen crowded around, trying to shake his hand. Russian tanks, he was told, had passed by on their way to the center of town. Citizens were plundering more than the Russians. It was the end of Old Vienna and Austria.

Skorzeny knew Hitler would want a personal report on the situation inside Vienna. The fact that Russian tanks were between him and the Inner City didn't discourage him. Following the side streets he knew so well, Skorzeny directed his driver through the blackness of the unlit city to Bünau's *Festung* headquarters. He told Bünau that he'd seen no German soldiers—but many Russians. "When I get out," he said, "I will report to the Führer that Vienna is lost."

Bünau asked if he wanted to see Baldur von Schirach, the defense commissioner; he was just down the hall.

Skorzeny walked into a large elegant room lit by candles. Schirach looked up from a desk and smiled. "You see, Skorzeny, I have only candlelight to work by."

"I haven't seen a single German soldier," Skorzeny complained. "The road blocks are unmanned! The Russians can walk in whenever they like."

"Impossible!"

Skorzeny told him to drive around and see for himself. The former Youth Leader still wouldn't believe it, and when Skorzeny advised him to escape, said, "No, I will never leave this post and I will die in this spot. But nothing is lost. One division is coming from the west and another will cross the Danube to reinforce us. We'll hold the Russians."

"You're a dreamer," Skorzeny replied. "I will report to the Führer that Vienna is lost."

It was dawn, April 11, as Skorzeny's car raced across the Floridsdorfer Bridge under heavy sniper fire from rooftops. He turned for a last look at his Vienna. It was in flames; guns thundered. Something inside him seemed to collapse.

At the nearest Gestapo headquarters he dictated a radio message to Hitler:

ON THE STREETS LEADING FROM VIENNA TO WEST I FOUND MORE OR LESS CHAOTIC SCENES AND I PROPOSE TO TAKE FORCEFUL ACTION THERE. VIENNA PRACTICALLY DEFENSELESS AND WILL FALL IN RUSSIAN HANDS THIS MORNING.

Bünau's troops were pushed back through the city across the Danube River to a final defense line. Four bridges were blown up, leaving only the Reichsbrücke as an escape route. When Bünau's last man had crossed the Danube, a demolition party approached to blow up the big structure, but the bridge guard, members of "0–5," suddenly turned their machine guns on the Germans and drove them off.

For three more days the hectic fighting dragged on, but by April 14 the battle of Vienna was over. The streets were littered with burned-out tanks and dead horses; thousands of dead Germans, Viennese and Russians lay side by side. Sick and wounded were trundled to emergency hospitals in baby carriages and wheelbarrows. Apartment buildings and homes were barricaded to keep away Russians, liberated slave laborers and Viennese—all bent on loot and rape. Children were trained to run to the nearest Russian district command post for help. If the patrol arrived in time, the plunderer or rapist was sometimes shot on the spot; or he might be arrested; but often as not he was merely let off with a warning.

Though the reservoirs were intact, water pipes all over the city had been destroyed by bombs and shells, and people stood for hours at the few springs still flowing. The food problem was even worse. Those storage houses not destroyed had been plundered by civilians. Almost nothing was available; ration cards were useless, and a barter system flourished.

The streets were ruled by the law of club and fist. Armed foreign workers seized weapons and assumed police powers themselves. Organized groups of civilian plunderers systematically swept through stores, shops and homes. Self-appointed civil authorities moved people out of their apartments and substituted their own families. In some districts it was an easy matter to claim that an empty apartment belonged to a Nazi—and simply take it over.

Already a number of political moves were under way. Ernst Fischer, a prominent Viennese Communist, arrived by air from Moscow. Dr. Karl Renner, the former Chancellor, was also brought to the city by the Soviets.

Major Szokoll was proclaimed civil commander of Vienna by the Russians and installed in the Rathaus (Town Hall). After two days in office he was told by a Russian colonel, "You have just been made chief of police of Vienna. Follow me; we've found some war criminals." Szokoll said he was too busy to leave but the colonel called for several Soviet guards, and Szokoll was escorted down the stairs of the Rathaus and into a waiting car.

Only then did the colonel reveal that he was an NKVD officer. He accused the major of being a spy of the Western Allies who had only come to Tolbukhin's headquarters to steal their plans. He was also charged with responsibility for the failure of the uprising, and threatened with execution.

That afternoon the NKVD locked Szokoll in a damp cellar. He curled up on a carpet atop an icebox and went to sleep.*

* Several weeks later Szokoll was sent to a prisoner-of-war camp. Posing as a janitor, he swept his way out the front door to freedom. He was rearrested, imprisoned for three more months, then released. Today he is a film producer and still a controversial figure in Vienna—to some a hero, to others the man who "betrayed" the city to the Communists.

# 21

## "Such Vile Misrepresentations"

**1.**

The many messages generated by Operation "Sunrise" seemed only to have aggravated the situation. On Good Friday, Roosevelt received another. In it Stalin charged that because of the talks at Ascona the Germans had felt free to send three divisions from Italy to the eastern front.* Stalin further complained that the agreement at Yalta to attack Hitler simultaneously from the east, west and south was not being observed by the Allies in Italy.

. . . THIS CIRCUMSTANCE IRRITATES THE SOVIET COMMAND AND ENGENDERS DISTRUST. . . . IN A SITUATION OF THIS KIND ALLIES SHOULD HAVE NOTHING TO CONCEAL FROM EACH OTHER.

In exasperation the President asked Marshall and Leahy to draft a reply. Concerned by Stalin's accusations, the Joint Chiefs feared that an open break with Russia was "the only miracle that would prevent the speedy collapse of the German armies" and composed an answer that somehow managed to be forceful and conciliatory at the same time.

. . . I MUST REPEAT THAT THE MEETING IN BERNE** WAS FOR THE

---

* Only one division was withdrawn from Italy, and that was transferred to the western front—and the move had nothing at all to do with the talks.
** In all messages, Berne is for some reason given as the locale of the historic meeting, not Ascona. Perhaps this was to fool the Soviets. It has also confused many historians.

SINGLE PURPOSE OF ARRANGING CONTACT WITH COMPETENT GER-
MAN MILITARY OFFICERS AND NOT FOR NEGOTIATIONS OF ANY KIND.
. . . THIS ENTIRE EPISODE HAS ARISEN THROUGH THE INITIATIVE
OF A GERMAN OFFICER REPUTED TO BE CLOSE TO HIMMLER AND
THERE IS, OF COURSE, A STRONG POSSIBILITY THAT HIS SOLE PURPOSE
IS TO CREATE SUSPICION AND DISTRUST BETWEEN THE ALLIES. THERE
IS NO REASON WHY WE SHOULD PERMIT HIM TO SUCCEED IN THAT
AIM. I TRUST THAT THE ABOVE CATEGORICAL STATEMENT OF THE
PRESENT SITUATION AND MY INTENTIONS WILL ALLAY THE APPRE-
HENSION YOU EXPRESSED IN YOUR MESSAGE OF MARCH 29.

Stalin's fears as to what might happen to Communist aspirations in
northern Italy if the Germans were allowed to surrender promptly were
well founded. Apparently inundated with misinformation from his agents
in Switzerland, Stalin again cabled Roosevelt on April 3. It was an astounding message for one ally to send another and quite openly accused
the Western Allies of playing a deceitful game.

. . . YOU AFFIRM THAT SO FAR NO NEGOTIATIONS HAVE BEEN
ENTERED INTO. APPARENTLY YOU ARE NOT FULLY INFORMED. AS
REGARDS MY MILITARY COLLEAGUES, THEY, ON THE BASIS OF IN-
FORMATION IN THEIR POSSESSION, ARE SURE THAT NEGOTIATIONS
DID TAKE PLACE AND THAT THEY ENDED IN AN AGREEMENT WITH
THE GERMANS, WHEREBY THE GERMAN COMMANDER ON THE WEST-
ERN FRONT, MARSHAL KESSELRING, IS TO OPEN THE FRONT TO THE
ANGLO-AMERICAN TROOPS AND LET THEM MOVE EAST, WHILE THE
BRITISH AND AMERICANS HAVE PROMISED, IN EXCHANGE, TO EASE
THE ARMISTICE TERMS FOR THE GERMANS.
I THINK THAT MY COLLEAGUES ARE NOT VERY FAR FROM THE TRUTH.
IF THE CONTRARY WERE THE CASE THE EXCLUSION OF REPRESENTA-
TIVES OF THE SOVIET COMMAND FROM THE BERNE [Ascona] TALKS
WOULD BE INEXPLICABLE.
NOR CAN I ACCOUNT FOR THE RETICENCE OF THE BRITISH, WHO
HAVE LEFT IT TO YOU TO CARRY ON A CORRESPONDENCE WITH ME
ON THIS UNPLEASANT MATTER, WHILE THEY THEMSELVES MAINTAIN
SILENCE, ALTHOUGH IT IS KNOWN THAT THE INITIATIVE IN THE MAT-
TER OF THE BERNE NEGOTIATIONS BELONGS TO THE BRITISH . . .

Eisenhower's recent co-operative message about Berlin might even
have added to Stalin's suspicions, and he went on to note sarcastically
that the "negotiations" in Switzerland enabled the Allies to advance "almost without resistance" into the heart of Germany, while the war in the
east raged on.
One American who felt strongly that the Russians should not be ap-
peased in this or other questions was Averell Harriman. As soon as Stalin's
message had passed through his hands, he cabled the State Department

that the Soviets were viewing all matters only from the standpoint of their own selfish interests.

> . . . THEY HAVE PUBLICIZED TO THEIR OWN POLITICAL ADVANTAGE THE DIFFICULT FOOD SITUATION IN AREAS LIBERATED BY OUR TROOPS, SUCH AS IN FRANCE, BELGIUM AND ITALY, COMPARING IT WITH THE ALLEGEDLY SATISFACTORY CONDITIONS IN AREAS WHICH THE RED ARMY HAS LIBERATED. . . . I THUS REGRETFULLY COME TO THE CONCLUSION THAT WE SHOULD BE GUIDED . . . BY THE POLICY OF TAKING CARE OF OUR WESTERN ALLIES AND OTHER AREAS UNDER OUR RESPONSIBILITY FIRST, ALLOCATING TO RUSSIA WHAT MAY BE LEFT.

The only way of supporting antitotalitarian peoples and stopping Soviet penetration, he said, was to help them attain economic stability quickly.

> . . . I THEREFORE RECOMMEND THAT WE FACE THE REALITIES OF THE SITUATION AND ORIENT OUR FOREIGN ECONOMIC POLICIES ACCORDINGLY . . .

These conclusions were passed on to the President and undoubtedly helped influence him to send Stalin, on April 5, the most aggressive, most indignant message since the war began:

> . . . IT IS ASTONISHING THAT A BELIEF SEEMS TO HAVE REACHED THE SOVIET GOVERNMENT THAT I HAVE ENTERED INTO AN AGREEMENT WITH THE ENEMY WITHOUT FIRST OBTAINING YOUR FULL AGREEMENT.

> . . . IT WOULD BE ONE OF THE GREAT TRAGEDIES OF HISTORY IF AT THE VERY MOMENT OF THE VICTORY, NOW WITHIN OUR GRASP, SUCH DISTRUST, SUCH LACK OF FAITH SHOULD PREJUDICE THE ENTIRE UNDERTAKING AFTER THE COLOSSAL LOSSES OF LIFE, MATERIAL AND TREASURE INVOLVED.

> FRANKLY I CANNOT AVOID A FEELING OF BITTER RESENTMENT TOWARD YOUR INFORMERS, WHOEVER THEY ARE, FOR SUCH VILE MISREPRESENTATIONS OF MY ACTIONS OR THOSE OF MY TRUSTED SUBORDINATES.

When Churchill received a copy of the message he was delighted. The last sentence, he thought, "seemed like Roosevelt himself in anger." He immediately wrote the President that he was "astounded that Stalin should have addressed to you a message so insulting to the honour of the United States and also of Great Britain," and cabled Stalin a long message which concluded:

> . . . I ASSOCIATE MYSELF AND MY COLLEAGUES WITH THE LAST SENTENCE OF THE PRESIDENT'S REPLY.

Harriman's next memorandum to the State Department, the following day, reported that America's continued "generous and considerate attitude" was looked on by the Soviets as a sign of weakness. "I cannot list the almost daily affronts and total disregard which the Soviets evince in matters of interest to us," he declared, and strongly urged reprisals to make the Soviets realize they could not "continue their present attitude except at great cost to themselves."

Harriman's conviction that only a tough policy would work with the Soviets was borne out by Stalin's answer to Roosevelt's "vile misrepresentations" message. Obviously disturbed by the President's injured, yet aggressive tone, he tried to ease the situation.

. . . I HAVE NEVER DOUBTED YOUR INTEGRITY OR TRUSTWORTHINESS, JUST AS I HAVE NEVER QUESTIONED THE INTEGRITY OR TRUSTWORTHINESS OF MR CHURCHILL.

But he still felt that the Russians should have been invited to the meeting in Switzerland and insisted that his point of view was "the only correct one." He also argued—with some validity—that the flagging German resistance in the west was not solely due "to the fact that they have been beaten."

. . . THE GERMANS HAVE 147 DIVISIONS ON THE EASTERN FRONT. THEY COULD SAFELY WITHDRAW FROM 15 TO 20 DIVISIONS FROM THE EASTERN FRONT TO AID THEIR FORCES ON THE WESTERN FRONT. YET THEY HAVE NOT DONE SO, NOR ARE THEY DOING SO. THEY ARE FIGHTING DESPERATELY AGAINST THE RUSSIANS FOR ZEMLENICE, AN OBSCURE STATION IN CZECHOSLOVAKIA, WHICH THEY NEED JUST AS MUCH AS A DEAD MAN NEEDS A POULTICE, BUT THEY SURRENDER WITHOUT ANY RESISTANCE SUCH IMPORTANT TOWNS IN THE HEART OF GERMANY AS OSNABRUECK, MANNHEIM AND KASSEL. YOU WILL ADMIT THAT THIS BEHAVIOUR ON THE PART OF THE GERMANS IS MORE THAN STRANGE AND UNACCOUNTABLE.

Stalin also wired Churchill an aggressive apology:

. . . MY MESSAGES ARE PERSONAL AND MOST SECRET. THIS ENABLES ME TO SPEAK MY MIND FRANKLY AND CLEARLY. THAT IS AN ADVANTAGE OF SECRET CORRESPONDENCE. BUT IF YOU TAKE EVERY FRANK STATEMENT OF MINE AS AN AFFRONT, THEN THE CORRESPONDENCE WILL BE GREATLY HANDICAPPED. I CAN ASSURE YOU THAT I HAVE NEVER HAD, NOR HAVE I NOW, ANY INTENTION OF AFFRONTING ANYONE.

Other messages to his Allies that day, though outwardly aggressive, also indicated a readiness to be more reasonable. He told Roosevelt, for instance, that the Polish question had reached an impasse because "the

U. S. and British ambassadors have parted from the instructions of the Crimean Conference," yet a moment later declared his eagerness to settle the matter "in a short time." If nothing else, the President's indignant cry of "vile misrepresentations" had created a healthy apprehension in the Soviet Union.

After Roosevelt read the message on Poland he cabled Churchill:

. . . WE SHALL HAVE TO CONSIDER MOST CAREFULLY THE IMPLICA-TIONS OF STALIN'S ATTITUDE AND WHAT IS TO BE OUR NEXT STEP. I SHALL OF COURSE TAKE NO ACTION OF ANY KIND NOR MAKE ANY STATEMENT WITHOUT CONSULTING YOU, AND I KNOW YOU WILL DO THE SAME.

Both men—at last of one mind—felt Stalin's attitude had changed enough to offer, as Churchill put it, "some hope of progress."

While the diplomats wrangled, Anglo-American-French forces were ripping up the entire western front. These successes did not quiet the British Chiefs' objections to the decision on Berlin. When Eisenhower's deputy, Marshal of the Royal Air Force Sir A. W. Tedder, attended the British Chiefs' meeting on April 3, he tried to rationalize his commander's action by proposing that Eisenhower had been forced to deal directly with Stalin only because Montgomery had issued a conflicting directive on troop movements.

"I am astonished Ike found it necessary to call on Stalin to control Monty" was Brooke's sarcastic retort.

In a long cable the following day, the British Chiefs asked their American counterparts to reconsider "the desirability of Anglo-American forces capturing Berlin as soon as possible." But Churchill wished to bring the argument to an end. He was convinced that the Americans would never change their minds, and on April 5 he cabled Roosevelt:

. . . I REGARD THE MATTER AS CLOSED, AND TO PROVE MY SINCERITY I WILL USE ONE OF MY VERY FEW LATIN QUOTATIONS: AMANTIUM IRAE AMORIS INTEGRATIO EST [lovers' quarrels are a part of love].

A few hours later, however, in a message to Roosevelt ostensibly about Operation "Sunrise," he could not resist bringing up the matter of Berlin again and said they should "join hands with the Russian armies as far to the east as possible, and, if circumstances allow, enter Berlin."

Eisenhower too was unable to let the matter drop. He continued to send lengthy explanations to Marshall, who needed no more ammunition to combat British objections. Even Montgomery had become convinced that further argument was fruitless and with good grace had wired Eisenhower:

. . . IT IS VERY CLEAR TO ME WHAT YOU WANT. I WILL CRACK ALONG ON THE NORTHERN FLANK 100% AND WILL DO ALL I CAN TO DRAW THE ENEMY FORCES AWAY FROM THE MAIN EFFORT BEING MADE BY BRADLEY.

General Simpson, whose Ninth Army was racing toward the Elbe and Berlin, had no idea that the German capital was no longer the final Allied objective, and therefore had no misgivings when Bradley ordered him to stop his advance "for a breathing spell." Several days later Bradley phoned again and said, "Go ahead." Simpson told his staff to go "hell-bent for Berlin" and decided to make the final assault along the Autobahn from Magdeburg, with Major General Isaac White's 2nd Armored Division and either the 30th or 83rd Infantry Division. He had plenty of supplies and ten-ton trucks, and his men were in good shape.

**2.**

Hitler's fronts were collapsing on all sides, but thousands of Allied prisoners of war were still being marched toward the Redoubt area in southern Bavaria. Early in the morning on April 5 the group from Hammelburg, wet and cold from a drizzling rain, marched into the spiritual home of National Socialism, Nuremberg.

They were impressed by the awesome damage from Allied air attacks. The I. G. Farben factories were a shambles, but still operating. Trolley cars, buses and trucks stood idle in the streets. People walked or rode bicycles; no children were in sight. As the column reached the other side of the city, the skies cleared. The prisoners were stopped and told to take an hour to eat. Father Cavanaugh's group sat under spruce trees in the warm sunshine, lunching from Red Cross boxes. Then they sprawled out to rest. Shortly before noon they could hear air-raid sirens from the city and a nervous shout went up, "Let's get going!" Suddenly the wailing changed to short, frightening blasts. The prisoners sat up, looked around. Half a mile to the south, across an empty stretch of sand, were railroad tracks on an elevated roadbed. Beyond was a long row of munitions buildings, chimneys and storage tanks.

Swarms of Germans, many of them soldiers, were scrambling over the railroad embankment toward the prisoners.

"Look at those Jerries run!"

Father Cavanaugh saw flyspecks high in the blue sky—two flights of fourteen bombers. Then two more flights appeared. As they approached in curves, two from the south, two from the west, thin white trails of markers began falling and a prisoner yelled, "My God, we're on the target!"

The priest leaped to his feet and shouted, "Make an Act of Contrition!"
As he repeated the short formula of General Absolution to the right and
left, bombs began to explode on the factories. Father Cavanaugh pulled
a blanket over his head and prayed. The earth shook under him. Finally
there was a lull and he looked up at clouds of smoke and flame erupting
from the factories. Figures like tiny dolls scattered from the holocaust.

"Keep down!" came a scream. Another flight was approaching to the
deafening roar of flak guns. More bombs skittered down, followed by a
rapid series of tremendous explosions. The munitions had been hit. The
roar of flames and crunch of falling walls drowned out the sound of the
third flight as it droned overhead and dropped its load.

"This must be the end," Father Cavanaugh thought, peering out from
under his blanket. It was strangely dark from the raining dust. The men
sprawled near by seemed to be clinging to the trembling earth. After the
fourth flight came a fifth. Geysers of earth and sand spouted closer and
closer. The heaving of the earth was staggering, the noise terrific. Sand,
gravel and dirt rained on the prisoners. Men were screaming, "Doctor!
Doctor!"

The priest got to his feet and began anointing every inert form he
found, running heedlessly from one to another, until he came to the head
of the column and collected his senses. "I must have missed some," he
thought and started back.

"Father, come and help us get this man out!" an officer shouted, staring
fixedly at a wounded American in a bomb crater filling with water. Five
other officers were just looking on, stupefied. Father Cavanaugh shook
them. "Come on, get busy! Help out. I have other work to do."

He went up to Johnny Losh, who was lying on his stomach. Beside him
sat his buddy, Jim Keough.

"Hello, Father," said Losh, smiling through his pain. "I'm glad you
didn't get hit."

"Johnny got hit in the side, Father," Keough explained.

The priest looked at the bloodstained shirt wrapped around Losh's
abdomen to hold in his vitals, and knew he was dying. He gave him Absolution and tried to console him.

"Do you think I'll be all right, Father?"

"I sure hope you will be, Johnny. We'll get a doctor here for you in
a few minutes."

The priest found Douglas O'Dell sitting in a bomb crater. Two men were
tying a tourniquet—a dirty, torn shirt—around what was left of one leg.

"Well, Father, it looks like I'm not going to make it." O'Dell smiled and
pointed to a severed leg, several yards away. "That's part of me over
there," he said, and added that for some reason he felt at ease with the
Father there.

Captain John Madden approached. "Father, one of the Protestant chaplains has been killed and the others want you to come over." The priest went with Madden and found the body of Chaplain Koskamp. As Father Cavanaugh stooped to anoint him, he saw an oily cross mark already on his soot-covered forehead.

Casualties were high. Many were wounded and twenty-four were dead. The guards gathered up those who could walk, about 400, and continued the march south. The four surviving chaplains, three doctors and seven officers stayed and took care of the wounded. Afterward they lined up the dead in orderly rows and sat down, completely exhausted.

The German sergeant of the guards asked Father Cavanaugh for a cigarette. He held out a pack, and suddenly felt the world spinning. The next thing he knew, someone was pressing a cup of water to his lips. It was the German, sitting beside him on the grass. The two men looked over the scene of carnage but found no words to say.

The companions Father Cavanaugh had left at Oflag XIIIB were about to be rescued by the U. S. 14th Armored Division, which was racing toward Hammelburg. At eleven o'clock the next morning, April 6, the camp commander, General von Goeckel, told the American doctor, Major Berndt,* that his countrymen were approaching in strength and would soon capture the camp. "I have orders from Berlin to retreat with my garrison troops. I now turn over the command of the American compound to you, and I charge you with the proper protection of your compatriots in the camp. I would also like to ask a favor." He pointed to a house several hundred yards away. "In that house I am leaving my wife and sister-in-law. I ask you to accept personal responsibility for their safety in my absence. I am concerned for their safety, mainly because of the Russian camp, which will be liberated soon after this camp."

As the sound of firing came closer, Berndt detailed two doctors to guard the general's home. From the second floor of the infirmary Berndt himself could see U. S. tanks pushing their noses over the edge of the hill. It was a lovely sight. The Americans advanced, guns blazing, but there was no answering fire. The tanks were about 100 yards away before two of Berndt's assistants managed to unfurl Red Cross and American flags—sheets painted with mercurochrome and methylene blue. The tanks stopped firing and rolled across the barbed-wire fences into the compound. Prisoners of a dozen nationalities rushed out, cheering frenziedly. Some wept for joy, and several even kissed the tanks.

Berndt sought out the task force commander, Lieutenant Colonel James Lann of the 47th Tank Battalion, and told him that Colonel Waters had to be taken immediately to a hospital. The news was relayed to Third

---

* After dismissing Major Berndt for "insubordination," Colonel Goode had reinstated him a few minutes later, and ordered him to remain in the camp with the other two doctors to tend the wounded.

Army, and at five o'clock Colonel Charles Odom left George Patton's head-quarters by air with orders to bring back his son-in-law.

The next morning, April 7, Patton visited Waters in the 34th Evacuation Hospital at Frankfurt am Main. Though thin and weak, the colonel was in high spirits—doctors said he would live and probably not be paralyzed. "Did you know I was at Hammelburg?" he asked.

"No, I did not," Patton replied. "I knew there were American PWs in the camp and that's why I went in."

About seventy-five air miles to the northeast, two German women in search of a midwife were stopped by MPs of the U. S. 90th Division near the Merkers salt mine. While they were all chatting, one of the women pointed at the mine and said casually, "That's where the bullion is hidden."

It wasn't long before Patton learned that over a $1,000,000,000 in paper money, as well as the sealed vaults of the German Reichsbank, had been found in the salt mine. Patton personally phoned Eddy, who said he thought the vaults contained the entire gold reserve of Germany. Patton ordered Eddy to blow them open and find out. If this really was the gold reserve, he said, and its capture was announced to the Germans, their paper money would become worthless.

Gay grabbed the phone from Patton and said, "Matt, don't break your back trying to carry out the gold!"

The following day Eddy reported that a large portion of the German gold reserve was indeed in the Merkers salt mine. He estimated that there was some $200,000,000 in gold, as well as 2,750,000,000 Reichsmark. The official count set the value at $84,000,000, which made it one of the greatest deposits in the world. There was another considerable treasure in the 2100-foot-deep vault, not even mentioned by Eddy: priceless works of art, including those evacuated from the Kaiser-Friedrich-Museum in Berlin.

Patton swept east toward Weimar, home of Schiller, Liszt, Goethe, the Weimar Republic—and Buchenwald. This concentration camp on the hills above the city was near the famous Goethe Oak where the poet liked to visit. Over its entrance gate were two slogans: RIGHT OR WRONG—MY FATHERLAND and TO EACH HIS OWN. In its eight years of existence, about 56,000 of its inmates had been liquidated. Its usual capacity of 70,000 had been reduced to 21,000 by recent evacuations. But many bodies still lay unburied in deep trenches.

As Patton drew closer, the camp commander vacillated between en-treaties and threats. "After all, I am not one of the worst," he told the inmates, and entreated them to tell the Americans of his kindness. At the same time, to discourage a possible revolt, he decided to execute forty-six political prisoners.

One was Dr. Petr Zenkl, former Lord Mayor of Prague and a stanch anti-Nazi for years. When his name appeared on the list Zenkl, like the others, decided to go into hiding. He buried his mementos from home, photos and letters, and wrote a farewell note to his wife and family. A friend cut his hair, shaved his mustache, trimmed his heavy eyebrows and took him to another barracks. For the rest of the night the sixty-year-old Zenkl was forced to find a variety of hiding places.

The order to execute the forty-six prisoners unified the two undergrounds in the camp—the Communists and anti-Communists. They agreed not to give up those destined to die. Secret orders were passed from barracks to barracks: no prisoner would answer the morning roll call. Tension rose as the 8 A.M. appell approached. It was eerily quiet. When the hour struck, not one of the 21,000 prisoners had entered the big courtyard. Then Zenkl, watching through a crack in the stone foundation, saw a solitary figure emerge. It was a French manufacturer. The guards sent him back, as if to show the other prisoners that nothing would have happened if all had obeyed.

The commander immediately ordered another roll call. This time no one appeared. Camp police were sent into the barracks to hunt out the forty-six. Outwardly the searchers were ridiculously thorough, even opening table drawers, but it was obvious they didn't mean to find anything; they too could hear the growing rumble of Patton's guns.

Some of those who had conspired to kill Hitler—Fabian von Schlabrendorff; Pastor Dietrich Bonhoeffer; Admiral Wilhelm Canaris, former chief of Intelligence of OKW; and his assistant, General Hans Oster—were facing death, with no hope of rescue. They had been brought to the Flossenbürg concentration camp, near the German-Czech border, along with a large group of "prominent" prisoners, including General Franz Halder; the former Austrian Chancellor Kurt von Schuschnigg; Dr. Hjalmar Schacht, the financial wizard; and Josef "Ochsensepp" Müller, who had persuaded the Pope in 1939 to act as intermediary between the British and an anti-Nazi regime.

On April 8 Müller was led to the gallows from his cell and told, "The last act is about to begin. You will be hanged right after Canaris and Oster." There was even more confusion here than in Buchenwald. Without explanation Müller was returned to his cell and almost immediately brought back to the gallows, where he was left standing. Finally he was told, "We'll have to forget you for today," and returned to his cell.

That night a puzzled Gestapo official came to Schlabrendorff's cell and asked if he was Dietrich Bonhoeffer. He said no; the official left but returned in a few minutes and asked again. The same question was shouted at Müller. He went back to sleep but was wakened around four o'clock by a child's voice. He thought he was dreaming or out of his mind. Dr. Schuschnigg's wife and child, along with Dr. Schacht and Generals

Halder and Thomas, were being loaded into a bus bound for Dachau.
A couple of hours later someone called out cell numbers and then
Müller heard Canaris asking to be allowed to write a few lines to his wife.
Two hours later a guard entered and took off Müller's handcuffs. "I don't
know what's going on," the guard said, perplexed. "I was told you were the
leading criminal and now we don't know what to do with you."

Müller went to his tiny cell window. Outside he saw two foreign officers
(one was a British secret agent, Peter Churchill, arrested in 1943) standing
in the exercise yard. "Are you one of these top officials to be hanged?"
Churchill's companion asked Müller.

"I think so."

"Your friends have been hanged already and are now being burned
behind their cells."

Pieces of flaky residue floated through the bars into Müller's cell. It took
several moments before he came to the horrifying realization that this
could be the charred skin of Canaris and Oster.

### 3.

In Berlin, Hitler's Minister of Finance—Count Lutz Schwerin von
Krosigk—knew that the war was irretrievably lost, and he wanted to save
the German people from further suffering. The count was a devout Catholic,
had been a Rhodes scholar at Oriel College, Oxford, and felt strong ties to
England. He decided to take his worries about the fate of Germany directly to Goebbels. Perhaps the Propaganda Minister would be able to
persuade Hitler to negotiate a peace with the West.

Goebbels shared this concern but said there was more hope for victory
than people realized. The split between the Bolsheviks and Anglo-Americans was deepening daily. "The only important thing for us to do is to
remain on the alert for the actual break that is bound to occur." This
should be in three to four months.

"I also believe in a forthcoming break," the count replied, but thought
it would come too late. "There is no time to lose," he said. The military
situation was desperate, and qualified unofficial representatives should be
sent abroad to negotiate through some intermediary like Dr. Burckhardt
or the Pope.

Surprisingly, Goebbels not only readily agreed but revealed that secret
steps had already been taken to make such a contact. All he knew so
far was that the Americans and Soviets were not too unfriendly to the
proposal but that the British were showing a completely negative attitude.* "Negotiations on our side, however," Goebbels noted, "are handicapped by Ribbentrop." Unfortunately, he couldn't criticize the Foreign

* No evidence to date has been uncovered that such negotiations took place.

Minister openly to the Führer, he said, since there were rumors in circulation that he himself wanted to take over the Foreign Office. "You have to understand that the Führer cannot and will not listen to unsolicited advice from outsiders. Besides, the Twentieth of July has affected him psychologically rather than physically. This betrayal was a terrible shock and has made him even more suspicious and lonely. But I know how greatly the Führer values your honesty and sincerity and how much he appreciates your advice, knowing you never wanted anything for yourself." Goebbels paused briefly, then asked, "Would you mind if I set up an appointment for you with the Führer?"

Without giving the astonished count a chance to answer, Goebbels said, "You should open the conversation with a short report within your bailiwick. The Führer will then begin discussing the general situation and give you an easy opening for the real subject. Remember, the Führer can't stand defeatism. You'll have to choose your words tactfully and with care." He looked at the count quizzically.

"You may speak to the Führer on my behalf." *

All at once Goebbels sparkled with his old enthusiasm. He described how he had recently read to Hitler Carlyle's description of the desperate days of the Seven Years' War: Frederick the Great, dejected by apparent defeat in Prussia, declared that if there was no change before February 15, he would take poison. "Brave King," wrote Carlyle, "wait a little while and the days of your suffering will be over; the sun of your luck is already hiding behind the clouds and will soon show itself to you." On February 12 the Czarina died and brought about the miraculous change in Frederick's fortunes. By the end of the story, said Goebbels, the Führer's eyes were filled with tears.

Expansively he revealed that Hitler's horoscope for January 30, 1933, had predicted victories until 1941, and then a series of reversals culminating in disaster in the first half of April, 1945. But there would be a temporary success in the second half of April, followed by a lull until peace in August. Germany would then have three years of hard times but in 1948 would begin rising again.

The next day Goebbels sent the count the horoscope, and while the predictions were not all evident to him, he was nevertheless intrigued by the speculation of what might happen in the second half of April.

### 4.

If an incredible reversal of German fortune was coming, it seemed most unlikely on the western front. Early in the morning of April 11 a spearhead

---

* The conversation never took place. "I don't know whether this was due to Goebbels, who hesitated to ask Hitler," Schwerin von Krosigk wrote recently, "or to Hitler, who refused to see me."

of Hodges' First Army, Combat Command B of the 3rd Armored Division, was rapidly converging on Nordhausen, in central Germany—site of the new assembly plant of a major Hitler wonder weapon, Wernher von Braun's missiles.

Braun, who was recovering from a serious automobile accident—his torso and left arm were still encased in a huge cast—heard a report on Easter Sunday that U. S. tanks were only a few miles to the south. He was afraid the SS would follow the Führer's "scorched earth" policy and destroy the tons of precious V-2 documents and blueprints. They had to be saved.

Braun instructed his personal aide, Dieter Huzel, and Bernhard Tessmann, chief designer of the Peenemünde test facilities, to hide the documents in a safe place. "Probably the best possibility is an old mine or cave, something of that sort. Other than that I have no specific thoughts. There is just no time to lose."

It took three Opel trucks to carry fourteen tons of papers. The little convoy headed north on April 3 toward the nearby Harz Mountains, famed for its spas and rich in mines. Tessmann and Huzel looked desperately all day long for a suitable hiding place, and finally found an abandoned iron mine in the isolated village of Dörnten. Thirty-six hours later all the documents had been hauled by a small locomotive into the heart of the mine and hand-carried into the powder magazine.

Mission accomplished, thought the exhausted Huzel. The following day he returned with his partner and dynamited the gallery leading to the magazine. Later the elderly caretaker carefully exploded another charge, completely sealing off the mine. Only Tessmann, Huzel and the caretaker knew the exact location of the invaluable papers. And the caretaker had no idea what they were.

On April 10, work in the great underground V-2 factory at Nordhausen stopped. The rocket specialists, engineers and workers—4500 of them— scattered to their homes and the slave workers were returned to the nearby concentration camp. Already 500 specialists had been sent about 300 air miles to the south, to Oberammergau—home of the Passion Play— by SS General Hans Kammler, special commissioner for the V-weapon program, in his private train, the Vengeance Express.

The next morning, April 11, Task Force Welborn of the 3rd Armored Division approached Nordhausen from the north as Task Force Lovelady came in from the south. Both commanders had been alerted by Intelligence to "expect something a little unusual in the Nordhausen area." They thought at first this meant the town's concentration camp, where about 5000 decayed bodies were lying in the open and in the barracks. But several miles northwest of Nordhausen, in the foothills of the Harz, they ran into other prisoners in dirty striped pajamas who told them there was "something fantastic" inside the mountain.

The two commanders peered into a large tunnel and saw freight cars and trucks loaded with long, slender finned missiles. With Major William Castille, the combat command's intelligence officer, they walked into the bowels of the mountain, where they found a complex factory. To Castille it was "a magician's cave." V-1 and V-2 parts were laid out in orderly rows, and precision machinery stood in apparently perfect working order.

When Colonel Holgar Toftoy, chief of Ordnance Technical Intelligence in Paris, learned of the amazing find he began organizing "Special Mission V-2." Its job was to evacuate 100 complete V-2s and ship them to the White Sands Proving Ground in New Mexico. But no one had bothered to tell Toftoy that the Nordhausen area would be in the Soviet zone once the war was over, and he proceeded at a routine pace.

About forty-five air miles to the southeast, a Patton armored spearhead finally rolled into Weimar. On the hill overlooking the city, the tension for the prisoners of Buchenwald was almost unsupportable. Liberation was only minutes away. At noon all SS men were ordered to leave. To Petr Zenkl, former Lord Mayor of Prague, the departure of the panicky Nazis was the most welcome sight of his life. As the last truck rolled away, the prisoners disarmed the hapless sentries who had been left behind, and seized the watchtowers. Then they hung out a white flag of welcome near the main gate.

That afternoon U. S. tanks pushed up the hill and entered the camp. The prisoners engulfed the tanks and grabbed at the Americans. Zenkl recognized Edward R. Murrow, the correspondent. "I know you from Prague!" he cried out, but at first Murrow had no idea who the skeletal figure was. "I'm Zenkl," he said, and within a few hours Murrow was broadcasting to London that the Lord Mayor of Prague had survived Buchenwald.

But Zenkl was far from safe. For the past few years Communists were the secret rulers of Buchenwald, as in many other camps, and Zenkl had been vigorously anti-Communist since 1920. Through their iron discipline, courage and ruthlessness the Communists had insinuated themselves into the best jobs in camps and finally held the power to decide where a man would work; who would head the kitchen, hospital and crematory; who would be sent to factories outside the camp. The Communists were even able to save their own members from the death chambers.

Zenkl had long clashed with the Buchenwald Communists and it was remarkable that he was still alive. They had no intention of letting him return to an important political post in Prague. During an interview Murrow discovered this and warned Zenkl. At dark he fled the camp and disappeared into the surrounding woods. Hours later he flagged down a civilian truck, and before dawn, arrived at an American military headquarters where, at last, he felt truly liberated.

Later that morning, sixty miles west of Buchenwald, Eisenhower, Patton and Bradley were in a primitive elevator operated by a German. They were being lowered into the Merkers salt mine to inspect the Reich gold reserve. Patton began counting the stars on his fellow passengers as the rickety freight hoist sped down the 2000-foot shaft. Then he looked up at the single cable overhead and remarked, "If that clothesline should part, promotions in the United States Army would be considerably stimulated."

"Okay, George," Eisenhower said. "That's enough. No more cracks until we are above ground again."

At the bottom they fumbled their way through a dimly lit tunnel into a vaulted area until they came upon sacks of gold coins, bars of bullion, paintings and crates filled with dental bridgework. Patton glanced at a few pictures—those from the Kaiser-Friedrich-Museum. As far as he was concerned they were worth about $2.50 apiece and belonged in saloons.

The mine custodian pointed to a dozen bales of money and explained that these 3,000,000,000 Reichsmark were the last paper reserves. "They will be badly needed to meet the Army payroll."

"Tell him," Bradley said to the interpreter, "that I doubt the German Army will be meeting payrolls much longer." He turned to Patton. "If these were the old freebooting days, when a soldier kept his loot, you'd be the richest man in the world."

Patton grinned.

Later, during lunch at XII Corps headquarters, Patton remarked that he was not at all perturbed by the uproar caused by correspondents protesting his news blackout on the Merkers story. "I knew I was right on that."

"Well, I'll be damned," said Eisenhower. "Until you said that, maybe you were. But if you're that positive, then I'm sure you're wrong."

Patton winked across the table at Bradley, who laughed and asked, "But why keep it a secret, George—what would you do with all that money?"

Patton broke into a broad smile and remarked that Third Army was divided into two schools of thought. Half wanted the gold made into medallions. "One for every son of a bitch in Third Army . . ." The rest wanted the loot hidden until Congress cracked down on peacetime military appropriations; then Third Army could drag out the money and buy new weapons.

Eisenhower shook his head and turned to Bradley. "He's always got an answer!"

After lunch the group left by observation planes for XX Corps headquarters at Gotha, near Erfurt. The commander, Major General Walton H. Walker, briefed them, then suggested that they all visit the concentration camp at Ohrdruf Nord.

"You'll never believe how bastardly these Krauts can be," Patton said, "until you've seen this pesthole yourself."

The stink of death was overwhelming even before the Americans passed into the stockade, where some 3200 naked, bony corpses lay in shallow graves. Others, covered with lice, were sprawled in the streets. Eisenhower paled at the sight. Until then he had only heard of such horrors. Aghast he said, "This is beyond the American mind to comprehend."

Bradley was too revolted to speak, and Patton walked off and vomited. Eisenhower, however, felt that it was his duty to visit every section of the camp. As the group solemnly waited for transportation at the entrance, a GI accidentally bumped into a former German guard and laughed almost apologetically. Eisenhower stared at the young GI and said icily, "Still having trouble hating them?" The general turned to his companions. "I want every American unit not actually in the front lines to see this place. We are told that the American soldier does not know what he is fighting for. Now, at least, he will know what he is fighting *against*."

At Third Army headquarters, Eisenhower dispatched messages to Washington and London urging both governments to send representative groups of legislators as well as newspaper editors. The evidence of Nazi barbarism, he felt, should be revealed at once to the American and British public.

After dinner Patton poured Eisenhower a drink. "I can't understand the mentality that would compel these German people to do a thing like that," Eisenhower said, still pale. "Why, our soldiers could never mutilate bodies the way the Germans have."

"Not all the Krauts can stomach it," said Patton's deputy chief of staff. "In one camp we paraded the townspeople through, to let them have a look. The mayor and his wife went home and slashed their wrists."

"Well, that's the most encouraging thing I've heard," Eisenhower replied. "It may indicate that some of them still have a few sensitivities left."

After dinner, when Eisenhower was alone with Patton, he divulged in confidence that the Ninth and First armies would have to halt soon but that Patton's Third Army would pivot to the south. Then he spontaneously revealed something he had told no other Army field commander. "From a tactical point of view," he said, "it is highly inadvisable for the American Army to take Berlin and I hope political influence won't cause me to take the city. It has no tactical or strategic value and would place upon the American forces the burden of caring for thousands and thousands of Germans, displaced persons and Allied prisoners of war."

Patton was dismayed. "Ike, I don't see how you figure that out," he said. "We had better take Berlin, and quick—and on to the Oder!" *

* Later at Third Army headquarters Patton, in the presence of General Gay, again urged Eisenhower to take Berlin. It could be done, argued Patton, in forty-eight hours. "Well, who would want it?" Eisenhower asked. Patton paused, then put both hands on Eisenhower's shoulders and said, "I think history will answer that question for you."

## 5.

Earlier that afternoon—it was April 12—Goebbels, his adjutant and Dr. Werner Naumann, his assistant, drove east to Ninth Army headquarters near the Oder River. Here he told Busse and his staff the same story about Frederick the Great that he had related to Schwerin von Krosigk. One skeptical listener asked caustically, "Well, what Czarina is going to die this time?"

"I don't know," Goebbels replied, "but Fate holds all kinds of possibilities."

In Warm Springs, Georgia, it was only 11 A.M. At the six-room clapboard cottage called the Little White House, two miles from the Warm Springs Foundation, President Roosevelt was trying to relax. Bad weather had grounded the courier plane from Washington and the morning mail would not arrive until noon. With no work to do, Roosevelt decided to stay in bed and read the Atlanta *Constitution*.

"I don't feel any too good this morning," he told Lizzie McDuffie, an elderly Negro maid, and laid the *Constitution* on top of the paperback mystery he was reading. It was *The Punch and Judy Murders* and was opened at a chapter entitled "Six Feet of Ground."

An hour later he was sitting in his leather armchair chatting with two cousins, the Misses Margaret Suckley and Laura Delano, and an old friend, Mrs. Winthrop Rutherfurd. He wore a dark gray suit, a vest and a red Harvard four-in-hand tie. He disliked vests and preferred bow ties but was about to have his portrait painted. His secretary, William Hassett, brought in the outgoing mail and the President began to sign letters. One prepared by the State Department tickled him. "A typical State Department letter," he told Hassett. "It says nothing at all."

A tall, dignified woman began setting up an easel near the windows. She was Madame Elizabeth Shoumanoff and had already painted one water color of the President. She was doing another, which Roosevelt planned to give to Mrs. Rutherfurd's daughter.

She draped a navy blue cape around the President's shoulders, and as he continued his work, began to paint. At 1 P.M. Roosevelt looked at his watch and said, "We've got just fifteen minutes more."

While Miss Suckley continued crocheting and Miss Delano began filling vases with flowers, Roosevelt lit a cigarette. Suddenly he touched his temple with his left hand; then the hand flopped down.

"Did you drop something?" asked Miss Suckley.

Roosevelt closed his eyes and said so quietly that only she heard it,

"I have a terrific headache." He slumped over and lost consciousness. It was 1:15 P.M. The fifteen minutes was up.

Moments later Commander Howard Bruenn, the Navy doctor attending the President, arrived and ordered Roosevelt carried to the bedroom. He was breathing heavily; his pulse was 104, his blood pressure above the last mark of 300. Bruenn knew it was a cerebral hemorrhage. He injected aminophyllin and nitroglycerin into Roosevelt's arm.

At 2:05 P.M. Bruenn phoned Admiral Ross McIntire, the President's personal physician, in Washington and reported that Roosevelt was still unconscious, after what looked like a cerebral stroke. McIntire phoned Dr. James Paullin, former president of the American Medical Association, in Atlanta and asked him to rush to Warm Springs at once.

It was about then that Laura Delano phoned Eleanor Roosevelt at the White House and said that Franklin had fainted while sitting for his portrait. A moment later McIntire also phoned the First Lady. He was not alarmed, he said, but thought they should both go to Warm Springs that evening. He advised her, however, to keep her afternoon engagements, since a last-minute cancellation to go to Georgia would cause too much comment. As scheduled, Mrs. Roosevelt was driven to the Sulgrave Club to attend the annual benefit for the Thrift Shop.

Dr. Paullin was racing over the back roads he knew so well and at 3:28 P.M. he reached the Little White House. He found the President "in a cold sweat, ashy gray, and breathing with difficulty." His pulse was barely perceptible, and by 3:32 P.M. his heart sounds disappeared completely. Paullin gave him an intracardiac dose of adrenalin. The President's heart beat two or three times, then stopped forever. It was 3:35 P.M., Central Time.

In Washington it was 4:35 P.M. Mrs. Roosevelt was still at the Sulgrave Club, sitting at the head table listening to a pianist, Evalyn Tyner. At 4:50 someone whispered that she was wanted on the telephone. It was Steve Early, the President's press secretary. In an agitated voice he said, "Come home at once."

Mrs. Roosevelt didn't ask why. She knew in her heart "that something dreadful had happened." But she felt "the amenities had to be observed" and went back to the party. After the pianist had finished her piece Mrs. Roosevelt applauded, then announced that she had to leave, since something had come up at home. As she was driven back to the White House she sat with clenched hands.

She went to her sitting room where Early and Dr. McIntire told her that the President had died in a coma. Reacting automatically, she at once sent for Vice-President Truman and then made arrangements to fly to Warm Springs that evening.

Harry S Truman was at the Capitol Building, presiding at a session of the Senate. Bored with a long speech by Senator Alexander Wiley of Wisconsin, he wrote a letter to his mother and sister:

Dear Mamma & Mary:

I am trying to write you a letter today from the desk of the President of the Senate while a windy Senator —————— is making a speech on a subject with which he is in no way familiar . . .

. . . I have to sit up here and make parliamentary rulings—some of which are common sense and some of which are not . . .

Turn on your radio tomorrow night at 9:30 your time, and you'll hear Harry make a Jefferson Day address to the nation. I think I'll be on all the networks, so it ought not to be hard to get me. It will be followed by the President, whom I'll introduce.

Hope you are both well and stay that way.

Love to you both.

Write when you can.

Harry

The Senate adjourned at 4:56 P.M. and Truman stepped into the office of Sam Rayburn for a drink. The House Speaker handed him a glass of bourbon and water, and suddenly remembered that Steve Early had just phoned and wanted Truman to call the White House. A minute later Early told Truman in an agitated voice, "Please come right over, and come in through the main Pennsylvania Avenue entrance."

That was all Truman remembered Early saying and later wrote that he was not at all upset—only imagined that Roosevelt had unexpectedly returned from Warm Springs. But Rayburn thought his face paled abruptly and a clerk in Truman's office claimed that he burst in greatly agitated and said, "I'm going to the White House."

Truman arrived at the White House at about 5:25 P.M. and was immediately brought up to Mrs. Roosevelt's second-floor study. It was only when he saw the President's daughter, Anna Boettiger, and Early that he finally realized—he wrote later—"something unusual has taken place."

Eleanor Roosevelt stepped forward with calm, graceful dignity and put an arm gently around Truman's shoulder. "Harry," she said quietly, "the President is dead."

The Vice-President couldn't speak for a moment. Finally he said, "Is there anything I can do for you?"

"Is there anything *we* can do for *you?*" she said. "For you are the one in trouble now." She told him how sorry she was for him and for the people of America.

Then she cabled her sons:

FATHER SLEPT AWAY. HE WOULD EXPECT<br>YOU TO CARRY ON AND FINISH YOUR JOBS.

At 5:45 P.M. Attorney General Francis Biddle, Secretary of the Navy James Forrestal and Stettinius were in a meeting near by when a message came for the latter to go to the White House. It was his duty as Secretary of State to proclaim the death of the President. By the time he walked into Mrs. Roosevelt's study, tears were flowing down his drawn cheeks. Truman told Stettinius and Early to summon the Cabinet immediately, and again asked Mrs. Roosevelt if he could do anything. She wondered if it was proper to fly to Georgia in a government plane. Truman assured her it was right and proper.

He walked to the Presidential Office at the West End of the building, where he telephoned his wife and daughter to come to the White House. He also phoned Chief Justice Harlan Fiske Stone, asking him to come at once to swear him in as President.

By now Secretaries Stettinius, Wallace, Stimson, Morgenthau, Perkins, Ickes, Wickard and Forrestal, as well as Attorney General Leo Crowley, Speaker Rayburn, House Majority Leader John McCormack, House Minority Leader Joseph W. Martin, and several others, had gathered in the Cabinet Room of the White House.

A few minutes after six Truman called the Cabinet to order and told them that it was his sad duty to report that the President was dead. "Mrs. Roosevelt gave me this news, and in saying so she remarked that 'he died like a soldier.' I shall only say that I will try to carry on as I know he would have wanted me and all of us to do. I should like all of you to remain in your Cabinet posts and I shall count on you for all the help I can get. In this action I am sure I am following out what the President would have wished."

All America was stunned that afternoon, and shared a momentary disbelief. When Robert E. Sherwood, the playwright and Presidential adviser, heard that FDR was dead he stayed by the radio "waiting for the announcement—probably in his own gaily reassuring voice—that it had all been a big mistake, that the banking crisis and the war were over and everything was going to be 'fine—grand—perfectly bully.' "

At the White House, hasty preparations for swearing in the new President were made. A few minutes after seven a Bible was finally found and placed near the end of the large, odd-shaped table given to Roosevelt by Jesse Jones. Truman, his wife and daughter at his left, faced Chief Justice Stone, who was wearing a blue serge suit. Mrs. Truman's eyes were red, and she looked frightened as her husband picked up the Bible with his left hand. But Truman failed to raise his right hand and the Chief Justice calmly reminded him to do so. Under the circumstances, Forrestal thought, Stone's firmness gave dignity to the scene.

Repeating after Stone, Truman said, "I, Harry S Truman, do solemnly swear that I will faithfully execute the office of President of the United

States, and will, to the best of my ability, preserve, protect and defend the Constitution of the United States." It was 7:08 P.M.

All left but the new President and his Cabinet. They took seats around the table in an atmosphere that seemed strangely subdued. Truman was about to speak when Early burst in and said the press wondered if the San Francisco Conference would take place as scheduled on April 25.

"The conference will be held as President Roosevelt has directed," Truman replied unhesitatingly. Peering levelly through his thick glasses, he told the Cabinet that he intended to "continue both the foreign and the domestic policies of the Roosevelt administration." Characteristically, he added that he was going to be President in his own right and would assume full responsibility for his decisions. He hoped they wouldn't hesitate to give their advice, but all final policy judgments would be his alone, Within the space of a few minutes Truman had shown that he was a man unafraid to declare himself. After the short meeting Stimson remained; he said he had to discuss a most urgent matter. "I want you to know about an immense project that is under way—a project looking to the development of a new explosive of almost unbelievable destructive power." Stimson said this was all he felt free to say at the time, and when the President left a few minutes later for his apartment at 4701 Connecticut Avenue, he was still puzzled.

The "All Clear" had just sounded in Berlin that night when Press Secretary Rudolf Semmler got a call at the air-raid shelter of the Propaganda Ministry. Someone from the Deutsches Nachrichtenbüro, the official German news agency, said, "Hello, listen, something incredible has happened. Roosevelt is dead!"

"Are you joking?"

"No, here's what the Reuters message says: 'Roosevelt died today at midday.' "

Semmler loudly repeated the message. The drowsy occupants of the shelter jumped to their feet, suddenly wide awake, and cheered. People laughed and shook hands. The Ministry cook crossed herself and cried, "This is the miracle that Dr. Goebbels has been promising us so long!"

Semmler called Ninth Army and was told Goebbels had left and should be in Berlin soon. Then the Reich Chancellery phoned and asked Goebbels to call the Führer as soon as he arrived. Fifteen minutes later Goebbels' car pulled up to the Ministry in the glow of fires from the recently bombed Adlon Hotel and Chancellery. Several staff members hurried down the steps to meet Goebbels. "Herr Reichsminister," a reporter said, "Roosevelt is dead."

Goebbels jumped out of the car and stood transfixed for a moment. At last he turned to Frau Inge Haberzettel and others from the office who had gathered excitedly around him, and said in a voice shaking with emotion, "Now, bring out our best champagne and let's have a telephone talk with the Führer!"

As he stepped into his office Semmler couldn't resist shouting the news at him. Goebbels, face pale, said, "This is the turning point!"; then he asked, incredulous, "Is it really true?"

Some ten people hung over him as he telephoned Hitler. "My Führer," he said feverishly, "I congratulate you! Roosevelt is dead. It is written in the stars that the second half of April will be the turning point for us. This is Friday, April the thirteenth!" It was just past midnight. "Fate has laid low your greatest enemy. God has not abandoned us. Twice he has saved you from savage assassins. Death, which the enemy aimed at you in 1939 and 1944, has now struck down our most dangerous enemy. It is a miracle!" He listened to Hitler for a while, and then mentioned the possibility that Truman would be more moderate than Roosevelt. Anything could happen now!

Goebbels hung up, his eyes shining, and began making an impassioned speech. Semmler had never seen him so excited; it was as if the war was nearly over.

Patton was just getting ready for bed in his trailer after a long evening with Eisenhower and Bradley. His watch had stopped, so he turned on the radio to get the BBC time signal; what he heard was the announcement of Roosevelt's death. He rushed into the house where the others were sleeping and knocked at Bradley's door.

"Anything wrong?" Bradley asked.

"Better come with me to tell Ike. The President has died."

The two went to Eisenhower's room, and the three of them sat there until two in the morning, gloomily wondering what effect Roosevelt's death would have on the future peace. They doubted that any other man in America was as experienced as FDR in dealing with Stalin and other leaders, and agreed it was a tragedy that America had to change leaders at such a critical point in history. Finally they filed off to bed, still sad and depressed.

When Churchill first heard that the President was dead he felt as if he'd been "struck a physical blow" and was "overpowered by a sense of deep and irreparable loss." He telephoned Baruch at the Claridge, and in a deeply grieved voice asked, "Do you think I ought to go to Washington?"

"No, Winston, I think you ought to stay here on the job." Baruch promised to see Churchill before he flew back to Washington, and when he arrived at No. 10 Downing Street, Churchill was still in bed, looking greatly upset. "Do you think I ought to go?" he asked again.

And once more Baruch assured him it would be wiser to stay at home.

He himself was leaving on *The Sacred Cow* with Judge Rosenman and others. It was noon by the time the plane took off on its long, sad trip to Washington. None of the passengers felt like talking, all were too occupied with their own memories of the President. Baruch remembered meeting Roosevelt first in Albany—he was a young, somewhat haughty State Senator then. And he recalled the great moment at the 1924 Democratic Convention when, as Governor of New York, Roosevelt propelled himself on crutches up to the podium and made his gallant "Happy Warrior" nomination speech for Al Smith. Whatever his defects and errors, Baruch thought—and they had disagreed a number of times—FDR "believed deeply in the ideas and ideals of democracy" and "thought of liberty, justice, equality of opportunity not in abstract terms, but in terms of human beings."

When Count Schwerin von Krosigk was told about Roosevelt he "felt the flutter of the wings of the Angel of History rustle through the room," and wondered if this could be "the long-desired change of fortune." He telephoned Goebbels and congratulated him on his recent prediction but advised him to "take the press into tow at once." It should neither revile the new President nor praise him and, above all, there should be no mention of the feud between Roosevelt and Goebbels. "New possibilities may now arise, and the press must not spoil them by clumsiness."

Goebbels agreed. "This news will provoke a complete change in the entire German people's morale, for one can and must consider this event a manifestation of fate and justice!"

The count was so stimulated that he immediately sat down and wrote Goebbels:

. . . I myself see in Roosevelt's death a divine judgment, but it is also a gift from God that we shall have to earn in order to possess.* This death eliminates the block that has obstructed all roads leading to contacting America. Now they'll have to exploit this God-sent opportunity and do everything to get negotiations started. The only promising way, it seems to me, is through the intermediary of the Pope. As the American Catholics form a strong, united block—in contrast to the Protestants, who are split into numerous sects—the Pope's voice would carry great weight in the U. S. A. Considering the seriousness of the military situation, we must not hesitate . . .

At a conference late that morning, Friday the 13th, Goebbels counseled the press to write very objectively and noncommittally about Truman; to say nothing to irritate the new President; and to hide any rejoicing at Roosevelt's death. But by afternoon the Propaganda Minister's elation

---

* He alludes to Goethe's *"Was du ererbt von deinen Vätern hast, erwirb es um es zu besitzen"* ("What you inherited from your forefathers you must earn before possessing").

was already beginning to wane. When General Busse called to ask if Roosevelt's death was the situation he had alluded to the day before, Goebbels replied half-heartedly, "Oh, we don't know. We'll have to see."

Certainly, the first reports from the front indicated that the change of Presidents had not at all affected the enemy's operations, and later in the day Goebbels told Semmler and others on his staff, "Perhaps fate has again been cruel and made fools of us. Perhaps we counted our chickens before they were hatched."

All Germans, however, did not rejoice at the President's death. Edward W. Beattie, Jr.—a captured American war correspondent imprisoned in Stalag IIIA at Luckenwalde, some thirty-five miles south of Berlin— thought a few guards seemed genuinely sorry. Beattie had never before realized what Roosevelt meant to the oppressed people of Europe. All day Poles, Norwegians and French sought out Americans and shook their hands in sympathy. Major General Otto Ruge, the former Norwegian commander in chief, wrote the senior American officer, Lieutenant Colonel Roy Herte, "The world has lost a great man, and my own country a true friend." And the senior British officer, Wing Commander Smith, wrote, "We of the British Empire have lost an ardent and loyal friend . . . had our desires been granted he would have lived to see the fruits of the labour for which he strove so wholeheartedly and gallantly."

At the American barracks Colonel Herte ordered the announcement of death read. As the men stood at attention for one minute, several wept openly.

It was a full day for Truman. On his way to the White House he gave Tony Vaccaro of the Associated Press a ride. "Few men in history," the President said, "equaled the one into whose shoes I'm stepping and I silently prayed to God that I could measure up to the task."

He summoned Stettinius and told him to prepare an outline of the problems with Russia, then went to the Capitol and asked a group of congressional leaders if they would arrange a joint session of the Senate and House so that he could address them in person on April 16.

"Harry," said one Senator, "you were planning to come, whether we liked it or not."

"You know I would have," he replied in his tart Midwestern twang. "But I would rather do it with your full and understanding support and welcome."

Page boys and reporters lined up outside the Senate office and the President shook hands with everyone.

"Boys," he said, "if you ever pray, pray for me now. I don't know whether you fellows ever had a load of hay fall on you, but when they told me yesterday what had happened, I felt like the moon, the stars, and all the planets had fallen on me. I've got the most terribly responsible job a man ever had."

"Good luck, Mr. President," a reporter called out.

"I wish you didn't have to call me that."

All day he received messages of condolence and encouragement, and the cable from Stalin read:

. . . THE AMERICAN PEOPLE AND THE UNITED NATIONS HAVE LOST IN THE PERSON OF FRANKLIN ROOSEVELT A GREAT STATESMAN OF WORLD STATURE AND CHAMPION OF POSTWAR PEACE AND SECURITY . . .

In Moscow, Roosevelt's death had caused genuine grief as well as apprehension for the future; the front pages of all newspapers were edged with wide black margins, black-bordered flags were displayed, and the Supreme Soviet stood in silence. (Even an enemy, the new Japanese Premier, Admiral Kantaro Suzuki, expressed his "profound sympathy" to the American people for the loss of a man who was responsible for "the Americans' advantageous position today." Some Japanese propagandists, however, started a story that Roosevelt had died in agony—and changed his last words from "I have a terrific headache" to "I have made a terrific mistake.")

Truman acknowledged Churchill's message of sympathy, and added that he was about to cable his "views and suggestions on this Polish matter." At three o'clock he received Stettinius and Bohlen, who briefed him on the Polish question. Truman began to compose another cable to Churchill:

STALIN'S REPLY TO YOU AND TO PRESIDENT ROOSEVELT MAKES OUR NEXT STEP OF THE GREATEST IMPORTANCE. ALTHOUGH WITH A FEW EXCEPTIONS HE DOES NOT LEAVE MUCH GROUND FOR OPTIMISM, I FEEL VERY STRONGLY THAT WE SHOULD HAVE ANOTHER GO AT HIM.

While Truman was still working on the message, Stettinius brought in a cable from Harriman. The ambassador had just seen Stalin, who hoped he could work as closely with Truman as he had with Roosevelt. Harriman had suggested to Stalin that the best way of assuring everyone of Soviet desire to continue collaboration would be to send Molotov to San Francisco. Stalin unhesitatingly told Harriman that this would be done if Truman made a formal request to have Molotov visit Washington and then San Francisco.

The President asked Stettinius to draft the request.

Harry Hopkins was telephoning Sherwood from St. Mary's Hospital in Rochester, Minnesota, just to talk to someone about FDR. "You and I have got something great that we can take with us all the rest of our lives," he said. "It's a great realization. Because we know it's *true* what so many people believed about him and what made them love him." The President sometimes seemed to be making too many concessions to expediency, he admitted. "But in the big things—all of the things that were of real, permanent importance—he never let the people down."

Mrs. Roosevelt was on a Washington-bound train with her husband's body. It had been "a long and heartbreaking day." All night long she lay in her berth, looking out at the passing country and "watching the faces of the people at stations, and even at the crossroads, who came to pay their last tribute all through the night."

At ten o'clock in the morning of April 14, the train arrived at Union Station, Washington. Anna Boettiger, accompanied by her brother Brigadier General Elliott Roosevelt and his actress wife, Faye Emerson, entered the car carrying the body. Then Truman, Henry Wallace and Byrnes went aboard to pay their respects to Mrs. Roosevelt.

A caisson drawn by six white horses carried the flag-draped coffin down Constitution Avenue toward the White House as hundreds of thousands watched. No President's death since Lincoln's had so affected the American people. Many wept quietly; some were grim and stoic or just stood staring in a daze. It was still hard for Americans to accept the fact that the man who had been their President since 1933 was dead. Truman noticed an old Negro woman, apron held to her eyes, sitting on the curb and crying as if she had lost a son.

As Rosenman and his wife passed under the White House portico, she whispered, "This is the end of an epoch in our lives!" It was the end of an epoch for the United States too and for the entire world, thought Rosenman, and remembered the Jefferson Day address Roosevelt was to have made the previous day—particularly the last sentence, which was in his own handwriting: "Let us move forward with strong and active faith."

A few minutes after Truman had returned to the Executive Office, Harry Hopkins arrived.

"How do you feel, Harry?" Truman asked, noting how pale he looked. "I hope you don't mind my calling you in at this time but I need to know everything you can tell me about our relations with Russia—all that you know about Stalin and Churchill and the conferences at Cairo, Casablanca, Teheran and Yalta."

Hopkins said he was glad to help, because he was confident that Truman would continue to carry out Roosevelt's policies. "And I know that you know how to carry them out." They talked for over two hours, eating their lunch from trays. "Stalin is a forthright, rough tough Russian," said Hopkins. "He is a Russian partisan through and through, thinking always first of Russia. But he can be talked to frankly."

When Hopkins mentioned that he planned to retire in May, Truman replied that he wanted him to stay, health permitting. Hopkins said he would give the matter serious thought.

Just before four o'clock Truman, his wife and daughter went to the East Room of the Executive Mansion for the funeral service. Flanked by flowers, the casket had been placed in front of the French doors. One of the 200 mourners, Robert Sherwood, felt a hand squeeze his shoulder. It was Hopkins, his face a "dreadful cold white." With Roosevelt dead, Sherwood thought, he seemed to have nothing to live for.

Nobody stood when Truman entered, and Sherwood felt sure "this modest man did not even notice this discourtesy or, if he did, understood that the people present could not yet associate him with his high office; all they could think of was that the President was dead." But as soon as Mrs. Roosevelt stepped through the doorway everyone rose.

After the service Hopkins asked the Sherwoods to come to his George-town home. Hopkins was so exhausted he went to bed. Sherwood sat beside him. "Goddamn it," Hopkins said, and fire shot out of his sunken eyes, "now we've got to get to work on our own. This is where we've really got to begin. We've had it too easy all this time, because we knew he was there, and we had the privilege of being able to get to him. Whatever we thought was the matter with the world, whatever we felt ought to be done about it, we could take our ideas to him, and if he thought there was any merit in them, or if anything that we said got him started on a train of thought of his own, then we'd see him go ahead and do it, and no matter how tremendous it might be or how idealistic, he wasn't scared of it. Well—he isn't there now, and we've got to find a way to do things by ourselves."

Obviously Harry Hopkins still had something to live for.

But he thought he and the whole Cabinet should resign. "Truman has got to have his own people around him, not Roosevelt's," he said. "If we were around, we'd always be looking at him and he'd know we were thinking, 'The *President* wouldn't do it that way!'"

# 22

# Victory in the West

**1.**

Almost at will the Allies were moving forward all along the front. In the north Montgomery drove steadily up toward Hamburg against token resistance. His chief obstacle was the army whose commander, General Günther Blumentritt, was determined to fall back in a leisurely manner with the least possible casualties to both sides. It was not a real war. Blumentritt had made a gentlemanly arrangement with the British, even going so far as to dispatch a liaison officer to warn the enemy of an area containing a cache of gas bombs.

On Montgomery's right Bradley's three armies were making much faster progress. Both Patton and Hodges had almost reached the Elbe River, and Simpson, who had already thrown two bridgeheads across it, was less than seventy-five air miles from the Reich Chancellery. But this did not panic Hitler, who had devised a plan not only to destroy Simpson but to save Model's troops in the Ruhr. It involved an army he had just created, the Twelfth, which was commanded by a man not yet fully recovered from a bad automobile accident, Walther Wenck.

Wenck, who was still strapped in a corset, had only a staff, a few maps, 200,000 troops—on paper—and Hitler's order to launch a tremendous counterattack from the very area now occupied by Simpson's bridgeheads. He was supposed to cut a 200-mile corridor straight through Simpson to the Ruhr pocket. If this could be done, it would relieve Model's trapped Army Group B as well as split Montgomery and Bradley.

On April 13 Hitler summoned Model's youthful operations officer,

Colonel Günther Reichhelm, and told him he was now Wenck's chief of staff. "The Twelfth Army must drive a wedge between the English and American troops and reach Army Group B. They must go all the way to the Rhine!" To one who had just seen the utter despair of the Ruhr pocket first-hand, it was a wild absurdity. Furthermore, Hitler went on to say, he wanted to steal a trick from the Russians. "They filter in through our lines in the night with little ammunition and no baggage." He told Reichhelm to gather 200 Volkswagens and use them to infiltrate the lines at night and cause such confusion in the enemy's rear area that Twelfth Army could then make a complete breakthrough.

Model did not even relay the Führer's optimistic messages about the new Twelfth Army to his troops. He knew Wenck could not possibly reach his lines. Army Group B's 300,000 men were now coralled in an area only thirty miles in diameter, with hardly enough food and ammunition for three more days. The situation was so hopeless that Model's new chief of staff, General Carl Wagener, urged Model to ask OKW for permission to surrender. A request coming from a soldier as dedicated as Model might influence the Supreme Command to bring a war already lost to an end.

"I could hardly make such a proposal" was Model's reply; even the idea of surrender was repugnant to him. By the end of the day, however, it was obvious that capitulation was inevitable. The three most important cities between his surrounded armies and Berlin—Hannover, Brunswick and Magdeburg—had fallen to the Americans. In a voice Wagener hardly recognized, Model said it was his personal responsibility to save his men and he had decided upon a course which had no precedent: he was going to dissolve Army Group B by order, and spare the troops the humiliation of surrender. But he first instructed Wagener to discharge the very young and old soldiers at once and let them return home as civilians. In seventy-two hours the others would have three choices: they could make their way home; surrender individually; or try to break through to a fighting front.

The next day, April 15, the Allies split the Ruhr pocket in two. When Hitler learned this he ordered the two smaller pockets to rejoin. Model only glanced at the message and did not bother transmitting such an impossible command. It was useless. By the end of the day the eastern pocket was overrun.

General Ridgway of the XVIII Airborne Corps had just sent his aide, Captain F. M. Brandstetter, to Model's headquarters under a white flag. The captain carried a chivalrous letter from Ridgway which should have swayed Model if anything could:

Neither history nor the military profession records any nobler character, any more brilliant master of warfare, any more dutiful subordinate of the state, than the American general, Robert E. Lee. Eighty years ago this month, his loyal command reduced in members, stripped of its means of effective fighting and completely surrounded by overwhelming forces, he chose an honorable capitulation.

The same choice is now yours. In the light of a soldier's honor, for the reputation of the German Officer Corps, for the sake of your nation's future, lay down your arms at once. The German lives you will save are sorely needed to restore your people to their proper place in society. The German cities you will preserve are irreplaceable necessities for your people's welfare.

Brandstetter brought back one of Model's staff officers with a verbal answer: the Feldmarschall could not surrender, since he was bound by personal oath to Hitler and it would violate his sense of honor even to consider Ridgway's proposal.

About 200 miles to the east Simpson was at his field headquarters near the Elbe River, making final plans to seize Berlin when he was called to the phone: Bradley wanted him to fly at once to 12th Army Group tactical headquarters at Wiesbaden. Simpson guessed Brad wanted to know when Ninth Army could kick off for Berlin. En route to Bradley, he again reviewed his plans. In forty-eight hours the 2nd Armored and 83rd Infantry divisions would attack as a team straight down the Autobahn to Berlin. He would issue the final orders as soon as he returned.

When he stepped out of the plane at Wiesbaden, Bradley was waiting. They shook hands and the first thing Bradley said was, "I want to tell you right now. You have to stop right where you are. You can't go any farther. You must pull back across the Elbe."

"Where in hell did this come from?" Simpson was stunned. "I could be in Berlin in twenty-four hours!"

"I just got it from Ike."

Simpson insisted that there was little opposition on the other side of the Elbe. In his opinion, there was a clear way to Berlin and he could close in so suddenly that he wouldn't meet any stiff defense until he got to the very outskirts of the city. But argument was useless and, disconsolate, he flew back to his headquarters. "Well, gentlemen, here's what happened," he told waiting correspondents. "I got orders to stop where we are. I cannot go on to Berlin."

"That's a hell of a shame!" one correspondent exclaimed.

Simpson tried to hide his disappointment. "These are my orders," he said tightly, "and I have no further comments to make."

In late March one of Eisenhower's reasons for deciding to by-pass Berlin had been that the Russians were much closer and would surely get there first. Little more than two weeks later, Simpson and Zhukov were almost equidistant from the Reich Chancellery, and Simpson's claim that he could get there in twenty-four hours was not just boasting. Except for isolated German units—and most of them would offer little or no resistance —there was nothing between him and Hitler except Eisenhower.*

## 2.

In Moscow Ambassador Harriman was practicing the methods he had long recommended to his superiors. He and General Patrick J. Hurley, U. S. ambassador to China, were in the Kremlin conferring with Stalin and Molotov. Harriman took the opportunity to protest the arbitrary grounding of 163 American airmen at Poltava merely because several other Americans had acted rashly on their own. One U. S. pilot, for example, was talked into stowing away a Pole who claimed he was a fellow citizen; another time a damaged American bomber which had landed at a Polish airfield for repairs took off again without permission. Stalin exclaimed that such cases only proved that the grounding was justified and that Americans "were conspiring with the Polish underground against the Red Army."

* Six days later Bedell Smith told a press conference at Hotel Scribe in Paris that Berlin was "no longer important." One reporter asked if Eisenhower had stopped at the Elbe because of some arrangement with the Russians. "No," Smith replied, "our only arrangement with the Russians was to select the area in which we expected to join hands with them. In our correspondence some time ago—well, I should say about seven or eight weeks ago—we agreed with the Russians that we should join in the Leipzig-Dresden area."

The following morning Drew Pearson wrote in the *Washington Post:*

Though it may get official denial the real fact is that American advance patrols on Friday, April 13th, one day after President Roosevelt's death, were in Potsdam, which is to Berlin what the Bronx is to New York City . . . [but] the next day withdrew from the Berlin suburbs to the River Elbe about 50 miles south. This withdrawal was ordered largely because of a previous agreement with the Russians that they were to occupy Berlin and because of their insistence that the agreement be kept.

Harry Hopkins wrote an indignant reply:

This story by Drew Pearson is absolutely untrue. There was no agreement made at Yalta whatever that the Russians should enter Berlin first. Indeed, there was no discussion of that whatever. The Chiefs of Staff had agreed with the Russian Chiefs of Staff and Stalin on the general strategy which was that both of us were going to push as hard as we could.

This was correct. But Hopkins' next words reveal an ignorance of the true situation on the Elbe.

It is equally untrue that General Bradley paused on the Elbe River at the request of the Russians so that the Russians could break through to Berlin first. Bradley did get a division well out towards Potsdam but it far outreached itself; supplies were totally inadequate and anyone who knows anything about it knows that we would have taken Berlin had we been able to do so. This would have been a great feather in the army's cap, but for Drew Pearson now to say that the President agreed that the Russians were to take Berlin is utter nonsense.

"You're impugning the loyalty of the American High Command and I won't allow it!" Harriman heatedly replied. Hurley tried to restrain him, but Harriman went on to accuse Stalin of "actually impugning the loyalty of General Marshall."

"I would trust General Marshall with my life," Stalin replied, somewhat chastened. "This isn't he, but a junior officer."

Hurley nervously turned the conversation to China. He said he had instituted negotiations between the Chinese Communist Party and Chiang Kai-shek's government, and asserted that both pursued the same objective: "the defeat of Japan and creating of a free, democratic, and united government in China." Roosevelt, Hurley said, had instructed him to see that China worked out her own destiny, under her own leadership, in her own way, and had authorized him to discuss the subject with Churchill. The Prime Minister and Eden had already endorsed the policy of letting China establish for herself a united, free and democratic government, thus unifying all armed forces in China to bring about the defeat of Japan.

After the meeting Hurley wrote an enthusiastic letter to Stettinius.

. . . The Marshal was pleased and expressed his concurrence and said in view of the over-all situation, he wished us to know that we would have his complete support in immediate action for the unification of the armed forces of China with full recognition of the national Government under the leadership of Chiang Kai-shek. In short, Stalin agreed unqualifiedly to America's policy in China as outlined to him during the conversation.

But Harriman thought Hurley had been too impressed by Stalin's surface cordiality and reported that "Stalin would *not* co-operate indefinitely with Chiang Kai-shek and that if and when Russia entered the conflict in the Far East he would make full use of, and would support, the Chinese Communists . . ." George Kennan, another American diplomat in Moscow experienced in the ways of the Soviets, also disagreed with Hurley's letter. He too reported that in his opinion Russia would only be satisfied with domination of Manchuria, Mongolia and northern China.

. . . It would be tragic if our natural anxiety for the support of the Soviet Union at this juncture, coupled with Stalin's use of words which mean all things to all people and his cautious affability, were to lead us into an undue reliance on Soviet aid or even Soviet acquiescence in the achievement of our long term objectives in China . . .

In the past three days Truman had felt the weight of the Presidency's "unbelievable burdens." On the way back from Roosevelt's burial at Hyde Park on Sunday, he had worked on the speech he would make the following afternoon at the joint session of Congress. As he went to bed he prayed he would be equal to the task of carrying on his work. Early the next morning, April 16, he read a summary of Harriman's latest report, which refuted "a number of Stalin's assertions regarding the work of the Polish Commission" and recommended that "we continue to insist that we cannot accept a whitewash of the Warsaw regime."

Eden and Lord Halifax, the British ambassador to the United States, arrived at midmorning, and the three went over their respective drafts of a message to Stalin regarding Poland. The joint message was polite, but insisted that Mikolajzcyk and two other London Poles be invited to Moscow for consultation regardless of the objections of the Warsaw government. Truman radioed the message to Harriman and told him to deliver it in person immediately.

Eden was "much heartened" by his first meeting with Truman and cabled Churchill:

MY IMPRESSION FROM THE INTERVIEW IS THAT THE NEW PRES-
IDENT IS HONEST AND FRIENDLY. HE IS CONSCIOUS OF BUT NOT
OVERWHELMED BY HIS NEW RESPONSIBILITIES. HIS REFERENCES TO
YOU COULD NOT HAVE BEEN WARMER. I BELIEVE WE SHALL HAVE
IN HIM A LOYAL COLLABORATOR . . .

It was 1:02 P.M. when Truman entered the House to a standing ovation. He looked up proudly at the galleries and finally spotted Mrs. Truman and Margaret.

"Mr. Speaker—" he began.

"Just a minute, Harry," Rayburn whispered. "Let me introduce you."

"It is with a heavy heart that I stand before you, my friends and colleagues," President Truman began his first speech to the nation. "Tragic fate has thrust upon us grave responsibilities. We *must* carry on. Our departed leader never looked backward. He looked forward and moved forward. That is what he would want to do. That is what America will do . . ."

He pledged to carry out the war and peace policies of Roosevelt, called for strong support of the United Nations and reaffirmed the demand for unconditional surrender and punishment of war criminals.

"The grand strategy of the United Nations' war has been determined —due in no small measure to the vision of our departed Commander in Chief . . .

"I want the entire world to know that this direction must and will remain—*unchanged and unhampered!*"

He also made it clear that Roosevelt's foreign policy would be continued. "Nothing is more essential to the future peace of the world, than continued co-operation of the nations which had to muster the force necessary to defeat the conspiracy of the Axis Powers to dominate the world."

After calling on assistance from all Americans he said, "At this moment, I have in my heart a prayer. As I have assumed my heavy duties, I humbly pray Almighty God, in the words of King Solomon:

" 'Give therefore thy servant an understanding heart to judge thy people, that I may discern between good and bad; for who is able to judge this thy so great a people?'

"I ask only to be a good and faithful servant of my Lord and my people."

It was evident that this dapper middle-class man, who could be cocky one moment and modest the next, was tied by personal and political bonds to all of Roosevelt's measures. Even if Truman had wanted to become more resolute with Russia, for example, it would have been extremely difficult. The American people had overwhelmingly supported Roosevelt's friendly policy, and the President's last telegrams to Stalin, Churchill and Harriman actually seemed to confirm this attitude: he had told Churchill that the general Soviet problem should be minimized as much as possible, since situations like Operation "Sunrise" seemed "to arise every day, and most of them straighten out." He had also instructed Harriman "to consider the Berne [Ascona] misunderstanding a minor incident," and had advised Stalin that "minor misunderstandings of this character should not arise in the future."

But these messages did not indicate Roosevelt's growing resolve to stand firmly with Churchill against Stalin. This was reflected only at the end of his message to the Prime Minister when he said, "We should be firm, however, and our course thus far is correct." But to a new President this was too subtle a directive.

As with all Vice-Presidents before him, Truman was not privy to many of the tremendous problems faced by the Chief Executive—for example, he had not been told of the existence of the secret White House Map Room until Roosevelt was leaving for Yalta, and he still hadn't visited it. The new Chief Executive, therefore, was poorly prepared to face such overwhelming responsibilities. Only his quick mind and down-to-earth common sense could save him from grievous mistakes in the coming days.

On the morning of April 17 Truman held his first press conference. A record number of about 350 newspaper, radio and magazine correspondents tried to crowd into his office, but many had to remain in the hall. In his typically brusque but affable manner Truman answered questions clearly or not at all.

One correspondent asked if he wanted to meet the other Allied leaders —Stalin and Churchill.

"I should be happy to meet them, and General Chiang Kai-shek also," he replied. "And General de Gaulle; if he wants to see me I will be glad to see him. I would like to meet all of the Allied heads of government."

On April 18 Truman first learned about the occupation zones in Germany when Churchill cabled him, urging that their armies push as far to the east as they could reach and firmly hold.* Here was another knotty problem about which he knew little or nothing. "I felt as if I had lived five lifetimes in my first five days as President. . . . It is a mighty leap from the vice-presidency to the presidency when one is forced to make it without warning."

That night he wrote his mother and sister:

. . . Before I was sworn in, I had to make two decisions of world-wide import—to carry on the war and to let the Peace Conference go ahead at San Francisco. Saturday and Sunday were spent on the last rites for the departed President. Monday, the Congress had to be told what I would do. It took all Sunday afternoon, half the night and until 11 A.M. Monday to get the job done on the speech. But I guess there was inspiration in it for it took Congress and the country by storm, apparently. Spent Monday afternoon seeing people and making all sorts of decisions, everyone of which would touch millions of people. Tuesday morning all the reporters in town and a lot more came to cross question me. They gave me a pretty hefty fifteen minutes, but even that ordeal seemed to click.

Had to spend all afternoon and evening preparing a five minute speech for the radio for the fighting men and women. It was after one o'clock when I turned in. This day has been a dinger too. I'm about to go to bed, but I thought I'd better write you a note. Hope you are both well.

Lots of love,                                      Harry

Truman recalled Harriman from Moscow for personal conferences and they met at noon, April 20. The President was anxious to know the ambassador's first-hand impressions of the Russians.

According to Harriman, the Soviet Union thought it could successfully pursue two policies simultaneously: co-operate with the United States and Britain while extending Soviet control over neighboring states by independent action. Some of Stalin's advisers mistook American generosity and desire to co-operate for weakness. "In my opinion, the Soviet government has no wish to break with the United States, because they need our help in their reconstruction," he said, and concluded, therefore, that America could stand firm on important issues without serious risk.

As Harriman began to point out specific difficulties, Truman interrupted. "I'm not afraid of the Russians," he said. He intended to be firm, but he would be fair. "Anyway, the Russians need us more than we need them."

"In my judgment, we are faced with a barbarian invasion of Europe," Harriman warned. "We must decide what our attitude should be in the face of these unpleasant facts." All this, he said, didn't mean he was

---

* Churchill also made a last appeal to take Berlin but Truman reacted as Roosevelt before him had—he completely supported Eisenhower.

pessimistic. A workable basis could be reached with the Russians. "But this will require a reconsideration of our policy and the abandonment of any illusion that the Soviet government is likely to act in accordance with the principles to which the rest of the world holds in international affairs."

Truman realized that there would have to be a certain amount of give-and-take. He wouldn't expect Stalin to give him 100 percent of what he asked. "But I feel we should be able to get eighty-five percent."

Harriman asked how important the President felt the Polish question was in relation to the San Francisco Conference and United States participation in the United Nations. Truman promptly replied that unless the Polish question was settled according to Yalta, the Senate would never approve entry into any U. N. organization. "I intend to tell Molotov just that, in words of one syllable," he said emphatically. "I intend to be firm in my dealings with the Soviet government."

At the end of their meeting Harriman said confidentially that one reason he was anxious to come back to Washington was the fear that Truman did not understand, as Roosevelt had come to understand, that Stalin was breaking his agreements. "My fear was inspired by the fact that you could not have had time to catch up with all the recent cables. But I must say that I am greatly relieved to discover that you have read them all and that we see eye to eye on the situation."

## 3.

In the meantime the battle in Europe was reaching a dramatic if predictable climax. On the morning of April 17 the unorthodox Model plan went into effect and the remnants of Army Group B ceased to exist by a stroke of his pen. The battle of the Ruhr pocket was over. The doughty little Feldmarschall turned to his chief of staff and said, "Have we done everything to justify our actions in the light of history? What is there left to a commander in defeat?" He paused, and his next words not only answered the question but indicated his own fate: "In ancient times they took poison."

Model had been right about Wenck. It was impossible for the newly formed Twelfth Army to break through to the Ruhr. Indeed, Wenck never even started the hopeless attack. He had all he could do to hold the Elbe line, and his left flank was already threatened by Hodges' steady advance. Wenck ordered General Max von Edelsheim to protect this flank by holding Halle and Leipzig. But by April 17 Hodges seized Halle and cut off Leipzig.

Leipzig was a historical shrine as well as one of Germany's most important industrial cities. It was here that Martin Luther preached his first sermon in the impressive St. Thomas Church—the same church where Bach played the organ for twenty-seven years and was buried, and where Wagner was baptized. Here also was one of Germany's most revered memorials, the massive monument of the *Völkerschlacht* ("Battle of the Nations"), honoring the war dead of 1813. It rose 300 feet, and German statisticians conscientiously figured it would take a freight car thirty-four miles long to haul the stone and cement that went into its bulk. It looked more like a fortress than a monument, and would, indeed, in a few days be one.

The paltry defenses of the city, under Oberst (Colonel) Hans von Poncet, consisted of about 750 men of the motorized 107th Infantry Regiment and one replacement motorized battalion of 250 men. There were also a few units of the 14th Flak Division, several battalions of Volkssturm troops, and the 3400 police personnel of Generalleutnant (Major General) Wilhelm von Grolmann, police chief of the city.

Grolmann was a policeman, not a military commander, and he strongly opposed the use of Volkssturm youth in a hopeless struggle. It was tantamount, he said, to the murder of children. "The police are under my command," he told Poncet, and he had no intention of releasing them to other agencies for other purposes. "Our own forces are much too weak for effective resistance, since they are completely without heavy arms." Therefore, he argued, efforts to defend the city were useless and only exposed its 750,000 citizens senselessly.

As Hodges began encircling the city with the 2nd and 69th U. S. Infantry divisions, Grolmann and Poncet continued to act at cross-purposes. While the colonel barricaded the Town Hall area with the bulk of his troops and then secretly occupied the huge monument with about 300 of his best men, Grolmann was preparing to surrender.

On April 18 Grolmann announced over the radio that he had taken over command and would represent the interests of the citizens to the best of his ability. At 4 P.M. he managed to reach Major General Walter Robertson of the 2nd Division by phone and offered to surrender Leipzig.

Robertson said Grolmann must induce Colonel von Poncet to lay down his arms and then radioed his commander, Clarence Huebner of V Corps, who in turn phoned Hodges that he was about to negotiate for the surrender of Leipzig. Hodges replied that only unconditional terms were acceptable. By this time Grolmann had finally made telephone contact with Poncet. He was inside the monument with his troops but Grolmann didn't know this. "I have absolutely no intention of surrendering," said Poncet and hung up.

Grolmann nevertheless sent one of his officers to the nearest U. S. troops with another offer to capitulate. It was dusk by the time this man was escorted to the command post of Captain Charles B. MacDonald, twenty-two-year-old commander of Company G, 23rd Regiment, 2nd Division.

"Does he know I'm just a captain?" MacDonald asked the interpreter. "Will he surrender to a captain?"

The answer was an enthusiastic *"Jawohl! Ist gut!"* and within an hour MacDonald's jeep was rolling down Leipzig's streets past groups of astonished civilians who stared in wonder or waved cordially. At police headquarters MacDonald encountered three immaculately groomed German officers. MacDonald rubbed his stubbly beard, suddenly conscious that he hadn't washed for two days. He wondered if he was supposed to salute. To be on the safe side, he saluted and then clicked his heels in imitation of the Germans.

MacDonald was escorted to Grolmann's office and the general came forward, hand extended, his round red face beaming, a monocle stuck in one eye. To MacDonald he looked like the Hollywood version of a high-ranking Nazi. After a cognac they settled down to a conference. Grolmann said he would gladly surrender the whole police force, but shook his head regretfully when MacDonald demanded that all Wehrmacht troops also lay down their arms. "I have absolutely no control over Colonel von Poncet and don't even know where his command post is," he said. He thought, however, that most of the Wehrmacht troops had already left the city and that Poncet would be no problem. The U. S. 69th Division was to discover otherwise. It was just entering the city from the southeast, spearheaded by the armored task force of Lieutenant Colonel Zwiebol.

As Task Force Zwiebol approached the monument, Poncet's men inside opened fire. Zwiebol's tanks, which normally traveled at 10 miles an hour, began careering down the streets toward the Town Hall at triple this speed, and at almost every corner some infantryman was flung off. At the last street before the Town Hall, Zwiebol learned from an Italian flier that there were at least 300 SS troops in the area. With only sixty-five infantrymen left—about 160 had fallen off the tanks in the wild dash or been hit by enemy fire—he wisely dug in for the night.

At dawn an infantry company of the 69th Division attempted an assault on the gingerbread Town Hall, but was quickly pinned down. Zwiebol moved forward to support them with his handful of tanks and tank destroyers.

Gabrielle Herbener and a girl friend, both in slacks, were standing at a main intersection when Task Force Z approached. They thought the armored vehicles were German until one of the tanks slowed down and someone inside shouted, "Stop, boys!"

A tanker stuck his head from the turret and said, "Go in a shelter or basement. The Town Hall is at the end of the square. We have to attack it." He smiled and disappeared, quickly emerging with candy. He tossed it to the girls. Still bemused, they went down into a shelter. What kind of an enemy was this?

Zwiebol moved up in two columns and together with the infantry company attacked the Town Hall. Again the Americans were stopped by panzerfaust, machine-gun and rifle fire. At about nine o'clock, after two more assaults were thrown back, the frustrated Zwiebol decided to use deception instead of force. He convinced a German fire chief that it would save lives if he took the following ultimatum into the Town Hall: unless the commander surrendered immediately, the Americans would attack in twenty minutes with heavy artillery, flame throwers and a full division of infantry.

In a few minutes 150 Germans poured out the doors with hands up. Inside, the Americans found the bodies of Bürgermeister Freyborg, his deputy and their families. They had committed suicide.

The only serious resistance left in Leipzig was at the monument, where Poncet now held seventeen American prisoners. However, 8-in. shells had little effect on the structure and some were simply bouncing off the granite. It looked like a long and costly siege. Captain Hans Trefousse, interrogator of the 273rd Regiment, had an idea. He told his regimental commander, Colonel C. M. Adams, that he thought he could "talk" Poncet into surrendering. Born in Frankfurt am Main, Trefousse had escaped to America with his parents in 1936 and six years later graduated Phi Beta Kappa from C. C. N. Y.

At three o'clock Trefousse, accompanied by Lieutenant Colonel George Knight, the regimental executive officer, and a captured German carrying a white flag, started up the steps toward the entrance to the souvenir shop at the rear of the monument. Poncet and two other German officers came out to meet the parliamentaries.

Trefousse told Poncet it was senseless to hold out. "There's no chance to win. The war is lost. It's wise to give up now and save men."

"I have orders from the Führer in person never to surrender," Poncet replied. He also refused to release the seventeen American prisoners or make an exchange for them. But a truce of two hours was arranged for the evacuation of wounded.

While American medics were removing more than a dozen casualties, Trefousse continued to argue with Poncet outside the souvenir shop, and by five o'clock finally persuaded him to continue the talks inside the monument.

In the rest of Leipzig the fighting was over except for occasional sniper fire, and American troops swarmed through the city. GIs were racing down the streets in jeeps and trucks, waving Nazi flags. One stood up in the back of a truck, making a Hitler mustache with a black comb and singing the Horst Wessel Song. Even the Germans laughed. For some it must have been the first laugh in years.

Günther Untucht and other children were hungrily watching one unit eat and then burn up the leftovers with gasoline. One boy deftly pulled out a half-filled can of rations but a GI took it away from him. Most of the Americans, however, were not as hostile and distributed chocolate to the children. Sometimes it was free; sometimes accompanied by the usual question, "Have you got a sister?"

Gabrielle Herbener was trying to exchange two bottles of brandy for food. She walked past parked tanks looking for a kind face, and by chance found the tanker who had given her candy that morning. "I have brandy," she said. "Would you give me something to eat?"

"Okay." He took the two bottles. "Take off your scarf."

Gabrielle took off her scarf and watched perplexed as he filled it with candy, soap and C-rations. On top of all this he put the two brandy bottles.

Trefousse and Poncet were still arguing at midnight. "If you were a Bolshevik," the German said, "I wouldn't talk to you at all. In four years you and I will meet in Siberia."

"If that's true," Trefousse argued, "wouldn't it be a pity to sacrifice all these German fighters who could help us against the Russians?"

"Yes, but I have orders never to surrender."

"I'm sure you're familiar with the story of the Prince of Homburg," Trefousse said, referring to the Heinrich Kleist play. "He won a battle for the Elector by disobeying orders."

Somewhat later Trefousse told Poncet and his officers that an offer had just been made by division headquarters: if Poncet walked out of the monument by himself and surrendered, his men would be allowed to follow, one by one. Poncet accepted, and at 2 A.M., April 20, strode out of the main door. The battle of the monument was over.

But as Trefousse was about to release the rest of the Germans, Colonel Knight said there had been a misunderstanding. Major General Emil F. Reinhardt, the division commander, had given permission only to release Poncet. The others would have to be temporarily interned inside the monument. Trefousse returned to the other German officers and tried to persuade them to accept the new conditions. As an inducement he said he would try to get them a forty-eight-hour leave in Leipzig if they promised not to escape. Only one German insisted that the original bargain be kept and Trefousse promptly released him. General or no general, Trefousse did not feel he could break his word of honor. He then persuaded Knight to approve the forty-eight-hour leave. "But," said Knight, "we've got to get these people in and out of the monument without Reinhardt's knowledge."

While the enlisted men were being disarmed, Trefousse spirited fifteen or so German officers out of the monument and to their homes. When he returned to pick them up forty-eight hours later, all were waiting except one and he had left behind an apologetic note.

Such strange surrenders were going on all over the western front; a number of times, for example, an American simply picked up a phone and arranged a peaceful capitulation of the next town with the Bürger-meister.

The war in the west, for all practical purposes, was over. But Kesselring felt he should still do his best to try and hold the Elbe River line in front of the capital so that Hitler would be free to throw every soldier in Berlin into the final battle with the Bolsheviks.

The man holding this line, however, had a different idea. Without orders and without even consulting Führer headquarters, General Walther Wenck ordered his Twelfth Army to do an about-face. His men turned their backs on the Americans and began marching toward the Bolsheviks.

# 23

## "On the Razor's Edge"

### 1.

For almost two months there had been relative quiet along the northeastern front while Zhukov prepared his final assault on Berlin, and Heinrici had been using this respite to try to ready the thin defenses of Army Group Vistula. From captured Red Army men he learned that the main attack would be preceded several days by smaller probing attacks in the Küstrin-Frankfurt area. When these began as scheduled on April 12 Heinrici's strategy, borrowed from the French, went into effect: Busse was ordered to wait three days and then pull back his Ninth Army—except for a skeleton force—under cover of darkness to the ridge behind the Oder.

Several hours before this surreptitious withdrawal, an unexpected visitor, Albert Speer, arrived at Army Group Vistula's command post near Prenzlau.

"I'm glad you're here," Heinrici greeted him. "My engineer officer has two conflicting orders."

"That's why I came," Speer replied, and explained why he had purposely made the orders unclear: he wanted to give field commanders an excuse to ignore Hitler's "scorched earth" policy.

Heinrici said he would not destroy any German property needlessly. "But what about the Gauleiters? They're not under my jurisdiction."

Speer nevertheless hoped the general would use his influence to prevent these Party officials from taking action. Heinrici promised to do his best, but said he himself might have to destroy some bridges—particularly those near Berlin—for military reasons. He suggested they go to the outer office, where, fortuitously, General (Lieutenant General) Helmuth Reymann, commandant of Berlin, was waiting. Heinrici had asked him to come to the front so that they could discuss the specific problems of Berlin's defense.

Reymann told them that the only troops he had in the capital were ninety-two poorly trained Volkssturm battalions. "I have quite a strong force of flak guns, two battalions of Guard troops, and the so-called Alarm troops." The last were units made up of clerks and cooks. "That's all there is. Oh, yes, I also have a handful of tanks."

"What will you do when the Russians attack?" Speer asked.

"I'll have to blow up the bridges in Berlin."

Speer frowned. "Herr General," he said, "do you realize that if you blow up these bridges you'll disrupt the entire public-utilities service for over two million people?"

"But what else can I do? It's that, or my head; I'm vouching for the defense of Berlin with my 'life and limb.' "

Speer reminded him that these bridges carried water pipes, gas mains and electric cables. If they were destroyed, doctors couldn't operate and life would come to a standstill; there wouldn't even be drinking water.

"But I've sworn an oath and I'm obliged to carry out this order." Reymann was distressed.

"I forbid you to blow up a single bridge," Heinrici said in his precise manner. "If there is an emergency, you must contact me and request permission."

"That's all very well, General, but what if I have to do something right away?"

"Let's take a look at the map," Heinrici suggested, and indicated several bridges that didn't carry gas or electric mains. "If worst comes to worst, you can blow up these. Any other bridges will have to be cleared with me."

Speer was satisfied and Reymann felt reassured. Someone else was taking the responsibility.

There was a special meeting in the bunker, where Hitler was revealing a bizarre strategy to save Berlin: German troops falling back toward the capital would create a hard nucleus of defense which would irresistibly draw Russian troops toward it. This attraction would relieve other German forces from pressure and enable them to attack the Bolsheviks from the outside.

"The Russians have overextended themselves so much that the decisive battle can be won at Berlin," he said confidently. "This will eliminate them as a negotiation factor in the coming peace." As for himself, he would remain in the city to inspire the defenders. Several of his listeners urged him to go to Berchtesgaden. But Hitler would not discuss the matter. As Commander in Chief of the Wehrmacht and as leader of all the people, it was his obligation to stay in the capital.

He composed an eight-page proclamation—the last he would write to the troops—and sent it to Goebbels. When the Propaganda Minister read the draft, even he thought its bombast was stupendous. He tried to revise it with a green pencil, but had to give up and threw it in the wastebasket. Then he pulled it out and went at the revisions again. Without bothering to clear the final version with the Führer, Goebbels had copies distributed along the front.

### SOLDIERS OF THE EASTERN FRONT!

Our mortal enemy—the Jewish Bolshevik—has begun his final massive attack. He hopes to smash Germany and wipe out our people . . .

If in the coming days and weeks every soldier on the eastern front does his duty, Asia's last assault will fail . . .

Berlin remains German, Vienna shall once more be German, and Europe shall never be Russian . . .

At this hour the entire German population looks to you, my fighters of the east, and hopes only that through your tenacity, your fanaticism, by your weapons and under your leadership the Bolshevik attack will drown in a bath of blood. At the very moment fate removed the greatest war criminal of all times [Roosevelt] from the world, the turning point of this war shall be determined.

Adolf Hitler

The night before Harriman flew from Moscow to see Truman, he met with Stalin. At the end of their long conference Harriman mentioned the German announcement that the Red Army was planning an immediate renewal of their attack on Berlin.

"We *are* about to begin such an offensive," Stalin admitted, trying to negate its importance by a deprecating tone of voice. "I don't know how successful it will be, but the main blow is to be in the direction of Dresden, as I have already told General Eisenhower."

Even as Stalin spoke, Zhukov was making final preparations for the all-out attack on Berlin. Big guns and mortars were massed just east of the Oder, ready to open one of the greatest artillery barrages of the war; 4000 tanks squatted on the east banks of the river, most of them poised to cross in the Küstrin-Frankfurt area; 1750 searchlight projectors with a range of three miles were emplaced on both sides of Küstrin—to light the way for the main force driving up the highway to Berlin, and to blind the defenders.

At Zhukov's field headquarters an important meeting of top-level officers of the First White Russian Front was about to begin. Lieutenant

Colonel Vladimir Yurasov was the lowest-ranking officer, and he was present by chance. He was an official in the Department of Construction Industry Material, a subsidiary of the Special Committee for Economical Disarmament of Germany and her Satellites. His job was to transport captured cement factories, complete and intact, to the Soviet Union for the postwar building program, and he had already shipped enough Polish factories back home to make a million tons of cement a year.

General Nikolai Bulganin (later Premier) was the first to speak: "The war is not over! We have defeated Hitler, but not Fascism. Fascism exists all over the world, especially in America. We needed the second front and the Capitalists refused to give it to us! And it cost us millions of our brothers!"

As Zhukov sat silent, general after general got up to exhort the listeners. "America is now the prime enemy," one of them said. "We have destroyed the base of Fascism. Now we must destroy the base of the Capitalists—America!"

Perhaps the most important single point in Heinrici's line of defense was the village of Seelow, located close to its southern end near the west bank of the Oder. Through the village, along the crest of the ridge, ran the Küstrin–Berlin highway, on which Zhukov was planning to launch his heaviest attack. Once the Red Army reached the top of the ridge, an almost open road would stretch before it all the way to Berlin.

Nothing could better illustrate the deplorable state of Army Group Vistula than the quality of the troops defending Seelow: young Air Force men of Göring's 9th Parachute Division with only two weeks' infantry training. Their company officers were former pilots, full of fighting spirit but with no knowledge of ground tactics.

Typical of the defenders was eighteen-year-old Gerhard Cordes, son of a grammar school principal. His hastily organized regiment had just dug positions at the east foot of the ridge. Armed only with hand grenades, machine pistols, rifles and bazookas, they were supported by half a dozen 4-in. flak guns and several antitank guns.

On the evening of April 15 sporadic Russian artillery fire began to fall in their positions, but they were told to dig in deeper. They had no inkling that the main German force was being clandestinely withdrawn to the ridge and that they were left out front only to put on a show of strength. At two o'clock in the morning 22,000 long-range Russian guns and mortars suddenly burst into a roar on a seventy-five-mile front. The heaviest concentration was just in front of Seelow, and it seemed to the terrified Cordes that every single square yard of earth was churned up.

The artillery fire stopped abruptly and a blaze of light hit either side of the Küstrin–Berlin highway. Hundreds of tanks roared toward the ridge. In the gray predawn light, men in the first foxholes, about 600 yards out front in the flat, marshy land, began to run back past Cordes, yelling, "The Russians are coming!" Cordes peered out of his foxhole and saw a horrifying sight: a swell of big tanks stretched as far as he could see. When the first wave loomed closer he saw a second, followed by hordes of loping infantrymen.

All at once there was a tremendous roar. From the top of the ridge hundreds of German flak guns, with lowered barrels, poured their deadly fire into the Russians. Tank after tank burst into flames, their riders blown off. The surviving infantrymen kept running forward with strident shouts. The airmen fired into their ranks and the Red Army men began to falter. A few T-34s broke through on the flanks, but were blasted as they tried to climb up the ridge along the road to Berlin. By dawn the attackers, savagely mauled, fell back.

The young airmen had suffered few casualties and were confident, almost cocky. This is not too bad at all, Cordes thought. But he and his comrades were grateful when an order was passed from foxhole to foxhole to crawl back to the ridge. Halfway up they were led to positions in the woods. Down front was a good field of fire, and behind was the protective covering of trees. They felt secure and didn't realize that even after this withdrawal they were still Heinrici's front line of defense—and within hours would again be Zhukov's principal target.

By pulling back his main force just before the opening barrage, Heinrici had not only saved thousands of lives but gained time. Finding almost empty foxholes and emplacements, the Russians apparently feared some trap and hesitated instead of pressing an attack up the ridge which would probably have succeeded.

In the afternoon Krebs called Heinrici and congratulated him on the first day's results at Seelow. But the little general was not at all optimistic. He said Busse had also been hit on both sides of Seelow and even heavier attacks could be expected. "Let's not praise the day before nightfall," he warned.

Göring's grounded airmen were dug in along the Berlin highway. On both sides of the village and halfway down the slope, a dozen 88s, eight 10.5 flak guns and several four-barreled flak guns trained their sights down at a seemingly impossible angle directly over the heads of the dug-in airmen.

Late that afternoon Cordes saw a single Red Army tank cautiously push its nose around a bend in the road and start up toward Seelow. It was obviously trying to draw fire to reveal the German positions. But nothing happened as it climbed farther and farther. It got so close that Cordes could see the grim expression on the tank commander's face as he stood resolutely in the hatch. All at once there was a screech, then an explosion, as an 88-mm. shell tore into the tank's tracks. The crew scrambled out the hatches and down the hill.

An order filtered down the slope from foxhole to foxhole: Hold your fire and keep quiet. As the minutes passed the men out front grew increasingly nervous and almost wished for something to happen. Then in the red glare of sunset Cordes saw a column of tanks snake out of the woods near the bottom of the ridge and start up the hill. A single German flak gun fired. The column turned around clumsily and hid among the trees.

There was an eery silence for two hours and Cordes felt as if all life on earth had somehow stopped. Suddenly, at seven o'clock, he heard the roar of tanks; it sounded like at least forty. The noise grew louder and he could tell that they were climbing up the left side of the road—his side. Through the din he heard another intense roar, this more distant, as if about twenty more tanks were starting up the other side.

The airmen somehow managed to hold their fire but they kept looking nervously at neighboring foxholes, wondering if they were doing the right thing. From an 88-mm. gun emplacement just behind him Cordes heard a gunner call out, "I want those bastards in front of my guns before the first round is fired!"

A monstrous form appeared; it was larger than any tank Cordes had ever seen. He shook all over.

"Don't worry," said an older man who had climbed into his foxhole. "You have nothing to do yet, unless they get up to us—then use your panzerfaust."

Now Cordes could see more shapes. The din of motors and clank of treads was tremendous. The earth trembled. He picked up a panzerfaust. From behind came an abrupt, heavy-throated chorus; 88-mm. shells screeched overhead and smashed into the first tanks. Flames shot up, parts of metal and shell fragments rained over the foxholes. At least six tanks were on fire, but others kept coming on and on. In the reddish glare they stood out with clarity and were helpless before the withering fire of big guns. Red Army infantrymen began erupting from the middle of this massive conflagration. There must have been 800, and they scrambled up the hill shouting, Cordes thought, like madmen.

The airmen fired rifles and burp guns, and hundreds of Russians toppled over. The rest came on, still yelling. More fell and at last, like a great wave that has shattered its strength against a jetty, the attackers fell back.

Cordes slumped back exhausted—at last he could rest. Suddenly a German tank destroyer passed in front of him and crossed the highway. It fired and in the glare Cordes could see the twenty tanks on the other side of the road. The first smoldered and awkwardly turned around, but the rest advanced slowly. Russian infantrymen darted from behind them and began to lead the way up toward the big German guns.

Cordes and the others on the left side turned and fired. Rounds from a four-barreled flak gun swished over his head with a piercing sound. They exploded in the middle of the Russian infantrymen and a dozen toppled over like tenpins. A second German tank destroyer crossed the road and began raking the survivors with its machine gun.

"Hell, there are four more!" Cordes' companion shouted and pointed at a cluster of tanks on the other side of the road.

"They're knocked out," someone from another foxhole called out. "They're not moving."

An orange flame spit out from one of the motionless tanks and the four-barreled gun just behind Cordes leaped into the air—crew and all.

"Get those damn tanks with a panzerfaust!" a voice shouted behind Cordes.

He and two others crawled down the hill. The four tanks were moving now, and as they rumbled up toward Seelow their silhouettes stood out boldly. A man to his left fired. The round flared across the highway like a toy rocket and splattered into the turret of the first tank. There was a flash, then a great roar as the ammunition inside exploded.

Cordes fired at the second tank. It burst into flames. Someone else hit the third tank; it too caught fire. The commander of the fourth tank gesticulated; the big machine swirled abruptly and started down the hill. Cordes raised his carbine, fired. The commander tumbled onto the road as the tank rumbled off.

At least fifteen of the forty tanks on Cordes' side of the road had broken through and were approaching the top. They began dueling with the emplaced guns at almost point-blank range, and the entire ridge seemed to erupt. There was wild confusion and Cordes had no idea what was going on. Other Red Army tanks appeared, but what with the roar of shells and motors he was so bewildered that he had no idea where they were going.

Forget the tanks and only shoot infantrymen! someone shouted. Cordes leaped back into his foxhole and fired at moving shapes. Suddenly a Russian hurtled into his hole. His eyes were wild and blood gushed out of a great hole that had once been a chin. Cordes held out his first-aid pack, but when the Russian realized he was with an enemy he scrambled out of the hole and stumbled down the hill.

"Let him go," said the older infantryman. "He won't bother us anymore. He'll never make it."

At eleven-thirty there was sudden silence. Not a rattle of gunfire, no clatter of tank tracks. When Cordes became accustomed to the relative quiet he heard moans of wounded out front and the faraway rumble of retreating tanks. It was incredible, but the line had held. To his left and right, foxholes were filled with the dead or dying. Just behind, it was almost as bad. At least 30 percent of the airmen had been killed, and of all the big guns only two 88s were left. There were no replacements for guns or men, but all Cordes and his comrades could do was wait in their foxholes for the next attack.

## 2.

Late that afternoon at Hela, a village at the end of the long, slender peninsula sticking out into the Bay of Danzig, the VII Tank Corps was loaded into half a dozen ships about a mile offshore. These survivors of the bitter battles around Danzig were now on their way to help defend Berlin.

Over 10,000 civilian refugees battled one another for the remaining places in the ships. They had been living a hazardous existence on the sand dunes of the narrow peninsula, targets of incessant bombing and artillery fire from the mainland. By dusk only a few more passengers could be taken on the biggest ship in the convoy, the *Goya*. The shipping officer for his division, Werner Jüttner, saw a young couple with a baby clamber aboard from a ferry. The husband turned to his aged parents and instead of helping them onto the deck roughly pushed them back into the ferry. "You're of no use any more!" he shouted. "You're too old!" As the ferry turned back for the shore, the parents stared in bewilderment at their son. He stood on the *Goya,* looking at them stonily, and did not even lift a hand in farewell.

At about seven-thirty in the evening the convoy, protected only by two destroyers, started northwest. It was a bright, cool night and Curt Adomeit, like so many other tankers, was so excited at escaping the Russians that he could not sleep. He wandered around the big ship. Soldiers and refugees crowded the hallways, compartments, rooms. There were, he guessed, at least 7000. He went to the upper deck and looked out into the night. At eleven o'clock he heard gunfire from the decks. Looking across the dark sea, he spotted the target—a ship. He couldn't make out what it was, but knew there was a good chance it was already reporting the position of the convoy to Russian submarines. But he was too tired to worry and went to sleep on top of some boxes. Just before midnight he was wakened by an explosion. Then came another. The lights went out and he heard several commands shouted in the darkness. There was a brief silence, followed by a great gurgling noise: it was water rushing into two gaping torpedo holes.

Jüttner was on patrol duty when he heard the two explosions. He checked his watch—it was exactly 11:56. The ship began to roll sharply to starboard and he heard someone call over the loudspeaker, "Save yourselves; we have been hit by two torpedoes."

The civilian passengers stormed the stairs, clawing at those ahead of them—there were only 1500 life belts for 7000. Sailors struggled with lifeboats, but it was obvious that the ship was going to sink before any could be launched. As the *Goya* tilted, anti-aircraft ammunition, boxes and baggage tumbled across the deck and plunged into the water. People hung desperately to the rails.

Above the screams of panic, Jüttner heard soldiers shooting themselves. He scrambled up a ladder to the top deck and saw hundreds of people leaping into the water. He was about to do the same, then figured someone might jump on him and climbed up toward the bridge. Halfway there a wave swept him over the quarter-deck and into the sea. Near by was a large life raft and he pulled himself aboard.

Adomeit felt the *Goya* tremble. All at once it seemed to snap in two and he found himself struggling in the water. It was icy cold and mothers were calling frantically for their children. Occasionally a yellow light flashed from a raft and he saw the shrieking mass of humanity in the water fighting for life. It was like a scene from hell. Those on rafts kicked and even shot would-be boarders. But Adomeit finally battled his way onto a large raft.

A huge bubble of flame leaped up from the water—it must have been the explosion of a boiler. In the sudden glare Jüttner saw hundreds of people in the sea, waving their arms, calling for help. After he had pulled five people aboard his life raft, he noticed water up to his ankles. Those in the sea shouted oaths he had never heard before—against Hitler and other leaders—even against God and the saints. Mothers cried in anguish as they saw their children sink out of sight. Jüttner didn't think he could stand it any longer and took out his pistol to kill himself. But he thought of his family and threw the gun into the sea before he could change his mind.

Jüttner vowed to change his way of life if only he were saved. People clinging to planks paddled up to his float and tried to get aboard. But by now the water had risen alarmingly and he knew he had to make a terrible decision. He joined others in beating off the boarders. If not, he told himself, they would all die. But even as he shoved off a man, he knew he would always feel guilty—he was no better than the young father who had pushed his parents back to the ferry.

The agonized cries of those in the Baltic soon died out and Adomeit could hear only the lapping of the waves against the raft. He had lost all hope—they were 100 miles from shore. Then a weak light gleamed not far away and Adomeit heard someone call out in German.

As Adomeit was dragged aboard he thought, Within twenty minutes a whole community had been wiped out, yet who would inform the next of kin? Nobody. For years women would wait hopefully for husbands; men for wives and children; mothers for sons. Out in the dark sea, he thought, nothing would remain to show that this night it had become the grave of almost 7000 human beings. In all, only 170 passengers survived.

## 3.

At five o'clock in the morning of April 17 it was still dark on the ridge at Seelow. The drowsy Cordes came to life when he made out dim forms coming up the right side of the highway. He waited for the comforting explosion of big guns behind him—but none came. The roar of oncoming tanks was suddenly deafening.

As the sky lightened he could see hundreds of T-34s, covered with infantrymen, crawling up both sides of the road. Dust rose in clouds. Cordes fired two panzerfausts. Behind he heard someone shout, "Get out of here! No more ammo!"

The airmen, who had fought so well in the dark, were seized with panic. As one, they swarmed out of their foxholes and fled back pell-mell to the top of the ridge. Cordes threw away his carbine, his belt, even his helmet, as he dashed through the empty village of Seelow.

Minutes later Red Army men stood on top of the ridge and looked west down the open highway to Berlin. Forty-five miles away lay Hitler's bunker.

Heinrici knew that Busse's lines were being hard hit not only at Seelow but also twenty miles to the south, below the Frankfurt *Festung,* and twenty miles to the north, at Wriezen. It wasn't until the next day, however, that he realized the enormity of the disaster at Seelow: the entire 9th Parachute Division had withdrawn from the ridge and left the highway to Berlin open. Russian tanks had already burst over the ridge in force and continued another fifteen miles down the main road toward the capital.

Before Heinrici could recover from this disastrous news, he was handed a dispatch from Busse: another catastrophe, and from an unexpected quarter. Two of Konev's tank armies—the Second and Fourth—had smashed a hole between Busse's right flank and Schörner's left, just south of Frankfurt. It was obvious that Konev was coming at Berlin from the south, to meet Zhukov west of the city in a pincers movement.

Heinrici called the bunker and asked permission to pull Biehler's troops out of the Frankfurt *Festung* and then throw them into the gap to the south. But Hitler said no: Frankfurt was to be held—and Heinrici would launch his counterattack with other forces. Heinrici hung up in dismay. How could he assault with troops that were running for their lives?

By April 19 the entire ridge from Seelow up to Wriezen was in Russian hands. At night Heinrici phoned Krebs, who had replaced Guderian, for permission to pull back Busse's entire army so that he might form a shield in front of Berlin.

Heinrici heard a gasp. "Hitler would never agree to that! Hold all positions." Heinrici hung up. It was useless arguing with Krebs. He was not only committed to Hitler, but had a dangerous tendency to minimize troubles. If he was informed that a Russian division was attacking, he would report it as "only a thousand people."

Strangely enough, Busse himself didn't want to withdraw. "We have to hold the Oder front until the Americans roll up our backs," he told Heinrici.

"But *will* the Americans come all the way?" Heinrici had heard of the demarcation line between east and west and wondered if it would really restrain the Americans.

On this point Busse seemed confident. "The United States," he said, "has great interest in keeping the Russians from Berlin."

## 4.

In his evening broadcast to the nation in celebration of Hitler's fifty-sixth birthday, Goebbels said that ". . . never before have matters been on the razor's edge as they are today." It was no time to celebrate the Führer's birthday with the traditional good wishes. "I can only say that these times, with all their somber and painful majesty, have found their only worthy representative in the Führer. We have him to thank—and him alone—that Germany still exists today, and that the West, with its culture and civilization, has not been completely engulfed in the dark abyss which yawns before us . . .

"Wherever our enemies appear, they bring poverty and sorrow, chaos and devastation, unemployment and hunger. . . . On the other hand, we have a clear program of restoration which has proved its worth in our own country and in all other European countries where it had a chance. Europe had the opportunity to choose between these two sides. She chose the side of anarchy and has to pay for it today."

He acknowledged that the war was nearing its end but prophesied that in a few years Germany would blossom again. "Her ravaged countryside will be studded with new and more beautiful towns and villages inhabited by happy people. We shall once again be friends with all nations of good will. . . . There will be work for all. Order, peace and prosperity will reign instead of the underworld."

Then he made an even more amazing prediction: Only the Führer could lead the way to this victory—and by a most curious means. "If history can write that the people of this country never deserted their leader and that he never deserted his people, that will be victory." To the faithful Nazi this was clear. If the nation kept faith with Hitler to the end, his spirit would at last rise triumphantly, like the phoenix, from the ashes of temporary defeat.

Unlike Goebbels, Hitler was thinking of a real victory on the eve of his fifty-sixth birthday. He was determined to drive all the way to the Rhine with Wenck's Twelfth Army—neither he nor OKW yet knew that Wenck had already turned around, on his own initiative, to face the Russians. To provide air cover for Wenck, Hitler had recently ordered all jet fighter-bombers put under the command of his favorite war hero, Hans-Ulrich Rudel—which would have wasted the unique capabilities of both.

A fortnight before, Rudel had tried to get out of the assignment; his experience, he said, was limited to dive bombing and tank combat. "I've always made a point of never giving an order which I couldn't carry out myself."

Hitler told him he was not to fly. "There are plenty of people with experience—that alone is not enough. I must have someone who can organize and carry out the operation with vigor." Hitler agreed, however, to reserve his decision and let Rudel return to his air base in Czechoslovakia where he was going out on daily combat missions, even though his right stump was far from healed.

Earlier Skorzeny had visited Rudel in a Berlin hospital, expecting to find him depressed. Instead Rudel was laughing and hopping around agilely on one leg. "I have to fly again!" he said.

"How will you do it?"

"My mechanics are making a steel band to go around my stump so I can reach the pedals."

"This is nonsense, Rudel. Think it over. First of all, your wound isn't healed—it's completely open. You can't go to the front like that. You'll get gangrene."

"I have to get out." Rudel flung himself on a chair, right on his stump, and put his full weight on it. "I have to train my short leg," he explained with a big grin. When Skorzeny called the hospital a few days later to inquire about Rudel the doctor exclaimed, "Oh, that madman escaped!"

Only a man of such spirit, Hitler thought, could successfully carry out the jet mission and he told General Karl Koller, Göring's chief of staff, who was appalled at his choice, that experience made no difference whatever. "Rudel is a fine fellow," he said. "All the others in the Luftwaffe are only clowns. They are actors, showmen, that's all they are."

Hitler had recalled Rudel to Berlin on April 19. As the flier limped into the conference room, the Führer rose to greet him affectionately. First Rudel was treated to a lecture about Germany's technological leadership in the past. This technical superiority, Hitler said, had to be exploited to the utmost in order to turn the tide of victory in German favor. Rudel was impressed by Hitler's memory for figures and his knowledge of technical matters, but noticed a feverish glint in his eyes; his hands trembled and he repeated certain trains of thought—something he had never done before.

Abruptly Hitler again told Rudel he wanted him to take command of all jet units at once and use them to clear the air space above Wenck's army. "It is my wish that this difficult task be undertaken by you, the only man who wears the highest German decoration for bravery."

For a second time Rudel refused to take the job and began making excuses. It was only a question of time, he said, before the Russians and Allies met, splitting Germany into two pockets. That would make jet operations impossible. Hitler complacently remarked that his various army commanders had assured him there would be no further retreats.

Rudel disagreed. He did not think the war could be ended victoriously on both the eastern and western fronts. "But it's possible on one front if we can get an armistice on the other."

The flier saw a tired smile flash across the Führer's face. "It's easy for you to talk. Time and time again I've tried to arrange a peace, but the Allies won't; ever since 1943 they have demanded unconditional surrender. My personal fate is naturally of no consequence, but any man in his right mind must see that I could not accept unconditional surrender for the German people. Even now negotiations are pending, but I've given up all hope of success. Therefore we must do everything to get past this crisis so that new weapons may yet bring us victory." Despite these confident words, Hitler said he would wait, and if the general situation developed favorably, he would recall Rudel to Berlin and expect him to accept the assignment.

It was late—after midnight—by the time Rudel was dismissed. As he entered the waiting room, he noticed that it was already filled with those eager to be the first to congratulate the Führer on his fifty-sixth birthday.

At Dr. Gebhardt's sanatorium Himmler and Schellenberg were just then toasting Hitler with a bottle of champagne. It was far from a happy occasion. The Reichsführer's face was lined with worry and he kept nervously twisting his snake ring around and around. Like Hitler, he too seemed to be near physical collapse. For the past month a dozen men had been endlessly urging him to make momentous decisions. He made promises on all sides; some he intended to keep, some he betrayed the next moment.

Perhaps his most important promise was to Kersten and Schellenberg: he at last agreed to meet with Gilel Storch, the World Jewish Congress official, to discuss the fate of the surviving Jews in the concentration camps.

But once he learned that Storch was about to fly to Germany, his resolve collapsed for fear that Kaltenbrunner would somehow find out and report it to Hitler. But Schellenberg reassured him by reminding him that Kaltenbrunner was going to Austria. The meeting with Storch could be held without anyone's knowledge on Kersten's estate, north of Berlin.

"You're the only one, besides Brandt [Himmler's aide], whom I can trust completely," he told Schellenberg. He admitted that a peace with the West could not be negotiated unless Hitler was out of power. But how could they get rid of the Führer? They couldn't shoot Hitler or give him poison or even arrest him—then the entire military machinery would collapse.

All that didn't matter, Schellenberg argued. There were only two possibilities: make Hitler resign, or remove him by force.

Himmler's new-found courage evaporated. He went pale. "If I said that to the Führer he would fall into a violent rage and shoot me out of hand."

All of Himmler's problems seemed to have come to a head on the eve of the Führer's birthday. Count Schwerin von Krosigk had urged him to persuade Hitler to seek a negotiated peace through the Pope or Dr. Burckhardt. "Isn't the Führer capable of evaluating the situation realistically, without illusions? I wonder what he is waiting for."

Himmler nibbled at his thumbnail and said, "It's just that the Führer has a different notion. But he won't reveal what this notion is."

The count was exasperated. "Then you must do away with the Führer whichever way you can."

"Everything is lost! And as long as the Führer lives there is no possibility of bringing the war to a proper end!" Himmler looked around in terror and put his fist to his mouth as if trying to hold back such treasonous words. The count wondered if he had "gone mad all at once." Then Himmler lowered his hand and hysterically repeated several times that he couldn't promise to do a thing.

No sooner had Himmler furtively left the count's office by a back entrance than Minister of Labor Franz Seldte was ushered in. Seldte said he had heard a rumor that the count was going to see Himmler, and he wanted to encourage this. When Schwerin von Krosigk explained that he had just talked to Himmler, Seldte proposed that they both see him again.

"It is better for you to speak to him alone," the count advised. "If there are two of us, he'll be so nervous he won't do a thing."

Seldte proceeded to Himmler's office, where he said, "You have to do something. The Führer must be made to negotiate a peace. This is no longer an individual matter, for the fate of the entire German people is at stake."

Himmler blustered about loyalty to the Führer. "My good Himmler," Seldte broke in, "you have only one thing to do—kill Hitler!"

Himmler instead fled to Dr. Gebhardt's sanatorium, where more problems awaited him. Kersten had just landed at Tempelhof with a representative of the World Jewish Congress, Norbert Masur (a substitute for Storch, who had decided not to make the trip, for a number of reasons.*) A Gestapo car was driving Masur and Kersten to his estate, Gut Harzwalde, only a few miles away. That was not all. Count Bernadotte was about to arrive in Berlin and wanted another meeting with the Reichsführer.

Himmler was completely unnerved and began to make feeble excuses. How could he meet two people at once? Couldn't both meetings be postponed? Finally, in desperation, he asked Schellenberg to drive over to Gut Harzwalde and "have a preliminary talk" with Masur. Schellenberg agreed, and since it was just past midnight, they toasted the Führer's birthday with champagne.

But Schellenberg was depressed by Himmler's latest vacillation, so he woke up Kersten to tell him what had happened. They talked on and on, trying to find some way of "getting around Himmler." Just before going to bed at four in the morning, they reluctantly concluded that there was no other choice but to make renewed efforts to force Himmler's hand.

Several hours later Schellenberg was wakened by the drone of Allied planes and the crump of a bomb. At breakfast Kersten introduced him to Masur. Today was Hitler's birthday, said Schellenberg, and Himmler would not be able to talk to Masur until late that night. Schellenberg said this confidently—and silently prayed he was right. Later Bernadotte called from the Swedish legation and said he would only be in Berlin for twenty-four hours. With the same show of confidence Schellenberg replied that Himmler would see him some time that night at Dr. Gebhardt's.

Masur spent the afternoon walking around the estate and talking with the people who worked there. They belonged to a religious sect—somewhat like Jehovah's Witnesses—and since they had refused to take up arms or to say "Heil Hitler" (to them, "Heil only comes from God"), they had been incarcerated once Hitler came into power. Three men told Masur of their ghastly experiences in Buchenwald for some years. Things had started to ease up in November, 1938, they said, "when the Jews were brought there in great numbers and the guards' sadism was satisfied through their treatment of the Jews."

* "I was prevented from leaving Sweden for several reasons," Storch wrote recently. "Firstly, I did not receive in the last minute the Swedish passport, but this was not the chief reason. Secondly, Kleist had learnt that I was to go and, therefore, I did not want to leave Stockholm. Thirdly, we had, in fact, already carried through our aims of delivering concentration camps and transferring 10,000 Jews to Sweden. The only motive was to prevent Kaltenbrunner from counteracting, as he had done in Buchenwald. . . . As I was prevented from going, I chose Masur in the last minute. I preferred him to the others because he had a moustache and looked older than the others. But, unfortunately, Masur was not familiar with our negotiations and, in view of the short notice (2 hours), I could not tell him about them."

While Kersten, Schellenberg, Schwerin von Krosigk, and others, were encouraging Himmler to negotiate with the West, Kaltenbrunner and SS General Heinrich Müller, head of the Gestapo, urged caution. In particular they disapproved of the Reichsführer's dangerous association with the Jews.

SS-Obersturmbannführer (Lieutenant Colonel) Karl Adolf Eichmann, in charge of "Jewish Problems" at the Gestapo, disapproved of such contacts even more openly than his chief. In a tone of reproach he told a Red Cross official that the Jews at the Theresienstadt camp were getting better food and medical care than many German citizens—all because of Himmler's recent secret order that Jews be treated "humanely." "I personally do not quite agree with such methods," Eichmann added self-righteously—it was disloyal to the Führer.

Shortly thereafter Eichmann indignantly strode into Müller's office. Like many other SS officials, Eichmann had just been given a certificate attesting that he had worked the last few years for a civilian firm.

"Well, Eichmann, what's the matter with you?" the Gestapo chief asked.

"Herr Gruppenführer, I don't need these papers." Eichmann pompously patted a Steyr army pistol. "This is my certificate. When I see no other way out, it will be my last remedy. I have no need for anything else."

Eichmann then bade farewell to Himmler, who seemed to be in an optimistic mood. "We'll get a treaty," he said, slapping his thigh. "We'll lose a few feathers, but it will be a good one." He did admit one big mistake. "If I had to do it over again, I would set up the concentration camps the way the British do."

After these duty calls, Eichmann went to his own office on Kurfürstendamm to say good-bye to his men. "If it has to be," he reportedly told them, "I will gladly jump into my grave in the knowledge that five million enemies of the Reich [Jews] have already died like animals."

Throughout April 20 Hitler continued to tell birthday visitors that he still believed the Russians were about to suffer their greatest defeat at Berlin. In the afternoon he received Artur Axmann and a group of his Hitler Youth in the Chancellery garden. With Göring and Goebbels in attendance, he thanked the boys for their gallantry in the battle for the capital, and passed out decorations.

He climbed down into the bunker and received Grossadmiral Karl Dönitz, who thought he looked like a man carrying a great burden. Then he greeted Keitel. "I will never forget you," he told the OKW chief and gripped his hand warmly. "I will never forget that you saved me at the time of the *Attentat* and that you got me out of Rastenburg—you made the right decisions and took the right actions."

Keitel could not bring himself to congratulate the Führer. He muttered a few words about Hitler's miraculous escape on July 20, and then blurted out that negotiations for peace should be initiated at once, before Berlin itself became a battlefield.

"Keitel," Hitler interrupted him, "I know what I want. I will die fighting either in or outside Berlin."

Those were only empty words, Keitel thought, but before he could make any comment, Hitler ended the conversation by extending his hand. "Thank you. Get Jodl, will you? We'll discuss this whole thing later."

After a personal talk with Jodl, Hitler then slowly passed down a line of military and civilian leaders—including Bormann, Ribbentrop and Speer—shaking hands and saying a few words to each man. Almost everyone expressed the opinion that the Führer should flee at once to Berchtesgaden while there was still an open road, but he brushed off their entreaties. From now on, he said, the Reich would be divided into two separate commands, with Dönitz in charge of the northern sector. Kesselring was the logical choice for the south, but Hitler had Göring in mind—perhaps as a political expediency—and said he would leave it to Providence to decide. He recommended that the various command staffs split in two, and those selected for the south should leave immediately for Berchtesgaden. Göring asked if he should go south or send his chief of staff, Koller.

"You go," said the Führer. Koller would stay in the north.

The two men, who had once been so close, parted politely but coolly. Göring headed for Karinhall, where his butler, Robert Kropp, was already waiting with fourteen carloads of clothing and art treasures. It was well into the early hours of the next morning by the time the caravan pulled away from Karinhall. Göring left orders to blow up the house so that the Russians couldn't enjoy his remaining treasures—including a huge room filled with miniature tracks and trains. The Reichsmarschall headed for Berchtesgaden, but he told Kropp to stop off at the old family home near Nuremberg so that he could get a last look at the paintings in the cellar.

## 5.

Himmler left the birthday party in the bunker and drove through the darkness toward his own headquarters where Schellenberg told him that Masur was at Kersten's and that Bernadotte was at Dr. Gebhardt's; both wanted interviews. The persuasive Schellenberg finally maneuvered Himmler into a car, and on the drive north to see Masur, Schellenberg urged Himmler not to dwell on the past or expound his astrological and philosophical theories. "Just tell him precisely what has to be done in the future."

Kersten came out in the beating rain to meet the car as it drove up to Gut Harzwalde at two-thirty in the morning. He drew Himmler aside and advised him to be magnanimous as well as amiable to the representative of the World Jewish Congress. It was a chance to show the world, he said, that humanitarian measures were now being undertaken in the Reich.

Himmler seemed eager to please. "I want to bury the hatchet between us and the Jews," he said with an unhappy choice of words. "If I'd had my own way, many things would have been done differently." He greeted Masur with an effusive "Guten Tag" instead of "Heil Hitler," and told him how happy he was to see him. While Kersten ordered tea and coffee, Masur covertly examined Himmler. He was elegantly dressed in a tailored uniform with insignia and decorations. He seemed well groomed and gave, in spite of the late hour, an impression of being vivacious. Masur thought he looked better in person than in photographs; perhaps his wandering gaze, his beady eyes, were a sign of sadism and cruelty, but Masur felt that if he hadn't known anything about him, he could not have believed that "this man was responsible for the most gigantic mass murders in history."

Himmler began to talk in generalities: "The Jews in our midst were a foreign element which had always caused friction. They had been driven out of Germany several times; they always returned. After we came into power we wanted to solve this problem once and for all, and I planned a humane solution through emigration. I negotiated with American organizations to carry out a quick emigration, but not even those countries which are considered friendly toward the Jews wanted to let them get in."

Masur—a tall, slender Swede of forty-four—coolly reminded Himmler in turn that it was contrary to international law to drive people from a country where their ancestors had lived for generations.

"Through the war," the obtuse Himmler continued as if Masur hadn't spoken, "we got into contact with the masses of the eastern Jewish proletariat, and this created new problems. We could not have such an enemy in our back. The Jewish masses were infected by severe epidemics, particularly typhus fever. I myself lost thousands of my best SS men because of these epidemics. And the Jews helped the partisans."

Masur asked how the partisans could possibly have been helped by the Jews, since they had been confined to ghettos.

"The Jews passed on information to the partisans," Himmler replied. "Furthermore, they shot at our troops from the ghettos." This, then, Masur thought, was Himmler's version of the heroic battle of the Jews in the Warsaw Ghetto!

"In order to curtail the epidemics," Himmler explained, "we had to build crematoriums where we could burn the corpses of the large number of people who died because of these diseases. And now they'll get us just for doing that!

"The war in the east was incredibly hard," Himmler continued. "We didn't want the war with Russia. But suddenly we discovered that Russia had twenty thousand panzers and then we had to act. It was a question of winning or becoming subjugated. . . . The German soldier could only survive by showing no mercy. If there was a shot from a village, the whole village might have to be burned down. The Russians are no ordinary enemies; we can't understand their mentality. They refused to surrender, even under the most desperate circumstances. If the Jews have suffered through the savagery of this fight, don't forget that the German people has not been spared, either."

Suddenly Himmler began to complain of distorted stories about the concentration camps. "The bad connotation of these camps is due to their inappropriate name. They should have been called 'reformatories.' There were not only Jews and political prisoners in those camps but criminal elements as well, who were not released after they had served their sentences. Because of this, in 1941—that is, during a war year—Germany had the lowest crime rate in decades. The prisoners had to work hard, but so did the whole German people. The treatment in the camps was harsh but just."

Masur could control himself no longer. How could one possibly deny that crimes had been committed in the camps?

"I concede that it occasionally happened, but I have also punished the persons responsible." Hadn't he executed SS-Standartenführer Karl Koch, commandant at Buchenwald, for ill-treatment of the prisoners?

"Much has happened which cannot be undone," Masur said, wishing to steer him away from this line of defense. "But if we are ever to build a bridge between our peoples for the future, then all Jews who are today alive in the areas dominated by Germany must remain alive." Masur requested specifically to get remaining Jews to Sweden and Switzerland, and Kersten supported him. Himmler informed them of the number of Jews in various camps, but Masur felt that these figures were grossly exaggerated. Himmler claimed, for instance, that 450,000 Jews had been left in Hungary. "But what thanks did I get for that?" he asked complainingly. "The Jews shot at our troops in Budapest." Masur pointed out that if 450,000 Jews were left in Hungary, then 400,000 out of the original number of 850,000 must have been deported or otherwise vanished. Himmler ignored this remark; it occurred to Masur that Himmler must have accepted a philosophy expressed by La Fontaine: *"Cet animal est très méchant, quand on l'attaque, il se défend* ["This is a very vicious animal; when it is attacked it defends itself"].

Himmler continued: "It has always been my intention to turn over the camps without resistance, just as I promised. I even turned over Bergen-Belsen and Buchenwald, but look what I got in return: in Bergen-Belsen a camp guard was tied up with a rope and photographed with some dead prisoners. And now these photographs are spread all over the world.

I was giving up Buchenwald, but the advancing American tanks started to shoot. The hospital caught fire, and then the corpses were photographed. Now they are using these photographs for their *Greuelpropaganda* [atrocity stories]. And last year, when I let twenty-seven hundred Jews go to Switzerland, that was used against me in the press; they claimed that I had only released these people to get myself an alibi. I don't need any alibi. I have always done only what I felt would fill the needs of my people, and I take full responsibility. It certainly didn't make me a rich man."

His indignation turned to the press. "Nobody has had so much mud slung at him in the last twelve years as I have, but it has never bothered me. Even in Germany anybody can write about me what he pleases. The news stories about the concentration camps have been used against us, which hardly serves as an inducement for me to continue handing over the camps."

Masur deftly stemmed this flow of self-pity by stating that the Jews had not been responsible for the newspaper stories. He went on to explain that not only the Jews but other countries were interested in the rescue of the surviving Jews and it would have a good effect on the Allies. A Jew himself, Masur "hated the very thought of having to plead with this man who was responsible for the cruelties to thousands of human beings." Moreover, one of his sisters and other members of his family had died in concentration camps, but he could not let his personal feelings interfere with the mission that might save thousands of lives.

Masur was particularly interested in the fate of the women prisoners in Ravensbrück, only eighteen miles away. He wanted to know what was really going to happen. When Himmler hesitated, Kersten suggested that the two of them go over a list of the women at the camp. Schellenberg knew Himmler would not want to do this in Masur's presence and led him to another room to discuss certain points on the agenda.

As they began shuffling through the long list, Kersten insisted that they had to stand by the agreement made in March. Suddenly Himmler asked Kersten if he would fly to Eisenhower's headquarters and discuss immediate cessation of hostilities.

"Make every effort to convince Eisenhower that the real enemy of mankind is Soviet Russia and that only we Germans are in a position to fight against her," the Reichsführer went on without waiting for an answer. "I will concede victory to the Western Allies. They have only to give me time to throw back Russia. If they let me have the equipment, I can still do it."

On Masur's return Himmler said he would release 1000 Jewish women from Ravensbrück at once but stipulated that their arrival in Sweden be kept secret. To this end he suggested that they be designated "Polish" instead of "Jewish." Such precautions, Masur thought, were typical of Himmler; he still wanted no trouble on a Jew's account.

At four-thirty Schellenberg began to worry that Bernadotte must be getting impatient at Dr. Gebhardt's sanatorium, where he had been waiting all night. At five o'clock Himmler said good-bye to Masur and walked outside with Kersten.

"*Ach,* Herr Kersten, we have made serious mistakes," he exclaimed with a deep sigh. "We wanted greatness and security for Germany and we are leaving behind us a pile of ruins, a crumbling world. But it is still true that Europe must rally to a new standard, else all is lost. I always wanted what was best, but very often I had to act against my real convictions. Believe me, Kersten, that went very much against the grain and it was bitter to me. But the Führer decreed that it should be so, and Goebbels and Bormann were a bad influence on him. As a loyal soldier I had to obey, for no state can survive without obedience and discipline. It rests for me alone to decide how long I have to live, since my life has now become meaningless. And what will history say of me? Petty minds, bent on revenge, will hand down to posterity a false and perverted account of the great and good things which I, looking further ahead, have accomplished for Germany. The blame for many things which others have done will be heaped on me. The finest elements of the German people perish with the National Socialists; this is the real tragedy. Those who are left, those who will govern Germany, hold no interest for us. The Allies can do what they like with Germany."

Himmler climbed wearily into his car, extending his hand as if for the last time. "Kersten, I thank you from the bottom of my heart for the years in which you have given me the benefit of your medical skill." There were tears in his eyes. "My last thoughts are for my poor family. Farewell!"

The sun was rising as Himmler and Schellenberg arrived at the sanatorium. Bernadotte thought Himmler looked spent and weary, yet agitated. The Reichsführer, as if guessing the Count's thoughts, said he had slept hardly a wink the past few nights. They sat down to breakfast. Himmler's exhaustion did not seem to affect his appetite, though he compulsively kept tapping his front teeth with his fingernails.

Unaccountably, Himmler objected to Bernadotte's modest request that the Scandinavian prisoners be allowed to continue from Denmark to Sweden, then spontaneously offered to let the Swedish Red Cross have all the women at Ravensbrück, when a few hours before he had limited the number to 1000—and retired to his bedroom.

Just after noon Himmler summoned Schellenberg. The Reichsführer looked up miserably from his bed and said he felt ill.

"There's nothing more I can do for you," Schellenberg said in exasperation. He had spent weeks arranging clandestine meetings and little had come of it.

Later, as their car crept along the jammed highway toward their nearby headquarters, Himmler said, "Schellenberg, I dread what is to come."

"That should give you courage to take action."

Himmler was silent.

After dinner Schellenberg began to criticize Kaltenbrunner's "blind and unrealistic attitude in insisting on the evacuation at all costs of all the concentration camps." It was, he said, a crime.

"Schellenberg, don't you start too," Himmler said like a scolded child. "Hitler has been raging for days because Buchenwald and Bergen-Belsen were not completely evacuated."

Of all the concentration camps, the International Committee of the Red Cross was presently most concerned with two which lay directly athwart the path of Zhukov's advance on Berlin—Sachsenhausen and Ravensbrück. The Red Cross delegate, Dr. Pfister, didn't reach Sachsenhausen—on the outskirts of Oranienburg, nineteen miles north of the bunker—until three o'clock in the morning of April 21. Already some of the inmates were being herded out of the barracks into the rain and lined up for departure; ten miles to the east Zhukov's guns roared ominously. Pfister immediately requested the camp commandant, SS-Standartenführer (Colonel) Keindel, to turn over Sachsenhausen to the Red Cross. But Keindel refused, on the grounds that he had standing orders from Himmler to evacuate everything but the hospital at the approach of the Russians— at Gut Harzwald, Himmler was just then assuring Masur that all evacuations had ceased.

Almost 40,000 prisoners—starved, sick, poorly clothed—were shoved into two great columns. The guards harried them through the pummeling rain in a northwesterly direction, and those who couldn't keep up the pace were shot and left in the ditches. Dr. Pfister followed the sad caravan and in the first four miles counted twenty bodies, all shot in the head.

"What can you do with a people whose men don't even fight when their women are raped!" It was Goebbels. In the twisted words of his birthday speech he had prophesied a strange victory coming out of apparent defeat. He had just taken the next logical step, and bitterly admitted to his aides that the war was irrevocably lost—not because of Hitler, but because the people had failed him. "All the plans, all the ideas of National Socialism are too high, too noble for such a people. . . . They deserve the fate that will now descend on them."

He surveyed his aides sardonically. "And you—why have you worked with me? Now you'll have your little throats cut!" He strode to the door and turned. "But when we step down, let the whole earth tremble!"

He also admitted defeat to a group of civil leaders, then called on them for personal sacrifice. "My family is now at home," he said with tears in his eyes. "We are staying here. And I demand of you, gentlemen, that you too remain at your posts. If necessary, we shall know how to die here."

The fitful Goebbels kept going from despair to resentment all day long. When two secretaries fled to the country on bicycles, he complained to his press officer, "Now I ask you, how could that ever have happened? How can there be any guarantee now of keeping regular office hours?"

On the eastern front rumors were passed from one headquarters to another that the leaders in Berlin had given up all hope and that OKW was packing up for Berchtesgaden. These stories only heartened Heinrici. They probably meant that Hitler would also go south, so an orderly withdrawal might be possible.

The Russians had broken through Army Group Vistula at half a dozen points. It was the final, all-out offensive the Red Army had been waiting for since the dark days at Moscow and Zhukov had kept himself and his staff awake the past six nights with cognac. His two deepest thrusts were at Seelow and two score miles to the north at Wriezen. The one through Seelow had continued west toward Berlin and was now twenty miles from its goal, the bunker; the one through Wriezen had driven twice as far and was already due north of Berlin. It was approaching the Sachsenhausen concentration camp and its goal was to encircle Berlin and reach from behind, southwest of Berlin. There it would meet the Konev column, which had moved up so unexpectedly from the south— and Berlin would be completely surrounded.

Heinrici told Krebs that he wanted to defend Berlin outside the city and ordered General Reymann to stop the Russians who had broken through Seelow. Reymann rushed his ninety Volkssturm battalions to the east by taxi, subway and elevated train, in imitation of the French taxi caravan to the Marne. Just before noon on April 21 Heinrici phoned Reymann again and asked how many of these battalions were in their new positions.

"Thirteen," Reymann replied. "But most of these people don't have weapons. Those who do have only five rounds. Besides, many aren't properly clothed."

By noon the Russians who had burst through Seelow were so close to Berlin that their heavy artillery began to land within the city limits. These explosions could be heard faintly in the bunker as Krebs and Jodl reported on Heinrici's situation. Busse and Manteuffel were both holding fairly well, they said, but Zhukov had succeeded in shoving a column between them at Wriezen and it had almost reached Oranienburg. This thrust threatened to encircle Manteuffel's army. To counter this,

Heinrici had placed his small reserve—the nucleus of a new panzer corps under SS General Felix Steiner—twenty-five miles north of Berlin.

Hitler jerked upright from his slump. To him Steiner was a magic name, like Skorzeny and Rudel; it was his desperate attack from Pomerania that had slowed Zhukov's advance in February. Hitler began poring over a map. Finally he looked up. His eyes glistened. Counterattack! he said with rising excitement. Steiner was to drive to the southeast and cut straight through the Zhukov spearhead: this would, with one bold blow, save Berlin and prevent Manteuffel from being encircled.

"Any commanding officer who keeps men back will lose his life within five hours!" he said.

No one raised any objections, and the order was passed to Heinrici, who reluctantly relayed it to the man who would have to carry it out.

Of all the impossible orders Steiner had received in the past few months, this was the most fantastic. His panzer corps was one in name only. In all, there were only 10,000 men, who had just arrived from Stettin and Danzig by ship. With these exhausted troops and a handful of tanks he was supposed to smash through a powerful armored force of at least 100,000 men.

By late afternoon Heinrici learned that the Konev thrust had made an alarming advance up toward Berlin. At six forty-five he called Krebs and said Busse's Ninth Army had to be pulled back during the night, or it might be completely cut off. "I owe it to my conscience and my troops," Heinrici added when there was only silence from Berlin.

"The Führer assumes the responsibility for his orders," Krebs said coolly.

"That's beside the point. I have a responsibility to my troops."

Later that night Krebs called and excitedly told Heinrici that Schörner had stopped the Konev drive toward Berlin. "The enemy has been cut off in the rear," he said. "The Führer wants you to note particularly that his decision to leave Ninth Army in its position still stands. He feels that only if they remain will it be possible for Schörner to mount another attack."

"When will Schörner continue his attack?"

"In two or three days."

Heinrici was sure that Busse would be completely cut off by then. "That will be too late," he said crisply and hung up.

He was right. Konev had only been momentarily delayed by Schörner's attack and was advancing toward Berlin with renewed energy.

# 24

# "The Führer Is in a State of Collapse!"

### 1.

Although Stalin had assured Harriman that the main Soviet drive was aimed at Dresden, his true intentions were obvious even to the most naïve by April 22. Konev, it is true, was aiming one column at Dresden, but a much stronger one had already smashed to the northwest, between Schörner and Heinrici, and by dawn had reached Luckenwalde, thirty-five miles south of the bunker. At six o'clock a miniature Russian armored car sped down the main street of the nearby prisoner-of-war camp, Stalag IIIA. The 17,000 half-dressed, wildly cheering Allied prisoners swarmed out of their barracks. When the tiny car stopped and the driver crawled out of the trap door, Russian prisoners grabbed him and flung him into the air again and again.

Four hours later a small Russian armored force pulled up to the gate. On the first tank a husky infantryman was playing an accordion and singing boisterously, and in a half-track a balalaika player strummed away as if it were natural to go into battle with music. The rugged Russians leaped down, shook hands and passed out wine, vodka and beer, and drank endless toasts to the Big Three as well as Eisenhower, Konev, Flying Fortresses, the Stormovik planes and Studebakers.

As the Red Army column roared off, one tank veered toward the fence and smashed down an entire length of the barbed wire. "You are free now!" the commander shouted in German.

Farther south Konev's drive to Dresden was meeting unexpectedly fierce opposition. It was here that Hitler had set up his strongest defenses —in the mistaken belief that this was Stalin's chief target. At some points the Russians could offer almost no resistance to a counterattack by Schörner. One stretch of almost a mile was held by an odd assortment of eighteen reserve officers, including Mikhail Koriakov, the Air Force correspondent who had been relegated to the infantry because of his religious beliefs. Captain Koriakov was now a humble runner.

At dawn of April 22 Koriakov leaned his rifle against the wall of the cottage serving as platoon command post and took out an enameled icon of the Holy Virgin. Kneeling, he began to pray. A fat German woman and her three equally stout daughters knelt behind him; Koriakov had just saved them from being raped by a Ukrainian lieutenant.

Koriakov then began to pass out food to the men lying in foxholes among the green shoots of winter wheat. Several hundred yards ahead lay a forest bisected by a road. It was quiet and peaceful. All at once figures appeared on the road.

"Runner!" the platoon commander called out. "Find out who those people are."

Koriakov went forward and saw a long line of refugees pushing baby carriages loaded with baggage, riding bicycles or walking behind heavily laden wagons. Suddenly clods of earth began to spurt at Koriakov's feet and he heard the quick, dry rattle of German automatic rifles from the forest. Horses leaped forward, upsetting several wagons. Children tumbled out. Shells were exploding. Koriakov hugged the ground, caught between two fires. Every time he tried to crawl away, a volley from the woods pinned him down. Flat on his stomach, he prayed in a loud voice, "We have no other help, no other hope but in you, Heavenly Mother . . ."

A powerful hand grabbed his collar and jerked him to his feet. A huge German was glaring down at him, his rifle butt raised. "Pole?" he shouted.

Koriakov tried to explain that he was a Russian captain. The German lowered his rifle and pushed him to another soldier, a boy of about fourteen. At a command post Koriakov was asked if he had molested any German women.

He shook his head.

"*Ja, ja!*" a captain said derisively. He slapped Koriakov's face, knocking his glasses to the ground, and began to shout angrily in German. Koriakov could only understand one word: *erschiessen*—"to be shot."

Four heavy German women hustled toward them. In the lead was the mother Koriakov had saved from rape. All four were shouting hysterically at the perplexed German captain. As the mother wiped away the tears flowing down her cheeks, she smiled at Koriakov. Her three daughters huddled together, nodding and smiling through tears.

An elderly German colonel, a silent witness, picked up Koriakov's glasses and without a word handed them to the Russian.

### 2.

In the bunker that morning Steiner was the main topic of conversation. Had his attack from the north been launched to relieve Berlin? If so, how far had it gone? Half a dozen times Hitler asked Krebs the same questions and each time was told there was nothing to report.

At eleven o'clock Krebs was finally connected by phone with Heinrici, but before he had a chance to speak the little general said, "Today is the last chance for Hitler to leave Berlin. I simply don't have the forces to rescue him."

What about Steiner?

Heinrici felt like laughing but politely said it was folly to pin the slightest hope on Steiner. Krebs's voice became frantic and he said it was Heinrici's duty to prevent Berlin from becoming surrounded. It was shameful to abandon Hitler!

This only exasperated Heinrici. "You tell me I must prevent the shameful encirclement of the Führer. Yet against my will, against my suggestions, yes, despite the fact that I've placed my command at your disposal, you still won't let me pull back forces from the front to protect him."

Before Krebs could answer, the connection was broken. When he managed to get through to Heinrici again he said, "The Führer has not given his consent to this withdrawal, because it would split northern and southern Germany."

"That split is already a fact," said Heinrici, then asked Krebs to make another appeal to the Führer and let him know the answer by one o'clock.

At three Krebs finally called to say that Busse could make a partial withdrawal.

Heinrici promptly phoned Busse, who was not at all pleased. "Those are halfway measures," he said. "Either I go with every man or I stay."

"Well, pull back," Heinrici decided. It was a deliberately vague order and could be interpreted by Busse as permission to withdraw his entire army.

But Busse could not let Heinrici assume such a burden. "I have a Führer order that binds me to stay here," he said stolidly. This was only an excuse. If he retreated now, he would have to abandon Biehler's men in the Frankfurt *Festung*. They were surrounded and for the past twenty-four hours had been trying vainly to smash a way through a

Russian cordon. Only when Biehler succeeded in joining the rest of Ninth Army would Busse pull back.

**3.**

Dr. Goebbels seemed to have forgotten yesterday's tirade against the German people. "Well, I must hand it to the Berliners for being a fine, brave bunch of people," he remarked to his press secretary as he looked out a window of his home at Allied planes swooping over the city. "They don't even go to their shelters but stare into the sky to see what's going on."

The streets were so clogged with debris and stalled cars that he canceled the daily press conference and began to record a speech to the people. But before he could finish, Russian shells exploded near by. One landed so close that it shattered the few remaining windows of the house. Goebbels calmly stopped the recording but continued a moment later. When the speech was over, he turned to the sound engineer and asked if the noise would be audible in the broadcast. "It would make a nice sound effect, don't you think?"

At lunch he was in a supercilious, almost gay mood, referring to Churchill as a "little man" and describing Eden as a "hoity-toity gent." But when his old friend Dr. Winkler called, Goebbels solemnly thanked him for past favors and said grimly, "We won't meet again."

With each passing hour Hitler was growing more nervous and irritable. He could not find out how the Steiner attack was progressing, and became increasingly upset every time Krebs told him there was nothing definite to report. (Steiner's pitiful "panzer corps" of 10,000 men had been able to drive only eight miles to the southeast and was already hopelessly stalled.)

There were a few new faces at the Führer conference that afternoon. Vize-admiral Erich Voss represented Dönitz, now in northern Germany setting up a separate command. Luftwaffe General Eckard Christian, who had married one of Hitler's secretaries, was there for Koller, whose new headquarters were northwest of Berlin. Bormann, of course, was present, as were Keitel, Jodl, Krebs and the aide he had inherited from Guderian, Major Freytag von Loringhoven, as well as other aides and secretaries.

Jodl overrode Krebs's routine optimism and told Hitler the truth: Berlin was three-fourths surrounded. One Zhukov column was just east of the city. Another was sweeping north down toward Potsdam and would probably be met there by a Konev column from the south within a week.

Agitated by Jodl's words, Hitler demanded to know once and for all how far Steiner had progressed in his attack. At last Krebs was forced to admit that the Steiner corps was still being organized and that there just wasn't anything to report.

Hitler's head jerked and he began breathing heavily. In a tight, hoarse voice he ordered everyone out of the room except his generals and Bormann. The rest stumbled over one another in their eagerness to get out. In the waiting room they stood in silent apprehension.

As soon as the door was closed Hitler lunged to his feet, his left arm flopping. He shouted that he was surrounded by traitors and liars as he lurched back and forth, swinging his right arm wildly. All were too low, too mean to understand his great purpose, he screamed. He was the victim of corruption and cowardice, and now everyone had deserted him.

His listeners had never before seen him lose control so completely. He flung an accusing finger at the generals and blamed their ilk for the disasters of the war. The only protest came from Bormann. The officers were surprised, but Bormann's words were undoubtedly meant not so much as a defense of the military as to calm the Führer.

Hitler shouted something about Steiner and abruptly flopped into his chair. In anguish he said, "The war is lost!" Then with a trembling voice he added that the Third Reich had ended in failure and all he could do now was die. His face turned white and his body shook spasmodically, as if torn by a violent stroke.

Suddenly he was still. His jaw slackened and he sat staring ahead with blank eyes. This alarmed the onlookers even more than his fury. Minute after minute passed—afterward no one could remember how many. Finally a patch of color came to the Führer's cheeks and he twitched. Bormann, Keitel and Burgdorf begged him to have faith. If *he* lost faith, then all indeed was lost. They urged him to leave for Berchtesgaden immediately, but he slowly shook his head and in a dead, tired voice said he would never leave the bunker. If they wanted to go they were free to do so, but he was meeting his end in the capital. He asked for Goebbels.

Those in the outer room had heard almost everything. Fegelein grabbed a phone and told Himmler what had happened. The shaken Reichsführer called Hitler and begged him not to lose hope. He promised to send SS troops at once.

"Everyone is mad in Berlin!" he told SS-Obergruppenführer (Lieutenant General) Gottlob Berger, chief of the SS head office. To the uncomplicated Berger, who had never for a moment doubted the great aims of National Socialism, there was only one thing to do. "You must go straight to Berlin, Herr Reichsführer," he said, "and your escort battalion, of course. You have no right to keep an escort battalion here, at a time when the Führer intends to stay in the Reich Chancellery." When Himmler didn't react, Berger said, disgusted, "Well, *I'm* going to Berlin and it's also your duty to go."

Instead, Himmler phoned the bunker again and implored the Führer to leave—in vain; Fegelein took the phone and urged his chief to come and make a personal plea. They argued until Himmler finally agreed to meet Fegelein at Nauen, a town twenty-five miles west of the bunker—in the middle of the one remaining escape corridor from Berlin.

Himmler waited for Fegelein at their rendezvous with Dr. Gebhardt, recently nominated the new president of the German Red Cross by Himmler, following the suicide of Professor Grawitz. After two hours Gebhardt suggested that he go on alone to see Hitler so that his appointment could be confirmed.

Himmler readily consented; he was relieved he didn't have to wait for Fegelein any longer and could go back to his headquarters. He told Gebhardt to be sure and tell Hitler that the Reichsführer's escort battalion was ready to defend the bunker to the end. Then he turned around and headed north in the darkness.

Goebbels was still at home when he learned of the Führer's collapse. He was told Hitler wanted him immediately. The catastrophic news probably struck him harder than anyone else. As he was preparing to leave, word came that the Führer also wanted to see Magda and the children. It was about five o'clock when Frau Goebbels told the nurse in a calm voice to get them ready to see the Führer. The children were delighted and wondered if Uncle Adolf was going to give them chocolate and cake. The mother guessed they might be going to their death. She put on a smile and said, "Each of you may take along one toy, but no more than that."

The Goebbels family left for the bunker in two cars. As Semmler watched them drive off, he noticed that his chief was calm and formal, but by now Magda and the children were weeping.

The family was installed in four tiny rooms not far from Hitler's own suite; then Goebbels and his wife went to the Führer. Goebbels announced that he too was going to stay in the bunker and commit suicide. Magda said that she would do the same, and would not be swayed even by Hitler. She also insisted that the six children die with them.

Keitel finally cleared the conference room so that he could talk alone with Hitler. He wanted to convince him to go to Berchtesgaden that night and initiate surrender negotiations from there. As had happened so many times before, the Feldmarschall only got the first words out when Hitler interrupted. "I already know exactly what you're going to say: 'The decision must be made at once!' " Hitler's voice rose. "I have already made a decision. I will never leave Berlin; I'll defend the city to my last breath!"

Keitel said that was "madness" and he felt impelled to "demand" that the Führer fly to Berchtesgaden immediately, where he could maintain command over the Reich and the Armed Forces. This could not be done in Berlin since communications would probably be cut at any moment.

"There's nothing to keep you from flying to Berchtesgaden at once," Hitler retorted. "As a matter of fact, I order you to do it. But I personally will stay in Berlin. Only an hour ago I announced this over the radio. I cannot retract it."

Jodl entered just as Keitel said, in an anguished voice, that he would leave only if Hitler did.

Hitler summoned Bormann and ordered all three to fly to Berchtesgaden, where Keitel would take command, with Göring as the Führer's personal representative.

"In seven years I've never disobeyed a single one of your orders," Keitel rejoined. "But this is one I refuse to execute." He reminded the Führer that he was still Supreme Commander of the Armed Forces. "It's unthinkable that after you have directed and led us for so long, you should suddenly send your staff away and expect them to do it themselves!"

"Everything is falling to pieces, anyway, and I can do no more," Hitler replied. The rest, he added, should be left to Göring.

"No soldier would fight for the Reichsmarschall," one of the generals said.

"What do you mean 'fight'? There's mighty little fighting to be done, and if it comes to negotiating, the Reichsmarschall can do it better than I can. I will either fight and win the battle of Berlin, or die in Berlin." He could not run the risk of falling into enemy hands, he said, and would shoot himself at the very last moment. "That is my final, irrevocable decision!"

The generals swore that the situation was not completely lost. Schörner was still strong and Wenck's Twelfth Army could be turned about and brought to the relief of Berlin; and in a few days Steiner would finally have enough men to launch a simultaneous attack from the north.

All at once Hitler's eyes brightened. Incredibly, hope returned and with it his determination. He began asking questions. Soon he was outlining in detail exactly how Berlin could be saved.

Keitel said he would go at once and give the orders to Wenck in person. Hitler was so much his old self that he solicitously insisted that Keitel stay and have a bowl of pea soup first. It was decided that Keitel and Jodl would set up new OKW headquarters a few miles west, near Potsdam, so that they could easily escape to Dönitz if Berlin was surrounded. Krebs would stay in the bunker as the Führer's military adviser.

With a picnic basket of sandwiches, cognac and chocolate—personally ordered by Hitler—Keitel and Jodl left the Reich Chancellery ruins in a staff car. It was dark. "There is only one thing I can tell Wenck," Keitel said grimly, "and that is: The fight for Berlin is on and the fate of the Führer is at stake."

It was just before midnight when, by pure chance, Keitel found Wenck's command post in a lonely forester's hut some sixty miles southwest of the bunker. Keitel ordered him to about-face and attack to the northeast through Konev's encircling thrust. At the same time Busse would attack to the northwest; together they would relieve Berlin. Wenck said that was impossible: Busse was surrounded and had only a small amount of ammunition.

Keitel resorted to pleas. The battle for Berlin had started, he said, and on it rested the fate of Hitler and Germany. It was the responsibility of the Twelfth and Ninth armies to go to Hitler's aid. He said that the Führer's life was now utterly dependent on Wenck and confessed something he had not even told Jodl: he was determined to abduct the Führer from the bunker, by force if necessary.

The plan to relieve Berlin was based on nonexistent divisions, Wenck protested, but Keitel continued to plead until the young general said he would do his best. As he watched Keitel's car disappear he thought of Berlin where he had grown up, and the fate of its women and children. He had fought the Russians and knew how they treated captives.

For some days Major Freytag von Loringhoven had been advising Krebs to do something so that they wouldn't both end up in the bunker. But his chief, unwilling or unable to act, had allowed himself to drift with the events. He told the young baron he certainly wasn't proud to be chosen the Führer's last military adviser. "But I can't change it now. I'm ordered to stay. So you must stay with me."

Just after midnight on April 23 Krebs finally got a concession from Hitler—at least he thought it was one. Busse could pull back. Krebs immediately phoned the good news to Heinrici. This was, of course, only so that Busse might join Wenck in the attack to relieve Berlin.

But Busse still refused to pull back. This time, however, he told Heinrici the real reason. "I can't retreat until all of Biehler's units are out of Frankfurt," he said. "I'm staying until Biehler has joined us."

Heinrici was exasperated—but he understood and hung up.

## 4.

A few hours after Hitler's breakdown, General Christian burst into Koller's headquarters just outside Berlin. "The Führer is in a state of collapse!" He gave a frightening account of what had happened.

Koller's first instinct was to phone Göring at Berchtesgaden—the Reichsmarschall was Hitler's legal heir. "The one we used to report to won't leave where he is," Koller told Göring's adjutant, Oberst (Colonel) Bernd von Brauchitsch. "But I must get out of here."

Brauchitsch knew Koller was referring to Hitler and said, "The Reichsmarschall wants you to come here immediately."

The line went dead. Koller turned to Christian and asked, "What is the OKW doing?"

"The OKW is leaving Berlin. It is assembling tonight at Krampnitz [a panzer training school between Berlin and Potsdam] and has decided to throw troops from the western front against the eastern front and continue the war."

Koller rang the bunker. "What's happening?" he asked Colonel von Below, Hitler's Luftwaffe adjutant. "Christian has told me various things. I'm appalled. Is it all true?"

"Yes, it's true."

Koller asked if he should stay up north.

"Yes."

But Koller wanted a different answer. "That's no good," he said in exasperation. "It's such a decisive moment." He said he must go south and personally report everything to the Reichsmarschall.

"Yes" was the answer.

"Is there any chance *he* [Hitler] will alter his decision again?"

This time Below said no.

Koller hurriedly drove to the new OKW headquarters and asked Jodl for confirmation of Christian's incredible story.

"What Christian told you is true," Jodl replied calmly.

Koller asked if the Führer would carry out his threat to commit suicide.

"The Führer is stubborn on that point."

"When the mayor of Leipzig killed himself and his family the Führer said, 'It was senseless, a cowardly evasion of responsibility.' " Koller was indignant. "Now he's doing the same thing!"

"You're right."

"Well, what are you going to do? Have you any orders for me?"

"No," said Jodl.

Koller said he had to leave at once to report in person to Göring. He had to be told that Hitler had said, ". . . if it comes to negotiating, the Reichsmarschall can do it better than I can." Such information, Koller said, could not possibly be explained in a radiogram. He simply had to go in person.

"You're right," said the laconic Jodl. "There's no other course open to you."

Just before dawn on April 23, Koller and his staff left for Munich in fifteen JU-52s.

At the Obersalzberg, a resort overlooking Berchtesgaden, Göring had already learned much of what had happened, from an unlikely source. That morning he had told Josef Zychski, his caretaker—and no one else—of a secret radio message from Bormann informing him that the Führer had suffered a nervous breakdown and that Göring was to take over command. Göring was torn between suspicion and credulity. What should he do? Act at once or wait?

Koller didn't reach Göring's comfortable but unostentatious house at the Obersalzberg until noon. Excitedly he told the Reichsmarschall and Philip Bouhler, a Party official, about Hitler's collapse. Göring, of course, knew most of this and to Koller's surprise showed little reaction. He asked if Hitler was still alive. Had he appointed Bormann as his successor? Koller replied that the Führer was alive when he left Berlin and that there was still one or perhaps two escape routes. The city would probably hold out for about a week. "Anyway," he concluded, "it is now up to you to act, Herr Reichsmarschall!"

Bouhler agreed, but Göring was still hesitating. Might not Hitler have appointed Bormann as his successor? he asked again. Bormann, an old enemy, could have sent the telegram to make him usurp power prematurely. "If I act, he will call me a traitor; if I don't, he will accuse me of having failed at a most critical time!"

He summoned Bormann's personal assistant, who happened to be in the neighborhood, and the commander of the SS detachment at the Obersalzberg. He also sent for Minister Hans Lammers, head of the Reich Chancellery and a legal expert, who was the custodian of the two official documents drafted by Hitler himself in 1941, establishing a successor to the Führer. In these documents Göring was appointed Hitler's deputy in case the Führer was prevented—permanently or temporarily—from performing his offices. He would also be Hitler's successor upon his death.

Göring wanted to know if the military situation in Berlin warranted his taking over—after all, the Führer was surrounded—but Lammers could make no decision.

Göring was well aware that his influence with the Führer had waned as Bormann's grew, and asked if Hitler had issued any orders since 1941 which might have invalidated his own succession.

Lammers answered no. "If the Führer ever issued any other orders, they would certainly have come to my attention." He had made sure from time to time that the documents had not been rescinded. The decree, he declared, had the force of law and didn't even need to be promulgated again.

Someone suggested that a radio message be sent asking the Führer if he wanted Göring to be his deputy. Everyone agreed and Göring began to write, but since it took quite a while, Koller interrupted to say that such a long message would never get through.

"Yes, that's right," Göring agreed. "You write another one."

Both Koller and Brauchitsch drafted separate messages and Göring chose the one that read: "My Führer, is it your wish, in view of your decision to stay in Berlin, that I take over complete control of the Reich, in accordance with the decree of June 29, 1941?"

Göring read it again and added: ". . . with full powers in domestic and foreign affairs," so that he might negotiate a peace with the Allies. Still concerned, he said, "Suppose I don't get any answer? We must give a time limit, a time by which I must receive an answer."

Koller suggested that they give Hitler eight hours and Göring scribbled down: "If no answer has been received by 10 P.M., I shall have to assume that you have been deprived of your freedom of action, and I will consider the terms of your decree as being in force and act for the good of our people and Fatherland." He paused, then added hastily, "You must realize what I feel for you in this most difficult hour of my life and I can find no words to express myself. God bless you and speed you here as soon as possible. Your most loyal, Hermann Göring."

He leaned back heavily. "It's frightful," he said. "If I don't get an answer by ten o'clock this evening, I must do something immediately—like send out a proclamation to the Armed Forces, issue a call to the population, and so on." His course of action was becoming clear. "I'll stop the war at once."

By coincidence, Hitler was being advised by Albert Speer to appoint Dönitz as his successor. Preoccupied, Hitler mulled over the idea, but said nothing.

Speer had flown to Berlin to say good-bye to Hitler in person and to make a confession. Without apologizing for it, he revealed that for weeks he had been obstructing Hitler's "scorched earth" policy by persuading leading generals and officials to spare bridges and factories. (He didn't confess, of course, that he had recently planned to assassinate Hitler by piping poison gas into the bunker through the ventilating system—only to find a protective chimney newly built around the funnel.) At twenty-nine, Speer had worked under Hitler's architect, Professor Paul Troost. Before long, the Führer had included the young man in his inner circle and now regarded him fondly as one of his closest friends. Speer expected to be arrested and possibly shot, but Hitler only seemed "deeply moved" by his minister's revelation.

Speer was still with Hitler when Göring's telegram arrived. Before the Führer could make a comment, Bormann indignantly branded the request for an answer by 10 P.M. an ultimatum. He seemed more outraged than anyone else and, with Goebbels, demanded Göring's execution.

Hitler hesitated, then admitted that he had been aware for some time of Göring's failure; moreover, the Reichsmarschall was corrupt—a drug addict. But his mood changed instantly and he said, "But he can still negotiate the capitulation; it doesn't matter who does." And though he refused to order Göring's death, he was persuaded to send this message:

YOUR ACTION REPRESENTS HIGH TREASON AGAINST THE FÜHRER AND NATIONAL SOCIALISM. THE PENALTY FOR TREASON IS DEATH. BUT

IN VIEW OF YOUR EARLIER SERVICES TO THE PARTY THE FÜHRER
WILL NOT INFLICT THIS SUPREME PENALTY IF YOU RESIGN ALL
YOUR OFFICES. ANSWER YES OR NO.

This message had been drafted by Bormann, and a little later Hitler
sent another:

DECREE OF 6.29.41 IS RESCINDED BY MY SPECIAL INSTRUCTION.
MY FREEDOM OF ACTION UNDISPUTED. I FORBID ANY MOVE BY YOU
IN THE INDICATED DIRECTION.

And then a third, which differed markedly from the first two and
perhaps more accurately expressed his own attitude:

YOUR ASSUMPTION THAT I AM PREVENTED FROM CARRYING OUT
MY OWN WISHES IS AN ABSOLUTELY ERRONEOUS IDEA WHOSE RI-
DICULOUS ORIGIN I DO NOT KNOW. I REQUEST THAT THIS BE STRONGLY
COUNTERED IMMEDIATELY, AND I SHALL, BY THE WAY, ONLY HAND
OVER MY POWER TO WHOM AND WHEN I CONSIDER IT TO BE RIGHT.
UNTIL THEN I SHALL BE IN COMMAND MYSELF.

Bormann must have feared that this message was a prelude to forgiveness; he clandestinely radioed the SS commandant at the Obersalzberg to
arrest Göring for high treason.*

## 5.

The catastrophes of the past few weeks had abruptly brought about
disintegration of the sanctity of command—so hallowed to the German
officer corps. Never in the history of the Wehrmacht had so many commanders become independent, to the point of mutiny. First, Guderian
had openly opposed Hitler and finally willed his own dismissal; then,
Heinrici took up face-to-face opposition and even sent out vague orders
in the hopes of forestalling Hitler; finally, Wenck ignored direct orders
and on his own decided to wage war in the east.

Rebellion ranged along the chain of command. While Heinrici was
obstructing Hitler, for example, Busse resisted Heinrici, and nowhere was
there more confusion than within Busse's own command. One of his

* Krebs phoned Keitel from the bunker and told him in detail about Göring's
dismissal. Keitel was "horrified" and kept insisting there must be "some misunderstanding." Suddenly Bormann's voice broke into their conversation and shouted that
Göring had been fired "even from his job as Reich Chief Hunter." Keitel did not
deign to reply. The situation, he thought, was "too serious for such sarcastic remarks." The Feldmarschall could not sleep after hearing such distressing news; it
suddenly dramatized "the desperate mood in the Reich Chancellery and particularly
the growing influence of Bormann." Only he could have driven the Führer to such
rashness, Keitel thought; then he wondered what would happen next. Had Hitler
decided to kill Göring and then himself at the last possible moment?

units, the LVI Panzer Corps, had become detached from the rest of Ninth Army and was now twenty miles east of Berlin, trying to stem the Russians who had broken through Seelow. Its commander, General Helmuth Weidling, had received conflicting orders: Busse was demanding that he drive southeast and join the main body of the army, and Hitler threatened to shoot him if he didn't move into the Berlin city limits at once—someone had falsely reported that Weidling had fled all the way back to Potsdam.

Nicknamed "Bony Karl" by his troops because of his rough skin and gruff manner, Weidling was a simple, professional field soldier who wanted only to do his duty. He decided to see Krebs personally and clear up the matter once and for all.

In the bunker he was greeted coolly by Krebs and Burgdorf. "Well, what's going on and why am I going to be shot?" Weidling blurted out.

Krebs stiffly replied that the Führer was infuriated because Weidling had moved his command post west of Berlin. Ridiculous! exploded Weidling, and brought out a situation map to prove that his command posts had never been more than two miles behind the Russian lines. It was obviously the truth and the other two assured Weidling they would go right in and set Hitler straight.

Krebs and Burgdorf returned to find a seething Weidling. He had just received a message from his own headquarters that he had been relieved of command by OKW. He denounced both generals as lackeys who were too cowardly to tell Hitler the truth about a fellow officer for fear of losing favor.

Krebs was not offended. He told Weidling that the order relieving him had already been canceled and that the Führer wanted to see him at once. They descended a flight of stairs and followed a corridor to the waiting room. Several men were sitting there on a bench, but the only one Weidling recognized was Ribbentrop.

Krebs and Burgdorf quickly escorted him into the main conference room, where Hitler was sitting behind a table, studying a map. As they entered Hitler turned, revealing his bloated face and feverish eyes. He smiled obliquely, extended a hand and asked in a low voice, "Have we met?"

Weidling said yes—a year before at the Obersalzberg, when he was awarded the Oak Leaf Clusters to the Knight's Cross.

"I remember the name," Hitler said, "but I don't recall your face." His own face was a smiling mask, Weidling thought, and noticed the Führer grimace with pain as he sat down.

At Krebs's suggestion Weidling revealed that he had already ordered his corps to move southeast to join the rest of Busse's army. If this move was not canceled, Krebs said, a gap would be opened east of Berlin through which the Zhukov column from Seelow could pour.

Hitler, his right leg trembling continuously, nodded his head in agreement and began a lengthy explanation of his operational plan for the relief of the city. Wenck's Twelfth Army was to attack from the southwest while Busse attacked from the southeast. Together these two forces would defeat the Russians south of Berlin. Simultaneously Steiner would attack from the northeast and contain the Zhukov column north of Berlin. As soon as Wenck and Busse had defeated the Russians in the south, they would drive north and help wipe out the enemy there in a massive joint attack.

If it made sense to Hitler, it was only confusing to a practical soldier like Weidling. Was this reality or just a dream?

Krebs suddenly announced that Weidling would now take charge of the defense of the eastern and southeastern sections of Berlin. As the bewildered Weidling rose, Hitler tried to stand up but dropped back in his chair. Instead he held out his hand. Weidling walked out deeply affected by the Führer's physical condition. He felt drunk. What was going on here? Was there still a Supreme Commander of the Wehrmacht? In the upper bunker he phoned his corps and ordered it repositioned to defend the eastern suburbs of Berlin. Then he asked Krebs, "Under whose command am I?"

"Directly under the Führer."

Weidling examined a map of Berlin and suggested that the responsibility of its defense be placed in one hand.

"There is such a hand," Krebs said. "The hand of the Führer."

"I have a feeling that I'm in a dream world!" Weidling exclaimed. His tank corps as well as all the other units in Busse's army were battered. Did Krebs think that the massive Russian forces could be pushed back in the twinkle of an eye? "If Berlin can't be defended at the Oder River," he said, "it must be declared an open city!"

But Krebs only smiled as if it were an old, old story, and said, "The Führer has ordered the defense of Berlin because he is positive the war will be over once it falls."

# 6.

Just before midnight several cars drove up to a small house near a park in Lübeck, the German port on the Baltic north of Hamburg. Himmler and Schellenberg, followed by several SS officers, entered the house—it was the Swedish consulate—and were met by Folke Bernadotte. He led Himmler and Schellenberg into a small room lit only by candles. As they began to talk there was an air-raid alarm, and Bernadotte wondered if Himmler would like to go down into the shelter with the others. Characteristically, Himmler couldn't make up his mind for quite a while, and when he found that the shelter was only an ordinary cellar he again hesitated momentarily before going down. During most of the hour underground Himmler went from person to person, asking questions as if he were taking a poll. Bernadotte thought that he looked utterly exhausted and that he was using all his will power to appear calm.

When the "All Clear" sounded they returned to the small room upstairs. Offered a drink, Himmler would only take soda. "I've come to realize that you're right," he said unexpectedly. "The war must end." He sighed resignedly. "I admit that Germany is defeated." The Führer might be dead, he said, and he was no longer bound by his personal oath.

The flickering light of two candles made Himmler's face look even more furtive and indecisive. It all depended on one thing, he went on: how the Allies treated the Germans. If they completely crushed the German people, Hitler would emerge as a hero and martyr. "In the present situation," he said, fastidiously sipping his soda water, "my hands are free. To save as much of Germany as possible from a Russian invasion, I'm willing to capitulate on the western front . . . but not on the eastern front. I have always been, and I shall always remain, a sworn enemy of Bolshevism." He asked if the Count was willing to forward this proposal to the Swedish Minister for Foreign Affairs for transmittal to the West.

Bernadotte did not like the idea. It was improbable, he said, that the Western Allies would make a separate peace with Germany if she continued to fight in the east.

"I'm well aware of how extremely difficult this is," Himmler answered, "but all the same, I want to make an attempt to save millions of Germans from a Russian occupation."

Bernadotte agreed to take the capitulation message to his government, but wondered what Himmler intended to do if his offer was turned down. "In that event I shall take over command on the eastern front and be killed in battle."

He said he hoped to meet Eisenhower and was willing to surrender unconditionally without delay. "Between men of the world should I offer my hand to Eisenhower?" he asked confidentially.

Upon leaving, Himmler said it was the bitterest day of his life and he had to leave at once for the eastern front. He strode purposefully into the darkness and got behind the wheel of his car. He stepped on the gas and the vehicle lunged through a hedge into a barbed-wire fence surrounding the building. The Swedes and the Germans managed to push the car clear and Himmler lurched off. There was, the Count remarked to several attachés, something symbolic about it all.

## 7.

The next morning, April 24, Krebs and his two aides, Major Freytag von Loringhoven and Hauptmann (Captain) Gerhard Boldt, were admitted to the Führer's conference room; Goebbels and Bormann were also there.

In the middle of Krebs's report Boldt was called to the phone to get a dispatch from the front. When he returned, Goebbels leaned across the table and whispered, "What is the news?" Boldt told him that a sudden thirty-mile tank thrust through Manteuffel's northern flank by Marshal Rokossovsky's Second White Russian Front not only was cutting off Manteuffel's army on the north, as Zhukov had already done in the south, but indicated that Stalin's major effort was toward Berlin. Three Russian fronts—about 2,500,000 men—were converging on the capital.

Hitler turned hopefully to Boldt. Rattled by the Führer's constantly wobbling head, the captain reported the new disaster. Hitler was silent for a moment, then began speaking in a harsh voice. "In view of the great natural obstacle that the Oder represents, this Russian success is simply the result of the incompetence of the German military leaders there!"

Krebs tried to defend Heinrici and Manteuffel. Their reserves—including Steiner's corps—had already been diverted to Manteuffel's heavily pressed right wing or withdrawn toward Berlin. This reminded Hitler of Steiner's abortive attack. He pointed shakily at a map and said that another drive from north of Berlin must be started the next day. "The Third Panzer Army is to use all available forces for this assault, with a ruthless weakening of other sections of the front not under attack. The north *must* re-establish connections with Berlin. Let that be passed on immediately."

Burgdorf's suggestion that Steiner lead the attack incensed Hitler. "I have no use for these arrogant, dull, undecided SS leaders! Under no circumstances whatever do I want Steiner to be in command."

As Krebs came out of the conference he saw Weidling waiting in the anteroom. "You made a very good impression on the Führer last night," he said. "He has now put you in command of the defense of all Berlin."

"It would be much better if you had me shot," Weidling replied, and accepted the command on the condition that only he issue orders for the defense of the city. He didn't want any interference from such as Goebbels, the Defender of Berlin.

That afternoon Jodl arrived at the headquarters of the one man— Steiner—who was supposed to have nothing to do with the new attack from the north. "By order of Hitler," Jodl announced, "you must start the attack at once."

"I don't want to move toward Berlin," Steiner replied with the unprecedented defiance that was becoming commonplace in the Wehrmacht. There was very little cover, he said, and most of his men would be killed. "I don't want to do it," he repeated.

Jodl glared at him and his bald patch turned pink, a sure sign of his mounting anger. But Steiner stared him down. His behavior was not quixotic. He was convinced that only a negotiated peace with the West could save Germany, and a week before had secretly agreed with Manteuffel to make contact with Eisenhower as soon as possible and tell him the Allies could pass through their lines and move all the way to the Oder.

In the middle of the argument with Jodl, Steiner was notified that 1000 Hitler Youth and 5000 pilots had just arrived. Mobilize them for the attack toward Berlin, Jodl ordered. Again Steiner was rebellious. They were untrained, he said, and would be murdered in battle. He sent them back to their home bases.

Jodl gave up and returned to OKW headquarters. A few hours later Keitel arrived and urged Steiner to start the attack.

Steiner was embarrassed. Had a German Feldmarschall ever humiliated himself like this before? But he could only say, "No, I won't do it. This attack is nonsense—murder. Do what you want to me."

Keitel too saw it was hopeless and left.

# 8.

The International Committee of the Red Cross had failed to stop the evacuation of prisoners from Sachsenhausen—despite definite promises from both Himmler and his Gestapo chief, Müller—but still hoped to save the 20,000 women in nearby Ravensbrück. They sent a delegate, Albert de Cocatrix, with an urgent letter to SS Colonel Rudolf Hoess, deputy chief of concentration camps and former commandant of Auschwitz.

Cocatrix was delayed on his way north by roads swelled with refugees and didn't arrive at Ravensbrück until after dark. He found SS-Sturmbannführer (Major) Fritz Suhrens, the camp commandant, and told him he had to see Hoess. But Hoess had been in an automobile accident and wasn't there.

Cocatrix described the atrocities that were being committed on the marching prisoners of Sachsenhausen and warned Suhrens that those responsible would be brought to account. He proposed that the Ravensbrück women be placed in charge of a Red Cross delegate and kept in their compounds until the Russians arrived.

But Suhrens said he had explicit instructions from Himmler himself to evacuate the camp. Besides, the military situation was not at all hopeless; the Russians would not only be stopped but thrown back to the steppes in a tremendous counteroffensive about to be launched.

"Only the fifteen hundred sick can remain in camp," he said. "Do you know that the Russian sick begged on their knees not to be left behind, to fall into their countrymen's hands, and cried out, *'Nix Bolscheviki!'*?"

At nine o'clock the following morning, April 25, several thousand women were lined up in front of the headquarters. Suhrens received Cocatrix at his office and spoke of the good morale of his "ladies," offering to show letters of recommendation they had written him.

An SS woman entered and announced, "The records have been destroyed."

The commandant surreptitiously motioned the woman to be quiet, then introduced her and asked how some prisoners recently evacuated had been treated.

"With humanity," she replied sententiously.

"You see, you see!" cried Suhrens. He raised his arms triumphantly and launched into a long apologia of the concentration camp system, lauding the remarkable results attained in education and training of the prisoners. The horrible things written about the camps, he claimed, were just "atrocity propaganda," and offered to let Cocatrix see Ravensbrück for himself.

What he saw resembled a Stalag, although the barracks were filled with three-deck cots. He visited the infirmary, the library and the surprisingly tidy detention building, but was not allowed to see several buildings in the eastern section which were, according to Suhrens, factories producing textiles for the Wehrmacht.

Suhrens stopped a prisoner, as if by chance, and asked if she had been badly treated or beaten. Did she have any complaints? The woman had only praise for her captors. Others were picked out—always by Suhrens—and interviewed with exactly the same results. Each time Suhrens turned to the Red Cross man and gravely said, *"Bitte!"* Suhrens called over a woman SS guard.

"Have you mistreated the prisoners?" he asked.

"But that's forbidden!" she said, as if scandalized.

"And if you beat them?"

"Then we would be punished."

The same questions brought the same answers from several other guards. Leaving the camp area, Cocatrix had an urge to ask Suhrens to show him the gas chamber and crematorium but restrained himself.

At the office he met SS Colonel Keindel, commandant of Sachsenhausen, who rather aloofly denied that any atrocities had occurred on the march from his camp. Cocatrix charged that two Red Cross drivers and a delegate had witnessed a number of murders.

Keindel shrugged his shoulders. "Perhaps some SS guards did such things to end their sufferings—as an act of humanity. I don't understand why so much fuss is made about a few deaths—not a word was said about the terror bombing of German civilians at Dresden." Certain SS soldiers might have acted too rashly, he admitted, but the ones who

usually mistreated prisoners were Hungarians, Rumanians, Ukrainians—
people of another mentality.

Cocatrix left with Suhrens, who took his arm familiarly and said in a
confidential manner that only was distasteful, "With me you don't have
to fear anything like that."

**9.**

The SS commandant at Berchtesgaden had acted immediately upon
receipt of Bormann's telegram and placed Göring and his family under
house arrest. The past forty-eight hours had been the most tempestuous
in the Reichsmarschall's dramatic career: his Führer had collapsed; he
thought he'd been called upon to inherit the Third Reich; then came
Hitler's three telegrams; and now he was sure he'd be executed.

The previous night an SS man laid a pistol with one bullet in it on
Göring's night table. "I won't do it," he told his caretaker, Zychski, and
threw the gun aside with contempt. "I'm going to face responsibility for
everything I've done."

The next morning, April 25, several SS officers tried to persuade
Göring, in the presence of his wife and his butler, to sign a document
stating that he was resigning all his positions because of poor health.
Göring refused; in spite of the telegrams, he could not bring himself to
believe Hitler really meant what he said. But when the SS men drew
their guns Göring quickly signed. Just then the drone of approaching
planes drove everyone into the shelter under the house.

Allied planes had often passed over Berchtesgaden on their way to
Salzburg, Linz and other targets, but as yet the Führer area at the
Obersalzberg was undamaged. Today, however, two large waves of Allied
bombers were bent on wiping out Hitler's mountain retreat. Though
Eisenhower was sure that the Führer was staying in Berlin, he was
equally sure that the rest of the Nazi government had moved to the
National Redoubt to establish headquarters at the Obersalzberg.

At ten o'clock the first wave swept over the Hohe Goell mountain and
dumped high explosives on the edge of the Führer area. Half an hour
later came an even bigger wave. For almost an hour plane after plane
unloaded blockbusters directly onto the Obersalzberg.

After the last bomber had disappeared, Air Force General Robert
Ritter von Greim, commander of Luftflotte 6 in Munich, drove up to the
Obersalzberg. Hitler's dream was a mass of twisted wreckage. Greim
looked around in dismay. The Führer's home, the famed Berghof, had
been hit directly; one side was demolished and the blasted tin roof hung
in mid-air. Several hundred yards away, black smoke still rose from

Bormann's badly damaged house and just beyond lay the shattered remains of Göring's house. The SS barracks, the Platterhof Hotel and the cottage where Hitler had written much of *Mein Kampf* were in flames.

A dedicated Nazi, Greim had received a telegram from Berlin to report to the bunker, and he now sought out Koller, who, he had been told, had a similar order. Greim began berating Göring for leaving the bunker and performing "treasonable" acts. At first Koller apologized for his chief, then burst into personal grievances long suppressed. "It's not for me to defend the Reichsmarschall," he said. "He has too many faults for that. He has made my life unbearable—he has treated me abominably, telling me he'd have me court-martialed and killed, for no reason at all, and threatening to shoot General Staff officers in front of the assembled General Staff." But he refused to go as far as Greim. "I know that the Reichsmarschall did nothing on the twenty-second and twenty-third of April that could be called treason."

Greim was not at all impressed. Göring's actions should not be defended, he declared, and headed for Berlin.

## 10.

Early that morning Schörner—recently promoted to Generalfeldmarschall—landed at an airport near Berlin and drove to the bunker. Hitler had summoned him, and he suspected that the Führer had somehow learned of his attempt to negotiate with the West. Like Himmler, Wolff and Steiner—all of them SS leaders—he had done this on his own. The initiative, however, had come from Dr. Hans Kauffman,* an official of the Foreign Office who had quarreled with Ribbentrop and been transferred to an Army Group Center machine-gun battalion. Dr. Kauffman had convinced Schörner that Czech nationalists could be used to arrange some sort of separate peace with the Allies. It was a complicated plan, but after many secret trips by Dr. Kauffman, two German army planes loaded with Czechs were sent off—one to Switzerland and the other to Italy—to open negotiations. But the British and Americans, unaware that Schörner was behind the plan, turned it down summarily.

Schörner need not have feared. Hitler greeted his favorite field commander with the usual enthusiasm and warmth. But Schörner was not at all prepared for Hitler's next words, "take over and organize an *Alpenfestung*." The mountain area between Austria and Germany would be fortified as quickly as possible and manned with the best available forces, Hitler explained; this was not aimed against the West but as the last bulwark against Bolshevism.

* Not his real name. He is still afraid of reprisals from certain of his own countrymen for attempting to negotiate independently with the Allies.

Schörner left the bunker for further briefing by Goebbels and Dr. Naumann. The Propaganda Minister explained that there was a similar "North Project" being built by Dönitz at the Kaiser-Wilhelm-Kanal (the Kiel Canal). Both redoubts had great political significance, he said, and stressed that it was most important to maintain strict military discipline in both areas. Then, if it became necessary to surrender to the West, the troops would be under such control that Eisenhower would undoubtedly let the German staff leaders keep command of them.

When the people of the West learned, Goebbels went on, as he had, of the scandalous agreement at Yalta—allowing the Russians to occupy most of eastern Europe—they would force Truman and Churchill to attack Russia. Allied military leaders knew that alone they could not conquer the Red Army and would gratefully accept the aid of German troops in the northern and southern redoubts.

The Red Army pincers around Berlin were about to close; the escape corridor between Zhukov and Konev was now only a few miles wide. The fighting was particularly fierce in the southern suburbs near Tempelhof Airport and it was almost suicide for any plane to attempt to land there.

"Bony Karl" Weidling spent the day rearranging his defenses around the city and it was near midnight when he arrived at the bunker to make a situation report. Hitler was hovering over his map-strewn table; Goebbels was perched like a bird on a bench across from him. Weidling walked past the others and pointed on a large map. The ring around Berlin would soon be completed, he said gruffly. Hitler's head jerked up; he scowled. Weidling ignored this, and said that it appeared on the map that the odds were equal: one German division was facing one Russian division. "Ours are divisions in name only," he said sarcastically, "and are outnumbered ten to one in man power, and more than that in fire power."

Hitler refused to acknowledge the odds. The fall of Berlin, he said, would be the ruin of Germany and he was going to stay in the bunker—win or lose. Only Goebbels spoke up—and he echoed everything Hitler said. Their thinking was so similar that one would often finish the other's sentences.

Weidling was galled that no one voiced a different opinion. Every word uttered by Hitler was tacitly accepted. Were they all too afraid to talk? He felt like shouting, "My Führer, what madness! A great city like Berlin cannot be defended with the weak forces and small supply of ammunition available. Think, my Führer, of the intolerable grief the people of Berlin will suffer during these battles!" But he too said nothing.

Heinrici's entire front was a shambles, but he had just received one heartening piece of information: Biehler had finally broken through the

Russian ring around Frankfurt to rejoin the main body of the Ninth Army—and Busse was at last retreating to the west toward Wenck.

Manteuffel was also close to encirclement by the combined thrusts of Zhukov in the south and Rokossovsky in the north, who had already driven a wedge across the Oder, twenty-five miles deep and forty-five miles wide. Despite all this, Hitler insisted that Manteuffel hold.

"Is it possible for you to carry out this order?" Heinrici asked.

"We can probably hold where we are the rest of the day" was the blunt answer. "Then we'll have to move back."

Heinrici pointed out that this meant mobile combat.

"We don't have much choice," Manteuffel answered. "If we stay where we are, we'll be encircled like the Ninth Army."

Heinrici agreed that a withdrawal in the near future was necessary, and drove southwest to see Steiner, who had told him on the phone that OKW still wanted him to make an attack toward Berlin.

Heinrici found Steiner in the midst of another heated argument with Jodl. The proposed attack, Steiner said, was out of the question. It would be a useless sacrifice of his men.

"This is a special mission," Heinrici urged. "A once-in-a-lifetime opportunity to liberate the Führer. At least you can try." There was tactical justification for the attack, he said. It would give Manteuffel a bit of flank protection. But Steiner still refused to promise anything definite.

As Heinrici and Jodl drove in the rain toward OKW headquarters, which had just been transferred near Dr. Gebhardt's sanatorium, Heinrici called attention to the masses of refugees on the road and the buildings burning from recent air attacks. "You see all this," he said. "What are we still fighting for? Take a look at all this suffering."

"We must liberate the Führer."

"After we've done that, then what?"

Jodl replied vaguely that, once liberated, the Führer was the only man who could master the situation.

This evasiveness proved to Heinrici that OKW had no effective strategy for the continuation of the war. As he entered his own command post after dark, the phone rang. Without bothering to take off his coat, he picked up the receiver.

"Manteuffel here," said a clipped voice. The Russians had penetrated into the marshes, his secondary defense area. "I request immediate permission to pull back into prepared positions. It's now or never."

Hitler's order, recently renewed, prohibited any large-scale retreats without approval by OKW, but Heinrici said without hesitation, "Start the retreat. Also abandon *Festung* Stettin." He hung up and told Colonel Eismann to inform OKW at once that he had personally ordered the Third Panzer Army to retreat—Hitler's order be damned.

# 25

## "We Must Build a New World, a Far Better World"

On the day of Hitler's breakdown a motorized column of the American 84th Division rolled into the town of Salzwedel, 100 air miles west of the bunker. Huddled in the houses, almost as frightened as the local citizens, were about 4000 concentration camp inmates and slave laborers abandoned by their guards.

Tadeusz Nowakowski was one of the first to venture into the street. In 1937, at the age of seventeen, he had won the Polish Academy of Literature's prize for young writers. Two years later he and his father, who had worked together with Paderewski at the time of the Versailles Treaty, were arrested for publishing the underground paper, *Poland Still Alive*. The elder Nowakowski never lived to see his concentration camp, Dachau, liberated; he was beaten to death with a shovel by an enraged guard. But his son endured a succession of Gestapo prisons and camps. He escaped in early February and fled west to Salzwedel, where he found refuge with Polish slave laborers at a sugar factory.

The streets of Salzwedel were jammed with U. S. motorcycles, jeeps, trucks and armored cars churning up clouds of smoke and dust. Nowakowski could hear the roar of planes. It was the scene of liberation he had dreamed of for so many years.

A jeep stopped and a huge Negro stepped out to wild applause and a deluge of flowers. He pushed the crowd aside and nailed a SLOW sign on a telephone pole. He fanned himself with his helmet, shoved his way back to the jeep and drove off with a blast of his horn.

The other Americans were just as bored and looked at the prisoners with indifference, even as they flipped out packs of Chesterfields. They were far from arrogant, yet their behavior suggested a barely concealed contempt at the sight of the miserable and helpless. Or perhaps, Nowakowski thought, they were just tired of it all.

Only a crew of cameramen showed special interest. They persuaded the emaciated prisoners to return to the nearby concentration camp so that they could be filmed behind barbed wire. Some of the children cried when asked to go back through the gate.

In town, mobs of slave laborers roamed the streets, looking for ways of revenge. Barefooted Rumanians emptied buckets of marmalade onto the sidewalk, enraged women smashed store windows with their hands, and a Russian tossed fistfuls of herrings into the air.

A wounded SS man was dragged out of a garage and trampled to death. Prisoners, whose bodies were bloated from hunger, moved painfully up to the corpse. They kicked at it feebly, then flung themselves down and began tearing the hated flesh with hands and teeth. Nowakowski wanted to join them, to shout, "Tear his eyes out! For my tortured father, for my companions, for my bombed city!" But the words stuck in his throat. He laughed hysterically, tears streaming down his cheeks. He thought, I am alive, you sons of bitches!

An American patrol in a jeep fired a burst just over the heads of the clawing mass, tooted a horn reprovingly and passed on. It was a surrealistic nightmare. In front of a department store Nowakowski saw two drunken Frenchmen, entangled in a shredded bridal gown, kissing each other on the mouth and stroking each other's hair. An old Polish woman was vomiting blood as gypsy children emptied a bag of flour on her.

Across the canal he saw prisoners clamber onto a railroad tank car full of alcohol. When no one could open the valve someone found an ax, and soon the liquid spurted out in a great jet. The shrieking mob held out mess tins, hats and shoes. A Czech boy shouted, "It's methyl alcohol! It's poison!" but no one would listen.

A group of Russians tied the Bürgermeister to a tombstone and stripped his wife and daughter of their clothes. The Bürgermeister reared up and screeched like a cock crowing. A red-faced Russian shouted that his own wife had suffered the same fate in Kharkov, and roughly pushed several young countrymen up to the daughter. The mother threw herself on the ground and in supplication tried to kiss their feet.

There was a moment's hesitation. Then a squat Kalmuck grabbed the girl and forced her down. Her father made a mighty wrench. He tore the tombstone out of the earth—and dropped dead. Nowakowski watched the prisoner who had started it all walk away, with hands in pockets; he sat down on the bank of the canal and buried his face in his hands.

The riot reached such proportions that the Americans were forced to pen up the prisoners again. With hundreds of others, Nowakowski was locked in the gymnasium of a former army camp. But the nightmare continued. A group of young girls sang the Polish song "All Our Daily Concerns," while a few yards away men poisoned by the alcohol writhed in agony and vomited violet liquid. Those suffering from diarrhea had to relieve themselves on the spot and were shoved away by angry neighbors.

A group of boys found the gymnastic equipment and began clambering up ropes and swinging on trapezes like monkeys. They did not even stop their yelling and laughing when one of them dropped onto a pile of scrap iron, screamed a few minutes, then died.

By midnight the situation had become intolerable. A mob of men broke into the huddles of sleeping Polish and Ukrainian women. Nowakowski heard scuffles, short cries, curses, laughing, crying and whimpering. One man lamented over and over, *"A ja ne mohu, no mohu!"* ("But I can't, I can't!")

An Italian poisoned by alcohol had a fit. Like an animal he crawled frenziedly over sleepers, meowing and barking. When he reached the wall he kept smashing his head against it until he slumped under a radiator, finally at peace.

It wasn't until dawn that the Americans unlocked the gymnasium and told the French, Dutch, Belgian, Luxembourgian and Czech prisoners to come out; they were to be transferred to the officers' quarters. This brought screams of outrage from those left, who began cursing the Americans and the day of liberation. "We're allies too!" an indignant Italian shouted.

A wave of hysteria swept the big room. A Ukrainian woman who thought a Polish woman had stolen her comb ripped off the offender's necklace. She screamed for help from fellow Poles and a cry went up: "Kill the Ukrainians!"

Suddenly a loudspeaker boomed "Hello, hello," and in five languages announced that the hall was going to be inspected. At eight o'clock several American officers peered in and, appalled, quickly withdrew. They ordered all children brought outside at once. A rumor started that Jewish women were being quartered in villas and given white bread, eggs and chocolate. Shouts of rage went up: "They take hot baths and walk around in kimonos!" "They sleep with Americans."

"You see how these sons of bitches look after their own people!" someone called out. "A Jew will always help a Jew, but the Christians are left to die like dogs!"

"Like dogs!" a hundred others repeated.

"That's because we're not dirty Jews like them!" screamed an old woman wearing a man's cap.

A girl angrily shouted back, "That's because they burned us in the crematorium ovens while you were screwing German farmers in barns!"

The room went quiet. Everyone stared at the girl. She was small and ugly, with a big head that looked like a pumpkin on top of a pole. Her red ears stuck out. "Go ahead, hit me!" she cried hoarsely.

"*Jüdin!*" someone screamed, and the mob rushed at the girl. An elderly bespectacled man who looked like a professor circled the girl with a protecting arm. "Don't touch her!"

The frenzied attackers threw them both to the floor and smothered them with sacks. The "professor" was overwhelmed; the women tore out the girl's hair in chunks and jabbed fingers in her eyes. "That's for the milk!" one shouted. "That's for the chocolate! That's for the farmers in the barn, you dirty Jew!"

Her defender stopped struggling, his body went limp.

"Oh, Jesus!" a woman cried. "They're dead!"

The women scattered, but two Russians wiped the blood off the victims' faces, dragged them to a corner and dumped them on top of several other corpses.

The loudspeaker boomed again, urging the prisoners to be patient; food was on the way and they would all be moved to new quarters. Within minutes food lines were established, and hot soup and white bread passed out. During the next hour the awed prisoners witnessed an incredulous transformation: the gymnasium was cleaned, and they were washed and given fresh clothes.

They were lined up to receive food parcels from a good-looking American sergeant who managed to carry out his duties while reading a comic book; each one approached his table as if it were an altar. Already the savage look on so many children's faces was gone. Everything now seemed so simple and logical and easy. Almost everyone was smiling and the loudspeaker played, "*I love you, I love you, I love you.*"

The American miracle was not over. Trucks drove up with four portable chapels and in half an hour services were being held in the football field by an Orthodox priest, a rabbi, a Catholic priest and a Protestant minister. Following hymns, a prayer thundered over the loudspeaker: " 'Alleluia! The Lord is victorious, and the spirit of unrighteousness has been reduced to dust and ashes! Alleluia! The chains that fettered the hands of the righteous have been removed, and the smoke of sacrifices is rising to heaven . . .' "

Leaflets of the prayer were passed out. Nowakowski grabbed several and walked to the latrine. He hadn't seen such soft paper in five years.

### 2.

At 2 P.M., April 23, President Truman held an important conference with his leading military and diplomatic advisers: Stimson, Forrestal,

Leahy, Marshall, King and Stettinius. Also present were Assistant Secretary of State James Dunn and three Soviet experts recently returned from Moscow—Harriman, Bohlen and General Deane.

Stettinius reported that Molotov, who was scheduled to meet the President in a few hours, was proving intransigent over the Polish question and kept demanding a seat for the Lublin government at the San Francisco Conference. "Our agreements with the Soviet Union have so far been a one-way street and this cannot continue," Truman said sharply. "It is now or never. I intend to go on with plans for San Francisco and if the Russians don't wish to join us, they can go to hell."

He asked each one to give his opinion. Stimson admitted he knew little about the problem but questioned the wisdom of too strong a policy. "I am very much troubled by it. . . . In my opinion we ought to be very careful and see whether we can't iron out the situation without getting into a head-on collision."

"This is not an isolated incident," Forrestal retorted, "but is one of a pattern of unilateral action on the part of Russia." The Soviets had taken similar positions in Bulgaria, Rumania, Hungary and Greece. "And I think we might as well meet the issue now as later on."

"The real issue is whether we are to be a party to a program of Soviet domination of Poland," Harriman said. "Obviously we are faced with the possibility of a break with the Russians, but I feel that, properly handled, it might still be avoided."

"I have no intention of delivering an ultimatum to Mr. Molotov," Truman said. He simply meant to make clear the position of the U. S. government.

Stimson was still concerned by the President's attitude. "I'd like to know how far the Russian reaction to a strong position on Poland will go," he said. It was a time, he told himself, to use all possible restraint on people like Forrestal and Harriman, who were apparently getting increasingly irritated with the Russians. But he felt very sorry for Truman, who had inherited a bad situation and might be pushed into rash decisions. "I would think that perhaps the Russians are being more realistic than we are in regard to their own security," he said. "And I am sorry to see this one incident project a breach between the two countries."

Leahy was also concerned. "I hope the matter can be put to the Russians in such a way as not to close the door to subsequent accommodation," he said. "I left Yalta with the impression that the Soviet government had no intention of permitting a free government to operate in Poland. I'd have been surprised had the Soviet government behaved any differently than it has." The Yalta agreement could be interpreted two ways and it was a serious matter, he felt, to break with the Russians. "But we should tell them that we stand for a free and independent Poland."

Marshall finally brought up what must have been on everyone's mind.

"I hope for Soviet participation in the war against Japan at a time when it will be useful to us," he said. "The Russians have it within their power to delay their entry into the Far Eastern war until we have done all the dirty work." Like Leahy and Stimson, he felt "that the possibility of a break with Russia is very serious."

"Is the issue an invitation to the Lublin government to San Francisco?" King asked.

"That's a settled matter and not the issue," Truman replied. "The issue is the execution of agreements entered into between this government and the Soviet Union." After listening to everyone's arguments, he had made up his mind—what Forrestal and Harriman said made the most sense. "I intend to tell Mr. Molotov that we expect Russia to carry out the Yalta decision, as we are prepared to do for our part."

At five-thirty Molotov arrived with Ambassador Gromyko and the interpreter, M. Pavlov. Stettinius, Harriman and Leahy stayed with the President—as did Bohlen, who was to interpret. After greeting his visitors, Truman said, "I am sorry to learn that no progress has been made in solving the Polish problem."

His direct and unhesitating manner must have jolted the Russians, who had become used to Roosevelt's suave persuasions. He said that the United States was determined to go ahead with plans for United Nations organization, no matter what difficulties or differences might arise. If no decision could be reached on Poland, he seriously doubted the success of postwar collaboration. "This applies in the field of economic as well as political collaboration . . . and I have no hope of getting such measures through Congress unless there is public support for them."

He handed Molotov a letter addressed to Stalin.

. . . In the opinion of the United States Government the Crimean decision on Poland can only be carried out if a group of genuinely representative democratic Polish leaders are invited to Moscow for consultation. . . . The United States and British Governments have gone as far as they can to meet the situation and carry out the intent of the Crimean decisions in their joint message delivered to Marshal Stalin on April 18th . . .

The Soviet Government must realize that the failure to go forward at this time with the implementation of the Crimean decision on Poland would seriously shake confidence in the unity of the three Governments and their determination to continue the collaboration in the future as they have in the past.

Harry Truman

Molotov took the letter and said with his usual convoluted formality, "It is my hope that I express the views of the Soviet government in stating that it wishes to co-operate with the United States and Great Britain as before."

"I agree," Truman shot back. "Otherwise there would be no sense in the talk we are having."

Startled, Molotov went on to say that the basis of collaboration had been established and the three governments had been able to find a common language to settle differences. Moreover, the three governments had always dealt as equal parties and there had been no case when one or two had tried to impose their will on another.

"All we are asking," Truman said, "is that the Soviet government carry out the Crimea decision on Poland."

His frankness was most refreshing, Harriman thought. Leahy was also impressed.

Molotov replied a bit stiffly that his government stood by the Crimean decisions. "It is a matter of honor for us." The good relations that existed, he said, offered bright prospects for the future. "The Soviet government is convinced that all difficulties can be overcome."

Truman's nasal voice broke in. "An agreement has been reached on Poland and there is only one thing to do and that is for Marshal Stalin to carry out that agreement in accordance with his word."

Molotov replied that Stalin had given his views in the April 7 message. "I personally cannot understand why, if the three governments could reach an agreement on the question of the Yugoslav government, the same formula can not be applied in the case of Poland."

"An agreement *has* been reached on Poland," Truman said sharply. "It only requires to be carried out by the Soviet government."

Molotov was visibly ruffled. His government, he said, supported the Yalta agreements. "But I cannot agree that an abrogation of those decisions by others can be considered a violation by the Soviet government. Surely the Polish question, involving as it does a neighboring country, is of great interest to the Soviet government."

Truman refused to be put off the main issue. "The United States is prepared to carry out loyally all the agreements reached at Yalta and only asks that the Soviet government do the same." The United States wanted the friendship of Russia. "But I want it clearly understood that this can be only on a basis of the mutual observation of agreements and not on the basis of a one-way street."

For the first time Molotov showed anger. "I have never been talked to like that in my life!" he exclaimed.

"Carry out your agreements," said Truman, "and you won't get talked to like that."

### 3.

After taking Leipzig, Hodges had continued to the Mulde River—and stopped to wait for the Russians. Patton's forces were also approaching their stop zone, and a meeting with the Red Army was expected momentarily. On the morning of April 23 Sergeant Alex Balter of the 6th

Armored Division was calling on his SCR 506 over Channel 4160: "American forces approaching South Germany. Listen, Russian forces! This is the voice of your American allies now at Mittweida awaiting a meeting with you."

At 8:20 A.M. he repeated the same message several times. All at once a Russian voice began saying over and over again, "Bravo *Amerikansky!*" but was jammed by a loud rendition of *"Ach du lieber Augustin."*

At 9:30 A.M. Balter, who understood the language since his mother was Russian, made the second contact with the Red Army and gave his co-ordinates. While he was asking the Russians for their whereabouts, German music again burst through, and a voice started to condemn the enemies of the Fatherland and curse all Jew-lovers. This jamming was so loud and persistent that it wasn't until 1:10 P.M. that Balter heard Russian voices shouting another greeting in chorus. Finally a single Russian voice said facetiously, "Where are the Germans? They all seem to wait until they get good and hungry, and then the bastards start surrendering in large groups." The Russian refused to divulge his position. "We are proceeding toward the American lines," he said, and asked Balter for better identification than Mittweida.

"Chemnitz."

The Russian corrected Balter's pronunciation.

"Our forces are intact," Balter said. "We have reached our destination. Happy greetings. Blessings to our friends."

"Comrades tomorrow. Brothers tomorrow." There was a pause. "The great moment is tomorrow. Be watchful. Tomorrow morning. God be with you, our friends. Tomorrow, eight o'clock. Wait where you are, we're coming!" A little later another Russian voice said, "Third Army, Third Army, we are getting closer to you right now. More than that cannot be said *now*. Your Russian comrades are not sleeping. Much work is being done by us."

"Americans, quit your worrying," a German broke in sarcastically. "You'll meet up with your hoodlum Russian friends."

When the excited Balter reported the conversations, his commander said, "Balter, you aren't crapping me, are you?"

"Colonel Harris," said the sergeant, "I have been with you for three years and I haven't crapped you yet."

In spite of the Russian promises to Balter, no Red Army troops came forward the next day to make contact with Patton's army. Hodges' troops were even more impatient; they had been on the banks of the Mulde for over a week. By midafternoon a number of eager First Army officers offered to lead patrols out to the east—but were warned to restrain themselves.

The first to get the go-ahead was 1st Lieutenant Albert Kotzebue, Company G, 273rd Infantry Regiment, 69th Division. He was to take seven jeeps and a patrol east of the Mulde. He was told there had been frequent reports of Russian patrols wandering in the narrow strip of land between the Mulde and Elbe rivers. If he found any he was to arrange a meeting between their commander and Colonel C. M. Adams, whose regiment had recently taken the monument at Leipzig. But he was *not, repeat, not* to go more than two miles to the east.

Lieutenant Kotzebue—son of a Regular Army colonel of Russian descent—collected thirty-five men, crossed the Mulde and headed for the Elbe. After several miles he ran into about seventy-five Germans who wanted only to surrender. They were disarmed and told to march to the rear. It was about 5:30 P.M. when Kotzebue reached the limit of his patrol, Kühren.

Kotzebue radioed back to "Tryhard," code name for his regiment, and was ordered to scout another three miles in all directions. He found nothing but several German soldiers, plus a few Allied prisoners of war—abandoned by their guards—who waved and shouted at the passing patrol. In one house he came upon a mother, father and two children slumped over the dining table—they had taken poison. Kotzebue returned to Kühren, and since it was dark, decided to stay overnight.

The next morning, April 26, Kotzebue again led the patrol east—he had been told to contact the Russians and he was determined to do just that. Even though he had orders to go only three miles farther, he kept moving east toward the Elbe over the rolling country, tempted by each successive rise to go to the next. He stayed well ahead of his radio jeep, afraid he might be ordered back.

At the bunker Heinz Lorenz of the official German news agency reported to Hitler that he had just heard an announcement from a neutral country that Russians and Americans had met on the Mulde River. Minor conflicts had broken out regarding the sectors to be occupied, with the Russians accusing the Americans of infringing on area agreements made at Yalta.

Hitler sat upright, his eyes gleaming. He leaned back stiffly in his chair and said, "Gentlemen, that is again striking proof of the disunity of our enemies. Wouldn't the German people and history brand me as a criminal if I called a peace today while there is still the possibility that tomorrow our enemies might have a falling-out?" He seemed to gather strength as he continued. "Isn't it possible that every day—yes, every hour—war could still break out between the Bolsheviks and the Anglo-Saxons over their prey, Germany?" He turned toward Krebs and nodded imperceptibly. The Army Chief of Staff launched into his report, twice interrupted by Hitler: Where was Wenck? Was Manteuffel's Third Army assault making progress? To both questions, Krebs sheepishly gave the same answer, "No report."

At 10:30 A.M. Lieutenant Kotzebue was halfway between the Mulde and Elbe rivers. He continued on secondary dirt roads. An hour later his little force drove into a settlement only a mile from the Elbe. The Americans suddenly saw a horseman in a fur hat turn into a courtyard. Kotzebue gave chase excitedly and soon had him cornered. It was a Red Army cavalryman, who looked at them suspiciously. Through an interpreter Kotzebue asked where his commander was, but the Russian would only wave an arm to the east.

Within minutes the Americans were at the Elbe. A mile upstream they came to the village of Strehla. It seemed abandoned, and Kotzebue could see the wreckage of a pontoon bridge. Across the river figures were milling about. He halted the patrol and examined the people on the east bank through his field glasses. From their uniforms and the glint of medals he was sure they were Russians. He looked at his watch. It was exactly 12:05 P.M.

Kotzebue tried to make radio contact with the Soviets. When this failed he turned to his driver, PFC Edward Ruff, and told him to send up the recognition signal between Russians and Americans. Ruff fired two green flares from the launcher on the end of his carbine. Curious, the figures across the river only walked to the water's edge and stared across.

Kotzebue yelled, *"Amerikansky!"* There was still no answer. He decided he had to get across somehow. Seeing four boats chained together near the bank, he carefully balanced a grenade on the knotted chains and pulled the pin. Within a few minutes he was in a sailboat with Ruff, PFC John Wheeler, a machine gunner; Private Larry Hamlin, a rifleman; T/5 Stephen Kowalski, a medic who could speak Russian; and PFC Joseph Polowsky, a rifleman who could speak German. They started paddling across the river with boards and rifle butts. The current was swift but they finally reached the end of the pontoon bridge sticking out from the east bank. As the Americans jumped out, three Russians moved cautiously toward them down the steep bank. Kotzebue identified himself, and said he would like to arrange a meeting between the Russian and American commanders as soon as possible. The Red Army men broke into smiles and began enthusiastically slapping the Americans on the back.

While a photographer was taking pictures, a Russian officer with a chest full of medals drove up. It was Lieutenant Colonel Alexander T. Gardiev of the 175th Rifle Regiment. He returned Kotzebue's salute and held out his hand. It was historic, he said, a proud moment for both countries. Kotzebue agreed. A pudgy public relations officer walked up to the Americans and told them to go back across the river with a Russian photographer and recross the Elbe farther upstream to meet the commanding general of the 58th Guards Infantry Division.

The party climbed into the sailboat and began paddling furiously, but the first joint effort of Russians and Americans failed—the strong current swept them downstream. On the west bank, American jeeps followed the tossing sailboat until it finally reached the shore.

The group loaded into five jeeps and headed back south to a hand-drawn ferry several miles upriver. At 1:30 P.M. Kotzebue wrote out a message to be sent to his regimental commanding officer:

TO: CO TRYHARD

MISSION ACCOMPLISHED MAKING ARRANGEMENTS FOR MEETING BE- ...
TWEEN COS [commanding officers] PRESENT LOCATION (87–17) NO
CASUALTIES.

They were pulled back to the east bank of the Elbe, and as photographers were taking more pictures, Kotzebue heard someone say in English, "My God, there are some Yanks!" He looked around to see three liberated prisoners, two Americans and a Scotsman, whooping with joy. Over Russian objections, Kotzebue insisted that the three join them. The whole party was brought back to a Russian regimental headquarters, a big farmhouse, where a banquet table was already set up. Kotzebue took off his soaking shoes and socks to dry, and a celebration started.

During the first toasts Major General Vladimir Rusakov arrived; the 58th Guards Division commander was reserved and seemed reluctant to sit next to a twenty-one-year-old barefoot American lieutenant. More toasts were drunk to Roosevelt, Truman, Churchill and Stalin. Finally Rusakov left and the party became more relaxed. In fact, one American (an Indian) wrestled a Russian MP (an attractive young lady) to the floor, and only after a clout over the head by Kotzebue could he be dragged off the girl.

It took almost two hours for Kotzebue's message to reach regimental headquarters. When Colonel Adams read it he saw that Kotzebue had obviously violated orders in his eagerness to contact the Russians. With mixed feelings, the colonel informed Division. Major General Emil F. Reinhardt was confounded and irate. His superiors had explicitly ordered him not to send patrols more than five miles beyond the Mulde River lest some rash incident mar the link-up. Kotzebue had gone at least twenty-five.

Reinhardt wanted to confirm the meeting before passing such information to his superiors—he knew they would be as angry with him as he was with Kotzebue. He ordered a news blackout and asked his operations officer to fly over the scene of the reported meeting and confirm the story (unfortunately, the co-ordinates in Kotzebue's message were incorrect and would lead him five miles south of the actual location).

At 4 P.M. Adams received a second message from Kotzebue:

ARRANGEMENTS NOT COMPLETE. WILL CONTACT YOU LATER.

Adams had no idea that another regimental patrol, with orders only to check refugees, had also gone all the way to the Elbe. Early that afternoon

2nd Lieutenant William Robertson, intelligence officer of the 1st Battalion —a short, quiet young man—reached Torgau, which was twenty miles north of Kotzebue's first crossing. He had just picked up two liberated American prisoners from a nearby PW camp when a hail of small-arms fire raked them from the other side of the river. Robertson broke into a drugstore where he found red and blue paint and a white sheet. He painted a crude American flag, climbed the tower of the city's castle and hung it over a parapet. Down below he could see a bridge crumpled into the Elbe like a crushed toy. He waved his arms and shouted, "Cease fire . . . *Tovarisch!* American! *Amerikansky!* Russia! America!" By mistake he once shouted, *"Kamerad!"* but quickly followed it with "Do you have anyone there who can speak English?"

The firing ceased and he saw men emerging from debris across the Elbe. It occurred to him that they might have been firing just for the hell of it; there was certainly no opposition from his side of the river. One of the liberated American prisoners—Ensign Peck, of Peck & Peck —joined Robertson on the tower and stuck his head up. This brought another fusillade. Robertson kept waving and shouting until the firing stopped again and a green flare shot up from the east bank, followed by another—the recognition signal. Then Robertson ordered two of his men to get a Russian prisoner at the PW camp.

He kept calling out invitations to cross the river, and when no one came, he apologetically yelled that he had no flares. The Russians began shooting again at 3:20 P.M. and one antitank shell almost hit Robertson. In the middle of the barrage the Russian prisoner arrived and shouted to his countrymen. Several Red Army men started toward the collapsed bridge. Robertson and the others ran down the tower and into the street. In the lead, the Russian prisoner scrambled nimbly along the bent girders that led up and down precariously all the way to the other side; behind him came Robertson and Peck. On the east side, the Red Army men waited near the river bank but one finally began crawling out to meet the Robertson party.

This man and the Russian prisoner met not far from the east shore. After exchanging a few happy greetings, they passed each other. On hands and knees Robertson crept cautiously forward. He suddenly came face to face with the Red Army soldier but couldn't think of anything appropriate to say. He grinned and pounded his ally on the knees.

At 5:30 P.M., still ignorant of the second meeting at Torgau, Adams radioed Kotzebue:

HOLD IN ABEYANCE ARRANGEMENTS FOR MEETING UNTIL FURTHER ORDERS. REPORT BY COURIER NOT REPEAT NOT BY RADIO SIZE AND IDENTITY OF RUSSIAN UNIT. TIME AND PLACE OF CONTACT, TYPE

OF COMMUNICATION RUSS. UNIT HAS WITH ITS NEXT HIGHER HEAD-
QUARTERS. MAINTAIN CONTACT AND INFORM ME OF ANY MOVEMENT.

The next message Adams received, however, was not from Kotzebue
but from Major Fred Craig, the executive officer of his 2nd Battalion:

HAVE CONTACTED LT. KOTZEBUE WHO
IS IN CONTACT WITH THE RUSSIANS.

Adams was completely puzzled. Had Craig also patrolled as far as
the Elbe? Did he mean he had made physical contact, or what? Had
everyone gone crazy?

Two other patrols had been sent out with the same mission as Kotzebue—and with the same warning not to go more than five miles east. One
of these was Craig's patrol—four officers and forty-seven men. Like
Kotzebue, Craig had been probing farther and farther east, in spite of
two radio messages from Adams ordering him to stop. At 3 P.M. he ran
into Kotzebue's communications jeep a few miles from the Elbe and
learned that contact with the Russians had already been made.

Craig decided to keep going east. Suddenly, on a parallel road to the
right, he saw a line of horsemen heading west. The Americans stopped
in a cloud of dust and almost everyone shouted spontaneously, "Russians!"

The cavalrymen in the distance, together with several bicyclists and
motorcyclists, wheeled abruptly and began galloping directly toward the
Americans. PFC Igor Belousevitch—born in Harbin, China, of Russian
parents—grabbed his camera and took a picture. The first Russian was
a bicyclist. He pedaled furiously to within a few yards of the Americans,
and fell off. He grinned and stuck out his hand. It was 4:45 P.M.

Horsemen pulled up like a Wild West posse amid shouts of *"Amerikansky"* and *"Russky."* Belousevitch stepped up to a Red Army lieutenant and said in Russian, "I greet you in the name of the American Army
and our commanders on this historic occasion. It is a privilege and honor
to be here."

"This is a historic occasion," the Russian replied, almost as if delivering
a prepared speech. "It is a moment for which both our armies have been
fighting. It is a great honor for me to be here. It is wonderful that we have
met in this place. It is a moment which will go down in history."

While pictures were taken and cigarettes exchanged, an American
leaped on a horse and cavorted around like a cowboy. The Russian
lieutenant said his patrol had to proceed on its mission and Craig decided
to continue to the Elbe. He found the primitive ferry used by Kotzebue and
crossed the river. Clambering up the east bank, he was met by a short,
stocky general—it was Rusakov. Belousevitch saluted, identified the patrol
and introduced Craig.

Rusakov said warily, "Show me your papers and I'll show you mine."

Craig handed over his identification card. Intrigued by Belousevitch's division insignia, Rusakov asked, "What is that?"

"It's the 69th Division patch." Belousevitch pointed out the intertwined "6" and "9." Such lax security startled the general. "After all, the war is over," Belousevitch said. "We just put them on."

By 8 P.M. the bemused Colonel Adams still wondered whether Craig had made actual physical contact with Kotzebue's patrol. And he still knew nothing of Robertson's meeting at Torgau. Robertson, however, was just driving up in his jeep to the 1st Battalion command post—with four Russians. Major Victor Conley, the commander, chanced to be standing outside, and he figured Robertson had brought back a jeepful of drunken Russian or Polish refugees. He was about to give Robertson hell when the lieutenant introduced him to three Red Army officers and a noncom.

At first Conley couldn't believe it. Then he felt "as if the world had fallen in" on him. His first impulse was to give the Russians a bottle of whiskey, a pat on the back and send them back with a "nice knowing you." But he figured he might as well be "hanged for a sheep as a lamb," and phoned Colonel Adams to say he had four Red Army men at his CP. What should he do with them?

"My God!" Adams exclaimed, and after a pause ordered them all brought to Regiment. It was almost 9 P.M. when the group entered Adams' excited headquarters, which had gone "into an uproar" at the news.

As soon as Reinhardt heard that four Russians had been brought back, he exploded. How could it have happened! Orders had been not to go out over five miles. There was something wrong with an officer that couldn't tell five miles from twenty-five. He ordered everyone involved, including the Russians, brought to his headquarters so he could interrogate them personally.

He called his corps commander, General Huebner, who was just as explosive with Reinhardt. The agitated Huebner got in touch with Hodges, who phoned the startling information to Bradley. He received it calmly.

"Thanks, Courtney, thanks again for calling," he said. "We've been waiting a long time. The Russians certainly took their own sweet time in coming those seventy-five miles from the Oder." He hung up, opened a Coke and circled Torgau on his wall map.

### 4.

In Washington, Ambassador Winant informed Truman after lunch that Churchill wanted to talk to him over the transatlantic telephone about an offer Himmler had submitted through the Swedish government, to surrender all German forces on the western front. The President phoned Marshall, who suggested that the call be taken at the communications center in the Pentagon.

Major General John E. Hull, chief of Marshall's Operations Division, set up arrangements for use of the scrambler system and phoned Acting Secretary of State Joseph Grew at the State Department to get some information, but he knew nothing more about it. He was unaware that a long radiogram from Minister H. V. Johnson of the U. S. embassy in Stockholm was being decoded in another part of the building.

Truman, Leahy, Marshall, King, Hull and Colonel Richard Park gathered in the Pentagon communications room, and at 2:10 P.M. everyone heard Churchill say, "Is that you, Mr. President?"

"This is the President, Mr. Prime Minister."

"How glad I am to hear your voice."

"Thank you very much, I am glad to hear yours," said Truman.

"I have several times talked to Franklin but . . . Have you received the report from Stockholm by your ambassador?" Churchill said he had received a detailed report from Sir Victor Mallet, the British ambassador to Sweden, and imagined Truman had received a similar one from Johnson. Truman thought he was referring to the information received from Winant and didn't know that Grew had just left the State Department with the decoded message from Minister Johnson. He said, "Yes, I have."

"On that proposal?"

"Yes. I have just a short message [the Winant message] saying that there was such a proposal in existence."

"Yes, of course," Churchill said, still thinking Truman had heard from Johnson. "We thought it looked very good."

"Has he anything to surrender?"

Puzzled by Truman's lack of comprehension, Churchill said Italy and Yugoslavia were mentioned, as well as the western front, ". . . but he [Himmler] hasn't proposed to surrender on the eastern front. So we thought perhaps it would be necessary to report it to Stalin. That is, of course, to say that in our view the surrender must be simultaneous to agree to our terms."

If Churchill was a bit vague, Truman was not. "I think he should be forced to surrender to all three governments—Russia, you and the United States. I don't think we ought to even consider a piecemeal surrender."

"No, no, no," Churchill said quickly. "Not a piecemeal surrender to a man like Himmler. Himmler will be speaking for the German state as much as anybody can. And therefore we thought that his negotiations must be carried on with the three governments."

"That's right. That's the way I feel exactly."

"I see, of course, that's local surrender on the front, Himmler's allied front. And then Eisenhower is still authorized to make the surrender—well, then he will wish to surrender."

"Yes, of course."

Truman at last realized that they were referring to two different messages and said, "I haven't received the message from Stockholm. This information that you are giving me now is the only information that I have on the subject, except that I was informed that your conversation was based on a message that you had from Stockholm."

"I see," said Churchill. He quoted the message he had received from Stockholm and said he felt it was their duty to tell Stalin about Himmler's offer.

"I think so too," said Truman. "Have you notified Stalin?"

"I held it up for about two hours, hoping to get an answer to the telegram I sent you . . ." That telegram was still being processed, but Grew was just approaching the Pentagon with the message from Johnson. "But I have now released the telegram. This is the telegram I have sent . . ."

Truman paid no attention to the fact that Churchill had acted on his own, and interrupted with "All right, then you notify Stalin, and I shall do the same immediately, of this conversation between us."

"Exactly. Here is what I have said to Stalin and I have telegraphed it over to you: 'THE TELEGRAM IMMEDIATELY FOLLOWING IS ONE I HAVE JUST RECEIVED EXACTLY FROM THE BRITISH AMBASSADOR IN SWEDEN. THE PRESIDENT OF THE UNITED STATES HAS THE NEWS ALSO.' I thought you had gotten it. Your telegram has not gotten through?"

"No, I haven't received my telegram as yet."

Churchill continued quoting his message to Stalin: " 'THERE CAN BE NO QUESTION AS FAR AS HIS MAJESTY'S GOVERNMENT IS CONCERNED, ARRANGING THUS AN UNCONDITIONAL SURRENDER SIMULTANEOUSLY TO THE THREE MAJOR POWERS.' "

"I agree to that fully," said Truman.

" 'WE CONSIDER HIMMLER SHOULD BE TOLD THAT GERMAN FORCES EITHER AS INDIVIDUALS OR IN UNITS SHOULD EVERYWHERE SURRENDER THEMSELVES TO THE ALLIED TROOPS OR REPRESENTATIVES ON THE SPOT. UNTIL THIS HAPPENS, THE ATTACK OF THE ALLIES UPON THEM ON ALL SIDES AND IN ALL THEATRES WHERE RESISTANCE CONTINUES WILL BE PROSECUTED WITH THE UTMOST VIGOUR. NOTHING IN THE ABOVE SHOULD AFFECT THE RELEASE OF OUR ORATIONS.' "

None of the Americans could make any sense out of the last sentence. By "orations" Churchill meant "announcements" and he had also neglected to add three words that ended the actual message—ON THE LINK-UP.*

* The message Stalin received was worded differently in half a dozen places. This entire phone conversation comes from an American transcript and the reception together with Churchill's lisp probably accounted for the mistakes.

"I sent it off a few minutes ago," Churchill continued. "And I was sending it to you with the following telegram from me, you see. That which I read you. I called the War Cabinet together at once and they approved of this telegram I've just read you."

"I approve of it too."

"The one I sent Stalin?"

"I approve of that telegram you sent to Stalin, and I shall immediately wire Stalin on exactly the same line."

"Thank you so much. That is exactly what I wanted." At least one of the listening Americans, General Hull, doubted this. He felt that Churchill was trying to sound out the President on a possible deal with Himmler without Russian participation. "I'm delighted," Churchill said. "I am sure we would be pretty well in agreement, and I hope that Stalin will wire back and say, 'I AGREE TOO.' In which case we could authorize our representatives in Stockholm to tell Bernadotte that you will pass on the message to Himmler. Because nothing can be done about that until we are all three agreed on it."

"All right."

"Thank you very much, indeed."

"Thank you," said the President.

"You remember those speeches we were going to make about the link-up in Europe?"

Truman was still puzzled. "I didn't understand that last statement, Mr. Prime Minister."

"You know what I am talking about—the speech, the statements that are written. Well, I think they should be let out just as they would be anyhow as soon as the link-up occurs."

"I think you're right on that," Truman replied, finally comprehending. "I agree with that. . . . I hope to see you someday soon."

"I'm planning to. I'll be sending you some telegrams about that quite soon. I entirely agree with all that you've done on the Polish situation. We are walking hand in hand together."

"Well, I want to continue just that."

"In fact, I am following your lead, backing up whatever you do on the matter."

"Thank you. Good night."


At 8 P.M. the President began his radio address to the delegates at the opening session of the United Nations Conference in San Francisco. Never had there been a more necessary meeting, he said. "You members of the conference are to be the architects of the better world. In your hands rests our future. By your labors at this conference we shall know if suffering humanity is to achieve a just and lasting peace . . .

"This conference will devote its energies and its labors exclusively to the single problem of setting up the essential organization to keep the peace. You are to write the fundamental charter.

"The essence of our problem here, is to provide sensible machinery for the settlement of disputes among nations.

"We must build a new world, a far better world—one in which the eternal dignity of man is respected . . ."

Two days later the Big Three announced simultaneously that the American and Russian armies had met, and the world was soon deluged with details of Lieutenant Robertson's meeting at Torgau. When he and his three enlisted companions presented Eisenhower with the homemade flag they had waved at the Russians, the Supreme Commander—in the belief that they had made the first contact—promoted them all one grade on the spot.*

* In *Crusade in Europe,* Eisenhower still calls Torgau the first meeting place. Those who made the historic first meeting at Strehla were not promoted. Lieutenant Kotzebue never even received the medal his superior officers announced he got.

# PART FOUR

❦❦❦

## *Wingless Victory*

═══════════════════════════════════

# 26

## "Pheasant Hunt"

**1.**

With the junction of U. S. and Russian forces, Hitler's Reich was cut in two. The southern segment, now under the command of Feldmarschall Kesselring, consisted of southeastern Germany, about half of Czechoslovakia, the bulk of Austria, the western corner of Yugoslavia and northern Italy. Kesselring's eastern front was holding remarkably well all the way from Dresden to the Adriatic Sea, but the entire western sector was on the verge of collapse.

The northern half of Germany was in an even more precarious situation. Hitler had put it in charge of the commander in chief of the Navy, Grossadmiral Karl Dönitz. It too covered a large area: Norway, Denmark, about half of Prussia, and a number of *Festungen* in the east. Berlin itself was about to become the last *Festung;* Konev and Zhukov were within hours of surrounding the old Prussian capital.

At two-thirty in the morning of April 26, Keitel radioed Dönitz at his headquarters in Plön, some fifty miles above Hamburg:

THE BATTLE FOR BERLIN IS TO BE A FIGHT FOR GERMAN DESTINY. . . . YOU ARE TO SUPPORT THE BATTLE FOR BERLIN. . . . SUCH SUPPORT IS TO BE MOVED BY AIR TRANSPORT INTO THE CITY ITSELF AND BY LAND AND WATER ROUTES TO THE FRONT BEFORE BERLIN . . .

Half an hour later Keitel radioed Schörner, whose troops were just south of where the Russians and the Americans had met:

ARMY GROUP CENTER, AFTER HAVING FIRST CLARIFIED THE SITUA-
TION, IS TO ATTACK NORTHWARD BETWEEN BAUTZEN AND DRESDEN
IN ORDER TO RELIEVE BERLIN . . .

What Keitel asked of both men was an impossibility, but by dawn reports that Berlin would soon be liberated spread through the city and
even the realistic General Weidling, now in charge of the defense of
Berlin, wrote in his diary, "The day of hope!"

Time and again Krebs called Weidling, always with "good news":
Army Wenck was driving to the rescue of Hitler; three strong, well-armed
battalions "had arrived"; and Dönitz was flying the best personnel from
the submarine training centers to the capital.

Weidling's optimism dissipated once he started his daily round of
inspection. At the huge anti-aircraft control tower near the Zoo, Oberst
(Colonel) Hans-Oscar Wöhlerman, the new artillery commander of Berlin, told Weidling he could only reach his sections by the regular telephone.
The walls of Wöhlerman's office were covered with detailed maps indicating the radius of action and maximum range of artillery, but they were
useless because he had no communications net. Wöhlerman said he had
few prime movers for his artillery, and the supply of ammunition was
dwindling. It was a lucky day when more than one shell per gun was
delivered by air.

Weidling found similar despair at almost every command post in the
city and he returned to his own headquarters after dark, exhausted and
disgusted. From recently captured prisoners he knew that he was now
being attacked by two or three Russian tank armies and at least two
infantry armies. He phoned Krebs and told him that the enemy had just
made deep penetrations into the city, in the west, southwest and east.
Even this didn't faze Krebs; he prophesied that Wenck would break
through in a few hours.

At dark Weidling made another tour of Berlin. The Potsdamerplatz
and Leipzigerstrasse were under such heavy artillery fire that dust from
pulverized brick and stone rose like heavy fog. The streets, littered with
rubble and pocked with huge craters, were deserted. Progress by car was
so difficult that the general got out and walked. When the artillery barrage increased in tempo, he descended to the U-bahn (subway) and followed the tracks to the next station, which was jammed with frightened
civilians.

Terrified or not, the Berliners still lived on hope. Wenck was coming
to the rescue! Their excitement rose as report after report over the radio
marked out his steady progress.

But, in truth, only one corps, the XXth, was attacking toward the
capital, and its limited mission was to reach Potsdam and provide a corridor of retreat for the Berlin garrison. The bulk of Wenck's army was still
driving east to save Busse.

"When we have done this," Wenck told Colonel Reichhelm, his chief of staff, "then we'll move back to the Elbe and turn our armies over to the Americans. That will be our last mission." U. S. and British air attacks on his troops had unaccountably stopped and Wenck hoped this meant that the West was about to join them in an attack against the Bolsheviks.

Thirty miles to Wenck's east Busse's surrounded Ninth Army was moving west slowly, painfully, the exhausted men spurred only by a responsibility for the crowds of refugees in their midst and the hope that they would soon meet Wenck.

Busse paid no attention to the OKW dispatch, either, ordering him to join Wenck in a drive to Berlin. They were a huge ambulating *Kessel* ("cauldron," here: surrounded group, or pocket) and it would be a miracle if they could even reach Wenck. Fortunately Busse knew the sandy, wooded territory south of Berlin from his youth and military training in the "Kaiser's Sand Box" and he deftly led the group through the trees, screened from enemy bombers and tanks.

Inside the *Kessel* was a mobile community—men, women, children, horses, trucks, carts, beds, sewing machines, cartons of food and baggage. Strangely, there was no panic. The civilians knew they were surrounded but they were alive, the weather was mild, there was enough to eat and they had complete confidence in the military leaders.

Among those in the great *Kessel* were survivors from Frankfurt an der Oder. Four days before, Biehler, recently promoted to general, had driven a corridor through the surrounding Russians, and 30,000 wounded and civilians from the *Festung* had escaped to the main body of the Ninth Army.

For two days General von Greim had been trying to get into besieged Berlin to report to Hitler. At six o'clock in the evening he guided a Fiesler-Storch down the bomb-pocked runway of Gatow Airport. In the rear was Hanna Reitsch, the famed test pilot, as ardent a National Socialist as Greim. The little plane took off again and, at treetop level, headed toward the Reich Chancellery, fifteen miles away. Overhead the sky raged with dogfights. Suddenly a gaping hole appeared in the flooring of the cockpit and Greim slumped over. As the plane plunged down, out of control, Hanna reached over the wounded Greim and grabbed the stick. Somehow she managed to right the Storch and make a safe landing on the broad avenue running through the Brandenburg Gate. She commandeered a car and helped Greim aboard.

First to greet her in the bunker was an old friend, Magda Goebbels, who embraced her affectionately, and tearfully expressed her astonishment that someone still had enough courage and loyalty to come to the Führer's side—all but a handful were deserting.

Hanna went to the dispensary, where Hitler's own doctor was ministering to Greim, whose right foot was shattered. A little later the Führer entered, his face exuding gratitude. "Do you know why I called you?" he asked Greim.

"No, my Führer."

"Because Hermann Göring has betrayed and deserted both me and his Fatherland. Behind my back he made contact with the enemy—that shows you what a sneak he is." His head was sagging, and his hands trembled. He showed Greim the telegram Göring had sent. "An ultimatum, a blatant ultimatum! Now there's nothing left. Look what I have to go through: no allegiances are kept, no honor lived up to; there are no disappointments, no betrayals, that I have not experienced, and now this above all." He stopped, unable to go on. He looked at Greim with half-closed eyes and said in a very low voice, "I hereby declare you Göring's successor as Oberbefehlshaber der Luftwaffe. In the name of the German people I give you my hand."

Both Greim and Hanna grasped his hands and begged to be allowed to remain in the bunker to atone for Göring's deceit. Moved, Hitler told them they could stay. Their decision to do so, he said, would long be remembered in the history of the Luftwaffe.

Later that evening Hitler summoned Hanna to his quarters. "Hanna," he said in a small voice, "you belong to those who will die with me. Each of us has a vial of poison such as this." He gave her two capsules, one for herself, one for Greim. "I don't want any of us to be captured by the Russians, nor do I wish our bodies to be found by them. Each person is responsible for destroying his own body so that nothing recognizable remains. Eva and I will have our bodies burned. You will devise your own method."

She burst into tears. "Save yourself, my Führer, that is what every German wants!"

But Hitler shook his head. "As a soldier I must obey my own command to defend Berlin to the last." He began to walk around the little room in quick, stumbling strides, his hands clasped behind him. "By staying, I believed that all the troops of the Fatherland would follow my example and come to the rescue of the city." He turned to her, his face suddenly buoyant. "But, my Hanna, I still have hope! The army of General Wenck is moving up from the south. He must and will drive the Russians back long enough to save our people. Then we will fall back to hold again!"

## 2.

By dawn of the following day, April 27, Berlin was completely encircled and the last two airports—Gatow and Tempelhof—were overrun by the Red Army. But a flurry of optimism swept through the bunker when a radiogram arrived from Wenck, announcing that his XX Corps had reached Ferch a few miles below Potsdam.

Goebbels' office immediately proclaimed over the radio that Wenck had reached Potsdam itself and predicted that he would soon be in Berlin. And if Wenck made it to Berlin, why not Busse?

"The situation has changed decisively in our favor," Berliners were told. "The Americans are marching toward Berlin. The great change of the war is at hand. Berlin must be held till Army Wenck arrives, no matter at what costs!" The daily Army communiqué, which was also broadcast in the clear, divulged further details:

"The Supreme Headquarters of the Army announces: 'In this heroic battle of Berlin, the fight for life against Bolshevism once more is illustrated before the whole world. While the capital defended itself in a way never known before in history, our troops on the Elbe River did an about-face and relieved the defenders of Berlin. These divisions from the west pushed back the enemy during heavy fights along a wide front and reached Ferch.' "

Wenck could hardly believe that his exact position was so flagrantly revealed. "We won't be able to move a single step farther tomorrow!" he exclaimed to his chief of staff. The Russians must have heard the same broadcast and would concentrate everything they had at Ferch. It was, he said, almost a betrayal.

After the noon conference Hitler pinned an Iron Cross on a small, heavy-eyed boy who had blown up a Russian tank. The youngster silently turned and walked to the corridor, where he crumpled to the floor. He was fast asleep. Krebs's two aides—Freytag von Loringhoven and Boldt—were so affected by the scene that they began to complain of the unbearable situation. Bormann came up behind them and draped his arms familiarly around their shoulders. He told them that there was still hope: Wenck was on the way and would soon relieve Berlin. "You, who stayed here and kept faith with our Führer through his darkest hours," he said unctuously, "you will, when this fight is victoriously ended, be invested with high rank in the Reich, and you will receive huge estates in reward for your faithfulness." The two aides gaped incredulously at him. They had "never before heard anything like this." As professional soldiers they had always been treated with the greatest suspicion by Bormann and his people.

Hanna Reitsch spent much of the day in Goebbels' suite. He seemed unable to forget Göring's treachery. "That bastard has always set himself up as the Führer's greatest supporter and now he doesn't have the courage to stand by him," he said as he limped about the room, waving his hands. He called Göring an incompetent: he had destroyed the Fatherland with his stupidity and now he wanted to lead the entire nation. "By this alone he proves that he was never truly one of us, that at heart he was always weak and a traitor."

He gripped the back of a chair as if it were a lectern, and proclaimed that those in the bunker were making history and dying for the glory of the Reich so that the name of Germany would live forever.

Hanna thought Goebbels was too theatrical, but she had only admiration for his wife. In the presence of her six children she was always cheerful; when she felt her self-control slipping she left the room. "My dear Hanna," she said, "you must help me to help the children out of this life. They belong to the Third Reich and to the Führer, and if those two things cease to exist, there will be no place for them. But you must help me. My greatest fear is that at the last moment I will be too weak."

Hanna told the children stories of her flying experiences and taught them songs which they later sang to "Uncle Führer," who assured them that the Russians would soon be driven away—tomorrow they could once more play in the garden.

Hanna also visited with Eva Braun, and thought she was a shallow woman who spent most of her time polishing her fingernails, changing her clothes and combing her hair. "Poor, poor Adolf," Eva would say over and over again, "deserted by everyone, betrayed by all. Better that ten thousand others die than he be lost to Germany."

The telephone conversation between Churchill and Truman was top secret but somehow it leaked out; American newspapers announced a reported offer of surrender to the West by "a group of highly placed Nazis acting without authority of Hitler but with the backing of the High Command." Himmler's name was not mentioned and the source of the story was not revealed.

In the evening Weidling tried to get Hitler to realize that Berlin was completely surrounded and that the circle of defense was fast shrinking. It wouldn't even be possible, he said, to get supplies by air any longer. He began talking of the misery of the civilians and the wounded, but Krebs interrupted and started his own report. Goebbels' assistant, Dr. Naumann, was called to the phone and informed of the alleged surrender offer to the West. He returned to the conference room and whispered something to Hitler, who then exchanged a few urgent but subdued words with Goebbels.

Weidling was dismissed and went to the anteroom, where he found Bormann, Burgdorf, Axmann, Hewel, the Führer's adjutants and two women secretaries chatting casually. Frustrated in the conference room, Weidling turned to the group and poured out all the things that Krebs and Hitler had refused to hear. Their only hope, he said, was to leave Berlin before it was too late. A breakout from this *Kessel* could only succeed if there was a simultaneous attack from the outside, and with

Wenck already near Potsdam it had to be executed within the next forty-eight hours. Everyone agreed, even Bormann.

This encouraged Weidling to repeat his suggestion to Krebs as soon as he came out of the conference room. Krebs too was receptive and said he could present the breakout plan in detail to the Führer the next evening.

Fifty-five miles away at Army Wenck headquarters a radio operator was tapping out a message to Weidling: COUNTERATTACK OF THE TWELFTH ARMY IS STALLED SOUTH OF POTSDAM. TROOPS ARE ENGAGED IN VERY HEAVY DEFENSIVE FIGHTING. SUGGEST BREAK THROUGH TO US. WENCK.

The operator waited for acknowledgment, but none came.

At Dönitz's headquarters in northern Germany, Count Schwerin von Krosigk made a long entry in his diary, which was, in effect, a postmortem of National Socialism. His views were of course private, but they reflected the conclusions of a great many Germans who longed for a solution to a war already lost.

It is a pity that a man with the talents, authority and popularity of Göring should not have utilized all those qualities during the war, instead of neglecting things and letting himself be dominated by his passion for hunting and collecting. . . . Meanwhile he was resting on the laurels his Luftwaffe had earned during the first years of the war. He alone was responsible for the failure to provide fighter planes in time to protect the Reich from the aerial terror. Warnings and remonstrances went unheeded. Since we lost the war militarily as a result of the Luftwaffe's failure, Göring must be regarded as responsible for the disaster that has befallen the German people. The main responsibility in the political field lies with Ribbentrop. It was he who by his conceit and lack of moderation alienated the neutral powers . . .

Others responsible are men like Erich Koch. His criminally false policies in the east made us appear not as liberators but as oppressors. As a result, those from the Ukraine and other parts of Russia refused to collaborate or even fight with us; instead, they became partisans and fought fanatically against us. Finally, men like Bormann, whom I consider the Führer's evil spirit, the shadowy "brown" eminence. . . . Bormann gave the Party too much prominence—the Party was even allowed to organize the Volkssturm, with the results known to everybody. Party rivalries sharpened the lust for power of the nonentities of the Party, and the political divergencies existing between Party members, often of doubtful character, grew boundless. . . . So finally, large parts of the loyal and brave German population hailed the invading armies of the Western Powers as liberators, not only from the bombing terror but from the terror of the big shots . . .

## 3.

Munich, the birthplace of National Socialism, was the most important German city left in the southern pocket. By late afternoon of April 27 it faced two threats: one from the outside and one from within. The U. S. Seventh Army of General Patch was fast approaching, and in the heart of the city itself, at Army District VII headquarters, a small band of German soldiers was preparing to seize Munich from the Nazis and turn it over to the Allies.

Their leader was Hauptmann (Captain) Rupprecht Gerngross, commander of a company of interpreters. He had returned from Russia with a second battle wound in the bitter winter of 1941, and became head of the 280 interpreters in the Munich area. Ever since then, he had cautiously been organizing a resistance group.

Gerngross was a large, heavy-set young man; he was also scholarly, cultured and good-natured—a most unlikely combination for a revolutionist. He was born in Shanghai but his family moved to Munich when he was eleven. He studied law at the University of Munich, then attended the London School of Economics under Professor Harold J. Laski and received his doctorate in 1939.

Using the 280 interpreters as a nucleus for his underground unit, which in the fall of 1944 had been given the name "Freedom Action Bavaria," Gerngross sought recruits from civilian intellectuals and professional men. He held regular meetings at his home. With the help of two collaborators, Leo Heuwing and Otto Heinz Leiling—like him, young officers who had been wounded in Russia—contact was established with similar circles in Munich whose members included lawyers, professors, judges, municipal officers, physicians and dentists.

In addition to his own interpreters company, Gerngross now controlled several other small military units as well as workers from the Agfa, Steinheil and Kustermann factories, but he knew that it would be difficult to overthrow the city: the Gauleiter of Munich, Kesselring's chief of staff and General Franz Ritter von Epp, the chief Reich executive in Bavaria, would all have to be captured, and radio stations and newspapers seized.

It was a complex plan, but Gerngross was convinced that it could be successful if carried out with the co-operation of General Patch. Two messengers had already been sent to Patch to inform him of the impending uprising and to request cessation of all air raids on Munich so that last-minute preparations for revolt could be more easily made. The air raids did stop, and Gerngross was sure Patch understood his plan and would enter Munich as soon as FAB seized it and declared it an open city.

On the evening of April 27 Gerngross sat deep in thought in his damp, stuffy barracks bedroom while a clerk typed out the last orders. Word had already been sent to outlying areas that "Pheasant Hunt," the military operation, would begin at 2 A.M. the next morning.

For months Gerngross and his family had been living in fear of discovery. Now his pregnant wife and child were hiding in a mountain cabin. Gerngross himself had taken special precautions. Under his bed was a rope so that he might be able to escape down the wall and reach a waiting car in seconds. Several times Heuwing had been tempted to give the alarm just to see the huge Gerngross clambering down the rope.

At 7 P.M. the interpreters company was assembled. The master sergeant, smiling broadly, looked into Gerngross's room and said, "Company ready to defend Munich, sir."

Gerngross walked out and surveyed his men. "The moment has come," he said. "We're going to do something to liberate ourselves. We are going to end the senseless fighting and devastation of our country." He said he would understand if anyone wanted to back out. "But whoever follows me now must stick it out to the end. I hereby release you from your oath to Hitler!"

The response was unanimous. Even the few Nazis who had been purposely kept in the company to allay suspicion were caught up in the enthusiasm and volunteered. Strips of white cloth were passed out. Just before 2 A.M. they were to be tied around the left arm.

All over the city the military groups in the conspiracy began moving into position. Leutnant Betz and a platoon of Battalion 61 started for Pullach to seize General Westphal; Leutnant Putz and his platoon from Battalion 19 headed for the main government building to arrest Gauleiter Paul Giesler. Other units set out for the Rathaus, the office of two newspapers—*Münchner Neueste Nachrichten* and the National Socialist organ, *Völkischer Beobachter,* and two radio stations: Radio Munich in the northern outskirts of the city, and one at Erding twenty miles to the northeast.

Heuwing and about twenty men drove south to Lake Starnberg in cars and an old truck; their mission was to destroy communication facilities of the High Command at Kempfenhausen. Just before midnight they reached the parking area near the enlisted men's quarters. Heuwing strolled into the barracks, said he was looking for someone and examined every floor to see how many soldiers were there; the building was almost empty. He returned to his convoy to wait until 2 A.M.

Just after midnight Gerngross and Leiling, followed by a platoon in trucks, drove up to the home of General von Epp in a Mercedes stolen from a high-ranking Nazi. They were stopped at a small guardhouse and Gerngross told the desk sergeant that he wanted to speak to Major Carraciola, Epp's adjutant—who was one of the conspirators; then he took out a knife and slashed the wires of the switchboard.

The startled guards put up no resistance; some even offered to join the uprising. When Carraciola came out he was aghast. "For God's sake—did you really do it?"

Gerngross walked into the big house with Leiling. Epp was in a meeting with civil officials. Carraciola brought the elderly, aristocratic general into the hall. In 1919 Epp had helped overthrow the brief Communist regime in Munich and was still a popular figure.

"You are a prisoner of Freedom Action Bavaria," said Gerngross.

The haughty Epp was unimpressed.

"Look here," Gerngross said impatiently. "You have a natural responsibility to wipe out your brown [Nazi] past and do something for the Bavarian people. We want you to sign a declaration of surrender for southern Bavaria."

Epp turned to his adjutant. "How could I possibly hand myself over to a captain?"

Gerngross, amused, suggested that they to go Freising, where there was a FAB major named Braun.

"And if I refuse to come along?" said Epp.

"Then we'll simply take you like a prisoner."

Gerngross put Leiling in charge of General von Epp and drove through a cold drizzle to his command post under a railroad bridge in the northern part of Munich. He was told that both radio stations had been seized intact, and left immediately for Radio Munich to make a broadcast. Just before dawn he took the microphone and read a prepared speech which outlined the major objectives of FAB and ended with an impassioned plea to join the uprising.

So far everything had gone as planned. At exactly 2 A.M. Heuwing and ten men entered the enlisted men's barracks at Kempfenhausen and said, "Hands up!" Again there was no resistance and several offered to help destroy the telephone and telegraph center.

But the early successes were misleading. By 9 A.M. reports coming in to Gerngross indicated that the conspiracy was running into serious difficulties. The platoon assigned to capture General Westphal had met with such fierce resistance from an SS unit that they had to flee. And when Leutnant Putz's platoon descended on the government building to kidnap Gauleiter Giesler they had been met by a barrage of hand grenades, and after a bitter fight they too were forced to withdraw empty-handed.

But there were also reports of widespread popular support—the crews at the Schleissheim airport had destroyed their planes, an entire division had offered to surrender and some troops were throwing weapons into the Amper and Glonn rivers. To the people of Munich the uprising was a success. The white-blue flag of Bavaria flew over the Marienplatz and thousands of civilians, upon hearing the Gerngross broadcast, began demonstrating in the streets. Many assumed Hitler was dead and telephoned the good news to friends. The streets were crowded with people shouting, "The war is over!"

But at 9:56 A.M. an announcer of the South Germany radio station interrupted its regular program to say, "You will now hear a message by the Gauleiter of München-Oberbayern." Then Giesler himself spoke: "Gauleiter Paul Giesler addresses the following explanation to all fellow

Germans concerning the activities of a treasonable transmitter in our area: Some contemptible scoundrels belonging to a company of interpreters under the command of a Captain Gerngross are trying to convey the impression that they have assumed power in Munich." It was all a lie, he said, and the traitors would soon be rounded up.

Fifteen minutes later Gerngross was back on the air again in an attempt to offset Giesler. He said General von Epp had surrendered all Bavaria and asked the people to help "the new leaders bring life back to normal as quickly as possible." Gerngross spoke in good faith, but the uprising had taken another bad turn. Epp had been on the verge of capitulating to Major Braun in Freising, when he heard Gerngross broadcast that FAB was pledged to abolish the military. It was more than the old general could stand and he absolutely refused to co-operate. Major Braun became so annoyed that he sent "the old fool" back to his home.

By noon the revolt, which had begun with such purpose, was at the point of disintegration. The South-West German Home Service flooded the air with announcements about traitors who had seized Radio Munich. "The criminal elements under the so-called leadership of a Captain Gerngross have been rendered harmless," one announcer said, and introduced Giesler, who told of the abortive attempt to seize him.

"Do not take this Gerngross nonsense seriously," he went on. "Not a word of it is true, but I call upon you to display your loyalty and love of our Fatherland, which you people of Munich in particular have shown to such a marked degree in the trying times of this war. . . . These contemptible scoundrels, who, during this hardest hour, want to besmirch the name of Germany, will soon be shot and wiped out. The people of Munich, however, will never turn against the brave soldiers who are fighting the enemy. The people of Munich will always think of the dead they have lost and will never be deflected from their loyalty to Germany and to Adolf Hitler! In this loyalty and love we abide! Long live Germany! Long live the Führer! Heil!"

Giesler was rapidly regaining his power over the city. Sixteen prominent members of FAB and the parents of Gerngross were jailed, and by 2 P.M. Gerngross himself admitted that further resistance was impossible. He sent out word that the uprising was over and that it was every man for himself. Gerngross and three accomplices escaped from the city in a car bearing SS plates.

The uprising was over, but the unrest created by FAB was not. Army barracks were scenes of disorder and near mutiny. It was almost impossible to organize any but the most stanch National Socialists. The situation was so chaotic that some front-line units were withdrawn. By midnight even Giesler was forced to abandon his own headquarters. The roads to the south and east were jammed with troops and officials trying to escape the three U. S. infantry divisions—the 3rd, 42nd and 45th—converging on the city.

And in the end Gerngross did attain his goal—although not in the way he had hoped. The Americans marched triumphantly into a city of cheering Germans, armed only with flowers.

# 27

# An "Italian Solution"

**1.**

With the enemy pushing into German soil from east and west, it finally became clear to more and more Germans that they could not possibly win the war. Attempts to capitulate became more numerous and the men involved, ranging from Himmler to Gerngross, were inspired by a variety of motives.

On March 1 a chief of state had endeavored to open negotiations with the West: Benito Mussolini sent his son Vittorio to Ildefonso Cardinal Schuster, the Archbishop of Milan, with a verbal proposition. The Cardinal asked that the offer be put in writing, and in mid-March young Mussolini returned to Milan with a document entitled "Proposals for Negotiations from the Head of the State." In it Mussolini offered to surrender to the Allied High Command "to avoid inflicting further sufferings on the population of northern Italy, to preserve what remains of the industrial and agricultural patrimony from total destruction . . ." and thus save his country from Communism. Mussolini further promised to dissolve the Republican Fascist Party, with the understanding that those who had taken the oath to the Italian Socialist Republic would not be persecuted "by the tribunal now functioning for this purpose in Rome."

The Vatican's interest in a surrender was three-fold: it wanted to spare the people of northern Italy from the horrors of a last desperate stand by the Germans and Fascists; to preserve the nation's industrial structure; and to prevent a Communist take-over. For some months Colonel Dollmann, who was acting on General Wolff's behalf, had been discussing the possibility of a negotiated peace with Cardinal Schuster, who was the channel to the Vatican. The Cardinal had promised to act as mediator between Wolff and the Italian partisans if the Germans spared industrial plants in northern Italy.

Cardinal Schuster forwarded the proposal to the Allies through the Apostolic Nuncio in Berne, but by April 6 Mussolini still had received no answer. On that day, however, he read a news report originating in Switzerland, of another peace move. This, of course, was Operation "Sunrise" and the report was remarkably close to the truth.

German troops in Milan received orders on Wednesday (April 4) not to leave their barracks. According to neo-Fascist and Nazi circles this measure is connected with negotiations initiated to determine the fate of the German Army in Italy. Two members of the partisan movement have been liberated and taken to the frontier. They allegedly carried definite proposals. One of these individuals is Ferruccio Parri, head of the military section of the National Committee of Liberation for Northern Italy. Parri had been arrested in Milan, and imprisoned by the SS at Verona.

Puzzled and perturbed, Mussolini summoned Dr. Rudolf Rahn, the German ambassador to Italy, and demanded an explanation. Rahn, of course, knew and approved of "Sunrise" but pretended ignorance. He warned Wolff of the Duce's uneasiness.

The next day Rahn and Wolff called on Mussolini at his headquarters on Lake Garda. The Duce began talking at length of a plan to stage a last desperate stand in the Valtellina, the mountainous area just north of Lake Como. Wolff listened with concern. Such a move could jeopardize the "Sunrise" negotiations. He told Mussolini it was not at all practical to fortify the Valtellina and suggested that he stay "in our immediate neighborhood."

After the Allied advance into Italy in July, 1943, the Fascist leaders had staged a coup, arrested and deposed Mussolini and reinstated King Victor Emmanuel. After his rescue by Skorzeny in September, Mussolini had set up a new Fascist Republican government in northern Italy on Lake Garda. But he was little more than Hitler's puppet, for German troops controlled the entire area. There was now a wide chasm between the Führer and Mussolini, whose last hope was to bring about some sort of "Italian political solution" to the disastrous war. Consequently, he never even reported to Hitler the peace negotiations in Switzerland.*

_____

* Several weeks earlier in one of his "private talks" Hitler had admitted to intimates that his "unshakable friendship" with Mussolini was probably a mistake. "It is in fact quite obvious that our Italian alliance has been of more service to our enemies than to ourselves. . . . If, in spite of all our efforts, we fail to win this war, the Italian alliance will have contributed to our defeat! The greatest service which Italy could have rendered to us would have been to remain aloof from this conflict." He still retained his "instinctive feelings of friendship" for the Italians, he said. "But I do blame myself for not having listened to the voice of reason, which bade me to be ruthless in my friendship for Italy."

On April 11, 1945, Mussolini received a message from the Vatican that the Allies had peremptorily turned down his proposal, and he sank into a state of apathy.

Ever since the failure of Hitler's gamble, the Battle of the Bulge, he had become noticeably manic. "He lives by dreams, in dreams and through dreams," remarked his youthful Minister of Popular Culture, Fernando Mezzasomma. "He does not have the least contact with reality. He lives and functions in a world which he creates for himself, a completely fantastic world. He lives outside time. His reactions, his fits of gaiety or depression, never have any relation to life. They come on suddenly and for no apparent reason."

When Ivanoe Fossani interviewed the Duce on an island in Lake Garda, Mussolini seemed to be in a semidelirious state. "If it were a summer's day," he told the journalist, "I would take off my coat and roll in the grass like an exuberant child." Fossani attributed this impetuous whim to the fact that Mussolini was momentarily out of sight of his guards, his ministers, his nagging wife, Donna Rachele, and his tearful mistress, Claretta Petacci.

He spoke of his own mistakes but accused others of far greater ones. He had been forced into war by "the diabolical foreign policy" of England, and Hitler had invaded Russia against his advice. He violently attacked the King, his reactionary court, the General Staff, selfish industrial and financial groups, then confessed in a sad, quiet voice that he had been a prisoner ever since his arrest in the King's palace. "I have no illusions about my fate. Life is only a short span in eternity. After the struggle is over they'll spit on me, but later perhaps they will come to wipe me clean. And then I'll smile because I will be at peace with my people."

Another journalist, Madeleine Moller, thought he looked like a convict, with his pale face, shaven head and empty black eyes. He seemed humble rather than resigned. "What do you want to know?" he asked. "Seven years ago I remember you came to Rome. I was an interesting person then. Now I'm obsolete. . . . This morning in my room a little swallow was trapped. It flew around desperately in the room until it fell exhausted on my bed. I picked it up carefully so I wouldn't frighten it, unlatched my window, then opened my hand. It didn't understand at first, and looked around before opening its wings and flying out to freedom with a little cry of joy. I'll never forget that cry of joy. But for me, the window will never open except to let me out to death . . .

"Yes, signora, I'm finished. My star has set. I still work, but I know that everything is a farce. I await the end of the tragedy, strangely detached from it all. I don't feel well and for a year have eaten nothing but slops. I don't drink. I don't smoke. . . . Perhaps I was, after all, only destined to show my people the way. But then, have you ever heard of a prudent, calculating dictator? . . .

"The agony is atrociously long. I'm like the captain of a ship in a storm;

the ship is wrecked and I find myself in the churning ocean on a raft which it is impossible to guide or to govern. No one hears my voice any more. But one day perhaps the world will listen to me."

On the night of April 13 Himmler phoned Wolff and told him to report to Berlin "posthaste"—he had just learned of his subordinate's repeated attempts to negotiate a peace. Wolff promised he would, then thought it over and wrote Himmler that he could not come to Berlin.

The next day Himmler phoned twice, again ordering Wolff to Berlin. Wolff ignored both messages and attended Mussolini's daily conference at Lake Garda as if nothing had happened.

The Duce still wanted to make a last heroic stand in the Valtellina, but almost everyone at the meeting was opposed. Marshal Rodolfo Graziani— the elderly, white-haired commander in chief of the Italian Army— was the most vociferous: it would be dishonorable, even if it were possible, to move his forces out of the front line without the full approval of their allies, the Germans.

"No one is obliged to go to the Valtellina," Mussolini said quietly. "Each one of you must decide for himself."

After the conference Wolff again tried to dissuade Mussolini from going to the Valtellina.

"What card is left for me to play?" Mussolini asked.

"Give up your plans for socialism and bargain with Western capitalism."

"Excellent!" the Duce replied, and Wolff felt he was being serious.

"Just be patient," Wolff said, and warned Mussolini not to make any more peace overtures of his own through Cardinal Schuster.

If Wolff had neutralized Mussolini for the moment, his own problems were mounting. What should he do about the orders from Himmler to fly to Berlin? He sent a message to Dulles asking for advice. Dulles warned him, through Parrilli, not to go to Berlin, and suggested that he immediately go to Switzerland with his staff and family.

Wolff nevertheless decided that he had to go to Berlin, risky as that might be, and face Hitler and Himmler. On the evening of April 16— the day Zhukov launched his ultimate attack on Berlin—Wolff landed at an airport some sixteen miles south of the capital, where Dr. Gebhardt was waiting for him. The cautious Himmler wanted Gebhardt to sound out Wolff. Gebhardt took him to the Hotel Adlon, close to the bunker, where they spent the night. The following morning they drove to the sanatorium and lunched with Himmler. By the time the meal was over, Wolff had convinced Himmler that he had done only what Hitler wanted him to.

Then Kaltenbrunner burst in and said he had to talk to the Reichs-führer privately: he had just received a radio message from an agent who reported that Wolff and Cardinal Schuster were carrying on secret negotiations and that the final signing of a cease-fire on the entire Italian front could be expected in a few days.

Wolff was summoned back to the room and faced with Himmler's furious accusation.

"I have never personally negotiated with Cardinal Schuster regarding the surrender!" Wolff swore. It was true; he had always delegated this duty to a subordinate. His indignation was so sincere that Himmler began to waver, but Kaltenbrunner was not so credulous. The quarrel went on for an hour, with Himmler believing first one, then the other. It was like a tug of war, Wolff thought, with Himmler the rope, and he wondered how this vacillating little man could ever have been his hero.

Wolff finally demanded that they all go to Berlin so that he could exonerate himself from Kaltenbrunner's accusation before the Führer himself. Himmler, of course, refused to go. Wolff insisted that Kaltenbrunner at least come along. He wanted him present, he said pointedly, when Hitler learned that all the negotiations in Switzerland had been properly reported to both Himmler and Kaltenbrunner—and that Himmler had specifically forbidden him to report the negotiations to the Führer.

It was blackmail, and all three knew it. But Kaltenbrunner was not cowed. He said he would go to the bunker, and it sounded like a threat. The two antagonists drove off at one o'clock in the morning of April 18, and for two hours sat side by side in bitter silence. But just before they entered the bunker, Wolff said something that made Kaltenbrunner turn white with anger: "If you repeat to the Führer the story of the radio message from your agent, I won't go to the gallows alone. You and the Reichsführer will hang beside me."

They encountered Hitler in the corridor. "Ah, you're here, Wolff," Hitler said, surprised. "Good! Please wait until the briefing is over."

At four o'clock the door to the conference room opened and Fegelein beckoned Wolff to enter. Hitler was cool and to the point. "Kaltenbrunner and Himmler have informed me of your negotiations in Switzerland with Mr. Dulles." He stepped up close to Wolff and stared at him. "What made you disregard my authority so flagrantly? In your duties as commander of the SS in Italy you are familiar with only a small section of the overall military and political situation. I do not have the time nor the opportunity to tell every individual commander what is happening on the other battle fronts or even on the political level. Is it clear to you just what an enormous responsibility you have thus taken on your shoulders?"

"Yes, my Führer."

"What made you do this?"

Wolff reminded Hitler of their meeting on February 6 with Ribbentrop. "You heard me suggest that if we could not be sure that these secret and special weapons would be ready in time, we should enter into negotiations with the Allies."

He spoke so rapidly that no one interrupted. Not once did he remove his eyes from Hitler's—he felt that if he did, he would lose his life. Wolff said he had interpreted the Führer's apparently favorable reaction during that talk as his "blessing" and had, therefore, acted accordingly. He described how he had met with Dulles on March 8, on his own initiative, since there was no time to get instructions from Berlin.

"Now I am happy to report to you, my Führer, that I have succeeded in opening doors, through Mr. Dulles, to the President, Prime Minister Churchill and Field-Marshal Alexander. I request instructions for the future."

When he stopped, Hitler continued to stare at him for a moment. "Good," he finally said, "I accept your presentation. You're fantastically lucky. If you had failed, I would have had to drop you exactly as I dropped Hess."*

Greatly relieved, Wolff gave him a whitewashed version of the negotiations in Switzerland, emphasizing the fact that unconditional surrender, in view of the military situation and Russia's attitude, could not be avoided.

"Good, I will consider it," Hitler said. "But I have to get some sleep first."

They met again late in the afternoon during a lull between air raids. Hitler decided to get a breath of fresh air and asked for his overcoat. He continued the discussion with Wolff, Kaltenbrunner and Fegelein as they strolled through the rubble of the Chancellery garden.

"I have considered the matter you brought up this morning," Hitler began, but immediately went off on a tangent. First he described the deeply echeloned antitank system he had set up to defend Berlin. Every day 250 Russian tanks were being destroyed, he said, and even the Red Army could not be bled like this. Its attack would soon stop, but he admitted that the Russians and Anglo-Americans would eventually join forces somewhere south of Berlin. At Yalta, he claimed, Roosevelt and Churchill had agreed to let the Russians penetrate into Europe, but he was sure the Russians would never stop at the line agreed upon.

"The Americans, however, cannot put up with this and will therefore be forced to push the Russians back by force of arms, and that"—Hitler stopped abruptly and fixed Wolff with a piercing, triumphant look—"and *that* will be the point at which I'll be offered a high price for my participation in the final war—on one side or the other!" He said he could hold out in Berlin against East and West for at least six weeks, possibly even eight weeks. "In the meantime this conflict will ensue, and then I'll decide."

* Perhaps Hitler was purposely misleading Wolff. If he was telling the truth, his words meant that he had secretly sent Hess on his mission to England and would have claimed credit if the negotiations had succeeded.

Wolff was dumfounded. "My Führer, isn't it clear which side you would take in such a war?"

Hitler turned again to Wolff and after a brief, thoughtful pause said, "I will decide in favor of the side that offers me the most." Rigidly still, he looked up at the sky. "Or the first side to establish contact with me."

All of Wolff's heroes were crumbling. What had happened to the "battle of the European Occident against the new Genghis Khan of this century"? he thought. Where was the idealism of the old days?

With President Roosevelt gone, Hitler went on, there could easily be a breakdown in the Allied ranks.

"Yes, my Führer," Wolff said, "but hasn't it been reported to you that we have from fifteen to twenty thousand enemy aircraft over us every day? Every day, every hour results in"—he almost said "inexcusable"—"losses of men and matériel. Shouldn't we bear this in mind?"

"I can't allow myself to be softened by these reports," Hitler replied curtly. The man who had to make the final decision could not let himself be moved by the horrors of war. "So do this: fly back; give my regards to General von Vietinghoff."

His mood changed and he began talking as if to himself. "Should this fateful battle of the German people under my leadership fail, then the German people don't deserve to exist." The race from the East would have proven itself "biologically superior" and there would be nothing left to do but "go down heroically." He looked up at Wolff as from a trance, and suddenly his optimism returned. "Go back to Italy, keep up your relationship with the Americans, but see that you get better terms. Stall a bit, because to surrender unconditionally on the basis of such vague promises would be preposterous."

A servant came up to them and announced, "My Führer, it's time for the evening briefing."

**2.**

Wolff was mistaken in his belief that Mussolini had been neutralized. The Duce was preparing to go to Milan, with the vague hope of finding his "Italian solution" to the war by somehow negotiating with the National Committee of Liberation (the partisans) or the Western Allies. If not, he could always go north to the Valtellina for the last stand. "After all," he told Marshal Graziani, "Fascism would fall heroically in such a place."

When Don Pancino, a priest, visited him that day he said, with an air of presentiment, "Say good-bye to me now, Father. Thank you for the prayers you say for me. Please go on with them, for I need them. I know I'll be shot."

At sunset he bade farewell to his wife in the garden of the Villa

Feltrinelli. He also said good-bye to his sister Edvige and added that he was prepared "to enter into the grand silence of death." Then he set out in a small convoy for Milan.

On April 20 Wolff was back at his headquarters, more determined than ever to surrender Italy unconditionally despite Himmler* and Hitler. After considerable debate General von Vietinghoff, Kesselring's replacement, had finally agreed that two officers should be sent to Field-Marshal Alexander's headquarters to conduct surrender negotiations.

Ironically, Truman and Churchill had just made up their minds to avoid further friction with Stalin by cutting off all further contact with Wolff or his representatives. Later in the day the Combined Chiefs of Staff radioed Field-Marshal Alexander at his headquarters near Naples:

. . . IT IS QUITE CLEAR THAT CIC ITALY [Vietinghoff] HAS NO INTENTION OF SURRENDERING HIS FORCES, ANYHOW AT THE PRESENT STAGE, ON TERMS ACCEPTABLE TO OURSELVES.

IN THE CIRCUMSTANCES, AND HAVING REGARD TO THE COMPLICATIONS THAT HAVE ARISEN WITH THE RUSSIANS OVER THIS MATTER, OUR TWO GOVERNMENTS HAVE DECIDED THAT OSS SHOULD AT ONCE BREAK OFF CONTACT WITH THE GERMAN EMISSARIES. U. S. CHIEFS OF STAFF ARE INSTRUCTING OSS ACCORDINGLY.

YOU SHOULD REGARD THE WHOLE MATTER AS NOW CLOSED, AND SO INFORM THE RUSSIANS . . .

On April 23 Wolff secretly crossed the border to Switzerland, now with the two men selected by Vietinghoff and himself to arrange surrender terms. Vietinghoff's representative was Oberstleutnant (Lieutenant Colonel) Viktor von Schweinitz, whose grandmother was a direct descendant of the first U. S. Chief Justice, John Jay. Wolff had chosen Major Wenner, who was now wearing the SS general's checked-tweed hunting jacket.

The trio was escorted to Lucerne by Major Waibel and Dr. Husmann, but not until they were settled in Waibel's home did he reveal that the Allies had broken off all negotiations. Waibel, who was almost as indignant as the Germans, tried to calm them down. Finally he phoned Dulles. "We are in an absolutely impossible situation!" he said. "We will be ridiculed for centuries if we don't manage this properly."

Dulles reiterated that he had strict orders to have nothing to do with Wolff. "But we just can't do that," Waibel pressed. "Here are German delegates to sign an unconditional surrender and the Allies just don't want to see them! It looks as if you want to end the war by killing people." Dulles at last gave in: he would send a cable to Alexander, who would

---

* Hours earlier Himmler had phoned Wolff, ordering him to make no more trips to Switzerland and adding ominously that he was moving the general's family from the Brenner area in Italy to the Tyrol "for their own safety."

in turn request the Combined Chiefs to let Dulles resume "contact" with Wolff.

But Waibel was not sure he could keep the three guests in his house until a positive answer was received. By the next morning they were pacing like tigers. Wolff said he couldn't stay away from his headquarters much longer because of a sudden change in the military situation. For months there had been little action on the Gothic Line, which ran from the Ligurian Sea to the Adriatic, just below Bologna, and was held by twenty-five German and five Fascist divisions. But Lieutenant General Mark Clark had just launched his 15th Army Group in a major assault, which had already broken through the German-Fascist defenses, to take Bologna and cross the Po River. Now Clark was in a position to loose his armor, and race unimpeded across the plains of the Po Valley.

To make matters worse, Wolff received a telegram from Himmler which was urgent enough to be phoned to him from the Swiss border, at Waibel's house.

IT IS MORE THAN EVER ESSENTIAL THAT THE ITALIAN FRONT HOLD AND REMAIN INTACT. NO NEGOTIATIONS OF ANY KIND SHOULD BE UNDERTAKEN.

Wolff, however, told Waibel that he was still willing to go through with "Sunrise." But as the day wore on, no word was received from Allied headquarters in southern Italy.

Wolff's position was even more precarious than he realized. He had also been negotiating a German surrender with the National Committee of Liberation—but these talks were only a smoke screen intended to keep the partisans quiet until "Sunrise" could be accomplished.

On the day Wolff entered Switzerland with the two emissaries, Cardinal Schuster warned Colonel Dollmann that all contact with the partisans would be broken unless Wolff himself came at once to Milan. Dollmann phoned Wolff about this newest crisis. He was instructed to "stall for time" and to tell the Cardinal that Wolff accepted the partisans' terms and would come to Milan "as soon as possible."

Cardinal Schuster told Dollmann that he had arranged a meeting with the partisans three days hence, April 25, at the Archbishopric in Milan, and that it was imperative that Wolff be present.

The Cardinal had also asked Mussolini to attend this meeting, but he was still undecided as to his course of action. A half-dozen means of escape had been suggested to him but he was apathetic to all of them, including an offer to fly him and Claretta Petacci to Spain.

On the morning of the meeting at the Archbishopric Marshal Graziani tried to get Mussolini's permission to withdraw the Italian troops retreating before Clark's attack, to new positions in the north, but he refused to discuss the matter. He said he had an appointment with Cardinal Schuster at six o'clock and was going to "spare the Army any further sacrifice" by surrendering to the National Committee of Liberation.

Early in the afternoon shrieking factory whistles proclaimed a general strike, and partisans were openly ranging the streets when Mussolini stepped out of his headquarters in the Prefecture and got into an old limousine to drive to the Archbishopric. The Duce didn't even bother to tell SS-Obersturmführer (Lieutenant) Fritz Birzer, his personal escort, that he was leaving. At the last moment Birzer rushed to the courtyard and pushed his way into the car. As it drove off, he was balanced precariously, half sitting on the Duce's knee.

When Mussolini walked into the reception room at the Archbishop's palace, Cardinal Schuster saw "a man benumbed by an immense catastrophe." The Cardinal tried to cheer him up, but he seemed lethargic and loath to talk. The Cardinal begged him to spare Italy needless destruction, by surrendering, but Mussolini said he would fight to the end in the Valtellina with 3000 Black Shirts.

"Duce," the Cardinal said, "do not have any illusions." He suggested that the figure might be more like 300 Black Shirts.

"Perhaps a few more," Mussolini replied, then added with a smile, "not many though. I have no illusions."

When the Cardinal reminded him of the fall of Napoleon, Mussolini's tired eyes came to life momentarily. "My empire of one hundred days is also about to expire. I must meet my destiny with resignation, like Bonaparte."

Three partisan delegates were ushered into the room: General Raffaele Cadorna, the senior military representative on the National Committee of Liberation; Achille Marazza, a Christian Democrat lawyer; and Riccardo Lombardi, an engineer from the Partito d'Azione (the Republican, or Action, Party). The newcomers kissed the Cardinal's ring and were introduced to Mussolini, who smiled and walked briskly toward them with extended hand. The delegates shook it uneasily.

The atmosphere grew even more awkward when the white-haired Marshal Graziani strode in, accompanied by two of Mussolini's ministers. The Cardinal indicated a large oval table in the center of the room. "Shall we sit down over there?"

"Well, then," Mussolini said impatiently, "what are the proposals?"

"My instructions are limited and precise," said the partisan spokesman, Marazza. "I have only to ask for and accept your surrender."

Mussolini bridled. "I'm not here for that! I was told that we were to meet and discuss conditions. That's why I came—to safeguard my men, their families and the Fascist militia. I must know what's to become of them. The families of the members of my government must be given protection. Also, I was assured that the militia would be handed over to the enemy as prisoners of war."

"Those are just details," another partisan interjected. "I believe we have authority to settle them."

"Very well," said the Duce. "In that case we can come to some agreement."

Marshal Graziani jumped up and said, "No, no, Duce! Let me remind you that we have obligations to our ally. We can't abandon the Germans and negotiate a capitulation independently like this. We can't sign an agreement without the Germans. We can't forget the laws of duty and honor!"

"I'm afraid the Germans don't seem to have been troubled by the same scruples," said the partisan general, Cadorna. "We have been discussing surrender terms with them for the past four days. We've already agreed on all details, and we are expecting news of the signed treaty at any moment."

Marazza noticed a look of pain on Mussolini's face and asked, "Haven't they bothered to inform your government?"

"Impossible!" the Duce exclaimed. "Show me the treaty!"

Mussolini, of course, knew more than he let on, but his surprise and indignation seemed real to those present. "The Germans have done this behind my back!" He sprang to his feet and announced that he wouldn't make a move until he talked to the German consul. "This time we'll be able to say that Germany has betrayed Italy!"

He threatened to make a radio broadcast to the world denouncing the Germans, and stamped out of the room.

At last Mussolini's mind was made up. At the Prefecture he jabbed a finger at a map and exclaimed, "We'll leave Milan immediately. Destination Como!"

Dressed in the uniform of the Fascist militia, he strode down the corridor, trailed by his ministers. One begged him not to go back to the Archbishopric, while another wanted to make sure that he would stay in Milan. Two others advised him to fly to Spain, and immediately a third shouted, "Don't go, Duce!" Through all this, his secretary was waving papers in front of him to sign. It was like a scene from an opera buffa.

A machine pistol slung over his shoulder, a bulging briefcase in each hand, Mussolini embraced two old comrades and cried, "To the Valtellina!"

It was about eight o'clock in the evening when ten cars, loaded with Mussolini's entourage, including Marshal Graziani and the German escort, pulled out of the courtyard amid frenzied farewells, and headed north for Como.

"Where are we going?" one of the ministers asked another.

"God knows, perhaps to our death."

In one of the cars, an Alfa-Romeo with Spanish license plates, was

Claretta Petacci. "I am following my destiny," she had written a friend "I don't know what will become of me, but I cannot question my fate."

## 3.

In Lucerne, Wolff had still received no word from Dulles. He told Waibel he could no longer stay in Switzerland. Clark was driving deeper into northern Italy and the partisans were demanding a showdown in Milan; moreover, Dollmann had reported that Mussolini was acting mysteriously and there was no telling what he might do.

Wolff returned to Italy about midnight, crossing the border at Chiasso. Exhausted by the trip, he decided to spend the night at the Villa Locatelli, headquarters of the SS border police on the west shore of Lake Como. As he was getting ready for bed Marshal Graziani suddenly appeared. He had deserted Mussolini's party at Como, less than five miles down the lake, and sought the protection of the SS.

The arrival of Marshal Graziani gave Wolff an unexpected opportunity to persuade the old man that surrender of his troops was the best way to save Italy. Graziani was bitter at first and accused him of betraying the Duce, but Wolff was so convincing in his protestations that he had always acted in the best interest of Italy that the Marshal wrote out a document granting Wolff authority to surrender the entire Italian Army.

Outside in the dark there were other Italians who did not look on the SS as protectors. They were armed partisans who had just learned of Wolff's arrival. Silently they began to surround the villa. By dawn, April 26, they had an iron ring around the entire estate. But they had neglected to cut the telephone wires.

Later in the morning Major Waibel received a report that a "big fish" would soon be caught at Lake Como; a few discreet inquiries verified Waibel's suspicion that this was Wolff. He arranged to meet an agent named Bustelli that evening at the Chiasso railroad station, where they would try to find some way to save Wolff.

Waibel then phoned Gaevernitz. "If we don't act promptly," he said, "Wolff will be killed and the show will be over."

Gaevernitz took the problem to Dulles, who said he was sorry. He knew how important Wolff was but he had definite orders to make no further contacts. "I can't do anything." Gaevernitz asked if he could at least get the assistance of Donald Jones, an OSS agent who posed as the American vice-consul in Lugano. Dulles shook his head and again said his hands were tied. Gaevernitz decided to act on his own and said impulsively, "I'm going on a little trip and will return in two or three days."

"Good-bye" was all Dulles said, but Gaevernitz was sure there was a twinkle in his eye. Eight hours later Gaevernitz and Waibel got off the train at Chiasso and to their surprise were met by Jones. "I've been waiting for you," he said. "I understand you want to liberate Wolff."

Waibel soon discovered that Jones knew nothing about this case and had become involved only through Bustelli. "There is considerable Swiss interest in saving Wolff," Waibel said, pretending it had nothing to do with the Dulles office. He asked Jones to help, and reminded him of the many favors he had been granted. "Now I want a favor in return."

Jones readily agreed and they all decided that the only way to do it was for Jones to make a bold dash through the partisan lines; he was well known to the partisans under the code name of "Scotti." They phoned the Villa Locatelli. Incredibly, the line was still open and Wolff was told that two cars would soon attempt to break through to rescue him.

At ten o'clock in the evening Jones's raiding party drove out of Chiasso, leaving Waibel and Gaevernitz waiting nervously in the small, dim-lit railroad restaurant. No sooner had Jones crossed into Italy than he was fired upon. He got out of his car and stood before the glare of its headlights.

*"L'amico Scotti!"* shouted a voice in the dark. The shooting stopped and "Scotti" was waved on.

Gaevernitz and Waibel remained in the restaurant for two hours. At midnight the tension became unbearable and they walked to the Swiss customs house, where the lights of any car coming from Italy would be visible. They saw nothing, but every so often heard a distant shot. What if Jones had become involved in a fracas at the villa and was discovered? Gaevernitz could visualize the headlines: AMERICAN CONSUL RESCUES GERMAN SS GENERAL WOLFF FROM ITALIAN PARTISANS. And at a time when Truman and Churchill had promised Stalin they were dropping all negotiations!

They went back to the restaurant and waited another restless hour. Again they returned to the border. Everything on the Italian side was completely blacked out. Several times they heard a car approach, then fade away. At two o'clock, pinpoints of light suddenly pierced the darkness. Two cars approached the border. It was Jones's party. Gaevernitz walked back toward his own car, intent on leaving inconspicuously as soon as he was sure Wolff was there.

But a bulky figure brushed past everyone and headed directly for Gaevernitz. It was Wolff. "I'll never forget what you have done for me," he said. Gaevernitz decided to take advantage of Wolff's gratitude. They all drove to a hotel in Lugano, and Gaevernitz suggested that Wolff write a letter to the SS commander in Milan ordering him to cease fighting the partisans.

Wolff not only wrote the letter but handed over the document signed by Marshal Graziani. He also promised to use his influence to prevent destruction of property and to protect the lives of political prisoners.

"What would you do," Gaevernitz asked, "if Himmler suddenly turned up and said, 'I'm taking over command and I arrest you'?"

"If that happened, I would of course turn around and arrest Himmler!"

In the afternoon of April 27 Wolff left alone to return to his new headquarters at Bolzano in northern Italy. To avoid the partisans he would have to take a route through Austria. Gaevernitz drove to his home in Ascona to get some sleep but he was almost immediately awakened by a phone call from Dulles: a wire had just come in from Washington permitting him to resume negotiations with the Germans;* and another had come from Alexander's headquarters ordering him to send Wolff's two emissaries to southern Italy at once.

* Apparently Stalin was told about this sudden reversal of Allied policy even before Dulles. The previous day Churchill had wired Stalin:
THE GERMAN ENVOYS, WITH WHOM ALL CONTACT WAS BROKEN BY US SOME DAYS AGO, HAVE NOW ARRIVED AGAIN ON THE LAKE OF LUCERNE. THEY CLAIM TO HAVE FULL POWERS TO SURRENDER THE ARMY IN ITALY. FIELD-MARSHAL ALEXANDER IS THEREFORE BEING TOLD THAT HE IS FREE TO PERMIT THESE ENVOYS TO COME TO ALLIED FORCE HEADQUARTERS IN ITALY. . . . WILL YOU PLEASE SEND RUSSIAN REPRESENTATIVES FORTHWITH TO FIELD-MARSHAL ALEXANDER'S HEADQUARTERS.
FIELD-MARSHAL ALEXANDER IS FREE TO ACCEPT THE UNCONDITIONAL SURRENDER OF THE CONSIDERABLE ENEMY ARMY ON HIS FRONT, BUT ALL POLITICAL ISSUES ARE RESERVED TO THE THREE GOVERNMENTS. . . .
WE HAVE SPENT A LOT OF BLOOD IN ITALY AND THE CAPTURE OF THE GERMAN ARMIES SOUTH OF THE ALPS IS A PRIZE DEAR TO THE HEARTS OF THE BRITISH NATION, WITH WHOM IN THIS MATTER THE UNITED STATES HAVE SHARED THE COSTS AND PERILS . . .

# 28

# Death Comes to a Dictator

**1.**

Not long after Mussolini had arrived at the Prefecture in Como, he sent a message to Donna Rachele, who had moved to the Villa Montero, not a mile from the Villa Locatelli, where Wolff was being surrounded by partisans. He told his wife that he was "at the last stages of my life, the last page of my book," and asked forgiveness "for all the harm I have unwittingly done to you." He begged her to take the two children, Anna Maria and Romano, to Switzerland where she could "build a new life."

Donna Rachele had no sooner finished the letter than her phone rang. It was Mussolini who had been trying all day to reach her. "I follow my destiny," he said in a quiet, resigned voice. "I'm alone, Rachele, and I realize quite well that all is over." After speaking briefly to the two children, he asked her to come to Como and see him for the last time.

They said good-bye in the dark courtyard of the Prefecture. He handed her some papers, including letters from Churchill which he hoped might get her across the frontier. "If they try and stop you or harm you," he said, "ask to be handed over to the English."

Just before dawn on April 26, Mussolini and a small party drove up the winding west shore of Lake Como, beautiful even in the heavy drizzle. At Menaggio, twenty-five miles from Como, he stopped at the villa of a local Fascist official and said he would wait there for his ministers and the 3000 Black Shirts that Alessandro Pavolini, the secretary of the Neo-Fascist Party, had promised to assemble. While Mussolini was sleeping, the rest of his entourage, including Claretta Petacci, escorted by two armored cars and several companies of Republican soldiers, caught up with them.

Mussolini awoke to find the large convoy parked along the main highway. It was too risky to wait there for the Black Shirts, he said, and ordered the whole party to turn off on a side road. Then he and Claretta got into an Alfa-Romeo and raced up a narrow mountain road to the west toward Switzerland—with the SS escort, Lieutenant Birzer, and the rest of the convoy in pursuit.

At the tiny settlement of Grandola, Mussolini and his followers descended on the Hotel Miravalle, where they lounged around listening gloomily to a radio broadcast news of the continuing triumphal advance of Clark, and the general uprising of partisans in the north.

Elena Curti Cucciati, the pretty daughter of one of the Duce's former mistresses, went to Mussolini and volunteered to bicycle back to Como and find out what was delaying Pavolini and the 3000 Black Shirts. When Claretta came upon the two talking in the garden, she screamed hysterically that the girl must be sent away. Embarrassed, Mussolini tried to restrain her; in the struggle she tripped on the carpet, fell and burst into tears.

During the afternoon three officials left the hotel without bidding Mussolini good-bye and headed for the Swiss border a few miles to the west. While others were wondering if they too should try to escape, one of the three returned, with the discouraging news that his companions had been captured by partisans at the frontier.

At dusk Mussolini impatiently told Birzer he was going to start immediately for the Valtellina, without Pavolini. The Black Shirts could meet him there. Birzer warned him that the partisans must have set up roadblocks; moreover, his men needed a night's rest before attempting the flight up the lake-front road. Mussolini promised to stay in the hotel until dawn.

Earlier in the day an eight-man partisan patrol had walked down the mountains skirting the west shore of Lake Como to Domaso, a town near the north end of the lake. Their leader was Count Pier Luigi Bellini delle Stelle, a handsome man of twenty-two, with a mustache, a Mephistophelian beard and a law degree from the University of Florence. His father, a Cavalry colonel, had been captured by the Germans in 1944 and had died of maltreatment in prison.

The partisans around Como were Communist-controlled but neither Bellini nor his second-in-command, twenty-year-old Urbano Lazzaro, were Party members and, in fact, were strongly opposed to Communism. Like so many others in similar Communist-dominated groups, their main objective was to fight Germans and Fascists and help bring peace again to Italy.

Bellini's patrol had come into town only to get tobacco, but were surrounded by a mob which hoisted them up in triumph. The war is over! a dozen voices shouted. Bellini went into an ice cream shop and heard a radio announcer say, "The Allies have crossed the Po; the German Army is in retreat. The Allies are in Brescia and are converging on Milan. Insurrection has broken out in Milan, and partisan units have occupied all the key points of the city and most of the barracks."

The enthusiastic townspeople clamored to join Bellini who had twenty more comrades up in the hills; they wanted Bellini to take over the whole Domaso section. But he had only enough arms to mount a force of fifty men and there were at least 200 well-armed enemy in the area.

Even so, Bellini decided to act. He wrote a letter to the commander of the nearby Fascist garrison at Gravedona, demanding surrender before 9 P.M., and then told a girl to ride her bicycle down the lakeside highway toward Como and give the ultimatum to the first soldier she met. Similar notes were sent to other Fascist and German garrisons.

In the afternoon the first definite good news came in: the garrison at Ponte del Passo had surrendered. A little later, however, Bellini learned that the Germans at Nuova Olonia, near the strategic bridge at the north end of the lake, were firing machine guns at any who dared approach. Bellini and Lazzaro walked boldly up to the German stronghold and demanded a parley. Bellini claimed that he was the Area Partisan Commander and threatened to blow the Germans to bits with mortars unless they surrendered. Their commander meekly handed over his revolver.

On his return to Domaso, Bellini found the townspeople about to lynch several Fascist prisoners. "We partisans can't make ourselves responsible for all the outrages the Fascists and Germans have committed!" he cried. "To answer evil with evil will only do harm to our cause and bring us down to the same level as our enemies."

By midnight Bellini controlled ten miles of lake-front road, from the bridge at the north to Dongo. Half a mile south of Dongo he set up a roadblock with a tree trunk, large stone blocks and barbed wire. It was a perfect cul-de-sac. On one side of the narrow highway, a bank fell off steeply to the lake. On the other side rose a huge wooded boulder—the Rock of Musso. Then, exhausted by the arduous events of the day, Bellini went to bed.

Pavolini had just arrived at the Hotel Miravalle in an armored car. Rain was still dripping from his face as he told Mussolini that most of the Black Shirts in Como had surrendered to the partisans. When the Duce asked how many men he had brought with him to fight in the Valtellina, Pavolini hesitated before saying, "Twelve."

At dawn Mussolini and what was left of his entourage joined a German convoy of twenty-eight trucks heading up the lakeside road. In the armored car were Pavolini, several government officials and two leather bags of papers and money. Near the end of the convoy in the yellow Alfa-

Romeo with Spanish license plates were Claretta, her brother and his family.

Mussolini, alone, was up front in his Alfa-Romeo. On the outskirts of Menaggio he called to a passer-by and asked if there were any partisans around. The answer was "Everywhere." Mussolini stopped the car, walked back to the armored car and climbed inside. It was almost six-thirty when the convoy passed through Musso, a mile away from Dongo. Suddenly, half a mile farther on, a huge tree trunk entwined with barbed wire loomed up ahead. It was Bellini's roadblock.

The partisan machine gunners loosed a warning burst into the air. Fire was returned from the armored car, killing an old laborer walking to Dongo. But a white flag fluttered from one of the convoy cars and the shooting stopped. Two partisans came from behind the roadblock and were met by a German officer who asked to see their commander.

In Domaso, Bellini was wakened and told a German column was advancing on Dongo. "Tell the advance roadblock to stop the column," he ordered. "No one is to move, whatever happens."

Bellini sent two messengers to the north for reinforcements, and accompanied by Lazzaro, drove at top speed to Dongo. On the way he instructed Lazzaro to place all their forces in strategic positions on the great rock overlooking the roadblock while he tried to negotiate.

At Dongo a *carabiniere* gave Bellini the last information about the roadblock. The count started walking down the highway and in a few minutes came upon three German officers standing near the armored car. The German commander introduced himself in fairly good Italian as Hauptmann (Captain) Otto Kisnatt. "I have orders to take my men to Merano [near the Austrian border] and I intend to go on there. From Merano we shall go into Germany and continue the fight against the Allies there. We have no intention of fighting the Italians."

"On the other hand, I have orders to halt all armed enemy columns and to let no one through," said Bellini, who had no orders but thought it would impress the Germans. "I ask you therefore to surrender, and I guarantee your safe-conduct and that of all your men."

"But our High Command and yours have come to an agreement." Kisnatt was bluffing. "We Germans are not to attack the partisans and the partisans are to let us go free."

"I have had no such orders."

"We've got as far as here from Milan and everyone has let us through without a shot being fired. That proves there *is* an agreement."

"If you've got as far as this, that simply means you haven't come across any partisans, or those you did meet weren't strong enough to attack you." Bellini decided to outbluff Kisnatt. "We are in control of the whole area; we are well placed and I have strong forces. You are covered by mortars and machine guns. I could wipe you out in fifteen minutes."

Lazzaro beckoned Bellini to one side and told him there were twenty-eight trucks full of German soldiers, an armored car, the German commander's vehicle and ten cars full of civilians. Each truck, Lazzaro said, contained a heavy machine gun, machine pistols and several light anti-aircraft guns.

Bellini knew he couldn't contain such a force if it came to a fight. He decided to mine the Vall'orba Bridge, a few hundred yards up the road toward Dongo. But to do this required time. The count returned to the three Germans. "First of all," he said, "we must know what men you have with you and if there are any Italians among them."

Kisnatt admitted there were Italians in the armored car and a few in the private cars. "I have no responsibility for them. I am concerned only with my own men. What is your decision?"

"We've decided that we can't take the responsibility of allowing you through without orders. Our headquarters is a mile or two away and we'll go there for instructions. It would be advisable for one of you to go with us and establish direct contact with them." Bellini had no idea where his division commander was. He only wanted to get Kisnatt away from his men so they would be unable to act.

When Bellini said it would take an hour and a half, Kisnatt said, "Too long. We have no time to lose! Make up your minds here and now."

"Impossible" was the curt reply. "I cannot let you pass."

Finally Kisnatt agreed to accompany Bellini to his HQ if they could all go in a German vehicle.

In a low voice Bellini told Lazzaro to make a show of strength up ahead: every armed man should be brought out to the road and civilians induced to wear something red to make them look like partisans.

As Bellini and Kisnatt entered Dongo in a German car, they passed crude barricades and crowds of suspicious-looking men wearing red bandannas. On the bridge at end of the lake Bellini called out to a partisan, "All men in position here? All mines ready?"

The partisan was puzzled until he saw the count wink, then said, "Everything is ready. Let me know when to light the fuses."

Bellini continued north. When Kisnatt had reached the limit of his patience, Bellini stopped the car and pretended he had to walk on alone to his HQ. He would return with the decision, he said.

At Musso, not far from the roadblock, Don Mainetti, the parish priest, was just going into his house when a bearded man ran up and said, "I must speak to you, Reverend! I'm giving myself up, but I don't want my capture to cause any fuss. It simply mustn't. I'll come to your house. You call a partisan and I'll give myself up." It was Nicola Bombacci. Thirty years before he and Mussolini had been revolutionary Socialists. He became a leading Italian Communist and a friend of Lenin's, but was expelled from the Party. Now he was one of Mussolini's closest advisers.

"I'm a victim of my own stupidity," he said. He revealed that the Duce was in the convoy down at the roadblock.

While they were talking, another civilian approached with a boy and said, "I am Romano, a government minister. I have my son with me. I am leaving him in your care because I don't know what will become of me."

The priest had no sooner taken the fifteen-year-old boy into his house than a group of government officials—including Ministers Mezzasomma and Paolo Zerbino—knocked at the door. "We are important people," one told the priest, "Speak for us, please."

Bellini returned to the roadblock with Kisnatt without revealing the imaginary orders he said he had received at his HQ. Everyone turned expectantly to Bellini and he knew he could stall no longer. He stared Kisnatt in the eye and said firmly, "Our decisions are: first, permission to proceed is granted only to German vehicles and German soldiers; all Italian and all civilian vehicles must therefore be handed over to us. Second, all German vehicles must halt at Dongo to be searched and all German personnel must show their identity papers. Third, you will stop again at Ponte del Passo to await further authorization to proceed."

Kisnatt hesitated, then said he could not abandon his Italian allies "in the moment of danger." But Bellini was adamant and the German asked for half an hour "to consult" with his officers.

Bellini nodded. As he sat on a wall and lit a cigarette, a priest whispered in a conspiratorial voice, "Come here!" It was Don Mainetti.

"What's the matter?"

"Mussolini's here! Don't let him get away, because we're sure he's here."

Bellini found it hard to believe. Nevertheless, he asked Lazzaro to investigate. Lazzaro started toward the convoy, but he didn't take the order seriously and never carried it out.

Kisnatt returned to Bellini and said that he would accept the conditions only if they were also acceptable to the occupants of the armored car.

Bellini walked up to a group standing near the armored car, which was in the middle of the road, blocking the convoy. "Who is in command here?" he asked.

An elderly civilian wearing a military gold medal indicating that he had been disabled in battle stepped forward. "My name is Francisco Barracu and I am Undersecretary to the Cabinet." He introduced two men standing next to him, Lieutenant Colonel Casalinovo, Mussolini's military aide, and a Black Shirt named Utimpergher.

Bellini answered their Fascist greeting with a military salute and asked, "What are your intentions?"

"To continue with the German column, of course," Barracu answered, somewhat surprised. "The question seems quite unnecessary." Bellini advised him to surrender. "No, we must get through at all costs. I repeat: we intend to follow the column."

Bellini was impressed by Barracu's soldierly attitude, but said he had made an agreement with the Germans to split up the column. "Don't delude yourselves into thinking that they will risk a fight for your sake. They don't want to fight any more—that's clear."

"Even so, we've got to move on."

Bellini repeated that it was out of the question. "Where would you possibly want to go?"

"You're a soldier and you appear to act like one," Barracu said persuasively. "So you will understand an old soldier like me." He said he had sworn to defend Trieste from Tito's Slavs. "If we can get there, I'm convinced that we'll be able to organize a resistance and at least try to save that piece of our country for which so many Italians have shed their blood."

Bellini listened politely and said that if he freed the party, another band of partisans would soon stop them. As for the future of Trieste, that would be settled by the Allies.

"What sort of Italians are you?" Utimpergher suddenly shouted excitedly. "Have you forgotten that our fathers died for Trieste?"

"As far as love of my country is concerned," Bellini answered bitterly, "I've nothing to learn from either you or the likes of you who welcomed the foreign invader, and deported and massacred your own countrymen!"

"I think everyone did his duty as he saw it," Barracu interrupted in a conciliatory manner, and once more asked permission to pass through.

"You can see that the Germans are getting nervous," Bellini said. "Since we still haven't reached an agreement, I think that it might be better to let them proceed at least as far as Dongo, then we can resume our discussions in peace."

To his surprise, Barracu too thought this was a good idea. Bellini told Kisnatt to move out, and the armored car pulled off to one side to let the convoy proceed. Sitting in one of the open trucks was Mussolini, huddled inside a German army overcoat.

A single civilian car was allowed to follow the trucks—the Alfa-Romeo with the Spanish license plates and diplomatic tag, flying the Spanish flag. In it were Marcello Petacci, posing as a Spanish consul, his wife and children, and his sister Claretta.

Again Barracu resumed his pleas, but Bellini was firm. Barracu finally asked if he could go back to Como and explain to his chief why he had been unable to proceed to Trieste.

"Your chief? Mussolini? And where do you hope to find him?" Bellini asked.

"I don't mean Mussolini. I mean Marshal Graziani and I do know where he is."

When Bellini also refused this request, Casalinovo and Utimpergher began to shout. "Shut up, for God's sake," Bellini shouted back. "Leave this to us. Listen if you want to, but keep your mouths shut!"

The two of them returned to the armored car and began talking so excitedly with someone inside that Bellini remembered what the priest had told him. Could Mussolini really be in there? He stepped through the rear door of the armored car and inspected those inside. "Had a good look?" Utimpergher asked sarcastically. "Whom did you expect to find?"

Bellini decided to let Barracu return to Como; after all, he was a disabled veteran. He told Barracu that the armored car could turn back in twenty minutes. "But I warn you—if you try to move forward we'll open fire."

The count sent word to the men on the big rock that the armored car was going to turn around. They were to fire only if it tried to go on toward Dongo instead.

At three-fifteen the armored car began moving ahead to turn around at a wider space in the road. Partisans on the big rock, however, thought it was bound for Dongo and opened fire. There was a brief flurry of shots before a grenade exploded under the armored car. A white rag fluttered from its turret. Pavolini jumped out the back and ran down the bank to the lake. The Black Shirt entrusted with Mussolini's papers followed with an armful of documents. Barracu was hit by shrapnel in the right arm, and Casalinovo and Utimpergher were captured on the road.

The Dongo town square would have made a perfect setting for a romantic opera. It was flanked on three sides by medieval buildings, with the snow-capped Alps as a dramatic backdrop and Lake Como at the open end.

Here Lazzaro was inspecting the German truck convoy when he heard the firing. It worried him, but he continued to check the identification papers of the German soldiers near the head of the column until he heard someone excitedly call out, "Bill!," his partisan name. It was Giuseppe Negri, a local clog maker who had recently been in jail for three months for helping the partisans.

"Well, what is it?" Lazzaro asked.

"We've got the Big Bastard!" Negri whispered.

"You're dreaming!" Lazzaro said.

"No, no, Bill, it's Mussolini. I've seen him with my own eyes."

"Where?"

"On a truck here, dressed as a German!"

This was too incredible, but Lazzaro's pulse quickened. "You must have made a mistake!"

"I've seen him and I recognized him at once. I swear it's him, Mussolini himself." He explained that while examining the papers of the Germans in one truck, he came to a man hunched up near the driver's cab, with a blanket over his shoulders. "I couldn't see his face because he had raised the collar of his greatcoat and pulled his German helmet down over his face. I went to him to ask for his papers, but the Germans in the truck stopped me and said, '*Kamerad* drunk, *Kamerad* drunk.' " The clog maker had sat beside the man and pulled down his collar. "He never moved. I only saw his profile but I recognized him at once. Bill, it *is* Mussolini. I swear it. I didn't let on I knew, and got down to come and tell you."

The two men went back along the line of open trucks until Negri stopped and pointed to a soldier with upturned collar and a German helmet pulled over his eyes. Lazzaro walked to the truck and reached up to tap the shoulder of the hunched man. *"Camerata!"*

When the man ignored this Fascist greeting, Lazzaro again tapped him on the shoulder and said ironically, *"Eccellenza!"* There was still no reaction, so Lazzaro shouted irritably, *"Cavaliere* Benito Mussolini!"

The figure stirred and Lazzaro was sure he recognized Mussolini. A crowd gathered as Lazzaro swung aboard the truck. He walked up to the huddled figure and took off his helmet, revealing a bald head. Lazzaro removed the man's sun glasses and turned down his collar. It was Mussolini, clutching a machine pistol between his knees, its butt under his chin.

Lazzaro took the gun from Mussolini and raised him to his feet. "Do you have any other arms!" Without a word, Mussolini unbuttoned his coat and handed over a 9-mm. long-barreled Glisenti automatic.

The two stared at each other, and Lazzaro felt momentarily at a loss. This was the man he had both revered and cursed. Mussolini, face waxen, seemed to be waiting for Lazzaro to say something. He did not look at all afraid, only utterly tired.

The crowd began shouting angrily—two days before, four local partisans had been murdered by the Fascists.

Lazzaro wanted to say something historic. All he could think of was "In the name of the Italian people, I arrest you!" He was surprised that his voice was so calm.

"I won't do anything," Mussolini said tonelessly.

"I give you my word that while you're in my personal charge no one shall touch a hair on your head!" As soon as the words were out, Lazzaro realized it was a silly thing to say to an almost completely bald man.

"Thank you," Mussolini said.

As Lazzaro escorted him across the square toward the Town Hall, formerly the Palazzo Mangi, the crowd surged forward, screaming insults.

A tall, lean man approached Mussolini. "Do you know who I am?"

"No," the Duce replied and shied away.

"I'm Rubini, Minister Rubini's son. You don't remember recalling me to Rome three times?" The towering Rubini hovered over the squat dictator, whose unbuttoned German overcoat almost touched the ground. "I'm the mayor of Dongo. Do you remember now?"

"Yes, yes," Mussolini said. "I remember now." The shouts of the crowd grew more menacing.

"Don't worry," Dr. Rubini reassured him. "No harm will come to you here!"

"I'm sure of that," Mussolini replied uncertainly. "The people of Dongo are generous."

As they entered the Town Hall Lazzaro asked, "Where is your son Vittorio?"

"I don't know."

"And Marshal Graziani?"

"I don't know. I think he is in Como."

Followed by a dozen curious townspeople who had pressed past the guards, Lazzaro escorted him into a long, simply furnished room overlooking the square. Mussolini took off the German coat and sat on a bench.

"Do you want anything?" Lazzaro asked.

"Thank you, a glass of water."

"Why were you in the truck with the Germans when your ministers were in the armored car?"

"I don't know. They put me there. Perhaps they betrayed me in the end."

Lazzaro ordered the room cleared. "No one must disturb the prisoner," he told a guard. "See that he is protected, and use your gun if necessary."

The door suddenly burst open and two partisans pushed in Barracu, Casalinovo and Utimpergher.

When they saw Mussolini they snapped to attention. *"Evviva Il Duce!"* He nodded absently.

A crowd jammed against the door, trying to get in. "Clear them all out!" Lazzaro ordered. He told a partisan to relay the news of Mussolini's capture to Bellini, and went back to the German convoy.

"There's a Spanish consul here who wants to leave at once," a partisan told him.

"Have you examined his papers?"

"Yes, they seem all right. He says he has to get back to Switzerland urgently for an appointment. Shall I let him go?"

"Just a minute, I'll come myself." Lazzaro walked up to a yellow Alfa-Romeo. The driver was large, fat, fair-haired and had a birthmark on his pudgy chin. Next to him sat a beautiful young lady who looked nervously at Lazzaro. In the back seat was another woman, face half hidden in a fur collar, and two children.

Lazzaro put his foot on the running board. "Are you the Spanish consul?"

"Yes," Marcello Petacci answered with a show of annoyance. "And I'm in a hurry."

His perfect Italian made Lazzaro suspicious. "May I see your papers, please?"

Petacci bristled but finally handed over three yellow-backed passports stamped "Consulado Español en Milan." Lazzaro didn't like the "Spanish official" and was secretly gratified to discover that the stamp on one of the photographs was printed, not embossed. "These passports are fakes," he said. "You are under arrest!"

In the back seat Petacci's wife looked imploringly at Lazzaro.

"What do you mean?" Petacci blustered. "You'll pay for this." He had an appointment at seven o'clock in Switzerland, he said, with a titled Englishman. "I've never heard such impudence!"

Lazzaro pocketed the passports and ordered the protesting Petacci to drive up to the Town Hall, and then went to look for Bellini.

He met the count on the road at the edge of town. "I have just captured Mussolini in Dongo," he said matter-of-factly.

Bellini's first thought was: What an extra load of trouble! "All right," he said. "Let's go and see."

Mussolini was still sitting on the bench, staring blankly into space. To Bellini he looked old and decrepit.

Bellini said he was in command. "I give you my word that no harm will come to you."

The Duce looked searchingly at the young count, then lowered his head and dejectedly mumbled, "Thank you."

Bellini went up to Barracu, whose right arm was being bandaged by the local druggist. "Why did you try to move forward?" Bellini asked, hurt that Barracu had gone against his word. "Why did you start firing?"

Barracu explained that the partisans had fired first and that "you mustn't think that I broke my word!"

Bellini inquired solicitously about Barracu's wound, and left to take a look at the "Spaniards," who had been taken to a small room in the Town Hall. Petacci rose from his chair at once, and extending his hand, introduced himself as the Spanish consul. "I'm in a tremendous hurry.

I'm attached to the embassy in Milan and have a most important diplomatic mission to undertake." He asked for permission to proceed at once with his wife and children.

Bellini said that would be impossible until their papers were verified. He nodded toward Claretta. "Is the other lady with you?"

Petacci looked at his sister. "No, we don't know her. She asked us for a lift and we have just brought her with us."

One of the children ran to Signora Petacci, a tall, fair-haired woman, and said in Italian, "Mommy, why are we waiting here? Won't these stupid partisans let us go?"

"You bring your children up well, signora," said Bellini.

She stammered an apology. "You know what children are . . . they pick up things, then repeat them."

"And who are you, signora?" Bellini asked, turning to Claretta. She was pretty, he thought, but looked exhausted.

"Oh, nobody in particular. I happened to be in Como during the disturbances, and to avoid being caught in any danger I asked these people for a lift so that I could get away to somewhere quiet. I've certainly landed myself into a mess now. What are you going to do with me?"

Bellini said that would be decided later. He saluted and left.

Lazzaro was in the long room examining the ministers' briefcases and leather portfolios. When he had finished he asked Mussolini, "What about you?"

"I only had one portfolio. It's there behind you."

Lazzaro put a large portfolio in brownish yellow leather on the table. As he was opening it the Duce said in a low, solemn voice, "Those are secret documents. I warn you: they are of great historical importance."

Lazzaro glanced hurriedly through the papers. They dealt with Trieste, the Verona trials* and a plan of escape to Switzerland; an entire folder contained correspondence with Hitler. Underneath the papers were 160 gold sovereigns.

"They were meant for my most trusted friends," Mussolini mumbled.

Lazzaro also found five checks, three were for 500,000 lire each. He put the money aside and handed Mussolini the rest of the contents: a pair of black leather gloves, a handkerchief and a pencil. He offered him a cigarette. The Duce declined with thanks, but Barracu accepted.

Bellini had just re-entered the small room when he heard a commotion outside. He saw three partisans escorting Pavolini from the jetty; he was dripping wet. Bellini feared the crowd might lynch a man so generally detested and rushed out to escort him into the Town Hall.

Pavolini's forehead was bleeding and he trembled. When he saw Mus-

---

* The trials held by Mussolini against those fellow Italians who had arrested him in the coup d'état of July 25, 1943.

solini he feebly raised his right forearm in salute. Mussolini nodded slightly.

Not until late that afternoon did Bellini fully realize the heavy responsibility Mussolini's capture entailed. He had to guard against two dangers: another German column might try to free the Duce or the townspeople might murder him.

With the approval of two Communist partisan leaders—Michele Moretti and Captain Neri (his real name was Luigi Canale)—it was decided to transfer the Duce to a safer place for the night. First he would be moved openly to the *finanzieri* (border guard) barracks of Germasino, about three miles up in the mountains. Then a few trusted men would secretly take him to a final hiding place.

The sun was just setting when Mussolini got into a car with a *finanzieri* sergeant; Bellini sat next to the driver. Followed by a truckload of partisans, they made a show of leaving town and headed up a steep, primitive road. Bellini watched Lake Como get smaller and smaller as the horizon widened, revealing ranges of snow-covered peaks. In those mountains he had endured a year of hardship and danger. It was almost all over now and he could return home—if he had a home, if his family were still alive.

He should hate the squat man in the back seat, but strangely, he didn't. He turned, held out a pack of cigarettes.

"No, thank you," the Duce said, explaining that he rarely smoked.

"I've always envied people who never start smoking. It's a terrible thing to want a smoke and then not have a cigarette." They were quiet. Then Bellini turned around again and said, "You have done a great many things in your life, some good, some bad . . . . But what I'll never understand—what I can never forgive—is that you let your men act in such an inhuman, bestial way against our comrades who fell in your hands . . ."

"You can't blame me for that!" Mussolini said passionately. "It's not true!" Beating a fist on his knee, he said he could prove it with documents.

At the barracks Bellini reassured Mussolini he was safe. "Everyone has been told to treat you with consideration and to attend to your wishes. Good-bye. We shall meet again soon. Do you want anything before I go?"

The Duce said no but changed his mind. "I should like you to give my regards to a lady you're holding in Dongo. The lady traveling with the Spanish gentleman."

"And what do you want me to say?"

"Oh, nothing in particular. Only that I am well, that I send her my regards and that she is not to worry about me."

"Certainly—but tell me, who is the lady?"

"Well, you see . . . she's a close friend."

"You could at least tell me her name if I'm expected to speak to her."

"What does her name matter," said the Duce, embarrassed. "She is simply a good friend and I wouldn't like to get her into any trouble, poor woman."

Bellini said he would eventually find out who she was.

Mussolini looked furtively around the room. "It's Signora Petacci," he whispered.

Like everyone else, Bellini knew she was the Duce's mistress. "I'll give the lady your message."

"I beg you not to reveal this to anyone!" said Mussolini. "I've trusted you, but it's a confidence which must stay between the two of us. I don't want any harm to come to her on my account. You must promise me that no one else will know."

Bellini saluted and left.

Mussolini relaxed, and during dinner he regaled the wide-eyed guards with stories of his visit to Russia to see Stalin and of the imminent collapse of the British Empire. "Youth is beautiful, beautiful!" he exclaimed, and when a young guard smiled he said, "Yes, yes, I mean it. Youth *is* beautiful. I love the young even when they bear arms against me." He held out his gold watch. "Take it in my memory."

In a small room of the Town Hall Claretta Petacci asked a guard for a brandy, but once it arrived she only took a sip. She still wore a turban-shaped hat and a mink coat; on her left hand was a gold wedding ring. She asked for coffee, tasted it daintily and said it was not good enough. She wondered if she could have another brandy.

The guard told her to drink the brandy he'd just brought.

"Dust has settled on it," she said a bit indignantly. "It might be harmful." But finally she picked up the glass of brandy, cleaned the rim and drank it. "I hope it won't make me ill," she said.

She pricked her finger with a pin and called for a doctor; then broke a fingernail and asked for a nail file.

When Bellini walked in she was alone. "Someone has asked to be remembered to you," he said quietly.

She looked up, surprised. "Remembered to me? Who?"

"Someone I have just left." He sat down next to her. "One of my prisoners." The only one she knew was the Spanish gentleman who had given her the ride. "No. This is another person whom you know well. Mussolini."

"Mussolini! But I don't know him . . ."

Bellini said it was no good pretending. "I know who you are, signora. Mussolini himself told me." He got up as if to leave. She was, he thought, only an adventuress.

"Please," she said. "Can you assure me this is true, that Mussolini himself gave you the message?"

"I tell you again I know who you are. You are Signora Petacci."

She sighed deeply. "Yes, it's true, I am Clara Petacci." Suddenly she was full of questions. What message did Mussolini send? Where was he? Was he in danger? Who was in command?

He begged her to calm down. He was in command, he said, and Mussolini was in no danger—for the moment.

"For the moment?" she cried in alarm. "Why for the moment? What could happen to him? Tell me, for pity's sake!"

He told her no harm would come to Mussolini if no attempts were made to rescue him.

"Rescue him? But who on earth is going to do that? If you only knew what I've seen these last few days! God, what wretches! It was a rout. They all ran away. All they thought of was saving their miserable skins. Nobody gave a thought to the man they professed to love and for whom they were supposed to lay down their lives . . ." She wept, and then was silent as Bellini sat watching her, wondering if he could be wrong about her. "What did he tell you to say to me?" she asked again.

"He simply wanted me to give you his regards and not to worry about him."

When she begged him to turn Mussolini over to the Allies, Bellini said, "The Allies have nothing to do with it. On the contrary, I'll do what I can to see that he *doesn't* fall into their hands. His future concerns Italians only . . ."

As he got up she asked a little hesitantly, "Tell me, what will you do with me?"

"I don't know. You've been very close to Mussolini and are too well known. The authorities will decide."

Suddenly she asked Bellini if he believed she had become Mussolini's mistress for selfish reasons.

He was too embarrassed to answer.

"Oh, God, you too! You believe everything they've said about me!" She began to sob. "I loved him so much that his life became mine, the only time I lived was when I was with him and that was never for very long. You must believe me!"

For a moment he thought she was acting; then he said gently that he believed everything she had told him.

She put a handkerchief to her eyes. "You are very kind," she said tremulously, and asked if he would grant her a favor.

He said he would first have to hear what it was. He drew his chair closer, lit a cigarette and waited while she seemed to be composing her thoughts, with eyes half closed. Finally, in a calm voice, she told him that she had met Mussolini in 1926, when she was only twenty. "He was still a very young-looking man who in every way belied his age." He was forty-three at the time; she had been struck not by his looks, but by his strong personality and the impression he gave of daring and firmness.

However, she had felt that his gaiety was forced, his mind uneasy and that not one of his many mistresses had ever given him true love. "But all *I* wanted was that he should think of me as a dear and trusted friend whom one turns to in order to escape for a brief time from the stresses of life."

She asked Bellini if she was boring him with the long story, and he truthfully replied that she certainly was not. She told about their love and her utter disinterest in politics and how even his former mistresses came to her for help. "And believe me, I often put in a good word for these women too. I always knew about all the women he'd had and even that didn't make me jealous. I understood and forgave. I was content to be the one who ruled his heart and feelings." For this reason she had never thought of leaving him at the end. She leaned forward, grasped Bellini's hand and said, "Let me go to him!"

Startled, Bellini freed his hand gently and said that the Fascists might attempt to liberate the Duce, which would endanger her own life.

"Now I know," she cried, and repeated over and over again, "you're going to shoot him!" She at last dried her tears with trembling fingers. "You must promise that if Mussolini is shot, I can be near him until that last moment and that I shall be shot with him. Is that too much to ask?"

"But, signora . . ."

"I want to die with him." Her voice still was shaking but she spoke more calmly. "My life will be nothing once he is dead. I'd die anyway, but more slowly and with greater suffering."

Her suppressed passion moved him even more than her outbursts. "Please don't upset yourself so. I swear to you I've no intention of shooting Mussolini."

She looked at him searchingly and he smiled to reassure her. She sighed. "I believe you," she said.

"I'll try to do whatever I can" were his parting words.

Bellini went into the long room and told the two Communist partisans, Captain Neri and Moretti, that the lady in the next room was Claretta Petacci. He repeated her request and added, "I can't see that it would do any harm. I've just about agreed to it, but I'd like your views first."

Both Neri and Moretti said they had no objections and Bellini went back to the other room. "Well, signora," he said cheerfully, "we're going to do what you ask. We've decided to let you be together. Are you happy?"

"Thank you! Thank you!" She tried to kiss Bellini's hand but he pulled it back in embarrassment.

By eleven o'clock at night Bellini, Neri and Moretti still had received no instructions from partisan headquarters in Milan. They decided to go ahead with their own plans to hide Mussolini. Bellini said he would leave at once for Germasino to get him.

It was raining hard when the count walked out into the town square. The lake looked spectral. It was a perfect night, he thought, to move the Duce. He told his driver to head for the *finanzieri* barracks.

The partisan in charge, Buffelli, led Bellini to a cell where Mussolini was lying on a cot.

"Are you asleep?" Buffelli asked softly.

The Duce pulled back the covers. "Oh, no, I was only dozing."

"I'm sorry to disturb you, but you have to get up. We're taking you somewhere else."

"This is only a move to a safer place," Bellini added.

"I was expecting it," said the Duce.

He was shivering and the count told him to wrap up well.

"I'll get your overcoat," Buffelli said and started toward the German coat lying on the chair.

"No, no," Mussolini said quickly. "I don't want that German greatcoat any more. I've finished with the Germans now. They have betrayed me three times. I don't want anything of theirs. I'd rather have something else."

Bellini helped him into a *finanzieri* coat and flung a military cape around his shoulders. He told the Duce it would be best to bandage his head to hide his face. "Do you mind?"

"Not if you think it's necessary."

The Duce's face was covered except for eyes and mouth, and they started back to Dongo. "Tell me, please," Mussolini asked hesitantly, "were you able to speak to the lady?" Bellini said he had. "And how is she?"

"Quite well, considering the circumstances. She is, of course, very depressed and worried about the future." The bandaged figure beside Bellini was silent. "Now I'll give you a surprise which I think will please you. The lady asked to be allowed to join you, and she begged and prayed so earnestly that we finally agreed."

"What!" Obviously moved, Mussolini silently fussed with his bandages a moment, then cleared his throat several times and said, "May I know where you are taking me?"

"Near Como, where you can be kept in the greatest security and secrecy."

In Como, Colonel Baron Giovanni Sardagna, the local partisan commander, had just received a telegram from Milan headquarters: BRING MUSSOLINI AND THE GERARCHI [ministers] TO MILAN AS SOON AS POSSIBLE.

Sardagna called Milan and said it was too risky to bring the Duce there. It was decided, instead, to take him by boat to Blevio, a village on the east coast of the lake about four miles north of Como, where he could be hidden temporarily at the secluded villa of Remo Cademartori, an industrialist.

Cademartori was informed that he would soon have a guest, a wounded English officer. He surmised that it was Mussolini and walked to his boathouse, where he waited on the steps with his aged gardener.

Mussolini and his two escorts were approaching Dongo. They rounded a bend, saw a car parked near a bridge and stopped. Moretti got out of the car and told the count that everything was ready. Bellini saw Captain Neri and Claretta getting out too and told Mussolini he could join them.

"Good evening, Eccellenza," Claretta greeted him formally.

"Good evening, signora," Mussolini replied. They looked at each other silently as the rain poured down. "Why have you followed me?"

"Because I wanted to. But what has happened to you? Are you wounded?"

"No, it's nothing." Mussolini nervously fingered his bandaged head. "Merely a precaution."

"We must go," Bellini said. "Please go back to your car, signora."

"But why can't we stay together?" Claretta asked. "You promised me."

Bellini said it was safer to be in separate cars. Gianna, a partisan girl who was to help guard Mussolini, swaggered up to Bellini. "Don't worry!" She flourished a big revolver. "He won't get away from me. If I see anything suspicious I'll shoot him." Bellini told her not to do any shooting unless he gave the word. "All right, but if anything happens to you I'll shoot him on the spot!"

They put Mussolini between them in the back seat. Captain Neri led the way in the other car; the partisans at every roadblock knew him. As they approached Menaggio, Mussolini predicted that there would be a wonderful harvest that year, especially of grain and grapes. Suddenly there was a machine-gun burst.

Bellini ordered the driver to pull over to the extreme right of the road under the shelter of a large overhanging rock. Neri jumped out, identified himself and the shooting stopped. But partisans at the next roadblock two miles farther on did not recognize him. One, however, cried "Pedro!" when he saw Bellini. It was the count's partisan name. "I can't believe it! You're still alive!"

Bellini explained that the "mummy" next to him was a badly wounded partisan. "We're taking him to Como and it's very urgent. See if you can get us through quickly."

At the Moltrasio square, five miles before Como, they heard shooting in the distance and a local man told them the Allies were fighting pockets of Fascists in the streets of Como.

They conferred and decided to go back. Neri said he knew a good hiding place in a village off the lake-front highway. They turned around and after fourteen miles came to Azzano.

"Everybody out, please," Neri said. "We have a little farther to go on foot."

In the downpour they started up a steep cobblestone path through the town. Soon they left the houses behind and there were only fields. The footing was slippery, particularly for Claretta, who wore high-heeled shoes. Bellini took a heavy bundle from her and gave it to a guard. Mussolini, wrapped in a blanket, took her by one arm and Bellini by the other. They trudged up the hill more than half a mile before coming to the outskirts of the village of Bonzanigo.

Neri turned toward the first house, a three-story white building, and knocked on the back door.

Giacomo de Maria came down the stairs, opened the door and blinked his eyes sleepily. Neri asked him to shelter a "wounded man" and the group was invited inside. Giacomo led them up narrow stairs to the kitchen on the next floor, where his wife, Lia, was already lighting the wood in a large fireplace.

The Marias agreed to keep Mussolini and Claretta for a few days in utmost secrecy and sent their sons up in the mountains to make room for the couple. Lia brewed a pot of ersatz coffee. Mussolini didn't drink it, but Claretta, who had refused better coffee at Dongo, drank hers eagerly.

Bellini and Moretti climbed to the top floor to inspect the sons' room. It was not large, with two small chests, a wash bowl, two chairs, a little wardrobe and a double bed with a garish religious print over it. Looking out the small window, Bellini saw a twenty-foot drop; escape was out of the question.

Mussolini and Claretta were sitting calmly near the kitchen fire, enjoying the warmth, when Bellini returned. He told two of the guards to stay on duty until he sent someone to relieve them. Bellini promised to have Claretta's suitcase sent from Dongo. As he went out he turned to get a final look of the couple. Mussolini, face still bandaged and hands in lap, was leaning back, staring at the flames while Claretta was bowed forward, elbows on knees, chin in hand.

A few minutes later Claretta asked to go to the bathroom and Lia took her to a rude shed. A guard stood watch. By the time Lia returned to the kitchen Mussolini had removed the bandages. His features were so familiar that she took her husband aside and whispered, "It looks like Mussolini, but it's impossible. What would the Duce be doing in the home of farmers?" They guessed he was a German prisoner, but they had no idea who the pretty woman was.

Lia showed Claretta the bedroom. "Come and see," she called down to Mussolini. "She has prepared a clean room for us."

The Duce dutifully tried the bed with his hand like any tourist and said to Lia, "It's nice. Thank you."

Claretta asked if they could have a second pillow. "He is used to sleeping with two," she explained. "I don't use any."

Lia brought in the second pillow and said goodnight. As she walked downstairs she thought, What nice people they are!

## 2.

In Milan a large group of partisan leaders decided to send Walter Audisio, whose *nom de guerre* was Colonel Valerio, to bring back Mussolini. The meeting was adjourned, but the Communists remained and were told that Palmiro Togliatti, head of the Italian Communist Party, had secretly ordered the summary execution of Mussolini and his mistress. Without dissent it was agreed that Colonel Valerio would shoot the prisoners as soon as they were properly identified. Valerio himself was a dedicated Communist who had fought in Spain.

To forestall any Allied attempts to capture Mussolini alive, the Communists telegraphed Allied headquarters in Siena:

THE COMMITTEE OF NATIONAL LIBERATION REGRET NOT ABLE TO HAND OVER MUSSOLINI WHO HAVING BEEN TRIED BY POPULAR TRIBUNAL HAS BEEN SHOT IN THE SAME PLACE WHERE FIFTEEN PATRIOTS WERE SHOT BY FASCISTS STOP.

Valerio left Milan soon after dawn, on April 28, with an escort of some fifteen well-armed partisans, but an hour later he was detained by Como partisans who opposed taking Mussolini to Milan. They wanted the honor of putting him in their own jail.

Finally Valerio—a tall, heavy-set, mustached man of about forty—brandished a pistol and insisted that he be allowed to telephone Milan headquarters. The call was made and a compromise was reached: Valerio could proceed to Dongo and get Mussolini, but he had to take along two Como partisans named Sforni and de Angelis.

At one-thirty a partisan ran in and breathlessly told Bellini that a truck and black car had just pulled into the Dongo square. Armed men claiming to be partisans were surrounding the Town Hall and their leader demanded to see the local commander.

Bellini feared they were plotting to free the prisoners. He phoned Lazzaro in Domaso and ordered him to bring help at once, then walked out into the square. Standing in line were fifteen men armed with machine pistols. In their new, pressed khaki uniforms they seemed strange partisans. A tall, brown-skinned man, slightly bald, introduced himself as Colonel Valerio, special envoy from GHQ of the Volunteers for Freedom

Corps. "I need to speak to you in private on matters of the greatest importance," he said imperiously.

Bellini told him to come to his office. "Leave your men here and follow me."

"My men must come with me," said Valerio.

Bellini asked the men if they were hungry. They were, of course, and Bellini sent them off to the kitchen.

Bellini found Valerio's identification papers in order, but something about the colonel bothered him. The count said he preferred handing over the important prisoners to his own HQ. "We captured them, after all."

"That's out of the question," Valerio said tersely. "I've come to shoot them."

Bellini was staggered.

"The sentence has been passed by the National Committee of Liberation and it's an order from general headquarters. I'm charged with carrying out that order and I intend to do so."

Bellini said he had to confer with his colleagues. Neri, Moretti and Gianna, the girl partisan—Communists like Valerio—felt the same as Bellini did. "We mustn't hand them over," Gianna repeated again and again. But nobody could think of an alternative.

"We will give you the prisoners," Bellini finally told Valerio. "But we're all against what you're going to do."

Valerio looked patronizingly at the count and asked for a list of prisoners. "Benito Mussolini," he read and made a cross with a pencil. "Death! Clara Petacci . . . death!"

Bellini said it was unthinkable to shoot a woman.

"She was Mussolini's adviser and behind his politics for years," Valerio said.

"She was only his mistress!"

In exasperation Valerio said he had his orders. "I know what I'm doing," he shouted. "And I'm the one to decide." He said he was in a hurry and had to get back to Milan before dark with the bodies. Bellini insisted that the sentences come from a properly constituted court but finally agreed to have all the prisoners brought to the Town Hall.

A partisan came in with the information that two men named Sforni and de Angelis claimed to have been sent by the Como National Committee of Liberation to stop Valerio and to take charge of Mussolini. But when they could not produce proper credentials, Bellini was compelled to stand by while Valerio ordered them locked up.

Claretta Petacci's brother was brought in.

*"Habla usted español?"* Valerio asked.

Petacci hesitated, then said, "No, but I speak French."

"What," Valerio said sarcastically, "a Spanish consul who doesn't speak Spanish!"

Petacci lamely explained that he had been living in Italy for twenty years but had seen his father in Spain six months before. "And when you speak to your father, you talk in French?" taunted Valerio. He jumped up and slapped Petacci's face. "I know who you are, you swine!" He grabbed a pistol. "You're Vittorio Mussolini! Don't you remember when you were strutting about in the film studios?"

Petacci stammered, "But . . . you're mistaken."

The enraged Valerio backed him against the wall and told Lazzaro, "Take him outside and shoot him—now!"

Lazzaro reluctantly took out his pistol and ordered Petacci to walk ahead of him. All the way down the stairs Petacci insisted he wasn't Vittorio Mussolini. As they passed through the square, the crowd pressed closer, shouting, "Look how fat he is!" "Kill him!"

Lazzaro held the mob off with his gun. He led Petacci toward the Capuchin monastery and sent for a priest. Then he lit a cigarette for his prisoner. "It's true that I am not the Spanish consul," Petacci admitted. "Nor am I Vittorio Mussolini. I'm head of the Italian Intelligence Service."

Lazzaro wished he would stop talking so he could think. How could he shoot a man just because he was Vittorio Mussolini?

The Capuchin priest came and Lazzaro walked off a few yards to give the two a half-hour's privacy. When the time was up, the priest begged Lazzaro for a few more minutes "to explain some facts of the greatest importance."

"I'm not the Spanish consul but I am not Vittorio Mussolini either!" Petacci shouted. "I'm Marcello Petacci."

"What of it?" Lazzaro replied, thinking he had said "Pertacci."

"Marcello Petacci," the prisoner repeated.

"Pertacci, Pertacci?"

"Not *Per*tacci, *Pe*tacci."

It was about four o'clock in the afternoon when Valerio, Moretti and Neri knocked at the door of the Maria house. Valerio charged up to the third floor and flung open the bedroom door. "I have come to rescue you!" he said.

"Really?" Mussolini was sardonic.

Claretta began pawing through a pile of clothes. Valerio asked impatiently, "What are you looking for?"

"My panties . . ."

The colonel told them to hurry up and herded them down the stairs.

From the upstairs window, Lia watched them go out the gate. She went into the bedroom. The pillows were stained with mascara.

Mussolini and Claretta were escorted through Bonzanigo to the little town square, where some women were pounding clothes against a stone water trough. They went through an ancient archway, and climbed into a parked car. With two men on the running board, the car started slowly down the steep hill toward Azzano. Two curious fishermen chased after it.

The car had only gone a few hundred yards when it stopped in front of a large iron gate leading to a villa.

Valerio got out. Acting as if he sensed danger, he whispered, "I heard a noise!" He cautioned Mussolini and Claretta to be quiet. "I'm going ahead to see." He moved stealthily down the road to a sharp curve, then came back and called softly for them to hide near the gate.

Mussolini was apprehensive but went to the gate. Claretta joined him. There was an awkward silence. Suddenly Valerio cried out, "By order of the general headquarters of the Volunteers for Freedom Corps I am required to render justice to the Italian people!"

Mussolini stood motionless but Claretta threw her arms around his neck and shouted, "No, he mustn't die!"

"Move away if you don't want to die too," Valerio said.

Claretta stepped to the Duce's right. With sweat running down his round face, Valerio aimed a machine pistol at Mussolini and pressed the trigger. Nothing happened. He grabbed his pistol. This too jammed and he called to Moretti, "Bring me your gun."

Moretti handed over a Mas 7.65 machine pistol given him by Bellini only a month before. From ten feet Valerio fired a burst of five shots. Mussolini crumpled to his knees and pitched forward to the ground.

Valerio swung the gun on Claretta.

Bellini had gone to pick up six other prisoners at the *finanzieri* barracks in Germasino. Coming back down the steep hill to Dongo, the prisoners chatted about the scenery. "A pity we're not in a position to enjoy it better," Pavolini said lightly.

"I wonder why we ended up here?" Casalinovo mused.

"Well, what do you expect," Pavolini joked, "Mussolini was always right."

As Bellini got out of his car at the Town Hall, Lazzaro was just approaching with Petacci. Lazzaro explained that his prisoner claimed to be Marcello Petacci, not Vittorio Mussolini. A partisan interrupted and said he had seen Vittorio many times. "I can assure you that Spanish consul isn't him."

When Petacci saw the other prisoners he cried, "They know me!" But Pavolini, Casalinovo and Barracu turned away. To them he was worse than a pimp.

"Do you know this man?" Lazzaro asked.

There was silence.

Lazzaro turned to Barracu. "Do you know this man?"

"No," said the Undersecretary, staring straight ahead.

"And you, Pavolini?"

"No."

Petacci yelled in rage, "Tell him who I am! Go on, tell him! You know me, all of you!"

"Do you know this man or don't you?" Lazzaro asked impatiently. Finally Barracu admitted that he did. "Well, who is he then?" yelled Lazzaro. There was a long silence. Barracu looked at Petacci and said scornfully, "We know him only as 'Fosco'."

Petacci's eyes widened in astonishment.

He was led away.

Minutes later another car careened up to the Town Hall. Valerio leaned out shouting excitedly, "Justice is done! Mussolini is dead!"

Bellini was appalled. "But I thought we had agreed . . ."

"I know, I know. But I couldn't waste any more time. Where are the others? Do you have them?"

Disgusted, Bellini took Valerio to the first floor of the Town Hall, where all the prisoners were held in the huge, high-ceilinged, ornate Golden Hall. On the landing Dr. Rubini intercepted Valerio and begged him not to shoot anyone else. The colonel refused and Rubini indignantly said he would resign as mayor.

A priest was summoned from the monastery and given three minutes to console the prisoners. It began to drizzle. The sky was dark, a somber backdrop to the theatrical setting of the square. Townspeople crowded around in an eager, almost festive mood. Valerio wanted to make up a firing squad of half of his men and half of Bellini's.

"We're against what you're doing," Bellini said. "I have to obey, so I'll hand over the prisoners to you. But that's all. I'll never order any of my men to take part in the execution. Not only that, but when I've handed over the prisoners, I'll withdraw from the square so I won't have to witness it and so I can show my disapproval."

"I command you to stay!" Valerio shouted. "Understand? That is an order!"

"If it's an order," Bellini said stiffly, "I shall obey."

Fifteen prisoners, flanked by partisans, started walking slowly across the square. Silently they lined up along the low parapet at the lake's edge, their backs to the lake. Valerio's firing squad, armed with machine pistols, stationed themselves about five yards away. While the priest was administering the last rites, Valerio remembered the Spanish consul and ordered him to be lined up with the others. Petacci was escorted from the Town Hall.

"We don't want him with us," the other condemned men cried out. "He's a traitor!" They shook their fists.

Petacci stumbled back in consternation.

"Put him with the others!" Valerio yelled. "Finish him off!"

"I don't see what difference it makes," Bellini said.

Valerio relented and Petacci was led to one side.

The commander of the firing squad called, "Prisoners, attention! About . . . face!" Several of the condemned men raised their arms in the Fascist salute and others shouted, "Long live Italy!" The others looked bewildered. But they all finally turned around to face the lake, except Barracu who stepped one pace forward and pointed to his decoration. "I hold the gold medal. I have the right to be shot in the chest."

Bellini asked Valerio to grant this request, but he answered, "In the back! You'll be shot in the back like the rest!"

Barracu briskly about-faced. The square was silent.

"Squad . . . load. Take . . . aim. Fire!"

There was a crackling of shots and again silence.

"Bring out Petacci!" someone shouted.

Struggling desperately, his face contorted with fear, Petacci was dragged forward by two partisans. "You can't shoot me!" he screamed. "You mustn't! You're making a terrible mistake. After all I've done for Italy!"

At the sight of the bodies he suddenly broke away from his guards and dashed through the crowd toward the Hotel Dongo to his wife and children. He was caught and carried back to the parapet kicking and thrashing. Again he gave a tremendous heave and freed himself. With a yell he leaped into the lake and began swimming frantically. Bullets from rifles smashed into him and he disappeared.

Guns were fired into the air in a wild, uncontrollable release of tension. When the shooting finally died down, Valerio asked Bellini to fish Petacci's body out of the lake. "Get someone else," said the count.

Early the next morning, a Sunday, the bodies of Mussolini, Claretta and the executed Fascists were carted to a half-built gas station in Milan, where nine months earlier fifteen hostages had been killed by the Germans. The bodies were dumped in a pile and it wasn't until dawn that someone arranged them in a row. Mussolini was pulled to one side so that his head rested on Claretta's breasts.

A large crowd gathered and the bodies were kicked and mutilated. Mussolini, mouth open, was strung up by his feet on an overhanging girder. His mistress was hung next to him. Her skirt fell over her head but a woman finally climbed on a box and tucked it between Claretta's roped legs. She looked strangely at peace, but Mussolini's battered, swollen face was cruelly distorted.

Twenty-three years before, armed with little more than an idea, Mussolini had marched on Rome to seize the government. Today he was reviled and dead, and so was Fascism.

# 29

## "The Chief Is Dead"

**1.**

By the morning of April 28 Army Group Vistula was almost completely disjointed and its leadership was on the verge of open rebellion.

Busse's Ninth Army was no longer a military force, only a surrounded group of exhausted men desperately trying to escape with thousands of civilians to the safety of Wenck's lines. The other half of Heinrici's army group, Manteuffel's Third Panzer Army, had also abandoned its fixed positions and was making a fighting withdrawal to the west. It too was trying to escape the Russians, and its goal was surrender to the Anglo-Americans.

In defiance of Hitler, Manteuffel had ordered this general retreat, and when Heinrici phoned Jodl at ten in the morning that one corps was already as far back as the Havel River, the usually temperate Jodl shouted, "They're lying to me from all quarters!"

Keitel phoned Manteuffel direct, and accused him of "sheer defeatism." He said he was coming up to Third Panzer Army headquarters at Neubrandenburg early that afternoon to find out personally what was going on.

Informed of this, Heinrici drove at once to Neubrandenburg and was waiting there with Manteuffel until two-thirty when a message came instructing them to meet Keitel at Neustrelitz, a town eighteen miles to the south. The two generals started off, but halfway to Neustrelitz they saw Keitel and his party approaching. Near a lake both groups turned off the road and a conference began in a small woods. Hiding near by were three of Manteuffel's staff officers. Armed with machine pistols, they were determined to seize Keitel by force if he made any move to arrest their commander.

"Army Group is only moving backwards!" Keitel cried. "The Group and Army leadership is much too soft. If you'd follow the example of other people and have the nerve to take rigorous steps and shoot a thousand deserters, Army Group would hold its ground."

Heinrici stiffly replied that he didn't "operate that way," and Keitel turned on Manteuffel, accusing him of withdrawing without orders. When Heinrici spoke up in defense of his subordinate, Keitel told him that he simply wasn't "tough enough."

Heinrici impetuously took Keitel's arm and led him to the highway, which was jammed with vehicles fleeing in obvious disorder. Heinrici pointed to a horse-drawn cart filled with battle-weary airmen. "Why don't you set an example for me yourself?" he asked.

Keitel stopped the cart and ordered the men to dismount. "Take them back to Third Panzer Army headquarters and have them court-martialed!" he said, and started toward his car. He stopped suddenly and angrily shook a finger at Heinrici. "Strictly follow OKW orders from now on!" he shouted.

But Heinrici was not cowed. "How can I possibly follow those orders when OKW isn't even properly informed about present conditions?"

Stung, Keitel yelled, "You will hear the results of this conversation!"

Manteuffel stepped forward, as defiant as Heinrici. "The Third Panzer Army will follow only orders given by General von Manteuffel!"

Keitel glared at the two rebellious generals and told them again to obey orders to the letter. "You will be responsible for the verdict of history!"

"I'm responsible for all the orders I give," Manteuffel said. "And I won't blame anyone else for them." His three staff officers edged forward, machine pistols at the ready.

But Keitel only spun around, and without saying good-bye, stepped into his car.

By nightfall the Russians had broken through the line that was shielding Manteuffel's withdrawal and were swarming toward Neubrandenburg itself. Heinrici phoned Keitel.

"That's what happens when you take it upon yourself to abandon positions!" Keitel snapped.

"I have never taken it upon myself to abandon any position," Heinrici replied coldly. "The situation has always warranted it." He asked permission to give up Swinemünde, which was being defended by an untrained division of recruits.

"Do you possibly think I could tell the Führer that the last stronghold on the Oder is going to be abandoned?"

"Why should I sacrifice those recruits for a lost cause?" Heinrici shot back. "I'm completely responsible for my men. And I have been in two world wars."

"You have no responsibility at all! The person who issues the order in the first place has the responsibility."

"I've always felt responsible to my own conscience and the people of Germany. I simply cannot squander lives." He again formally requested the withdrawal.

"You must hold Swinemünde."

"If you insist, you'll have to get someone else to carry out your orders."

"I warn you," Keitel sputtered. "You're old enough to know what it means to disobey an order in battle."

"Herr Generalfeldmarschall, I repeat, if you want this order carried out, find someone else."

"I warn you a second time. Disobeying an order means court-martial."

Now it was Heinrici who lost his temper. "This is an impossible situation —the way I'm being treated!" he cried. He struggled to regain control of himself. "I've done my duty to the best of my ability and with the complete approval of my fellow officers. I'd lose my self-respect if I allowed myself to be forced to do something I felt was wrong. I will inform Swinemünde that Feldmarschall Keitel insists that it be defended. But since I can't concur in this order, I place my command at your disposal!"

"With the authority invested in me by the Führer, I herewith relieve you of your command! Turn over all your official business immediately to General von Manteuffel."

But Manteuffel was in no mood to play a compliant role. He radioed Keitel that he refused to accept either the command or the promotion that went with it. He ended the message with a defiant: HERE ALL ORDERS ARE GIVEN BY MANTEUFFEL.

It was, in effect, the end of Army Group Vistula.


## 2.


The disintegration of the military hierarchy was even evident in the bunker. Just before dawn on April 28, Bormann, Krebs and Burgdorf, Chief of Army Personnel, were embroiled in a drunken argument. "Nine months ago I approached my present task with all my strength and idealism!" railed Burgdorf. "I tried again and again to co-ordinate the Party and the Armed Forces." And because of this, he said, his fellow officers came to despise him and even called him a traitor to the officers' caste. "Today it's clear that these accusations are justified, and my labors were for nothing. My idealism was misplaced, and not only that, it was naïve and stupid!"

Krebs tried to quiet him but the noise had already wakened Freytag von Loringhoven in the next room. He shook young Boldt in the bunk above him. "You're missing something, my friend," he whispered. They could hear Burgdorf shout down the conciliatory Krebs. "Let me alone, Hans—all this has to be said! Perhaps it'll be too late to do so in another forty-eight hours. . . . Young officers with faith and idealism have gone to their death by the thousands. For what? The Fatherland? No! They have died for you!"

Burgdorf turned his attack on Bormann. Millions, he shouted, had been sacrificed so that Party members could further themselves. "For your life of luxury, for your thirst for power. You've annihilated our centuries-old culture, annihilated the German nation. That is your terrible guilt!"

"My dear fellow," Bormann said in a soothing voice, "you shouldn't be so personal about it. Even if all the others have enriched themselves, I at least am blameless. That much I swear on everything I hold sacred. Your health, my friend!"

In the next room the two eavesdroppers heard the clink of glasses. Then there was silence.

All that morning General Weidling worked on his plan to break out of Berlin in three echelons. It was obvious that the Russians would reach the Reich Chancellery in a day or two, and Weidling was so sure that he could get approval from the Führer at the evening conference that he ordered all his commanders to report at the bunker by midnight.

In her quarters Frau Goebbels was writing her son by a previous marriage, Harald Quandt, who was now an Allied prisoner of war. She told him that the whole family, including the six children, had been in the Führer bunker for the past week "so as to give our National Socialist life the only possible and honorable end."

The "glorious ideas" of Nazism were coming to an end "and with them everything beautiful and noble and good I have known in my life." A world without Hitler and National Socialism, she went on, was not worth living in. That was why she had brought the children to the bunker. They were too good for the life that was coming after defeat "and a merciful God will understand my reasons for sparing them that sort of life."

She told how, the night before, the Führer had pinned his own Party badge on her, and how proud and happy it made her. "May God give me the strength for my last and most difficult duty," she wrote. "There is only one thing we want now: to be true to death to the Führer and to finish our lives with him." Such an end was a "blessing of fate" she and "Papa" had never dared hope for.

"My darling son," concluded Frau Goebbels, "live for Germany!"

## 3.

At San Francisco, where the conference to set up a United Nations organization was still in session, Anthony Eden was holding his first meeting with the British delegation on the eighth floor of the Mark Hopkins Hotel.

"By the way," he said after briefing his colleagues on the Polish question, "there's one item of news from Europe that may interest you. We've heard from Stockholm that Himmler has made an offer through Bernadotte to surrender Germany unconditionally to the Americans and ourselves. Of course, we are letting the Russians know about it."

His manner was so casual that most of his listeners were scarcely impressed. But Jack Winocur, a young press official, thought, My God, what a story! and when he returned to his headquarters at the Palace Hotel and found no mention of the surrender offer in the papers, he assumed someone in London had "fallen asleep at the switch."

This is *the* story, he told himself. It could end the war overnight, but it would be the end of his government service if he disclosed it and was found out. Frustrated, he went to bed.

Around one o'clock in the morning of April 28, he was wakened by a phone call from Paul Scott Rankine of Reuters. "Anything going on?" Rankine asked. "I need something for the afternoon paper."

Winocur hesitated, then decided to take a chance. Every paper would carry a Reuters dispatch and BBC would pick it up. Winocur gave Rankine the details of Himmler's proposal and asked him not to reveal the source.

"Of course," Rankine assured him, and filed his story from the wireless desk in the lobby of the Palace:

IT WAS AUTHORITATIVELY STATED IN OFFICIAL CIRCLES HERE YESTERDAY THAT ACCORDING TO INFORMATION SENT TO STETTINIUS EDEN MOLOTOV A MESSAGE FROM HIMMLER GUARANTEEING GERMAN UNCONDITIONAL SURRENDER BUT NOT TO RUSSIA HAS BEEN CONVEYED TO BRITISH AND U. S. GOVERNMENTS STOP HIMMLER AUTHORITATIVELY STATED HAVE INFORMED WESTERN ALLIES HE IS IN POSITION ARRANGE UNCONDITIONAL SURRENDER AND HE HIMSELF IN FAVOUR OF IT RANKINE

The telegram got through to Reuters without censorship. When Jack Bell of the Associated Press in San Francisco learned that he had been scooped on one of the biggest stories of the war, he cornered Senator Tom Connally, a delegate to the conference, and asked for confirmation. Within minutes an A. P. bulletin, headed SURRENDER, was released.

SF APRIL 28 (AP) GERMANY HAS SURRENDERED TO THE ALLIED GOV-
ERNMENTS UNCONDITIONALLY, AND AN ANNOUNCEMENT IS EXPECTED
MOMENTARILY, IT WAS STATED BY A HIGH AMERICAN OFFICIAL TODAY.

The San Francisco *Call-Bulletin* issued an extra with the banner line:
NAZIS QUIT. Copies were taken into the Opera House, where Molotov
was presiding at a meeting of the conference. Delegates began rushing
around congratulating one another but Molotov, after a glance at a copy
of the paper, merely adjusted his pince-nez and rapped the gavel for
order.

In Washington the White House was flooded with phone calls and an
excited crowd quickly gathered and sang "God Bless America." Across
the street, at Blair House, Truman phoned Admiral Leahy at his home
and told him to check the truth of the report with Eisenhower. Leahy
phoned Bedell Smith at SHAEF headquarters. "We have a report that
Germans have asked Eisenhower for an armistice," he said. "We have
nothing official on it. What are the facts?"

Smith said no such request had been received; and Truman's suspicion
that the report had been based largely on Himmler's offer to Bernadotte
was confirmed.

It was dark when Truman left Blair House and walked across to the
White House. "Well, I was over here, as you can see, doing a little work,
and this rumor got started," he told the correspondents. "I had a call from
San Francisco, and the State Department called me. I just got in touch
with Admiral Leahy and had him call our headquarters Commander in
Chief in Europe, and there is no foundation for the rumor. That is all I
have to say."

## 4.

In the upper level of the bunker, in the little office of the Deutsches
Nachrichtenbüro, the official German news agency, Wolfgang Boigs, assistant to Heinz Lorenz, was listening to enemy broadcasts. Shortly before
nine o'clock he heard a BBC version of Rankine's dispatch. He translated
it and brought it immediately to "The Golden Cage," the DNB's nickname
for Hitler's quarters.

Hitler read the message without emotion, as if resigned that the end
had come. He asked someone else to check the translation, and once
assured that it was correct, quietly dismissed Boigs.*

Hitler called in Goebbels and Bormann, and the three conferred behind

* Trevor-Roper states that Lorenz delivered the dispatch through Hitler's valet,
Heinz Linge, and that the Führer was "white with indignation." The above version
comes from Boigs, who is at the present time working for the U. S. Army at
Berchtesgaden.

locked doors. All day long Bormann had been making wholesale charges of treason and only an hour earlier had radioed Dönitz: TREACHERY SEEMS TO HAVE REPLACED LOYALTY. The bunker was seething with rumors by the time the door finally opened and Hitler ordered Fegelein brought down from the upper level, where he was being held under armed guard. The previous day Himmler's liaison officer had deserted the bunker for his house in the suburb of Charlottenburg, only to be fetched back and placed under arrest on Hitler's personal order.

Hitler suspected everyone connected with Himmler—even Eva's brother-in-law. In the space of an hour Fegelein was court-martialed, found guilty of treason and condemned to death. He was taken to the Chancellery garden and shot.*

The bunker was still in a turmoil when Weidling arrived for the evening conference. He informed Hitler of the latest Russian advances and told him that all ammunition, food and supply dumps were either in enemy hands or under heavy artillery fire. In two days his troops would be out of ammunition and no longer able to resist. "As a soldier, I suggest therefore that we risk the breakout at once." He immediately launched into the details of his plan before Hitler could comment.

Pure hysteria! Goebbels ridiculed. But Krebs said it was feasible from a military viewpoint. "Naturally," he added quickly, "I must leave the decision to the Führer."

Hitler was silent. What if the breakout succeeded? he finally asked. "We would merely flee from one *Kessel* to another. Am I, the Führer, supposed to sleep in an open field or in a farmhouse or something like that, and just wait for the end? No, it would be far better for me to remain in the Chancellery."

Weidling left the conference at midnight. In the anteroom his commanders gathered around and he told them of his failure. "There is just one course left for us," he said grimly. "To fight till the last man is killed." But he promised he would try once more to persuade the Führer.

Hitler left the conference to visit the wounded Greim. Hanna Reitsch was there. Hitler slumped down on the edge of Greim's bed, his face white. "Our only hope is Wenck," he said, "and to make his entry possible we must call up every available aircraft to cover his approach."

---

* The last two days of Fegelein's life are still clouded in mystery. It is commonly believed that when he was arrested in his house he phoned Eva Braun, asking her to intercede with Hitler, and that she indignantly refused. Otto Günsche categorically states that there was no such phone conversation; he monitored all incoming calls. Moreover, says Günsche, Eva came to him in tears on the night of April 28 and insisted that "dear Hermann" could not possibly have betrayed the Führer.

Kempka states he was told by SS-Brigadeführer (Brigadier General) Johann Rattenhuber, in charge of the police guarding Hitler, that Fegelein was found hiding not in his house but in a coal bin on the upper level. Fegelein was wearing a long leather coat, house slippers, sport cap and scarf; in his briefcase were documents with details of Himmler's negotiations with Bernadotte.

Wenck's guns, he declared, were already shelling the Russians in the Potsdamerplatz. "Every available plane must be called up by daylight." He ordered Greim to fly to the Rechlin airport, which was not far from Dr. Gebhardt's sanatorium, and muster his planes from there. Only with Luftwaffe support would Wenck get through. "That's the first reason you must leave the shelter. The second is that Himmler must be stopped." His lips and hands trembled, his voice became unsteady. "A traitor must never succeed me as Führer. You must get out to make sure he will not."

Greim said that it would be impossible to reach Rechlin and that he preferred to die in the bunker.

"As soldiers of the Reich it is our holy duty to exhaust every possibility," Hitler said. "This is the only chance of success that remains. It is your duty and mine to take it."

"What can be accomplished now, even if we should get through?" Hanna asked.

But Greim was impressed by Hitler's last words. "Hanna, we are the only hope for those who remain here. If there is the smallest chance, we owe it to them to take it. . . . Maybe we can help, but whether we can or cannot, we will go."

This brought a burst of sentiment from Hitler. "The Luftwaffe fought best of all the armed forces from beginning to end," he said. "For its technical inferiority, others are to blame."

Painfully Greim began to dress. In tears, Hanna went up to Hitler, "My Führer, why, why, don't you let us stay?"

Hitler looked at her. "God protect you."

Frau Goebbels gave Hanna two letters to her son. She took off a diamond ring and asked Hanna to wear it in her memory. Eva Braun also gave Hanna a letter, for her sister, Frau Fegelein. Later Hanna couldn't resist reading it; she thought it was "so vulgar, so theatrical and in such poor, adolescent taste" that she tore it up.

The dark night was lit up by flaming buildings, and Greim and Hanna could hear intense small-arms fire as an armored car brought them to an Arado 96 trainer, hidden near the Brandenburg Gate. Hanna taxied the little plane down the East-West Axis and took off in a hail of fire. At rooftop level Russian searchlights picked up the Arado, and flak explosions began tossing it about like a feather. With full power she climbed out of the maelstrom—below lay Berlin, a sea of flames. She headed north.

## 5.

Himmler's betrayal had brought an end to Hitler's hesitation and hope. In spite of his show of confidence to Greim, he now realized that Wenck too was a lost cause and that the time had come at last to prepare for the end. This began in the little map room of the bunker with an extraordinary act of normalcy—a wedding. Hitler had often told friends he couldn't undertake "the responsibility of marriage." Perhaps he had also feared that it might diminish his uniqueness as Führer; to most Germans he was almost a Christlike figure. But now all that was over and his bourgeois impulse was to reward his faithful mistress with the long-delayed sanctity of matrimony.

A minor official was found in a nearby Volkssturm unit and brought underground to officiate—appropriately, his name was Wagner. With Goebbels and Bormann present as witnesses, both Hitler and Eva swore they were of pure Aryan descent. After the brief ceremony Eva started to sign the register "Eva B . . ." Corrected, she crossed out the "B" and wrote "Eva Hitler, née Braun."

Then Hitler invited Bormann, the Goebbels, two of his secretaries, Frau Christian and Frau Junge, to his quarters for champagne, and for over an hour he reminisced. Others joined the party from time to time— Günsche, Krebs, Burgdorf, Below, even Fräulein Manzialy, the vegetarian cook. Finally Hitler said it was the end of his life and National Socialism; death would be a relief after the betrayal of his closest comrades. He went to another room and began dictating his political testament to Frau Junge.

He charged that neither he nor anyone else in Germany wanted war and that it had been "provoked exclusively by those international statesmen who either were of Jewish origin or worked for Jewish interests." He blamed the English for forcing him to invade Poland "because the political clique in England wanted war, partly for commercial reasons, partly because it was influenced by propaganda put out by international Jewry."

He declared that he had stayed in Berlin "to choose death voluntarily at that moment when I believe that the position of the Führer and the Chancellor itself can no longer be maintained," and that he would die "with a joyful heart" but had ordered his military commanders "to continue to take part in the nation's struggle." Surrender of any district or town, he said, was out of the question and he called on his commanders to "set a shining example of faithful devotion to duty until death."

He expelled both Himmler and Göring from all their offices for "secretly negotiating with the enemy without my knowledge and against my will, and also by illegally attempting to seize control of the state."

As his own successor—both as President of the Reich and Supreme Commander of the Armed Forces—Hitler appointed Admiral Dönitz. Goebbels was made Chancellor, Bormann Party Minister and Schörner Supreme Commander of the Army; the first two, Hitler said, had asked to die with him, but they were ordered to "put the interests of the nation above their own feelings" and save themselves.

The testament ended, as it began, with an attack on the Jews. "Above all, I enjoin the government of the nation and the people to uphold the racial laws diligently and to fight mercilessly the poisoner of all nations, international Jewry." To the death he remained true to his obsession.

Frau Junge dated the document: 29 April 1945, 0400 hours. Hitler scratched his signature at the bottom and Goebbels, Bormann, Burgdorf and Krebs signed as witnesses.

The Führer then dictated his personal will. He left his possessions to the Party "or if this no longer exists, to the state," and appointed "my most faithful Party comrade, Martin Bormann," the executor of his will. "He may give to my relatives everything that is of value as a personal memento or can be used to maintain their middle-class standard of living; especially to my wife's mother and my faithful fellow workers of both sexes, who are well known to him—particularly my former secretaries, Frau Winter, et al., who helped me for many years by their work.

"My wife and I choose to die in order to escape the shame of overthrow or capitulation. It is our wish that our bodies be burned immediately in the place where I have performed the greater part of my daily work during the twelve years of service to my people."

These somber preparations eventually led to a violent argument. When the Führer told Goebbels to leave the bunker with his family, Goebbels took this as a slight, not a privilege. How could the Defender of Berlin possibly leave! he shouted. Hitler insisted, and the wrangle became so heated that he finally said, "Not even the most faithful of my followers will obey me!" and went off to bed.

In tears, Goebbels retired to his quarters, and not to be outdone, began composing his own last words under the title "Appendix to the Führer's Political Testament."

The Führer has ordered me, should the defense of the Reich capital collapse, to leave Berlin and to take part as a leading member in the government appointed by him.

For the first time in my life I must categorically refuse to obey an order of the Führer's. My wife and children join me in this refusal. Apart from the fact that feelings of humanity and loyalty forbid us to abandon the Führer in his hour of greatest need, I would instead appear for the rest of my life as a dishonorable traitor and common scoundrel, and should lose my self-respect along with the respect of my fellow citizens, a respect I should need in any further attempt to shape the future of the German nation and state.

In the nightmare of treachery which surrounds the Führer in these most critical days of the war, there must be at least one person who will stay with him unconditionally until death, even if this conflicts with the formal and, materially speaking, entirely justifiable order which he has given in his political testament.

I believe that I am thereby rendering the best service to the future of the

German people. In the hard times to come, examples will be more important than men. Men will always be found to lead the nation forward into freedom; but a reconstruction of our national life would be impossible if it were not developed on the basis of clear and obvious examples.

Together with my wife and on behalf of my children, who are too young to be able to speak for themselves but who would unreservedly agree with this decision if they were old enough, I express, for this reason, my unalterable resolution not to leave the Reich capital even if it falls, but rather, at the side of the Führer, to end a life that for me personally will have no further value if I cannot spend it in the service of the Führer, and at his side.

British Spitfires were sweeping over the burning ruins of Berlin. The stink of death below reminded Wing Leader Johnnie Johnson of Falaise during the Normandy campaign. He could see Russian tanks rolling into the city. Suddenly a large group of Yak fighters appeared. He was afraid there'd be a mix-up. "All right, chaps, stick together. Don't make a move."

As more than 100 Yaks began turning slowly behind the Spitfires, Johnson swung his planes to the right, turning over the Russians. When his wingman warned there were more above, Johnson said, "Tighten it up. Don't break formation."

Both groups circled each other suspiciously. Johnson drew as close as he dared, then waggled his wings at the Russian leader, but there was no answer. Abruptly the Russians turned back east in ragged order. As the undisciplined pack darted off, rising and falling, Johnson was reminded of a wheeling, tumbling pack of starlings. Every so often a few broke off and pounced on something in the rubble below.

By midmorning Russian ground forces were driving toward the bunker in three main attacks: from the east, south and north. The circle around the dying city tightened as advance Soviet units infiltrated the Zoo. From the hippopotamus house and planetarium they began to fire on the two huge anti-aircraft towers which were the command posts of several divisions, as well as the artillery center. The artillery commander of Berlin, Colonel Wöhlerman, watched in fascination from the fourth floor of one tower as Russian tanks again and again tried in vain to hit his windows. He could see the great city sprawled all around him— burning, smoldering, almost completely wrecked. The steeple of the Gedächtniskirche (the Kaiser Friedrich Memorial Church) blazed in terrible beauty like a giant torch.

A mile away in the bunker Martin Bormann was making preparations to send Hitler's testament as well as his personal will to his successor, Admiral Dönitz. To help guarantee their delivery, Bormann decided to dispatch two separate emissaries: SS-Standartenführer (Colonel) Wilhelm Zander, his own personal adviser, and Heinz Lorenz. Goebbels also wanted his testament to reach the outside world and gave a copy to Lorenz.

A third copy of Hitler's political testament was entrusted to Major Willi Johannmeier, the Führer's Army adjutant, by Burgdorf, who ordered it taken to Feldmarschall Schörner. Burgdorf also gave Johannmeier a handwritten covering note explaining that the will had been written "under the shattering news of Himmler's treason," and was the Führer's "unalterable decision." It was to be published "as soon as the Führer orders it, or as soon as his death is confirmed."

When Freytag von Loringhoven, Boldt and Oberstleutnant (Lieutenant Colonel) Weiss, Burgdorf's aide, learned that three couriers were leaving the bunker with copies of Hitler's testament, they too decided to ask permission to leave. "Now that it's all over," they told Krebs, "let us fight with the troops or give us the chance to get to General Wenck's army." Krebs understood and went to Hitler, who had no objections, but said he wanted to see the three young men before they left.

At noon Hitler chatted with them at length. How did they expect to get out of Berlin? Boldt pointed out a route along the Tiergarten to the Picheldorf Bridge, where they would find a boat and row down the Havel River.

"Near the bridge!" Hitler broke in. "I know where there are some electric boats that make no noise!" He spent the next fifteen minutes giving them a step-by-step escape route down the river. It was a *tour de force* of memory but the three officers only listened perfunctorily. Like so many of Hitler's military plans it was perfect in theory but impossible to execute. They donned camouflage jackets and steel helmets and armed themselves with machine pistols. They left the oppressive atmosphere of the bunker and emerged into Hermann Göringstrasse.

The man in whose honor this street was named was being sentenced to death by Bormann, who dispatched a telegram to his agents at the Obersalzberg:

THE SITUATION IN BERLIN IS MORE TENSE. IF BERLIN AND WE SHOULD FALL, THE TRAITORS OF 23RD APRIL MUST BE EXTERMINATED. MEN, DO YOUR DUTY. YOUR LIFE AND HONOR DEPEND ON IT.

But Göring had already persuaded his SS guard to take him, his wife, daughter and butler to the family castle in nearby Mauterndorf, Austria. As Göring drove off he held in his lap a stovepipe; rolled up inside was one of his favorite paintings—worth 2,500,000 Mark.

## 6.

The afternoon of April 29 was a time of morbid preparation in the bunker. The Führer's favorite Alsatian wolf dog, Blondi, was poisoned by Dr. Haase, Hitler's former surgeon, and the other two dogs were shot. Hitler himself supplied poison capsules to his two secretaries, Frau Junge and Frau Christian. It was a poor parting gift, he said apologetically, and praised their courage; it was unfortunate, he added, that his generals weren't as reliable.

Kempka saw Hitler at six o'clock, not long after a report arrived that Mussolini had been assassinated by partisans. In his right hand was a map of Berlin; he wore his gray jacket and black trousers. Though his left hand shook slightly, he seemed composed. "How are things with you, Kempka?" he asked.

The chauffeur said he was going back to his emergency defense positions at the Brandenburg Gate.

"How are your men?"

"Their morale is good and they're waiting for relief from Wenck."

"Yes . . . we're all waiting for Wenck," Hitler said quietly and held out his hand. "Good-bye, Kempka, and take care of yourself."

As they were shaking hands, one of Kempka's men shouted down the corridor, "Hurry, the Russians are coming!"

Weidling's heart was heavy as the Führer conference started at 10 P.M. He told of the bitter, hopeless battles in the streets. His divisions, he said, were little more than battalions. Morale was poor and ammunition was almost exhausted. He brandished an Army field newspaper filled with optimistic stories of the imminent relief of Berlin by Wenck. The troops knew better, he charged, and such deceptions only embittered them.

Once more Goebbels was unable to listen to such a realistic appraisal. He accused Weidling of defeatism and another argument erupted. It took Bormann to calm them down so that Weidling could continue. He concluded his report with the devastating prediction that the battle would be over the next evening.

There was a stunned silence. In a tired voice Hitler asked SS-Brigadeführer (Brigadier General) Mohnke, commandant of the Citadel (Chancellery) area, if he had observed the same conditions. Mohnke said he had.

Weidling again pleaded for a breakout. Hitler raised his hand for quiet. He pointed to his map, and in a resigned but sarcastic tone, said he had marked down the positions of the troops according to information from foreign radio announcements, since his own troop staffs were not even bothering to report to him any longer; his orders were not executed any more and so it was useless to expect anything.

As he rose painfully from his chair to say good-bye to Weidling, the general once more begged him to change his mind before the ammunition ran out. Hitler murmured something to Krebs, then turned to Weidling.

"I will permit a breakout of small groups," he said, but added that capitulation was out of the question.

Weidling walked down the passageway wondering what Hitler meant. Wasn't the breakout of small groups actually a capitulation? He radioed all his commanders to congregate at his headquarters in the Bendlerblock the next morning.

At midnight Colonel von Below and his orderly left the bunker with a letter from Hitler to Keitel about the appointment of Dönitz as his successor. The Führer praised the Navy for its brave performance and excused the Luftwaffe for failures caused by Göring. But he castigated the entire Army General Staff and said it could not be compared with the General Staff of World War I. "The efforts and sacrifices of the German people in this war," he concluded, "have been so great that I cannot believe they have been in vain. The aim must still be to win territory in the east for the German people."

Below and his companion followed the route the others had taken out of the bunker. In the darkness their progress was easier, and just before dawn they caught up with the Freytag von Loringhoven party at the Reich sport stadium.

In the main dining room on the upper level Hitler was bidding good-bye to a group of twenty officers and women secretaries. His eyes were covered by a film of moisture, and to Frau Junge, he seemed to be looking far away. He passed down the line shaking hands, then descended the curving staircase to his suite.

A strange new atmosphere of conviviality suddenly ensued. Barriers dropped and high-ranking officers chatted familiarly with junior officers. In the canteen where soldiers and orderlies ate, a dance began spontaneously. It became so boisterous that a messenger brought a warning to hold the noise down from the lower level, where Bormann was trying to concentrate on a telegram he was writing to Dönitz. In the message Bormann complained that all incoming reports were "controlled, suppressed or distorted" by Keitel, and ordered Dönitz "to proceed at once, and mercilessly, against all traitors."

## 7.

That midnight Father Sampson stood on the hill overlooking Neubrandenburg and listened to the growing rumble of Red Army tanks. Manteuffel had already withdrawn his headquarters from town and had left only a rear guard.

For the past week Russian planes had showered the town and Stalag IIA with leaflets warning that Rokossovsky was "at your gates!" He was indeed. Dozens of Soviet tanks smashed down the camp's barbed-wire fences and guard towers. Multiple rockets mounted on American trucks rolled up and began firing into Neubrandenburg three miles away. Within an hour the city was in flames and even the prisoners on the distant hill could feel the heat. The lure of freedom was too much for many French, Italian and Serbs who straggled toward the blazing city to loot—and be shot at by the Russians. But the Americans under the leadership of Sergeant Lucas, their Man of Confidence, and Father Sampson remained in camp as instructed by coded BBC broadcasts.

Liberation was only a word to the 3000 surviving Russians in the camp. Those even suspected of collaborating with the Germans were summarily shot; the rest were given rifles and sent to the front lines.

A Russian general asked Father Sampson if he had any complaints about the Germans. The priest remarked that the camp doctor had refused to help the Americans, and the general held out his pistol. "Shoot him," he said simply.

Prisoners returning from Neubrandenburg brought back such revolting stories of murder, pillage and rape that the fifty-year-old French abbé with the youthful face and Father Sampson were impelled to visit the town to see what they could do to help. In the woods between the camp and town they came upon the raped and murdered bodies of German girls and women. Several, throats slit, were hanging from trees by their ankles.

Neubrandenburg, once a beautiful little city, was still burning, its street piled with debris. Soviet women in uniform directed the heavy military traffic. The stench of burned flesh was intolerable, but the abbé moved purposefully through the carnage, praying and giving solace. To Father Sampson he seemed to be a symbol of the Church in a devastated world. They found their friend, the local priest, sitting dazed on the steps of the gutted rectory. Inside, the priest's mother and his two sisters, who were nuns, cowered on a sofa. All three women had been raped before his eyes by a gang of Russians. The mother, clutching her rosary, looked dead. The abbé asked if he could do anything. The two nuns shook their heads.

On the way back to camp the two priests approached an overturned wagon. Near by were half a dozen hastily buried bodies. A shepherd dog lay over one of the graves. Sampson tried to coax him to come along but the dog refused to budge. Most of the family possessions had been stolen, but the looters had left a little doll and an old family Bible. The abbé opened the book, glanced at Confirmation and Communion pictures pasted inside and scanned the carefully penned recordings of baptisms, marriages and deaths. The French priest suddenly seemed utterly worn and tired of life; he looked every day his age.

## 8.

By late morning of April 30 the Tiergarten was overrun by the Soviets and one advance unit was even reported in the street next to the bunker. But it was difficult to see that this news had any effect on Hitler. During lunch with Frau Junge, Frau Christian and Fräulein Manzialy, he chatted as if it were just another "inner circle" gathering without problems.

But it was no ordinary day, and soon after the ladies had left Hitler asked Günsche to call them back, as well as Bormann, Goebbels, Burgdorf, Krebs, Voss, Hewel, Naumann, Rattenhuber and Fräulein Else Krüger, Bormann's secretary. Hitler shook hands with everyone and said good-bye. Eva embraced the ladies. Hitler took Günsche aside and said that he and his wife were going to commit suicide and that he wanted their bodies burned. "After my death," he explained, "I don't want to be put on exhibition in a Russian *Panoptikum* [wax museum]."

Günsche phoned Kempka's quarters at the bunker, just as he was returning from his command post at the Brandenburg Gate. "Erich, I need something to drink," he said. "Do you have a bottle of schnapps?" There was a strange quality in Günsche's voice that Kempka couldn't quite define. "Don't you have anything to drink?" Günsche persisted, and said he was coming over.

Kempka knew something was wrong. In the last days no one had thought of alcohol. He found a bottle of cognac and waited. The phone rang. It was Günsche again. "I need two hundred liters of gasoline immediately," he said hoarsely.

Kempka thought it was some kind of joke. "Impossible," he replied. "Gas! Gas, Erich!"

"What do you need two hundred liters for?"

"I can't tell you on the phone, I want it at the entrance of the Führer bunker without fail."

Kempka said the only gasoline left—about 40,000 liters—was buried in the Tiergarten. "It's under artillery fire and means sure death. Wait until five o'clock when the artillery lets up."

"I can't wait a single hour. See what you can siphon out of the wrecked cars."

At 3:30 P.M. Hitler picked up a Walther pistol. He was alone in the anteroom of his quarters with Eva Braun. She was already dead. She was on a couch, slumped over the arm rest, poisoned. A second Walther lay on the red carpet, unfired.

Hitler sat at a table. Behind him was a picture of Frederick the Great. In front, on a console, was a picture of Hitler's mother as a young woman. He put the pistol barrel in his mouth and fired. He pitched forward and sent a vase flying. It hit Eva's body, soaking part of her dress with water, and dropped to the carpet.

In the conference room Bormann, Günsche and Linge heard the shot. They hesitated momentarily, then broke into Hitler's anteroom. Günsche saw him sprawled face-down across the table. Unnerved, Günsche stumbled back into the conference room and was accosted by Kempka.

"For God's sake, Otto," the chauffeur said, "what's going on? You must be crazy to have me send men to almost certain death just for two hundred liters of gasoline."

Günsche brushed past him and slammed the door to the cloakroom so that no one else could wander in. Then he closed the door to the Führer's suite and turned, eyes wide. "The Chief is dead!"

Stunned, the only thing Kempka could think of was that Hitler had had a heart attack.

Günsche lost his voice. He pointed a finger like a pistol and put it in his mouth.

"Where is Eva?"

Günsche indicated Hitler's anteroom and was finally able to say, "She's with him." It took Günsche several minutes to stammer out the whole story.

Linge peered out of Hitler's anteroom. "Gasoline," he cried, "where is the gasoline?" Kempka said he had about one hundred seventy liters in jerricans at the garden entrance.

Linge and Dr. Stumpfegger carried out Hitler's body in a dark brown army blanket. The Führer's face was half covered, his left arm hung down. Bormann followed, carrying Eva. She wore a black dress and her blond hair was hanging down loose. The sight of her in Bormann's arms was too much for Kempka. She had always hated Bormann and he thought, "Not one more step." He called to Günsche, "I'll carry Eva." Kempka silently took her away from Bormann. The left side of her body was moist and Kempka thought it was blood; it was water from the spilled vase. Halfway up the four flights of stairs to the garden, her body almost slipped out of his grasp. Kempka stopped, unable to continue, but Günsche quickly moved to his aid and together they carried Eva into the garden.

Another Russian barrage had begun and shells smashed into the rubble. Only the jagged walls of the Chancellery remained and these trembled with every shattering explosion.

Through a cloud of dust Kempka saw Hitler's body not ten feet from the bunker entrance. It was in a shallow depression next to a large cement mixer. His trousers were pulled up; his right foot was turned in—the characteristic position he had always assumed on a long auto trip.

Kempka and Günsche stretched out Eva's body on Hitler's right. The artillery barrage suddenly increased in tempo, forcing them to take cover in the entrance. Kempka waited a few minutes, then seized a jerrican of gasoline and ran back to the bodies. He placed Hitler's left arm closer to his side. It was an unnecessary gesture but he could not bring himself to drench the body with gasoline. A gust of wind moved Hitler's hair. Kempka opened the jerrican. A shell exploded, showering him with debris; shrapnel whizzed past his head. Again he scrambled back for refuge.

Günsche, Kempka and Linge waited in the entrance for a lull in the shelling. When it came they returned to the bodies. Shivering with revulsion, Kempka sprinkled them with gasoline. He thought, I can't do it but I'm doing it. He saw the same reaction in the faces of Linge and Günsche, who were also pouring gasoline on the bodies. From the entrance Goebbels, Bormann and Dr. Stumpfegger peered out with morbid concern.

The clothing became so soaked that even the strongest gusts of wind couldn't stir it. The shelling resumed, but the three men emptied can after can until the shallow depression in which the bodies lay was filled with gasoline. Günsche suggested igniting it with a hand grenade but Kempka said no. The idea of blowing up the bodies was too repugnant. He saw a large rag lying near a fire hose at the entrance. He pointed it out to Günsche, who grabbed it and doused it with gasoline. "Match!" called Kempka.

Goebbels handed him a pack. Kempka lit the match and put it to the rag. Günsche ran with the burning rag, tossed it onto the bodies. A boiling ball of fire mushroomed above the bodies, followed by dark clouds of smoke. Against the background of a burning city it was a small blaze, but it was the most horrifying. They watched, hypnotized.

The fire slowly began to consume the bodies. Shaken, they stumbled back into the entrance. More jerricans of gasoline were delivered, and for the next three hours Günsche, Linge and Kempa kept pouring the liquid on the burning bodies.

Within nineteen days three of the world's leaders had died—one by a stroke, one by his own hand and one at the hands of his own people. Two of them—Roosevelt and Hitler—had assumed leadership of their countries in the same year, 1933, and both had been called "The Chief" by their intimates—but there the similarities ended.

It was about seven-thirty in the evening before the exhausted Günsche and Kempka staggered down into the bunker, the long task of cremation done. There was bedlam in the conference room. The chief of the body-guard, Rattenhuber, and the commander of the Citadel area, Mohnke, were openly weeping; others were arguing over minor matters in near hysteria. They all seemed lost without the Führer to lead them. Finally Goebbels gained control of himself. As the new Chancellor he called a meeting to order and asked Bormann, Mohnke, Burgdorf and Krebs to attend. One of Goebbels' first decisions was to order Rattenhuber to bury the remains of Hitler and Eva next to Kempka's little house in the garden. They began discussing the possibility of sending Krebs, who spoke some Russian, through the lines to negotiate some sort of treaty.

Weidling still did not know that Hitler was dead. Late that afternoon he had received a message from Krebs ordering him to report to the bunker at once and forbidding any breakout from Berlin, even in small groups. It was madness and Weidling was tempted to disobey; in another twenty-four hours any breakout at all would be impossible. Enemy columns were already driving deep wedges into the Potsdamerplatz area and another group had advanced along Wilhelmstrasse all the way to the Air Ministry.

It took Weidling almost an hour to work his way to the Chancellery less than a mile away and it was dark by the time he climbed down into the bunker. He was puzzled by the hectic atmosphere in the corridors, but the first intimation he had that there was something wrong was when he saw Goebbels sitting at Hitler's desk. In a somber voice Krebs pledged him to secrecy, then revealed that Hitler had committed suicide.

The thunderstruck Weidling was told that Stalin and only Stalin had been informed of the Führer's death. Krebs said he was going in person to tell Zhukov about the suicide and the new regime. He would then request a truce and start negotiations for the capitulation of Germany. With Hitler gone, his desire to fight to the last man against the Bolsheviks had suddenly vanished.

Weidling couldn't believe Krebs was serious, and looked at him incredulously. "As a soldier, do you think that the Russian Supreme Command will agree to negotiate a truce just as they are about to gather the ripe fruit?" Unconditional surrender must be offered, he said. Only that could end the useless battle of Berlin.

Capitulation is absolutely out of the question, cried Goebbels.

"Herr Reichsminister," Weidling said, "do you really believe that the Russians will negotiate with a German government that has you for Chancellor?"

For perhaps the first time in his life Goebbels could find no ready answer. When he did speak, the words were of a man who had warped reality to his own needs. The last wish of Hitler, he declared, was a sacred duty, and Krebs should only ask for a truce.

On the way back to his battle station, Kempka passed Dr. Stumpfegger's room and saw Magda Goebbels sitting at a desk. Her face was vacant.

She recognized Kempka and asked him to come in. "I begged the Führer on my knees not to commit suicide," she said tonelessly. "He picked me up gently and said quietly that he must leave this world. It was the only possibility to pave the way for Dönitz to save Germany."

To distract her, Kempka said there was a real possibility of escape. He told her he had three armored personnel carriers and could possibly bring them all out safely.

She gave a great sigh and brightened. Then Goebbels walked in and said Krebs was going to see Zhukov personally and urge "a free departure from the bunker." He had pledged to die with Hitler, but the instinct to save himself and his family was stronger. Even this instinct, however, had its limits. "In case the negotiations turn out negative," he added grimly, "my decision has already been made. I shall remain in the bunker because I do not choose to play the role of a perpetual refugee in the world." He turned to Kempka. "Naturally, escape for my wife and children is open to them."

"If my husband stays," Frau Goebbels said hastily, "I'll stay. I'll share his fate."

Admiral Dönitz was not informed of Hitler's death, only that the Führer had named him his successor. Bormann had radioed that confirmation in writing would follow and the Admiral was "hereby authorized to take any measures which the situation demands."

Perhaps Bormann had withheld the whole truth so that he could bring the news in person. Unlike Goebbels, he was determined to escape from Berlin whatever happened and undoubtedly hoped to be the first from the bunker to reach Dönitz. Then, by his presence, he could perhaps retain his power.

The Admiral was a military man without political aspirations and the appointment was completely unexpected. He guessed that Hitler must have named him to clear the way for an officer of the Armed Forces to end the war honorably. He radioed Hitler that his loyalty was without qualification and that he would do everything possible to relieve him in Berlin. "But if Fate forces me to rule the Reich as your successor, I shall carry on the war to an end worthy of the unique, heroic struggle of the German people."

Dönitz had always feared that Hitler's death might lead to the end of central authority and that chaos would follow, with hundreds of thousands needlessly losing their lives. Now if he acted swiftly and surrendered unconditionally, he might be able to prevent such a catastrophe. But first he had to find out if his appointment would be accepted peaceably by Himmler, who had armed forces all over the country, while he had none. It took a personal phone call from Dönitz before Himmler reluctantly promised to come to Plön to discuss "an important matter."

Dönitz put a pistol with the safety off under some papers on his desk. It struck him as melodramatic but necessary. Himmler arrived with six armed SS orderlies, but he walked alone into the Admiral's office. Dönitz brought out the telegram announcing his appointment as Hitler's successor. "Please read this," he said and watched Himmler closely. The Reichsführer's face went pale and he seemed to shrink "as if punctured by a pin." Even after the exposure of his attempted negotiations with Churchill and Truman, Himmler was convinced he would be named Hitler's successor. After an embarrassing silence he stood up and bowed clumsily. "In that case," he said, "please let me become the second man in your state."

Himmler's plaintive tone gave Dönitz confidence, but he edged a hand near the hidden gun. "That is impossible," he said firmly. "I have no job for you."

Himmler cleared his throat as if to say something, then rose resignedly. Dönitz also got up and escorted Himmler to the door. Himmler walked out of the building, head low, trailed by his six bodyguards.

# 30

---

# "And Now You Stab Us in the Back"

---

**1.**

Since 1939, when the Polish government-in-exile went to London, there had been continual arguments over the fate of that tragic country. At Yalta the Big Three seemed to have found a solution; then Stalin changed his mind, which led not only to scores of acrimonious messages but a disagreement between Churchill and Roosevelt as to how to cope with Stalin. Soon after Roosevelt had come around to Churchill's point of view in late March, he died, and Truman was forced to deal with a situation he knew little about. Consequently, it was not until late April that Churchill and Truman were finally ready to present a strong united front.

For several days Churchill had pondered Stalin's latest message, which categorically stated that the only answer to the problem was to adopt the Yugoslav example for Poland. On April 29 Churchill dispatched a 2509-word rejoinder that was as impassioned at it was long.

Churchill said that their 50-50 agreement on Yugoslavia had not worked out at all well: Tito had become an absolute dictator. Moreover, there was no connection between Yugoslavia and Poland; the Big Three had come to a definite agreement about the latter at Yalta. Churchill went on to say that both he and Truman felt they had been "rather ill-treated about the way the matter has been handled since the Crimea Conference."

The whole affair, Churchill charged, had become aggravated because of stories coming out of Poland, such as the reported disappearance of fifteen Poles who had left Warsaw a month before to negotiate with the Russians. Churchill asked how he could contradict such stories when Britons and Americans were not allowed into Poland to find out the true state of affairs.

There was not much comfort in looking into a future, he said, where Stalin and the countries he dominated, plus the Communist parties in many states, were all drawn up on one side, and the English-speaking democracies and their associates on the other.

. . . IT IS QUITE OBVIOUS THAT THEIR QUARREL WOULD TEAR THE WORLD TO PIECES AND THAT ALL OF US LEADING MEN ON EITHER SIDE WHO HAD ANYTHING TO DO WITH THAT WOULD BE SHAMED BEFORE HISTORY. EVEN EMBARKING ON A LONG PERIOD OF SUSPICIONS, OF ABUSE AND COUNTER-ABUSE AND OF OPPOSING POLICIES WOULD BE A DISASTER HAMPERING THE GREAT DEVELOPMENTS OF WORLD PROSPERITY FOR THE MASSES WHICH ARE ATTAINABLE ONLY BY OUR TRINITY. I HOPE THERE IS NO WORD OR PHRASE IN THIS OUTPOURING OF MY HEART TO YOU WHICH UNWITTINGLY GIVES OFFENCE. IF SO, LET ME KNOW. BUT DO NOT, I BEG YOU, MY FRIEND STALIN, UNDERRATE THE DIVERGENCIES WHICH ARE OPENING ABOUT MATTERS WHICH YOU MAY THINK ARE SMALL TO US BUT WHICH ARE SYMBOLIC OF THE WAY THE ENGLISH-SPEAKING DEMOCRACIES LOOK AT LIFE.

Churchill's frankness only nettled Stalin, who replied that if the Lublin government was not "taken as a basis for a future government of national unity" it would be "impossible to count on successful fulfillment of the task set by the Crimea Conference."

Previously Stalin had denied any knowledge of the missing fifteen Poles. Now he blandly admitted that they were in Soviet custody. Furthermore, the Allies were wrongly informed—there were "16, not 15, persons."

. . . THE GROUP IS HEADED BY THE WELL-KNOWN GENERAL OKULICKI. THE BRITISH INFORMATION SERVICES MAINTAIN A DELIBERATE SILENCE, IN VIEW OF HIS PARTICULAR ODIOUSNESS, ABOUT THIS POLISH GENERAL, WHO, ALONG WITH THE 15 OTHER POLES, HAS "DISAPPEARED." BUT WE HAVE NO INTENTION OF BEING SILENT ABOUT THE MATTER. THIS GROUP OF 16, LED BY GENERAL OKULICKI, HAS BEEN ARRESTED BY THE MILITARY AUTHORITIES OF THE SOVIET FRONT AND IS UNDERGOING INVESTIGATION IN MOSCOW. GENERAL OKULICKI'S GROUP, IN THE FIRST PLACE GENERAL OKULICKI HIMSELF, IS CHARGED WITH PREPARING AND CARRYING OUT SUBVERSIVE

ACTIVITIES BEHIND THE LINES OF THE RED ARMY, SUBVERSION WHICH HAS TAKEN A TOLL OF OVER A HUNDRED RED ARMY SOLDIERS AND OFFICERS; THE GROUP IS ALSO CHARGED WITH KEEPING ILLEGAL RADIO-TRANSMITTERS IN THE REAR OF OUR TROOPS, WHICH IS PROHIBITED BY LAW. ALL, OR PART OF THEM—DEPENDING ON THE OUTCOME OF THE INVESTIGATION—WILL BE TRIED. THAT IS HOW THE RED ARMY IS FORCED TO PROTECT ITS UNITS AND ITS REAR-LINES AGAINST SABOTEURS AND THOSE WHO CREATE DISORDER.

These charges, which were in fact unfounded, were followed by an accusation that the British Information Service was spreading lies, claiming that it was the Russians who had murdered the Poles in the Katyn Forest. The message ended on an ominous note:

IT APPEARS FROM YOUR MESSAGE THAT YOU ARE UNWILLING TO CONSIDER THE POLISH PROVISIONAL GOVERNMENT AS A BASIS FOR A FUTURE GOVERNMENT OF NATIONAL UNITY, OR TO ACCORD IT THE PLACE IN THAT GOVERNMENT TO WHICH IT IS ENTITLED. I MUST SAY FRANKLY THAT THIS ATTITUDE PRECLUDES THE POSSIBILITY OF AN AGREED DECISION ON THE POLISH QUESTION.

## 2.

Upon one issue, however—the surrender of Italy—Churchill and Stalin were at long last in agreement. Once Dulles got approval to resume Operation "Sunrise," he asked Gaevernitz to take the two German emissaries by car and plane to Alexander's headquarters at Caserta, near Naples. At first Major Wenner and Oberstleutnant von Schweinitz objected to the Allied terms of unconditional surrender; but in an all-night private session Gaevernitz persuaded them that every minute meant further destruction and loss of life.

Even so, Schweinitz insisted that a message be sent to Generaloberst von Vietinghoff outlining the terms. When no answer had been received by April 29, Schweinitz was persuaded to sign the surrender—set for noon, May 2—so that he and Wenner could deliver the documents to Vietinghoff in time for him to issue cease-fire orders to front-line units.

At the impressive ceremony, which was held in the presence of Soviet Major General A. P. Kislenko, Schweinitz caused momentary consternation when he said he was personally going beyond his powers. "I presume that my commander in chief, General von Vietinghoff, will accept, but I cannot be entirely responsible." There was a surprised murmur from the witnesses, but Lieutenant-General William Morgan, Alexander's chief of staff, said unhesitatingly, "I accept," and signed for the Allies, at 2:17 P.M.

The next day Churchill wired Stalin: WE MUST REJOICE TOGETHER AT THIS GREAT SURRENDER. His jubilation was premature. Gaevernitz had managed to bring the two Germans back into Switzerland but could not get them across the border again to Austria. The Bundesrat, the highest Swiss governmental body, had ordered all borders closed. The world-wide publicity of the secret negotiations had apparently become too embarrassing to a nation priding itself on strict neutrality.

Now Allen Dulles stepped in. He abandoned protocol, and even before breakfast went to the home of a Swiss official. While the official was shaving, Dulles interrupted and persuaded him to authorize passage for the Germans. Finally, at eleven o'clock in the morning on April 30, Wenner and Schweinitz were allowed to leave Switzerland for Italy. Soon they were driving in a rickety car toward German headquarters at Bolzano, in the Dolomites, along out-of-the-way Austrian roads not yet cleared of a recent snowfall. They were using this roundabout route because Kaltenbrunner was reportedly blocking the main roads to prevent them from delivering the surrender papers to Vietinghoff.

When Wolff returned to his headquarters in Italy on the night of April 27, he found confusion and vacillation. Kesselring, recently put in charge of all German troops in the south, had just been informed by Gauleiter Hofer in Innsbruck that a treaty had been signed at Caserta. He ordered Vietinghoff to meet him at Innsbruck, where he forcefully reiterated that any capitulation was out of the question. Thereupon he summarily relieved Vietinghoff and his chief of staff, General Hans Roettiger, of their duties and ordered them to report to the military retreat area in the Dolomites, northeast of Bolzano, for further orders and possible court-martial.

Vietinghoff dutifully left for the Dolomites, completely disillusioned both with Wolff and "Sunrise," but Roettiger would not accompany him. Instead, he joined Wolff in pressuring the new commander of German forces in Italy, General der Infanterie F. Schulz, to join the conspiracy. Schulz, however, was a stolid career officer and refused to act without Kesselring's complete approval.

Wenner and Schweinitz finally arrived in Bolzano at midnight, April 30, and the situation looked hopeless. The surrender was supposed to take place in thirty hours and Schulz still would not honor the treaty. Wolff and Roettiger talked until dawn and finally concluded that the only solution was to arrest Schulz. At seven o'clock they imprisoned the indignant general and his chief of staff in the Army Group's central command post, a spacious underground shelter blasted out of a huge rock.

This isolated Schulz but led to a new complication. Generals Herr and Lemelsen, who commanded the two German armies in Italy and had been persuaded against their better judgment to go along with "Sunrise," considered Schulz's arrest an insult to the entire officer corps, and reversed their decision: under these circumstances, they said, they could neither subordinate themselves to Roettiger, nor surrender their troops.

At noon Field-Marshal Alexander radioed Wolff, urgently requesting information. Had Vietinghoff and Wolff ratified the terms signed at Caserta? Would the armistice still take place on May 2? The message was received on equipment secretly located in a small dressing room next to Wolff's bedroom at his headquarters in the palace of the Duke of Pistoia. The operator, Vacalr Hradecky—Wally for short—was a Czechoslovakian working for Dulles who was hidden in the palace, and for the past week had been living on trays of food ordered for Wolff as camouflage.

Wolff was left with the task of trying to reason with a man he had just locked up. Schulz quite naturally was "bitterly hurt" by his arrest the day after he arrived at his new command, and it took the persuasive Wolff two hours before Schulz reluctantly admitted that surrender in Italy was probably for the good of the Fatherland. "All right, we are with you," he finally said. "We shall raise no personal or official objections, but we cannot capitulate without Kesselring's approval."

But Wolff needed allies, not neutrals. "Look here, don't let's waste any more time. It's Germany that's at stake and not individuals. Please see this thing through with me. Tell the Army commanders that the orders for surrender are to be strictly carried out."

Though not completely convinced, Schulz phoned Lemelsen and Herr and got their promise to attend a conference of the leading German commanders in Italy at six o'clock in the evening, May 1. Wolff himself called on General Ritter von Pohl, commander of the Luftwaffe in Italy. "My God, we really are in a mess," Pohl exclaimed. "And you got us all into it!"

"No, Pohl, I didn't get you into it, and however difficult this step is, I'm sure you realize that it's the only sensible and possible way to carry it out. Leave it to me."

"All right," Pohl sighed, "I'm with you."

The generals were by nature conservative and their reluctance to act independently was understandable. Equally understandable was the attitude of the young, ardent pro-Nazi officers at Army Group headquarters. As soon as they learned of the proposed surrender, they threatened revolt. Roettiger called them to his office: it was senseless to continue fighting and he could no longer bear that responsibility.

A young captain stepped forward. "Then, sir, why don't you relinquish command to one of your subordinate officers who is willing to shoulder the responsibility—in accordance with the Führer's order?"

Roettiger said he was familiar with that particular order. "At this moment, however, I regard the carrying out of the cease-fire as my greater responsibility, since further useless bloodshed will be avoided by it. Captain, think of the hard fate of your comrades at the front, some of whom, even at this moment, are fighting for positions already lost and who, sooner or later, will be faced with the same individual decision which I, thinking of the *entire* Wehrmacht in Italy, have just made." Roettiger said he would assume the responsibility for making this decision for all of them. "If I'm no longer able to bear it, I will let you and the staff know, Captain."

At six o'clock Wolff opened the meeting of commanders. There was no time to waste, he said. Less than twenty hours remained before the armistice deadline. Vize-admiral Löwisch, who represented the commander of the German naval forces in Italy, stood in the corner, dolefully saying over and over, "The Admiral will never give his consent, and for heaven's sake, we shouldn't force him to do it!" Pohl took the floor and said the Luftwaffe would honor the surrender. Herr and Lemelsen both hesitated, then declared that further fighting could not be justified.

It was now up to the Supreme Commander in Italy, Schulz. "I agree fully," he said, and Wolff thought he had won. Then Schulz added that he could still do nothing without the consent of Kesselring.

A call was put through to the Feldmarschall but he was unavailable. Half an hour later they again failed to reach him. The air in the deep shelter was getting uncomfortably close. At eight o'clock another radiogram from Alexander arrived: Would the signatures on the surrender be honored? If an affirmative reply was not received soon, the Allies would resume their attack.

Wolff replied that he would try to answer by ten o'clock, and made a third phone call to Kesselring's headquarters. His chief of staff, General Westphal, said he could not be disturbed. "This is our last chance!" Wolff shouted. "But neither you nor General Schulz are willing to take the responsibility. There are four commanders standing here who demand that you give us power to do what is necessary. Not one of us has any personal ambition; none of us has any intention of seeking protection from the enemy. We're prepared to defend our action and will submit to the Feldmarschall's judgment. But a decision must be made now, before it's too late and the fighting continues." Westphal said that he would talk it over with Kesselring and phone back in half an hour.

At ten o'clock Westphal still had not called and Wolff knew he must convince those in the room to act on their own, particularly Schulz. "Schulz is shirking the issue!" the exasperated Wolff exclaimed. "There seems to be no one with enough guts to make an independent decision, even if it concerns the lives of tens of thousands of soldiers and misery for thousands of German families. Therefore, the rest of us here in this room must make the decision. Let Schulz do what he wants about it—and Kesselring too!"

There was a shocked silence. General Herr suddenly turned to his chief of staff and said with quiet authority, "Issue orders to all units in Tenth Army to lay down their arms tomorrow at noon."

It was the turning point. Lemelsen and Pohl issued similar orders.

At ten o'clock that night Wolff radioed Alexander that the cease-fire would take place as planned. But his words implied a confidence he did not feel. He knew Kesselring and Schulz could still sabotage the surrender. An hour later someone rushed in: the news of Hitler's death had just come over the radio. Tears of relief came to Wolff's eyes. Now Kesselring and Schulz were freed from their personal oath to the Führer. But Hitler's death had an unexpected effect on Schulz. "Gentlemen," he exclaimed, "up to now I have been quite amenable! I have given my qualified consent to your decision and I've tried to make the best of a bad bargain. But don't forget the scandalous way I was treated this morning and that in spite of it I gave you my moral support I was ready to fall in with your ideas. But I'm bound to obedience. The Feldmarschall told me that he trusted me and I cannot abuse his trust. I cannot and may not—and you've got to understand that." His face became red. "How dare you come here and threaten me? Now get out!" He pointed to the door. "I'm tired of all this! I'm still the Supreme Commander in this place. If you choose to go your own way, well and good. But that's your own responsibility. But for God's sake, don't expect me to do the same!"

Wolff stormed from the room, followed by Herr, Lemelsen and Pohl. There were heavily armed guards at the two main exits, and fearing arrest, Wolff led the group out a secret tunnel to the safety of his own headquarters.

Wolff's suspicions were well founded. Shortly after midnight a message arrived ordering the arrest of Roettiger, who had fled the tunnel separately, and of Oberst Moll. "The fight goes on," Kesselring declared. Hitler's death had apparently not changed a thing.

Pohl, Lemelsen and Herr decided it was safer in their own headquarters and urged Wolff to go with them. But he wanted to stay at the palace to save "Sunrise" if he could. He ordered his reliable SS troops to defend the grounds. His new fear was that Kaltenbrunner might send Otto Skorzeny on an airborne commando operation to arrest him.* Seven tanks were lined up in front of the main gate, ready to defend him.

He had no idea what was on Kesselring's mind: he could countermand the orders to surrender; he could arrest all the conspirators and shoot them as traitors; or he could give tacit consent to the surrender by doing nothing at all.

* When told of this, Skorzeny sarcastically said, "It's nonsense to think these SS troops would have fought against me."

Wolff didn't have to wait long to find out exactly what Kesselring thought. At two o'clock in the morning of May 2, Kesselring shouted over the phone, "How dared you act on your own, without orders?"

Wolff reminded Kesselring that he had known about the plot for over a month. "If you'd joined us then, a lot of human blood need not have flowed and a great deal of destruction could have been avoided." Wolff said he could get the same surrender terms for all of Kesselring's forces. "I need only send a signal and the thing is done. And you seem to have forgotten that I kept you in the picture from the beginning. You knew what was at stake and now you stab us in the back by removing Vieting-hoff!" Wolff said that the agreement already made at Caserta had to be honored; he was convinced that history would vindicate them. "You'll do well to follow my advice. You don't seem to realize what's at stake."

Kesselring interrupted; he was no longer angry but excited. "You mean you made a deal with the Anglo-Americans to join in the fight against Tito and Russia?"

"Herr Generalfeldmarschall, I don't know where you got such a wild idea. That's entirely out of the question!" Wolff explained that he had negotiated a simple military surrender. "I've managed to save a lot of our men. They won't go to Siberia or North Africa or God knows where else, and I could probably do the same for many of the others." It was irre-sponsible to continue a losing fight. "Particularly now that the Führer's death has become known and you too are released from your oath, it's your duty to refuse to transfer this oath to anyone else. No oath of personal loyalty is transferable anywhere. I'm not in the least interested in Grossadmiral Dönitz. I feel in no way bound to Dönitz. Dönitz means less than nothing to me. Whoever goes on fighting now is nothing but a war criminal."

He stopped at last and Kesselring took up the debate with equal fervor. Their close relationship only made the argument more bitter. They shouted at each other until both were exhausted. They were spelled by Westphal and Wenner. For two hours the violent conversation raged, and when it at last ended Wolff sat dazed.

At four-thirty the phone range again. It was Schulz. The exasperated Wolff was about to say, "I don't give a damn what's on your mind," when the Supreme Commander in Italy announced that Kesselring had just phoned and given him permission to approve the surrender.

To hear these words, Wolff had made several dangerous trips to Switzerland; narrowly missed capture and death by partisans at Lake Como; and directly faced the fury of Himmler and Hitler. Moreover, he had humiliated himself, been forced to arrest a fellow officer, and endured numerous insults. But success was an anticlimax; he felt nothing. He told Wally to wire Alexander that "Kesselring too has accepted the terms." Then he flopped on his bed and fell asleep.

# 31

## "The Iron Curtain in the East Moves Closer and Closer"

### 1.

By midnight of April 30 Busse's huge wandering *Kessel* was at the point of disintegration. Only fear that the Bolsheviks might massacre them all kept the exhausted soldiers struggling west toward Wenck's Twelfth Army.

Oberst (Colonel) Hans Kempin, whose task it was to prevent the Russians from breaking through the north side of the *Kessel,* had left the Oder with 20,000 troops. Now, after ten days of almost constant running combat, his heavily reinforced 32nd SS Panzer Grenadier Division had been reduced to 400. He didn't have a single tank left. Kempin—a huge man, the size of Skorzeny—had never seen so much suffering in his years of battle. Many of his men were so fatigued that he could not rouse them from the ground. "If you want to get out of here," Kempin told a group of women, "you'll have to do it yourselves," so they picked up rifles and machine pistols lying on the ground and headed west. Most of the soldiers near by struggled to their feet and followed.

Toward the south of the *Kessel* there had been few civilian casualties in the long trek from the Oder. But just before dawn the civilians heard wild shouts and saw dim figures approach—Russians. They ran frantically into the woods until they came to the Dahme River; it was only twenty-five feet wide but ice-cold. Soldiers improvised rafts, then stripped off their clothes and began towing women across.

Elisabeth Deutschmann, whose husband had lost a leg in Russia, had just reached the west bank when the first Russians burst into view. The two naked soldiers who had ferried her to safety were unable to move and begged her to escape before the Russians crossed the river. But she rubbed their frozen bodies and covered them with her fur coat.

Across the river they could hear hysterical screaming and shooting. Then there was silence and they thought the Russians had left. Suddenly a huge Red Army enlisted man with a bloody bandage around his forehead loomed out of the mist and poked a pistol at them. "Don't be afraid," he said in German and grinned.

A Soviet officer grabbed Elisabeth, but the big Russian jammed a pistol in his ribs. "No, no, the woman belongs to that man." He indicated one of the Germans. As he led his prisoners through the woods, they passed a German whose nose was brutally gouged out; another had been castrated. But the Russian kept assuring the Germans that they were safe, and gave them hunks of bread and ham.

With the Red Army threatening to break through on all sides, Busse called on the spearhead to make one last desperate attempt to pierce the enemy lines and reach Wenck. There were only two Tigers left in the entire *Kessel*. Fueled from abandoned vehicles, they led the final assault.

In the darkness they were met by withering fire from Russian submachine guns and mortars, but somehow the two Tigers kept moving, shooting till their gun barrels were red hot. Behind them surged the infantry, accompanied by hundreds of women and girls carrying extra machine pistols, rifles and ammunition.

Only ten miles to the west Wenck was waiting for them; he had driven up to his front lines on a motorcycle. His commanders had warned him that the Red Army was about to smash through their lines; the Twelfth Army must pull back. But he could not forget the thousands of women and children in the *Kessel*. "We must stand," he radioed his commanders. "Busse is not yet here. We must wait for him."

In the first light of day, May 1, Wenck's outposts saw fireballs shooting in the air; then shadowy figures approached. They were bedraggled Ninth Army men. They shouted, "We made it!" "We are free!" then dropped to the ground, so spent that they could not be moved.

### 2.

Weidling, of course, had been correct in thinking that the Russians would not negotiate with those in the bunker. That noon a grim-faced Krebs returned from the Soviet lines at Tempelhof to report that he had talked with General Vasili Chuikov, commander of the Eighth Guards Army. He in turn phoned Zhukov, who demanded unconditional surrender to the Big Three.

Goebbels accused Krebs of misrepresenting his proposals and a bitter argument erupted. Goebbels shouted down the others and demanded that they send another messenger to the Russians, canceling all the proposals set forth by Krebs and declaring "war to the death."

Weidling urged that they stick to their breakout plan. "To continue the battle of Berlin is absolutely impossible!"

Krebs said he couldn't authorize this, then changed his mind. "Give the orders immediately," he said, "but wait here for possible modifications."

While the others made their various plans for escape, Goebbels prepared for death. He asked Dr. Stumpfegger to inject his six children with poison. But Stumpfegger said he could not have this on his conscience—he had children of his own—and Goebbels began looking for another doctor among the civilian refugees on the upper level.

At the Zoo flak tower an intelligence officer named Fricke took Colonel Wöhlerman aside and in a trembling, almost inaudible voice said that he had just heard Hitler was dead and that the government was going to announce it to the world. Like so many others, Wöhlerman refused to believe the news at first. He told Fricke to keep his information to himself.

## 3.

On May 1 at Plön, Dönitz received another enigmatic telegram from Bormann:

THE TESTAMENT IS IN FORCE. COMING TO YOU AS SOON AS POSSIBLE. TILL THEN YOU SHOULD IN MY OPINION REFRAIN FROM PUBLIC STATEMENT.

By now Dönitz felt certain that Hitler was dead and that for some reason Bormann wanted to hold back the truth. Personally he believed that the German people as well as the Armed Forces should be told at once what had happened, before a garbled account from other sources caused confusion. But he had little reliable information and decided to abide by Bormann's request, for the time being. It was clear, however, that the war was lost. Since there was no possibility of a political solution, it was his duty as Head of State to bring an end to hostilities as quickly as possible to prevent useless bloodshed.

"In my opinion," he told Keitel and Jodl, "Schörner's armies should evacuate the positions they are firmly holding and retire in the direction of the American front." Thus, when surrender came they could turn themselves over to the West.

He decided to surrender northern Germany to Montgomery, and to this end wired Generaladmiral Hans-Georg von Friedeburg, a skillful negotiator, to be prepared for a special mission. Once this had been accomplished, he would attempt to surrender the rest of the western front while holding off the Russians. But these negotiations must be stretched out as long as possible for the mass evacuation to the west to succeed.

He issued his first declaration to the Armed Forces the same day, with the assurance that it was his firm intention to continue "the fight against the Bolsheviks until our troops and the hundreds of thousands of German families in our eastern provinces have been saved from slavery or destruction," and that the "oath of allegiance which you took to the Führer now binds each and every one of you to me, whom he himself appointed as his successor."

He had also sent for the Reichskommissars for Czechoslovakia, the Netherlands, Denmark and Norway and now instructed them to do all they could to avoid further bloodshed in those countries. To Ribbentrop he said over the phone, "Think about a successor, and if you come up with someone call me back." An hour later Ribbentrop called on Dönitz in person. "I've thought about this problem over and over, and I can propose only one man capable of doing the job—myself."

Dönitz felt like "laughing in his face," but politely declined the offer. He asked Schwerin von Krosigk to accept the post. "You can expect to win no laurels, but both you and I are duty-bound to accept our tasks in the interests of the German people."

As soon as Himmler learned about this appointment he summoned Schwerin von Krosigk to his quarters. "I hear you're going to be the new Foreign Minister," he said. "I can only congratulate you. Never has a Foreign Minister had greater opportunities!"

The count stared at him. "What do you mean?"

"In a few days the Russians and Americans will clash and then we, the Germans, will be the decisive force. Therefore, never has the aim to get to the Ural Mountains been closer to fulfillment than at this moment."

"Do you still think that you personally have a task to fulfill?" Schwerin von Krosigk asked with mild sarcasm.

"Oh, yes! I am the rock of order. And Eisenhower and Montgomery are going to recognize me as such. All I need is an hour's talk with either of them, and the matter will be settled."

Late that afternoon Dönitz finally received official confirmation from Bormann and Goebbels of Hitler's death:

FÜHRER DIED YESTERDAY, 1530 HOURS. IN HIS WILL DATED APRIL 29 HE APPOINTS YOU AS PRESIDENT OF THE REICH, GOEBBELS AS REICH CHANCELLOR, BORMANN AS PARTY MINISTER, SEYSS-INQUART AS FOREIGN MINISTER. THE WILL, BY ORDER OF THE FÜHRER, IS BEING SENT TO FELDMARSCHALL SCHÖRNER AND OUT OF BERLIN FOR SAFE CUSTODY. BORMANN WILL TRY TO REACH YOU TODAY TO EXPLAIN THE SITUATION. FORM AND TIMING OF ANNOUNCEMENT TO THE ARMED FORCES AND THE PUBLIC IS LEFT TO YOUR DISCRETION. ACKNOWLEDGE.

But Dönitz had no intention of bringing either Goebbels or Bormann into his government and gave orders to arrest them if they set foot in Plön.

He also decided that it was time to inform the people of Hitler's death.* At 9:30 P.M. Hamburg Radio interrupted its program to announce that "a grave and important announcement" would follow. There was a selection from Wagner operas, followed by the slow movement of Bruckner's Seventh Symphony. Then a solemn voice said, "Our Führer, Adolf Hitler, fighting to the last breath against Bolshevism, fell for Germany this afternoon [it was the previous afternoon] in his operational headquarters in the Reich Chancellery. On April 30 [the testament was dated April 29] the Führer appointed Grossadmiral Dönitz to take his place. The Grossadmiral and successor to the Führer now speaks to the German people."

Dönitz said that Hitler had died "at the head of his troops" and that his own first task was "to save German men and women from destruction by the advancing Bolshevik enemy."

### 4.

Soon after dark that day Colonel Wöhlerman was told to report at once to Weidling's headquarters at the Bendlerblock. The breakout had been canceled.

Wöhlerman asked his first staff officer to accompany him with a machine pistol, and his driver volunteered to act as an additional guard. It was almost impossible to cross the Tiergarten diagonally, since the Russians already held the Lichtenstein Bridge. The three waited at the base of the flak tower until a fire fight ended, and then started down the East-West Axis. Shells exploded over their heads and they jumped into

---

* Dönitz thought Hitler had died in a bombing raid. Recently he said, "I am glad now that I didn't know he committed suicide, because then I'd have been obliged to tell the people, and many soldiers would immediately have put down their arms."

a bomb crater. It reminded Wöhlerman of Verdun. When the firing persisted, they crawled out of the crater and continued moving east. At Friedrich Wilhelmstrasse they dashed across the wide street under heavy fire. The Neue Siegesallee (New Victory Avenue) was a shambles: the monuments of the rulers of Brandenburg-Prussia, from Albrecht the Bear to Kaiser Friedrich III of Hohenzollern, had been blasted from their pedestals. Carefully they picked their way through the debris to the courtyard of the War Department, where Stauffenberg and others had been shot on July 20.

In the bunker there was an oppressive, doomsday atmosphere. Goebbels summoned his adjutant, Günther Schwägermann, and briefed him on the momentous events of the last few hours. "Everything is lost," he said. "I shall die, together with my wife and children. You will burn my body." He handed Schwägermann a silver-framed photograph of Hitler and bade him farewell.

Others in the bunker were getting last-minute instructions for escape. They were divided into six separate groups. At 9 P.M. the first group would make a run for the nearest subway entrance and walk along the tracks to the Friedrichstrasse station. Here they would emerge, cross the Spree River and head west or northwest until they reached the Western Allies or Dönitz. The other five groups would follow the same course, at intervals.

Kempka was put in charge of one group of thirty women. At 8:45 P.M. he went to the Goebbels' suite to say good-bye. The children were already dead, poisoned. Frau Goebbels asked Kempka in a calm voice to send greetings to her son Harald, and tell him how she had died.

The Goebbels' left their room, arm in arm. Utterly calm, Goebbels thanked Dr. Naumann for his loyalty and understanding; Magda could only hold out her hand. Naumann kissed it.

Goebbels wryly said that they were going to walk up the steps to the garden so that their friends wouldn't have to carry them. He shook hands with Naumann and escorted his silent, pale wife toward the exit. Naumann, Schwägermann and Rach, Goebbels' chauffeur, watched enrapt as they disappeared up the steep concrete stairway.

There was a shot, then a second. Schwägermann and Rach ran up the stairs and came upon the Goebbels' sprawled on the ground. An SS orderly was staring at them—he had shot them. Schwägermann, Rach and the orderly poured four jerricans of gasoline on the bodies and ignited it. Without waiting to see the effect of the blaze, they returned to the bunker, which they were ordered to set afire. They dumped the last can of gas in the conference room and put a match to it.

As the flames licked around the table that had been the center of such bitter arguments, Mohnke and Günsche led the first group from the bunker. It included Ambassador Hewel, Vize-admiral Voss, Hitler's three secretaries and the cook. Most of them had not been outside for days, and they emerged to find a conflagration far greater than they had imagined. All Berlin seemed to be on fire. It was night but the wreckage of the Chancellery stood out starkly in the leaping flames. A shell exploded near by and a cloud of pulverized rubble enveloped them. The sharp crack of rifles and the stutter of machine guns seemed to grow louder, as one by one they crawled through a narrow hole in the Chancellery ruins near the corner of Wilhelmstrasse and Vosstrasse. In single file they scurried 200 yards across the rubble and disappeared into the subway entrance opposite the Hotel Kaiserhof.

They came out at the Friedrichstrasse station amid a barrage and raced across the Spree River on an iron footbridge.

About 100 men—NCOs as well as high-ranking officers—crowded into Weidling's room in the Bendlerblock. The general stood behind his desk, his gnarled face serious. "Gentlemen," he began in a sharp, forceful voice, and informed them of Hitler's marriage and suicide. "According to his last will, his body was burned in the Chancellery garden. Therefore, we are released from our sworn oath."

He told about Krebs's unsuccessful negotiations with the Russians and Goebbels' subsequent order to defend Berlin to the last man. "Therefore, with heavy heart but unable to carry any more the responsibility for more victims in this hopeless battle, I have decided to surrender." He was going to send his chief of staff, Oberst (Colonel) Theodor von Dufving, to meet the Russians and negotiate. "And thus the terrible drama will end!"

The listeners stood silent. They knew it was the worst hour of Weidling's life as a soldier. No one uttered a word in rebuttal.

Just before midnight Weidling's first signals to the Russians went out but it was an hour before they answered, "We await you." Weidling told Dufving he could offer surrender on the following conditions: honorable capitulation for the troops; an immediate cease-fire; protection of civilians against terrorism; necessary food and personal belongings to be kept by each soldier; officers and men to remain with their units.

Dufving started toward the Russian lines.

Kempka had brought his group out of the Friedrichstrasse subway station but then decided to wait in a theater, the Admiral's Palace, before trying to cross the Spree. At two o'clock he cautiously crept out of the theater and saw a small group approaching in the darkness. It was led by Bormann in the uniform of an SS-Gruppenführer, and included Dr. Naumann, Dr. Stumpfegger, Rach, Schwägermann, Axmann and SS-Standartenführer (Colonel) Beetz, one of Hitler's personal pilots.

Bormann was looking for tanks to help them break through the Russian lines. Just then three German tanks and three armored personnel carriers loomed out of the dark. Kempka stopped the first vehicle. Its commander said that he was SS-Obersturmführer (1st Lieutenant) Hansen and that this was the last of an armored company of the Nordland Division.

Kempka ordered him to proceed slowly toward Ziegelstrasse so that the group could follow under armored cover. Bormann and Naumann walked to the left of one tank, with Kempka a few steps behind. Suddenly there was a volley of Russian antitank and small-arms fire. The tank near Kempka exploded and a huge flame boiled out. He saw Bormann and Naumann blown aside and was sure they had both been killed.* Then he felt Stumpfegger slam into him and he lost consciousness.

When Kempka came to, he couldn't see. He crawled ahead blindly for about forty yards, until he bumped into something. He stood up slowly, feeling his way along the obstruction—it was a roadblock. Slowly his vision cleared. In front of him Beetz stood in a daze, scalp torn open to the base of his skull. Supporting each other, they staggered back toward the Admiral's Palace until Beetz said he couldn't go another step. Kempka glanced around and saw Frau Dr. Haussermann, the assistant of Professor Blaschke, Hitler's dentist. She promised to take Beetz to her apartment.

It was obvious to Kempka that there was no chance to lead his group safely out of Berlin. He ordered them to split up and get out as best they could. Kempka himself made a dash across the Spree on a footbridge and hid in a railroad building with four slave laborers. One, a pretty Yugoslav girl, led Kempka to the attic and gave him a pair of soiled coveralls. He was wounded in the right arm, but he was too exhausted to care and slumped to the floor.

By this time Colonel von Dufving had safely penetrated the Red Army lines and negotiated the surrender. Russians were sending out messages to individual German units all around the perimeter calling for immediate capitulation: "We promise honorable treatment. Each officer can keep his side arms. Each officer and man can take his luggage with him."

All over the smoldering city German soldiers began emerging from

---

* But Werner Naumann was alive—and still is. He, Bormann and four others walked on to the Lerter station, where they separated. One man—Arthur Axmann, head of the Hitler Youth—has claimed that he saw Bormann's corpse later that night. But this testimony is unsupported. A good percentage of those who fled the bunker that night got out alive. Of all the Nazi leaders, Martin Bormann would have had the best chance to avoid capture, because even in Germany his face was known to few. He was an anonymous man and could easily have escaped into obscurity. An authoritative SS source has recently testified that Bormann was seen in South America. If any of the high-ranking Nazis escaped, Bormann did; he was a born survivor.

cellars and bunkers with white flags. Weidling's own surrender was without incident. He crossed the Landwehrkanal on a rope suspension bridge and handed himself over to a Russian division. He was taken to Chuikov's headquarters, where he wrote out a personal message ordering his men to lay down their arms at once.*

Just before dawn in the Tiergarten, Colonel Wöhlerman, wearing all his decorations, stepped out of the flak tower, followed by his men. The air was thick with fog. Suddenly German machine-gun bullets from within the park ricocheted off the building. But the Russian parliamentary kept his head; he restrained his own men from answering the fire. Wöhlerman shouted an order. The German firing ceased, and his 2000 men formed a long line. They started north through the park, climbing over fallen trees until they reached the East-West Axis. Near the Tiergarten railway viaduct the fog lifted slightly and Wöhlerman saw hundreds of Soviet tanks in review order, stretched along Hitler's traditional parade avenue. It was a frightening but impressive display.

At the sight of the surrendering Germans, Russians leaped off their tanks and held out cigarettes. *"Voyna kaputt!"* they shouted. *"Voyna kaputt!"* ("The war is over!")

Their open camaraderie prompted Wöhlerman to point to a group of twenty Hitler Youth and shout, *"Domoi?"* ("Back home?")

*"Domoi!"* the Russian parliamentary shouted back.

Wöhlerman put both hands to his mouth and called, "Boys, you can all go home!"

As the youngsters, shouting excitedly, scattered to freedom, the older German soldiers experienced a sense of gratitude, almost of joy, at the unexpected show of Russian compassion.

Kempka was wakened by the sound of boisterous Russian voices. From the attic he saw Red Army soldiers affectionately pummeling the slave workers. The Yugoslav girl beckoned and, apprehensive, Kempka climbed down. The smiling young woman led him to a commissar who looked suspiciously at him until the girl said, "This is my husband." The commissar hugged Kempka and shouted, *"Tovarisch,* Berlin kaputt, Hitler kaputt! Stalin is our hero!"

---

* On May 9 Weidling, Dufving, five generals, three colonels and a lone PFC were put on a plane bound for Moscow. The PFC was a middle-aged tobacconist from Potsdam, whose name was Trumann. After his capture he was asked if he was a relative of President Truman. He surmised he might be, since a granduncle had emigrated to the United States. He was put under heavy guard.

Trumann shared Dufving's cell in Moscow. One day, after many interrogations by the NKVD, he told Dufving, "The commissar just told me that I'm not related to the President of the United States and I have to tell everyone." Three months later he was removed from the cell and Dufving never saw him again.

Dufving was finally returned to West Germany in December, 1955, but Weidling died in a Russian prison in November of that year.

The Russians produced food and vodka, and with dawn a wild, boisterous party began.

## 5.

Except for sporadic firing from diehard Germans, the battle of Berlin was over, and the city's defenders were resigned to captivity.

But only sixty-five air miles west of the bunker, thousands of German soldiers and civilians crowded the east bank of the Elbe River at Tangermünde, waiting their turn to escape to the west. The bridge had been destroyed, but German engineers had erected a flimsy span for foot traffic over the wreckage. Americans watched approximately 18,000 soldiers and civilians daily make their way across to the west shore. Thousands more forded the river at other points in wooden rafts, rubber boats and river craft.

On the morning of May 2, Russians broke through Wenck's left flank, and his chief of staff suggested that negotiations be started at once with the Americans. Wenck said he was willing to surrender, but he wanted a week's delay so that the civilians east of the Elbe could also escape to the west.

General Max von Edelsheim was sent across the river as a parliamentary. The Americans agreed to let troops cross the Elbe at three points but refused to admit any more civilians.

North of Berlin Manteuffel's army—almost all that was left of Army Group Vistula—was withdrawing in a desperate effort to reach the Anglo-American lines before Rokossovsky caught up with them. Rokossovsky, however, was more interested in taking the key Baltic port of Lübeck than collecting prisoners. Eisenhower prodded Montgomery to hasten his drive to the Baltic before the Russians seized Schleswig-Holstein and perhaps even Denmark.

Montgomery quite tartly replied that he was well aware of what had to be done; when Simpson's army had been taken from him the tempo of his attack had, naturally, slowed. Eisenhower's response was to lend him the four divisions of Ridgway's XVIII Airborne Corps.

Only Blumentritt's depleted army stood between Montgomery and the Baltic. For the past few weeks Blumentritt had been waging a gentleman's battle with the British, pulling back with as little bloodshed as possible. Since mid-April an informal liaison had been maintained between the adversaries, and that morning one of the liaison officers from the Second British Army came to Blumentritt unofficially and said that since the Russians were closing in on Lübeck, His Majesty's forces wondered if the Germans would allow them to take the Baltic port ahead of the Russians.

Blumentritt too preferred to keep Lübeck out of Russian hands and issued immediate orders not to fire on the advancing British.

The British 7th Armoured Division immediately raced north, while German refugees continued to flee west, their movements so neatly co-ordinated that by late afternoon thousands were safely west of the Elbe-Trave Canal and the British were in Lübeck, ahead of the Red Army.

## 6.

That day Hanna Reitsch and Greim encountered Himmler as they were coming out of Admiral Dönitz's command post.

"One moment, Herr Reichsführer," Hanna said. "A matter of extreme importance, if you can spare the time?"

"Of course." He seemed almost jovial.

"Is it true, Herr Reichsführer, that you contacted the Allies with proposals of peace without orders to do so from Hitler?"

"Why, yes!"

"You betrayed your Führer and your people in the very darkest hour? Such a thing is high treason, Herr Reichsführer!"

Perhaps Himmler was getting accustomed to such attacks because his reactions were more apologetic than indignant. He explained that Hitler was "mad with pride and honor" and, in fact, was insane and "should have been stopped long ago."

"Insane? I came from him less than thirty-six hours ago. He died for the cause he believed in. He died bravely and filled with the 'honor' you speak of, while you and Göring and the rest must now live as branded traitors and cowards."

"I did as I did to save German blood, to rescue what was left of our country."

"You speak of German blood, Herr Reichsführer? You speak of it now? You should have thought of it years ago, before you became identified with the useless shedding of so much of it."

The debate was cut off by a crackle of machine-gun fire as Allied planes swept low, strafing the area.

At his new headquarters near Kiel, Himmler received Léon Degrelle, who was deeply affected by the news of Hitler's death. The Belgian said that he was going to Denmark, then on to Norway, where he would continue the fight against Bolshevism to the end. He asked what Himmler's plans were.

Himmler morbidly displayed a cyanide capsule inside his cheek, then almost in exultation said that he thought something could still be done with the Dönitz government. "We must gain six months' time! By then the Americans will be at war with the Russians."

"Herr Reichsführer," Degrelle replied grimly, "I believe it will take six years."

At dusk Dönitz and Schwerin von Krosigk met Admiral von Friedeburg, the man chosen to negotiate with Montgomery, on a bridge near Kiel. Dönitz instructed him to offer the military surrender of all of northern Germany while emphasizing the dire condition of the refugees and soldiers trying to escape to the British lines.

Then Dönitz and Schwerin von Krosigk drove on to Flensburg, their new headquarters at the northernmost tip of Germany, near the Danish border. On the way Dönitz approved a policy speech written by his recently appointed Foreign Minister; the Admiral wanted it broadcast as soon as possible.

In Flensburg, Schwerin von Krosigk went at once to the radio station. "German men and women," he began, and told them about the stream of terrified people trying to escape to the west. "The iron curtain in the east moves closer and closer; behind this, hidden from the eyes of the world, all those people caught in the mighty hands of the Bolsheviks are being destroyed." The conference at San Francisco, he said, was trying to draw up a constitution to guarantee the end of war—of a third world war that would use horrible new weapons "and bring death and destruction to all mankind." But a Bolshevik Europe, he predicted, would be the first step toward the world revolution so systematically planned by the Soviets for the past twenty-five years. "Therefore, we do not see in San Francisco what anxious mankind is longing for. And we also believe that a world constitution must be established, not only to prevent further wars but to remove the tinderboxes which start war. But such a constitution cannot be established if the Red incendiary helps establish it . . .

"The world now must make a decision of the greatest consequence to the history of mankind. Upon that decision depends chaos or order, war or peace, death or life."

# 32

## Beginning of a Long Surrender

**1.**

The British had already beaten the Russians to the Baltic and it was apparent that a meeting with the Red Army could come at any moment. Matthew Ridgway, whose XVIII Airborne Corps had been lent to Montgomery for the northern German campaign, instructed the U. S. 7th Armored Division to probe forward and make an orderly contact.

A recent graduate of West Point, 1st Lieutenant William A. Knowlton of the 87th Cavalry Reconnaissance Squadron, was selected to lead this force. He was told that the Russians were "somewhere to the east—between fifty and a hundred miles, according to rumor." He was to give the Soviet commander a few bottles of three-star Hennessy and persuade him to return to the American lines.

Late in the afternoon of May 2 Knowlton led ninety men in eleven armored cars and some twenty jeeps across his own lines, and headed northeast. The little task force struck out boldly down the main highway as if spearheading an entire army, and within a few miles began passing surprised German soldiers who were so eager to surrender that they threw their arms away and marched unescorted toward Allied captivity.

Knowlton's troops entered Parchim—twenty miles behind enemy lines —more like liberators than conquerors. German MPs had already cleared the main street, and the sidewalks were six lines deep with cheering soldiers and civilians who thought Knowlton was heading east to join in the fight against Bolshevism.*

Darkness caught the Americans nine miles farther east, in Lübz; they were beyond radio contact. Knowlton set up a command post in a beer hall with such authority that some 200,000 Germans surrendered during the night. Early the next morning he started east to meet the Russians, with two German officers perched on the front of his armored car. "Now, gentlemen," he told them, "if my car hits a mine, you will be just as dead or slightly more so than anyone in the car."

After fifteen cautious miles through mine fields, they approached the town of Reppentin. "There is our artillery!" One of the Germans pointed ahead at a long column of horses, vehicles and marching men.

Knowlton handed his field glasses to the German. "Look again, Herr Hauptmann, and then tell me for how long the German Army has had Cossacks in high fur caps riding the column!"

The military procession was beyond Knowlton's wildest imagination. It was an unruly collection of farm wagons, droshkies, rusty old field pieces, buses, German delivery trucks, bicycles and motorcycles. The wagons were filled with mothers and children; herds of cattle jogged down the fields alongside the column. It was, Knowlton thought, like some great caravan of nomads. The Russians yelled and waved at the Americans.

A two-horse wagon approached with a man and woman. They looked like farmers to Knowlton, but the driver was the colonel in command of the unit, and the woman a stocky nurse.

The colonel and Knowlton shook hands, slapped each other's backs and shouted, *"Tovarisch!"* and *"Ya Amerikanyets!"* They signed each other's maps and Knowlton handed over a bottle of three-star Hennessy.

Russian soldiers were already swarming over the U. S. armored cars, trying the guns, opening and closing the hatches, talking to one another on the radios and acting, Knowlton thought, like school children at an army exhibit. One accidentally tripped a machine gun and bullets kicked

* The next day a German major radioed his division commander, Ernst von Jungenfeld, that he had just met an American captain in command of twenty tanks, at a road junction six miles east of Parchim.
. . . BOTH OF US TANK LEADERS, WITH 40 GOOD TANKS REQUEST YOU PERSONALLY ORDER AN ATTACK AGAINST THE EAST, TO START THE MORNING OF MAY 4. WE BELIEVE THAT WITH HITLER DEAD, IT IS THE MOMENT TO FINALLY DEFEAT AND CRUSH THE RUSSIANS AND THEREBY, COMMUNISM. THEREFORE WE REQUEST YOU AND EXPECT FROM YOU A CLEAR ATTACK ORDER AGAINST THE EAST AND WE ARE CONVINCED THAT WE WILL DEFEAT AND DRIVE OUT THE RUSSIANS AND WE ARE ALSO SURE THAT EVERYWHERE OTHER COMRADES WILL IMMEDIATELY FOLLOW OUR EXAMPLE.
Jungenfeld radioed American headquarters for information and instructions on the joint attack, but when he failed to make contact, refused to give the order on his own initiative.

up dust all around the colonel. His staff bellowed with laughter and thumped one another on the back.

The colonel pointed an imperious finger at a large house. Several Cossacks galloped over and broke inside. There was a shatter of glass, then a great crash of splintering wood, followed by screams. Two elderly Germans shot through the front door. A Cossack carried out a boy by the seat of the pants and tossed him over a hedge. The colonel turned to Knowlton and invited him to enter his new command post.

The usual toasts were drunk to Stalin, Truman, Churchill and anybody or anything else that came to mind. Just before noon, the division commander arrived and told Knowlton he would meet the American commander that evening in a church halfway to Parchim.

Knowlton noticed a Russian task force leader reel drunkenly out of the house and go up to a group of young officers alertly poised with notebooks. He poked a finger vaguely at a map and mumbled something. The young officers looked at each other with resigned good humor, folded their notebooks and shouted commands. There was an answering roar from several thousand men who started riotously toward the west, firing their weapons in the air like Mexican revolutionaries.

As Knowlton pulled out of Reppentin, he looked back at one of his armored cars. A Russian major was poking out of the assistant gunner's seat like a jack-in-the-box. Towel over arm and rocking with drunken laughter, he began shaving the gunner with an old-fashioned straight razor.

## 2.

That morning Admiral von Friedeburg, accompanied by three officers, was led to Montgomery's headquarters on Lüneburger Heide (heath), some thirty miles southeast of Hamburg. Montgomery emerged from a trailer, his home for the past few years. He strode up to them and asked, "Who are these men? What do they want?"

As the Union Jack fluttered overhead, Friedeburg read a letter from Keitel offering to surrender all German troops in the north, including those who had been fighting the Red Army. The latter should surrender to the Russians, Montgomery replied briskly. "Of course, if any German soldiers come towards my front with their hands up they would automatically be taken prisoner."

It was unthinkable to surrender to the "Russian savages," said Friedeburg. Montgomery replied that the Germans should have thought of all these things before they began the war, and particularly before they attacked the Russians in June, 1941.

Friedeburg finally asked if some arrangement couldn't be made to allow the bulk of their troops as well as civilians to escape to the west. Montgomery refused, and asked for surrender of all forces in northern Germany, Holland,* Friesland with the Frisian Islands and Heligoland, Schleswig-Holstein and Denmark.

"I do not have the authority, but I'm sure that Admiral Dönitz would accept this," Friedeburg replied, and once again brought up the refugee problem.

Montgomery said he was "no monster" but refused to discuss the matter. The Germans had to surrender unconditionally. "If you refuse, I shall go on with the battle."

The distraught Friedeburg got permission to return to Dönitz with Montgomery's stipulations.

## 3.

The first Americans to enter Berlin were two civilians: John Groth, a combat artist and correspondent for the *American Legion Magazine,* and Seymour Freidin of the New York *Herald Tribune.* They had inveigled their way to the capital without American or Soviet sanction; a jeepload of enlisted U. S. Army photographers had tagged along. Just after lunch Freidin, who spoke Yiddish, had convinced a Soviet captain to let them proceed to the heart of the city. Under a "sick yellow rain" they passed the gutted Tempelhof airdrome. The great white administration building was black with smoke, and dozens of crumpled planes lay in the cratered field.

Walls were scrawled in whitewash with Nazi slogans: *"Heil Werwolf!"* and *"Mit unserem Führer zum Sieg!"* (With our Führer toward victory!). Here and there Russian propagandists had countered with neat signs of just one slogan: HITLERS COME AND GO, BUT THE GERMAN PEOPLE AND THE GERMAN STATE GO ON. STALIN.

Red Army men cheered the two American jeeps as they headed up Berlinerstrasse and approached the Blücherplatz, which was a junk yard of crushed tanks "with burnt bodies still sticking to them." The square was strewn with abandoned German equipment—socks, underwear, rifles,

---

* On September 17, 1944, a call for a general railway strike in occupied Holland was issued by the government-in-exile. In retaliation, the Germans prohibited all building-up of food supplies in western Holland until the end of October, and confiscated all means of transport. The daily calorie unit issued to each person dropped to 450 and people started dying from starvation by the end of November. Early in April, 1945, the Germans offered to let the Allies send food to the occupied area under certain conditions. Finally an agreement was reached between Dr. Artur Seyss-Inquart, Reichskommissar for the Netherlands, and Eisenhower's chief of staff, Bedell Smith. On April 29, 253 aircraft of Bomber Command dropped over 500,000 rations near Rotterdam and The Hague. By the end of May 8 over 11,000,-000 British and American rations had been dropped.

shells, mines. The "honey-on-herring" stink of death rose from every pile of rubble.

The jeeps slowly circled craters to Wilhelmstrasse. The glare from burning buildings silhouetted the "broken soda-cracker edges" of the ruins. In the distance they could hear the thump of artillery, and the closer typewriter chop of machine guns.

The Wilhelmplatz looked to Groth like Roquefort cheese. On his left, charred walls encompassed a huge heap of rubble—the Reich Chancellery. Fastened high on the east wall, overlooking the craters of the square was a large black-and-white photograph of Stalin. An oil painting of the Führer hung askew on the south wall. Bright red Russian flags, looking black-purple in the drizzle, sprouted all over the jagged ruins.

The Americans parked the jeeps and began investigating the ruins. Freidin poked around the Reich Chancellery, looking for Hitler's body, but it would take a crew of bulldozers a week to reach the bottom of the debris.

The Americans returned to their jeeps and started down Unter den Linden, a vast panorama of gray, smoking ruins. Up ahead, Red Army men swarmed past the Brandenburg Gate to wipe out the last stubborn Germans in the Tiergarten. The only bright note was the scarlet row of banners over the Brandenburg Gate. The chariot of victory on top was twisted beyond recognition, with three of its four horses tipped over. To the left, the Adlon Hotel was gutted, and a large Red Cross flag draped from an upper window gave the area its only touch of white.

Groth climbed over the roadblock built into the columns of the impressive gate and followed Russians into the Tiergarten. It reminded him of the Hürtgen Forest battlefield the year before, with trees lying "like scattered matches" over foxholes and slit trenches. From behind a blasted wall he watched the Soviets charge into the smoke.

A few minutes after three o'clock an awesome silence enveloped the park. Suddenly there were exultant cheers. A Russian officer, lying in the mud, looked over at Groth. He smiled. "Berlin kaputt!"

## 4.

There was nothing Dönitz could do but accept Montgomery's conditions. He told Admiral von Friedeburg to sign the tactical surrender of North Germany, including Holland and Denmark. Friedeburg would then fly to Rheims and offer Eisenhower the separate surrender of all other German forces on the western front.

Late that afternoon on the Lüneburg heath Montgomery jauntily entered a tent filled with newsmen. Over his battle dress he wore a camel's-hair naval duffel coat with hood. "Sit down, gentlemen," he said perkily and everyone squatted on the ground. He preened himself—a sign to correspondent Richard McMillan that he was in special form.

"There is a certain gentleman called Blumentritt," Montgomery began, "who, as far as I know, commands all forces between the Baltic and the Weser River. On Wednesday he sent in and said he wanted to come in on Thursday and surrender what they call the Army Group Blumentritt. It was not an army group as we know it, but a sort of brigade group. He wanted to surrender it. That was done to Second British Army.

"He was told: 'You can come in. That's O.K. Delighted!' But the next thing that happened was yesterday morning, Blumentritt did not come. He said: 'As far as I know, there is something going on just above my level and therefore I am not coming in.'

"He did not come in. But instead there arrived here to see me four German people." He told them about the meeting with Friedeburg the previous day.

A staff officer signaled that Friedeburg had at last returned, and Montgomery went back to his trailer. Friedeburg and his four comrades waited, drawn and nervous, in the rain. Through the open door of the trailer they could see Montgomery fiddling with some papers. At last he came out and stood under the Union Jack. The Germans saluted. Montgomery delayed before answering their salute. Friedeburg was escorted into the trailer and Montgomery asked if he would sign the full surrender. The admiral nodded dejectedly and was sent outside.

Again the five Germans waited, fidgeting, clasping and unclasping their hands. Just before six o'clock Montgomery emerged once more. As he swaggered past the correspondents he said with the hint of a smile, "A great moment this," and gave them a quick look as if seeking their approval.

The field-marshal led the Germans into another tent, set up for the ceremony. He read the terms matter-of-factly and turned to Friedeburg. "You will sign first." Montgomery watched, hands in pockets, like a placid hawk.

He called over his photographer. "Did you get that picture—under the Union Jack?" The photographer had. "Good. A historic picture—historic!"

At Rheims, Eisenhower had given up waiting for news of the surrender at Lüneburg. He said he was going home.

"Why don't you wait just another five minutes?" said his personal secretary, Lieutenant Kay Summersby. "The call may come."

Just about five minutes later the phone did ring. "Fine, fine," said Eisenhower. "That's fine, Monty."

Captain Harry Butcher, Eisenhower's naval aide, wondered if the Supreme Commander would personally sign the surrender when Admiral von Friedeburg arrived the next day at Rheims. Eisenhower replied that he didn't "want to bargain"; he would tell his staff exactly what to do but did not want to see the German negotiators until after they had signed.

The Big Three had agreed on the terms of surrender not long after D-Day. Following Yalta, however, these terms were revised in a second instrument of surrender, to include the dismemberment of Germany. The American ambassador in London, John Winant, feared that the existence of these two different documents might cause confusion and phoned "Beetle" Smith at Rheims to remind him of possible complications. Smith said he didn't even have an authorized copy of the second surrender document. Moreover, the Big Three and France had not yet delegated SHAEF the power to sign it.

More concerned than ever, Winant phoned the State Department in Washington and urged that the necessary authorization to sign be cabled to SHAEF at once.

## 5.

Early that morning two German officers led an armed unit up to the salt mine near Bad Ischl, not far from Berchtesgaden, where the finest art objects from the Vienna Kunsthistorisches Museum and the Österreichische Galerie were stored. They claimed that Baldur von Schirach had ordered them to save the most valuable objects from the approaching Russians; then threatened to shoot anyone who objected.

They selected 184 valuable paintings—including five Rembrandts, two Dürers, eight Brueghels, nine Titians, and seven Velázquez'—as well as forty-nine bags of tapestries and several boxes of sculpture, and drove off with them in two trucks toward Switzerland.

The little convoy stopped several hours later at the Goldener Löwe, an inn in a small Tyrolean village. They hid the works of art in the cellar of an adjoining guest house and told the unhappy occupant—his name was God—that it was now his personal responsibility to save Austria's treasures from the Russians.

As the two Allied fronts drew closer together there was a scramble between East and West for art treasures, gold, military weapons and scientists. An American MFA&A (Monuments, Fine Arts and Archives) lieutenant discovered the cellar hideaway at the Goldener Löwe and fellow officers found Göring's fabulous art treasure in nearby Berchtesgaden. Many masterpieces were still in crates at the railroad station but even more were stored in freight cars at a siding.

Other American specialists were picking up more than their share of German scientists. In a cloak-and-dagger episode straight out of fiction,

Father Sampson was persuaded by a U. S. captain, who suddenly turned up at Stalag IIA, to help him smuggle a noted German fuse expert from the next city through the Russian lines. To get a pass for the entire party at the final Soviet check point, the priest was forced to match vodka, glass for glass, with the local Russian commandant. He barely accomplished his mission and staggered off to freedom.

The most clandestine of these operations, "Alsos," was brought to a successful conclusion, largely through the persistence and derring-do of a Californian of Russian lineage, Colonel Boris Pash. His special task force struck out in advance of combat troops and captured an experimental uranium pile in the Black Forest, as well as three noted physicists involved in Germany's atomic program.

But America's prize acquisition was a windfall. Dr. Wernher von Braun and his leading V-2 scientists had decided France and England could not afford a major rocket program, and voluntarily surrendered to the U. S. 44th Division. Almost as important was the recovery of the fourteen tons of V-2 documents hidden in the Dörnten iron mine by Tessmann and Huzel.

Despite a slow start, Colonel Holgar Toftoy's "Special Mission V-2," under Major James Hamill, also succeeded in its mission. One hundred complete V-2s from Nordhausen were evacuated only hours before the Russians occupied the area. Hamill had been ordered to remove the rockets "without making it obvious that we had looted the place," yet, curiously, was not even told that Nordhausen would be in the Soviet zone. Consequently it never occurred to him to destroy the remaining rockets.

Lieutenant Colonel Vladimir Yurasov arrived at Nordhausen soon after Hamill's departure. He was there to evacuate a cement plant to the Soviet Union and only by accident discovered the remaining V-2s in the great tunnel. "It's strange," remarked his chauffeur, Nikolai. "This was the most secret German weapon, and the Americans left it for us. Americans are not bad fellows, but somehow too trusting." Later Yurasov escorted a fellow colonel through the cave. He laughed, incredulous. "The Americans gave us this! But in five or ten years they will cry. Imagine when our rockets fly across the ocean!"

## 6.

Bedell Smith's answer to the problem of two surrender documents was to draw up a third—one which provided only for military surrender in the field. This obviated the necessity of getting authorization from the Big Three, since it was only a tactical capitulation. In a phone call to Churchill he argued that the Germans would more readily sign such a simple document, and this would save lives.

It was after five in the afternoon by the time Friedeburg finally arrived at Rheims. The German hopes for a surrender only on the western front were dashed when Smith told the admiral that Eisenhower demanded immediate and unconditional surrender on all fronts. This meant that Friedeburg had to find some way to delay as long as possible, to give the people in the east more time to escape to the west. He told Smith he was authorized only to parley, not to surrender, and would have to communicate with Dönitz. And this would take time, since he had brought no code, nor had he arranged frequencies for radio communication with Dönitz's headquarters. Moreover, because of poor communications it would take at least forty-eight hours before all German front-line units could be informed of the signing.

While he was talking, Friedeburg kept glancing furtively at a situation map spread out on the desk. Smith pushed it over to him and said, "Obviously you do not entirely realize the hopelessness of the German positions."

The admiral stared at the map. Germany was punctured from east and west by attack arrows. He couldn't take his eyes off two particularly large ones—both of which Smith had imaginatively added to frighten Friedeburg. Tears came to the admiral's eyes and he asked if he could send a message to Dönitz.

Winant only learned late that night that Smith had actually composed a third instrument of surrender. He told Smith over the phone that this new document was a purely military instrument, which under the Geneva and Hague conventions would legally force the Allies to uphold National Socialist laws, thus forestalling the trials of war criminals. It could also deny the Allies an unconditional *political* surrender and would ultimately question their supreme authority over Germany. Furthermore, arbitrarily replacing the document agreed upon by the Big Three without informing the Russians could create justified protests in Moscow.

Winant felt so strongly about the problem that he took it personally to Churchill, who decided not to interfere. Winant's persistence led to only one concession: Smith added a new paragraph to his own simple document, stating that it would be "superseded by any general instrument of surrender" later drawn up by the United Nations. Winant assumed, of course, that Smith had already cleared his document with the Combined Chiefs of Staff and the U. S. War Department; he radioed the State Department that agreement had at last been reached. But the War Department and the Combined Chiefs—like the Russians—didn't even know that the third instrument of surrender existed.*

* Three days later, on May 9, the State Department radioed Winant that the War Department still had no idea why the version agreed on by the Big Three had not been signed at Rheims and that they had known nothing about Smith's document.

### 7.

With Berlin already in the hands of the Red Army, Prague was the only great capital in central Europe still held by Germans. Bismarck's dictum that whoever held Prague, held central Europe still made sense to Churchill. He had radioed Truman the last day of April that the liberation of Prague by Patton "might make the whole difference to the post-war situation in Czechoslovakia, and might well influence that in near-by countries." He warned that Czechoslovakia would "go the way of Yugoslavia" if the West hung back.

The U. S. Department of State urged Truman to heed these words, and Acting Secretary of State Joseph Grew added that a drive to the Moldau River, which ran through Prague, would give America a bargaining edge in future negotiations with the Soviets. Truman asked his Joint Chiefs for an appraisal and they turned to Eisenhower, who replied that the Red Army was "in perfect position" to occupy Czechoslovakia and would "certainly reach" Prague before Patton.

. . . I SHALL NOT ATTEMPT ANY MOVE I DEEM MILITARILY UNWISE MERELY TO GAIN A POLITICAL PRIZE UNLESS I RECEIVE SPECIFIC ORDERS FROM THE COMBINED CHIEFS OF STAFF.

The argument that the Soviets would reach the goal first—as had been stated about Berlin—was punctured when Patton, against little opposition, suddenly rolled across the border of Germany into Czechoslovakia.

"Thank God, thank God!" exclaimed Dr. Eduard Beneš, President of the Czechoslovakian government-in-exile, on receiving the news. "Haničko, Haničko," he called in a choked voice to his wife. "The Americans have just entered Czechoslovakia! Patton is across the border!"

Even a few weeks before, his enthusiasm would have been just as great if it had been the Russians who were approaching Prague. At that time he still trusted Stalin. In 1943 he had gone to Moscow and "in the utmost harmony, friendship, and cordiality," signed a Treaty of Friendship, Mutual Aid, and Postwar Co-operation with the Soviets. He reassured his countrymen that Stalin had guaranteed Czechoslovakia's integrity. "The Soviet Union believes that the Republic will remain democratic and progressive. . . . The Soviet Union does not request anything special from us. Our policy will simply be the policy of our democratic majority."

This faith was not even shaken after the Red Army entered his country in late 1944 and local Communists began seizing control. There were demands for secession of Subcarpathic Russia to the U.S.S.R.; then with the help of Soviet political commissars and the NKVD, "national committees" were set up to take over the administration of towns and villages.

Those who tried to resist were imprisoned as German collaborators. Stalin wrote Beneš that it was all a "misunderstanding" but what could he do if secession was the will of the people of that area? At the same time he reassured Beneš that he had no intention of breaking his agreement with Czechoslovakia.

But alarming reports of increased Communist activities as well as acts of terrorism by the Red Army finally convinced Beneš by mid-March, 1945, that his exile government could no longer afford to remain in London. En route to Czechoslovakia he stopped off in Moscow, where Stalin gave a state dinner in his honor. The Marshal toasted Slav solidarity and remarked that the Red Army was not "an army of angels" and should be forgiven for its bad behavior. He called for the independence of every nation, good or bad. "The Soviet Union will not interfere in the internal affairs of its allies. I know that even among you there are some who doubt it." He turned to Beneš. "Perhaps even you are a little dubious, but I give assurance that we will never interfere in the internal affairs of our allies. Such is Lenin's neo-Slavism, which we Bolshevik Communists are following."

In the shadow of the Kremlin the delegates from London began meeting with the Czechoslovak Communist delegates, and a government was created which ostensibly gave equal representation to the six Czech and Slovak parties. But six "unpolitical" members were included as "personalities of national repute and experts without regard to their political membership," though most of these, in fact, were Communists or fellow travelers. The result was that the Communists could control every major decision of the new government.

In German-occupied Czechoslovakia, underground groups which had operated more or less independently were being organized for joint action. The common goal was to prevent the destruction of property by the Germans and to ensure that postwar Czechoslovakia would be truly democratic.

Unlike other east and central European cities, Prague itself was almost untouched by the war; its picturesque castle, churches and bridges—which looked like something out of a fairy tale—were still intact. On the afternoon of May 4, impatient citizens of Prague endangered the underground timetable for open revolt by removing German signs or painting them over with patriotic slogans. Radio Prague threatened heavy penalties for such vandalism, but these warnings had no effect. Early the next morning, street peddlers were openly selling little black-framed death notices reading: "The Third Reich—Curse of Humanity." Across the bottom was an old Czech proverb: "If you blow up a balloon too much, it will burst."

A false report that Patton was only eighteen miles away led to widespread public demonstrations. A trolley car festooned with Allied flags rolled full speed through Wenceslaus Square, the center of the city, its bell clanging wildly while its conductor leaned out the rear, shouting slogans of liberation.

By noon, Czech flags flew from many windows, and stores displayed pictures of Beneš, Masaryk and Stalin in their windows. Karl Hermann Frank, the Nazi State Minister of Bohemia and Moravia, ordered the streets cleared, but only a few SS troops fired on the demonstrators.

The Revolutionary Czech National Council hastily assembled in an insurance office and voted unanimously to lead the premature revolution. Its own plan for an uprising had depended largely on an airdrop of arms from the British which had been postponed again and again. The Council's first task was to find a figurehead with wide popular appeal. Dr. Albert Pražák, a sixty-four-year-old professor at Charles University, was chosen. He was anti-Communist but politically naïve, and the Communists in the Council were sure they could control him because his daughter was a Party member.

At three o'clock the Council broadcast an appeal to the people to build barricades in the streets. At every strategic corner, citizens began erecting obstructions in the cold rain. Men dug out heavy cobblestones from the streets while women piled them up. Trolley cars were lifted bodily from their tracks and turned sideways.

A jeepload of Americans suddenly appeared in Wenceslaus Square. It was an OSS team led by Lieutenant Eugene Fodor, who was of Hungarian descent. The Americans were embraced by the enthusiastic Czechs, who thought they were the vanguard of Patton's army, and taken to the joint headquarters of the political (the Council) and the military command of the uprising. The Americans were told they could march in and easily take the city. Then Major Nechansky, of the military command, suggested he return with Fodor and see General Patton. He was anxious to transmit a formal request to the Americans in the name of General Kuttelwaser, the titular military head of the uprising, to come to the aid of Prague.

A Communist on the Council vehemently objected—undoubtedly he wanted the Red Army to arrive first—but he was outvoted.

Fodor took Nechansky back to U. S. headquarters in Pilsen, fifty miles to the west, and found Patton there with General Huebner. Patton was so impressed by Fodor's account of the desperate situation in the capital that he begged Bradley to let him seize Prague. Bradley said it wasn't his decision to make. It was up to Eisenhower.

Bradley phoned Eisenhower, who told him that the halt line through Pilsen was mandatory. Patton was, under no circumstances, to march on Prague.*

---

* The previous day Eisenhower had reconsidered his decision not to seize Prague —perhaps because of continued pressure from Churchill and Grew. But he chose to ask final permission to take the Czech capital from the Russians themselves. He

In Prague it was reported that two German divisions were approaching the city. The promised arms had still not been dropped and in desperation one group of Czech officers, without informing the Council, turned for aid to a group of Russians dressed in German uniforms. This was a division of the so-called Vlasov Army, which in the last three weeks had wandered defiantly from its battle position on the Oder just below Frankfurt to within thirty-five miles of Prague.

Almost three years before, Lieutenant General Andrei Andreevich Vlasov—former military adviser to Chiang Kai-shek and one of the heroes of the Moscow defense—had been captured by the Germans near Leningrad. He was then so disillusioned with the state of affairs in the U.S.S.R. that he wrote an impassioned open letter to other Soviet prisoners, denouncing Stalin and calling for the overthrow of Communism. Nazi propagandists were sure they could use such a man as a tool and sent him on a tour of prison camps to enlist other Red Army men in Hitler's crusade against Bolshevism.

To his captors' chagrin, however, Vlasov also began criticizing the Nazis themselves for treating Russia as a slave state and terrorizing its citizens. "Today the Russian people can still be won for the great struggle," he wrote. "Tomorrow will be too late." A number of important Wehrmacht officers endorsed Vlasov's views and the tall, bony man with heavy horn-rimmed glasses grew in importance, becoming the rallying point for over 1,000,000 Russian prisoners of war who wanted to drive Bolshevism out of their country.

But Hitler remained suspicious of Vlasov. "We will never build up a Russian army, that's a phantom of the first order," he said. "You will not get men for the fight against Russia, but rather an army to proceed against Germany, if the opportunity presents itself. For every nation thinks of itself and of nothing else. . . . Above all, one thing must not happen —we can't give these units to a third man who gets them under his thumb and says, 'Today you work with them, tomorrow you don't.' One day we would get a sort of strike slogan that will run along the entire front. Then, suddenly, they're organized and ready to start extorting."

But Himmler believed that such troops could still be a potent political factor, and when the man-power shortage became desperate he sent for Vlasov and gave him permission to organize an initial force of 50,000 men. In one day alone, November 20, 1944, 60,000 tried to enlist. But

radioed General Deane in Moscow to tell Colonel General Alexei Antonov, Chief of Staff of the Red Army, that U. S. troops were now able to advance as far as the Moldau River.

Antonov's reaction was immediate and foreseeable. To avoid "a possible confusion of forces," he requested Eisenhower not to move beyond Pilsen. The Red Army had already stopped its advance in northern Germany at Eisenhower's request, and Antonov hoped that the Supreme Commander "in turn will comply with our wishes."

because of continued skepticism on Hitler's part, and lack of equipment, only two units were activated: the 1st and 2nd R.O.A. divisions (Russkaia Osvobitel'naia Armiia, Russian Army of Liberation).

Hitler's prophecy began to materialize only hours after the 1st R.O.A. Division was turned against the Red Army on Busse's front. After a day of senseless attacks against far superior Soviet forces, General Sergei K. Bunyachenko, the 1st Division commander, pulled his troops out of the front line without orders. He reasoned that the war was almost over and that one division more or less wouldn't alter the situation; his main concern was to save lives. Determined to link up with the other R.O.A. division and Vlasov himself, Bunyachenko ordered his men to march to Czechoslovakia. The men ripped the swastikas from their uniforms and mimeographed 30,000 leaflets in German denouncing Hitler. The R.O.A. was now "organized and ready to start extorting."

The German High Command pleaded and even sent truckloads of food as a peace offering, but the 20,000 Russians continued marching south. Schörner sent two delegations urging Bunyachenko "to conciliate this conflict," and when their efforts failed, made a personal visit to the rebel division. He pleaded for an hour with Bunyachenko and Vlasov, then gave up in disgust and flew back to his own headquarters.

The Russians didn't stop till they reached the region of Beroun, some twenty-five miles southwest of Prague. From there they wanted to march farther south to rendezvous with the 2nd R.O.A. Division.

About midnight, May 4, a delegation of Czech officers, wearing civilian overcoats to cover their uniforms, brought an unusual request to Bunyachenko's headquarters in the village of Shukomasty: they wanted these Russians to help support the uprising in Prague. Bunyachenko excused himself and returned with Vlasov, who questioned the Czechs; then he asked Bunyachenko and his regimental commanders, "So, Sergei Kuzmich? So, gentlemen? What are we going to do now?"

There was a long silence. Suddenly Bunyachenko bellowed, "I think we must help our Slavic brothers!"

Turning to the Czechs, Vlasov said, "We will support your uprising. Go ahead."

German tanks were already converging on the capital to help the ground troops. "The Nazis are coming!" partisan-held Radio Prague announced, and urged the people to reinforce the barricades. "We hope for help from our brothers, the Vlasovites!" The Czechs again appealed directly to the Allies. "We need urgent assistance." They asked for planes, tanks and an airdrop. "The Germans are suppressing the uprising mercilessly. For God's sake, send help!"

It was past dawn before the first elements of the Vlasov Army, wearing the emblem of the R.O.A. on their German uniforms, started toward

Prague on foot. The march became almost a festive parade. In every village, lines of cheering Czechs cried out, *"Naz dar!"* ("Long life!") Weeping women joyously offered food to the passing men, and girls strewed flowers in their path. At dusk they would enter Prague.

# 33

# "The Flags of Freedom Fly All Over Europe"

## 1.

Dönitz was not sure he could comply with Eisenhower's demand for unconditional surrender on all fronts. Even if he agreed to such conditions, he could not control the men on the eastern front; they were so afraid of the Russians that they would probably ignore the order and flee to the west. He decided to try again to convince Eisenhower that the German soldiers and civilians in the east should not be abandoned to the Bolsheviks. On May 6 he asked Jodl to fly to Rheims and present new proposals, and handed him written instructions.

Try once again to explain the reasons why we wish to make this separate surrender to the Americans. If you have no more success with Eisenhower than Friedeburg had, offer a simultaneous surrender *on all fronts,* to be implemented in two phases. During the first phase all hostilities will have ceased, but the German troops will still be allowed liberty of movement. During the second phase this liberty will be withheld. Try and make the interval before the introduction of Phase Two as long as possible, and if you can, get Eisenhower to agree that individual German soldiers will in any case be allowed to surrender to the Americans. The greater your success in these directions, the greater will be the number of German soldiers and refugees who will find salvation in the west.

Dönitz also gave him a power of attorney to sign a surrender for all fronts. "Use this authorization only if you find that your first object of separate surrender cannot be reached," he said, and cautioned him not to sign anything without getting final approval by radio.

Later in the day Dönitz received an unexpected offer of help in the negotiations. Göring, who had just been released from SS captivity by Luftwaffe troops, radioed:

ARE YOU AWARE OF THE INTRIGUES, ENDANGERING THE SECURITY OF THE STATE, CARRIED ON BY REICH LEADER BORMANN TO ELIM- INATE ME? ALL MOVES AGAINST ME AROSE OUT OF THE LOYAL REQUEST SENT BY ME TO THE FÜHRER, ASKING IF HE WISHED HIS ORDER ON SUCCESSION SHOULD COME INTO FORCE . . .

I HAVE JUST LEARNED THAT YOU PLAN TO SEND JODL TO EISEN- HOWER TO NEGOTIATE. IN THE INTERESTS OF OUR PEOPLE, I BE- LIEVE THAT I ALSO SHOULD SEE EISENHOWER, AS ONE MARSHAL TO ANOTHER. MY SUCCESS IN IMPORTANT FOREIGN NEGOTIATIONS EN- TRUSTED ME BY THE FÜHRER BEFORE THE WAR IS GOOD ENOUGH GUARANTEE THAT I COULD PROBABLY CREATE A PERSONAL ATMOS- PHERE HELPFUL TO JODL'S NEGOTIATIONS. BESIDES, GREAT BRITAIN AND AMERICA HAVE SHOWN . . . IN THE REMARKS OF THEIR STATES- MEN THE PAST FEW YEARS THAT THEIR FEELING TOWARD ME IS MORE FAVORABLE THAN TOWARD OTHER POLITICAL LEADERS IN GER- MANY. AT THIS MOST DIFFICULT HOUR I FIRMLY BELIEVE THAT WE SHOULD ALL COOPERATE AND OVERLOOK NO STEP WHICH COULD BEST SERVE THE FUTURE OF GERMANY.

Dönitz tossed the message aside.

Many of those whose lives had been dominated for years by Hitler were suddenly thrust into an uneasy freedom. In a final interview with Adolf Eichmann at a mountain villa in Austria, Ernst Kaltenbrunner said almost idly, "What are you going to do now?" He was playing solitaire and sipping cognac.

Eichmann said he was going to the mountains and join other stalwart Nazis in a final struggle.

"That's good. Good for Reichsführer Himmler too," Kaltenbrunner said with a sarcasm that apparently went over the literal-minded Eichmann's head. "Now he can talk to Eisenhower differently in his negotiations, for he will know that an Eichmann in the mountains will never surrender— because he can't." Kaltenbrunner snapped down a card. "It's all a lot of crap," he said quietly. "The game is up."*

* Kaltenbrunner was hanged after the Nuremberg Trials. Eichmann went to the mountains, but instead of fighting, he surrendered peaceably to an American unit under the name of Luftwaffe Corporal Barth. In prison camp he promoted himself to SS lieutenant and assumed the name of Otto Eckmann. He escaped in 1946 without difficulty and fled to South America, where, fourteen years later, he was captured by Israeli agents in Buenos Aires and smuggled to Jerusalem for trial— and execution.

Himmler's reaction to the problems confronting him was to flee Flensburg.

"You can't just walk out," protested SS-Oberstgruppenführer (General) Otto Ohlendorf, chief of Bureau III of the RSHA Sicherheitsdienst (Security Office). "You must make a radio speech or send some declaration to the Allies that you take responsibility for what's happened. You must give the reasons."

Himmler acquiesced, but only to avoid argument. He accosted Schwerin von Krosigk and anxiously asked, "Please tell me what is going to become of me?"

"I'm not interested in the least what will happen to you or any other man," said the exasperated count. "Only our mission interests me, not our personal destinies." He told Himmler he could commit suicide or disappear with a false beard. "But if I were you I'd drive up to Montgomery and say, 'Here I am, Himmler the SS general, and ready to take responsibility for all my men.'"

"Herr Reichsminister . . ." Himmler couldn't finish the sentence. He turned away.

That night he cryptically told his best friends that an important new mission remained. "For years I have borne a great burden. This new great task I shall have to undertake alone. One or two of you perhaps can accompany me."

He shaved off his mustache, put a patch over one eye, changed his name to Heinrich Hitzinger, and—with half a dozen followers, including Dr. Gebhardt—went into hiding. Within two weeks he was captured by the British. A doctor conducting a routine examination noticed something in Himmler's mouth, but when he reached in to pull out the object Himmler bit down on the cyanide capsule he had once shown Degrelle, and died almost instantly.

**2.**

In Paris, seventeen correspondents were selected by SHAEF to cover the story of the surrender. On the afternoon of May 6 their plane left for Rheims. En route Brigadier General Frank A. Allen, chief of Eisenhower's Public Relations Division, said that premature disclosure of the negotiations could have disastrous results, and asked everyone to sign a pledge "not to communicate the results of this conference or the fact of its existence until it has been released by the Supreme Headquarters."

At Rheims the correspondents were driven to Eisenhower's headquarters in the École Professionnelle et Technique de Garçons, a modern three-floor, red brick building. Allen led them to a classroom on the ground floor and told them to wait.

In the meantime another group of correspondents, including Raymond Daniell of the *New York Times* and Helen Kirkpatrick of the Chicago *Tribune,* had arrived from Paris by jeep. Angry at the arbitrary selection of those who would have exclusive access to the big story, they attempted to enter the schoolhouse but were barred by orders from Allen. They remained on the sidewalk, accosting everyone leaving or entering the building. Lieutenant-General Frederick Morgan sympathized with their plight and told Allen something should be done about the locked-out correspondents. Allen thought he was complaining of their presence and ordered MPs to chase them away.

About five-thirty Jodl and his aide, accompanied by two British generals, entered the schoolhouse and were taken to Admiral von Friedeburg. Jodl greeted his countryman with a noncommittal "Ah-ha" and closed the door. Shortly Friedeburg came out, with a request for coffee and a map of Europe.

The Germans were escorted to Bedell Smith's office by Major-General Kenneth Strong, Eisenhower's chief of intelligence, who spoke German fluently. Here Jodl doggedly argued the German position: they were willing to surrender to the West but not to the Russians. At seven-thirty Strong and Smith left the Germans. They went down the hall to Eisenhower's office to report their progress, and then returned.

A moment later Captain Butcher walked into Eisenhower's office to remind him of the two pens—one gold and one gold-plated—which an old friend of Eisenhower's, Kenneth Parker, had sent him for the occasion. Eisenhower told his naval aide to hang on to the pens "for dear life"— one would be sent to Parker and the other to Truman.

When Butcher asked, What about Churchill?, Eisenhower said, "Oh, Lord, I hadn't thought of that."

Down the hall, Jodl had at last agreed to surrender to the Russians also but requested a forty-eight-hour delay. "You'll soon be fighting the Russians yourselves. Save as many as you can from them."

Jodl was so persistent that Strong went again to see Eisenhower and told him of the German's firm stand. "Give it to them," Strong advised.

Eisenhower didn't want to delay the signing. "You can tell them that forty-eight hours from midnight tonight, I will close my lines on the western front so no more Germans can get through. Whether they sign or not. No matter how much time they take."

The words were threatening but, in effect, gave Jodl what he asked— two days' grace. Even so, he was dejected as he dictated a radiogram for Dönitz and Keitel:

GENERAL EISENHOWER INSISTS WE SIGN TODAY. OTHERWISE ALLIED LINES WILL BE CLOSED EVEN TO PERSONS ATTEMPTING TO SURRENDER INDIVIDUALLY AND NEGOTIATIONS BROKEN OFF. SEE NO AL-

TERNATIVE TO CHAOS OR SIGNATURE. REQUEST IMMEDIATE RADIO
CONFIRMATION WHETHER AUTHORIZATION FOR SIGNING THE CAPITU-
LATION BE PUT INTO EFFECT. HOSTILITIES WILL THEN CEASE ON
9 MAY 0001 HOURS OUR TIME.

It was almost midnight before Dönitz received the uncoded message and
by that time Jodl had sent another: REPLY TO RADIOGRAM MOST URGENTLY
AND IMMEDIATELY REQUESTED. The Grossadmiral thought the terms were
"sheer extortion" but he had no other choice. The forty-eight hours Jodl
had won would at least save thousands from slavery or massacre. He
authorized Keitel to send an acceptance, and not long after midnight the
OKW chief radioed Jodl:

FULL POWER TO SIGN IN ACCORDANCE WITH CONDITIONS
AS GIVEN HAS BEEN GRANTED BY GROSSADMIRAL DÖNITZ

At one-thirty in the morning Major Ruth Briggs, Smith's secretary,
phoned Butcher. "The big party is on," she said, and told Butcher to
hurry over with the two pens. How could the war be ended without
pens?

The war room where the ceremony would take place had once been a
recreation hall where students played ping-pong and chess. It was approximately thirty square feet and the walls were covered with maps. At
one end of the room stood a large table used by teachers to grade papers.

When Butcher arrived he found the room already crowded with participants and witnesses, including the seventeen selected correspondents,
Major General Ivan Susloparov and two other Russian officers; Commandant (Major General) François Sevez, the French representative;
three British officers—General Morgan, Admiral Harold Burrough and Air-
Marshal Sir James Robb; and General Carl Spaatz, commander of the
U. S. Strategic Air Forces in Europe.

Bedell Smith strode in, blinking unhappily at the glare of floodlights
set up for movies. He checked the seating arrangements and briefed
everyone on the procedure. A moment later Jodl and Friedeburg stepped
in and halted uncertainly when the lights hit their eyes.

The principals sat down at the big table and Butcher placed the gold
pen before Smith and the gold-plated one before Jodl, who was sitting directly across the table. Smith told the Germans that the documents were
ready for signature. Were they prepared to sign?

Jodl nodded slightly and signed the first documents, which called for
a complete cessation of all hostilities the next day at 11:01 P.M., Central
European Time. His face was impenetrable but Strong noticed that his
eyes were moist. Butcher took the gold pen and gave Jodl his own
Sheaffer—it would be a nice souvenir—to sign the second document.
Finally Smith, Susloparov, and Sevez signed. It was exactly 2:41 A.M.,
May 7, 1945.

Jodl leaned across the table and said in English, "I want to say a word." Smith said, "Yes, of course."

Jodl picked up the single microphone on the table and began speaking in German: "General, with this signature the German people and the German armed forces are, for better or worse, delivered into the victor's hands. In this war, which has lasted more than five years, both have achieved and suffered perhaps more than any other people in the world. In this hour I can only express the hope that the victor will treat them with generosity."

Eisenhower was impatiently pacing from his room to his secretary's office and back. To Kay Summersby the silence "was heavy."

Smith strode in—half grinning, half grim—to announce that the surrender had been signed. Outside in the hall Lieutenant Summersby heard the clomp of heavy boots and instinctively stood up. Jodl and Friedeburg marched past her without a glance and headed into Eisenhower's office, where they came to a sharp halt, clicked their heels and saluted smartly. She thought they looked like "the exact prototypes of filmland Nazis, sour-faced, glum, erect and despicable."

Eisenhower stood stock-still, more military than she had ever before seen him.

"Do you understand the terms of the document of surrender you have just signed?"

Strong interpreted and Jodl said, "*Ja, ja.*"

"You will get details of instructions at a later date. And you will be expected to carry them out faithfully."

Jodl nodded.

"That is all," Eisenhower said stiffly.

The Germans bowed, saluted and marched back past Lieutenant Summersby. Eisenhower's face suddenly broke into a broad grin. "Come on, let's all have a picture!" he said as photographers pushed in. Everyone in the office crowded around the Supreme Commander, who held up the two gold pens in a V for Victory.

He sent a message to the Combined Chiefs of Staff:

> THE MISSION OF THIS ALLIED FORCE WAS FULFILLED AT 0241, LOCAL TIME, MAY 7, 1945. EISENHOWER.

He phoned Bradley at the Fürstenhof Hotel in Bad Wildungen. Awakened from a four-hour sleep, Bradley turned on a light and heard the Supreme Commander say, "Brad, it's all over. A TWX is on the way."

Bradley called up Patton, asleep in his trailer in Regensburg. "Ike just called me, George. The Germans have surrendered. It takes effect at midnight, May eighth. We're to hold in place everywhere up and down the line. There's no sense in taking any more casualties now."

Bradley opened his mapboard and with a china-marking pencil wrote down, "D plus 335." Then he went to the window and ripped the blackout blinds apart.

In the classroom the seventeen correspondents had just finished writing the biggest story of the war—peace in Europe. Their dispatches had already been passed to the censor when General Allen walked in and announced that the news could not be released for a day and a half. General Eisenhower was sorry but his hands were "tied at a high political level" and nothing could be done.

There was a concerted cry of protest from the correspondents. "I personally think this story should be released," Allen said. The date he had just given was purely arbitrary; the Big Three had not yet agreed on any date to announce the surrender. "I will try my best to get it released before the time set but I don't know how effective I shall be. In any case, there is nothing for us to do now but return to Paris."

In Moscow, word of the signing had not yet been received. Soviet General Nikolai Vasilevich Slavin walked into the office of the U. S. Military Mission and handed General Deane a letter from General Antonov, complaining that in spite of the surrender negotiations at Rheims, Dönitz was "continuing his announcements over the radio calling upon Germans to continue the war against the Soviets . . . and not to resist Allied forces in the west. . . . This infers to the public that Dönitz has made a separate peace with the West and is continuing war against the East. We can't give public opinion in Europe the excuse to claim there is a separate peace."

Antonov had also just learned that the new surrender document, which had been prepared by Smith, differed from the one approved by the Big Three, and refused to accept its validity.

Then, to Deane's consternation, Antonov added, "The Soviet High Command prefers that the signing of the 'Act of Military Surrender' take place in Berlin." Marshal Zhukov would sign for the Red Army.

General Slavin explained that the Soviets wanted only one signing of the document—and that in Berlin. They definitely did not want Susloparov to sign any document at Rheims. "The Berlin ceremony could be quickly arranged," Slavin said. "And wouldn't cause any delay."

In Rheims, Robert Murphy, Eisenhower's political adviser, was just as perturbed by the surrender document as Antonov. He had never seen it before. He got Bedell Smith out of bed and asked what had happened to the approved text, which he had personally turned over to the Chief of Staff late in March.

Smith couldn't recall even getting such a document.

"But don't you remember that big blue folder which I told you were the terms approved by everybody?" Murphy asked.

Smith—who only a few days before had argued at length with Winant about this very document—now said he "remembered," and soon the two were in his office searching for it. They found the blue folder in the personal top-secret cabinet and Murphy was convinced that Smith had merely "suffered a rare lapse of memory and had been under the impression that the E.A.C. never had approved a surrender agreement."

About nine-thirty in the morning Butcher came into Eisenhower's bedroom. He was in bed. Near by was a Western paperback, *Cartridge Carnival*. The message from Moscow had arrived and Eisenhower was writing Antonov that he would be delighted to come to Berlin the next day at any hour specified by Zhukov.

Half an hour later at the Hotel Scribe in Paris, General Allen repeated to a press conference what he had told the seventeen correspondents at Rheims: no stories about the surrender could be released before 3 P.M. the next day. Already infuriated by the way they had been treated, the frustrated newsmen milled about in the hotel lobby, threatening to draw up a resolution against SHAEF Public Relations. Edward Kennedy—one of the original seventeen and chief of the Paris Bureau of the Associated Press—went up to his office on the fourth floor to check the latest reports: de Gaulle's office announced he was preparing a V-Day address and General Sevez had told a *Figaro* reporter that he had signed for France at Rheims.

The noon Paris papers carried dispatches from London that loudspeakers were being set up at No. 10 Downing Street. It appeared that Churchill was about to formally announce the surrender.

The announcement came, but not from Churchill. A little after three o'clock Kennedy heard the BBC broadcast an English translation of a speech Schwerin von Krosigk had just made over Radio Flensburg: "German men and women! By order of Grossadmiral Dönitz, the Supreme Headquarters of the Army announced today the unconditional surrender of all troops." He called on Germans to make sacrifices. "In the darkness of the future we must be led by the light of the three stars which were always the pledge of real German character: *'Einigkeit und Recht und Freiheit'* [Unity and Justice and Liberty] . . ."

It was inconceivable to Kennedy that the Dönitz government would have made the broadcast without the consent of SHAEF. He phoned Allen's office, only to be told that the general was too busy to speak with him. He rushed to the office of Lieutenant Colonel Richard Merrick, the chief U. S. censor, and said he no longer felt obliged to hold the news, since SHAEF had already released it through the Germans. "I give you warning now that I am going to send the story."

"Do as you please," said Merrick.

Kennedy wrote a condensed version of the story and put a call through to the London A. P. office by military phone. From the Hotel Scribe anyone could simply call "Paris Military" and be connected to any number in London. An enemy agent could have strolled into the hotel and done the same.

"This is Ed Kennedy, Lew," he shouted to Lewis Hawkins in the London office. "Germany has surrendered unconditionally. That's official. Make the date Rheims, France, and get it out." Kennedy's voice kept fading and forced Hawkins to copy down ten "takes."

Since the story originated in Paris and was only to be relayed through London, the British censors allowed it to be transmitted as dictated to the New York office of the A. P. Here it was held up eight minutes at the foreign desk for possible corrections. There were none, and the news was sped throughout the Allied world at 3:35 P.M., London time (9:35 A.M., Eastern War Time), by press and radio.

Repercussions were almost immediate. Around four o'clock Churchill, who had called Eisenhower half a dozen times that day trying to get the story released, phoned Admiral Leahy in the Pentagon for information.

"In view of agreements already made," Leahy replied, "my Chief asks me to tell you that he cannot act without the approval of Uncle Joe. Did you understand, sir?"

"Will you let somebody with a younger ear listen to it?" said Churchill. "My ears are a bit deaf, you know."

Leachy began to repeat the message to the Prime Minister's secretary, but Churchill impatiently cut in, "Hello. The German Prime Minister [Foreign Minister Schwerin von Krosigk] has given out an hour ago, on the radio—"

"I know that."

"—an address stating that they had declared the unconditional surrender for German troops."

"We know that."

"What is the use of me and of the President looking to be the only two people in the world who don't know what is going on?" He said he would have to release the news himself at 6 P.M.

"You have not asked the approval of Uncle Joe?" Leahy re-emphasized that Truman would make no announcement without Stalin's approval.

"The whole world knows it, and I do not see why we should put our news off until . . . it is an idiotic position." Churchill repeated that he simply could not delay his announcement any longer. "The whole world knows about it."

"They know about it now, that's quite true, sir. Everybody knows it."

Churchill called back an hour later. "We have communicated with Eisenhower and we have talked with him," Leahy stated. "He says no announcement has been made from his headquarters, and that no announcement will be made until after the announcements are made in London and Moscow and the United States."

Churchill replied that the London crowds were gathering. "The thing must go forward . . ."

"I know your difficulties and I cannot say what you ought to do," Leahy replied, "but the President said that he would not make any announcement until he would hear from Stalin." He promised to let Churchill know as soon as word from Moscow arrived.

"Do tell the President how sorry I am. I hope we will do it at the same time."

"I will give the President your message."

"I feel I can delay no longer."

"I am sorry about this," said Leahy.

The people of London waited with growing impatience for official word from Churchill. A few minutes past six o'clock three Lancasters flew low over the city, dropping red and green flares, and flags of the Allied countries began appearing in shops and homes as thousands poured into the streets.

For almost two hours the crowds milled around. Then the announcement they had awaited for years came from the British Ministry of Information: tomorrow would be V-E Day. But for Londoners the war was over that night. Riotous celebrations broke out. From Piccadilly to Wapping, bonfires blazed, coloring the sky red. Tugs, motorboats and small craft raced noisily up and down the Thames. Piccadilly Circus was a frenzied mass of dancing, cheering people. Strangers embraced as rockets streaked into the sky and crowds sang—in harmony and in discord— "Roll out the Barrel," "Tipperary," "Loch Lomond," and "Bless 'em All." Long processions snaked through the streets to the Palace, chanting in unison, "We want the King!"

In New York the celebration was muted. A war was still to be won in the Pacific. There was also wide skepticism over the authenticity of the news because of the premature peace rumor ten days earlier. Moreover, many remembered the false armistice of 1918.

By now the American who had started it all, Edward Kennedy, had been indefinitely suspended from further dispatching facilities by SHAEF, but this did nothing to assuage the other correspondents in Paris. Drew Middleton typified their mood when he cabled the *New York Times* that the entire affair was "the most colossal 'snafu' in the history of the war. I am browned off, fed up, burnt up and put out . . ."

In Oslo, the Norwegians were celebrating in open defiance of German occupation troops. Vidkun Quisling, the man whose name had become a synonym for traitor, was still in the royal palace. He was listening to Léon Degrelle, who had escaped from Germany through Denmark to continue his fight against Bolshevism. Quisling's face was bloated, his eyes darting nervously as he tapped the table with his fingers. To Degrelle he looked like a man completely crushed by events, consumed within. For the next half-hour Quisling talked only about the weather and Degrelle left completely disillusioned. He had done everything he could, holding out to the bitter end. But where could he fight now?

He went to the palace of Crown Prince Olaf to see Dr. Josef Terboven, the Reichskommissar of Norway.* A uniformed maître d' served them drinks as if it were an ordinary day. Terboven, his little eyes blinking like Himmler's, said gravely, "I've asked Sweden to give you asylum, but she refuses. I hoped to send you to Japan by submarine, but the capitulation is so absolute that submarines can't leave the harbor." However, there was a private plane belonging to Minister Speer. "Do you want to take a chance and try to fly to Spain tonight?"

The distance from Oslo to the Pyrenees was 2150 kilometers and the plane only had a range of 2100 kilometers, but fuel could be saved at high altitudes. At eight o'clock that evening, a pilot wearing a high German decoration picked up Degrelle, who was still in his SS uniform. They drove through the jammed streets of Oslo, noticed by a few curious celebrants but never stopped.

A few minutes before midnight they took off. They flew safely over enemy-occupied Holland, Belgium and France, only to run out of gas and crash in the surf off a Spanish beach at San Sebastián, thirty-five miles from Biarritz. Five of Degrelle's bones were broken, but he had reached the sanctuary of Franco.

## 3.

Distracted as Churchill was by the problems of the surrender, he could not forget the besieged people of Prague and radioed a final appeal to Eisenhower:

I AM HOPING THAT YOUR PLAN DOES NOT INHIBIT YOU TO ADVANCE TO PRAGUE IF YOU HAVE THE TROOPS AND DO NOT MEET THE RUS-SIANS EARLIER. I THOUGHT YOU DID NOT MEAN TO TIE YOURSELF DOWN IF YOU HAD THE TROOPS AND THE COUNTRY WAS EMPTY. DON'T BOTHER TO REPLY BY WIRE, BUT TELL ME WHEN WE NEXT HAVE A TALK.

But Eisenhower had no intention of moving a single mile east of Pilsen. As far as he, the Joint Chiefs of Staff and Truman were concerned, the fate of Prague was not their business.

Only Vlasov had come to its aid and one R.O.A. regiment was already locked in furious street-fighting with German troops. On the evening of May 7 General Bunyachenko learned that an SS division was approaching

---

* Terboven later shot himself. Quisling tried to escape but was captured.

Prague from the south. He ordered a reserve regiment to dig in on a hill eight miles from the city and stop the enemy "at all costs."

By midmorning the next day the Germans appeared to be contained. A few hours later, however, the victorious R.O.A. troops began pulling out of Prague. Bunyachenko explained to a regimental commander that the Czechs had asked them to leave: their help was no longer needed; the tanks of Marshal Konev were about to enter the city.*

The Vlasovites feared that their counrymen would show them no mercy, and turned away from the city they had helped to save. Bewildered and embittered, they started back toward the southwest. This time it was no festive procession. There were no flowers thrown at their feet, no food handed out, no joyous shouts of *"Naz dar!"*\*\*

Just after noon General Rudolf Toussaint, the German military commander in Prague, was led blindfolded into the Revolutionary Czech National Council headquarters, where his son was held prisoner. General Toussaint was a tall, handsome man of fifty, impeccably dressed. A freedom fighter ripped off the general's blindfold; it was hanging rather ridiculously on one ear, but he retained his straight, formal bearing until it was removed.

Although he represented a beaten army, Toussaint argued for more than four hours, until the Czechs finally agreed to let his men march west and surrender to the Americans. Even so he was despondent. "Who am I now—a general without an army!" His son, head bandaged, was led into the room. "All I can do is go home and sit in the ditch and look up at the blue sky," Toussaint said. "But we deserved it."

It was a day of retribution. All over the city, Czechs were battling German soldiers and civilians with a fury engendered by years of oppression.

Soon Prague was once again free, and by the time the Red Army finally arrived, the streets were almost completely cleared of Germans. But the

---

* Dr. Otakar Machotka, a member of the Revolutionary Czech National Council, emphatically denies that the Vlasovites were dismissed by the Czechs.

\*\* Of the 50,000 armed Vlasovites about half escaped across the Anglo-American lines. The rest were rounded up by the Red Army, and those who didn't commit suicide were brought back to the Soviet Union as captives. Vlasov himself was tried in Moscow with Bunyachenko and eight other leaders for "espionage-diversionary and terrorist activity against the Soviet Union." A military board announced that "all accused admitted their guilt." They were hanged.

At Yalta, Churchill and Roosevelt had agreed to return Soviet citizens in their respective occupation zones, and most of those who had fled to the West were ultimately handed over to the Russians—occasionally with brute force on the part of their Anglo-American guards. At Lienz, Austria, a group of Cossacks refused to load into trucks for evacuation. They formed a protective circle around their families and barehanded fought off British troops. At least sixty were killed by the British, and others leaped into the Drava River to drown rather than be brought back to the U.S.S.R.

Russians began to take credit for liberating Prague and western Czechoslovakia, and their claim was to become a strong weapon in the subsequent power struggle for the country.

By the morning of May 8 the only heavy fighting on the eastern front was in Yugoslavia, where Tito's partisans had practically surrounded the 200,000 remnants of Generaloberst Alexander Löhr's battered Army Group F. In the past two months almost 100,000 had been killed.

To Löhr's right, Army Group South under Dr. Rendulic, the Austrian historian, held a continuous line from southern Austria to the border of Czechoslovakia; Rendulic's four armies had seen little action since the fall of Vienna. Confident that the Americans and British would join him in a fight against the Bolsheviks, Rendulic sent an envoy to Major General Walton H. Walker of the U. S. XX Corps asking permission to move German reserve troops through the American lines to the eastern front. Walker caustically refused, and the disillusioned Rendulic, who knew nothing of the negotiations at Rheims, took it upon himself to order hostilities to stop against the West at nine that morning. The four armies facing the Soviets were told to disengage and retreat to the west.

To Rendulic's north, Feldmarschall Schörner, who had already ordered his army group to turn around and escape to the American lines, got a wire from Dönitz informing him that a general unconditional surrender would take effect at midnight. From that moment Schörner was to stop fighting and stay in place. Some of his staff felt they had been betrayed, but Schörner accepted the situation philosophically. He ordered his troops to split up in small groups and flee to the west as best they could, taking along as many civilians as possible.

At ten o'clock in the morning a colonel from OKW, Wilhelm Meyer-Detring, arrived at Schörner's command post, some sixty air miles north of Prague. Meyer-Detring, accompanied by four Americans, told Schörner he was relieved of all command functions once the capitulation went into effect at midnight.

Schörner sent out his last messages, then made plans to fly to the Tyrol in a Storch so that he could carry out Hitler's order to take command of the *Alpenfestung.**

* By the time he arrived there was no *Alpenfestung,* and the war was over. A week later he surrendered to the Americans and was sent to the Soviet Union, where he was tried and sentenced to 25 years' imprisonment. While he was in Russia his chief of staff, General Oldwig von Natzmer, accused him of deserting his men; when Schörner returned to Munich after nine years he found himself the symbol of cowardice to many Germans. He was tried again, on another charge, this time by the West German government, and convicted on circumstantial evidence. A score of fellow officers recently volunteered convincing information that Schörner did indeed fly off to the Tyrol to assume command of the *Alpenfestung*— not to save his life.

. . .

Hans-Ulrich Rudel, Hitler's favorite flier, learned that the war was over late that morning when he returned from a mission to his air base north of Prague. He assembled his men, thanked them for their gallantry and loyalty, and shook hands with everyone.

With six other pilots he flew in three Junker 87s and four Focke-Wulf 190s toward the American lines, where he hoped to get medical attention for his amputated leg. Over the big Kitzingen airfield in Bavaria, Rudel could see American soldiers parading, and he led his group in a low sweep toward the runway. As his wheels touched down he braked violently on one side while kicking the rudder bar, and the undercarriage ripped off. When he opened the canopy an American soldier poked a revolver at him and grabbed for his golden oak leaves. Rudel shoved him back and slammed shut the canopy. A jeep pulled up with several American officers who took him to a first-aid station to dress his blood-drenched stump. Then he was escorted to an officers' mess where his colleagues sprang to their feet and gave the Führer salute. An interpreter told Rudel that the U. S. commandant objected to this salute, and asked if he spoke English.

"Even if I can speak English, we are in Germany and here I speak only German," Rudel said. "As far as the salute is concerned, we are ordered to salute that way, and being soldiers, we carry out our orders. Besides, we don't care whether you object to it or not." He glared defiantly at a group of American officers at the next table. "The German soldier has not been beaten on his merits but has simply been crushed by overwhelming masses of matériel. We have landed here because we did not wish to stay in the Soviet zone. We should also prefer not to discuss the matter any further but would like to clean up and have something to eat."

The Americans let the prisoners wash, and while they were eating the interpreter told them that the U. S. commanding officer wondered if they would like to have a friendly talk with him and his officers.

Like Rudel, millions of Germans from the eastern front were trying to reach American sanctuary. Many were funneling into Enns, Austria, hoping to cross the river into the lines of the U. S. 65th Division.

Late in the afternoon, lines of weary Germans from the 12th SS Panzer Division approached the bridge, where a heavy log barricade had only been cleared enough to let a single truck squeeze through. Someone cried, *"Russky!"* and there was a stampede toward the bridge. Trucks ground into the surging mass of men. At least fifteen were killed instantly and countless others mangled. The bridge approach was hopelessly jammed and the terrified Germans fanned out along the river bank for a mile, shouting, *"Russky! Russky! Russky!"*

A squat medium tank clanked toward the bridge. A Red Army lieutenant stood in the turret, laughing at the sight of 6000 men frantically scrambling to escape his single gun.

## 4.

Early in the morning of May 8, Truman wrote his mother and sister:

Dear Mama & Mary:—

I am sixty-one this morning, and I slept in the President's room in the White House last night. They have finished the painting and have some of the furniture in place. I'm hoping it will all be ready for you by Friday. My expensive gold pen doesn't work as well as it should.

This will be a historical day. At 9:00 o'clock this morning I must make a broadcast to the country: announcing the German surrender. The papers were signed yesterday morning and hostilities will cease on all fronts at midnight tonight. Isn't that some birthday present?

Have had one heck of a time with the Prime Minister of Great Britain. He, Stalin and the U. S. President made an agreement to release the news all at once from the three capitals at an hour that would fit us all. We agreed on 9 A.M. Washington time which is 3 P.M. London and 4 P.M. Moscow time.*

Mr. Churchill began calling me at daylight to know if we shouldn't make an immediate release without considering the Russians. He was refused and then he kept pushing me to talk to Stalin. He finally had to stick to the agreed plan—but he was mad as a wet hen.

Things have moved at a terrific rate here since April 12. Never a day has gone by that some momentous decision didn't have to be made. So far luck has been with me. I hope it keeps up. It can't stay with me forever however and I hope when the mistake comes it won't be too great to remedy.

We are looking forward to a grand visit with you. I may not be able to come for you as planned but I'm sending the safest finest plane and all kinds of help so please don't disappoint me.

Lots & lots of love to you both.

Harry

*Stalin, in fact, still protested such an early announcement and had stated his reasons in a recent radio message to Truman:

. . . THE SUPREME COMMAND OF THE RED ARMY IS NOT SURE THAT THE ORDER OF THE GERMAN HIGH COMMAND ON UNCONDITIONAL SURRENDER WILL BE EXECUTED BY THE GERMAN ARMIES ON THE EASTERN FRONT. WE FEAR, THEREFORE, THAT IF THE GOVERNMENT OF THE U.S.S.R. ANNOUNCES TODAY THE SURRENDER OF GERMANY WE MAY FIND OURSELVES IN AN AWKWARD POSITION AND MISLEAD THE SOVIET PUBLIC. IT SHOULD BE BORNE IN MIND THAT THE GERMAN RESISTANCE ON THE EASTERN FRONT IS NOT SLACKENING BUT, JUDGING BY INTERCEPTED RADIO MESSAGES, A CONSIDERABLE GROUPING OF GERMAN TROOPS HAVE EXPLICITLY DECLARED THEIR INTENTION TO CONTINUE THE RESISTANCE AND TO DISOBEY DÖNITZ'S SURRENDER ORDER.

FOR THIS REASON THE COMMAND OF THE SOVIET TROOPS WOULD LIKE TO WAIT UNTIL THE GERMAN SURRENDER TAKES EFFECT AND TO POSTPONE THE GOVERNMENTS' ANNOUNCEMENT OF THE SURRENDER TILL MAY 9, 7 P.M. MOSCOW TIME.

At 8:35 A.M. the press crowded silently into the Executive Office of the White House, where Truman was waiting with his wife and daughter and a group of political and military leaders. "Well," said the President, "I want to start off by reading you a little statement here. I want you to understand, at the very beginning, that this press conference is held with the understanding that any and all information given you here is for release at 9 A.M. this morning, Eastern War Time."

He said he was going to read a proclamation. "It won't take but seven minutes, so you needn't be uneasy. You have plenty of time." The correspondents laughed.

" 'This is a solemn but glorious hour. General Eisenhower informs me that the forces of Germany have surrendered to the United Nations. The flags of freedom fly all over Europe.' " He interrupted himself. "It's celebrating my birthday, too—today, too."

"Happy birthday, Mr. President!" several voices called out and there was another burst of laughter.

Truman finished the proclamation, which ended with a plea for "work, work and more work" to finish the war; the victory was only half over. He then read a release calling for relentless war against Japan until it surrendered unconditionally, and enumerating clearly to the Japanese people exactly what unconditional surrender meant:

"It means the end of the war.

"It means the termination of the influence of the military leaders who brought Japan to the present brink of disaster.

"It means provision for the return of soldiers and sailors to their families, their farms, and their jobs.

"And it means not prolonging the present agony and suffering of the Japanese in the vain hope of victory.

"Unconditional surrender does not mean the extermination or enslavement of the Japanese people."

[A similar statement to the Germans in 1944 might have brought an earlier end to that conflict.]

Departing from his script Truman said, "You remember, it has been emphasized here all the time that we want a peace of justice and law. That's what we are trying to get, at San Francisco—what we are going to get—the framework for a peace in justice and law. We have got terrific problems facing us."

He declared Sunday, May 13, a day of prayer and noted that it was "exceedingly fitting that that is Mother's Day, too."

At 9 A.M. he was in the Radio Room of the White House, broadcasting to the people. "This is a solemn but a glorious hour," he began and spontaneously added a sentence not read to the correspondents. "I only wish that Franklin D. Roosevelt had lived to witness this day . . ."

At exactly the same moment Churchill addressed the British people from the Cabinet Room at No. 10 Downing Street. He reviewed the past five years, then said somberly that he wished he could now say all their toil and troubles were over. But there was much to do.

"On the continent of Europe we have yet to make sure that the simple and honorable purposes for which we entered the war are not brushed aside or overlooked in the months following our success, and that the words 'freedom,' 'democracy,' and 'liberation' are not distorted from their true meaning as we have understood them. There would be little use in punishing the Hitlerites for their crimes if law and justice did not rule, and if totalitarian or police governments were to take the place of the German invaders. We seek nothing for ourselves. But we must make sure that those causes which we fought for find recognition at the peace table in facts as well as words, and above all we must labor to ensure that the world organization which the United Nations are creating at San Francisco does not become an idle name, does not become a shield for the strong and a mockery for the weak. It is the victors who must search their hearts in their glowing hours, and be worthy by their nobility of the immense forces that they wield. . . ."*

After his speech Churchill went to the House of Commons, but the short walk took him half an hour because of the great, surging crowds. When he finally strode into the Chamber every member stood and cheered. He moved that the House adjourn and give "humble and reverent thanks to Almighty God for our deliverance from the threat of German domination," and led the way to Westminster Abbey throught the boisterous mob.

Following lunch at Buckingham Palace he drove to the Ministry of Health in Whitehall. He stepped onto a balcony, but the cheering crowd would hardly let him speak. "This is your victory," he shouted. "It is the victory of the cause of freedom in every land. In all our long history we have never seen a greater day than this!"

## 5.

At ten o'clock in the morning Marshal Vasili Sokolovsky and the rest of Zhukov's staff were at Tempelhof Airport watching an American transport plane come in for a landing. They assumed it was Eisenhower but the plane did not even come from Rheims; it was from Moscow and carried General Deane. The Russians were obviously bewildered and somewhat affronted. It was Deane's awkward task to explain that Eisenhower wasn't coming. After Eisenhower had radioed Moscow that he

* While Churchill and Truman were speaking, the Soviet radio broadcast a story about two rabbits and a bird on the "Children's Hour." Stalin was determined not to make his own announcement until the next day.

would be delighted to go to Berlin for the second signing, Smith and others advised him to send his deputy, Marshal of the Royal Air Force Sir Arthur Tedder, in the interests of Allied prestige. The man signing for the Soviets, Zhukov, was only an army group commander, considerably below Eisenhower's rank.

An hour later Tedder and a party from Rheims arrived and were driven in a motley caravan of captured German vehicles to a suburb of Berlin, and installed in cottages. In the group were three WACs, including Kay Summersby. As she sat in her cottage, waiting hour after hour for something to happen, she thought it was a good thing Eisenhower had not come. She was sure he'd have returned to Rheims "in a huff" at such an "insulting delay."

But the Russians were not wasting time. In another part of the city Lieutenant Colonel Vladimir Yurasov, in charge of sending cement factories back to the Soviet Union, and other officers were being lectured by the Deputy for Economical Problems for the Soviet Commander of Berlin. "Take everything from the western sector of Berlin," the deputy said. "Do you understand? Everything! If you can't take it, destroy it. But don't leave anything for the Allies. No machinery, no bed to sleep on, not even a chamber pot to pee in!"

Even when Zhukov finally met the Tedder delegation five hours after their arrival, it seemed to a number of Allied observers as though the marshal was only trying to delay the signing—which, in truth, he was. He was waiting for Vishinsky, who at that moment was flying to Berlin with instructions from Moscow.

During this meeting, however, one important conflict was cleared up. Since Eisenhower was not present to represent all the West, de Gaulle had sent instructions that Général Jean de Lattre de Tassigny would sign for France. Some Americans as well as British thought this was just another example of de Gaulle's chauvinism.* The impasse was solved when everyone, including Zhukov, agreed that Tedder would sign for the British, General Spaatz for the Americans, and de Lattre for the French.

* De Gaulle on his part had been treated cavalierly by both Churchill and Roosevelt. Besides open ridicule, they had refused to let him attend Yalta and then told him nothing about the results until it was all over. Most Americans were incensed when the French were loath to evacuate Stuttgart after conquering it. Truman himself radioed de Gaulle that he was "shocked by the attitude of your government in this matter and its evident implications," and threatened "an entire rearrangement of command" if the French Army carried out "the political desires of the French government."

The American closest to the situation, General Jacob L. Devers, commander of the 6th U.S. Army Group, recently said that the entire Stuttgart matter was blown up out of proportion by his fellow countrymen. "The trouble was an absurdity. They made it a problem." Devers himself always sympathized with French aspirations. Much of this understanding Devers credits to a colonel on his staff who spoke French fluently, Henry Cabot Lodge.

De Lattre soon discovered that there was no French flag in the hall where the ceremony would take place. Russian girls hastily made a tricolor from a Nazi flag, a sheet and a pair of blue serge overalls, but they sewed the blue, white and red horizontally. De Lattre diplomatically told them they had made a Dutch flag and the girls had to tear apart the colored strips and sew them vertically.

But Eisenhower's failure to appear had further repercussions. Tedder entered the hall with a worried expression. "Everything has broken down," he told de Lattre. "M. Vishinsky has just arrived from Moscow and will not agree to the formula we have settled with Zhukov. He willingly agrees that you sign so that the resurrection of France will be publicly affirmed, but he is categorically opposed to Spaatz signing too. His argument is that the United States is already represented by me, since I have to sign in Eisenhower's name. Now Spaatz demands to sign if you sign."

De Lattre only repeated his implicit orders from de Gaulle. "If I return to France without fulfilling my mission," he replied, "that is to say, having allowed my country to be excluded from signing the capitulation of the Reich, I deserve to be hanged. Think of me!"

"I shan't forget you," said Tedder with an understanding smile, and went off to see the Russians. For two hours the debate went on, Zhukov now arguing that there was no logical need for any witnesses to sign and Tedder asserting just as vigorously that the surrender document must have one name to represent the 40,000,000 Frenchmen, and another the 140,000,000 Americans.

It was Vishinsky who finally found the solution: Spaatz and de Lattre would sign a bit lower than Tedder and Zhukov.

Just before eleven-thirty at night Keitel, Friedeburg and Generaloberst Hans Jürgen Stumpff of the Luftwaffe stepped into the surrender room, momentarily blinded by the floodlights. Keitel strode forward, impressive in his full-dress uniform. He jerked up his baton in a crisp salute and sat down stiffly across from Zhukov, head rigid, chin high. "Ah, the French are here too!" Vishinsky heard him mutter upon seeing de Lattre. "That's all we need!"

Friedeburg, dark circles under his eyes, sat on the Feldmarschall's left and Stumpff on the right.*

Zhukov stood up. "Have you taken cognizance of the protocol of capitulation?"

"*Ja,*" Keitel replied loudly.

"Do you have authority to sign?"

"*Ja.*"

"Show me your authority."

Keitel did.

* Fifteen days later Friedeburg committed suicide.

"Do you have any observations to make about the execution of the act of capitulation which you are about to sign?"

After Keitel in clipped tones asked for a twenty-four-hour delay, Zhukov looked around inquiringly and said, "That request has already been rejected. No modifications. Do you have any other observations to make?"

*"Nein."*

"Sign, then."

Keitel got up, adjusted his monocle and walked to the end of the table. He sat down next to de Lattre, placing his cap and baton in front of the Frenchman. De Lattre motioned to take them away and the Feldmarschall pushed them aside. Then he pulled off one gray glove with deliberation, picked up a pen and began to sign several copies of the surrender instrument.

Photographers and correspondents surged forward, even climbing on tables to get a better view. One Russian, a movie cameraman's assistant, tried to force his way through and someone hit him on the jaw. He swung back.

Tedder faced the Germans and in his thin, high voice said, "Do you understand the terms you have just signed?"

Keitel shot to his feet again, saluted with his baton and strode out the room, his chin still high in the air.

In Flensburg, Hitler's successor, Grossadmiral Karl Dönitz, sat at a desk finishing his farewell address to the officers corps.

Comrades. . . . We have been set back for a thousand years in our history. Land that was German for a thousand years has now fallen into Russian hands. Therefore the political line we must follow is very plain. It is clear that we have to go along with the Western Powers and work with them in the occupied territories in the west, for it is only through working with them that we can have hopes of later retrieving our land from the Russians . . .

Despite today's complete military breakdown, our people are unlike the Germany of 1918. They have not yet been split asunder. Whether we want to create another form of National Socialism, or whether we conform to the life imposed upon us by the enemy, we should make sure that the unity given to us by National Socialism is maintained under all circumstances.

The personal fate of each of us is uncertain. That, however, is unimportant. What is important is that we maintain at the highest level the comradeship amongst us that was created through the bombing attacks on our country. Only through this unity will it be possible for us to master the coming difficult times, and only in this manner can we be sure that the German people will not die. . . .

But these words gave no hint at what had been haunting him ever since Jodl returned from Rheims with a copy of *Stars and Stripes* containing pictures from Buchenwald. At first Dönitz had refused to believe that such atrocities had ever taken place. But as incontrovertible evidence mounted he was forced to face the truth—the horror of the concentration camp system was not merely Allied propaganda.

This revelation struck at the core of his faith in National Socialism and he wondered if Hitler's achievements had been won at too frightful a cost. He thought of his two sons who had died in battle for the Führer.

Like so many other Germans, Dönitz was just beginning to see the perils of the *Führerprinzip,* the principle of dictatorship; perhaps human nature was incapable of using the power arising from dictatorship without succumbing to the temptations of its abuse of power.

As he finished the speech to the officers, the Admiral was beset by doubts. He glanced through it again, then slowly folded the paper and locked it away in his desk drawer.

# Acknowledgments

To gather material for this book my wife Toshiko and I traveled more than 100,000 miles in twenty-one countries (including five behind the Iron Curtain): to a prison in Munich to see SS General Wolff; to the Bernadotte home near Stockholm; to the site of the Shell House in Copenhagen; to the Citadel in Budapest; to the Warsaw Ghetto; to Dachau, Buchenwald, Auschwitz and Sachsenhausen; to the site of Stalag Luft III, which is now an empty field except for a monument erected by the Polish government in memory of the men of Sagan; to the site of Stalag IIA overlooking Neubrandenburg, which is now a training ground for the East German Army.

We traveled on both sides of the Oder River to visit the battlefields near Frankfurt an der Oder, Küstrin and Seelow. We walked through the streets of Danzig (now Gdansk), Stettin (Szczecin) and Breslau (Wraclaw), where the damage of war is still visible. We listened to Major Szokoll's story (of the Vienna uprising) in the bar of the Hotel Sacher; W. Averell Harriman's in his Georgetown home; Clement Attlee's in the dining room of the House of Lords; Bernard Baruch's in "Little Hobcaw" in South Carolina; and Admiral Dönitz's in his home near Hamburg.

Libraries contributed greatly to the book: the National Archives and Records Service, Alexandria, Virginia (Wilbur Nigh and Lois Aldridge); the Library of Congress; the Air University Library at Maxwell Air Force Base (Margo Kennedy); the main branch of the New York Public Library; the U. S. Army Infantry School Library at Fort Benning, Georgia (Ruth Wesley); The Chatham House Library, London, England (Kenneth Younger, Miss Campbell and Miss Hamerton); and the British War Museum (Dr. Noble Frankland and Rose Coombs). Two libraries in Germany were particularly helpful: the Bibliothek für Zeitgeschichte (Dr. Jürgen Rohwer, Joachim Röseler and Werner Haupt); and the Ostdokumentation des Bundesarchivs in Koblenz, which, out of some 13 million pages, selected the most authoritative and significant personal accounts of German refugees from the east.

This book could not have been written without the full co-operation of the U. S. departments of Defense, Army, Navy and Air Force, as well as the governments of East and West Germany, Poland, Hungary, Denmark, Austria and Yugoslavia. Numerous agencies, organizations and individuals made substantial contributions to the book. To list them all would be impossible, but here are a few:

*Washington, D. C.*: Lieutenant Colonel C. V. Glines, Lieutenant Colonel Charles Burtyk, Jr., Major Robert Webb, Major B. J. Smith and Anna C. Urband of the Magazine and Book Branch, Office of the Assistant Secretary of Defense; Martha Holler, Public Affairs, O A S D; Brigadier General

Hal C. Pattison, Judge Israel Wice, Charles B. MacDonald, Martin Blumenson, Charles Romanus, Mrs. Magna Bauer, Detmar H. Finke and Hannah Zeidlik of the Office of the Chief of Military History, Department of the Army; Major General J. C. Lambert, the Adjutant General; Dr. G. Bernard Noble, Chief, Historical Division of the State Department; Major General G. V. Underwood, Jr., Chief of Information, Department of the Army; Alice Martin and Edith Midgette.

*New York City:* Free Europe Committee; Dr. Jaan Pennar, American Committee for Liberation; Mike Land and Robert Meskill, *Look* magazine; Monty Jacobs, World Jewish Congress.

*San Antonio:* Colonel and Mrs. Hurley Fuller, Hurley Fuller, Jr., Mr. and Mrs. James Haslam.

*Austria:* Dr. and Mrs. Friedrich Katscher, Dr. Fritz Meznik, Dr. Hans Kronhuber and Dr. Otto Zundritsch of the Bundeskanzleramt. Dr. Zundritsch's efficiency and zeal were primarily responsible for our successful research in Austria.

*Denmark:* Kai Johansen, Bengt Petersen and Mrs. Kirsten Rode of the Ministry for Foreign Affairs. Mr. Johansen not only arranged our interviews and gathered pertinent information on his country's participation in the war but was a most hospitable host.

*East Germany:* Edgar Oster, Informations- und Organisations-Büro, and Frau Wera Bayer, Press Section, of the D.D.R. Mr. Oster escorted us on our tour of East Germany, taking us everywhere we wished to go.

*England:* James T. Pettus and William Clarke of the American Embassy; Major-General David Belchem; and Colonel A. E. Warhurst, Historical Section, Cabinet Office.

*France:* Robert Calmann-Levy and Miss Lolay Bloch of Calmann-Levy, Editeurs; Mrs. Edith Bohy and M. Roland Mehl.

*Hungary:* Dr. Elek Karsai; Lieutenant Colonel Sandor Mucs, editor of *Military History Review;* Dr. György Ranki; Paul A. Nyiri and László Hingyi of the Institute for Cultural Relations; Dr. Foti, Foreign Affairs Office; and Tibor Ormos, Budapest Filmstudió, who showed us films of the battle of Budapest. The general hospitality throughout Hungary was extraordinary. For example, Mr. Nyiri prevented our trip through eastern Europe from ending in disaster by somehow, over the telephone, arranging our re-entry to Hungary from Yugoslavia—without visas.

*Italy:* Dr. Pier Luigi Bellini delle Stelle, Dr. Luigi Ronchi, Dr. Gianfranco Bianchi and Generale Almerico Jacobucci.

*Japan:* Yatsuji Nagai, Mr. Sakomizu, Rolland Gould, Norizane Ikeda, Colonel Hisashi Nishi, Colonel Etsu Endo, Rear Admiral Tadao Yokoi, Tokiji Matsumura, Dr. Keigo Okonogi.

*Netherlands:* Dr. L. de Jong, Rijksinstituut voor Oorlogsdocumentatie (Netherlands State Institute for War Documentation), H. M. Van Randwijk, Dr. W. Drees, Col. J. J. F. Borghouts, Col. Pieter Jacob Six, Dr. L. Neher.

*Poland:* Edward Kowalski, Secretary, Związck Bojowników o Wolność i Demokrację (Association of Fighters for Liberty); H. Malinowski, Secretary, Związek Literatów Polskich (Polish Writers' Guild); Lidia Wanda Gall; Professor Bernard Mark, Director General, and Boris Szacman, curator, of Jewish Historical Institute, Warsaw.

*Sweden:* Dr. Ragnar Svanström and Countess Estelle Bernadotte.

*Spain:* Mr. and Mrs. Otto Skorzeny; Luis de Pedroso, Secretario de Embajada; Don Fraga Irribarne, Ministerio de Información.

*Switzerland:* Ambassador August Lindt; Dr. Carl J. Burckhardt, membre de l'Institut Ministre Plénipotentiaire; Henrik Beer, Secretary General, League of Red Cross Societies; Pierre Vibert and Roger du Pasquier of the Comité International de la Croix Rouge.


*West Germany:*

Berchtesgaden—Wolfgang Boigs.

Bonn—Dr. Arthur Henry Moehlman, Cultural Attaché, American Embassy; Mr. Petzold, the Bundespress Amt; Dr. Karl Hans Hermann, Historical Division, Ministry of Defense; Claus Amthor, Frederic George Adams, Generalmajor Adolf Galland and Count Gerhard Grasen von Schwerin.

Frankfurt am Main—Colonel Louis Gershenow, Commanding Officer, Lieutenant Colonel Allen C. Deming, Public Affairs Officer, Major Ruby Rose Stauber, Troop Information Officer, Major William J. Daniels, Civil Affairs Officer, Heidi Düppe and Freddy Ploecker of U. S. Army Hq. Northern Area Command. Major Stauber acted most efficiently as our liaison during our visits to other countries.

Koblenz—Dr. Vogel, Frau Eva Tiebel and Hans von Spaeth-Meyken.

Munich—Lieutenant Colonel Charles E. Gilbert, Public Affairs Officer, Major Henry Covington, Frau Karola Gillich and Herta Wiegel of Public Section, U. S. Army Hq. Southern Area Command; Ernst Langendorf and Tadeusz Nowakowski of Radio Free Europe; Hyman Busch, Radio Liberty; Dr. Heinrich Schulz, Dr. Oliver Frederickson and Leon J. Barat of the Institute for the Study of the USSR; Professor Alexander von Stauffenberg, Munich University; Count Ludwick Lubienski, Polish-American Immigration & Relief Committee; Dr. Helmut Krausnick, Institute for · History; Dr. Paul Schmidt, Director, Language and Interpreters Institute; Minister President Dr. Wilhelm Högner, Ambassador Eugen Ott, Erich Kernmayr, Major General Gustav Lombard and Günther Daum.

Nuremberg—Captain Kurt Gabel.

Oberammergau—Lieutenant Colonel Frederick Sanders, Commandant, Hawkins Barracks.

Stuttgart—Lieutenant General Hugh P. Harris, Commanding General, Colonel Joel B. Stephens, Information Officer, Sergeant Gerhard Cordes, Frau Elisabeth Hirzel and Reinhard Pradel of Seventh U. S. Army; Dr. J. Rohwer and Werner Haupt of the Bibliothek für Zeitgeschichte.

West Berlin—Major General James H. Polk, U. S. Commander Berlin, Major Edward P. Endres, Deputy Information Officer, and Gertrand Blum of Hq. Berlin Command; John Koehler, Berlin Bureau Chief, Associated Press; and Hans Wallenberg, Generalbevollmächtigter, Ullstein GmbH.

Würzburg—Alexander Spuhl, U. S. Verbindungsbüro (Civil Affairs Office); and Dr. Hans Schneider, Verkehrsdirektor.

Others include Dr. Albert Simpson of the Air University; Major James F. Schildt; Mikhail Koriakov; Richard T. Alexander, Jr., Associate Professor of Education, Ball State Teachers College; Alfred J. Betar; David Englander; General Hasso von Manteuffel; Dr. Gero von S. Gaevernitz; Gregor Dorfmeister; Lothar Greil; Professor Dr. Percy Ernst Schramm; Hubertus Freiherr von Humboldt; General Erwin Jollasse; and Hubert Schröder.

Finally I would like to thank those who contributed most outstandingly to the book: my chief assistant, Toshiko Toland; my representative in Germany, Karola Gillich; my typists, Edith Lentz and Helen Toland; my copy editor, Mrs. Barbara Willson, for her many invaluable suggestions; John Barkham and John Jamieson for their constant encouragement and advice; and two men without whom this book could not have been written—my editor, Robert Loomis, and my agent, Paul Reynolds.

# Notes

The main sources for each chapter are listed below with explanatory details. Those books which proved of great overall value, and which will not be listed again, are: *The Supreme Command* by Forrest C. Pogue; *Roosevelt-Churchill-Stalin* by Herbert Feis; *Die Niederlage 1945,* edited by Percy Ernst Schramm; *Kriegstagebuch des OKW 1944–1945* (OKW War Diary), kept by Percy Ernst Schramm; *Hitler—A Study in Tyranny* by Alan Bullock; *Mein Kampf* by Adolf Hitler; *Grand Strategy* by John Ehrman (*History of the Second World War,* Vol. VI); *The War in Eastern Europe,* Department of Military Art and Engineering, U. S. Military Academy, West Point, N. Y.; *Correspondence Between the Chairman of the Council of Ministers of the U.S.S.R. and the Presidents of the U. S. A. and the Prime Ministers of Great Britain during the Great Patriotic War of 1941–1945,* Vols. I and II; *The Testament of Adolf Hitler: The Hitler-Bormann Documents, February–April 1945,* edited by H. R. Trevor-Roper; *The Rise and Fall of the Third Reich* by William Shirer; *Es Begann an der Weichsel* and *Das Ende an der Elbe* by Jürgen Thorwald; *The Last Days of Hitler* by H. R. Trevor-Roper; *The Struggle for Europe* by Chester Wilmot; *Triumph and Tragedy* by Winston S. Churchill; *Panzer Leader* by Heinz Guderian; and *War As I Knew It* by George S. Patton, Jr.

Also of great value were more than 200 manuscripts prepared for the Office of the Chief of Military History, Department of the Army, by German officers; the forty-two-volume record of the main Nuremberg trial, *Trial of the Major War Criminals before the International Military Tribunal;* the fifteen volumes of subsequent trials, *Trials of War Criminals before the Nuremberg Military Tribunals;* and thousands of documents from the National Archives in Alexandria, Virginia. Unless otherwise specified, all material on German refugees from the east, including the stories of the *Wilhelm Gustloff* and the *Goya,* comes from the files of the Bundesarchiv in Koblenz.

Otto Skorzeny read the entire first draft of this manuscript and made numerous corrections and suggestions. He also showed pertinent parts to a number of people close to Hitler, such as Frau Christian, for their comments and corrections.

## Chapter 1. Floodtide East

The description of the Allied prisoners' march from Sagan and other camps in the east is based primarily on interviews or correspondence with General Vanaman, Colonels Spivey, Clark and Lockett, Lieutenant Phelan, Major Charles Lenfest, 2nd Lieutenants James F. Schildt and Stratton

Appleman. Also *History of Center Compound Stalag Luft III, Sagan, Germany;* and *Kriegie* by Kenneth W. Simmons. Colonel Yardley's story comes from an official report.

The poem by Larry Phelan originally appeared in *The Oflag 64 Bulletin,* a two-page daily published by the prisoners. "The flag of the *Bulletin,* done in tasteful Old English, was one of our favorite jokes of long standing on the protecting power," Phelan wrote. "For the *Bulletin* had a slogan, all but hidden in scrolls and flourishes. The slogan was patterned after that of the *Völkischer Beobachter,* the Nazi party organ, which claimed to be for '*Freiheit und Brot*' or 'Freedom and Bread.' We, who had been subsisting on small quantities of a rocklike pumpernickel liberally laced with sawdust, proclaimed ourselves for '*Freiheit und Weissbrot*' (white bread)—two commodities which had been conspicuously lacking in our lives as unwilling guests of the Third Reich. The censor who daily read every inch of the *Bulletin* never caught it and we were able to enjoy it as a private family joke for almost two years."

The Führer conference is excerpted from the transcription of the January 27 meeting; further details came from interviews with Baron Freytag von Loringhoven and two others who attended but wish to remain anonymous.

The events which took place at Wugarten in this and following chapters come from interviews with Colonel Fuller, Lieutenant Hegel, 1st Lieutenant Francis Richwine, 2nd Lieutenant Henry Cronin, Captain Donald Gilinski, and others. Also: *Neve Ross a Selchew* by Generale Almerico Jacobucci; numerous Italian records; Hegel's private diary; and the official diary, *Journal of American Prisoners of War* (January 27, 1945–March 18, 1945).

Other material is based on interviews with Feldmarschall Schörner and SS Colonel Kempka; correspondence with Dr. von Braun; a report by Josefine Schleiter; and the following books: *The Final Solution* by Gerald Reitlinger; *Crossbow and Overcast* by J. McGovern; and *V-2* by Walter Dornberger.

Chapter 2. "Five Minutes Before Midnight"

Based on interviews with General Wolff; correspondence with Dr. von Braun; an official report of Stalag IIIC; and *The Bormann Letters; The War and Colonel Warden* by Gerald Pawle; *Eisenhower's Six Great Decisions* by Walter Bedell Smith; *Foreign Relations of the United States, The Conferences at Malta and Yalta 1945; Triumph in the West* by Arthur Bryant; and *Crossbow and Overcast* by McGovern.

The informal meeting with Hitler was related by two officers who were present but wish to be anonymous. For confirmation of Hitler's convictions, see entry for February 6 in *The Testament of Adolf Hitler.*

Chapter 3. "This May Well Be a Fateful Conference"

The Yalta Conference is based on interviews with Ambassador Harriman, Freeman Matthews, Ambassador Bohlen and Denys Myers, and on the following books: *Foreign Relations of the United States, The Conferences at Malta and Yalta 1945; Fleet Admiral King* by Ernest J. King; *The Memoirs of Anthony Eden, Earl of Avon, The Reckoning; Roosevelt and Hopkins* by Robert E. Sherwood; *Roosevelt and the Russians* by Edward R. Stettinius, Jr.; *As He Saw It* by Elliott Roosevelt; *Working with Roosevelt* by Samuel I. Rosenman; *Speaking Frankly* by James F. Byrnes; *The Meaning of Yalta* by John L. Snell, Forrest C. Pogue, Charles F. Delzell and George A. Lensen; *Airman at Yalta* by Laurence S. Kuter; and *I Was There* by Fleet Admiral William D. Leahy.

The official version of the private conversation between Churchill, Eden and Bohlen at the end of the dinner on February 4, as it appears in the Yalta report, was recently amended by Ambassador Bohlen in a letter. Churchill and Eden, he says, did *not* leave "obviously in disagreement on the voting procedure on the Security Council of the Dumbarton Oaks organization."

The material on Poland in this and following chapters comes primarily from interviews with twenty-eight Polish leaders of varying political affiliations, including Prime Minister Mikolajczyk; Jan Ciechanowski, Ambassador to the United States; Count Edward Raczynski, Ambassador to the Court of St. James; and Zbigniew Stypulkowski. It is also based on *Defeat in Victory* by Jan Ciechanowski; *The Communist Party of Poland* by M. K. Dziewanowski; *Rape of Poland* by Stanislaw Mikolajczyk; *I Saw Poland Betrayed* by Arthur Bliss Lane; *The Secret Army* by T. Bor-Komorowski; *An Army in Exile* by Lieutenant General W. Anders; and *Allied Wartime Diplomacy* by Edward J. Rozek, which contains many hitherto unpublished documents.

Other material: interviews with Bernard Baruch, Annedore Leber, Fabian von Schlabrendorff, Generals Hull, Hodges and Simpson. Also *They Almost Killed Hitler,* prepared and edited by Gero von S. Gaevernitz; *Conscience in Revolt* by Annedore Leber; *The Public Years* by Bernard M. Baruch; and a report by Friedrich Paetzold.

Chapter 4. "Bread for Bread, Blood for Blood"

Based on interviews with Father Sampson, Generals Wolff and Thomale, Colonel Rudel, Baron Freytag von Loringhoven and Captain Karl Hans Hermann. Also *The Bormann Letters; Look Out Below!* by Chaplain Francis L. Sampson; *Stuka Pilot* by Hans-Ulrich Rudel; and *Russia At War 1941–1945* by Alexander Werth.

Since the war Rudel has become a noted mountain climber and was in the party that first ascended Mt. Llullay-Yacu in the Andes.

## Chapter 5. "Judge Roosevelt Approves"

See Chapter 3 for Yalta. Also: *The Kremlin and World Politics* by Philip E. Moseley, and an article in *Life* magazine, September 6, 1948 by William C. Bullitt.

I am indebted to a number of those close to Churchill for an insight into his character; these include Bernard Baruch, Clement Attlee and Alan Bullock. Other material: interviews with Generals Craig, Horrocks, Huebner and Simpson; and *Battle for the Rhine* by R. W. Thompson; *Escape to Action* by Lieutenant-General Sir Brian Horrocks; and *The Victory Campaign,* Vol. III of the official history of the Canadian Army in World War II.

## Chapter 6. The Balkan Cockpit

Information on Yugoslavia derives from interviews with Brigadier Maclean; Colonel Jack Churchill; twenty-five partisans, from privates to generals; and seven Yugoslav political leaders. Also: *The Heretic* and *Eastern Approaches* by Fitzroy Maclean; *Tito* by Vladimir Dedijer; *The War and Revolution of the Peoples of Yugoslavia 1941–1945;* and *Oslobodilački Rat, Naroda Jugoslavije 1941–1945,* Vol. II.

In an interview Alexander Botzaris—an anti-Comintern specialist for the Balkans on Goebbels' staff—told an intriguing story about Mikhailovich. Early in February, 1945, Botzaris was summoned by Kaltenbrunner and given a verbal message from Hitler which was to be transmitted to Mikhailovich, who in turn was to pass it on to the British: The Führer promised to withdraw all troops from the Balkans, provided that England and the United States agreed to start occupying the abandoned area in twenty-four hours; after the Balkans had been completely occupied by the West, Hitler would pull out of Hungary and Czechoslovakia.

Kaltenbrunner warned Botzaris that he would be shot if word of the mission was ever divulged. Botzaris flew to Sarajevo, rode a horse to Mostar and then proceeded by mule to the Chetnik mountain headquarters. When Mikhailovich read Hitler's message he leaped to his feet and shouted, "The war for us is over!" The message was coded and transmitted to the British radio station at Bari. Some twenty-four hours later Botzaris was summoned to Mikhailovich. "It's unbelievable," he said, holding out a message, "The Allies refuse the offer and say the Germans should take it to Stalin!" He began to weep.

Information on Hungary: interviews with Otto Skorzeny; Lothar von

Greelen; Erich Kernmayr; Kemal Oltayli; General Hermann Balck; General Hubert Lanz; and twenty-two Hungarians, including Lieutenant Litteráti and Joseph Nemeš, the artist who carried the written authorization from Horthy to the Russians. Other material: *Skorzeny's Special Missions* by Otto Skorzeny; *Liberated Hungary,* edited by Ferenc Baktai and György Máté; *October Fifteenth* by C. A. Macartney; and numerous reports collected especially for this book by Dr. György Ranki, Deputy Director of the Institute of Historical Sciences of the Hungarian Academy of Sciences, and Dr. Karsai Elek, head of scientific research on the end of World War II for the Hungarian National Archives.

Chapter 7. Operation "Thunderclap"

The Dresden bombing is based on interviews with Sir Arthur Harris; Lord Portal; Sergeant Skiera; and thirty-two survivors, including Bodo Baumann, Hans Köhler, Joachim Weigel, Franz von Klepacki, Ingrid Günnel, Joachim Barth and Annemarie Friebel. Also: *Victory,* Vol. III of *The Strategic Air Offensive against Germany 1939–1945* by Sir Charles Webster and Noble Frankland; *The Destruction of Dresden* by David Irving; a number of official reports; and the USAF study, *Historical Analysis of the 14-15 February 1945 Bombings of Dresden.*

Other material: interviews with Count Raczynski, Baron Freytag von Loringhoven, Generals Wolff and Wenck. Also: *Himmler* by Roger Manvell and Heinrich Fraenkel; *Himmler* by Willi Frischauer; and *Goebbels—the Man Next to Hitler* by Rudolf Semmler.

Chapter 8. War and Peace

Interviews with Generals Wenck, Steiner, Hausser and Wolff, Colonel Degrelle, Captain Koriakov, Bodo Baumann, Hans Köhler, Dr. Kleist, Dr. Ragnar Svanström, Ambassador Torsten Brandel and Countess Bernadotte. Also: *I'll Never Go Back* by Mikhail Koriakov; *Russia At War* by Werth; *La Campagne de Russie* by Léon Degrelle; *The Gestapo* by Jacques Delarue; *Himmler* by Manvell and Fraenkel; *Goebbels—the Man Next to Hitler* by Semmler; *The Labyrinth* by Walter Schellenberg; *The Man with the Miraculous Hands* by Joseph Kessel; *The Curtain Falls* by Count Folke Bernadotte; and *Between Hitler and Stalin* by Dr. Peter Kleist; also correspondence with Dr. Werner Naumann.

Chapter 9. "An Iron Curtain Will Go Down"

Interviews with Generals Airey, Simpson, Horrocks and Lemnitzer, Brigadier Maclean, Colonel Thayer and Ambassador Harriman. Also *This I Remember* by Eleanor Roosevelt; *The Roosevelt I Knew* by

Frances Perkins; *Working with Roosevelt* by Rosenman; *Battle for the Rhine* by Thompson; *Triumph in the West* by Bryant; *Conquer: the Story of the Ninth Army; Patton—Ordeal and Triumph* by Ladislas Farago; *The Memoirs of Field-Marshal Montgomery; Escape to Action* by Horrocks; *Joseph Goebbels* by Curt Reiss; an undated Führer conference that took place at the end of February or in the first days of March, 1945; and twenty-four after-action reports.

## Chapter 10. Ebb and Flow

Based on interviews with Generals von Manteuffel, Balck, Dietrich, Hodges and Collins, SS Colonel "Fritz Hagen," Colonel Kimball, Lieutenant Kernmayr and Jan Krok-Paszkowski. Also *Dance of Death* by Erich Kern; *Timberwolf Tracks* by Leo A. Hoegh and Howard J. Doyle; a monograph by General Köchling; and a number of after-action reports.

## Chapter 11. "What If It Blows Up in My Face?"

Based primarily on interviews with Generals von Zangen and Westphal, Colonel Reichhelm, SS Colonel Skorzeny, Captain Bratge and Sergeant Rothe; Major General Edwin Parker, Jr., Generals Hodges, Hoge, Leonard, Bull, Gay and Craig, Colonel George Smythe, Colonels Carter and Maness, Major Cothran, Captain I. J. Newman, 2nd Lieutenant Fred Mitchell, Lieutenant Miller, Sergeant Nicholas Brdar, Sergeants Sabia and De Lisio; and correspondence with General Ridgway, Colonels Coker and Engeman, Captain Soumas, Lieutenants Richard T. Alexander, Jr., and McCurdy. Also based on thirty-eight combat interviews; twenty-three German monographs; forty-seven U. S. and German after-action reports; General Gay's war diary; *Kesselring—A Soldier's Record* by Albert Kesselring; *The German Army in the West* by General Siegfried Westphal; *Three Years with Eisenhower* by Harry C. Butcher; *Crusade in Europe* by Dwight D. Eisenhower; *A Soldier's Story* by Omar N. Bradley; and *The Bridge at Remagen* by Ken Hechler. I am indebted to Congressman Hechler for putting his material at my disposal.

The reader will note that my account of the conversations between Generals Bradley and Bull (which was based not only on *A Soldier's Story* but also on an interview and correspondence with General Bull) differs in some instances from that in General Bradley's book.

## Chapter 12. "I Am Fighting for the Work of the Lord"

Interviews with Dr. Burckhardt, Count Schwerin von Krosigk, SS Colonels Skorzeny and Kempka, SS General Hausser, General Hodges, Bernard Baruch and Ambassador Harriman. Also: *Mein Kampf; Ma*

*Mission à Dantzig* by Carl J. Burckhardt; *The Labyrinth* by Schellenberg; *The Public Years* by Baruch; *This I Remember* by Eleanor Roosevelt; the diary of Count Schwerin von Krosigk; *The Kersten Memoirs* by Felix Kersten; *An Army in Exile* by Anders; *Drive* by Colonel Charles R. Codman; four confidential reports from the files of the International Committee of the Red Cross; and five after-action reports. *The Pursuit of the Millennium* by Norman Cohn, subtitled *Revolutionary messianism in medieval and Reformation Europe and its bearing on modern totalitarian movements* was particularly useful.

Chapter 13. Operation "Sunrise"
The information on Operation "Sunrise" in this and following chapters came from interviews with Allen Dulles, Gero von S. Gaevernitz, Lieutenant-General W. D. Morgan, Generals Airey, Lemnitzer and Wolff, and Major Waibel. Also: *Germany's Underground* by Allen Dulles; *Kesselring—A Soldier's Record* by Kesselring; *Call Me Coward* by Colonel Eugen Dollmann; *Burn After Reading* by Ladislas Farago; *Spying for Peace* by Jon Kimche; and a number of reports. I am indebted to Dr. von Gaevernitz, not only for letting me interview him five times and at great length, but for the numerous corrections and suggestions he made after reading the second draft of this book.

Other material: interviews with General Hodges and Ambassador Harriman; the Gay diary; and *The Kremlin and World Politics* by Moseley.

Chapter 14. The Shell House
Interviews with Professor Fog, J. Jalser, Ole Lippmann, Stig Jensen, Kai Johansen, Christian Lyst Hansen and Frode Jakobsen. Also: *The Danish Resistance* by David Lampe; *Secret Alliance* and *From Occupied to Ally* by Jørgen Haestrup; reports; and excerpts from the underground newspaper, *Information*.

Chapter 15. Between Two Rivers
Interviews with Generals Canine, Simpson, Horrocks, Wolff, Busse, Biehler and Heinrici. There were seven interviews with General Heinrici, several lasting a full day. The general dictated from his personal notes and message books for the first time in any interview, correcting a number of dates and incidents that had appeared in other books. Also based on *Hitler's Paper Money* by Wilhelm Höttl; *Conquer: the Story of the Ninth Army;* the Gay diary; *A Soldier's Story* by Bradley; *Escape to Action* by Horrocks; *The Memoirs of Field-Marshal Montgomery; Miracle Before Berlin* by Richard McMillan; *American Civil-Military Decisions,* edited

by Harold Stein; *Triumph in the West* by Bryant; *Crusade in Europe* by Eisenhower; *Kesselring—A Soldier's Record;* and *Roosevelt and Hopkins,* in which Mr. Sherwood states that he had lunch with Roosevelt on March 24. Unless the President had lunch twice that day, Sherwood is mistaken. The President's secretary, William Hassett, made the following note for March 24: "There were three off-the-record callers today— Bernard Baruch, General Pat Hurley and Anna Rosenberg for lunch." Some of the details came directly from Anna Rosenberg.

## Chapter 16. "We Have Had a Jolly Day"

Operation "Varsity" is based on interviews with General Miley, Colonel Miller and Lieutenant Paul McGuire; correspondence with Generals John L. Whitelaw, General Ridgway and Sergeant Pete Hulewicz. Also: *Soldier: the Memoirs of Matthew B. Ridgway; Wing Leader* by Group Captain J. E. Johnson; and sixteen after-action reports.

Other material: interviews with Generals Simpson, Heinrici and Busse; *Triumph in the West* by Bryant; *The Memoirs of Anthony Eden, The Reckoning; Drive* by Codman; *Crusade in Europe* by Eisenhower; and the transcript of the Führer conference of March 23.

## Chapter 17. Task Force Baum

Interviews with Generals Hoge and Canine, Colonels Abrams and Waters (both now four-star generals), Majors Baum, Berndt and Boyer, Lieutenants John W. Collins, Robert Westbrook, L. J. Weigel, Oliver Patton, Kern Pitts, Howard Richards, Alexander Bolling, Jr., and Alan Jones, Jr.; Ernst Langendorf and Pavle J. Javanovic; and correspondence with Father Cavanaugh, Sergeant Yoerk, Reverend Matthews, Lieutenant Matthew J. Giuffre and Norman Smolka. Also the diary of the prisoners from Szubin; sixteen German and U. S. after-action reports; Baum's report, *Notes on Task Force Baum;* nine combat interviews; two monographs from the Infantry School, Ft. Benning, Georgia; an account by Major Berndt; and Father Cavanaugh's unpublished book, *American Priest in a Nazi Prison.*

Thirty-two of Baum's men were wounded, nine killed, sixteen missing in action. There are no definite casualty figures for the Hammelburg prisoners.

## Chapter 18. Decision at Rheims

The material on Eisenhower's decision comes from *Crusade in Europe* by Eisenhower; *Command Decisions,* prepared by the Office of the Chief of Military History, Department of the Army; *Great Mistakes of the War* by Hanson W. Baldwin; and, particularly, *The Soldier and the State* by

Samuel P. Huntington. Of great help were a number of secret messages which are published here for the first time.

Other material: interviews with Ambassador Oshima, Generals Onodera, Busse and Thomale, Baron Freytag von Loringhoven, Colonels Richardson and Hogan, and Mr. Stypulkowski. Also reports of the last days of Danzig by Frau Seidler and Friedrich von Wilpert; *Invitation to Moscow* by Zbigniew Stypulkowski; *Triumph in the West* by Bryant; and *The Strange Alliance* by John R. Deane.

## Chapter 19. The Rose Pocket

Interviews with Generals von Zangen, Simpson and Collins, Colonel Richardson, Mr. Baruch and Father Sampson. Also *Kesselring—A Soldier's Record; The Public Years* by Baruch; *The Strange Alliance* by Deane; Father Cavanaugh's manuscript; *Look Out Below!* by Father Sampson; a number of German and American after-action reports; *Kampf und Ende der Heeresgruppe B im Ruhrkessel* by Carl Wagener; also interviews with Colonels Brown, Garton, Major Bellinger and Sergeant Owen.

Several paratroopers who were scheduled to make the airdrop on Berlin in Operation "Eclipse" felt so sure that some high-level conspiracy aborted the plan that I put the question to more than twenty high-ranking officers, including Generals Simpson, Hodges and Ridgway. Some recalled nothing of "Eclipse" and others only that it was some vague plan for the administration of Germany after its occupation. General Ridgway wrote, "I can recall nothing about Operation 'Eclipse' except dimly that among many airborne schemes which were advanced in the closing days of hostilities, there was one for putting a force into Berlin. . . . I never heard a word of any high-level conspiracy in connection with the Berlin scheme."

## Chapter 20. "0–5"

Material on Vienna comes from interviews with Major Szokoll, Sergeant Käs, Colonel A. Podhajsky, Dr. and Mrs. Friedrich Katscher; Mr. and Mrs. Max Slama; Otto Skorzeny; Paula Schmuck-Wachter, Frau Thea Jung, Otto Molden, Franz Sobek, Emil Oswald, Dr. Karl Gruber and Leopold Figl. Also: *Als Wien in Flammen Stand* by West; *Skorzeny's Special Missions;* and a number of newspaper articles and reports.

Other material: interviews with Generals Dietrich, Bittrich, Balck, Heinrici, Busse, SS Colonel "Hagen," Colonel Biehler and Lieutenant Kernmayr.

## Chapter 21. "Such Vile Misrepresentations"

Material on Roosevelt's death from *When F. D. R. Died* by Bernard

Asbell; *Off the Record with F. D. R.* by William D. Hassett; *Year of Decision,* Vol. I of *Memoirs by Harry S. Truman; All in One Lifetime* by James F. Byrnes; *This I Remember* by Eleanor Roosevelt; *The Public Years* by Baruch; *Russia At War* by Werth; the diary of Schwerin von Krosigk; *Roosevelt and Hopkins* by Sherwood; *The Forrestal Diaries; On Active Service in Peace and War* by Henry L. Stimson and McGeorge Bundy; *Working with Roosevelt* by Rosenman; *A Soldier's Story* by Bradley; *Crusade in Europe* by Eisenhower; *Diary of a Kriegie* by Edward W. Beattie, Jr.; *Goebbels—the Man Next to Hitler* by Semmler; and a number of magazine articles and newspaper stories. Also interviews with Mr. Baruch, Count Schwerin von Krosigk and General Busse.

Other material: interviews with Ambassador Harriman, General Simpson, Colonel Waters, Major Berndt, Fabian von Schlabrendorff, Dr. Müller, Dr. Schacht and Dr. Zenkl. Also correspondence with Dr. von Braun; *Triumph in the West* by Bryant; Father Cavanaugh's manuscript; *Crossbow and Overcast* by McGovern; Major Berndt's account; a letter from 1st Lieutenant Henry R. Heyburn; six after-action reports; the Gay diary; and *Buchenwald—Mahnung und Verpflichtung.*

Curiously, I was unable to get any confirmation from Japanese sources of Admiral Suzuki's message of sympathy to the American people. Nothing was mentioned in any Japanese newspapers at the time and even the admiral's son had never heard of the incident.


Chapter 22. Victory in the West

Interviews with Generals Simpson, Blumentritt and Wenck; Ambassador Harriman, Colonel Reichhelm, Captains MacDonald and Trefousse, Gabrielle Herbener and Günther Untucht. Also: correspondence with General Ridgway; *Year of Decision* by Truman; *The Memoirs of Anthony Eden, The Reckoning; Kampf und Ende der Heeresgruppe B im Ruhrkessel* by Wagener; *Company Commander* by Charles B. MacDonald; a monograph by General von Grolmann; nine after-action reports; and three State Department reports.


Chapter 23. "On the Razor's Edge"

Interviews with Admiral Dönitz, Generals Steiner, Heinrici and Busse, Colonels Rudel and Yurasov, Robert Kropp and Gerhard Cordes, who, incidentally, was interpreter in three of the interviews with General Heinrici. Also *Stuka Pilot* by Rudel; *The Labyrinth* by Schellenberg; *The Kersten Memoirs; En Jude Talar Med Himmler* by Norbert Masur; *The Curtain Falls* by Count Bernadotte; *Goebbels—the Man Next to Hitler* by Semmler; *Dr. Goebbels* by Manvell and Fraenkel; *Memoirs—Ten Years and Twenty Days* by Admiral Karl Dönitz; four confidential reports of the International Committee of the Red Cross; Eichmann's own story in *Life,* December 5, 1960; and correspondence with Mr. Storch and Dr. Naumann.

Chapter 24. "The Führer Is in a State of Collapse"

Interviews with Feldmarschall Schörner, Generals von Manteuffel, Wenck, Steiner, Busse and Heinrici; Captain Koriakov, Baron Freytag von Loringhoven, Countess Bernadotte, Ambassador Brandel, Dr. "Kauffman," Josef Zychski and Robert Kropp. Also *Diary of a Kriegie* by Beattie; *Goebbels—the Man Next to Hitler* by Semmler; Keitel's interrogation at Nuremberg; *Generalfeldmarschall Keitel, Verbrecher oder Offizier?* edited by Walter Görlitz; *Dr. Goebbels* by Manvell and Fraenkel; *The Curtain Falls* by Count Bernadotte; *Notes* of Colonel Hans-Oscar Wöhlerman; *Der Endkampf in Berlin,* the diary of General Helmuth Weidling; *Berlin 1945* by Werner Haupt; *In the Shelter with Hitler* by Gerhard Boldt; *Der letzte Monat* by General Karl Koller; *I'll Never Go Back* by Koriakov; two reports from the International Committee of the Red Cross; and a report by Dr. Naumann.

Chapter 25. "We Must Build a New World, a Far Better World"

Interviews with Generals Hodges, Hull and Reinhardt, Captain George Morey, Lieutenant Kotzebue, and PFC Belousevitch. Also *Year of Decision* by Truman; *On Active Service in Peace and War* by Stimson and Bundy; *The Forrestal Diaries; I Was There* by Admiral Leahy; a report by Sergeant Balter; and *The Russian-American Linkup,* a lengthy report prepared by the 69th Division, including combat interviews with the various commanders. The Truman-Churchill phone conversation is excerpted from the complete transcript, which appears in President Truman's *Year of Decision.*

The account of Salzwedel comes from interviews with Mr. Nowakowski and from his novel, *The Camp of All Saints,* which was translated into a number of languages and was described by the *New York Times* as a "bitter, brilliant book."

Chapter 26. "Pheasant Hunt"

Interviews with Admiral Dönitz, Generals Wenck and Busse, Colonels Wöhlerman, Reichhelm and Biehler, Baron Freytag von Loringhoven, Drs. Gerngross and Heuwing; Ursula Wilzopolski, Herta Wiegel and Rolf Wiegel. Also *Memoirs* by Dönitz; the Weidling diary; *Berlin 1945* by Haupt; *Notes* by Wöhlerman; U. S. Army interrogation of Hanna Reitsch; *In the Shelter with Hitler* by Boldt; the Schwerin von Krosigk diary;

Conclusive Report about the Activities of F. A. B. by Dr. Rupprecht Gerngross and Otto Heinz Leiling; two Seventh U. S. Army reports; German radio broadcasts monitored by the Allies; and German newspaper stories.

Chapter 27. An "Italian Solution"
Interviews with General Wolff. Also The Brutal Friendship by F. W. Deakin; Gli Ultimi Tempi di un Regime by Ildefonso Cardinal Schuster; the Graziani Processo; Mussolini Confessa alle Stelle by Ivanoe Fossani; and Il Duce by Christopher Hibbert, which was particularly useful.
For sources on Operation "Sunrise," see Chapter 13.

Chapter 28. Death Comes to a Dictator
Interviews with Count Bellini and Lia de Maria. Le Ultime Ore di Mussolini by F. Bandini; Il Duce by Hibbert; and The Brutal Friendship by Deakin. I am indebted to Count Bellini and Urbano Lazzaro for allowing me to use liberal portions of their book, Dongo—the Last Act, which contains, I believe, the most authoritative and comprehensive account of Mussolini's last hours.

Chapter 29. "The Chief Is Dead"
The last few days of Hitler are based on interviews with Wolfgang Boigs, Baron Freytag von Loringhoven, Colonel Kempka and three other members of the Führer's inner circle who wish to be anonymous. Also: In the Shelter with Hitler by Boldt; the Weidling diary; the Wöhlerman Notes; Goebbels—the Man Next to Hitler by Semmler; the interrogation of Hanna Reitsch; and correspondence with Dr. Naumann.
Other material: interviews with Admiral Dönitz, Generals Heinrici and von Manteuffel, General Burkhardt Müller-Hillebrand, and Father Sampson. Also: Generalfeldmarschall Keitel, Verbrecher oder Offizier? edited by Görlitz; Keitel's interrogation; Year of Decision by Truman; Look Out Below! by Father Sampson; Wing Leader by Johnson; and Amateur Agent by Ewan Butler.
Following the serialization of this book in Look magazine I received a letter from Texas offering Hitler's body for sale. It had been smuggled out of Germany, said the writer, and is hidden "under the name of John Dough in the Western Hemesphier."

Chapter 30. "And Now You Stab Us in the Back"
For sources, see Chapter 13. Also: a report by General F. Schulz. Soon after the successful conclusion of Operation "Sunrise," Major

Waibel's key role in the negotiations was uncovered and a number of high-ranking Swiss officials demanded his court-martial. General Henri Guisan, the elderly Commander in Chief of the Swiss Armed Forces, summoned Waibel and asked for an explanation. Waibel gave a detailed report and then said, "If I had asked your permission, sir, you would never have given it." Guisan made no comment. He dismissed Waibel, then had the court-martial quashed. Today Oberstdivisionär Waibel is Chief of Infantry with a rank equivalent to major general.

Recently Allen Dulles, General Lemnitzer and Gero von Gaevernitz met in Ascona to commemorate the twentieth anniversary of the surrender of the German armies in Italy. The German most responsible for this historic capitulation could not take part; General Wolff was in jail in Munich, awaiting the outcome of his appeal for a new trial. Earlier he had been tried by a German court and sentenced to fifteen years of hard labor.

Ironically, it was his efforts in behalf of "Sunrise" that helped bring him to trial. Field-Marshal Alexander, General Lemnitzer and Allen Dulles all felt that if he was tried at Nuremberg, due consideration should be given to what he had accomplished in Italy. But since there was also comparatively little evidence against Wolff at that time, he was not brought to trial by the Allies.

The so-called *Überleitungsvertrag* (treaty between the Allied powers and the new German government) provided that German war criminals who had been tried and sentenced by Allied courts could not be tried by German courts. This provision was originally included in the treaty because the Allies feared that the German courts might reopen these trials and reduce the sentences. But it worked out quite differently. After Germany's sovereignty was restored, the Allies pardoned all but three of the imprisoned war criminals (Hess, Schirach and Speer). Today the others are free and cannot be tried by German courts.

At Wolff's trial Dr. von Gaevernitz testified for the defense, trying for two hours to impress upon the court what Wolff had done. Gaevernitz later wrote that the "entire atmosphere was unfavorable to Wolff. This phenomenon may be explained by the fact that Wolff is the only one of the high Nazi hierarchy still alive. . . . He is the only big fish left against whom the anger of certain sections of the population can be unloaded.

"Also, it seems that it was a trial of the younger generation in Germany against the older one. The prosecuting attorney, who is an able, intelligent and sympathetic fellow, is a man of forty years or less and, like most people of his age (or like younger people), never experienced the Nazi terror or the terror of a totalitarian police state. Quite naturally, the younger generation feels no responsibility for National Socialism and its crimes, and has a justified grudge against the older generation. This because the young people are now suffering—and probably will suffer for many years to come—from the shadows that have been cast over everything which is German, due to the faults or crimes committed by their fathers.

"The prosecutor, as well as many other persons, are judging the events of the Nazi reign from the point of view of the legally sound and stabilised atmosphere presently prevailing in Germany. They do not realize that in those days a person rarely could act as he wanted and was forced to do what he was told. It was impossible to come out in open opposition. It was even extremely difficult to resign from any important position.

"I am not trying to whitewash Wolff. As one of the top men in the Nazi hierarchy, he bears a historic responsibility for the crimes of the system. But he was never policy-making, as some have charged. You might say that he was an obedient servant, believing for a long time in his master's voice.

"Wolff began to 'see the light' in 1943 and tried not to extricate himself but to extricate the nation out of its tragic situation.

"Late in 1943 Wolff received a high command in Italy. For the first time he was in a position to take action on his own. And what did he do? He spared the Jews, as far as any of them were left in Italy; he spared the partisans and, finally, without the knowledge of Hitler and Himmler, established contact with the Allies in Italy at a tremendous personal risk, in order to end the war. The rest is known. Again, I want to say that if he had been interested in saving himself, he could have had a much easier way!"

Chapter 31. "The Iron Curtain in the East Moves Closer and Closer"
Interviews with Admiral Dönitz, Lieutenant-General Miles Dempsey, Generals Blumentritt and Wenck, Count Schwerin von Krosigk, Colonels von Dufving, Degrelle, Kempka, Kempin, and Wöhlerman, Frau Deutschmann, and others close to Hitler who do not wish to be mentioned. Also: the Weidling diary; *Berlin 1945* by Haupt; the Wöhlerman report; *Memoirs* by Dönitz; the Schwerin von Krosigk diary; the Hanna Reitsch interrogation; *La Campagne de Russie* by Degrelle; *Goebbels—the Man Next to Hitler* by Semmler; and *Dr. Goebbels* by Manvell and Fraenkel. Also correspondence with Dr. Naumann.

Chapter 32. Beginning of a Long Surrender
Czechoslovak material in this and the following chapter is based on interviews with General Arthur Schmidt, Dr. Petr Zenkl, Frank Meloun, Dr. Otakar Machotka, Eugene Fodor and Emil Horyna. Also: *The Communist Subversion of Czechoslovakia* by Josef Korbel; *Who's Next?* by John Brown; *Anatomy of a Satellite* by Dana Adams Schmidt; *Czechoslovakia in European History* by S. Harrison Thomson; *Oh My Country*

by Josef Josten; *Czechoslovakia Enslaved* by Robert Ripka; and an article by Joseph Wechsberg in the August 11, 1945 issue of *Collier's*.

Material on the Vlasov movement in this and the following chapter comes from interviews with Colonel Konstantin Kromiadi; Misbach Miftachoglu, Eugen Kuzminsky, Valentin Pischwanoff, Constantine A. Krylov, Yury Harkusha, Dr. Heinrich Schultz, Grigoriy Tapeshko, Dr. Muzychenko-Pismenny, Lieutenant Colonel Vyacheslav P. Artemiev, Dr. George Kohlik and Peter Kruzhin. Also: correspondence with Nikolai Gallay; *Soviet Opposition to Stalin* by George Fischer; *German Rule in Russia* by Alexander Dallin; an interrogation of General Ernst Köstring; and a pamphlet by Vlasov, "In Memory of Russian Fighters for Freedom Who Perished in Their Struggle Against the Tyranny of Stalin."

Other material: interviews with Admiral Dönitz, Colonels Yurasov and Pash, Major Hamlin, Father Sampson and John Groth. Also: correspondence with Lieutenant Knowlton, Dr. von Braun and Dr. L. de Jong, director of Rijksinstituut voor Oorlogsdocumentatie, Amsterdam; *Memoirs* by Dönitz; *The Memoirs of Field-Marshal Montgomery; The Kremlin and World Politics* by Moseley; *Three Years with Eisenhower* by Butcher; *Crusade in Europe* by Eisenhower; *Eisenhower's Six Great Decisions* by Smith; *Eisenhower Was My Boss* by Kay Summersby; *Crossbow and Overcast* by McGovern; *Miracle Before Berlin* by McMillan; *The Strange Alliance* by Deane; *Report of the American Commission for the Protection and Salvage of Artistic and Historic Monuments in War Areas; Survival* by James J. Rorimer; *Studio in Europe* by John Groth; an article in the August, 1945 issue of *Reader's Digest* by William A. Knowlton; an article by Ernst von Jungenfeld in the September, 1961 issue of *Der deutsche Soldat;* and a story by Seymour Freidin in the May 8, 1945 issue of the New York *Herald Tribune*.


Chapter 33. "The Flags of Freedom Fly All Over Europe"

Interviews with Admiral Dönitz, Count Schwerin von Krosigk, Feldmarschall Schörner, Generals Devers, Morgan and Strong; Colonels Degrelle, Yurasov and Rudel. Also: *Memoirs* by Dönitz; *Himmler* by Frischauer; *Himmler* by Manvell and Fraenkel; diary of Schwerin von Krosigk; *Eisenhower Was My Boss* by Kay Summersby; *Crusade in Europe* by Eisenhower; *My Three Years with Eisenhower* by Butcher; *A Soldier's Story* by Bradley; *The Strange Alliance* by Deane; *Diplomat Among Warriors* by Robert Murphy; *I Was There* by Leahy; *La Campagne de Russie* by Degrelle; *Stuka Pilot* by Rudel; *Russia At War* by Werth; *The History of the French First Army* by Marshal de Lattre de Tassigny; Eichmann's own story in the December 5, 1960 issue of *Life* magazine; and an article by Edward Kennedy in the August, 1948 issue of *The Atlantic Monthly*.

# INDEX

Abrams, Lt. Col. Creighton, 287, 288
Adams, Col. C. M., 394, 451, 453, 454–5, 456
Adlon, Hotel, 376, 478, 559
Adolf Hitler Bridge, 194
Adomeit, Curt, 404, 405–6
Airey, Maj.-Gen. Terence, 179, 244
Alexander, Field-Marshal Harold, 53, 122, 175–6, 179, 180, 342, 482, 488, 537, 539, 540, 542
Alexandrov, G. F., 156
Allen, Brig. Gen. Frank A., 572–3, 576, 577
Alpenfestung (National Redoubt), 262–3, 312, 439, 440, 582
"Alsos," Operation, 562
Anders, Lt. Gen. W., 131, 233
Andrews, Lt. Gen. Frank M., 41
Antonov, Col. Gen. Alexei, 62, 567, 576, 577
Arciszewski, Tomasz, 131
Arnold, Gen. H. H. ("Hap"), 135, 318
Ascona, 244, 246, 356–7
Associated Press, the, 158, 219, 518–19, 578
Atlantic Charter, 44
Attlee, Clement, 96–97
Audisio, Walter (Col. Valerio), 508–10, 511, 512–13
Auschwitz (concentration camp), 9–10
Axmann, Artur, 412, 468, 549–50
Bach-Zelewski, SS-Gruppenführer Erich von dem, 45
Balck, General Hermann, 337–8
Balter, Sgt. Alex, 449–50
Barracu, Francisco, 494–6, 498, 499, 500, 511–12, 513
Bart, Inge, 302
Barth, Joachim, 157
Baruch, Bernard, 52, 55, 234, 324–5, 377–8
Bateson, Group Capt. Bob, 250, 251
Baum, Task Force, 288–99
Baum, Capt. Abraham, 287–91, 293–7
Baumann, Bodo, 141, 143–4, 147, 157
Bayerlein, Generalleutnant Fritz, 222
BBC, 4, 519
Beattie, Jr., Edward W., 379
Beetz, SS-Standartenführer, 549–50
Belgrade, 119, 122, 123
Bell, Jack, 518
Bellinger, Maj. Robert, 323

Bellini, Count Pier Luigi delle Stelle, 490–6, 498–509, 511
Belousevitch, PFC Igor, 455–6
Below, Oberst Nicolaus von, 76, 270, 271, 429, 522, 527
Beneš, Eduard, 564–6
Berchtesgaden (the Obersalzberg), 271, 413, 425, 426–7, 429, 439
Berg, Generalleutnant Kurt von, 219
Bergen-Belsen (concentration camp), 415
Berger, SS-Obergruppenführer Gottlob, 425
Berlin, 28, 136–7, 307–8, 312, 325–9, 332, 345, 360, 385–6, 390, 399, 427–8, 463–4, 576, 577, 586–9
Bernadotte, Countess Estelle Manville, 164
Bernadotte, Count Folke, 162, 163, 164–7, 168, 333–4, 411, 413, 417, 434–5, 459
Berndt, Maj. Albert, 293, 363
"Bernhard," Operation, 262, 263
Bertin, Alex, 24, 68
Best, Werner, 162, 249
Biddle, Francis, 375
Biedermann, Major Karl, 348, 349, 352
Biehler, Generalmajor Ernst, 258–9, 343, 344, 346–7, 406, 423, 424, 428, 441–2, 465
Bierut, Boleslaw 45, 93, 94
Birzer, SS-Obersturmführer Fritz, 484, 489
Blaskowitz, Generaloberst Johannes, 321, 333
Blumentritt, Generalleutnant Günther, 383, 552–3, 560
Boettiger, Mrs. Anna, 29, 56, 177, 374, 381
Bohlen, Charles ("Chip"), 59, 60, 61, 64–5, 89, 92, 99, 115, 116, 268, 380, 447, 448
Boigs, Wolfgang, 519
Boldt, Hauptmann Gerhard, 435–6, 517, 525
Bolling, Jr., Lt. Alexander ("Bud"), 295
Bols, Gen. Eric, 280
Bolzano, 488, 538
Bombacci, Nicola, 494
Bonhoeffer, Pastor Dietrich, 365
Bor, General, see Komorowski
Bormann, Gerda, 30, 66–7, 73, 74
Bormann, Martin, 30–1, 66–7, 73, 74, 76, 81–3, 333, 343, 413, 424, 425,

427, 429–30, 431, 432, 436, 467, 468, 469, 516–17, 519–20, 522, 523, 524, 525, 526, 527, 529, 530, 531–2, 533, 545, 546, 547, 549–50
Botsch, Generalleutnant Walther, 196
Bottomley, Air-Marshal Sir Norman, 135–6
Bouhler, Philip, 430
Boyer, Maj. Don, 297
Boyle, Hal, 219
Bradley, Lt. Gen. Omar, 27, 28, 40, 53–54, 106, 174, 214–16, 220, 224, 245, 264, 267, 282, 320, 331, 361, 369–71, 377, 383, 385, 456, 566, 575
Brandstetter Capt. F. M. 384–5
Brandt, Dr. Karl, 12
Bratge, Hauptmann Willi, 197–8, 200, 205–6, 209, 210, 223
Brauchitsch, Oberst Bernd von, 428–9, 430
Braun, Eva, 13, 73–4, 304, 466, 468, 520, 521, 522, 529, 530–1, 532
Braun, Gretl, 13
Braun, Wernher von, 10, 37, 368, 562
Briggs, Maj. Ruth, 574
Brilon, 310, 311
British Military Units:
    21 Army Group, 27, 28, 176, 331
    Second Army, 28, 254, 265, 553
    XII Corps, 265
    XXX Corps, 97, 172, 265
    6th Airborne Division, 255, 273, 279, 280
    7th Armoured Division, 553
    15th Division, 279
    51st Highland Division, 279
Brooke, Field-Marshal Alan, 28, 29, 40, 41–2, 48, 61, 106, 176, 265–6, 274, 278, 279, 282, 283–4, 311, 327, 328, 360
Brown, Col. Frederic, 322–3
Broz, Josip, see Tito
Bruenn, Comm. Howard, 373
Bucharest, 181
Buchenwald (concentration camp), 364–6, 369, 411, 415–6
Budapest, 125, 126–9
Bulganin, Gen. Nikolai, 400
Bulgaria, 118
Bull, Maj. Gen. Harold ("Pink"), 29, 214–15
Bullitt, William C., 91
Bünau, General der Infanterie Rudolf von, 348, 350, 351, 352, 354
Bunyachenko, Gen. Sergei K., 568, 580–1
Burckhardt, Carl J., 230, 366, 410

Burgdorf, General Wilhelm, 15–16, 270–1, 272, 281, 304, 347, 425, 433, 436, 468, 516–17, 522, 523, 525, 529, 532
Burrough, Adm. Harold, 574
Burrows, Lt. Emmet, 201, 202
Busse, General Theodor, 260, 261, 262, 281, 304, 372, 397, 406, 407, 419, 420, 423–4, 428, 432–3, 434, 442, 465, 514, 543, 544
Butcher, Capt. Harry, 215, 216, 560, 573–4, 577
Byrnes, James, 63, 114, 313, 314, 381
Cademartori, Remo, 505–6
Cadorna, Gen. Raffaele, 484, 485
Caffery, Jefferson, 131
Campbell, Lt. Craig, 24
Canadian First Army, 28, 97
Canale, Luigi (Capt. Neri), 501, 504, 506–7, 509, 510
Canaris, Admiral Wilhelm, 59, 365–6
Canine, Brig. Gen. Ralph, 287
Carpenter, Iris, 192
Carter, Col. William, 224
Caserta, 537, 542
Castille, Maj. William, 369
Catoctin, U.S.S., 116, 129
Cavanaugh, Father Paul, 291–2, 293–4, 295, 296, 330, 361–3
Chemnitz, 136, 137, 146
Chernyakhovsky, Marshal Ivan Danilovich, 4, 5, 9
Chevasse, Noel, 274, 279
Chiang Kai-shek, Generalissimo, 100, 107, 115, 387, 389
Chiasso, 240, 486, 487
Chinchar, Sgt. Mike, 207, 208
Christian, Frau, 522, 526, 529
Christian, General Eckard, 424, 428
Christian X, King of Denmark, 249
Chuikov, Gen. Vasili, 545, 551
Churchill, Peter, 366
Churchill, Sarah, 53
Churchill, Rt. Hon. Winston S., 26, 29, 42, 43, 45, 46–47, 48, 51, 53, 54–55, 56, 57, 60, 61, 62, 63–65, 85, 86–91, 92–95, 96–97, 101–5, 107–12, 113–16, 117, 118, 120–1, 123–4, 136–7, 158, 175, 176–7, 233, 234–5, 246, 265–6, 274, 278, 279, 282–4, 308, 312, 324–6, 327, 328, 329, 332, 358, 359, 360, 377, 380, 388, 390, 456, 457–9, 482, 488, 535–7, 538, 562, 563, 564, 566, 577–9, 580, 581, 584, 586
Clark, Lt. Col. Albert, 19
Clark, Lt. Gen. Mark, 483
Clark Kerr, Sir Archibald, 233, 245, 246
Clay, Gen. Lucius D., 313–14

Cleve, 97, 98, 105, 106, 172
Codman, Col. Charles, 237, 280, 288
Cohen, Lt. Col. Harold, 288
Coker, Lt. Col. Sears Y., 210, 217, 218
Collins, Lt. Gen. J. Lawton ("Lightning Joe"), 191, 192, 331
Cologne, 191, 192
Como, 485, 505
Concerzowo, Margarite, 132
Coningsby, 137, 138
Conley, Maj. Victor, 456
Copenhagen, 248, 249, 251–3
Cordes, Gerhard, 400, 401–4, 406
Cothran, Maj. Ben, 197, 199–200, 203, 218
Coutts, Col. James, 277–8
Cowan, Howard, 274, 278
Craig, Maj. Fred, 455–6
Craig, Maj. Gen. Louis, 99, 105, 220, 224
Crerar, Lt.-Gen. H. D. G., 97, 98
"Cricket," see Malta Conference
Crimean Conference, see Yalta Conference
Croy, Princess Agathe, 351
Cucciati, Elena Curti, 490
Czech National Council, Revolutionary, 566, 581
Czechoslovakia, 564–7, 580–2
Dahme River, 543–4
Danich, Col. Radovan, 298
Daniell, Raymond, 573
Danzig (Gdansk), 4, 23, 31, 151, 300–3, 404
Deakin, Capt. F. W., 120
Deane, Maj. Gen. John, 308, 312, 327, 329, 447, 567, 576, 586
Decker, Lt. Col. Harold, 19
de Cocatrix, Albert, 437–9
Deevers, Maj. Murray, 204–5, 207
de Gaulle, Gen. Charles, 60, 61, 87, 131, 389, 577, 587
Degrelle, Col. Léon, 152–3, 553–4, 579–80
Delano, Laura, 372, 373
de Lattre de Tassigny, Gen. Jean, 587–9
De Lisio, S/Sgt. Joseph, 201, 202–3, 205, 206, 207–8
de Maria, Giacomo, 507
de Maria, Lia, 507–8, 510
Dempsey, Lt.-Gen. Miles, 254
Denmark, 248–53
De Rango, Lt. Fred, 202
Deutschmann, Elisabeth, 544
Devers, Lt. Gen. Jacob L., 28, 40, 214, 587

Dietrich, SS-Oberstgruppenführer Josef ("Sepp"), 38, 187, 337, 338, 340, 350–1
Dollmann, SS-Standartenführer Eugen, 238, 240–2, 244, 475–6, 483, 486
Domaso, 491, 492
Dongo, 492, 494, 495, 496, 508, 511
Dönitz, Grossadmiral Karl, 343, 344, 346, 412, 413, 441, 463, 469, 520, 522, 524, 527, 533–4, 542, 545–7, 548, 554, 558, 559, 563, 570–1, 573–4, 577, 589–90
Donovan, Maj. Gen. William J., 239, 243
Dooley, 1st Lt. William, 331–2
Dorn, Hermann, 154
Dornberger, Generalmajor Walter, 11
Drabik, Alex, 208, 218
Dresden, 135, 136, 137–49, 157–8, 386, 471
Dufving, Oberst Theodor von, 549, 550, 551
Dulles, Allen W., 239–40, 241, 242–4, 478, 482–3, 486, 488, 537, 538
Dumbarton Oaks Conference, 94
Dunn, James, 268, 447
E.A.C. (European Advisory Commission), 85
Early, Steve, 268, 373, 374, 375, 376
"Eclipse," Operation, 329
Eddy, Maj. Gen. Manton S., 256, 285, 287, 364
Edelsheim, General Max von, 391, 552
Eden, Anthony, 43, 48, 51, 53, 54, 61, 64–5, 88, 92, 96, 100, 108, 110, 113, 114, 117, 246, 284, 387, 388, 518
Ehrenburg, Ilya, 71–2, 156
Eichmann, SS-Obersturmbannführer Karl Adolf, 412, 571
Eisenhower, General of the Army Dwight D., 10, 27, 28–9, 40, 41–2, 91–2, 106, 171, 174, 175, 214, 215–16, 219, 220, 221, 225, 236–7, 245, 266–7, 282, 283, 307–8, 311–12, 315–16, 325, 326, 327, 328–9, 332–3, 360, 369–71, 377, 385–6, 416, 437, 439, 458, 460, 519, 552, 560–1, 563, 564, 566–7, 570, 573, 575–7, 578, 580, 586, 587, 588
Eismann, Oberst Hans-Georg, 261, 343, 442
Elbe River, 325, 326, 385, 386, 451, 452–3, 454, 455, 552
Embry, Air Vice-Marshal Basil, 250
Engeman, Lt. Col. Leonard, 199, 201, 202, 203–4, 206, 211, 216, 217
Epp, General Franz von, 470, 471–2, 473

Erpel, 204, 209, 218
Erpeler Ley (Flak Hill), 198, 200, 204, 216, 218, 220
Fabian, Richard, 31, 32, 36
Faust, Feldwebel, 206
Fegelein, SS-Brigadeführer Hermann, 13–14, 16, 163, 425, 426, 428, 479, 480, 520
Ferch, 467
Fischer, Ernst, 355
Flensburg, 554, 589
Flynn, Edward, 114
Fodor, Capt. Eugene, 566
Fodor, Capt. Oscar, 277
Fog, Mogens, 251–2
Forrestal, James, 317, 375, 447
Fossani, Ivanoe, 477
Frank, Karl Hermann, 566
Frankfurt an der Oder, 71, 75, 258, 343, 344, 397, 399, 406, 423, 428
Freidin, Seymour, 558–9
Freisler, Roland, 58–59
French First Army, 28
Freytag von Loringhoven, Major (Baron) Bernd, 11, 17, 78, 303–5, 424, 435, 467, 517, 525, 527
Friebel, Annemarie, 145–6, 147
Friedeburg, Generaladmiral Hans-Georg von, 546, 554, 557–8, 559–61, 563, 573–5, 588
Friesenhahn, Hauptmann Karl, 198, 203, 205–6, 209
Fuchs, Hauptmann, 292, 293
Fuller, Col. Hurley, 21–22, 23–24, 25, 36, 67–68, 184–5
Gadermann, Hauptmann Ernst, 79, 80–81
Gaevernitz, Gero von S., 239–40, 242–3, 244, 486–8, 537, 538
Gardiev, Lt. Col. Alexander T., 452
Garton, Col. George ("Seafood"), 322
Gavin, Maj. Gen. James, 215
Gay, Maj. Gen. Hobart ("Hap"), 223–4, 237, 264, 364, 371
Gebhardt, Dr. Karl, 133, 150, 165, 257, 409, 426, 478, 572
Gehlen, General Reinhold, 345
Gemünden, 289
German Military Units:
  Army Group B, 236, 320, 332, 384, 391
  Army Group Center, 6, 343, 463
  Army Group F, 582
  Army Group G, 236, 320
  Army Group H, 13, 273, 320
  Army Group Kurland, 38, 78
  Army Group North, 5, 78
  Army Group South, 188, 348, 582
  Army Group Vistula, 7, 78, 133–4, 151, 257, 260, 281, 343, 397, 400, 419, 514, 516
  First Panzer Army, 187
  Third Panzer Army, 151, 154, 168, 261, 436, 442, 514
  Fourth Army, 5
  Fifth Panzer Army, 195
  Sixth Army, 337
  Sixth Panzer Army, 38, 187, 337
  Seventh Army, 17, 289, 290, 298
  Ninth Army, 262, 304, 372, 397, 420, 424, 442, 465, 514
  Eleventh Army, 151
  Twelfth Army, 384, 391, 396, 408, 427, 434, 469, 543, 544
  Fifteenth Army, 195, 196, 321
  Seventeenth Army, 17
  VII Tank Corps, 404
  XX Corps, 464, 467
  LIII Infantry Corps, 320–1
  LVI Panzer Corps, 433
  LXVII Corps, 196
  LXXI Corps, 191
  7th Parachute Division, 282
  8th Parachute Division, 282
  9th Panzer Division, 191, 192
  9th Parachute Division, 262, 400, 406
  10th SS Panzer Division, 262
  11th Panzer Division, 212, 213
  12th SS Panzer Division, 583
  14th Flak Division, 392
  25th Panzer Division, 262
  32nd SS Panzer Grenadier Division, 543
  84th Infantry Division, 282
  363rd Infantry Division, 191
  Führer Grenadier Division, 262
  Panzer Lehr Division, 212
Gerngross, Hauptmann Rupprecht, 470–2, 473, 474
Gestapo, 6
Gibble, Chaplain William T., 207, 218
Giesing, Dr. Erwin, 12
Giesler, Paul, 471, 472–3
Gilinski, Capt. Donald, 184
Goch, 98, 172
Goebbels, Josef, 10, 37, 81–2, 83, 130, 149, 150, 157–9, 181, 259, 262, 270, 366–7, 372, 376–7, 378–9, 399, 407–8, 412, 418–9, 424, 425, 426, 431, 436, 441, 467–8, 519, 520, 522, 523–5, 526, 529, 531–2, 533, 545, 546, 547, 548
Goebbels, Magda, 426, 465, 468, 517, 521, 522, 532–3, 548
Goeckel, Generalleutnant Günther von, 286, 291, 292, 363
Goerdeler, Karl, 58

Goode, Col. Paul ("Pop"), 286, 291, 293, 294, 363
Goodrich, Col. C. G. ("Rogo"), 18
Goodson, Sgt. William ("Speedy"), 216–17
Göring, Reichsmarschall Hermann, 11, 13, 14, 15, 16, 76, 78–79, 81, 149, 344, 345, 346, 412, 413, 427, 429–32, 439, 440, 466, 522, 525, 561, 571
Gotenhafen (Gdynia), 300-1
*Goya*, the, 404–6
Graziani, Marshal Rodolfo, 478, 481, 483, 484, 485, 486
Greim, General Robert von, 439–40, 465–6, 520–1, 553
"Grenade," Operation, 98, 105, 106, 172, 173
Grew, Joseph, 268, 457, 564, 566
Grierson, C. M., 158
Grimbull, Lt. John, 202, 203, 204
Grolmann, Generalleutnant Wilhelm von, 392–3
Gromyko, Andrei, 109, 448
Groth, John, 558–9
Growdon, Col. John ("Pinky"), 199
Groza, Petru, 179, 181
Guardini, Romano, 242
Guderian, Generaloberst Heinz, 5, 6–7, 11, 12, 13, 14, 15, 17, 38, 77–79, 131–2, 133–4, 152, 173–4, 256–8, 259–60, 271, 281, 303–5
Günsche, SS-Sturmbannführer Otto, 38, 270, 520, 522, 529, 530–1, 548
Günther, Christian, 163
Gurney, Maj. Edward, 190, 191
Haberzettel, Frau Inge, 376
Halder, Generaloberst Franz, 59, 365
Halifax, Lord, 388
Hamill, Maj. James, 562
Hamlin, Pvt. Larry, 452
Hammelburg, 285, 291; see also Oflag XIIIB
Hamminkeln, 279
Hannover, 384
Hansen, Christen Lyst, 250, 252
Hanslick, Leutnant Walter, 349
Harkins, Col. Paul, 256
Harriman, W. Averell, 45, 46, 56, 59, 87, 92–3, 99, 107, 109, 111, 115, 118, 178, 181, 233, 245, 246, 327, 357–8, 359, 380, 386–7, 388, 389, 390–1, 399, 447, 448, 449
Harris, Air Chief Marshal Sir Arthur T. ("Bomber"), 134, 135, 136, 137
Harsch, Joseph C., 130
Harz Mountains, 368
Hassett, William, 372

Hauenschild, Generalleutnant Bruno von, 83
Haushchild, Sgt. Arthur, 323
Hausser, SS-Obergruppenführer Paul, 13, 14, 133, 236, 320, 333
Hawes, Capt. Cecil, 70
Hawkins, Lewis, 578
Hegel, Leutnant Paul, 21, 22, 24, 68, 184
Heinrici, Generaloberst Gotthard, 257, 259–62, 281–2, 343–6, 347, 397–8, 400, 401, 406, 407, 419–20, 421, 423, 428, 436, 441–2, 514–16
Herbener, Gabrielle, 393, 395
Hermann, Hauptmann Karl Hans, 83
Herr, General, 538–9, 540–1
Herte, Lt. Col. Roy, 379
Hess, Rudolf, 480
Heuwing, Leo, 470, 471, 472
Hewel, Walter, 270, 271, 468, 529, 549
Heydrich, Reinhard, 6, 230
Himmler, Reichsführer-SS Heinrich, 6, 7, 10, 30, 37, 132–4, 150–1, 152, 159–61, 163–7, 168, 173, 229–30, 231, 257–8, 259, 261, 269, 333–4, 343, 346, 409–11, 412, 413–18, 425–6, 434–5, 456, 457–8, 459, 478–9, 482, 483, 518, 520, 521, 522, 533–4, 553–4, 567, 571, 572
Hindenburg, President Paul von, 29
Hinds, Col. Sidney, 194
Hiss, Alger, 59, 100
Hitler, Adolf, 5, 6–7, 11–16, 17, 37–39, 58, 72–73, 74, 75–76, 77, 78–79, 81, 82, 83–84, 119, 124–5, 133–4, 153, 159, 173–4, 182, 183, 187, 188, 212, 213, 221–2, 226–9, 231–2, 249, 257, 258, 260, 262, 263, 270–3, 281–2, 300, 303, 304–5, 334, 338, 343–7, 351, 377, 383–4, 398–9, 408–9, 412–3, 420, 423, 424–7, 431–2, 433–4, 436, 440, 441, 442, 451, 466, 467, 468, 476, 479–81, 519–23, 525, 526–7, 529–32, 547, 567–8
Hitzfeld, General Otto, 196, 198–9, 211
Hodges, Lt. Gen. Courtney, 54, 98, 99, 106, 109, 174, 191, 195, 196, 211, 213–14, 220–1, 224, 225, 235–6, 245, 265, 309, 320, 368, 383, 391, 392, 449, 456
Hoess, SS-Standartenführer Rudolf Franz, 10, 437
Hogan, Lt. Col. Sam, 309, 331
Hoge, Brig. Gen. William, 197, 199, 203–4, 205, 206, 210–11, 213, 218, 220, 285, 286–7
Hohenlychen, 150, 257
Hohenzollern Bridge, 192

Home Army (Poland), 45, 46, 185
Hopkins, Harry, 42, 43, 48, 54, 85, 86, 88, 92, 95, 108, 109, 111, 116, 317, 324, 380–2, 386
Horrocks, Lt.-Gen. Brian, 97–9, 106, 172, 265
Horthy, Adm. Miklós von, 124, 125–6
Hossbach, General Friedrich, 5
Hottelet, Richard C., 275
Höttl, Wilhelm, 262–3
Howze, Col. Robert, 309
Hradecky, Vacalr (Wally), 539, 542
Hübner, SS-Gruppenführer Rudolf, 222, 223
Huebner, Maj. Gen. Clarence, 99, 392, 456, 566
Hull, Cordell, 41, 117, 316, 317
Hull, Maj. Gen. John E., 457, 459
Hungary, 124–29
Hurley, Gen. Patrick J., 386, 387
Husmann, Max, 239, 240–1, 242
Huth, Hauptmann Alfred, 348, 352
Huzel, Dieter, 368
Irshko, Lt. Col. Theodocius, 36
Irwin, Maj. Gen. S. Leroy ("Red"), 256
Ismay, Gen. Sir Hastings, 57, 158
Issel Canal, 274, 278
Jacobsen, 2nd Lt. Donald E., 332
Jalser, J., 252–3
Janert, Oberst Felix, 223
Japan, 92, 99-100, 107, 111, 387, 448, 585
Jeanne d'Arc School (Copenhagen), 251, 253
Jodl, Generaloberst Alfred, 11, 14, 16, 213, 221, 281, 304, 343, 413, 419, 424, 427, 429, 436–7, 442, 514, 545, 570, 573–5
Johannmeier, Major Willi, 270, 271, 525
Johnson, H.V., 457
Johnson, Col. Harry, 210–11
Johnson, Wing Leader Johnnie, 275, 524
Jones, Jr., Lt. Alan, 295
Jones, Donald, 486–7
Junge, Frau, 522, 523, 526, 527, 529
Jungenfeld, Ernst von, 556
Jüttner, Werner, 404–5
Kaiserbrücke, 174
Kaltenbrunner, SS-General Ernst, 6, 160, 161, 162–3, 164–5, 167, 230–1, 243, 262–3, 269, 410, 411, 412, 478–9, 480, 538, 541, 571
Kammler, SS-Obergruppenführer Hans, 37, 368
Kannenberg, Artur, 303
Käs, Feldwebel Ferdinand, 340–2, 347, 348, 349
Karinhall, 76, 413

Katyn Forest, 131
Keitel, Generalfeldmarschall Wilhelm, 7, 11, 12, 13, 15–16, 134, 183, 221, 281, 305, 338, 343, 412–13, 424, 425, 426–8, 432, 437, 463–4, 514–16, 528, 545, 557, 573–4, 588–9
Kelley, Capt. David, 190
Kempin, Oberst Hans, 543
Kempka, SS-Obersturmbannführer Erich, 12, 232, 520, 526, 529, 530–1, 532–3, 548–51
Kennan, George, 387
Kennedy, Edward, 577–8
Kerley, S/Sgt. Herman, 37
Kernmayr, Leutnant Erich, 188
Kersten, Dr. Felix, 159, 160, 161, 163, 229–30, 231, 409, 411, 413–14, 415, 416, 417
Kesselring, Feldmarschall Albrecht, 213, 221, 222, 223, 236, 241, 243, 244, 267, 320, 321, 333, 396, 463, 538, 540, 541–2
Keuch, Lotte, 9
Kimball, Col. Edward, 189–91
King, Fleet Adm. Ernest, 52, 57, 318, 447, 448, 457
Kinzel, General der Infanterie Eberhard, 261
Kirkpatrick, Helen, 573
Kislenko, Maj. Gen. A.P., 537
Kisnatt, Hauptmann Otto, 492–3, 494
Kittredge, Capt. T. B., 318
Kleist, Peter, 161–3, 164, 168, 230, 411
Kleist-Schmenzin, Ewald von, 58, 59
Knight, Lt. Col. George, 394, 395
Knowlton, 1st Lt. William, 555–7
Knox, Frank, 317
Koblenz, 174, 245
Koch, Gauleiter Erich, 9
Koch, SS-Standartenführer Karl, 415
Köchling, General Friedrich, 191–2
Köhler, Hans (John Koehler), 141–2, 144–5, 147–8, 157
Koller, General Karl, 408, 413, 424, 428–9, 430, 431, 440
Komatsu, Lt. Gen. Mitsuhiko, 306
Komorowski, Gen. Tadeusz (Bor), 45, 46
Konev, Marshal Ivan, 5, 6, 9, 17, 182, 406, 419, 420, 421, 422, 424, 463
Königsberg, 4, 78
Koriakov, Capt. Mikhail, 155–7, 422–3
Kortzfleisch, General Joachim von, 212–13
Kostow, Lt. Peter, 194
Kotzebue, 1st Lt. Albert, 450–2, 453, 454, 455, 460
Kowalski, T/5 Stephen, 452

Krampnitz, 429
Krebs, General Hans, 258, 260, 305, 343, 344, 345, 347, 401, 407, 419, 420, 423, 424–5, 427, 428, 432, 433, 434, 435–6, 451, 464, 468, 469, 516–17, 520, 522, 523, 525, 526, 529, 532, 544–5
Krok-Paszkowski, Jan, 185–7
Kropp, Robert, 76, 413
Krüger, Fräulein Else, 529
Kurland, 78, 79, 151, 303, 304
Küstrin, 36, 75, 258, 260, 261, 281–2, 304, 397, 399
Lammerding, SS-Brigadeführer Heinz, 257
Lammers, Hans, 430
Landsberg, 36, 72
Lanford, Lt. Col. Willie, 19
Langendorf, T/3 Ernst, 290
Lann, Lt. Col. James, 363
Larsen, Lt. Harold, 200
Lazzaro, Urbano, 490, 491, 492, 493, 494, 496–9, 500, 508, 510, 511–12
Leahy, Fleet Adm. William, 59, 96, 102–3, 108, 131, 268, 314, 316, 317–18, 356, 447, 448, 449, 457, 519, 578–9
Leiling, Otto Heinz, 470, 471, 472
Leipzig, 136, 327, 386, 391–6
Lemelsen, General, 538–9, 540–1
Lemnitzer, Maj. Gen. Lyman, 180, 244
Leonard, Maj. Gen. John, 196–7, 199–200, 210, 211
Linge, Heinz, 12, 530, 531
Litteráti, 1st Lt. Gyula, 128
Livadia Palace, 56, 59, 60, 62, 85, 103, 107, 116
Lockett, Lt. Col. James, 8
Lodge, Col. Henry Cabot, 587
Löhr, Generaloberst Alexander, 582
Lombardi, Riccardo, 484
Lorenz, Heinz, 451, 519, 524 5
Löwe, the, 33, 35
Lübeck, 434, 552–3
Lublin Polish Committee of National Liberation, 45, 46, 59, 91, 101, 246, 447, 448, 536
Lucerne, 244, 482, 486, 488
Ludendorff Bridge (Remagen), 195, 196, 198, 199, 202, 213, 214–18, 219, 220, 221, 224, 235
Lund, Jens, 251
Lüneburg, 557, 559
Luqa Airport, 55
MacArthur, Gen. Douglas, 268
MacDonald, Capt. Charles B., 393
Maclean, Brig. Fitzroy, 120, 121, 180
McCurdy, 2nd Lt. William, 225

McDuffie, Lizzie, 372
McGuire, Lt. Paul, 275–6
McIntire, Adm. Ross, 373
McLain, Maj. Gen. Raymond, 254–5
McMillan, Richard, 266, 560
Maas River (Meuse), 97, 106
Madden, Capt. John, 362–3
Main River, 285, 288, 289
Mainetti, Don, 493–4
Maisky, Ivan, 88, 113
Malinovsky, Marshal Rodion Yakovlevich, 124, 126–7, 338
Malinski, Frank, 289
Malta Conference ("Cricket"), 26, 27, 40
Maness, Lt. Col. Lewis, 218
Manteuffel, General der Panzertruppen (Baron) Hasso von, 182–3, 261, 419, 420, 436, 437, 442, 514–16, 527, 552
Marazza, Achille, 484, 485
Marshall, General of the Army George C., 26–27, 28, 40–1, 48, 52, 53, 57, 59, 61, 62, 91–2, 106, 107, 312, 316, 317–18, 325, 356, 360, 447–8, 457
Massie, Pfc. Art, 207, 208
Masur, Norbert, 410, 411, 413, 414–17, 418
Matthews, Lt. Bruce (chaplain), 295
Matthews, Freeman ("Doc"), 59, 87, 92, 116
Menaggio, 489
Merrick, Lt. Col. Richard, 577
Meuse River, see Maas River
Meyer-Detring, Oberst Wilhelm, 582
Mezzasomma, Fernando, 477, 494
Michael, King of Rumania, 118, 178–9, 181
"Micky Mouse," Operation, 125
Middleton, Drew, 579
Mikhailovich, Col. Draja, 119–20, 121
Mikolajczyk, Prime Minister Stanislaw, 44–45, 46–47, 93, 388
Milan, 508
Miley, Maj. Gen. William ("Bud"), 279, 280
Miller, Lt. Col. Allen C., 274, 275, 276–8
Miller, 1st Lt. C. Windsor, 216–17
Millikin, Maj. Gen. John, 195, 197, 210–11, 235–6
Model, Generalfeldmarschall Walther, 195–6, 211, 212, 213, 221, 222, 236, 320–1, 331, 332, 333, 383, 384–5, 391
Mohnke, SS-Brigadeführer, 526, 531–2, 548
Moller, Madeleine, 477
Molotov, Vyacheslav M., 46, 56, 57, 60, 61, 63, 94, 95, 99, 100, 102, 107, 109,

110, 112–13, 122, 178, 233, 245, 246, 269, 284, 380, 386, 391, 447, 448–9, 519
Mönchen-Gladbach, 175
Montgomery, Field-Marshal Bernard, 27, 28, 29, 40, 53, 54, 97, 98, 106–7, 171–2, 175–6, 219, 220, 221, 236, 254, 255, 264, 265, 279, 282–3, 308, 320, 325, 331, 360–1, 383, 552, 557–8, 559–60
Moore, T/5 Lemoyne, 37
Morell, Dr. Theodor, 12, 304
Moretti, Michele, 501, 504, 506, 507, 509, 510, 511
Morgan, Lt.-Gen. Frederick, 215, 573
Morgan, Lt.-Gen. William, 537
Morgenthau, Henry, 89, 92, 267, 375
Moseley, Philip, 247
Mott, Lt. Hugh, 204, 207, 211
Mulde River, 449, 451
Müller, SS-Gruppenführer Heinrich, 167–8, 412
Müller, Josef ("Ochsensepp"), 365–6
Munich Uprising, 470–4
Murphy, Robert, 576–7
Murrow, Edward R., 369
Mussolini, Anna Maria, 489
Mussolini, Benito, 475, 476–8, 481–2, 483–5, 489–90, 491–2, 494, 496–8, 499, 500–2, 504, 505–7, 508, 510–11, 513
Mussolini, Donna Rachele, 477, 482, 489
Mussolini, Romano, 489
Mussolini, Vittorio, 475
Musy, Jean-Marie, 161
Myers, Lt. Col. Henry T., 55
National Redoubt, see Alpenfestung
Naumann, Werner, 83, 372, 441, 468, 529, 548, 549–50
Negri, Giuseppe, 496–7
Neisse, 186
Netherlands, 558
Neubrandenburg, 69, 514, 528; see also Stalag IIA
Nijmegen, 97–8, 105, 106
Nordhausen (also concentration camp), 368, 562
Nordic News Service, 253
Nowakowski, Tadeusz, 443, 444–5, 446
Nuremberg, 361
Nutto, Lt. William, 290
Oder River, 7, 17, 60, 75, 79, 151, 256, 258, 399
Odom, Col. Charles, 364
Oflag XIIIB (Offizierslager, Officer Prisoner of War Camp, Hammelburg), 285, 286, 287, 291–2, 293–6, 297, 298, 330, 361–3

Ohlendorf, SS-Oberstgruppenführer Otto, 572
Ohrdruf Nord (concentration camp), 370–1
Olson, Ivar, 162
Olson, Sidney, 172
O'Malley, Sir Owen, 131
Onodera, Maj. Gen. Makoto, 306, 307
Oppenheim, 256, 270, 273, 280
Orion, H.M.S., 29, 43, 48, 51
Oseth, Maj. Fred, 294
Oshima, Amb. Hiroshi, 306–7
OSS, 239, 482, 566
Oster, General Hans, 365
Owen, Sgt. Bryant, 323–4
Paderborn, 309, 311, 321, 331
Paetzold, Friedrich, 49–50
"Panzerfaust," Operation, 125, 126
Parchim, 555–7
Park, Col. Richard, 457
Parri, Ferruccio, 241–2, 476
Parrilli, Baron Luigi, 239, 240, 241
Pash, Col. Boris, 562
Patch, Lt. Gen. Alexander, 236, 237, 470
Patterson, Robert, 317
Patton, Lt. Gen. George S., Jr., 27, 29, 54, 106, 107, 173, 174, 175, 196, 220–1, 223, 225, 236–7, 245, 255–6, 264, 267, 273, 280–1, 285, 287, 288, 299, 320, 364, 369–71, 377, 383, 449, 564, 565, 566, 575
Paul, Prince (Yugoslavia), 119, 121
Paullin, Dr. James, 373
Pavlov, M., 87, 99, 448
Pavolini, Alessandro, 489, 490, 491, 496, 500–1, 511
Pearson, Drew, 386
Peenemünde, 10, 11
Perkins, Frances, 177–8, 313, 375
Petacci, Claretta (Clara), 477, 483, 486, 489–90, 492, 495, 500, 502–4, 506–8, 510–11, 513
Petacci, Marcello, 495, 499–500, 509–10, 511–13
Peter the Second, King of Yugoslavia, 121
Peters, Leutnant Karl, 223
Pfeffer-Wildenbruch, SS-Obergruppenführer Karl von, 127, 128
Phelan, Lt. Larry, 8
Phillips, Col. James, 210–11
Pilsen, 566, 567
Plön, 463, 545
"Plunder," Operation, 254, 255, 264, 265, 273, 282
Podewils, Countess Mechtilde, 242
Pohl, General Ritter von, 539, 540–1

Poland, 43–48, 59, 90–91, 92–93, 94, 95, 100–1, 108–9, 111–12, 115, 176–7, 233–4, 312, 388, 447, 448–9, 535–7
Polowsky, PFC Joseph, 452
Pomerania, 31, 79, 151
Poncet Oberst Hans von, 392, 393, 394, 395
Portal, Sir Charles, 135, 158
Posen (Poznán), 5, 161
Potsdam, 386, 424, 464
Prague, 312, 345, 564–9, 580–1
Pražák, Albert, 566
Prince, Lt. Col. William R., 199
Quandt, Harald, 517
*Quincy*, U.S.S., 29, 51, 53, 54
Quisling, Vidkun, 579-80
Raczkiewicz, President Wladyslaw, 131
Raczynski, Count Edward, 131
Radescu government, 178, 179
Raff, Col. Edson, 275
Rahn, Rudolf, 238, 476
Rankine, Paul Scott, 518
Raschke, SS-Oberleutnant Rudolf, 348, 349–50, 352
Rattenhuber, SS-Brigadeführer Johann, 520, 529, 531–2
Ravensbrück (concentration camp), 416, 417, 418, 437
Rayburn, Sam, 177, 374, 375, 388
Reber, R. W., 131
Red Cross, the International Committee of the, 418, 437
Red Cross, the Swedish, 165, 166, 417
Rehberg, Dr. Brandt, 252
Reichhelm, Oberst Günther, 211–12, 383–4, 465
Reichswald, 97, 98, 106
Reif, Gefreiter Johann, 341, 348
Reilly, Michael, 56, 112
Reinefarth, SS-Oberstgruppenführer Heinz, 258
Reinhardt, Maj. Gen. Emil F., 395, 453, 456
Reinhardt, Generaloberst Georg-Hans, 5
Reitsch, Hanna, 465–6, 467–8, 520, 521, 553
Remagen, 196, 199, 200, 201, 224
Remer, Generalmajor Otto, 12
Rendulic, Generaloberst Lothar, 5, 6, 582
Renner, Karl, 355
Reppentin, 556-7
Reuters, 518
Reymann, General Helmuth, 398, 419
Rheims, 215, 220, 245, 325, 560, 563, 572, 577, 578
Rheinberg, 189–91

Rhine River, 29, 40, 60, 97, 173, 174, 191, 254–5, 265, 275
Ribbentrop, Foreign Minister Joachim, 14, 73, 126, 159, 163, 164, 165, 168, 306–7, 413, 433, 546
Richardson, Lt. Col. Jack J., 174
Richardson, Lt. Col. Walter, 309–11, 321, 331
Ridgway, Maj. Gen. Matthew, 215, 216, 255, 279–80, 282, 384–5, 552, 555
Robb, Air-Marshal Sir James, 574
Roberts, Brig. Gen. W. L., 287
Robertson, Maj. Gen. Walter, 392
Robertson, 2nd Lt. William, 454, 455, 460
Roer dams, 98, 99, 105–6
Roer River, 98, 105, 106, 172
Roettiger, General Hans, 538, 539–41
Rokossovsky, Marshal Konstantin, 4, 5, 23, 151, 300, 436, 442, 527–8, 532
Roosevelt, Eleanor (Mrs. Franklin Delano), 51, 177, 234, 268–9, 313, 373, 374, 375, 381, 382
Roosevelt, Elliott, 51, 381
Roosevelt, Franklin Delano, 29, 43, 44, 45, 51–52, 53, 55–56, 57, 59, 60–62, 63–64, 85, 86–93, 94–95, 96, 99–100, 101–2, 103, 104, 107–12, 113–16, 117–18, 123, 129, 131, 162, 177–8, 233, 234, 246, 247, 267–9, 284, 312–14, 316, 317–18, 319, 324, 328, 356, 357, 358, 359–60, 372–3, 374–82, 387, 388, 389, 581
Rose, Maj. Gen. Maurice, 310, 321, 322, 323–4
Rosenberg, Anna, 268–9
Rosenman, Judge Samuel, 177, 178, 378, 381
Rothe, Feldwebel Gerhard, 203, 205
Rudel, Oberst Hans-Ulrich, 75–77, 79–81, 408–9, 583
Ruff, PFC Edward, 452
Ruge, Maj. Gen. Otto, 379
Ruhr, the, 28, 221, 309, 320, 331, 332, 333, 383, 384, 391
Rumania, 117, 118, 178–9, 181
Rundstedt, Generalfeldmarschall Gerd von, 173, 213, 221, 222
Rusakov, Maj. Gen. Vladimir, 453, 455–6
Russkaia Osvobitel'naia Armiia (Russian Army of Liberation), 568, 580–1
Rust, Lt. Col. Clayton, 235
Rutherfurd, Mrs. Winthrop, 372
Sabia, Sgt. Carmine, 201, 205, 207–8, 209
Sachsenhausen (concentration camp), 262, 263, 418, 419, 437

Sack, Carl, 59
Sagan, *see* Stalag Luft III
Saki Airport, 55
Salzwedel, 443–6
Samele, Sgt. Anthony, 207, 208
Sampson, Captain Francis (chaplain), 69–71, 330–1, 527, 528, 562
San Francisco Conference, 112–13, 267–8, 284, 447, 459, 518, 554, 585, 586
Sardagna, Baron Giovanni, 505
Saundby, Air-Marshal Sir Robert, 137
Schacht, Hjalmar, 365
Schellenberg, SS-Brigadeführer Walter, 160, 161, 163–6, 167, 333, 409, 410, 411, 413, 416, 417–18, 434
Scheller, Major Hans, 198–9, 200, 205–6, 209, 213, 221, 223
Schirach, Baldur von, 340, 354, 561
Schlabrendorff, Fabian von, 58–59, 365
Schleiter, Josefine, 23
Schmuck-Wachter, Paula, 351–2
Schneider, Irwin, 71
Schörner, Generalfeldmarschall Ferdinand, 5, 6, 17, 182, 343, 345, 353, 406, 420, 421, 422, 427, 440–1, 463, 522, 545, 547, 568, 582
Schulz, General der Infanterie F., 538, 539–42
Schulz, Oberst Rudolf, 212, 213
Schuschnigg, Kurt von, 365
Schuster, Ildefonso Cardinal, 73, 475, 476, 478–9, 483–4
Schwägermann, Günther, 548, 549
Schweinitz, Oberstleutnant Viktor von, 482, 537, 538
Schwerin von Krosigk, Count Lutz, 366–7, 378, 410, 469, 546, 554, 572, 577, 578
Seelow, 281, 400–3, 406, 407, 419
Seely, Col. Theodore, 295
Seidler, Frau Klara, 301–3
Seldte, Franz, 410
Semmler, Rudolf, 150, 158–9, 376, 377, 426
Sevez, Commandant François, 574, 577
Shaunce, T/5 Glen, 323
Shell House, the (Copenhagen), 249–53
Sherwood, Robert E., 268, 375, 380, 382
Shoumanoff, Elizabeth, 372
Siegfried Line, *see* West Wall
Simpson, Lt. Gen. William, 54, 98, 105, 106, 171–2, 175, 176, 194–5, 254, 255, 266–7, 282, 283, 309, 320, 331, 361, 383, 385–6
Sinclair, Sir Archibald, 136, 158
Sinn River, 290

Sinzig, 199, 202
*Sirius*, H.M.S., 43, 48
Skiera, S/Sgt. Joe, 146
Skorzeny, SS-Obersturmbannführer Otto, 125, 126, 213, 236, 353–4, 408, 541
Slavin, Gen. Nikolai Vasilevich, 576
Smith, Wing Comm. Maurice A., 137, 138, 140, 141, 143
Smith, Lt. Gen. Walter Bedell ("Beetle"), 28, 29, 40, 41–2, 245, 386, 519, 561, 562–3, 573–7, 587
Smolka, Norman, 292
Sokolovsky, Marshal Vasili, 586
Soumas, Capt. George, 216, 217, 218-19
Spa, 53, 213, 235
Spaatz, Gen. Carl, 574, 587–8
Speer, Albert, 76–77, 182–3, 231–2, 258, 397–8, 413, 431
Spivey, Col. Delmar, 19, 20–21
SS (Schutzstaffel), 6
Stalag IIA (Prisoner of War Camp, Neubrandenburg), 69–70, 330–1, 527–8
Stalag IIIA (Prisoner of War Camp, Luckenwalde), 379, 421
Stalag IIIC (Prisoner of War Camp, Küstrin), 37
Stalag Luft III (Air Prisoner of War Camp, Sagan), 3, 4, 5, 7–8, 12, 16, 17–21
Stalin, Joseph, 45–46, 60–61, 62, 63–64, 85–91, 92–93, 94, 95, 99–100, 101–3, 104, 107, 108–12, 113–16, 118, 122–3, 156, 178, 233, 234, 246–7, 269, 284, 308, 312, 327, 329, 356, 357, 358, 359–60, 380, 386–7, 388, 391, 399, 448, 458, 482, 488, 535–7, 538, 564–5, 584, 586
Stargard, 152, 153
Stauffenberg, Count Claus von, 11
Steiner, SS-Obergruppenführer Felix, 151–2, 153, 154, 168, 182, 420, 423, 424–5, 427, 434, 436–7, 442
Stettin, 442
Stettinius, Jr., Edward, 42–43, 48, 53, 54, 56, 59, 61, 62, 63, 86, 88, 89, 94, 95, 102–4, 109, 110, 112–14, 116, 118, 375, 379, 380, 387, 447, 448
Stiller, Maj. Alexander, 280, 286, 287, 288, 298
Stimson, Henry, 95, 234, 316, 317, 375, 376, 447
Stirbey, Prince, 179
Stockholm, 305, 306, 457, 458
Stokes, Richard, 158
Stone, Chief Justice Harlan Fiske, 375
Storch, Gilel, 161–2, 163, 230, 231, 409, 411

Straughn, T/Sgt. Charles, 37
Strehla, 452, 460
Strobel, Major Herbert, 218, 219, 223
Strong, Maj.-Gen. Kenneth, 573, 575
Student, Generaloberst Kurt, 13
Stumpfegger, Dr. Ludwig, 304, 530, 531, 545, 549-50
Stumpff, Generaloberst Hans Jürgen, 588
Stypulkowski, Zbigniew, 315
Suckley, Margaret, 372
Suhrens, SS-Sturmbannführer Fritz, 437-8, 439
Summersby, Lt. Kay, 560, 575, 587
"Sunrise," Operation ("Sunrise Crossroad"), 243-4, 269, 284, 356-7, 389, 476, 478-80, 482-3, 486-8, 537-42
Susloparov, Maj. Gen. Ivan, 574
Suzuki, Adm. Kantaro, 380
Sweat, Lt. Col. Wesley, 323
Swinemünde, 515-16
Szokoll, Maj. Carl, 339-41, 347-53, 355
T-36, the, 33, 35, 36
Tannenberg, 4
Taylor, Maj. Gen. Maxwell, 215
Tedder, Marshal of the RAF Sir Arthur W., 176, 360, 587-9
Tessmann, Bernhard, 368
Textor, Katherina, 36, 72
Thayer, Lt. Col. Charles W., 179-81
Thomale, General Wolfgang, 79
Thompson, Comm. C. R., 26, 57, 265, 279
"Thunderclap," Operation, 135-7
Timmermann, 2nd Lt. Karl, 201, 202, 204-5, 206-7, 208
Tito (Josip Broz), 118, 119-23, 582
Toftoy, Col. Holgar, 369, 562
Tolbukhin, Marshal Feodor Ivanovich, 124, 126-7, 179-80, 181, 337-8, 340, 342, 347, 351, 352
Torgau, 454, 460
Toussaint, General der Infanterie Rudolf, 581
Trefousse, Capt. Hans, 394, 395-6
Trier, 174, 175
Truelsen, Svend, 250
Truman, Harry S, 177, 178, 373-4, 375-6, 379-80, 381-2, 387-91, 447, 448-9, 456-60, 482, 519, 535, 551, 564, 580, 584-5, 586, 587
Truman, Mrs. Harry, 375, 382, 388
Truman, Margaret, 375, 382, 388
Tucker, Capt. Kimball, 189, 190
United Nations, 89, 94, 100, 114, 178, 391, 586
Untucht, Günther, 395
U.S. Military Units:
6th Army Group, 28, 214

12th Army Group, 28, 220, 331, 385
15th Army Group, 483
First Army, 28, 224
Third Army, 27, 28, 224, 236, 256, 264, 371
Seventh Army, 28, 236, 237, 470
Eighth Air Force, 58, 146
Ninth Army, 28, 54, 98, 105, 171, 172, 175, 265, 266, 385
III Corps, 210
V Corps, 99, 392, 566
VII Corps, 191
XII Corps, 256
XVIII Airborne Corps, 255, 552, 555
XIX Corps, 254
XX Corps, 370, 582
2nd Division, 392
2nd Armored Division, 172, 193-4, 309, 331, 361, 385
3rd Division, 474
3rd Armored Division, 191, 309, 321, 331, 332, 368
4th Armored Division, 285, 296
5th Division, 256
5th Armored Division, 172
6th Armored Division, 449-50
7th Armored Division, 555-7
8th Armored Division, 189
9th Division, 99, 105, 214, 224, 235
9th Armored Division, 196, 220
10th Armored Division, 174, 175
14th Armored Division, 363
17th Airborne Division, 255, 273-4, 275, 277, 278, 280
29th Division, 175
30th Division, 172, 266
42nd Division, 474
44th Division, 562
45th Division, 474
65th Division, 583
69th Division, 392, 393
78th Division, 99, 214, 218, 224
79th Division, 266
83rd Division, 385
84th Division, 443
90th Division, 364
94th Division, 175
99th Division, 214, 224
104th Division, 191, 192
U.S.S.R. Military Units:
First Ukrainian Front, 5, 182
Second Ukrainian Front, 124, 126
Third Ukrainian Front, 124, 126, 179, 341
First White Russian Front, 5, 399
Second White Russian Front, 4, 300, 436
Third White Russian Front, 4
Second Tank Army, 406

Fourth Tank Army, 406
Sixty-eighth Army, 153
58th Guards Infantry Division, 452
Uschdraweit, Paul, 31–36
V-2 (Vengeance Weapon-2), 10, 37, 235, 368, 369, 562
Valerio, Col., see Audisio
Valletta, 27, 29, 51
Van Houten, Lt. Col. John, 190
Vanaman, Brig. Gen. Arthur, 3, 4, 19
"Varsity," Operation, 255, 273–4, 275–9, 282
Veesenmayer, SS-General Edmund, 124, 125, 126
"Veritable," Operation, 97, 98, 99, 105–6, 172, 173
Victor Emmanuel, King of Italy, 243, 476
Vienna, 339–42, 347–50, 351, 352, 353–5
Vietinghoff, Generaloberst Heinrich von, 244, 481, 482, 537, 538, 542
Viktoriaberg, 198
Vishinsky, Andrei, 178–9, 181, 587–8
Vistula River, 7, 151
Vlasov, Lt. Gen. Andrei Andreevich, 272, 567–8, 580–1
Vorontsov Palace, 57, 60, 92, 112
Voss, Vize-admiral Erich, 424, 529, 549
Wagener, General Carl, 384
Waibel, Maj. Max, 239–40, 242, 243, 244, 482–3, 486–7, 488
Walker, Maj. Gen. Walton H., 370, 582
Wallace, Henry, 375
Warm Springs, Ga., 178, 372
Warsaw Uprising, 45–6
Warthe River, 72, 151, 152
Waters, Lt. Col. John Knight, 286, 287, 292, 293, 298, 363–4
Watson, Maj. Gen. Edwin ("Pa"), 52
Weichs, Generalfeldmarschall Maximilian von, 6
Weidling, General der Artillerie Helmuth ("Bony Karl"), 433, 434, 436, 441, 464, 468–9, 517, 520, 526–7, 532, 544–5, 547, 549, 551
Weigel, Joachim, 141
Weimar, 364, 369
Welborn, Col. John, 321, 322, 368–9
Wenck, General Walther, 131–2, 133–4, 150–1, 154, 271, 383, 384, 391, 396, 407, 427, 428, 434, 464–5, 466, 467, 469, 520–1, 522, 543, 544, 552
Wenner, Major, 482, 537, 538, 542
Wesel, 254, 265, 266
West Wall, 54, 105, 176

Westphal, Generalleutnant Siegfried, 222, 333, 471, 472, 540, 542
Wheeler, PFC John, 452
White, Maj. Gen. Isaac, 361
Wiener Neustadt, 341
Wietersheim, General Wend von, 212
Wilhelm Gustloff, the, 31–34
Wilson, Woodrow, 91
Winant, John, 324, 456, 561, 563, 577
Winocur, Jack, 518
Winter, General der Gebirgstruppen August, 304
Wirtz, Generalleutnant Richard, 219
Wöhler, General Otto, 188, 338
Wöhlerman, Oberst Hans-Oscar, 464, 524, 545, 547–8, 551
Wolff, SS-Obergruppenführer Karl, 29–30, 73, 238, 239, 240, 241–3, 244, 269, 475–6, 478–81, 482–3, 486–8, 538, 539, 540–2
World Jewish Congress, 161–2, 231
Wriezen, 406, 407, 419
Wugarten, 21, 22, 23, 24–25, 36, 68, 151, 184
Xanten, 274
Xylander, Generalleutnant Wolfdietrich von, 17
Yalta Conference (Crimean Conference), 51, 52–3, 54–7, 59–65, 85–96, 99–105, 107–116, 130, 176–7, 178
Yardley, Lt. Col. Doyle, 22
Yoerk, Sgt. Donald, 289, 290
Youngblood, Capt. George, 194–5
Yugoslavia, 118–23, 582
Yurasov, Lt. Col. Vladimir, 400, 562, 587
Zander, SS-Standartenführer Wilhelm, 524
Zangen, General Gustav von, 195–6, 211, 213, 222, 321
Zenkl, Petr, 365, 369
Zheltov, Col. Gen. Alexei Sergeievich, 341, 342
Zhukov, Marshal G. K., 5, 6, 7, 36, 78, 79, 151, 152, 153, 154, 182, 256, 258, 314, 315, 397, 399, 400, 406, 419, 420, 424, 434, 442, 463, 532, 545, 576, 587–9
Zimmer, SS-Obersturmführer Guido, 238–9, 240
Zonhoven, 171
Zossen, 17, 259, 347
Zürich, 239, 242
Zwierzynski, Alexander, 314
Zychski, Josef, 429, 439

# About the Author

JOHN TOLAND was born in LaCrosse, Wisconsin and worked his way through Williams College, where he graduated Phi Beta Kappa in 1936. During World War II he served in the Special Services Division of the United States Army. After the war he came to New York and launched a successful career as a freelance writer, contributing to almost all national magazines.

Then he turned to non-fiction and books, where he gained fame as one of the most popular and respected historians in the world. He won the Pulitzer Prize for *The Rising Sun*, as well as critical acclaim for *The Last 100 Days, Infamy, But Not In Shame, Battle: The Story of the Bulge* and *Ships in the Sky*. Currently his first novel, *Gods of War*, is appearing on national bestseller lists.

Mr. Toland and his interpreter-researcher wife, Toshiko, make their home in Connecticut, where Mr. Toland is busying writing the sequel to *Gods of War*.